HERMAN RIDDERBOS

PAUL

An Outline of His Theology

Translated by
JOHN RICHARD DE WITT

WILLIAM B. EERDMANS PUBLISHING COMPANY

Printed in the United States of America

First printing, August 1975

Reprinted, May 1987

Translated from the Dutch edition, *Paulus: Ontwerp van zijn theologie,*
© Uitgeversmaatschappij J. H. Kok N.V., Kampen, The Netherlands, 1966.

Library of Congress Cataloging in Publication Data

Ridderbos, Herman N
   Paul: an outline of his theology.
   Translation of Paulus.
   1. Bible. N.T. Epistles of Paul — Theology.
I. Title
BS2651.R513   227'.06'6   73-2292
ISBN 0-8028-3438-8

Author's Preface

It is with great pleasure and gratitude that I present to the English-speaking world my studies on the teachings of Paul. This work is a translation with minor corrections of the foregoing Dutch editions of *Paulus* (Kampen: Kok, 1967, 1969, 1972). Although discussions of Pauline themes continue, my basic thesis and argumentation remain unchanged and hence I did not feel it necessary to prepare a new redaction of the work or make any special additions to set forth or defend my position more clearly.

The burdensome task of translation was undertaken by Dr. John R. de Witt, a friend and relative who while studying in the Netherlands lived at my home. He has both grasped and expressed in English the sense and content of my Dutch edition. It has been a long and arduous task, involving numerous difficult details which required understanding of two or more languages and awareness of varied theological traditions. Words cannot adequately express my gratitude and appreciation to Dr. de Witt for his skill, theological acumen, and devoted service demonstrated in this translation. I also want to express my thanks to Dr. Richard Gaffin of Philadelphia and Rev. Marvin Hoff of New York for their willing assistance, helpful advice, and useful suggestions to Dr. de Witt as he prepared this translation.

Finally, to the Wm. B. Eerdmans Publishing Company I owe this opportunity to present in English this work on the Apostle Paul. I wish to thank the editorial staff for many hours of editing, checking the proofs, and preparing indexes to make this work more meaningful and useful to English readers. May this book contribute to the ongoing theological reflection about Paul's incomparable message in the closing quarter of the twentieth century.

— Herman Ridderbos

Pentecost, 1975

Translator's Preface

It has been a great privilege to translate Professor Herman N. Ridderbos's monumental work on the theology of the Apostle Paul, and I am thankful for the opportunity of making it accessible to readers in the English-speaking world. It will be understood that there are certain difficulties involved in executing a task of this kind. Many technical terms are employed which it is not at all easy to reproduce exactly in another language. Then, too, the author has not confined himself to a given translation of the Bible in his quotations from the Pauline epistles; and had he done so it would have been of course in the Dutch version. I can only say that I have done my best to utilize standard English terminology so as to make the text itself and the footnotes self-explanatory. In only two or three instances did I add a word of elucidation, where it seemed particularly necessary to do so. In the matter of Bible versions, I have sometimes used one, then another of the existing English translations, and sometimes followed none of them, giving instead an English rendering of Professor Ridderbos's own translation, when it appeared imperative to seek to preserve the precise nuance he was attempting to bring out.

I must here express my gratitude to three persons who have been particularly helpful to me in the course of the work. Dr. Richard B. Gaffin, Jr., of Westminster Theological Seminary, has been unwearying in his assistance, and even went to the length of reading through the whole typescript before the final revision, offering innumerable suggestions for improvement. I am likewise indebted to the Rev. Marvin D. Hoff, of Ridgewood, New Jersey, who generously offered his own comments and suggestions. My warm thanks also to Miss Ann Mims, of Kingstree, South Carolina, who typed the final draft of the translation.

— John Richard de Witt

Contents

Abbreviations

ET   English Translation
NICNT   *New International Commentary on the New Testament*
NTD   *Das Neue Testament Deutsch*
NTS   *New Testament Studies*
PRE   *Realencyclopädie für protestantische Theologie und Kirche*
RGG   *Religion in Geschichte und Gegenwart*
TDNT   *Theological Dictionary of the New Testament*
TLZ   *Theologische Literaturzeitung*
TZ   *Theologische Zeitschrift*
ZNW   *Zeitschrift für die neutestamentliche Wissenschaft*
ZST   *Zeitschrift für systematische Theologie*
ZTK   *Zeitschrift für Theologie und Kirche*

COMMENTARIES FREQUENTLY CITED

Althaus, *Rom.* — P. Althaus, *Der Brief an die Römer* (Das Neue Testament Deutsch, 6), 6th ed., 1949.

Dibelius, *Th.* — M. Dibelius, *An die Thessalonicher* (Handbuch zum Neuen Testament), 3rd ed., 1937.

Dibelius, *Col.* — M. Dibelius (rev. Greeven), *An die Kolosser, Epheser, An Philemon* (Handbuch zum Neuen Testament, 12), 3rd ed., 1953.

Greijdanus, *Rom.* — S. Greijdanus, *De Brief van den apostel Paulus aan de Gemeente te Rome*, I, 1933; II, 1933.

Grosheide, *1 Cor.* — F. W. Grosheide, *De eerste brief van den apostel Paulus aan de kerk te Korinthe* (Commentaar op het Nieuwe Testament), 2nd ed., 1957.

Lietzmann, *Cor.*, or Lietzmann-Kümmel, *Cor.* — H. Lietzmann (rev. W. G. Kümmel), *An die Korinther* (Handbuch zum Neuen Testament, 9), 4th ed., 1949.

Lietzmann, *Rom.* — H. Lietzmann, *An die Römer* (Handbuch zum Neuen Testament, 8), 4th ed., 1933.

Michel, *Rom.* — O. Michel, *Der Brief an die Römer* (Kritisch-exegetischer Kommentar über das Neue Testament, 4), 1955.

Oepke, *Gal.* — A. Oepke, *Der Brief des Paulus an die Galater* (Theologischer Handkommentar zum Neuen Testament, 9), 1937.

Ridderbos, *Col.* — H. N. Ridderbos, *Aan de Kolossenzen* (Commentaar op het Nieuwe Testament), 1960.

Ridderbos, *Rom.* — H. N. Ridderbos, *Aan de Romeinen* (Commentaar op het Nieuwe Testament), 1959.

Rigaux, *Th.* — B. Rigaux, *Saint Paul: les épitres aux Thessaloniciens* (Études bibliques), 1956.

Schlier, *Gal.* — H. Schlier, *Der Brief an die Galater* (Kritisch-exegetischer Kommentar über das Neue Testament, 7), 10th ed., 1949.

Wendland, *Cor.* — H. D. Wendland, *Die Briefe an die Korinther* (Das Neue Testament Deutsch, 7), 5th ed., 1948.

PAUL

An Outline of His Theology

I
MAIN LINES IN THE HISTORY OF PAULINE INTERPRETATION

SECTION 1. INTRODUCTION

It is not surprising that with respect to so profound and complicated a phenomenon as the manner in which the Apostle Paul has given form and expression to the gospel of Jesus Christ, a great variety of conceptions is to be traced in the history of Pauline investigation. Although this history demands a study in itself,[1] and to treat it at all exhaustively would take us far beyond the proportions of an introductory chapter, it is nevertheless profitable and necessary to acquaint oneself with the main lines along which this investigation has moved, particularly in the last hundred years. Our concern in this connection is above all to gain an insight into the fundamental structure of Paul's preaching and doctrine or, in other words, where the entrance is to be sought into the imposing edifice of Paul's theology. It is clear that there are all sorts of doors by which one can enter. But which is the main entrance that governs the whole building? That question has been answered very differently, particularly in the last hundred years of the inquiry. And this difference has in the nature of the case been bound up with the views scholars have held of the architectonic structure and arrangement of the building as a whole.

The theology of the Reformation, broadly speaking, has long found this entrance in Paul's preaching of justification by faith. In the great struggle with Roman Catholic legalism and mysticism the forensic statements in the epistles to the Romans and the Galatians were of fundamental significance. The result was that the Reformation view of the epistles of Paul came to be determined primarily by this doctrine of justification. This is especially apparent in Luther. For him, that which "preaches and inculcates Christ" (*Preface to James and Jude*), in

---

1. See, e.g., A. Schweitzer, *Paul and His Interpreters*, ET 1912; P. Feine, *Der Apostel Paulus*, 1927, pp. 158ff.; R. Bultmann, "Zur Geschichte der Paulus-Forschung," *Theol. Rundschau*, New Series, 1929, pp. 26-59; by the same writer, "Neueste Paulus-Forschung," *Theol. Rundschau*, New Series, 1934, pp. 229-246; 1936, pp. 1-22; A. M. Denis, "Saint Paul dans la Littérature récente," in *Ephemerides Theologicae Lovanienses*, 1950, pp. 383-408; my *Paul and Jesus*, 1952, ET 1957, pp. 3-20; W. G. Kümmel, *The New Testament: The History of the Investigation of Its Problems*, ET 1972; G. Delling, "Zum neueren Paulusverständnis," in *Novum Testamentum*, 1960, pp. 95-121; B. Rigaux, "L'interprétation du paulinisme dans l'exégèse récente," and the surveys mentioned there, in *Littérature et Théologie Pauliniennes (Recherches Bibliques*, V), 1960; and by the same writer, *The Letters of St. Paul: Modern Studies*, ET 1968; E. E. Ellis, *Paul and His Recent Interpreters*, 1961. For the ancient church see E. Aleith, *Paulusverständnis in der alten Kirche*, 1937; K. H. Schelkle, *Paulus. Lehre der Väter. Die altkirchliche Auslegung von Römer 1-11*, 2nd ed., 1959.

the sense of Paul's doctrine of justification by faith, was the only principle and criterion for the whole New Testament doctrine of salvation,
the canon within the canon, as appears, for example, from Luther's
critique of the Epistle of James. Later Lutheran theology continued to
exhibit traces of this point of departure in the Pauline doctrine of
justification. It has not infrequently gone further still and projected
Luther's struggle to arrive at assurance of faith back into Paul's conversion on the road to Damascus, and in this respect has not only understood Luther *sub specie Pauli,* but also indeed Paul *sub specie Lutheri.*[2]

In the theology emanating from Calvin these matters lie from
the very beginning in decidedly better balance. For Calvin Paul's doctrine of justification by faith did not become a *principium canonicitatis.*
Nevertheless, in opposition to Rome the Pauline doctrine of justification
in the tradition originating with Calvin, too, acquired a dominant
significance as the key to understanding the whole gospel.[3] The entire
Reformed concept of faith, which bears Calvin's stamp, also testifies to
the same effect. The gospel of justification by faith alone without the
works of the law appeared anew to be the only and powerful means to
liberate the burdened conscience and to replace the spirit of legalistic
servitude with the certainty of reconciliation and of the adoption as
children of God. No wonder, then, that because of this all-controlling
antithesis, for the Reformation consciousness of faith Paul was above
everything else the preacher of justification, and all his theology came
to be regarded from this point of view.

In the degree to which the force of the original Reformation idea
slackened, change came about with respect to it in the traditions emanating both from Calvin and from Luther. Questions about the order
of salvation, having reference to the personal appropriation of redemption *(ordo salutis),* came increasingly to receive attention in preference
to questions about the history of salvation *(historia salutis).* While in
Luther and Calvin all the emphasis fell on the redemptive event that
took place with Christ's death and resurrection,[4] later under the influence of pietism, mysticism, and moralism, the emphasis shifted to the
process of individual appropriation of the salvation given in Christ and
to its mystical and moral effect in the life of believers. Accordingly, in
the history of the interpretation of the epistles of Paul the center of
gravity shifted more and more from the forensic to the pneumatic and
ethical aspects of his preaching, and there arose an entirely different
conception of the structures that lay at the foundation of this preaching.

This shift acquires scholarly significance and force, however, only
in the theology deriving from the Enlightenment, without which the
whole history of the *Paulusforschung* during the nineteenth and twentieth centuries is inconceivable. On the one hand, it initiated historical-
critical exegesis and made a powerful contribution to a better distin-

---

2. Cf., e.g., O. Kietzig, *Die Bekehrung des Paulus,* 1932, pp. 51-72; E. Pfaff,
Die Bekehrung des hl. Paulus in der Exegese des 20. Jhrh., 1942.
3. Cf. G. C. Berkouwer, *Faith and Justification,* ET 1954, pp. 72ff.
4. For Luther see also J. T. Bakker, *Eschatologische Prediking bij Luther,* 1964.

guishing and understanding of the great theological motifs of Paul's preaching in their original, historical significance. On the other hand, the extent to which this so-called free and critical investigation into Paul's preaching has again and again come to be determined by the religious and philosophical premises of the spirit of the time, and continues to be so determined to the present day, is apparent in a very striking (and, we may certainly say, shameful) manner from a survey of this newer interpretation of Paul. This comes to our attention with particular clarity when we observe a number of the pictures of Paul that have played a very prominent part in the scientific investigation of the last hundred years: the Hegelian Paul of the Tübingen school, the liberal Paul of liberal theology, the mystical Paul of the history of religions school, and the "existentialist" Paul now presented with great ability and acumen by the school of Bultmann. It is not difficult to see in this succession of interpretations the reflex of a theological-philosophical development such as may be pointed out in the past hundred years.

Now it would be one-sided and unfair to choose to consider and judge the history of the investigation exclusively from the viewpoint of changing philosophical and theological conceptions. Calling attention to this history would then have only a negative significance. It does not, however, in any way have only this negative significance, as may appear from what follows. For it is not only evident from this history how much the investigation of so tremendous and many-sided a phenomenon as that of the preaching of Paul is threatened by the influence of the constantly changing spirit of the time; there is in it also the proof that the Word of God which sounds through that preaching is not bound, but, both in spite of and with the help of the changing results of human investigation, again and again maintains itself and commands reverence in the unmistakableness of its purpose.

Since Albert Schweitzer wrote his *Geschichte der Paulinischen Forschung* in 1911, the fascinating and extremely instructive picture of the development of the inquiry into the general purport of Paul's preaching has been described time and again, and it may be regarded as superfluous, at least as far as the period that extends from c. 1840 to 1940 is concerned, to repeat this in every detail. Nevertheless, a short sketch of the history as background to that which will concern us constantly in the following chapters is indispensable. In the main we have to do here with four successive basic conceptions, namely, that of the Tübingen school, the liberal, the history of religions, and the eschatological interpretations. To be sure, these exist in pure form only partially or not at all. Particularly the second and the third, and the third and the fourth, exhibit all kinds of connections and hybrids. Even so the basic types are clearly distinguishable, and a short delineation of these four main streams can be serviceable the better to catch sight both of the problems involved in the matter of the general character of Paul's preaching (the "main entrance") and of the background of the investigation of the present day.

SECTION 2. F. C. BAUR (THE TÜBINGEN SCHOOL)

The struggle concerning the significance of the Apostle Paul in the history of the New Testament revelation began in recent times with the works of F. C. Baur, the father of the so-called Tübingen school (d. 1860).[5] Baur attempted to interpret the history of Christianity according to the philosophical tenets of Hegel. Also guided by them he sought the center of Paul's preaching, not in Christology, but in the Pauline conception of the Spirit and the antithetical motif of Spirit and flesh bound up with it. Baur takes this in the Hegelian sense as the infinite and absolute in opposition to the finite (the flesh). In the spirit man has a share in the Spirit of God himself, by which he is freed from the finite and relative and attains absolute freedom. In this idealistic scheme Christianity for Baur is the absolute religion and Paul is the one in whose doctrine of freedom and reconciliation the absolute consciousness of the unity of man with God in the Spirit has been embodied.

According to Baur this consciousness in Paul developed in antithesis with the primitive Christianity that was still bound to the law and to particularistic Judaism. In this conflict, which was resolved in later synthetic Catholicism under the pressure of rising Gnosticism, Paul became the champion of the universalistic Christian faith detached from the law. In the later synthesis this universalism, then bound up with the ecclesiastical hierarchical idea, retained the mastery.

Historically considered, both lines can be traced to the appearance of Jesus, in which according to Baur the universal, generally human and moral and therefore absolute makes itself known, as well as the particularistic, namely, in his assessment of Israel as the people of God and of his own person as the Messiah. Nevertheless, Baur interprets Paul, not out of his following of the historical Jesus, of whom after all Paul seldom speaks in his epistles, but out of the miracle of his conversion when God revealed his Son in him, that is, by confronting him with the tremendous fact of Jesus' death. It was in that experience surely that the idea of absolute truth and freedom stripped of all national and legalistic ties entered his mind, and he came to the development of the ideas that are characteristic of him and henceforth also determinative for the whole of his view of the person of Christ. On this account Paul does not need any historic argumentation for his doctrine. "Why should he ask whether what he is teaching agrees with the original teaching of Jesus . . . when in the Christ who lives and works in him he hears the voice of the Lord himself? Why should he draw from the past what the Christ who is present in him has made to be the direct utterance of his own consciousness?"[5a]

---

5. The principal writings of Baur, in which he sets forth his ideas about Paul's teaching, are: *Paul, the Apostle of Jesus Christ*, ET 1876; *The Church History of the First Three Centuries*, ET 1878; *Vorlesungen über Neutestamentliche Theologie*, 1864. On Baur's significance and his interpretation of Paul, in addition to the literature cited above (p. 13), see the full discussion by H. Schmidt (J. Hausleiter), *PRE*, II, 3rd ed., 1897, pp. 467-483, *s.v.* Baur; M. Tetz in *RGG*, I, 3rd ed., 1957, cols. 935ff., and the monographs listed there; and K. Barth, *Protestant Theology in the Nineteenth Century*, ET 1972, pp. 499-507.

5a. Baur, *The Church History of the First Three Centuries*, p. 50.

This reconstruction of the origin of Christianity functions at the same time for Baur as the criterion for the genuineness of Paul's epistles, and in general for the dating of the New Testament writings. Baur thinks only the four principal epistles (Romans, Galatians, 1 and 2 Corinthians) can be accepted as genuine, because in them the antithetic motif is still visible in all its sharpness. The others he considers as already dominated by a unionistic tendency and therefore of a later date.

Baur's conception is entirely governed by the Hegelian view of history and the idea of Spirit. This *pneuma*-idea is not, however, Pauline. Also, by his exclusively antithetic interpretation of Paul's doctrine, Baur has not only barred his own way to arriving at a correct appreciation of the picture of original Christianity drawn for us in the Acts of the Apostles, but also to an understanding of the full significance of Paul in the history of New Testament revelation. This led to a massive amputation of the *corpus Paulinum,* for which (after the radical consequences of Baur's conception were drawn by the Dutchmen Pierson, van Manen, and Loman, and the Swiss Steck, who finally rejected the genuineness of all the Pauline epistles) no agreement could be found at a later time even in the most advanced historical criticism. Nevertheless, Baur's critical and idealistic-universalistic conceptions of original Christianity have continued to exercise great influence, and the distance he created between Paul's doctrine and that of the other apostles who associated themselves with Jesus has continued to be one of the chief motifs of the later inquiry. The formulations, the manner in which he stated the problems with respect to the place of Paul in the New Testament and his relationship to Jesus and original Christianity, have been of incalculable influence, even though the total construction of Baur has been accepted in unaltered form only by a few even in the so-called Tübingen school (e.g., by Schwegler).

SECTION 3. THE LIBERAL INTERPRETATION AND ITS DECLINE

After Baur another explanation of the theological significance of Paul's preaching of the gospel found acceptance, which likewise took its point of departure from what Paul had to say about the Spirit, but which attempted to interpret this from Greek anthropology. Among others Holsten, Lüdemann, Pfleiderer, and H. J. Holtzmann are to be mentioned as the most prominent representatives of this period.[6]

While Reformation theology viewed justification by faith as the center of Paul's doctrine and associated sanctification, the struggle between flesh and spirit, and the like very closely with it, in this period scholars proceeded to distinguish beside the juridical-forensic "line," which they explained from Judaism, an ethical (or mystical-ethical)

---

6. K. Holsten, *Das Evangelium des Paulus,* I, 1880; II, 1898; H. Lüdemann, *Die Anthropologie des Apostels Paulus,* 1872; O. Pfleiderer, *Paulinism,* ET 1891; *Primitive Christianity,* ET 1906-1911; H. J. Holtzmann, *Lehrbuch der neutestamentlichen Theologie,* 1897, 2nd ed., 1911.

line, which was said to find its expression in the contrast of flesh and
spirit and to be oriented, not to Judaism, but to Greek-Hellenistic
thinking. Thus "spirit" is no longer taken here as the antithesis of the
finite and the human (as with Baur), but as the antipode of the sensual.
"Spirit" and "flesh" is an antithesis that is actualized in man himself:
the spirit as the leading rational principle in man must gain the victory
over the lower sensual nature *(sarx)* and hold it in subjection. This
Greek idea is supposed to appear in a Christianized form in Paul and
to constitute in many respects that which is distinctive in his proclamation of the gospel, whereby at one time the emphasis is placed on the
ethical, at another on the mystical significance of the antithesis of flesh
and spirit. It is in this sense accordingly that all that Paul writes about
believers as being "with Christ" and "in Christ" is also understood.
This communion is thought of as an ethically oriented mysticism, not
as an objective inclusion of believers in Christ, but as a spiritual and
mystical connection, out of which then, understood in a general religious
sense, a life of love and spiritual freedom would flourish.

     These ideas place us in the heyday of the so-called liberal the-
ology. The ethical view men had of Jesus' preaching is also dominant
in their assessment of Paul's theology. A fundamental contrast between
Jesus and Paul is not made as yet, inasmuch as scholars attempt to
reduce Paul's proclamation, too, to a rationalistic-idealistic morality.
It is true indeed that other tendencies are discovered in Paul, for example, his eschatological, demonological, and angelological pronouncements. These are regarded, however, as the contemporary framework of
Paul's real teaching, just as Jesus' preaching of the kingdom of God
was also interpreted. To be sure, it is assumed that Paul's conversion
played a great part in the development of these ideas.[7] In this way he
came to be entirely detached from the Jewish scheme of thought, and
there came into him the possibility of an entirely new attitude toward
life in which then, as has been said, Greek thought was of great
influence.

     Yet the liberal school cannot deny that, alongside this ethical-
mystical religiosity in Paul, other motifs occupy an important place, in
particular the juridical doctrine of justification, which Paul bases on
faith in the death and resurrection of Christ. Although liberal theology
attempts to hide the significance of these redemptive facts in Paul behind the moral-rational conception of religion (i.a., by explaining
Paul's doctrine of justification from tradition and polemic), it nevertheless cannot ignore the place all this occupies in Paul's epistles. It is

---

7. Holsten especially, in a rationalizing and psychologizing manner, related
the genesis of the Pauline gospel to Paul's conversion (*Das Christusvision des Paulus
und die Genesis des paulinischen Evangeliums,* 1861 and 1868). In Michel's words,
"He began precisely at the point where Baur did not draw the consequences of the
modern view of the world. He contended against any supernatural explanation of
the Damascus experience and of the development of Pauline Christology ... and sought
[in Paul's own spiritual individuality and in the Christ-worship of the primitive
church] sure foundations on which he could construe Paul's experience of Christ
as a necessary outgrowth" ("Die Entstehung der paulinischen Christologie," *ZNW,*
1929, pp. 324, 325).

now supposed that no consistent theological thinking was present in Paul; that his religious ideas at any rate do not receive adequate expression in his theology; that for him Jewish and Greek elements remained in an internal discord. While a writer like Lüdemann regards the contrast between spirit and flesh taken in a Greek sense as dominant in Paul, Pfleiderer, for example, comes to the conclusion that in Paul's mind two kinds of representation stood unreconciled next to each other (the juridical and the ethical), and that he often leaped from the one to the other without sensing the contradiction.

The zenith and at the same time the terminal point of this interpretation of Paul is found in the grand master of liberal theology, H. J. Holtzmann. For Holtzmann the event at Damascus is of fundamental significance for understanding Paul's theological position. He interprets that event as the first subjective experience of what Paul will shortly proclaim as his objective doctrine of salvation.[8] Even before the experience at Damascus Paul is said to have become an "ethical bankrupt" (which is then supposed to be described in Rom. 7) and to have received the correct light concerning this condition through his vision of the exalted Christ. He then discovered another way of salvation than that of the law, the haughty Pharisee in him was conquered, the proud particularism in him shattered, he came to grasp what it means "to die and rise with Christ," new powers and tasks came flooding in upon him. What in his preaching Paul afterwards teaches on this matter would thus be in the deepest sense an objectivizing and generalizing of his inner and personal experience.[9]

Holtzmann assumes, moreover, that in the shaping of these experiences and ideas Paul exhibits strong Greek influences. This is so, for example, in the metaphysical dimensions of his Christology.[10] These are to be explained from a Greek-Alexandrian influence, particularly the speculations of Philo; likewise the contrast of spirit and flesh is typically Greek,[11] and one must relate his doctrine of the sacraments to the Greek teaching of the mysteries. Yet Holtzmann, too, cannot deny that many Jewish ideas and influences continue to be at work in Paul. In the remarkable conjunction of the Greek and the Jewish, whereby antinomies are often to be encountered, Holtzmann sees that which is in many respects distinctive of Paul's theology.[12] Alongside the ethical stands the juridical, alongside the idealistic the realistic conception of man, alongside the Greek idea of the soul detaching itself from the body the realistic Jewish eschatology. Though all this may in itself

---

8. *Lehrbuch der neutestamentlichen Theologie*, II, 1911, p. 238: "The whole of St. Paul's 'doctrine' will only be intelligible and transparent from the point of view that it is the generalization of what its author had gone through in his own person and what he therefore enjoins on all who follow the same path, as something they should share. It simply means the explication of the content of Paul's conversion, the systematization of the Christophany" (tr. from Ridderbos, *Paul and Jesus*, p. 133, n. 13).

9. At length, *ibid.*, pp. 256, 257.

10. *Ibid.*, pp. 73ff.

11. *Ibid.*, pp. 21ff.

12. *Ibid.*, pp. 238, 239.

yield a combination in many respects heterogeneous and a theology full of internal contradictions, behind it all stands the great religious personality of Paul, and his deep experience on the road to Damascus, by which everything is supported.[13]

Holtzmann's conception is thus an extending of the lines drawn by Holsten, Lüdemann, and Pfleiderer. The vision at Damascus, the Greek influence, and, not to be forgotten, their own religious-ethical view of Christianity form for these authors the constituent elements in their interpretation of Paul. They are not able to achieve a unity. Everything, however, is directed toward an effort to reduce Paul's theology and religion to a general, ethical-rational religiosity not dependent on redemptive facts.[14] In Jesus this piety is said to exhibit its noblest appearance and flowering. Paul ranks behind Jesus in this respect because with him all manner of juridical and metaphysical speculations play a greater role. Fundamentally, however, the same thing lives in Paul as in Jesus,[15] and it was he who first came to the Christian world of ideas with Hellenistic forms of thought and made the transition from the Semitic to the Greek and by this avenue also to the modern world.[16]

After Holtzmann this liberal picture of Paul was not able to maintain itself for long. Investigation began more and more to grasp the fact that it was not possible, for example, to spiritualize in the manner of Holtzmann the so-called metaphysical Christology, the significance of the redemptive facts, the juridical doctrine of satisfaction, and eschatology, or to consider them as a "theological" element foreign to Paul's real religion. The contrast in Paul between spirit and flesh understood by Holtzmann and his predecessors in the light of dualistic Greek thinking was also subjected to serious criticism, by Gunkel, among others, who considered the Pauline pneuma-concept to be not of Greek but rather of Jewish origin and in consequence rejected the rational-ethical character of the flesh and spirit antithesis.[17] Even so early a writer as R. Kabisch had already directed attention to eschatology as the dominating factor in the Pauline theology and in this way pointed to Jewish theology, especially to late Jewish apocalyptic, as the origin of the so-called Pauline doctrinal system.[18] Further, more than had been the case with Holtzmann, the emphasis came gradually to be placed on the significance of the sacraments in Paul's teaching, to which, in contrast to the spiritualizing conceptions of Holtzmann, a realistic naturhaft significance was ascribed, and it was thought possible to explain them from the eastern mystery religions. The result of this increasingly accepted history of religions method of interpretation was that scholars came to reject the ethical-idealistic interpretation of liberal

---

13. *Ibid.*, pp. 255-262.
14. *Ibid.*, pp. 257ff.
15. *Ibid.*, pp. 235ff.
16. *Ibid.*, p. 243.
17. H. Gunkel, *Die Wirkungen des heiligen Geistes nach der populären Anschauung der apostolischen Zeit und nach der Lehre des Apostels Paulus,* 1888.
18. R. Kabisch, *Die Eschatologie des Paulus in ihren Zusammenhängen mit dem Gesamtbegriff des Paulinismus,* 1893.

theology as completely inadequate and to place the emphasis on the "alien" character of Paul's theology, on precisely that which is not assimilable for modern man. Along with that emphasis, however, the possibility fell away of preserving the unity between the picture of Jesus still accepted by many as the teacher of the fatherhood of God and lofty morality and the supernatural Christ as Paul preached him in his epistles. The problem of the Jesus-Paul relationship becomes acute for modern theology when it comes to recognize that one cannot understand the Pauline Christology psychologically (as the objectivizing of Paul's religious experience at Damascus) and in a spiritualized manner, as did Holtzmann, nor separate it from Paul's "religion" as a "theological" construction, but that it ought to be interpreted precisely as the great central datum of Paul's theology as well as of his religion.

Nowhere does this disintegration of the liberal picture of Paul and along with it of the connection of Jesus and Paul come to light more clearly than in the very radical and to the present day very in-fluential exposition of Wrede.[19]

Wrede will have nothing to do with a separation between Paul's "religion" and his "theology" (e.g., as in Holtzmann). Paul's "theology" is the adequate expression of his religion.[20] And this theology is funda-mentally Christology. The whole Pauline doctrine is a doctrine of Christ and his work; that is its essence. That which is peculiar to Paul and also new in him is this, that he made redemptive facts — the in-carnation, the death, and the resurrection of Christ — the foundation of religion. Redemptive history is the backbone of Pauline Christianity.[21]

When one inquires into the origin of this doctrine, then neither Paul's conversion experience, nor the impression of the personality of Jesus (whom Paul probably never knew), nor Paul's own theological construction can constitute the explanation for it. One can only unravel the problem as to how it was possible that within one human lifetime the figure of Jesus was so completely changed into the Pauline Christ if one supposes that Paul the Pharisee was already in possession of "a number of ready-made conceptions of a divine being," which he then transferred to the historical Jesus under the impact of his conversion.[22] His christological preaching thus has little to do with the historical Jesus, but is to be understood from the mythological redeemer- and redemption-speculations of his time, which he applied to Jesus of Nazareth without being conscious of this radical transformation.[23]

Wrede's criticism has had such an influence because he was able to give a much more self-contained picture of Paul's preaching than that of liberal theology. He designated Paul's Christology of redemptive facts as the essence of his preaching, and broke the bond between Paul's preaching and the liberal picture of Jesus. This criticism had to prevail because it did much greater justice to Paul's preaching — if only

19. W. Wrede, *Paul*, ET 1908. On Wrede in detail see my *Paul and Jesus*, pp. 3ff.

20. Wrede, *Paul*, p. 48.

21. *Ibid.*, pp. 103-104.

22. *Ibid.*, p. 87.

23. *Ibid.*, p. 95.

in an historical-exegetical sense — than did those who viewed as the heart of his preaching not the great Christ-event, but a timeless religious-ethical truth. At the same time, however, the gap between Paul's preaching and the modern-liberal conception of Jesus and his proclamation of the kingdom of God was hereby indicated, a gap that was and is unbridgeable so long as one is able to discover in Jesus of Nazareth only a human figure, no matter what the spiritual height to which he rose.

SECTION 4. THE HISTORY OF RELIGIONS APPROACH

At the end of the last century and the beginning of the present one the *religionsgeschichtliche* interpretation of Paul's epistles and of the Christian kerygma contained in them demanded increasingly greater attention. In contrast with earlier attempts to derive various leading motifs in Paul's preaching from the literature and world view of Greek philosophical thinking (as that had been attempted, for example, with the spirit-flesh antithesis), scholars now turned to the popular religious views and phenomena of the Hellenistic period, in particular to the religious syncretism of that time as this had arisen under the influence of eastern on western religiosity and manifested itself in the mystery religions and cultus. The knowledge of these religious phenomena has greatly increased since the investigations of such noted philologists and historians as Cumont,[24] Rohde, Dieterich,[25] Reitzenstein,[26] *et al.*

In general it may be said of these mystery religions that approximately at the beginning of the Christian era they form a combination of mystical-transcendent eastern thinking and the more concrete immanent religiosity of the West. At a time in which a marked religious lassitude emerges in the West, the eastern ideas of redemption pour in and lay hold of the spirit of the time which is looking for deeper religious satisfaction and deliverance from the transitoriness of time-bound human existence.

All these mystery religions have a so-called cultus-myth, that is to say, a mythological story concerning the deity worshipped in the cultus, whether it be that he dies and comes to life again or that he gains the victory over the powers or gods that fight against him, but always with a tendency toward redemption from the transitory. Already in ancient Greece there were the

---

24. Cumont wrote, i.a., *The Oriental Religions in Roman Paganism*, ET 1911. He himself was very cautious about making Christianity dependent on the heathen cults.

25. Well known, i.a., is his writing *Eine Mithrasliturgie*, 1923, a fragment from the so-called "great Paris magic papyrus," which Dieterich takes for a liturgy used in the Mithras cultus. This has been disputed by others (among them Cumont).

26. Reitzenstein much occupied himself with later gnostic literature (e.g., with the Corpus Hermeticum), from which he then thought himself able to reconstruct earlier syncretistic views and practices already prevalent in Paul's time. Reitzenstein was a great authority on this eastern Gnosticism and by his comparison of gnostic and Pauline texts convinced many of the terminological and conceptual connection between the two. He wrote, i.a., *Poimandres*, 1904; *Die hellenistischen Mysterienreligionen*, 3rd ed., 1927.

Eleusinian mysteries; and the deliverance of Cora, daughter of Demeter, who, brought to Hades by Pluto, was restored to her mother by the intervention of Zeus, was celebrated annually. A vegetation cultus is spoken of here, because the myth represents the dying and rising of nature. Very important at a later time were the Serapis mysteries stemming from Egypt, in which the worship of Isis and Osiris was fused. The original myth speaks of the union of Osiris (the masculine) and Isis (the feminine) in which the victory over death is symbolized. Osiris is robbed of life by an opponent hostile toward him (his brother Seth), and when found by the grieving Isis he is again overpowered by his adversary and hacked in pieces. The scattered limbs are once more sought out by Isis. They come to new life, whereupon the union of Osiris and Isis and the dominion of Osiris follow. From this, then, the general idea of victory over death and the hostile powers and belief in immortality are derived. Syria, too, contributed its share to the mystery religions in the Adonis cultus (the Baal of Byblos). Adonis also makes his appearance as the god who dies and rises again, the savior from death. The cultic myth speaks of the mortal wound that is inflicted by a wild boar on Adonis while hunting. From his blood roses (or anemones) begin to flourish. The whole of nature participates in the mourning. The festival of the dying and coming to life again of Adonis is celebrated annually. Very well known, too, is the cultus of the Phrygian god Attis, closely related to the worship of the Thracian Dionysus-Sabazius. In the Phrygian cult the mother goddess Cybele, held in high respect in Rome, appears next to Attis. Here again the myth speaks of the death of the god Attis and his subsequent resurrection. The festival is attended with wild orgies, emasculations, etc. Finally the cult of Mithras, very important especially at a later time, deserves to be mentioned. It is of Persian origin and was imported into the West particularly by Roman soldiers. In accordance with its derivation the Mithraic religion is dualistic in character. Its fundamental motif consists in the struggle between the world of good and that of evil, in which Mithras achieves the victory.

These different cultic myths, which came to a common blending in all sorts of ways, are now in one way or another transferred to the initiates in the cultus belonging to these mystery religions. In this cultus they receive a share in the victory, resurrection, and immortality of the deity worshipped by them. In the cultus, in which one can participate in various ways according to the depth to which he has been initiated, one comes to deification. This takes place in the manner of mysticism and of the magical-materialistic idea "sacrament," which works *ex opere operato,* consisting in the immersion in or the sprinkling with water or blood, the putting on of holy clothing, and the eating of certain foods. The highest objective is to arrive at a beholding of the deity, transcending all sense experience. Naturally, in the various mystery religions all kinds of differences exist at this point, too. In some it is a wild and ecstatic sort of thing, as, for example, in the cults of Attis and Dionysus; others exhibit a much more sober and subdued type, as, for example, the cult of Mithras. In them all, however, lives the consciousness that those who are admitted to the secrets of the cult thereby receive immortality. In the mystery religions a fixed doctrinal system is wanting. The myths themselves are recited in all sorts of ways. To be sure, one needs *gnosis* in order to reach redemption, but this is not to be understood as a clearly defined quantum of religious or theological tenets, but rather as the initiation into certain ceremonies described with secret language, the knowledge of which must be kept in strict secrecy.

It is these mystery religions, the "sacramental" acts that occur in them, and especially the mystical approach to the deity centrally placed in them, with which some have related that which is distinctive in Paul's preaching and "religion" and have wanted in part to interpret it.[27] For a time the relationship was sought above all in the former, namely, the sacramental acts in the mystery religions on the one hand, and on the other the communion of baptism and the Lord's Supper, connected by Paul with Christ's death and resurrection.[28] Further consideration has made it increasingly apparent, however, that this way was impassable. So far as the sacred meals are concerned, it has become evident that as soon as one goes beyond the general phenomenon of a sacral eating and drinking, the parallel or analogy with the Lord's Supper as described by Paul becomes dubious or even ceases altogether.[29] Some have thought to find at least in baptism a fixed point of agreement, inasmuch as Paul related baptism to Christ's death (burial) and resurrection (Rom. 6:3, 4; Col. 2:11ff.); and this "baptismal death," it is said, could not have developed from the Jewish symbolism of purification and therefore must be viewed as a "Hellenistic commodity."[30] But it has come to be seen with increasing clarity that (a) nowhere in the mystery religions is such a symbolism of death present in the "baptismal" ritual,[31] and that (b) in Romans 6 and Colossians 2 Paul does not portray baptism itself as a symbolic or sacramental representation of the going down into death (the so-called "death by drowning," about which Lietzmann speaks) and rising up again to life.[32] Thus in the area of the sacraments every deeper link with the ritual acts in the mystery religions has become illusory.

It is often alleged, to be sure, that a realistic, *naturhaft* conception of the sacraments is to be found in Paul, and that he must have borrowed this from the mystery religions. Specifically, it has been supposed that evidence could be found for this in 1 Corinthians 15:29 (baptism for the dead). It is noteworthy, however, that in the heathen religions there is nowhere mention of

---

27. See also G. W. Ittel, *Urchristentum und Fremdreligionen im Urteil der Religionsgeschichtlichen Schule,* 1946.

28. Cf., e.g., W. Heitmüller, *Taufe und Abendmahl bei Paulus,* 1903. One may find a valuable summary of the data to which appeal is made, e.g., in J. Hoek, *De Sacramenten bij Paulus en de hellenistische mysterie-religies,* 1925, p. 95; see also Lietzmann, *Cor.,* pp. 44ff., and now especially G. Wagner, *Pauline Baptism and the Pagan Mysteries,* ET 1967.

29. Against Lietzmann's view that the idea is present both in the mystery religions and in Paul that the deity (in Paul: Christ) is not only the dispenser but also the object of the sacral eating and drinking, see, e.g., Kümmel in the "Anhang" to Lietzmann, *Cor.,* pp. 181ff.

30. Thus Lietzmann still (*Rom.,* pp. 67, 68); cf. also R. Bultmann, *Theology of the New Testament,* ET 1959, pp. 135ff., 140, 144ff.

31. In the Isis mysteries, to which appeal is made indeed, sprinkling with water has only a preparatory character. It does not accomplish the real initiation (*myēsis*), much less the beholding (*epopteia*) that follows it, but only fulfills the function of a preparatory purification (*katharsis*). There is nowhere any question of a connection between baptism and a "dying and coming to life of the deity" (cf. Hoek, *De Sacramenten,* pp. 117ff.). For this "dying and rising of the deity" in the cultus-mysteries and the so-called connection with the Pauline dying and rising with Christ see my *Paul and Jesus,* pp. 10ff.

32. See my *Rom.,* pp. 132-134; further below, pp. 402ff.

a baptizing in behalf of the dead, so far as we know. There is mention in an Egyptian papyrus of the baptism of a dead person,[33] which is represented as an act to be performed by the deity, but this is something other than in behalf of or in place of the deceased.[34] For the rest, it does not follow from 1 Corinthians 15:29 as a whole that Paul starts from a magical conception of the sacrament. For the passage is very obscure and has long been understood in the most widely varying ways.[35] Perhaps Paul alludes to a practice followed by some Corinthians who had themselves baptized in behalf of the dead. That could then speak of a certain magical notion of baptism. But if it must be so understood, there are numerous arguments that tell against any such conception on the part of Paul himself. It is possible that he could be appealing to a custom among his opponents that he does not himself sanction, but which argues against their denial of a future resurrection. Yet the whole idea of such a vicarious baptism is uncertain.[36] Others interpret this not as a baptism in behalf of, but in the place of the dead. One would then have submitted to baptism not in behalf of, but, by way of a testimony of faith, in the place of (prematurely deceased?) unbaptized believers, in order in this way to bear witness to the faith of these believers in the resurrection.[37] The passage is too obscure, however, and the materials for comparison too inadequate to reach conclusions that are in any degree well founded.

Without doubt the high point of the *religionsgeschichtliche* assessment of Paul's preaching against the background of the mystery religions accordingly lay elsewhere: not in the appeal to Paul's doctrine of the sacraments, but in the appeal to his Christology. Here in particular the grandiose attempt by W. Bousset[38] to explain Paul's preaching of Christ as a mystical reinterpretation of the "eschatological" Christ of the primitive church deserves mention. And here then, by way of the cultus communion of the Hellenistic churches, the influence of the mystery religions is supposed to be perceptible.

This conception of Bousset — which we have described at length elsewhere[39] — represents a noteworthy transition in the history of the investigation into the fundamental structures of Paul's preaching. On the one hand, the history of religions method is here wielded with consummate skill — with an enormous knowledge of the materials of the Hellenistic religions and with great circumspection, in order to throw light on the specific character of the pneumatic *Kyrios* of the Hellenistic church and especially that of Paul. It is true indeed that in the Hellenistic church and in Paul the *Kyrios* with whom one enters into

---

33. Cf. Reitzenstein, *Die hellenistischen Mysterienreligionen*, 3rd ed., pp. 220ff.; J. Leipoldt, *Die Urchristliche Taufe im Lichte der Religionsgeschichte*, 1928, pp. 47ff. See also the materials cited in Lietzmann-Kümmel, *Cor.*, pp. 82, 194, and M. Rissi, *Die Taufe für die Toten*, 1962, pp. 62ff.

34. See Hoek, *De Sacramenten*, pp. 88ff.; Rissi, *Die Taufe*, pp. 62ff.; and G. Wagner, *Pauline Baptism*, pp. 268ff., and the literature referred to there.

35. Cf. Rissi, *Die Taufe*, pp. 10-51.

36. See, e.g., Bachmann's ten arguments against it in *Der erste Brief des Paulus an die Korinther*, 3rd ed., 1921.

37. So Rissi, *Die Taufe*, pp. 85ff.

38. In his book *Kyrios Christos: A History of the Belief in Christ from the Beginnings of Christianity to Irenaeus*, ET 1970; cf. *Jesus der Herr*, 1916.

39. *Paul and Jesus*, pp. 12ff., 80ff.

mystical communion in the cultus takes the place of the Son-of-Man Christology of the Palestinian church that represented Christ above all as the future world judge. This is the fundamental Greek idea of God, which takes the place of the Palestinian-Jewish: the Christology becomes pneumatic and mystical instead of eschatological. In Paul, however, this Christ-mysticism develops into the intensive feeling of a personal belonging to and of a spiritual connection with the exalted *Kyrios*, which for him constitutes the basic fact of the Christian life and the Christian ethic. The *Kyrios* is the Spirit (2 Cor. 3:17), and where the Spirit is there is liberty, and likewise the principle of the Spirit-governed life in Christian love.

On the other hand, Bousset's conception of Paul's Christology, however much the model of a well-balanced application of the history of religions method, is at the same time the typical intellectual product of around the time of the First World War. The rational-ethical Christ figure of liberal theology gave way to a deeper, more sensitive conception of religion; such words as Christ-experience, Christ-mysticism, Christ-communion everywhere made their appearance.[40] It may be posited, moreover, that the history of religions school was the appropriate agency to furnish from the history of religious life and experience the evidence for this deeper element focused more on the divine mystery and the divine hiddenness and to indicate its forms. But it is another question whether Paul, in accordance with Bousset's conception of it, can be summoned as the star witness for this Christ-mysticism.

The day when scholars believed this is long since past. On the basis of historical argumentation and criticism light has not only been cast on the untenableness of the antithesis Bousset supposed himself able to point out between the Messianic-eschatological Christology of the primitive Palestinian church and the worship of the pneumatic *Kyrios*, in which Paul's epistles were said to bear their distinctive Hellenistic mark;[41] but it is also acknowledged, even by those who have otherwise followed in the footsteps of Bousset, that the fundamental structure of Paul's preaching and Christology is other than the mystical and pneumatic sketch of it given by Bousset. Paul's kerygma is not to be reduced to a christological projection of religious feeling. It is rather the explication of the absolutely unique, one-time-only redemptive event that was enacted in Christ's advent, his suffering, death, and resurrection.[42] However much this event finds its outworking and application in the life according to the Spirit, in putting on the new man

40. The widely read book by A. Deissmann, *St. Paul: A Study in Social and Religious History*, ET 1912, is also to be mentioned in this connection.

41. For the older literature see my *Paul and Jesus*, p. 148, n. 3. Furthermore, O. Cullmann, *The Christology of the New Testament*, ET 1959, pp. 205ff.; E. Schweizer, *Erniedrigung und Erhöhung bei Jesus und seinen Nachfolgern*, 1955, pp. 93ff. (cf. ET revised, *Lordship and Discipleship*, 1960, pp. 56ff.).

42. Cf., e.g., R. Bultmann, "The Christology of the New Testament," in *Faith and Understanding*, I, ET 1959, pp. 273ff.; also his "Zur Geschichte der Paulus-Forschung," *Theol. Rundschau*, 1929, pp. 50ff. Otherwise Bultmann, too, is of the opinion that the Christianity represented by Paul is something new over against Palestinian Christianity, belongs in the sphere of the mystery religions and *gnosis*, and as such is characterized by the name *Kyrios*. See the text below.

and standing in the liberty that is not of the law but of the Spirit, the point of departure and the matrix even of the pneumatic character of Paul's preaching is not to be sought in the mystical cultus experiences of contemporary Hellenistic religiosity, but in the historical revelation of Christ in the fullness of time, that is to say, in the Christocentric fulfillment of the redemptive promise given to Israel.

In view of the above it is no wonder that, in order to trace the history of religions backgrounds of Paul's preaching, scholars began to orient themselves on a broader terrain than that of the mystery cults. To be sure, they continued to seek these backgrounds in Hellenistic religiosity, particularly as this was experienced and brought to expression in the mystery religions. But more than in the specifically cultic, they sought the connection between Paul and Hellenism in the general character and attitude toward life of this religiosity. They came more and more to speak of Gnosticism as the common denominator for this world of thought, a name formerly used for a syncretistic heresy in the second century of the Christian era, whose roots came to be sought in a universally dispersed pre-Christian complex of ideas, partly of Greek, partly of eastern origin, and of a distinctly dualistic character.[43] It is supposed to have been the influence of this Gnosticism by which Paul's world of ideas in general and his Christology in particular, both in a positive and in a negative sense, were profoundly conditioned, and in which the explanation is to be sought for those "elements" in his teaching for which no correspondence is to be found in the tradition of the primitive Palestinian church.

The writer who was especially responsible for this turn in the history of religions approach to Paul's preaching was the classical literary scholar R. Reitzenstein. He appealed, at least in the first instance,[44] primarily to the so-called Hermetic literature,[45] a motley mixture of speculative religious non-Christian tracts from the second and third centuries (A.D.) that announce themselves as revelations of Hermes Trismegistos, i.e., of the Egyptian god Thoth. Greek, Egyptian, eastern, and Jewish influences have here come together. Hermes, sometimes also called Poimandres or Asklepios, gives secret revelations that have reference to astrological and magical as well as to religious subjects. The religious ideas are dualistic-gnostic. The soul, imprisoned in matter, ascends once again to God in the way of *gnosis*. Along with this then, according to Reitzenstein, the so-called *Anthropos*-myth makes its appearance, the representation of original man in whom the divine *pneuma* finds its highest manifestation and who once more shows the scattered particles of light the way to God.

According to Reitzenstein a strong immediate influence of this gnostic Hellenism on Paul is to be assumed. The absolute proof for this

---

43. On the various theories concerning the origin of Gnosticism see, e.g., Colpe, *RGG*, 3rd ed., II, 1958, col. 1651.

44. *Poimandres*, 1904.

45. See, e.g., the great work by A. J. Festugière, *La Révélation d'Hermès Trismègiste*, 4 vols., 1945-54, and the introduction included in it; further, G. van Moorsel, *The Mysteries of Hermes Trismegistus* (an Utrecht dissertation), 1955.

he finds in the technical use of all kinds of gnostic words and ideas in Paul, as, for example, *psychikos* and *pneumatikos* (being or not being in possession of *gnosis*), *gnosis* and *agnosia, photizein* and *doxa, morphousthai* and *metamorphousthai, nous,* in the sense of *pneuma,* as the divine effluvium that is conferred on the elect as *charisma*.[46] And Paul is said to have had not only the terminology but also the notions and concepts bound up with it in common with Hellenistic mysticism and Gnosticism. Reitzenstein views Paul not as the first, but as the greatest Gnostic.[47] For this he refers particularly to 1 Corinthians 2, where Paul appeals for his knowledge to the *Pneuma,* the Spirit, who searches even the deep things of God. The psychical man is not in a position to grasp this, nor can he judge the pneumatic man. He is still a man; the pneumatic is that no longer.[48] It is to this *Pneuma,* which finds its highest expression in the beholding of the Risen One, that Paul also appeals for his apostleship and his independence of others, as no longer bound to any tradition (Gal. 1). This also provides the explanation, it is said, for the fact that Paul does not ground his teaching on the deeds and words of the historical Jesus. According to Reitzenstein, Paul thought, not historically, but pneumatically. It was not what would have reached him from the tradition concerning Jesus of Nazareth, but what he had beheld and inwardly experienced as a Gnostic that constituted the source of his Christology.[49]

The sweeping conclusions drawn by Reitzenstein have been rejected. Almost no one believes any longer that Paul was a mystic who, detached from the Christian tradition, gave out his pneumatic speculations for the gospel of Jesus Christ. The deep-lying material differences between the Pauline and gnostic conceptions, notwithstanding terminological similarity, have also been demonstrated from more than one side with a profusion of evidence.[50] Even so, Reitzenstein's fundamental proposition that Paul's world of thought was profoundly conditioned by what is then termed his pre-Christian Gnosticism became the real foundation of the history of religions interpretation of Paul's preaching and doctrine, and has remained so to the present day. And this influence is the more radical according to the extent to which it is the more closely connected with the views propagated by Reitzenstein in his later writings,[51] that Paul's Christology, too, was conditioned in a decisive way by pre-Christian Gnosticism, especially by what is termed the Iranian myth of the redeemed Redeemer.[52] It is in this mythological interpretation of Paul's Christology that the transitions are to be found

---

46. Reitzenstein, *Die hellenistischen Mysterienreligionen,* 2nd ed., 1920, p. 65.
47. *Ibid.,* p. 62.
48. *Ibid.,* p. 52; cf. p. 193.
49. *Ibid.,* p. 226.
50. Cf., e.g., the careful writing by K. Deissner, *Paulus und die Mystik seiner Zeit,* 2nd ed., 1921; for the later period especially the great work of J. Dupont, *Gnosis, La connaissance religieuse dans les Épitres de Saint Paul,* 1949.
51. Above all in *Das iranische Erlösungsmysterium,* 1921.
52. For the whole genesis of this hypothesis see the full and penetrating sketch by C. Colpe, *Die religionsgeschichtliche Schule. Darstellung und Kritik ihres Bildes vom gnostischen Erlösermythus,* 1961, pp. 10-57.

to the presently influential school of Bultmann and the history of religions interpretation of Paul's Christology advocated by it.

Before we attempt to trace this development further,[53] however, we shall have to include in our range of vision the fourth or eschatological method of interpretation of Paul's gospel. For without its radical influence the whole of the subsequent history, even that of the present-day history of religions method of interpretation, is incomprehensible.

SECTION 5. THE ESCHATOLOGICAL INTERPRETATION

Diametrically contrary to the endeavor of the history of religions school, of which he was a decided and formidable opponent, Albert Schweitzer pointed to the basic eschatological motif as the key to the whole of Paul's preaching.

Already in his *Geschichte der Paulinischen Forschung* (English translation, 1912, *Paul and His Interpreters*), which appeared in 1911 as a sequel to his great work on the *Geschichte der Leben-Jesu-Forschung,* Schweitzer had proved himself to be a very consistent and well-equipped adversary of the *religionsgeschichtliche* interpretation of Paul. He did not set forth his ideas in a positive way, however, until the publication in 1930 of his book *Die Mystik des Apostels Paulus* (English translation, 1931, *The Mysticism of Paul the Apostle*). Here he attempted to achieve unity between his consistent-eschatological conception of Jesus' life and preaching and the theology of the Apostle Paul.

According to Schweitzer, the center of Paul's teaching lies in what he describes with the easily misunderstood term, Christ-mysticism. By that he means the way in which the church is involved in the death and resurrection of Christ, being with Christ and in Christ. One must understand this communion, however, not in a Greek-dualistic, but in a Jewish-eschatological sense. Paul's doctrine rests entirely on the eschatological preaching of Jesus concerning the nearness of the kingdom of God. While for Jesus, however, this kingdom was still a matter of the (imminent) future, Paul was faced with a completely new situation. With the death and resurrection of Christ the future continually expected by Jesus but not fulfilled has reached the stage of fulfillment. A radical alteration of the eschatological situation has entered in. The *eschaton* has become present time in the resurrection of Christ. Paul is said now, however, to have been confronted with the question as to how this breakthrough of the *eschaton* was to be related to the unmistakable fact that the resurrection of the dead, to be expected with the consummation, the judgment of the world, and the like, had not yet come to pass. He is supposed now, in order to overcome this discrepancy between the "already" (of Christ's resurrection) and the "not yet" (of the final consummation), to have associated himself with the eschatological "schema" in the apocalypse of Baruch and the fourth book of Ezra and, in divergence from Jesus' expectation, to have conceived of

---

53. Below, pp. 32ff.

the Messianic kingdom as coming before the full revelation of the kingdom of God.[54] In the Messianic kingdom the natural and the super-natural worlds meet one another — telescope, as it were, into each other.[55] The resurrection of Christ signifies the beginning of this over-lap. With Christ, however, the sharers in the Messianic kingdom (the elect church) also participate in his resurrection.[56] The elect have risen with Christ. They are with him sharers in the "mode of being of the resurrection." This "mysticism" is to be taken as realistically as possible. With the resurrection of Christ the resurrection of the elect has already been begun in its entire corporeality. They are no longer natural men, but, as Christ, supernatural beings, although this is not yet manifest.[57] This is also expressed as the "being-in-Christ." This "mysticism" is thus not one of feeling, inner, spiritual, but an "objective mysticism of facts."[58] This union with Christ, sharing in his new corporeality, comes about by baptism. Together with Christ the elect form a "joint personality"[59] of which the *pneuma* is the vital force. Therefore all that they henceforth do, think, experience, will, can be characterized as "in Christ." The primary idea, however, lies in the words "with Christ."

Schweitzer speaks repeatedly in this connection of the *actual*. The mysticism of Paul is not Greek in character, not a symbolically ex-pressed experiencing of reality, but it is realistic, corporeal. It is, how-ever, the new, pneumatic corporeality that is operative here, and it does not make rising with Christ, being in Christ, with all its hidden-ness, an inward, mental occurrence, but a reality into which one is taken up automatically by the sacramental event.[60]

Schweitzer attempts to elucidate all the facets of Paul's teaching from the eschatological Christ-mysticism thought of in this way. Thus it becomes clear that the law no longer has any power over man.[61] The commencement of the new aeon signifies the end of the law. Thus the power of sin is also destroyed. It has place only in the body, in which the elect have died with Christ. As far as justification is con-cerned, Schweitzer speaks here of a "subsidiary crater, which has formed within the rim of the main crater — the mystical doctrine of redemption through the being-in-Christ."[62] Paul no longer has any need for this juridical line. Because with the dying and rising of Christ God has made sin to be destroyed with the flesh, those who have died and risen with Christ are considered before God in fact as sinless beings. The doctrine that God forgives sins on the basis of Christ's expiatory death is the doctrine handed down to Paul. He holds fast to it. The other is more his own, however, and springs from the mysticism of being in Christ. It is also this doctrine alone which establishes the right relation-

---

54. *The Mysticism of Paul the Apostle,* ET 1931, pp. 89ff.
55. *Ibid.,* p. 86; cf. p. 37.
56. *Ibid.,* p. 90.
57. *Ibid.,* pp. 109f.
58. *Ibid.,* p. 100.
59. *Ibid.,* p. 118.
60. *Ibid.,* pp. 117, 227ff.
61. *Ibid.,* pp. 177ff.
62. *Ibid.,* p. 225.

up a clear picture and to reach sweeping conclusions with respect to the manner in which, for example, Paul may be said already to have been dependent on them. This applies particularly to what is termed the gnostic mystery of redemption in the figure of the primal-man redeemer. For many scholars who have occupied themselves with these questions it is regarded as definitely established that wherever in this literature there is mention of such a redeemer, this representation is not antecedent to Christianity, but rather is borrowed from it.[75] Colpe in his extensive discussion of this so-called gnostic redeemer-myth especially stressed the unwarranted generalization in the talk about this myth, as if it were a uniform thing that were to be found ready to hand in all the relevant texts. He demonstrates with great exactitude how complicated and differentiated the whole gnostic idea of redemption is and with how little justice one constructs for himself from it a "model" of a mythical redeemer figure (which then comes to function as "the" gnostic Redeemer) and in this way suggests a general gnostic myth of redemption that has perhaps never existed.[76] And all this becomes still worse when one infers from this a precursor in the older gnostic traditions not known to us in which, it is said, the background of certain Pauline (and other New Testament) redemption and redeemer ideas must be discovered.

As more comes to be known about this *gnosis* from the newly discovered gnostic writings of the early Christian period, the correctness of this criticism is more and more corroborated. It becomes ever more apparent how cautiously one ought to speak of "gnosis," "gnostic myth," etc., as soon as one intends to denote something more than a general dualistic philosophy of life and to arrive at a comparison with that which, for instance, may be said to be characteristic of Paul. Thus van Unnik, for example, on the basis of the examination of newly discovered gnostic texts, writes: "Anyone who has made a study of the speculative passages on Adam in the *Apocryphon of John,* for example, will not so easily get away with explaining Paul's exposition in Rom. 5 and 1 Cor. 15 in terms of similar ideas of a Gnostic type: and anybody who has seen here how the Gnostics handle the concept of the 'Son of Man' will not be inclined to try to shed light on this term in the Gospels by reference to such ideas of 'primeval man.' An understanding of the history and growth of Gnosticism, such as now becomes possible, must make us cautious about drawing so freely on very late Manichaean and Mandaean sources — as has happened often enough — in order to explain something in the New Testament. We may also expect that when these documents have been properly studied, academic myth-making will be a more sober business, and some of the myths will be up for sale."[77]

---

75. Cf., e.g., E. Schweizer, *Erniedrigung und Erhöhung,* pp. 157ff. (cf. *Lordship and Discipleship,* pp. 117ff.); M. Black, "The Pauline Doctrine of the Second Adam," in *The Scottish Journal of Theology,* 1954, p. 177.

76. *Die religionsgeschichtliche Schule,* pp. 203ff.; see also pp. 171ff.

77. W. C. van Unnik, *Newly Discovered Gnostic Writings,* ET 1960, p. 93. See also R. M. Wilson, *The Gnostic Problem,* 1958.

In the light of all the foregoing it is not strange that interest in the Greek-Hellenistic religiosity as background of the Pauline formulation of the gospel has diminished in recent years, and that its place has been taken by a vigorous revival of the study of the Jewish premises of Paul's preaching.[78] All sorts of *a priori* considerations would seem to make this method of approach plausible.[79] Is it not in the nature of things that a writer be judged above all according to the milieu from which he comes and which provides his frame of reference? Must not, then, the Pauline ideas be viewed in the light of the Old Testament and rabbinic Judaism, which are known, rather than in that of the Hellenistic Gnosticism of the second century or later, which is not, or scarcely, known? Paul himself appeals again and again to the Old Testament and to his Jewish origin (Phil. 3:5; 2 Cor. 11:22; cf. Acts 23:6; 26:5). The thesis often advanced that Paul was reared in Tarsus and even in his youth must have been deeply impressed by Hellenistic heathenism has been strongly contested on the basis of a closer examination of Acts 22:3 and been replaced by another, namely, that Paul not only received his Pharisaic training in Jerusalem, but also spent his youth there.[80] This is not, of course, to deny that at a more advanced age Paul will have become thoroughly acquainted with the Hellenistic religions; nor either that, by the frequent use of the Septuagint, he gives evidence of his affinity with the Greek-speaking Jewry in the Diaspora; but there has indeed been a return from seeking the fundamental structures of Paul's preaching and doctrine, as well as that which was distinctive in his world of ideas and mode of expression, elsewhere than in his Jewish origin. Very characteristic of this new view is surely, for example, the very detailed and magnificently constructed book of J. Dupont on *gnosis*.[81] Although this author, too, does not deny that in certain respects Paul draws on the vocabulary of the popular Hellenistic philosophy, he strongly posits on the other hand that what is said to be *gnosis* in Paul is not borrowed from Hellenism, but must be interpreted from the Old Testament. In order to understand Paul, therefore, one must not call in the assistance of the gnostic systems, the mystery religions, or the Hermetic writings, but rather seek in the knowledge of God in the Old Testament the source from which Paul has drawn even for the formulation of his proclamation.

This emphasis on the Jewish character of Paul's preaching and doctrine is then developed further in a great many different ways. While Dupont attempts to appeal especially to the Old Testament, the thesis has been defended, notably by the Jewish scholar H. J. Schoeps, that Paul must be understood entirely as a Hellenistic Jew, and as such

---

78. Against the *religionsgeschichtliche* interpretation see the early work of H. A. A. Kennedy, *St. Paul and the Mystery Religions*, 1913; later, i.a., C. A. A. Scott, *Christianity according to St. Paul*, 1939; now especially G. Wagner, *Pauline Baptism and the Pagan Mysteries*.

79. Cf. E. E. Ellis, *Paul and His Recent Interpreters*, pp. 30, 31; see further his *Paul's Use of the Old Testament*, 2nd ed., 1960, pp. 38ff.

80. W. C. van Unnik, "Tarsus or Jerusalem: the City of Paul's Youth," ET in *Sparsa Collecta*, I, 1973, pp. 259ff.

81. J. Dupont, *Gnosis*.

exhibited a type to be distinguished clearly from the Old Testament and Palestinian Judaism.[82] Others have posited, on the other hand, that Paul's dependence on the literature of the Jewish Diaspora nowhere directly appears and that his writings reflect only so much of it as was proper to Palestinian Judaism.[83] And some have gone so far as to have pointed specifically to Pharisaic rabbinism as the matrix of the Pauline ideas and mode of expression and have wished to deny any dependence on Hellenism.[84]

In the meantime there are also cautious voices that warn that one must not conceive of the Palestinian Judaism of Paul's day as a self-contained intellectual world[85] and that therefore, even if one chooses to seek Paul's spiritual background in it, other influences are not thereby excluded but must rather be presupposed. In this context the Qumran literature is very often taken into consideration. However one thinks these writings can be characterized — here, too, the word *gnosis* crops up repeatedly, though usually in a much more restricted and less pregnant sense than that in which, for example, Bultmann and his school are accustomed to speak of it — they represent the Jewish world of thought again in another way than, for example, the rabbinic writings, and they also show, more clearly perhaps than any other contemporaneous Jewish writings, the influx of other than originally Jewish ideas.

Now it is these writings, and the motifs that predominate in them, to which it is thought that Paul's preaching, too, can be related. To be sure, the essence of the Pauline kerygma, the historical-eschatological character of his Christology in which Christ's death and resurrection occupy the central place, cannot in any sense be connected with the data of the Qumran literature. But this does not alter the fact that with respect to secondary (although not unimportant) motifs in Paul's preaching striking analogies are to be observed: motifs which, it is true, have been thoroughly transformed by the use that Paul makes of them precisely because he presses them into the service of a new and entirely original kerygma, but which nevertheless are able to throw light on the backgrounds that until now have been sought in vain not only in the Greek, but also in the Jewish thinking of his time. Among others certain themes are mentioned that are highly characteristic of Paul, such as the struggle between light and darkness, the revelation of the mystery, justification from pure grace.[86] One can add to this that in the heresies combatted by Paul, as in the Epistle to the Colossians (heresies that frequently have had to do service as witnesses for the gnostic interpretation of Paul's preaching), motifs stand out that seem to fit

---

82. H. J. Schoeps, *Paul, the Theology of the Apostle in the Light of Jewish Religious History*, ET 1961, pp. 27ff.

83. E. E. Ellis, *Paul's Use of the Old Testament,* 1957, pp. 76-84.

84. Cf. W. D. Davies, *Paul and Rabbinic Judaism. Some Rabbinic Elements in Pauline Theology,* 2nd ed., 1955.

85. Cf., e.g., B. Rigaux, in *Littérature et Théologie Pauliniennes,* 1960, p. 37.

86. For the above see the well-balanced article by P. Benoit, "Qumrân et le Nouveau Testament," *NTS,* 1961, pp. 276-296. Cf. also K. G. Kuhn, "Qumran," in *RGG,* 3rd ed., cols. 745-754, and the literature mentioned there.

much better in the framework of the Judaism represented in the Qumran
literature than in that which it has been thought possible to reconstruct
on the basis of the later gnostic writings as pre-Christian *gnosis*. Indications are accordingly seen here, especially in the epistles to the Ephesians[87] and the Colossians, that Paul's preaching with respect to its
formulation must be viewed especially against the background of these
newly unlocked sources.

This whole development admits finally of being demonstrated at
a single point, although for the understanding of Paul's preaching a
very important one: the frequently occurring formula "in Christ," "with
Christ," and what is related to it. Although formerly appeal was often
made to these formulae and ideas in order to show the mystical character
of Paul's proclamation of the gospel and experience of faith (dying,
rising, etc., "with Christ") and attempts were made to cite all sorts of
parallels from the Greek world, since scholars have become more aware
of the Jewish and Semitic background of Paul an entirely different
view has come to predominate in this respect, that of the Old Testament
idea of the "all-in-one," frequently denoted with the term "corporate
personality." Although it is questionable whether this term, in the
special sense with which it has been stamped notably by Wheeler Robinson for certain relationships observed in the Old Testament,[88] is
applicable in every respect to the epistles of Paul,[89] yet the idea one
intends to typify with the aid of this expression is undoubtedly of great
significance for insight into the fundamental structures of Paul's preaching. It is that of the representation by Christ of those who belong to
him, the inclusion of "the many" in the One and on this ground the
application to these many of what has taken place, or will yet take
place, in and with the One, Christ. It is a matter here not only of a
certain formula ("in Christ," "with Christ"), but of a way of thinking
that understands the relationship between Christ and his own in an
entirely different, much more "objective" manner than the method of
interpretation that moves in the Greek-mystical direction. Along with
this the Adam-Christ parallel has appeared to be of a much broader
purport than has often been assumed on the basis of the few explicit
pronouncements (in Rom. 5 and 1 Cor. 15). The whole specifically
Pauline idea of the church as the "body" of Christ is bound up with
it, as also the all-embracing significance of Christ's redemptive work
with respect to "all things."[90] Later we shall return to all this in greater

---

87. Cf., e.g., K. G. Kuhn, "Der Epheserbrief im Lichte der Kumrantexte," *NTS*,
1961, pp. 334-346.

88. His writings date already from the beginning of this century; see also,
however, his *Inspiration and Revelation in the Old Testament*, published in 1953
(1946), pp. 70ff. and passim.

89. In Paul it is not so much the representation of the whole by every part
("an identity of the individual and the group to which he belongs"; W. Robinson,
ibid., p. 70), as of the whole having been included in and being represented by a
specific figure standing at the head (Abraham, Noah, Moses; cf. also *ibid.*, p. 82).

90. See, e.g., E. Percy, *Der Leib Christi in den paulinischen Homologoumena
und Antilegomena*, 1942; S. Hanson, *The Unity of the Church in the New Testament*,
1946, pp. 67ff.; J. A. T. Robinson, *The Body. A Study in Pauline Theology*, 1952, pp.

detail. Here it can already be established, however, what a radical change this new approach has involved, an approach that some retrospectively have once again wished to press into the service of the gnostic interpretation of Paul's preaching,[91] but which, even so, obviously finds support in the first place in the Old Testament and Semitic character of Paul's world of ideas and thought.

If we now return finally to our starting point and ask ourselves where it is that continuing investigation sees the confluence of the main architectonic lines of Paul's preaching and where it supposes that the main entrance to this imposing building can be found, then surely one can speak of a growing consensus insofar that scholars are more and more finding the point of departure for an adequate approach to the whole in the *redemptive-historical, eschatological character of Paul's proclamation*. The governing motif of Paul's preaching is the saving activity of God in the advent and the work, particularly in the death and the resurrection, of Christ. This activity is on the one hand the fulfillment of the work of God in the history of the nation Israel, the fulfillment therefore also of the Scriptures; on the other hand it reaches out to the ultimate consummation of the parousia of Christ and the coming of the kingdom of God. It is this great redemptive-historical framework within which the whole of Paul's preaching must be understood and all of its subordinate parts receive their place and organically cohere.

If it is possible to speak in this sense of a growing consensus, such must undoubtedly be done with great reserve, as has already been evident in part from the preceding. For while there is agreement that what lies at the root of Paul's preaching is not the theological system, nor the philosophical idea, nor religious feeling, but the eschatologically understood activity of God in Jesus Christ, yet just with respect to this eschatological character of Paul's preaching strongly divergent opinions are once again to be pointed out, so that it is not without justice that Rigaux speaks of "eschatology and eschatologies."[92]

As we have seen, Schweitzer applied his consistent-eschatological conception to Paul's preaching in such a way that this is defined on the one hand by the expectation,[93] unaltered in all his epistles, of the imminent return of Jesus and of the Messianic glory, and on the other by the certainty that with Jesus' death and resurrection the *eschaton* and with it the eschatological mode of being of believers (by virtue of their being-in-Christ) has broken through into this aeon. For Schweitzer and his followers this means that the first is an illusion rendered out

---

13ff.; E. Best, *One Body in Christ*, 1955; E. Schweizer, *Erniedrigung und Erhöhung*, pp. 76ff. (cf. *Lordship and Discipleship*, pp. 46ff.); by the same writer, "Die Kirche als Leib Christi in den paulinischen Homologoumena," *TLZ*, 1961, cols. 168ff.; and "Antilegomena," cols. 255ff.; C. K. Barrett, *From First Adam to Last, A Study in Pauline Theology*, 1962; and many others.

91. See, e.g., Haenchen, *RGG*, 3rd ed., II, col. 1653, and the authors mentioned above, p. 34.

92. Rigaux, *Littérature et Théologie Pauliniennes*, 1960, p. 30.

93. *The Mysticism of Paul the Apostle*, p. 52.

of date by the course of events, but that the abiding significance of
Paul's teaching is situated in the Pauline pneumatology attending the
second motif.[94] Not unjustly has it been said of the latter position that
Schweitzer, by making the Spirit a timeless element, in the end shows
more kinship with the theology of the nineteenth century than with
that of Paul.[95]

But while Schweitzer always recognized the great significance that
the continuing future expectation had for Paul, however much this
proved to have been an illusion, others wish to see the real core of
Paul's eschatological preaching in the eschatological event realized in
Jesus' death and resurrection. Here the conception of C. H. Dodd[96] and
of the literature that has emerged under his influence should be mentioned especially.[97] According to Dodd also, it is the eschatological
framework within which the death and resurrection of Christ must be
understood and from which this event derives its specific significance
in Paul's preaching. This eschatological context, in which everything
is placed in Paul, is said to be the expression of Paul's belief that
history has reached its fulfillment in Christ's death and resurrection;
that is to say, these events have the absolute significance of the final
goal that God has set for himself in history.[98] To be sure, this belief
among the first Christians and also in Paul was coupled with the expectation of a speedy return of Christ, but his interest in it is said to have
decreased more and more and the "futurist eschatology" of the first
period to have been replaced by his "Christ-mysticism," that is to say,
by the consciousness of spiritual unity with Christ and the contemplation
of all the riches of the divine grace that even now are the portion of
those who are in Christ.[99] The church is accordingly the place in which
the promise of the great future is fulfilled. It is the sphere of divine
grace and supernatural life.[100] The supra-natural order of life that the
apocalyptic writers had foretold "in terms of pure fantasy" is now described as an actual fact of experience. In this way Paul brought the
principle of realized eschatology to full development. After the resurrection of Christ the church became the sphere of the eschatological
miracle.[101]

Although Dodd cannot of course deny that Paul's preaching is
full of references to the future, yet in his spiritual development[102] the

---

94. *Ibid.*, pp. 160-176, 385-388.
95. Thus N. Q. Hamilton, *The Holy Spirit and Eschatology in Paul*, 1957,
pp. 51ff.
96. E.g., in his *The Apostolic Preaching and Its Developments*, 7th ed., 1951
(1936). On Dodd see also E. E. Wolfzorn, "Realised Eschatology. An Exposition of
Charles H. Dodd's Thesis," in *Ephemerides Theologicae Lovanienses*, 1962, pp. 44-70.
97. See, e.g., J. A. T. Robinson, *Jesus and His Coming*, 1957.
98. *The Apostolic Preaching*, p. 44.
99. *Ibid.*, p. 63.
100. *Ibid.*, p. 64.
101. *Ibid.*, p. 65.
102. Paul's interest in the speedy return is said to have diminished especially
in the period after he wrote 1 Corinthians (*ibid.*, p. 63). See also Dodd's article cited
there: "The Mind of Paul: Change and Development," in *Bulletin of the John
Rylands Library*, I, 1933, II, 1934, included in his *New Testament Studies*, 1953.

presence of the salvation given in Christ is said more and more to have defined the eschatological character of his preaching. That Dodd very one-sidedly shifts the accents here, and that this whole hypothetical development in Paul from "futuristic" to "realized" eschatology can be constructed in Paul's epistles in no other way than by means of a strongly selective arrangement of texts, has been frequently demonstrated.[103] One is certainly permitted to take into consideration here Dodd's own philosophical-religious premises, in which the temporal aspects of salvation entirely recede into the background in comparison with the "eternal issues of life." It has consequently been said, not unjustly, that Dodd's interpretation of the Pauline eschatology has a certain Platonizing tendency.[104] Eschatology is ultimately nothing other than the expression of the absolute, timeless significance and value of the realities proclaimed by Paul. The futural element of this eschatology may not entirely disappear, but it does become withered. And with that Paul's preaching is deprived of a dimension that pertains to its essence no less than the realized eschatology Dodd posits so emphatically.

In this connection the name of Bultmann is once more to be mentioned. As we have seen, while on the one hand he considers Paul's preaching in a positive as well as in a negative sense to have been profoundly determined by motifs from the religions of the heathen world, for Bultmann, too, its starting point lies in the eschatological interpretation of Christ's death and resurrection. More clearly than Dodd, Bultmann recognizes the essential significance of the futural dimension in Paul's eschatology.[105] Paul interprets eschatology, however, on the basis of his anthropology, that is to say, the eschatological present and future is for him the expression of a specific understanding of human existence. To be sure, according to Bultmann Paul does not abandon the apocalyptic picture of the future of resurrection, judgment, glory, etc., but the real salvation is righteousness, liberty, joy in the Holy Spirit. The idea of salvation is thus oriented to the individual. On the one hand this salvation is already present time, on the other it is still future, for it is, by virtue of "the historicity of man," to be obtained only in the way of existential decisions. In order to attain to his authentic existence man must let himself be crucified with Christ over and over again, that is to say, renounce that which is ready to hand, which he has at his disposal, and choose for that which is not ready to hand and which he does not have at his disposal. In this he is again and again brought to the end of the possibilities at his disposal and led to the liberty of true humanness. It is therefore not the eschatological notions, but rather the anthropological insights given expression in them, which constitute the very core of Paul's preaching. Not the idea of the end of the world but the manner in which man is confronted

---

103. I.a., in the full and penetrating critique by N. Q. Hamilton, *The Holy Spirit and Eschatology in Paul*, pp. 53ff.

104. Ellis, *Paul and His Recent Interpreters*, p. 32; cf. also Hamilton, *ibid.*, p. 59; G. C. Berkouwer, *The Return of Christ*, ET 1972, pp. 87f., 103ff.

105. In addition to the writings of Bultmann already mentioned, for what follows see his *History and Eschatology*, ET 1957, pp. 33ff., 40ff.

existentially with the acting and speaking of God in Jesus Christ is the demythologized substance of this eschatology. In the nature of the case there can be no question in this interpretation of an eschatological redemptive history in the sense of a train of events advancing toward the consummation which have already taken place and are still to be anticipated in Christ. Such a conception presupposes, in Bultmann's judgment, a conception of history and *Naherwartung* that has long since been rendered out of date by the course of events. It is precisely the great significance of Paul that, by interpreting eschatology out of his anthropology, he has already given *in nuce* the solution to the problem of history and eschatology, as this was posed by the failure of the parousia to arrive.[106]

It is clear that this demythologizing interpretation covers the content of Paul's preaching only very incompletely — and at that according to the prior understanding of an existentialistic hermeneutic.[107] All of theology, and thus also Christology, is treated from the viewpoint of anthropology. Accordingly the anthropological categories of which Paul makes use form the real framework in which Bultmann in his *Theology of the New Testament* analyzes and brings together Paul's preaching. It is not difficult to recognize that along with this approach a great narrowing makes its appearance insofar as here — otherwise than in Paul! — all of the divine redemptive activity in Christ is regarded *sub specie hominis*.[108] Yet Bultmann's interpretation is so far an advance with respect to his radical predecessors, in that he seeks the heart of Paul's preaching, not in timeless notions concerning God or in a new experience of religious feeling, but in the decisive significance of the divine redemptive work in Christ. For this reason the analyses of Bultmann, even though they all bear the signature of his existentialistic interpretation (and reduction!) of the gospel, still have a greater value for the understanding of Paul, even for those who cannot follow him on his philosophical pathways, than those of his radical-critical predecessors.

Finally, then, it remains to mention that interpretation of Paul's eschatological preaching — to our mind the most adequate interpretation — which does justice both to the present and the future significance of this "eschatology" and which does not attempt to dissolve the historical backbone of Paul's preaching, with respect to what has already taken place as well as to that which must yet take place, in an idealistic or existentialistic fashion. There is no specific school in the investigation to be spoken of here, but rather a widespread group of interpreters, highly differentiated among themselves, who endeavor to understand the Pauline gospel in its original meaning and purport without subjecting its content to a previously determined hermeneutical principle. On the one hand this redemptive-historical interpretation (as it has been given expression in a very representative manner, for example, in

---

106. *Ibid.*, p. 49.
107. Cf. Bultmann's essay, "The Problem of Hermeneutics," in *Essays Philosophical and Theological*, ET 1955, pp. 234-262.
108. For this "narrowing" see my *Bultmann*, 1960, pp. 38ff.

the work of O. Cullmann, *Christ and Time*[109]) is marked by a strong accentuation of the element of fulfillment, in the preaching of Jesus as well as in that of Paul. It has in this way offered a powerful counterpoise to the one-sided significance that is ascribed by the so-called consistent eschatology to the *Naherwartung* in the New Testament, and has constantly pointed to the fact that the primitive church precisely because of this consciousness of fulfillment was not thrown off the track when its expectation of the speedy return of the Lord was not realized. In this sense the truth of the so-called realized eschatology is fully recognized in this interpretation. On the other hand, however, it has understood the essential significance of continuing future expectation in Paul's preaching and laid full emphasis on the reciprocal dependence of the "already" and the "not yet," as an integral component element of the Pauline eschatology. There are not only two poles here, between which there would only be tension and no connection. The church has already been included in Christ's death and resurrection, and it also shares in the future resurrection. While it is still in the present world and its temporal existence is subject to death, it is no longer to be regarded in it from the viewpoint of the first Adam and of the natural body but as included in the second Adam, under the regime of the Spirit. And this Spirit is not only the principle of the new life, in the spiritual and ethical sense of the word, but also of the renewal of the whole man in all the functions and potentialities of his existence and of the whole cosmos, just as Christ, too, has a predominating position in Paul's preaching with respect to all things and the whole of history. It is this all-embracing significance of Christ's death and resurrection, understood on the foundation of faith in God as the Creator and Consummator of heaven and earth, in which this interpretation has located the heart and therewith the hermeneutical presuppositions of Paul's eschatological preaching. And it is in the footsteps of the redemptive-historical method of interpretation intended in this sense that the following inquiry into the nature and content of Paul's preaching, as this comes to us in his epistles,[110] will move.

---

109. ET 1951; and by the same author the general work *Christology of the New Testament*, while reference is now to be made especially to his *Salvation in History*, ET 1967, where the whole problem surrounding the redemptive history of the New Testament is treated at length; as regards Paul, see pp. 248-268. In his footsteps on Paul, e.g., J. Munck, *Paul and the Salvation of Mankind*, ET 1959; Hamilton, *The Holy Spirit and Eschatology in Paul*, 1957.

110. By these I understand the thirteen canonical epistles. On the authenticity of Colossians (and Ephesians) see the Introduction to my *Col.*; on that of the Pastoral Epistles my *De Pastorale Brieven*, 1967.

II
FUNDAMENTAL STRUCTURES

SECTION 7. THE FULLNESS OF THE TIME.
THE REVELATION OF THE MYSTERY

From the history of the investigation it has become evident how easily the entrance to Paul's preaching is blocked or narrowed when one comes to place in the center and absolutize certain facets of his proclamation of salvation at the expense of others. It may undoubtedly be said to be a result of the more recent investigation that, although it has not in its own turn escaped all kinds of one-sidedness and dogmatism, it has succeeded in arriving at a broader conception of Paul's preaching. It has no longer sought the basic motif of this preaching in one particular soteriological aspect, whether in justification by faith or in victory over the flesh through the Spirit, but, transcending all these partial viewpoints and antecedent to them, in the eschatological or redemptive-historical starting point of Paul's proclamation. The whole content of this preaching can be summarized as the proclamation and explication of the eschatological time of salvation inaugurated with Christ's advent, death, and resurrection. It is from this principal point of view and under this denominator that all the separate themes of Paul's preaching can be understood and penetrated in their unity and relation to each other.[1]

Naturally, only the continuation of our inquiry will throw further light on this thesis in all its implications. The extent, however, to which Paul saw the advent and work of Christ as revelation of the fulfilling activity of God in history and as the breaking through of the great time of salvation can immediately be demonstrated on the basis of a number of typical pronouncements from his epistles.

What is said in Galatians 4:4 of "the fulness of the time" and in Ephesians 1:10 of "the fulness of the times" is surely of special importance:

> ...but when the fulness of the time came, God sent forth his Son....
> ...the mystery of his [God's] will..., unto a dispensation of the fulness of the times, to sum up all things in Christ, the things in the heavens, and the things upon earth....

What is meant by this "fulness of the time" is not only the maturation of a specific matter in the great framework of redemptive history, but the fulfillment of the time in an absolute sense. The time

---

1. See, e.g., H. D. Wendland, *Die Mitte der paulinischen Botschaft*, 1935, pp. 5ff.; also my *When the Time Had Fully Come, Studies in New Testament Theology*, 1957, pp. 44-61.

of the world[2] has come to a conclusion with Christ's advent. However much this fulfillment still bears a provisional character and the *perfectum* is followed yet again by a *futurum*,[3] nevertheless the *pleroma* of the time or of the times is here spoken of as a matter that has already taken effect[4] and thus in principle has been settled.

This commencement of the great time of salvation is no less clearly attested in 2 Corinthians 6:2, where the apostle as with finger extended points to its presence: "Behold, now is the acceptable time; now is the day of salvation!"

Here, too, what is to be understood by "the acceptable time" and "the day of salvation" is not merely a certain saving event or opportunity that one must embrace and which may perhaps presently disappear again. Nothing less is intended than that the decisive, long-expected coming of God has dawned, the hour of hours, the day of salvation in the fulfilling, eschatological sense of the word.[5] This is apparent as well from the preceding context where Paul writes of the great change that has entered with the death and resurrection of Christ as follows: "Wherefore if any man is in Christ, he is new creation; the old things have passed away; behold, the new have come" (2 Cor. 5:17).

When he speaks here of "new creation," this is not meant merely in an individual sense ("a new creature"), but one is to think of the new world of the re-creation that God has made to dawn in Christ, and in which everyone who is in Christ is included. This is also evident from the neuter plural that follows: "the old things have passed away, the new have come," and from the full significance that must be ascribed here to "old" and "new." It is a matter of two worlds, not only in a spiritual, but in a redemptive-historical, eschatological sense.[6] The "old things" stand for the unredeemed world in its distress and sin, the "new things" for the time of salvation and the re-creation that have dawned with Christ's resurrection. He who is in Christ, therefore, is

---

2. In Gal. 4:4 there is mention of the *plērōma tou chronou*, that is, the fullness of the time in its extensiveness, as world time. In Eph. 1:10 it is *plērōma tōn kairōn*, that is, the fulfillment of all antecedent redemptive-historical interventions and turning points in the extensiveness of the time.

3. See below, p. 52.

4. *Ēlthen to plērōma* (Gal. 4:4). In Eph. 1:10 there is mention of the *oikonomia* ("management of a household," "arrangement," "administration"—not "preparation," as the Dutch Bible Society translation has it) of the fullness of the times in which God sums up all things anew in Christ as under one head. Although the fullness intended here is still a matter of the future, it has already found its initial fulfillment with Christ's exaltation (Phil. 2:10; Col. 1:20), and it is certainly meant in that sense here as well.

5. Cf. Stählin, *TDNT*, IV, pp. 1118f., *s.v. nyn*. He writes that the apostle believed "that the long-expected day of the Lord had come in this *nyn....* In the NT *nyn* there is in fact expressed the certainty of eschatology already realized." See also Wendland, *Cor.*, p. 37: "The great 'now' is the onset of the time of salvation."

6. Cf., e.g., Kümmel, too, in the "Anhang" to Lietzmann, *Cor.*, p. 205. In a sweeping manner Kümmel here corrects Lietzmann, who still wholly followed the mystical interpretation and by "from now on" (v. 16) understood, not the redemptive-historical revolution that has dawned with Christ's resurrection, but the point of time of conversion.

new creation: he participates in, belongs to, this new world of God.[7]

The qualification of this event as the "revelation of the mystery," or the "making known" of that which until now was "kept secret" or "hidden," for which the apostle has a predilection, is also indicative of this eschatological character of the redemptive dispensation that has dawned in Christ and of its proclamation by Paul. What a dominant place this expression occupies throughout all of Paul's epistles may appear from the following survey:

> ... the revelation (apokalypsis) of the mystery (to mystērion) which was kept secret for long ages (sesigēmenon), but is now disclosed (phanerō thentos) (Rom. 16:25, 26).

> ... the mystery (to mystērion) which has been hidden (apokekrymmenon) for ages and generations, but now has been revealed (ephane-rōthē) to his saints (Col. 1:26; cf. 2:2, 3).

> ... making known (gnōrisas) unto us the mystery (to mystērion) of his [God's] will, according to his good pleasure which he purposed in him unto a dispensation of the fulness of the times (Eph. 1:9, 10).

> ... my insight into the mystery (to mystērion) of Christ, which was not made known (egnōristhē) to the sons of men in other generations as it has now been revealed (apekalyphthē) to his holy apostles and prophets ... (Eph. 3:4, 5; cf. v. 3).

> ... but we speak God's wisdom in a mystery (en mystēriō), even the wisdom that has been hidden (apokekrymmenēn), which God foreordained before the ages ... (1 Cor. 2:7).

> ... the grace which was given us in Christ Jesus before times eternal, but has now been manifested (phanerōtheisan) by the appearing of our Saviour (2 Tim. 1:9, 10; cf. also Tit. 1:2, 3).

The attempt has often been made to understand "mystery" by analogy with the significance of this word in the ancient mystery religions in the sense of a kind of secret teaching that is "revealed" to only a few intimates. In Paul, however, it has a completely different sense, as is apparent also from a comparison with the newly unlocked Jewish sources:[8] "mystery," that which has been "hidden," is to be understood, as a few of the texts cited say in so many words, in connection with the hidden counsel of God in relation to his redemptive work in history. "Hiddenness," "mystery," etc., has, therefore, in addition to a noetic a plainly historical connotation: it is that which has not yet appeared,

---

7. That ktisis here does not simply mean "creature" in the sense of individual man or being, but must be understood in the full sense as the new life called forth by God's omnipotence, is clearly evident from a comparison with such passages as Eph. 2:10, 15; 4:24; Col. 3:10; cf. also Foerster in TDNT, III, p. 1034, s.v. ktizō. To the same effect G. Vos, The Pauline Eschatology, 1930, pp. 46, 47: "... not merely individual, subjective conditions have been changed, but ... there has been created a totally new environment, or, more accurately speaking: a totally new world, in which the person spoken of is an inhabitant and participator."

8. It is a matter here of the equivalent of mystērion, namely, the Hebrew word rz, rāz, which occurs frequently in the Qumran literature; cf. E. Vogt, " 'Mysteria' in Textibus Qumran," in Biblica, 1956, pp. 247-257; J. Coppens, "Le Mystère chez Paul et à Qumran," in Recherches Bibliques, V, 1960, pp. 142-165; see also P. Benoit, "Qumran et le Nouveau Testament," in NTS, 1961, pp. 290ff.

that which still exists in the counsel of God and has not yet been realized in history as fulfillment of that counsel.[9]

Accordingly the corresponding word "reveal" not only means the divulging of a specific truth or the giving of information as to certain events or facts, but the appearance itself, the becoming historical reality of that which until now did not exist as such, but was kept by God, hidden, held back.[10] As such, namely, as the realized redemptive plan of God, this mystery is consequently the object of Paul's proclamation and of the revelation of God to his saints, and so forth.

From the way in which this expression — certainly very characteristic for Paul — is used, the eschatological nature of the content of his preaching is apparent once again. For this mystery has reference to the purpose of God with a view to the fullness of the times (Eph. 1:9, 10). Standing over against the "kept secret for long ages," "hidden for ages and generations," etc., is again and again the "now" of the revelation, the end of the waiting ages, the ultimate intervention[11] of God according to his counsel and promise. What is here called in various nuances the revelation of the mystery is nothing other than that which the fullness of the time brings to view; it is the fulfillment of the eschatological promise of redemption in the times appointed for it, its "own times,"[12] that is denoted in this fashion.

This revelation of the mystery is the real content of Paul's gospel (Rom. 16:26), the object of "the ministry which was entrusted to him" (Col. 1:25, 26; cf. Eph. 3:2). Therefore Paul's preaching itself is taken up into the great eschatological event;[13] it is rightly and in the full sense kerygma of the gospel, that is, announcement, proclamation of the coming of salvation. That Paul's epistles give what is no longer the first announcement of this gospel, but rather the further exposition and application of it,[14] does not detract from the fact that this gospel is the sole and constant subject of his epistles also; and that therefore, if one

9. Cf., e.g., Bornkamm, *TDNT*, pp. 819ff., s.v. *mystērion;* Grosheide, *1 Cor.*, pp. 179ff.; on 1 Cor. 2:7, Wendland, *Cor.*, p. 18; C. Masson, *l'Épitre de Saint Paul aux Colossiens*, 1950, p. 112; my *Paul and Jesus*, p. 58.

10. The usage is also very clear, e.g., in 1 Cor. 1:7, where "the revelation" of our Lord Jesus Christ is spoken of in the sense of his advent, his appearing (cf. Rom. 8:18ff. [twice]; 1 Cor. 3:13, *et al.*). Rom. 1:18 is also characteristic of the Pauline usage, where Paul speaks of the wrath of God. What is meant is not the announcement that God is wrathful, but the coming into operation of that wrath, even though this is not recognized as such. Cf. Bultmann, *Theology*, I, pp. 275f.

11. Oepke states that the concept of revelation has "its true *locus* ... in eschatology" (*TDNT*, II, p. 583).

12. Thus Tit. 1:2, 3, where the hope of eternal life is spoken of, which the veracious God promised before times eternal, but revealed in its own time *(kairois idiois)*. The same expression is found in 1 Tim. 2:6; 6:15. One can take it as a synonym of *plērōma tou chronou* or *tōn kairōn*. The adjective *idios* speaks of the proper, fitting, appropriate, which, just as *plērōma*, finds its determination in God's counsel; cf. O. Cullmann, *Christ and Time*, ET 1964, pp. 40f.

13. See also J. Munck, *Paul and the Salvation of Mankind*, pp. 36-80. His thesis, acceptable in itself, is diminished by dubious exegesis in several subordinate parts. See below, pp. 524f.

14. On this at greater length see my *The Authority of the New Testament Scriptures*, ET 1963, pp. 72ff.

has to characterize their general content not only as kerygma, but also as doctrine and paraenesis, yet this doctrine, too, has no other object and this admonition no other starting point and ground than the ful-filling and redeeming activity of God in the advent of Christ.

It is plain that this general character of Paul's preaching is materially altogether in harmony with the great theme of Jesus' preach-ing of the coming of the kingdom of heaven. What Jesus proclaims as the "fulfillment of the time" (Mark 1:15) is almost word for word identical with what Paul terms "the fulness of the time." And the beatitude Jesus addresses to his disciples: "To you it has been given to know the mysteries of the kingdom of heaven; ... many prophets and righteous men desired to see the things which you see, and saw them not ..." (Matt. 13:11, 16, 17) finds its echo in Paul's word of the revela-tion of the mystery that has been hidden for ages and generations. However much the preaching of Jesus and that of Paul in a formal sense (that is, in choice of words, way of representing things, type of teaching) may be distinguished, and however much the time after the resurrection of Christ represents a stage of the revelation that has advanced further than Jesus in his earthly self-revelation,[15] this does not alter the fact that the coming of the kingdom as the fulfilling eschato-logical coming of God to the world is the great dynamic principle of Paul's preaching, even though the word "kingdom of heaven" does not occupy a central place in it.[16] That this deeper unity of the New Testa-ment kerygma is once again being recognized in a broad circle[17] is among the great gains of the eschatological approach to Paul's preaching as well.

And this applies not only to the relation of Jesus and Paul. In this general character of his preaching Paul in his fashion also carries on what the apostles and the early Christian church at Jerusalem be-lieved and proclaimed as the gospel of Christ. For them, too, the advent of Christ, his appearance, death, and resurrection, as well as the gift of the Holy Spirit, were above all the fulfillment of the promise, the dawning of the consummation of the history of redemption, eschato-logical event. Thus Peter at once expounded it on Pentecost in the light of the prophecy of Joel (cf. Acts 2:17), and the church lived in the consciousness of having seen the breaking of the day of salvation and of being itself the people of God of the great end time.[18] One can understand the nature and origin of this peculiar consciousness, called forth by Jesus' advent and confirmed by his resurrection, in no other way than against the background of Israel's expectation of redemption and view of history. Paul stands in the same life stream, and the funda-

---

15. Cf. in detail my *Paul and Jesus*, pp. 64ff.

16. See also H. J. Westerink, *Het koninkrijk Gods bij Paulus*, 1937.

17. Thus Bultmann, e.g., in the footsteps of A. Schweitzer, speaks of the es-chatological preaching as "the proclamation in which Jesus and Paul are in com-plete accord" ("Jesus and Paul," in *Existence and Faith*, p. 186); see also his *Faith and Understanding*, I, p. 232.

18. Cf. H. D. Wendland, *Geschichtsanschauung und Geschichtsbewusstsein im Neuen Testament*, 1938, pp. 5ff.; W. G. Kümmel, *Kirchenbegriff und Geschichtsbe-wusstsein in der Urkirche und bei Jesus*, 1943.

mental motif of his preaching is not different from that of the other apostles and of the primitive Christian church. But he unfolded it in a wealth of aspects and with a depth of ideas that is unequalled in the rest of the apostolic preaching preserved to us, and therefore has repeatedly opened new perspectives in the history of investigation and for the faith of the Christian church.

SECTION 8. THE MYSTERY OF CHRIST. ESCHATOLOGY AND CHRISTOLOGY

It follows directly from what has just been said that this general eschatological character of Paul's preaching is entirely defined and explained by the advent and the revelation of Jesus Christ. Paul's "eschatology" is "Christ-eschatology," and "the Pauline approach to history is faith in Christ."[19] The fundamental structure of Paul's preaching is consequently only to be approached from his Christology.

This can be seen in various ways from the already quoted eschatological pronouncements themselves. It is the advent of Christ, the sending of the Son of God, that brings to light the fullness of the time[20] (Gal. 4:4); similarly, the revelation of the mystery that has now dawned consists of the fact that "the mystery of Christ" has been revealed (Eph. 3:4). It is the "appearing of our Saviour" that is the proof of the great turning point of the times (2 Tim. 1:9, 10). For this reason the whole content of the mystery that has now been revealed can be qualified and summarized in the one word — Christ (Col. 2:3), just as the gospel of the inaugurated time of salvation, of which Paul is the herald, is again and again called the gospel of Christ (Rom. 15:19; 1 Cor. 9:12; 2 Cor. 2:13), or the gospel of our Lord Jesus (2 Tim. 1:8), or the gospel of God's Son, whereby the words "of Christ," etc., if not always and exclusively, then certainly for the most part, have the sense of (the gospel) *concerning* Christ.[21]

This interdependence between the "eschatological" and the "christological" ground motif of Paul's preaching is of the highest importance for the understanding of both.

On the one hand, it is determinative for insight into the real nature of Paul's preaching of Christ. This has in principle a redemptive-historical, eschatological content. It is decisively defined by what has taken place in Christ, by the acts of God that he wrought in him for the fulfillment of his redemptive plan and of which the death and resurrection of Christ constitute the all-controlling center. Paul's Christology is a Christology of redemptive facts. Here lies the ground of the whole of his preaching, and it is with the historical reality of this event, in the past as well as in the future, that both the apostolic kerygma

---

19. Wendland, *Geschichtsanschauung*, p. 26.

20. Thus Luther, too, on Gal. 4:4: "For the time did not cause the Son to be sent, but on the contrary the sending of the Son placed the time in the category of fullness"; quoted in Schlier, *Gal.*, p. 138.

21. Cf. Friedrich, *TDNT*, II, pp. 730f., and the literature cited there.

and the faith of the church stand or fall (1 Cor. 15:14, 19). This historical-eschatological character of Paul's Christology also places it in organic relationship with the revelation of the Old Testament. What has taken place in Christ forms the termination and fulfillment of the great series of divine redemptive acts in the history of Israel and the presupposition of the progress and consummation of the history of the world. Therefore the still-to-be-expected future of the Lord and the continuing activity of God in history are never to be detached from the fulfillment of God's promises to Israel, but rather must be understood in the light of them (cf. Rom. 11:15ff.; 15:8-12). In this connection the thesis of Bultmann that Paul's eschatology is entirely determined by his anthropology, and that the history of the people of Israel and the history of the world have disappeared from his sight and been replaced by the "historicity of man," is also to be rejected.[22] It is true indeed that Paul does not develop a well-defined historical picture of the new dispensation of history that has begun with Christ.[23] In that sense Paul is no philosopher or theologian of history. But this does not mean that his eschatology may be said to be only an eschatology *sub specie hominis,* whereby world history would have the significance of the wings and properties of the stage on which the small history of the individual man is enacted. Paul's eschatology bears a theocentric character; that is to say, in it past, present, and future occur *sub specie Dei,* under the viewpoint of that God who is the Creator of heaven and earth and who conducts all things to their consummation in accordance with the prophetic revelation of the Old Testament. And this is reflected in his eschatological, redemptive-historical Christology. This Christology is not only directed to and determined by the fact that Christ brings man to his "authenticity" and destiny — here the great narrowing[24] of every theology that makes the knowledge and redemption of the individual man its all-controlling hermeneutical starting point becomes perceptible — but also that God in Christ has brought to fulfillment and will yet bring to fulfillment his man- and world- and history-encompassing redemptive work in a conclusive way. This all-embracing character of Paul's eschatology and Christology comes to the fore, as we shall see still further, especially in the epistles to the Ephesians and the Colossians. But it forms the great presupposition of all of Paul's preaching. For the Christ in whose death and resurrection the new aeon dawns is the Messiah of Israel (Rom. 1:2-4; 9:5), in whom God gathers and saves his people (2 Cor. 6:16ff.), and whom he has exalted and appointed Savior and *Kyrios* of all things (Phil. 2). However much the name Christ in the Pauline usage seems to have acquired the sense of a proper

---

22. Bultmann, *History and Eschatology,* p. 43.
23. See further below, Section 74.
24. Cf., e.g., the critique of Delling, "Zum neueren Paulusverständnis," *Novum Testamentum,* 1960, pp. 100ff.; and N. A. Dahl's great objection against Bultmann's interpretation of Paul, which Delling quotes: that in it "the *heilsgeschichtlich*-eschatological setting is subordinated." See also the rising criticism in the school of Bultmann itself, e.g., of E. Käsemann, "On the Subject of Primitive Christian Apocalyptic," *New Testament Questions of Today,* ET 1969, pp. 108ff., and of his pupil C. Müller, *Gottes Gerechtigkeit und Gottes Volk,* 1964.

name, this does not mean that this designation has lost its official, historic-Israelitic significance.[25] Paul proclaims Christ as the fulfillment of the promise of God to Abraham, as the seed in which all the families of the earth shall be blessed (Gal. 3:8, 16, 29), the eschatological bringer of salvation whose all-embracing significance must be understood in the light of prophecy (Rom. 15:9-12), the fulfillment of God's redemptive counsel concerning the whole world and its future. This redemptive-historical significance of Paul's Christology also comes to light in the pronouncements, so characteristic of him, concerning Christ as the revelation of the mystery. Here the past is not described only as a time of darkness and ignorance, but rather as the preparation of the work of God in the course of the centuries. The grace that has now been revealed "was given us in Christ Jesus long ages ago" (2 Tim. 1:9), in the purpose and promise of God and in their initial realization; it was promised by God who cannot lie, before times eternal (Tit. 1:2). Therefore the mystery that has been revealed with the advent of Christ must also be made known and understood "by means of the prophetic writings" (Rom. 16:26). The nature of that which has taken place in Christ is rightly known only from prophecy, just as, on the other hand, it becomes clear in the light of the fulfilling action of God how much the Old Testament is the book of Christ (2 Cor. 3:14; 1 Cor. 10:4; Gal. 3:16). For this reason one of the leading motifs of Paul's preaching is that his gospel is according to the Scriptures (Rom. 1:17; 3:28; cf. Rom. 4; Gal. 3:6ff.; 4:21ff.; 1 Cor. 10:1-10; Rom. 15:4; 1 Cor. 9:10; 2 Tim. 3:16, et al.). However this use of the Old Testament by Paul is further to be judged in detail,[26] a most basic conception of Christ's advent and work lies at the root of this whole appeal and use, that of the divine drama being realized and fulfilled in his advent and work; this fulfillment was not only foretold by the prophets, but signifies the execution of the divine plan of salvation that he purposed to himself with respect to the course of the ages and the end of the times (Eph. 1:9, 10; 3:11). This is the fundamental redemptive-historical and all-embracing character of Paul's preaching of Christ.

On the other hand — and this is of no less importance — Paul's eschatology is entirely determined by the realized and still-to-be-realized redemptive work of God *in Christ.* However much he gives expression to the significance of Christ's advent with the help of the conceptual materials of the Old Testament and Jewish eschatology, this does not mean that the eschatological "setting" in which he describes this advent and significance can simply be reduced to an Old Testament or Jewish "schema" lying ready to hand, from which Paul's Christology may be said to have borrowed its composition and from which it would thus be easy to extract this form. What is so remarkable about Paul's eschatology is that although he avails himself of all kinds of traditional terms and

25. See also C. Masson, *Le Christ Jésus et l'ancien Testament selon saint Paul,* 1941, p. 10, and especially the rich essay of N. A. Dahl, "Die Messianität Jesu bei Paulus," in *Studia Paulina,* 1953, pp. 83-95.

26. See in particular O. Michel, *Paulus und seine Bibel,* 1929, and E. E. Ellis, *Paul's Use of the Old Testament,* 1960.

ideas, yet it is distinguished from all forms of the contemporaneous Jewish eschatological expectation and bears a completely independent character. Now this has its origin in the fact that Paul's eschatology is not determined by any traditional eschatological schema, but by the actual acting of God in Christ. This is the fundamental christological character of his eschatology.

This distinctive character emerges most plainly in the peculiar tension that is to be ascertained between the aspects of fulfillment and expectation in Paul's eschatology and which already finds expression in the eschatological terminology. For while, on the one hand, the apostle speaks of the fullness of the time that has taken effect and of the new creation that has begun, on the other hand he is clearly conscious of still living in the present world (ho aiōn houtos) and the time corresponding with it (ho nyn kairos; cf., e.g., Rom. 8:18; 11:5; 12:2, et al.). Of the new world, denoted in the Jewish usage as the world to come (ho aiōn mellōn), he makes mention exclusively in a future sense (Eph. 1:21; cf. 2:7). And he does speak of the present world time in which the church is living as "the end (literally, the ends) of the ages" (ta telē tōn aiōnōn; 1 Cor. 10:11), "the last times" (en hysterois kairois; 1 Tim. 4:1), but sometimes the expression "in the last days" (en eschatais hēmerais) has reference to a period that has not yet been entered upon (2 Tim. 3:1). Finally, to mention still another example, in one place Paul can speak of "the present evil aeon" (ek tou aiōnos tou enestōtos ponērou) as of a situation from which Christ has snatched his people (Gal. 1:4),[27] and he can reproach the church for having subjected itself to all manner of commandments "as if still living in the world" (Col. 2:21; cf. also Eph. 2:2),[28] while elsewhere he speaks of the present aeon and of the world as the place where the believers must live godly lives (Tit. 2:12), and must shine as stars (Phil. 2:15). The result is that in certain contexts he qualifies the unredeemed life prior to the redemptive time as a "once," "in that time," etc., which has now been overcome (cf. Eph. 2:2, 12), in contrast with the present "now" of the new creation, the time of redemption and fulfillment (2 Cor. 6:2; Eph. 2:13; Rom. 3:21, et al.). Elsewhere, however, the "at present" or "now" indicates the continuance of the mode of existence defined by the world, over against the "then" or "once" of the perfection still to be expected (1 Cor. 13:10, 12, et al.).[29]

It is this remarkable ambivalence of the "now," which can have the sense of the "already now" of the time of salvation that has been entered upon as well as of the "even now" of the world time that still continues, which imparts to Paul's eschatology its wholly distinctive character. The attempt has been made indeed to recover in certain Jewish eschatological notions the "fundamental schema" of this "already" and "not yet" eschatology (namely, in those writings in which the

27. In Col. 1:13 this is expressed as being delivered out of the power of darkness and transferred into the kingdom of Christ.
28. Here kosmos is used in the same sense as aiōn.
29. On this variously qualified nyn see Stählin at length in TDNT, IV, s.v. nyn.

Messianic time of salvation is placed before the end of the world, as in Baruch and IV Ezra),[30] but in doing so one must establish that for Paul's consciousness, otherwise than is the case in these apocalypses, the *eschaton* in a certain sense has already dawned; and furthermore, in order even so to be able to lay this schema at the foundation of Paul's eschatological pronouncements, one must come to highly dubious and untenable exegeses of certain Pauline pronouncements.[31]

It is very striking that Paul, at least in the epistles that have been preserved to us, makes no attempt whatever to present the church with a balanced eschatological timetable. It may perhaps be said by way of conclusion that in Paul a "mingling of the two ages" takes place[32] and that the advent of Christ is to be viewed as the "breaking through of the future aeon in the present."[33] For him the future has become present time, and even when he speaks of the groaning of the creation and of the church in the present world, that is for him not a reduction, but a confirmation of the coming redemption (Rom. 8:13).[34] But Paul himself gives no explanation of this tension between the "even now" and the "already now" in the categories of an eschatological system. For he was not a "theologian who thought in terms of the aeons,"[35] but a preacher of Jesus Christ, who has come and is yet to come. Here is the reason why this eschatology is ambivalent and fits into no single schema, and why he can employ the eschatological categories at one time in a present, and at another time in a future sense, apparently without concerning himself about the "unsystematic" character of it. The revelation of Jesus Christ as the Messiah promised by God to Israel determines and creates Paul's historical consciousness and eschatological thought, and not the reverse. Who Christ is and what he does, what the relationship is between the time of salvation that has been entered upon with him and the future still to be expected, all this is not determined by eschatological-theological presuppositions, but is only gathered by the apostle from the unexpected and overwhelming manner in which God in Jesus Christ has given and will yet give the fulfillment of the redemptive promise.

SECTION 9. THE FIRSTBORN FROM THE DEAD. THE LAST ADAM

When we attempt to analyze further what we have met with in the preceding sections and ask ourselves why and in what respect, according

---

30. In addition to A. Schweitzer see also H. J. Schoeps, who associates himself very closely with Schweitzer, *Paul, The Theology of the Apostle in the Light of Jewish Religious History*, ET 1961, pp. 97ff.

31. E.g., of the double doctrine of the resurrection that Paul is said to have held (*ibid.*, p. 104). See further Chapter XII.

32. *Ibid.*, p. 99; cf. Wendland, *Geschichtsanschauung*, p. 26: "Two epochs are present simultaneously"; see also his *Die Mitte der paulinischen Botschaft*, pp. 12ff.

33. Thus, e.g., Schlier, *Gal.*, p. 138.

34. See also my *Rom.*, p. 188.

35. As Schoeps wants to typify him (*Paul*, p. 99).

to Paul, the fullness of the time has been entered upon and the new creation has dawned with the advent of Christ, it is clear at once that we have to do with a total vision of the whole redemptive action of God in Christ. The breakthrough of the new does not begin only at a specific point in Christ's life on earth or at his exaltation, but the fullness of the time takes effect with the sending of God's Son, born of a woman, born under the law (Gal. 4:4). The Christ-hymn of 1 Timothy 3:16, in which "the great mystery of godliness" finds its expression, accordingly begins with the words: "who was manifested in the flesh."[36] This does not alter the fact that it can be said of Paul's gospel in particular that it has its starting point and center in the death and resurrection of Christ, and that only from thence does the proper light fall on the whole of the fulfilling and consummating activity of God, both "retrospectively" in the incarnation and pre-existence of Christ and "prospectively" in his continuing exaltation and anticipated parousia.

That the center of Paul's gospel may rightly be sought in Christ's death and resurrection can be confirmed in all sorts of ways from his own pronouncements. Thus, for example, in the important words of 1 Corinthians 15:3, 4: "For I delivered to you [as tradition] as of first importance that which I also received: that Christ died for our sins according to the Scriptures, and that he was buried, and that he was raised on the third day according to the Scriptures."

Paul speaks here of the apostolic tradition,[37] as this has been laid by him and the other apostles as the foundation of the whole of their preaching and which he admonishes the church to preserve in the same words as those in which they have received it. This tradition consists above all[38] in that Christ has died, was buried and raised. And that: according to the Scriptures. The fulfillment of God's prior redemptive promise, the fullness of the time, has therefore become manifest above all in Christ's death and resurrection. It is thus, he emphatically adds in verse 11, that we preach and that you have come to believe. In this gospel lies the starting point and foundation both for preaching and for faith.

It is, moreover, of the greatest importance to see the significance of Christ's death and resurrection, which are the center of Paul's proclamation, as an inseparable unity; and particularly to keep in view how the significance of Christ's resurrection is determined by that of his death and vice versa. On the one hand the eschatological significance Paul ascribes to Christ's resurrection is not that of a general belief in redemption or immortality that may be said to have found its firm

---

36. See further below, Section 11.

37. For this idea of tradition in more detail see my *The Authority of the New Testament Scriptures*, pp. 17ff., and the literature cited there.

38. *En prōtois*. Lietzmann translates it "als Hauptstück," and he explains these words with the synonyms "*in primis*, 'hauptsächlich,' vom Rang" (*Cor.*, p. 76). Robertson-Plummer translate "in the foremost place," and annotate thereby: "Foremost in importance, not in time; the doctrine of the Resurrection is primary and cardinal, central and indispensable" (*A Critical and Exegetical Commentary on the First Epistle of St. Paul to the Corinthians*, 2nd ed., 1929, p. 332; cf. Grosheide, *1 Cor.*, p. 386.

basis in Christ's resurrection. The eschatological significance of Christ's resurrection is determined by the special character of his death, which does not merely consist in that Christ was abandoned to the transitoriness of human life as a fate or necessity or tragedy that is not to be qualified further, with his resurrection being characterized as a vanquishing of that transitoriness. For Paul Christ's death is determined primarily by its connection with the power and guilt of sin. It is characteristic of this emphasis that again and again he relates Christ's death to the cross and can therefore qualify the whole of his gospel as "the word of the cross" (1 Cor. 1:17, 18; cf. Gal. 3:1). He declares that in the church he will know nothing other than Jesus Christ and him crucified (1 Cor. 2:2), and he calls the enemies of the gospel "enemies of the cross of Christ" (Phil. 3:18). It is this special death of Christ, qualified by the cross, which further determines the significance of Christ's resurrection and the new life that has come to light with it, in its forensic, ethical, and cosmic aspects, into which we shall have to go further in what follows. As often, therefore, as Paul mentions the resurrection as the great central redemptive fact (Rom. 1:4; 2 Cor. 4:13, 14), calls it the content of "the word of faith, which we preach," "that Jesus is Lord," and "that God has raised him from the dead" (Rom. 10:8, 9), and describes the faith itself by which man is justified as "faith in him that raised Jesus our Lord from the dead" (Rom. 4:24; cf. v. 17),[39] this is only to be understood adequately if the specific significance of Christ's death, as that is developed by the apostle in a great variety of ways, is never for an instant detached from this eschatological gospel of the resurrection.

On the other hand, it is to be maintained no less vigorously that in Paul's proclamation the resurrection of Christ in fact means the breakthrough of the new aeon in the real, redemptive-historical sense of the word, and therefore cannot be understood only in forensic, ethical, or existential categories. This all-embracing significance of the resurrection of Christ is in Paul likewise not only the fruit of his profound theological reflection, but above all of divine revelation. For, as he himself expresses it, when it pleased God to reveal his Son to him (Gal. 1:15), that was first and foremost the evidence for him that Jesus of Nazareth, who was crucified and had died and whom he himself had persecuted, was the Son of God and the Messiah of Israel. And it was this certainty, entirely foreign and even offensive to Jewish thinking,[40] which determined his insight into the redemptive-historical significance of Christ's death and resurrection in a decisive manner. Because Jesus was the Christ, his resurrection is not, as previous raisings of the dead, an isolated occurrence, but in it the time of salvation promised in him, the new creation, dawns in an overwhelming manner, as a decisive transition from the old to the new world (2 Cor. 5:17; cf. v.

---

39. Cf. Dodd, *Apostolic Preaching*, pp. 9ff.

40. Cf., e.g., Strack-Billerbeck, *Kommentar zum Neuen Testament aus Talmud und Midrasch*, II, 1924, pp. 273ff.; W. Bousset, *Die Religion des Judentums im späthellenistischen Zeitalter*, 3rd ed., 1926, p. 231.

15). It is in this light too, that those passages are to be understood where Paul calls Christ the Firstborn, the Firstfruits, the Beginning:

> ...that he might be the Firstborn *(prōtotokos)* among many brethren (Rom. 8:29).
> ...but now Christ has been raised from the dead, the Firstfruits *(aparchē)* of those who have fallen asleep (1 Cor. 15:20).
> ...who is the Beginning *(archē),* the Firstborn from the dead, that in everything he might be the First (Col. 1:18).

In connection with the name Firstborn one is not to think here merely of an order of birth but, as may appear from a comparison with certain Old Testament pronouncements (as, for example, Exod. 4:22; Ps. 89:22),[41] of an order of rank or dignity. To be sure, this name also indicates the relationship to others who in Romans 8:29 are called "many brethren." As the Firstborn among those many, however, Christ not only occupies a special place and dignity, but he also goes before them, he opens up the way for them, he joins their future to his own. Now, while in Romans 8:29 the thought is of the glorification that is still to be expected, in Colossians 1:18 this position as Firstborn is related specifically to the resurrection, and this pronouncement is amplified still further with the words "who is the Beginning." We shall have to understand both qualifications in close relationship with each other, and must thus see in "the Beginning" a denotation of the significance of Christ's resurrection as well. Our word "beginning" is no adequate translation of it. For what is intended is not merely that Christ was the First or formed a beginning in terms of chronological order; he was rather the Pioneer, the Inaugurator, who opened up the way. With him the great Resurrection became reality. And very similar is the meaning of Firstborn from the dead: he ushers in the world of the resurrection.[42] He has brought life and incorruptibility to light (2 Tim. 1:10). In a somewhat different way the same idea is given expression by "Firstfruits" (of those who have fallen asleep). Here the picture of the harvest is in the background. The firstfruits are not only its beginning, but its representation. In the firstfruits the whole harvest becomes visible. So Christ is the Firstfruits of them that slept. In him the resurrection of the dead dawns, his resurrection represents the commencement of the new world of God.

Nowhere is this more clearly voiced than in the passages in which Christ is set over against Adam. Paul speaks in 1 Corinthians 15:45ff. of Adam as "the first man," and of Christ as "the last *(ho eschatos)* Adam," the "second man." The expression "the last Adam" is again highly typical of the eschatological character of Paul's preaching: Christ is thereby designated as the Inaugurator of the new humanity. And it is once more his resurrection from the dead that has made him this last Adam:

> For as by a man came death, by a man has come also the resurrection

---

41. Cf., e.g., Michaelis, *TDNT,* VI, pp. 876ff.; and also my *Col.,* p. 137.
42. *Ibid.,* p. 143.

of the dead. For as in Adam all die, so also in Christ shall all be made alive (1 Cor. 15:21, 22).

... the first man, Adam, became a living soul; the last Adam a life-giving spirit.... The first man is from the earth, earthy; the second man is from heaven.... And as we have borne the image of the earthy, we shall also bear the image of the heavenly (1 Cor. 15:45ff.).

The intention of the apostle is here again not merely to point to the resurrection of Christ as the token or as the possibility of the future resurrection of all believers. Rather, Christ as second man and last Adam is the one in whose resurrection this new life of the re-creation has already come to light and become reality in this dispensation. This is also the clear purport of Romans 5:12ff. As Adam is the one through whom sin entered into the world and death through sin, so Christ is the one who gives righteousness and life. Christ and Adam stand over against one another as the great representatives of the two aeons, that of life and that of death. In that sense, as representing a whole dispensation, a whole humanity, Adam can be called the type of "him who was to come" (v. 14), i.e., of the second man and of the coming aeon represented by him.[43] For as the proto-father brought sin and death into the world, so Christ by his obedience (that is, by his death) and his resurrection has made life to dawn for the new humanity.

In summary we can say, therefore, that Paul's kerygma of the great time of salvation that has dawned in Christ is above all determined by Christ's death and resurrection. It is in them that the present aeon has lost its power and hold on the children of Adam and that the new things have come. For this reason, too, the entire unfolding of the salvation that has dawned with Christ again and again harks back to his death and resurrection, because all the facets in which this salvation appears and all the names by which it is described are ultimately nothing other than the unfolding of what this all-important breakthrough of life in death, of the kingdom of God in this present world, contains within itself. Here all lines come together, and from hence the whole Pauline proclamation of redemption can be described in its unity and coherence. Paul's preaching, so we have seen, is "eschatology," because it is preaching of the fulfilling redemptive work of God in Christ. We might be able to delimit this further, to a certain extent schematically, by speaking of Paul's "resurrection-eschatology." For it is in Christ's death and subsequent resurrection that the mystery of the redemptive plan of God has manifested itself in its true character and that the new creation has come to light.

SECTION 10. IN CHRIST, WITH CHRIST. THE OLD AND THE NEW MAN

Before inquiring further into the basic christological-eschatological struc-

---

43. Cf. A. Nygren, *Commentary on Romans*, ET 1949, pp. 20ff., 217: "When Paul speaks about the new aeon, it is not usual for him to refer to it as 'the

ture of Paul's preaching, an important implication of what has been
dealt with in the previous section should be pointed out separately. It
relates to the highly important question of how that which once took
place in Christ also concerns others (his own, the church, etc.) and by
virtue of which principle what took place in him and was accomplished
by him is applicable to them and benefits them. Here is one of the
most typical motifs of Paul's preaching, which has come to be seen as
most closely connected with the significance he ascribes to Christ as the
last Adam and Inaugurator of the new humanity.[44] For this reason we
now purpose to go further into this relationship — an important link
in the fundamental structure of Paul's preaching — first by way of an
interlude.

     Undoubtedly one cannot say that Paul derives the redemptive
significance of Christ for his own exclusively from his position as the
last Adam and gives expression to it only in these "Adam-categories."
The apostle not infrequently speaks of this in a less pregnant fashion
and adopts the usage frequently followed elsewhere in the New Testament that Christ has executed his redemptive work "for us," i.e., in our
behalf. This is so particularly when his suffering, death, and resurrection
are spoken of. It is not Paul but Christ who has been crucified for his
people (1 Cor. 1:13). God made Christ to be sin for us (2 Cor. 5:21).
He has become a curse for us (Gal. 3:13). He gave himself for our sins
(Gal 1:4; cf. 1 Tim. 2:6; Phil. 2:14); in due season died for the ungodly
(Rom. 5:6); died for us when we were yet sinners (Rom. 5:8); died for
our sins according to the Scriptures (1 Cor. 15:3). In these and other
pronouncements Paul gives expression to the redemptive significance of
Christ's death in a more traditional fashion, at the basis of which
terminology lie various ideas that are still to be discussed more fully
(e.g., of sacrifice, ransom, etc.).[45]

     It is typical of Paul's preaching, however, that he joins this
general formula "for us" (in the sense of "in our behalf"[46]) with another,
the purport of which is that Christ forms such a unity with those for
whom he appears that it can be said that they are "in him" (2 Cor.
5:17), and that on this account what once took place "in Christ" is
applicable to them. While the formula "in Christ," "in him," etc.,
appears in various connections and even exhibits something of the
character of a stereotype, the application to his own of what once took
place and is yet to take place with Christ often occurs with the words
"with Christ," "with him," etc. In connection with the latter one is to
think particularly of those pronouncements so typical of Paul's preaching which speak of being crucified, dead, buried, and raised with Christ

coming aeon' *(ho aiōn ho mellōn)*. But here we glimpse the idea in his characterization of Christ as He 'who was to come'; for as *ho mellōn* He is the head of *ho
aiōn ho mellōn*."

     44. Cf. E. E. Ellis, *Paul and His Recent Interpreters*, pp. 31ff.; J. de Fraine,
Adam and the Family of Man, ET 1965; see also the literature cited above, p. 38, n. 90.
     45. See, e.g., below, Section 34.
     46. Usually indicated by *hyper* with the genitive, but also by *peri* with the
genitive (cf. 1 Cor. 1:13; 1 Thess. 5:10); likewise in the combination *peri hamartias*
(Rom. 8:3); cf. also Riesenfeld, *TDNT*, VI, pp. 54f.

(Rom. 6:3ff.; Gal. 2:19; Col. 2:12, 13, 20; 3:1, 3), of having been made to sit with him in heaven (Eph. 2:6), and of appearing with him in glory (Col. 3:4).[47]

In the course of the later investigation all kinds of explanations have been given as to the nature of this connection between Christ and his people which is denoted by the formulae "in Christ" and "with Christ." For a long time scholars have proceeded from the idea that "being in Christ" denotes communion with the pneumatic Christ, out of which then the speaking of dying, rising, etc., "with Christ" is said to have developed as a description of the closest personal experiences.[48] Some choose to think here only in a general sense of influences of Hellenistic mystical thought.[49] Others have gone much further. At the root of "being in Christ," "dying, rising with him," is supposed to be the idea of an absorption with the deity, indeed of a physical unification with the divine being. Over against the religious-ethical interpretation of oneness with Christ all the emphasis was placed on the *naturhaft* character of this mysticism, which one must take, not in an ethical or symbolical, but in a proper and real sense as union with the deity and which is effected in particular through baptism and the Lord's Supper in a magical way as in the rites of the mystery religions.[50]

It has come to be understood increasingly, however, that with this "mystical" explanation of "in Christ" and "with Christ" one is on the wrong track. This is evident even from the fact that "being in Christ," "crucified, dead, raised, seated in heaven with him," obviously does not have the sense of a communion that becomes reality only in certain sublime moments, but rather of an abiding reality determinative for the whole of the Christian life, to which appeal can be made at all times, in all sorts of connections, and with respect to the whole church without distinction (cf., for example, Col. 2:20ff.; 3:1ff.). Rather than with certain experiences, we have to do here with the church's "objective" state of salvation, for which reason an appeal is repeatedly made to baptism (Rom. 6:4; Col. 2:12). It is precisely this which has been seized upon in order to interpret the co-dying and rising of believers with Christ by analogy with the initiatory rites in the mystery religions. But in addition to what may be urged against this interpretation even from a purely historical-phenomenological point of view,[51] the unmistakable fact is passed over that in Paul dying, being buried, etc., with

---

47. See also below, Chapter VI.

48. In this sense still, e.g., K. Deissner, *Paulus und die Mystik seiner Zeit*, 2nd ed., 1921, in which he places the emphasis, over against the history of religions interpretation, on the "spiritual-personal character of communion with Christ" in Paul, pp. 115ff.; cf. also E. Sommerlath, *Der Ursprung des neuen Lebens nach Paulus*, 2nd ed., 1927, pp. 97ff.

49. So, e.g., A. Deissmann, *St. Paul*, p. 132: "It is justifiable, I think, to speak of Hellenistic influence here, when we remember the importance in Greek mysticism of inspired persons who are filled with their god, and gifted with power in their god." Deissmann goes on to emphasize strongly the distinctive character of Paul's mysticism.

50. For a survey of these older *religionsgeschichtliche* interpretations, such as those of Heitmüller, Brückner, Wrede, Reitzenstein, *et al.*, see, e.g., Deissner, *Paulus und die Mystik seiner Zeit*, pp. 1-17.

51. Cf. above, pp. 23ff.

Christ does not have its ultimate ground in the ceremony of incorporation[52] into the Christian church, but rather in already having been included in the historical death and resurrection of Christ himself. Of particular significance is the pronouncement of 2 Corinthians 5:14ff., where a clear transition becomes perceptible from the "Christ for us" to the "we with [or in] Christ":

> ...we have come to the insight that one died for all. Therefore they all have died. And he died for all, that those who live might no longer live for themselves, but for him who died and was raised for them. Wherefore we henceforth know no man after the flesh.... Wherefore if any man is in Christ, he is new creation....

From this it is to be concluded that "having died," "being in Christ," "being new creation," the fact that his own are no longer judged and "known according to the flesh" (namely, according to the worldly mode of existence), has been given and effected with the death of Christ himself. Of this determination by and involvement of his own in that which once took place with Christ the formula "in Christ" now gives the expression so typical of Paul's preaching.[53]

Accordingly, it becomes increasingly apparent that the expression "dying and rising with Christ" does not have its origin in the sphere of the individual mysticism of experience, nor in the automatism of the initiatory rites of the Hellenistic mysteries, but is of an entirely different nature. The attempt has been made to give expression to this "objectivity" of being in Christ and with Christ in all sorts of ways.[54] It has become more and more apparent, however, that the Adam-Christ parallel not only casts a clear light on the significance that Paul ascribes to Christ himself, but also on the way in which he sees his own as involved in him and with him in his redemptive work. This is very clear, for example, from the words of 1 Corinthians 15:22: "... for as in Adam all die, so also in Christ shall all be made alive."

The concern here (as distinguished from what is intended in 2 Cor. 5) is with the resurrection of the dead at the parousia. What really matters, however, is that here "in Christ" is paralleled with "in Adam." Herewith the character of this "in" becomes plain. As the decision has fallen in Adam with respect to the "all" who pertain to him, that they should die, so in Christ that they shall live. Adam and Christ

---

52. For the question whether baptism symbolizes dying and rising (with Christ) see below, pp. 401ff.

53. Cf. the important essay of F. Neugebauer, "Das Paulinische 'In Christo,' " *NTS*, 1958, pp. 124-138.

54. Thus Schweitzer, e.g., has pointed to the notion also occurring in the Jewish writings of the unity of the Messiah with the predestinated congregation of the saints, calling this the germ cell of Paul's "Christ-mysticism." Materially this exegesis harks back to the old Reformation interpretation. Thus, e.g., Zanchius, in his commentary on Ephesians 2:5, writes: "God has made us alive in the person of Christ, since through Christ's death, sin having been expiated, he liberated all the elect, howsoever many had been from the foundation of the earth and would be to the end of it, so many he considered the members of Christ in his selfsame head" (*Hieron. Zanchii Comment. in epistolam sancti Pauli ad Ephesios*, I, ed. A. H. de Hartogh, 1888, p. 160).

here stand over against each other as the two great figures at the entrance of two worlds, two aeons, two "creations," the old and the new; and in their actions and fate lies the decision for all who belong to them, because these are comprehended in them and thus are reckoned either to death or to life.[55] This is now expressed by "in Adam" and "in Christ." And it is therefore in this sense that Adam can be called the type of him who was to come.[56]

In Romans 5:12ff. this is explicated still further. There Paul elucidates what he has posited in verses 1-11 as the certainty of salvation for believers, that those who have already been reconciled to God by the death of Christ shall live by him in the future. For that purpose he points to the bond that joins all the descendants of Adam with their progenitor, as the pattern and type of the communion between Christ and his own. Here there is no mention of "in Adam," but (still more "realistically"!) the transgression of Adam is called the sin of all: ". . . as through one man sin entered into the world, and death through sin; and so death passed unto all men, for the reason that all sinned . . ." (Rom. 5:12).

On what this unity rests, whether it must be viewed, for example, as "realistic" or as "federal,"[57] is not further elucidated. Adam and Christ are spoken of here as "universal personalities . . . construed cosmically and eschatologically," who comprehend within themselves all the members of the generations of men pertaining to them,[58] or, with a term that has found still more acceptance, as a "corporate personality,"[59] which points to the figure (which also appears in the Old

---

55. As a variant of the future in 1 Cor. 15:22, the aorist is elsewhere to be found: "He *has* made you alive with Christ" (Col. 2:13; cf. Eph. 2:5). That it is evident from these aorists that these pronouncements in Ephesians and Colossians are from a later hand, as C. Masson supposes (*l'Épitre de Saint Paul aux Colossiens,* pp. 126, 127), is without foundation. It is a matter in 1 Cor. 15:22, too, of an accomplished decision; cf. also E. Percy, *Die Probleme der Kolosser- und Epheser-Briefe,* 1946, pp. 110ff.

56. With this the conception of K. Barth is in conflict, that "it is Christ who vouches for the authenticity of Adam, and not Adam . . . for Christ" (*Christ and Adam,* ET 1956, pp. 8ff.). Still less acceptable is the conclusion Barth attaches to it, that Adam in Rom. 5 is only apparently as Christ a First, the Head of humanity, that in truth, however, he is "one among others" and thus represents humanity (*ibid.,* pp. 9, 24, 44). As has been clearly shown by Bultmann, "Adam and Christ in Romans 5," in *The Old and New Man in the Letters of Paul,* ET 1967, pp. 49ff., in no respect whatever is justice done to the significance Paul here ascribes to Adam. The relationship of Adam and his descendants is here not that of "one among all" but of "all in one."

57. See in detail G. C. Berkouwer, *Sin,* ET 1971, pp. 436-465. On Rom. 5:12 see further below, Section 16.

58. Thus Oepke, *TDNT,* II, pp. 541-542. He elucidates this as follows: "The first and the second Adam are progenitors initiating two races of men. Each implies a whole world, an order of life or death. Each includes his adherents in and under himself.

59. For this term and its applicability see above, p. 38. Further still, e.g., C. H. Dodd, *The Epistle of Paul to the Romans,* 1947, p. 80, cf. p. 86; S. Hanson, *The Unity of the Church in the N.T.,* 1946, pp. 68ff., 84ff. The term was apparently introduced in the Old Testament studies of H. Wheeler Robinson. See also J. de Fraine, *Adam and the Family of Man;* Berkouwer, *Sin,* pp. 512ff.

Testament) of the progenitor or leader or king or spokesman who represents a whole people or societal relationship and with whom the members of this nation, etc., in virtue of the relationship in which they stand to him, can be identified. It is this corporate connection of the all-in-One that Paul applies to Christ and his people, and from which the pronouncements concerning (dying, etc.) "with Christ" must be interpreted, at least as to their origin,[60] as is plainly evident as well from the close connection between Romans 5:12-21 (Adam and Christ) and Romans 6:1ff. (being buried with Christ, etc.).[61] We have to do here with one of the fundamental motifs of Paul's preaching of redemption, which occurs again particularly in his conception of the church.[62] In that sense Christ and believers can be spoken of as the one seed of Abraham (Gal. 3:16), and it can be said of them that they, although many, are one body in Christ (Rom. 12:5), indeed that they are one *(heis)* in Christ (Gal. 3:28).[63]

In close connection with the above there is another point still to be indicated in which in an oblique fashion the Adam-Christ parallel comes to still further elaboration. It is the manner in which not only Christ as the second man, but also in a more general sense the old and the new man are spoken of. The following pronouncements are of particular importance here:

> ... knowing this, that our old man was also crucified, that the body of sin might be rendered powerless (Rom. 6:6).
> But they who are of Christ have crucified the flesh with its passions and lusts (Gal. 5:24; cf. Col. 2:11).
> ... that you put away, as concerning your former manner of life, the old man ... and put on the new man, that has been created in accordance with God (Eph. 4:22ff.).
> ... seeing that you have put off the old man with his desires, and have

---

60. On the working out of this corporate unity between Christ and believers, see further below, Section 37. With a view to this Oepke correctly writes: "On the other hand, a place must be found for the plenitude of pneumatic interconnections which are here felt by Paul and which may even be comprehended psychologically and empirically" (*TDNT*, I, p. 542, *s.v. baptō*).

61. For the rejection of the "mystical" interpretation see also the clear exposition of Nygren, *Commentary on Romans*, pp. 236f.

62. Cf. below, Chapter IX.

63. One should observe the masculine *heis* and not *hen*. S. Hanson, *The Unity of the Church in the N.T.*, pp. 81f., writes: "This expression has, so to say, a personal character; it means: 'You are all one man in Christ Jesus.' After *heis* we must add *anthrōpos* or a similar word. 'In Christ Jesus,' in the New Aeon, all are one man." In this connection see also the interesting views of the biblical "root-thinking" of H. Hofer, *Die Rechtfertigungsverkündigung des Paulus nach neuerer Forschung*, 1940, pp. 26ff. He writes: "It is not the individual that is the fundamental, the first, the original, the primary datum, but it is also not society; rather it is the ancestral father, as type and mediator of life, as the one who comprises his followers and disciples in himself. ... Therefore it is the case with respect to the *church* that it is not to be construed in the first place as a community, but in its roots as the embodiment and unfolding of its progenitor Christ. It is not primarily congregation, community of believers, but it is, as 1 Cor. 12:12 says, 'Christ' *(ho Christos)*, or, as Paul, expanding, says elsewhere, 'the body of Christ.'" See further below, Chapter IX.

put on the new man, that is being renewed . . . in accordance with the
image of his Creator (Col. 3:9f.).

Frequently the old man is taken in an individual sense and the
crucifying and putting off of the old man as the personal breaking with
and fighting against the power of sin.[64] "Old" and "new" then designate
the time before and after conversion or personal regeneration, and the
corresponding manner of life. But we shall have to understand "old"
and "new man," not in the first place in the sense of the *ordo salutis,*
but in that of the history of redemption; that is to say, it is a matter
here not of a change that comes about in the way of faith and conversion in the life of the individual Christian, but of that which once
took place in Christ and in which his people had part in him in the
corporate sense described above. This is at least the obvious meaning
of Romans 6:6: our old man was crucified (namely, with Christ), that
is, on Golgotha. Christ's death on the cross was their own (cf. Rom.
6:2; Col. 3:3) and affected them in their existence. The old man, the
old mode of existence of sin, was then judged and cursed. For although
Christ himself was free of sin, he was nevertheless "in the likeness of
sinful flesh" and united himself with them in their existence; and their
sin, their old man, was condemned in his flesh (Rom. 8:3; cf. 7:4). Here
again, therefore, "the old" stands over against "the new"; not first of
all in a personal and ethical sense, but in a redemptive-historical, eschatological sense. It is not as yet a matter here, therefore, of that which
must come about and be changed in the believer, but of that which
was done "objectively" to the old man in Christ, of the *einmalig*
crucifixion of the old man on Golgotha with Christ. Hence, the words
can follow in Romans 6:6: "that the body of sin might be rendered
powerless." Because the old man was condemned and put to death in
Christ's death on the cross, the body of sin, the flesh, the old mode of
existence of sin, has lost its dominion and control over those who are
in him. In Christ's death and resurrection they have been transferred to
the new order of life — the life order of the new creation, the new man.[65]

Undoubtedly there is also mention of the putting off of the old
and the putting on of the new man by believers themselves (Eph. 4:22ff.;
Col. 3:9ff.), just as it is said that they have crucified the flesh (Gal. 5:24),
and that they have put off the body of sin. This refers, as will be demonstrated still further,[66] to the transition that has come about in their
life by baptism. Yet even understood in this way the expression old
and new man retains a supra-individual significance; this transition has
been effected in their life because they have been incorporated into the

---

64. Cf., e.g., Greijdanus (*Rom.,* I, p. 299) on Rom. 6:6: ". . . the apostle means
that the old man, the sinful corruption in the believer, was also struck by God's
curse and underwent death," namely, "at his connection or union with Christ"; cf.
also his exegesis of *apethanomen* (v. 2): "speaking of that which has taken place
with having been joined to and having become a believer in Christ" (p. 293).

65. Cf. N. A. Dahl, "Christ, Creation and the Church," in *The Background
of the New Testament and Its Eschatology,* 1956, p. 436: "In a similar way, 'the
new man' is not simply the converted individual, but an eschatological entity, personal, corporate and pneumatic, nearly identical with Christ himself. . . ."

66. See below, Chapter VI, Section 37.

body of Christ by baptism, and they may thus apply to themselves in faith that which has taken place in Christ. They have put off the old man, as crucified and buried in Christ (Col. 2:11), and have put on the new man, the new creation of God that has come to light in Christ's resurrection. This renewal is a continuing process (Col. 3:9), just as the mortification of the old man is a continuing process (Eph. 4:22). But it is the redemptive-historical transition, effected in Christ's death and resurrection, that is working itself out in this process. And it all rests on their being-in-him, as the second Adam. For this reason the new man can be spoken of as being created in accordance with God (Eph. 4:24), or being renewed in accordance with the image of his Creator (Col. 3:9ff.). These are all Adam-categories, for they have been (re-)created in him (Christ) as in the new Adam (Eph. 2:10), and as they have borne the image of the first (earthly) Adam, so, by virtue of this same corporate relationship, they will bear the image of the last (heavenly) Adam (1 Cor. 15). Indeed, this corporate unity with Christ dominates the idea of the new man so strongly that believers, as the body of Christ, even in their totality can be called "the one new man" (Eph. 2:15; cf. Gal. 3:28), and that it can be said of them that they together, in the building up of the body of Christ, will be permitted to attain to "the perfect man," the mature man in Christ (Eph. 4:13).[67]

The corporate idea of the all-in-One derived from the significance of Adam — thus we may conclude — works itself out in all sorts of ways in the Pauline explication of the redemptive event that made its appearance in Christ. It teaches us to understand the redemptive-historical character not only of that which has once occurred in Christ, but also of the way in which those who belong to Christ participate once and continuously in the salvation wrought in Christ.

SECTION 11. REVEALED IN THE FLESH.
FLESH AND SPIRIT

If in the preceding sections Christ's resurrection has rightly been shown to be the beginning of the new creation for Paul, the question naturally arises as to what significance must be ascribed to Christ's life on earth before his death and resurrection. It has frequently been observed that Paul goes into very few details in his epistles as to Jesus' life on earth, his miracles and preaching, and the meaning of all this. Now, one will have to take into full account the fact that Paul's epistles build on a foundational preaching in which he has made known the apostolic tradition to the church. This is evident from specific references to what he had already said and which the church may thus be considered to know (cf., e.g., 1 Cor. 15:1, 2; Gal. 1:11; 2 Thess. 2:5; 3:10). Only in certain connections in his epistles does he repeat fragments of this tradition because there was a particular occasion for it (1 Cor. 11:23ff.; 15:2ff.). In the same sense he appeals only incidentally

---

67. In addition see below, Chapter XI, pp. 435ff.

to specific pronouncements of Jesus (1 Cor. 7:10; cf. v. 25; 9:14; 1 Thess. 4:15), from which it appears that in general the point of departure for his instruction lay in them. If one looks more closely, it becomes apparent that his epistles contain all kinds of conscious or unconscious reminiscences of and allusions to words of Jesus (cf., e.g., Rom. 12:14; 13:9; Gal. 5:14; 1 Cor. 13:2).[68]

This does not alter the fact that in Paul's epistles the significance of Jesus' advent and life on earth before his resurrection is usually not drawn from specific words or works of the Lord, but is approached more from a general redemptive-historical point of view. It is typical of this approach that the apostle prefers to characterize Jesus' life on earth before his resurrection as his existence "after the flesh," or "in the flesh." One has only to think of the following pronouncements:

> . . . who was born of the seed of David according to the flesh (Rom. 1:3).
> . . . God sent his Son in the likeness of sinful flesh (Rom. 8:3).
> . . . of whom is Christ as concerning the flesh (Rom. 9:5).
> . . . even though we have known Christ after the flesh, yet now we know him [so] no more (2 Cor. 5:16).
> . . . who made both one, and . . . abolished in his flesh the enmity (Eph. 2:14ff.).
> . . . but now he has reconciled you in the body of his flesh through death (Col. 1:22).
> . . . who was revealed in the flesh (1 Tim. 3:16).

On the one hand, in several of these pronouncements the accent is laid on the wholly unique, eschatological character of Christ's advent and his life on earth. He was even then the Son sent by God (Rom. 8:3), the evidence that the time was fulfilled (Gal. 4:4). His advent was revelation (1 Tim. 3:16) of what till that moment had been hidden, fulfillment of God's counsel.[69] He was the Christ out of Israel (Rom. 9:5), the long-expected Son of David (Rom. 1:3). But his revelation took place "in the flesh," that is, he assumed the mode of existence of the present world. "Flesh" does not refer only to the physical, nor merely to the human as such, but to the human in its weakness, transitoriness, that which Paul elsewhere terms being "of the earth, earthy" (1 Cor. 15:47), and what in Galatians 4 is called being "born of a woman." In Romans 8:3 he speaks of "the likeness of sinful flesh," in which God sent his Son. "Flesh" and "sinful flesh" need not coincide. But sin in the nature of the case takes place in the flesh and stamps the human mode of existence as "the sinful flesh." It is in "the likeness" of this that God sent his Son, a phrase with which Paul elsewhere expresses the difference between correspondence and identity (cf. Rom. 6:5). Christ came, therefore, in the weak, transitory human state, without sharing in the sin of the human race. It was in that way, in that mode of existence, that he was "known" before his resurrection (2 Cor. 5:16). In this "flesh" he lived and he died, or as it is also called: "in the body

---

68. On this and on the whole question of Paul's knowledge of the "historical" Jesus see my *Paul and Jesus*, pp. 50ff., and the literature referred to there.
69. Cf. above, pp. 46ff.

of his flesh" (Col. 1:22), which expression likewise refers not only to the physical as material organism, but to the whole of Christ's existence as a man subject to transitoriness, dishonor, frailty (cf. 1 Cor. 15:42ff.). And it was also in this flesh, i.e., his human existence delivered up to the death of the cross, that the enmity was abolished, the church reconciled, and sin condemned (Eph. 2:14, 15; Col. 1:2; Rom. 8:3).

It is Christ's being revealed in the flesh (to be understood in this way) that is the specific significance of Christ's life before his resurrection, and which is to be adored (cf. 1 Tim. 3:16a). The revelation, the sending of the Son, the fullness of the time, already took effect with it. But the new creation is that of Christ's resurrection. For this reason the death of Christ is a turning point in the mode of existence of the old aeon. Christ dies to it, through death he dies to the flesh, to the old aeon (cf. Rom. 6:7, 9ff.). It is this turning point to which Paul orients himself and to which he wants believers to orient themselves (Rom. 6:11; 8:10; Col. 3:3). Not only does Christ's life in the flesh come to an end, but an all-important and all-embracing Transition takes place, namely, from the existence of the old to that of the new, from the old aeon to the new creation. By dying Christ has thus snatched his people away from the present aeon (Gal. 1:4). From this moment on faith no longer "knows," that is to say, judges, "after the flesh" (2 Cor. 5:16). It regards all things from another point of view, namely, that the aeon of the sole dominion of the flesh is done away with and the mode of existence of the Spirit has been entered upon.

For in Paul it is the Spirit who stands over against the "flesh" described in this way:

> ...of the seed of David according to the flesh, designated the Son of God in power according to the Spirit of holiness in virtue of his resurrection from the dead (Rom. 1:3, 4).
> ...who was revealed in the flesh, justified by the Spirit (1 Tim. 3:16).
> ...the body is dead, ...the Spirit is life (Rom. 8:10).

Flesh (body) and Spirit do not stand over against one another here as two "parts" in the human existence or in the existence of Christ. There is no question here (nor in Rom. 8:10!) of a dichotomistic distinction in an anthropological sense. Nor is the contrast ethical, as is indeed the case in other contexts (Gal. 5:13, *et al.*), even though there, too, on the foundation to be further indicated here. Rather, "flesh" and "Spirit" represent two modes of existence, on the one hand that of the old aeon which is characterized and determined by the flesh, on the other that of the new creation which is of the Spirit of God. It is in this sense that the difference is also to be taken between the first Adam as "living soul," i.e., flesh, and the second as life-giving Spirit. The contrast is therefore of a redemptive-historical nature: it qualifies the world and the mode of existence before Christ as flesh, that is, as the creaturely in its weakness; on the other hand, the dispensation that has taken effect with Christ as that of the Spirit, i.e., of power, imperishableness and glory (1 Cor. 15:42, 43, 50; Phil. 3:21). It is within this redemptive-historical contrast of flesh and Spirit as the mode of existence of the old and new creation that Paul now views the life of Christ before and after his resurrection. In virtue of his resurrection from the dead, Christ, "according to the Spirit of holiness,"[70] is declared to be the Son of God in power (Rom. 1:4); he is "justified" (i.e., vindicated, disclosed in his true significance) by the Spirit (1 Tim. 3:16). It is in that new existence of the resurrection and of the Spirit that the church may now know Christ (2 Cor. 5:16), and may also judge itself as joined with him. The body, that is to say, life, insofar as it still belongs to the old aeon, is (subject to) death because of sin, but the Spirit, the Author of the new creation, gives life because of the righteousness accomplished in Christ[71] (Rom. 8:10). For this reason the church is no longer "in the flesh," i.e., subject to the regime of the first aeon and the evil powers reigning in it, but "in the Spirit," brought under the dominion of freedom in Christ (Rom. 8:2ff., 9, 13; 2 Cor. 3:6; Gal. 3:21). All the facets of the contrast of flesh and Spirit, which are to be treated still further in what follows,[72] become transparent and luminous out of this basic eschatological structure of Paul's preaching and constitute a highly important element of it.

In the history of the investigation — as we have seen — the "flesh and Spirit" contrast has frequently been viewed as a proof that Paul withdrew from the original eschatological consciousness of the primitive Christian church and became dependent on Hellenistic thinking. The contrast of flesh and Spirit was, moreover, at one time interpreted in an idealistic sense, as that between the Absolute and the historical and therefore relative; at another as the "ethical" struggle between the higher and the lower in man.[73] Without regard, however, to the fact that one is compelled thus to come to accept all manner of mutually contradictory basic motifs in Paul's preaching, one also in this way misjudges the real nature of the work of the Spirit in Paul. For this nature is not to be understood as a Christianizing of the Greek or Hellenistic *pneuma*-concept, however understood, but finds its clear and "natural" background in the Old Testament thinking and speaking about the Spirit. There the Spirit appears repeatedly in the closest relationship with the acting of God in history. The Spirit represents the creating and re-creating power of God that governs the world and history and conducts them to their final goal.[74] He is the Creator and the Precursor of the great future, he equips the coming Messiah-Savior for his task, and he will pour out his gifts without measure on the eschatological people of God (cf., e.g., Isa. 32:15; 11:2; 59:21; 61:1; Joel 2:28, 29; Zech. 4:6; 12:10, *et al.*).[75] In the New Testament the Spirit is consequently spoken of, by Paul too, in all sorts of ways in connection

---

70. The uncommon expression "Spirit of holiness" (*pneuma hagiōsynēs*) will have to be judged simply as an equivalent, resting on Old Testament usage, of "Holy Spirit"; cf. Procksch, *TDNT*, I, pp. 114-115.

71. For this exegesis see also below, p. 113, n. 57.

72. Cf., e.g., Chapter VI, Section 38.

73. Cf. above, Chapter I, Sections 2, 3, 4.

74. Cf., e.g., Baumgärtel, *TDNT*, VI, pp. 365ff.; also Ingo Hermann, *Kyrios und Pneuma, Studien zur Christologie der paulinischen Hauptbriefe*, 1961, pp. 126ff.

75. Cf. Sjöberg, *TDNT*, VI, pp. 383ff.

with and in terms of this promise (cf., e.g., Acts 2:16; Rom. 2:29; 5:5; 8:15; 2 Cor. 3:3, 6; Gal. 3:14; Eph. 1:13). It has rightly been observed, therefore, that the content of the *pneuma*-concept in Paul admits of being most sharply defined and filled in when he is understood as the gift of the end time[76] (see further below, Section 14).

SECTION 12. CHRIST, THE SON OF GOD AND THE IMAGE OF GOD

However much Paul's Christology finds its point of departure in Christ's death and resurrection and to whatever degree he draws the lines from thence on the one hand to the incarnation and on the other to the future of the Lord, all this does not alter the fact that the whole of his preaching of the historical and future revelation of Christ is supported by the confession of Christ as the Son of God, in the supra- and prehistorical sense of the word. It can even rightly be said that the sending of the Son by the Father in the fullness of time presupposes his pre-existence with God (cf. Gal. 4:4; Rom. 8:3 with such passages as 2 Cor. 8:9; Phil. 2:6ff.; Col. 1:15ff.; Rom. 8:32).[77] This pre-existence of Christ with the Father so emphatically declared by Paul underlies his whole Christology and makes it impossible to conceive of all the divine attributes and power that he ascribes to Christ exclusively as the consequence of his exaltation. It is true that he often speaks in this sense of the *Kyrios* exalted by God, to whom he prays (2 Cor. 12:8, 9), whose name is to be "called upon" in the church (1 Cor. 1:2; Rom. 10:13), from whom one may expect that which God alone has the power to grant (Rom. 1:7; 1 Cor. 1:3; Rom. 16:20; 2 Cor. 13:13), before whose judgment seat all will appear (2 Cor. 5:10; cf. Rom. 14:10), and whose gospel, kingdom, and Spirit are spoken of as those of God (cf. Rom. 1:1; 15:16; Eph. 5:5; Rom. 8:9, *et al.*).[78] But this "exaltation Christology" is at the same time not for a moment to be divorced from the significance of Christ's person as such. This is also evident from the (few) places where Paul calls Christ himself God, to be blessed forever (Rom. 9:5; cf. 2 Thess. 1:12; Tit. 2:13),[79] whereby one cannot, of course, think of a conferred or acquired dignity or mode of existence; but then further in particular from the pronouncements on his pre-existence. It is this pre-existence of Christ with the Father that we must take fully into account in the interpretation of the name frequently and continuously employed by Paul of Christ as the Son of God (Rom. 1:3, 4, 9;

---

76. Hermann, *Kyrios und Pneuma*, p. 144; cf. also N. Q. Hamilton, *The Holy Spirit and Eschatology in Paul*, pp. 17ff.

77. Cf. G. Delling: "The assertion of the incarnation includes, for Paul, preexistence"; "Zum neueren Paulusverständnis," *Novum Testamentum*, 1960, p. 102.

78. Cf. G. Sevenster, *De Christologie van het Nieuwe Testament*, 1946, pp. 144ff.; F. Prat, *The Theology of Saint Paul*, II, ET 1964, pp. 132ff.

79. Cf. also Bultmann, *Theology*, p. 129; for a further discussion of these passages see my *Paul and Jesus*, pp. 72, 73, and the literature cited there; Cullmann, *Christology*, pp. 312ff.

5:10; 8:3, 29, 32; 1 Cor. 1:9; 2 Cor. 1:19; Gal. 1:16; 2:20; 4:4, 6; Eph. 4:13; Col. 1:13; 1 Thess. 1:10). For this reason, too, we cannot accept Cullmann's thesis that "it is only meaningful to speak of the Son in view of God's revelatory action, not in view of his being."[80] However true it is that the name Son of God again and again denotes the entirely unique relationship of Christ to the Father in the divine redemptive work revealed in him, one cannot, precisely because of this pre-existence (that is, the existing prior to the revelation) of the Son, permit the being of the Son to be lost in his revelation as the Son of God. God sent his Son (Rom. 8:3; Gal. 4:4), and this sending does not create the Sonship, but presupposes it.[81] For the same reason, on the other hand, where there is mention of the consummation of Christ's work of redemption, in the words of 1 Corinthians 15:28 (when the Son has subjected all things to the Father, then will he himself be subjected to him, that God may be all in all), this cannot mean the end of the Sonship.[82] One will rather have to judge the "post-existence" of the Son intended here in the light of what is elsewhere so clearly stated of his pre-existence.

All this does not alter the fact — and this is the element of truth in Cullmann's argument — that when he speaks of Christ's pre-existence, Paul regards and designates this not as separate from, but precisely in its bearing on Christ's revelation in redemptive history. So far as the latter is concerned, it can be said that he makes the line of redemptive history go back to Christ's pre-existence and represents his pre-temporal divine Sonship to the church from the viewpoint of Christ's revelation in redemptive history. As the Pre-existent One, too, the Son of God is the Christ, the object of God's election (Eph. 1:4), and as such the one in whom the grace of God has been given to the church before times eternal (2 Tim. 1:9; cf. Eph. 1:9); likewise the one in whom the church itself had already been comprehended, chosen, and sanctified (Eph. 1:4; 2:10; cf. Rom. 8:29).

In this connection those pronouncements are to be mentioned in particular which describe Christ as the Image of God:

... Christ, who is the Image of God (2 Cor. 4:4).
... who [Christ] is the Image of the invisible God (Col. 1:15).
... who, being in the form of God (Phil. 2:6).

These formulations are so important because Paul gives expression in them to the divine glory of Christ in a way that is very significant

---

80. *Christology*, p. 293.

81. For that matter, in answer to the criticism brought against him at this point, Cullmann has denied that he sees the functional character of the Sonship as excluding the ontological (*Scottish Journal of Theology*, 1962, pp. 36ff.); cf. also his formulations on pp. 306ff. of his *Christology*. For this discussion (with Roman Catholic theologians) see also G. C. Berkouwer, *The Return of Christ*, pp. 427-428.

82. For his conception Cullmann appeals specifically to 1 Cor. 15:28, which he terms "the key to all New Testament Christology" (*ibid.*, p. 293). We are brought here, so he says elsewhere, "to the very threshold of a complete eschatological absorption of the Son in the Father" (*ibid.*, p. 248; cf. p. 268; see also below, pp. 560ff.).

and highly characteristic for his Christology. In the context of 2 Corinthians 4:4 Paul speaks of his gospel as an irradiation of the divine glory. He motivates this by calling Christ, whose glory is seen in the gospel, the Image of God, and then speaks further of this glory as the light that God, who through the word of his power once brought light forth out of darkness, has made to shine in the hearts of the church by the knowledge of the glory of God in the face of Christ. We shall, as is also apparent in 2 Corinthians 3:18, have to think in connection with this glory especially of the glory of the exalted Lord. When in this context he is called at the same time the Image of God, this is to say nothing less than that in him the glory of God, indeed God himself, becomes manifest. By calling Christ the Image of God he thus identifies Christ's glory with that of God himself.[83] And the same thing applies to Colossians 1:15 and the definition of "Image of God" in Philippians 2:6, which is to be discussed still further. There is, however, special mention of Christ's glory as the Pre-existent One in these passages. As such, by the designation Image of God he is on the one hand distinguished from God, and on the other identified with God as Bearer of the divine glory. It is evident here anew, therefore, to what extent the divine glory of Christ, even already in his pre-existence with the Father prior to his redemptive revelation, determines and underlies the Pauline Christology.

On the other hand, precisely in this description of Christ's divine glory a new indication can be seen of the redemptive-historical character of Paul's Christology. Surely this name in itself recalls the manner in which Adam is spoken of in Genesis 1:27; 5:1ff.; 9:6, when he is there said to be created "after" or "in the Image of God."[84] The question now is whether a connection has rightly been made between the one and the other,[85] in other words, whether the description of the glory of Christ as Image of God is derived from the manner in which the creation of man is spoken of in Genesis 1 as after God's image. And a second question is quite naturally linked with this, as to the extent to which the Pauline conception of Christ as the second Adam here again plays a definite part.

Some scholars deny any direct connection between 2 Corinthians 4:4 and Colossians 1:15 on the one hand, and Genesis 1:27 on the other.[86] But it has rightly been observed that both 2 Corinthians 4:4

83. For this interpretation of 2 Cor. 4:4, in addition to the commentaries, see the extensive explications of J. Jervell, *Imago Dei, Gen. 1.26f. im Spätjudentum, in der Gnosis und in den paulinischen Briefen*, 1960, pp. 173ff., 214ff.

84. *Kat' eikona Theou* or *en eikoni Theou* (LXX).

85. Thus, e.g., Kittel in *TDNT*, II, 396, *s.v. eikōn*, following Schlatter. In the more recent literature increasingly greater emphasis is placed on this connection; see, e.g., the title of the work of Jervell referred to above; also N. A. Dahl, "Christ, Creation and the Church," in *The Background of the New Testament and Its Eschatology*, pp. 434ff.

86. E.g., by F. W. Eltester, *Eikon im Neuen Testament*, 1958, p. 148. He is of the opinion that one must explain *eikōn* in 2 Cor. 4:4 from the notion of *Sophia* in later Judaism, and in Col. 1:15 from a combination of the latter with the *Urmensch* idea in the *gnosis* (*ibid.*, pp. 133ff., 140, 149). It is possible, then, that later

and Colossians 1:15 are in all sorts of ways directly reminiscent of the creation story. So far as 2 Corinthians 4:4 is concerned, Genesis 1:3 is cited in 2 Corinthians 4:6. Further, in this context there is repeated mention of "glory" (*doxa*; 3:18; 4:4, 6), an idea that both in later Judaism and by Paul himself is closely linked with Genesis 1:26ff. (cf. 1 Cor. 11:7; Rom. 1:23; 3:23; 8:29ff.). Furthermore, in the context of 2 Corinthians 4:4 the image (of God) is attributed not only to Christ, but also to the church (2 Cor. 3:18), which is obviously reminiscent of Genesis 1:27.[87] And with respect to Colossians 1:15 (of Phil. 2:6 we shall speak still further), the whole of the so-called hymn in that passage speaks of the creation. The expression Image of God is here clearly rooted in Genesis 1:27. This is further corroborated by the fact that Christ is here likewise called the Beginning (*archē*) and the Firstborn (*prōtotokos*; 1:15, 18), and is set forth as World Ruler, an idea to be met with as well in the late Jewish Adam-theology. The conclusion is: "We have before us [in Col. 1], therefore, a christological interpretation of Genesis 1."[88]

However, everything has not herewith been said. The question remains as to whether this connection — which it is difficult to deny — also means that Christ is in this way again described by Paul as (the last) Adam (1 Cor. 15; Rom. 5). Here the paths of the interpreters diverge once more. While some do in fact conceive of the connection with Genesis 1:27 in this sense, it is denied by others. Paul, by naming Christ here Image of God in the absolute sense (and not created "after" God's image), is said to distinguish in the manner of Philo and Gnosticism between the heavenly prototype (*Urbild*) and its earthly representation (*Abbild*). Christ represents the former, while in Genesis 1:27 there is mention of the latter.[89] In the expression Image of God as a description of Christ we are accordingly said not to have to do with a creation of Paul's, but with an even older usage in the Hellenistic church.[90]

Now the matter is indeed a complicated one. When Paul speaks of Christ as Image of God, he describes him thereby not, as is the case when he calls him the last Adam (1 Cor. 15:45ff.), as the second or last man, but, at least in Colossians 1:15 (and Phil. 2:6), as the Pre-existent One in his divine glory. It can even be maintained that by the name Image of God in the passages in question Paul intended to elucidate precisely "the eternal relationship of the Father to the Son."[91] On the other hand, the idea that in 2 Corinthians 4 and Colossians 1:15ff. Paul has indeed established a direct connection with Genesis 1:27, but in so doing has not started from the image of God intended in Genesis 1:27, but from a traditional Philonic-gnostic speculation concerning an *Urbild* (distinct from that of Gen. 1:27), is certainly not very credible. If one

---

this gnostic *anthropos*, who already bore the name *eikōn Theou*, was connected with Gen. 1:27. But in 2 Cor. 4:4 and Col. 1:15 this is said not yet to have been the case.

87. Jervell, *Imago Dei*, pp. 174ff.

88. *Ibid.*, pp. 200ff.

89. Thus Jervell, *ibid.*, pp. 217f., 219.

90. *Ibid.*, p. 209.

91. A. Schlatter, *Die Theologie des Neuen Testaments. 2. Die Lehre der Apostel,* 1910, p. 299.

wishes, as in our opinion is inescapable, to establish a direct relationship between Genesis 1:27 and the Pauline pronouncements concerning Christ as the Image of God, one will not be able at the same time to rob this connection of its force by slipping in between them a gnostic speculation entirely alien to this connection. Paul himself gives no evidence of such a "re-interpretation" of Genesis 1:27 in the relevant passages in any fashion whatever, and on the other hand can hardly be regarded as having silently applied so fundamental an operation to Genesis 1:27. We can come to no other conclusion, therefore, than that in the above-mentioned passages Paul has denoted the divine glory of Christ both in his pre-existence and in his exaltation with a qualification that also held for the first Adam, although, of course, in another sense appropriate to the first Adam.

This conclusion is the only acceptable one for the reason that the connection to be assumed in 2 Corinthians 4 and Colossians 1 with Genesis 1:27 on further reflection appears to rest on a much broader foundation in the Pauline epistles than on that of these two texts. It is true that the apostle, so far as the creation of man after God's image is concerned, only once explicitly refers to Genesis 1:27, namely, in 1 Corinthians 11:7, where he calls the man the image[92] and glory of God. In this context he then mentions the woman, because she is of the man, the glory of the man, and the man the head of the woman. He joins to this, however, the pronouncement that Christ is the Head of the man, and God is the Head of Christ (cf. v. 3). To be Head, to shed forth glory, is therefore a consequence of being the image of God. And when God, Christ, the man, and the woman are here mentioned successively, it may be concluded that Christ, too, derives this Headship and glory from the fact that he, in a still higher sense than the man, is the Image of God. This same parallel of the headship of the man over the woman and the Headship of Christ over the church recurs in Ephesians 5:23, even though here there is no mention of the image of God. We do, however, find the linking of the Image of God and the Headship of Christ in Colossians 1:15 and 17. Thus there are obvious connections between the glory of Christ and that of the first man as the image of God.

Other pronouncements corroborate this. In 1 Corinthians 15:45ff. in the comparison between the first and the last Adam this pronouncement also occurs: "And as we have borne the image of the earthy, we shall also bear the image of the heavenly" (v. 49).

It is true that the words "image of the earthy" (ton eikona tou choikou) do not here allude so much to the glory of the first man as image of God, but rather to his having been taken from the earth; it first of all reflects Genesis 2:7 (cf. 1 Cor. 15:45) and not Genesis 1:25ff. Even so, it is difficult to think of the expression "image" here apart from the manner in which the first man is called the image (of God)

---

92. From this absolute qualification of man as "image of God" it may also appear with how little justice Jervell thinks himself able to distinguish between Christ as eikōn and man as created kat' eikona (Imago Dei, p. 217; see above).

in Genesis 1ff.[93] He bore this image as the earthy man, the man taken from the earth. But he nevertheless bore this "image," and it can be said of him as bearer of the image of God that he begot his descendants after his own likeness and his own image (Gen. 5:1, 3[94] — the passage to which 1 Cor. 15:49 perhaps also refers). In any case — and this is for us the most important thing — Christ's image as the Heavenly is here spoken of in the closest relationship to the image of the first man. The "image" that Christ represents and which he gives to his own is thus very clearly thought of here as parallel to the image of the first man and to that which he communicated to his descendants. In this context such passages as Ephesians 4:24 and Colossians 3:10 also come to stand in a clearer light.

On the basis of all these materials it is difficult to deny that the absolute use of the Image of God as a qualification of Christ must be connected with what is said in Genesis 1ff. of the first Adam. In the nature of the case Christ is not herewith put on a level with the first Adam. The glory of the second Adam is incomparably greater than that of the first. But it must certainly be ascertained that Christ's divine power and glory, already in his pre-existence,[95] are defined in categories that have been derived from his significance as the second Adam (cf. further Section 13).

All this finds expression in a still more direct and pregnant way in the well-known christological passage of Philippians 2:6ff.:[96] ". . . who, being in the form of God, thought it not robbery to be equal with God, but emptied himself and took upon him the form of a servant, and was made in the likeness of men. And being found in fashion as a man, he humbled himself, and became obedient unto death, even the death of the cross."

In the history of the investigation the initial words (*en morphē Theou hyparchōn*) in particular have frequently been subjected to an abstract conceptual definition.[97] Here again, however, the Pauline conception of Christ as the Image of God on analogy with Genesis 1:27 appears to offer the key for a clearer insight. To be sure, this has often been hidden from view because there is mention here of the "form" and not the "image" of God, as in 2 Corinthians 4:4 and Colossians 1:15. Some have wanted indeed to oppose the interchangeableness of

93. Jervell, too, acknowledges this (*Imago Dei*, p. 258).

94. Cf. Von Rad, *TDNT*, II, p. 391.

95. In any case one cannot eliminate the element of pre-existence from these pronouncements. In Col. 1:15 this is, in our view, incontrovertible, as appears from the whole context. In 2 Cor. 4:4 Grosheide wants to understand the expression Image of God only of Christ's mode of existence after his incarnation. Berkouwer, *Man: The Image of God*, ET 1962, pp. 107f., writes that Paul calls Christ the Image of God in a context which goes beyond the dilemma (pre-existence or incarnation), in my opinion correctly. But even so this means that in 2 Cor. 4:4, too, one cannot eliminate the pre-existent significance of the Image of God. See further below in connection with Phil. 2:6ff.

96. See also already my article "Nieuwere beschouwingen over Phil. 2:6-11," in *Eeuwfeest-Almanak F. Q. I.*, 1963, pp. 133ff.

97. Cf., e.g., the detailed and forceful discussion by S. Greijdanus, *De brief van den apostel Paulus aan de gemeente te Philippi*, 1937, p. 188.

these two ideas.[98] However, even various church fathers understood the expression "being in the form of God" as a parallel of "Image of God" in 2 Corinthians 4:4 and Colossians 1:15, and Philippians 2:6 as an interpretation of Genesis 1:27.[99] In the more recent literature[100] the view that "form" (morphē) has no other meaning in this context than image (eikōn) has once again gained ground, and, along with this, the conclusion that the expressions in 2 Corinthians 4:4; Colossians 1:15 and that in Philippians 2:6 are to be regarded as synonyms. In addition to the evidence that can be drawn from the usage of the Septuagint, Paul's own epistles afford more than one illustration for such an interchangeableness of morphē and eikōn. And this is of the greater importance because these examples repeatedly bring us into the sphere of thought of the first and second man.[101] We have to do here with a combination of concepts and ideas (to which here again the concept "glory" also belongs; cf. 2 Cor. 3:18; Phil. 3:21) that are all closely bound up with the creation and significance of the first Adam and thus cast a clear light on the initial words in Philippians 2:6.

Now, this interpretation is furthermore corroborated by the fact that in what immediately follows Christ is spoken of as being "equal with God," in which phrase it is easy to discover an allusion to that with which the serpent deluded the first man: "you shall be as God" (Gen. 3:5). Likewise the idea hidden in the words "thought it not robbery" then admits of being more easily understood. While the first Adam wanted to appropriate to himself the being on an equality with God in an unlawful manner, Christ did not regard this equality, in which he already shared, as a privilege that had come to him for his own advantage,[102] on the ground of which he could have refused the

---

98. See, e.g., Behm, *TDNT*, IV, p. 752.

99. Cf. F. Loofs, "Das altkirchliche Zeugnis gegen die herrschende Auffassung der Kenosisstelle (Phil. 2,5-11)," in *Theol. Stud. und Kritiken*, 1927-28, pp. 28ff.; quoted in Jervell, *Imago Dei*, p. 204.

100. Cf. J. Héring, *Le Royaume de Dieu et sa Venue*, 1937, pp. 162ff.; and, in conjunction therewith, Cullmann, *Christology*, p. 176. See also M. Black, "The Pauline Doctrine of the Second Adam," in *The Scottish Journal of Theology*, 1954, pp. 170ff.; E. Käsemann, *Exegetische Versuche und Besinnungen*, I, pp. 65ff.; Eltester, *Eikon im Neuen Testament*, p. 10; R. P. Martin, *An Early Christian Confession*, 1960, pp. 17ff.; Jervell, *Imago Dei*, pp. 204ff.

101. Thus it is said in 2 Cor. 3:18 that we shall be transformed (*metamorphoumetha*) after the same *image (eikona)*, namely, of Christ. Similarly it is said in Rom. 8:29, once again with an obvious application to Christ's "Adamitic" significance, that God has destined us to be conformed (*sym-morphous*) to the image (*eikōn*) of his Son; cf. also Phil. 3:21; Gal. 4:19, pronouncements which contain the same thought as that of 1 Cor. 15:49, in which it is explicitly said that we shall bear *the image (tēn eikona)* of the Heavenly, namely, of the last Adam (v. 45).

102. In the well-known dispute as to whether *harpagmos* must be taken as *res rapienda* or *res rapta*, we herewith opt, therefore, for the latter. Others, who choose the former, proceed from the idea that Christ had not yet acquired the being-equal-with-God and give this exegesis, that he, other than Adam, did not strive for the being-equal-with-God as a status of glory to be drawn (by way of "robbery") to himself; so, e.g., Cullmann, *Christology*, p. 180; cf. W. Michaelis, *Der Brief des Paulus an die Philipper*, 1935, p. 36. But we must undoubtedly start from the fact that Christ already possessed this being-equal-with-God in his pre-existence; that he did not, however, regard this as a *harpagmos*, in the sense of something

way of self-emptying and humiliation. Even here he manifests the disposition, which in verse 8 is called his obedience, to accept suffering, a word once again striking in this context, which apart from this passage is elsewhere applied by Paul to Christ only in Romans 5:19, where he again points out the difference between the first and second Adam. And herewith has been given the third indication of the extent to which the composition of Philippians 2:6ff., especially where this pericope deals with the pre-existent Christ, is determined by Paul's view of Christ as the second man and the last Adam.[103]

All this can only confirm our initial conviction that, when he calls Christ the Image of God, Paul once again relates Christ to the first Adam. But this must not tempt us to the conclusion drawn by some that Paul here represents Christ as the man come from heaven. So, for example, Cullmann writes that Christ is here "the pre-existent Heavenly Man, the pre-existent pure image of God, the God-man already in his pre-existence."[104] He then relates this to the significance of Christ as the Son of Man, a title which, to be sure, does not occur in Paul, at least in the form known to us from the Gospels, but which is said to be met with once again in Paul's pronouncements concerning Christ as Adam.[105] Others, as we have already seen, seek the background of this notion not in the Old Testament, but in pre-Christian Gnosticism.[106]

So far as this last is concerned, we have already pointed out the

---

that had fallen to him and in which he could thus have rested, *res rapta*. For this explanation see Martin, *An Early Christian Confession*, pp. 21ff., 50ff., and the literature cited there; see also E. Käsemann, *Exegetische Versuche und Besinnungen*, I, pp. 69ff. The ground for seeing in *to einai isa Theō* an allusion to Gen. 3:5 (Käsemann) does not herewith fall away. Only it becomes clear that one must not overdraw the parallel (temptation of Adam—temptation of the pre-existent Christ). The allusion extends no further than that, with respect to the being-equal-with-God, Christ acted differently from Adam. It is indeed a matter of the description of an "attitude," not of a "decision" in a temptation situation (thus, rightly, Käsemann, *ibid.*, p. 70).

103. For this explanation see, i.a., the writings cited above (n. 100) of Héring, Cullmann, Martin. Jervell, *Imago Dei*, p. 227, says that it is "quite possible," but even so will know nothing here or in 2 Cor. 4:4 of a connection with the Pauline thought of Christ as the second Adam (cf. p. 215). He asks how then the contrast between God and man in Phil. 2:6 and 7 is to be explained, and points to the fact that while in Rom. 5:12ff.; 1 Cor. 15:20ff., 45ff. Christ is the man of the end time, the concern in Phil. is with his pre-existence (p. 228). These differences between Phil. 2 (2 Cor. 4; Col. 1) on the one hand and Rom. 5 and 1 Cor. 15 on the other, however, are denied by no one. The question, however, is this, whether the idea of the second Adam in Rom. 5 and 1 Cor. 15 does or does not receive a further application and extension. The conception of Jervell himself is that here again we have to do with a gnostic *Vorlage* which was altered only so far that the pronouncement now involves Christ and not an *Urmensch* (p. 229). We are accordingly obliged to accept a gnostic interpretation of Gen. 1:27 of a heavenly primal-man, which was not applied by Paul himself, but with the hymn of Phil. 2 was implicitly taken over from the Christian church (cf. pp. 204ff.). How this admits of being reconciled with the Pauline idea of Christ as the second Adam in Rom. 5 and 1 Cor. 15 is not explained. With Paul all sorts of notions concerning *eikōn* are said to run through each other (p. 209).

104. *Christology*, p. 177.

105. *Ibid.*, p. 177; cf. pp. 166ff.

106. See, e.g., Käsemann, who thinks he is able to point out in the "hymn"

problems with which one is faced when he has Paul at work here with gnostic materials (adopted by him from the Hellenistic church). Without regard to the fact that the whole idea of a pre-Christian primal-man redeemer appears to be encountering ever greater objections in the continuing investigation,[107] one is confronted with not inconsiderable difficulties when he has Paul at one time relate Christ with the Adam of the Old Testament and at another with the primal man of Gnosticism. That for his reflection on the connection between Adam and Christ Paul, at any rate in 1 Corinthians 15, appeals to explicit pronouncements of Genesis 1-3 is undeniable. That in Philippians 2 he is working with an entirely different Adam, or with an entirely different interpretation of Genesis 1-3, would be, to say the least, very surprising. It is much more plausible, therefore, to seek the background of Philippians 2 (with Cullmann, et al.), not in the conceptuality of later Hellenistic Gnosticism, but in the Old Testament, specifically in Genesis 1-3.[108]

When Cullmann, however, wishes to find in Philippians the representation of Christ's *human* pre-existence, at least that of Christ as (divine) "man from heaven," we are convinced that he is moving on the wrong track. For in Philippians it is said with great clarity that by emptying himself Christ became man and made his appearance as man in contrast to his previous "being in the form of God."[109] However much the description of Christ's pre-existence in Philippians occurs, therefore, in terms that relate him to the first Adam, this may not mislead us to the conclusion that according to Paul Christ was already man in heaven,[110] or must be regarded as the pre-existent Son of Man.[111]

---

of Phil. 2 the so-called Hellenistic "myth of the *Urmensch*-redeemer," for which he appeals in particular to statements in the Hermetic literature (*Exegetische Versuche und Besinnungen*, pp. 69ff.).

107. Cf. above, pp. 34ff.

108. *Christology*, pp. 177f.

109. *En homoiōmati anthrōpōn genomenos* undoubtedly speaks of incarnation, in contrast to *en morphē Theou hyparchōn*. The construction with *homoiōma* does not in one way or another limit this incarnation, but has its explanation in the fact that Christ distinguished himself from all other men because he was and remained obedient (cf., e.g., Schneider, *TDNT*, V, p. 197). The kenosis *(heauton ekenōsen;* v. 7) does not thus mean only that from a divine man he became a slave-man *(morphē doulou;* v. 7). The transition is that from the divine to the human. For the rest, the expression *heauton ekenōsen* says no more than that Christ laid aside his divine glory, described in the preceding words (cf. 2 Cor. 8:9). That with that he did not cease to be who he was in his pre-existence is just as much presupposed as that the human mode of existence for him began therewith and was not merely continued in another manner; see also Oepke, *TDNT*, III, p. 661, *s.v. kenoō*, and my *Paul and Jesus*, pp. 75ff., and the literature referred to there.

110. When in 1 Cor. 15:47 Christ is called *ho deuteros anthrōpos ex ouranou*, the words *ex ouranou* are intended predicatively and not as an attribute of *anthrōpos*. They do not speak of the heavenly origin of his humanness by virtue of his pre-existence, but of the spiritual, heavenly nature of his humanness by virtue of his resurrection (cf. v. 45). Therefore his own can also be called *hoi epouranioi* (v. 48), which, of course, alludes not to their descent, but to their new humanness in Christ; see further below, p. 544.

111. Against the whole conception, as though in Paul's parallel between the

We are thus faced here with the remarkable, in some degree paradoxical, phenomenon that Paul describes Christ's pre-human, divine mode of existence and his "disposition" shown in it (Phil. 2:5) with features that make him known to us already in his pre-existence as the second Adam. To want to join to this the speculative idea of Christ as the pre-existent heavenly man brings us into conflict with the text itself and finds no support elsewhere in Paul's preaching. What takes place here is the extension of the redemptive-historical outlook to Christ's pre-existence. Starting from the risen Christ as second man or last Adam (1 Cor. 15), and from his glory as Image of God (2 Cor. 4), Paul regards the whole of the divine Sonship from this point of view.

There is in all this something highly characteristic of Paul's "Christology." Without any doubt Christ is for him the Son of God, not only in virtue of his revelation, but from before the foundation of the world, God, to be blessed forever. But as such he is from before the foundation of the world and to all eternity God-for-us. It is not the Godhood of Christ in itself, but that he is God and God's Son for us which is the content and foundation even of the most profound of his christological pronouncements. He is God, who became man and was to become man. He is called Image of God as the one who was pre-destined to become man, and as the Firstborn of many brethren to make others share in this image (Rom. 8:29; 1 Cor. 15:49; 2 Cor. 3:18). He is the Son of God, who was sent (Rom. 8:3; Gal. 4:4), who was not spared by God (Rom. 8:32), who was born of the seed of David (Rom. 1:3), who died (Rom. 5:10), who by his resurrection was declared to be the Son of God in power (Rom. 1:4). In a word, his Sonship and his Redeemership are in Paul's preaching nowhere abstracted. For this reason even in the glory of his pre-existence he can be designated by the name of the last Adam and he can already be ascribed the disposition that would characterize him as the second man.

It has often been supposed that in the manner in which Paul speaks of the destining, the sending, the glorification of the Son of God, tendencies are to be discovered that would later be called sub-ordinationistic or adoptionistic. But this is an illusion. Paul is nowhere engaged in limiting Christ's divine glory, whether in his pre-existence or in his exaltation, with respect to that of God himself. For him Christ's being the Son of God is none other than being God himself. And if it has been thought necessary to subtract anything from that assessment on the basis of certain expressions, it is due to the trans-position of redemptive-historical into ontic categories. Indeed, it is characteristic of Paul that he speaks of Christ's divine Sonship in no other way than in direct connection with his redemptive work. His whole "Christology" rests on the manner in which he has learned to

first and the second man the idea of the Son of Man also played a role, see G. Delling, *Zum neueren Paulusverständnis*, pp. 104ff. That is not, of course, to assert that this qualification of Christ was unknown to Paul, nor either that the ideas that attend it could have had no influence on his description of Christ's exaltation and parousia (cf., e.g., 1 Thess. 4:17). But this is surely not very clearly demonstrable, and when contrasted with Adam Christ is not described with the features of the Son of Man from Dan. 7.

understand Christ in his cross and resurrection as the Sent One of the Father. For this reason he delineates even the glory of Christ in his pre-existence and in his divine exaltation with features drawn from redemptive history, and the image of the second Adam can be clearly recognized in the pronouncements of Christ's "riches" in heaven and his "being equal with God."

SECTION 13. THE FIRSTBORN OF EVERY CREATURE

It may be that what has just been said can furnish us with the key to a better understanding of a series of pronouncements that describe a still wider sphere of Christ's redemptive significance and of his corresponding glory as the Image of God: those which speak of Christ's position with respect to the whole creation. The following passages in particular are to be considered here:

> Yet to us there is one God, the Father, of whom are all things, and we unto him; and one Lord Jesus Christ, through whom are all things, and we through him (1 Cor. 8:6).
> . . . according to his [God's] good pleasure which he purposed in him with regard to the dispensation of the fulness of the times, to gather together all things in Christ, the things in heaven as well as the things on earth (Eph. 1:10).

Of special importance is the great passage of Colossians 1:15ff.:

> Who [Christ] is the Image of the invisible God, the Firstborn of every creature.
> For in him were all things created, in the heavens and upon the earth, things visible and things invisible, whether thrones or dominions or principalities or powers; all things have been created through him, and unto him;
> And he is before all things, and all things have their existence together in him. And he is the Head of the body, the church; who is the Beginning, the Firstborn from the dead, that in all things he might be the First.
> For the whole Fulness was pleased to dwell in him, and through him to reconcile all things to himself, he [God] having made peace by the blood of his cross, through him, whether things upon the earth, or things in the heavens.

Scholars have attempted in a great variety of ways to clarify the backgrounds of these so-called "cosmic" dimensions of Paul's Christology or — if they think it necessary to deny such ideas to Paul — of the Epistle to the Colossians (and to the Ephesians), which are dated (much) later. One explanation that was long in vogue makes reference to the well-known notions concerning "Wisdom" in Proverbs 8:22 (cf. Prov. 3:19), modified still further in the book of Wisdom (7:21, 25ff.) and in Ecclesiasticus (1, 4). Paul is said in Colossians 1:15ff. to have invested the Messiah Jesus with the aureole of the Jewish wisdom figure.[112] Others

---

112. This explanation is defended in particular by H. Windisch, "Die göttliche

are of the opinion that this explanation, although it contains much
that is valuable, is not adequate and that the *anthropos*-speculations in
Philo and in the Hermetic literature must also be taken into consideration.[113] The most radical standpoint is occupied by those who see in
Colossians 1:15-20 a pre-Christian hymn of gnostic origin that with a
few slight alterations and additions has been adopted here and applied
to Christ.[114] Others suppose that this obtains only for the first part of
Colossians 1:15-20, namely, for verses 15-18a. To this first "gnostic"
strophe of the song in Colossians 1 the second, Christian strophe (vv.
18b-20) is then said to have been subjoined, with the intention of
making it plain that "the first *anthropos*" (of the *gnosis*) is identical
with Christ.[115]

To be sure, one must properly distinguish here between the
terminology and the matter itself. So far as the former is concerned,
one could assume that Paul found occasion in the pretension of the
heresy at Colosse (that it had the true "knowledge," "wisdom" at its
disposal) to transfer certain features of the Old Testament Wisdom to
Christ. Thus he says in Colossians 2:3, in his rejection of the *"philo-sophia*
of men"* (v. 8), that all the treasures of wisdom and knowledge are hidden
in Christ. In the sequence of such terms as insight, knowledge, wisdom
(Col. 2:2ff.), one is surely to observe a certain reaction to the heresy.
Yet on further reflection this appears to be of a very general nature. If
one compares the pronouncements concerning Wisdom in the chokmatic
literature with what is said of Christ in Colossians 1:15ff., then only a
vague similarity is to be noted here. Wisdom is indeed called the "image
of God's goodness," "master builder of all things" (Sap. 7:21ff.), and
"of all things the first created" (*protera pantōn ektistai sophia;* Sir. 1:4),
and "the beginning of his [God's] way" (*Kyrios ektisen me archēn
hodōn autou eis erga autou;* Prov. 8:22); but with all that, it is and
remains a creature of God, pertaining to that which is created; while
Christ, precisely distinguished from all that is created, stands on the
side of God (Col. 1:15). If one remembers, moreover, that Wisdom in
the passages quoted is a personification, while Christ is the divine
person himself, not the means or the Mediator God employs, and that
no connection between Wisdom on the one hand and the Messiah on
the other can be shown either in the Jews or in Paul, then it is surely
evident that Colossians 1:15ff. very definitely cannot be understood as
a christological interpretation of Wisdom. There are terminological
points of contact here, vague reminiscences of the Wisdom literature,

Weisheit der Juden und die paulinische Christologie," in *Neutest. Studien für
Heinrici,* 1914, pp. 220-234, and he has been followed by many. For the materials see
in addition my *Col.,* p. 134.

113. Cf., e.g., Eltester, *Eikon,* p. 140; also Dibelius, *Col.,* p. 16.

114. Käsemann, *Essays on New Testament Themes,* 1964, pp. 149ff.; cf. also
Bultmann, *Theology,* I, p. 176.

115. Jervell, *Imago Dei,* p. 211. Jervell is of the opinion, other than Käsemann,
et al., that the pre-Christian *gnosis* did know a divine *Urmensch,* but not an *Urmensch*-
redeemer. He thinks then that it is in the combination of Col. 1:15-20 (of primal-
man and redeemer) that the point of contact lies for the later (post-Christian) gnostic
Urmensch-redeemer myth *(loc. cit.).*

but as an interpretative principle for the "cosmic" significance of Christ the pronouncements concerning Wisdom can function neither terminologically nor — a fortiori! — materially. In no respect whatever was this notion of Sophia sufficient for Paul to have arrived at these very radical pronouncements concerning Christ.[116]

As regards the materials from Philo and the Hermetic literature,[117] the case is weaker still. Undoubtedly in the speculations of Philo about the Logos as the totality of divine ideas such terms occur as "the Son of God," "protogonos," "beginning and name of God," "the man-after-the-image," and the like. And in the Hermetic literature, whether or not with reference to Genesis 1, it is said of the hypostatized cosmos that he is the image of God, and the divine primal man is spoken of in similar terms.[118] One can speak here of terminologically comparable materials, which with respect to these speculations concerning creation is not particularly surprising. One must also take into consideration the fact that such words as image, firstborn, and beginning have had a wide circulation in the Jewish literature.[119] Thus there is no necessity whatever that Paul must have been specifically dependent on the Philonic or Hermetic terminology. And this is even less the case because there is a fundamental difference materially between the speculations of Philo concerning the Logos, etc., and of the Hermetic literature concerning the primal man on the one side, and the christological pronouncements of Colossians 1:15ff. on the other. In this whole epistle Paul is speaking of the person of Jesus Christ in conformity with the gospel that has been given to the church, and he admonishes it to adhere to this and not to suffer itself to be led astray by strange doctrine, tradition of men, rudiments of the world (cf. 2:6ff.). He intends this Christ in Colossians 1:15ff. as well, not an abstract Logos-idea or a mythological anthropos. Can one nevertheless assume that, in the form of a hymn, he incorporated into his gospel and simply identified with Christ such an absolutely non-Christian speculation, as Käsemann wants to do? And if one cannot — for this reason! — regard Paul as the writer of the epistle, can one then expect this of another writer, who wrote this epistle and whom one must therefore surely term at the least a disciple of Paul? Moreover, if for verses 18b-20 such a gnostic Vorlage is regarded as unacceptable (a) because one cannot speak of a pre-Christian gnostic Redeemer upon good grounds, and (b) because verses 18b-20 are altogether too characteristic of the Pauline Christology,[120] is it then to be considered at all probable that this second, Christian strophe was simply attached to a first, non-Christian, gnostic strophe, with the theological purpose of demonstrating that this gnostic anthropos is identical with Christ?[121] If it is here to be a matter not only of stringing together the most

---

116. Cf. Michaelis, *TDNT*, VI, p. 879, s.v. prōtotokos; also H. J. Schoeps, *Paul, The Theology of the Apostle in the Light of Jewish Religious History*, p. 156.
117. See, e.g., Dibelius-Greeven, Eltester, Jervell.
118. See the tabular survey of the comparable materials in Eltester, *Eikon*, pp. 142/143.
119. See the relevant surveys in Kittel, *TDNT*.
120. Thus Jervell, *Imago Dei*, p. 211.
121. Jervell, *loc. cit.*

heterogeneous quantities, but further in some degree of explaining the background of this "cosmic" Christology, is not one permitted to make the demand that this deep and far-reaching idea concerning Christ's relationship to the whole creation be in some measure placed in organic connection with the central motifs of the early Christian preaching in general and that of Paul in particular? And this the more so because, as is evident from the passages cited above, the ideas elaborated in Colossians 1:15ff. also appear to be present in essence elsewhere in Paul's epistles, both in Ephesians 1 and in 1 Corinthians 8:6.

As has already been shown in the examination of the significance of the christological name "Image of God,"[122] we undoubtedly have to do in Colossians 1:15ff. with creation categories, and therefore also with a clear reflection of Genesis 1. The crucial question now, however, is whether the connection of "Christology" and "protology" here is different from the Pauline conception, familiar from 1 Corinthians 15, of Christ as the second Adam; or whether it is organically related to it. With respect to the qualification of Christ occurring here again in the opening words, ". . . who is the Image of the invisible God," we have already attempted in the preceding section to vindicate such an organic relationship. In what follows this phrase, the conceptual material connected with the creation is much more extensive still. And therein in a certain sense the answer is to be found to the problem as to whether the explanation given earlier of the Image of God is the correct one.

What follows the pronouncement concerning the Image of God is at once of special importance: the Firstborn of every creature. That this designation in general contains an allusion to Adam is obvious. Even the fact that in the Jewish writings, although not in a conspicuous manner, Adam is called the Firstborn may argue for this.[123] Likewise the connection Firstborn of every creature points in this direction. It does not denote temporal order merely, but order of rank, position of rulership, in which it is easy to discover a reminiscence of the position Adam occupied among all of creation, likewise in virtue of his creation after God's Image (Gen. 1:28ff.). It is of more importance, however, that this name functions in the Pauline conception of the second Adam. For this name recurs in Colossians 1:18, when Christ is called the Firstborn from the dead, just as Christ is termed already in Romans 8:29, once more in connection with the Image of God, the Firstborn among many brethren. And it is surely this function of Firstborn and Image of God in virtue of his resurrection from the dead which leads Paul in 1 Corinthians 15:45 to place Christ over against Adam as the second over against the first man. What happens in Colossians 1:15,

---

122. Cf. above, pp. 70ff.
123. Cf., e.g., Strack-Billerbeck, *Kommentar zum Neuen Testament*, III, pp. 256ff., 626, and Michaelis, *TDNT*, VI, p. 875. Michaelis is indeed of the opinion (p. 878, n. 46) that the designation of Adam in the Jewish writings as "firstborn of the world" "is not a close par.," because Christ, in distinction from Adam, cannot be called "first creature." But the expression *prōtotokos* points, even when it is applied to Adam, not to the manner of origin—Adam was not born either—but to the position of authority; cf. also Michaelis himself, p. 875, n. 30. The genitive *tēs ktiseōs* is not a partitive genitive but a relative or comparative genitive.

therefore, is this, that Paul applies the same "Adamitic" categories (Image, Firstborn) with which he describes Christ's significance in "eschatology" to his place in "protology" as well.

The sequel to Colossians 1:15 confirms this. It gives a further explication of Christ's glory as Image of God and Firstborn of every creature in the profound words, that in him all things were created, in the heavens and upon the earth . . . , that all things have been created through him and unto him, that he is before all things, and that all things have their existence together in him. Here again it is easy even in general to discover a reminiscence of what is said in Genesis 1 of the first Adam; the summing up of what is "in heaven" and what is "upon earth" (Gen. 1:26ff.), the creation of all things for the sake of man (however much the place of Christ transcends this ruling position of the first man as the Image of God). It is again the case here, however, that Paul denotes the relationship of Christ to all creation with concepts with which he elsewhere gives expression to Christ's relationship as second Adam to the church.[124] The "corporative" ideas that the apostle employs are here to be pointed out in particular: the gathering together of all things in Christ and their existing together in him, as the church in its Head. It is in that sense that one will have to interpret the statement: "in him were all things created" (Col. 1:16). A whole series of explanations has been given of this[125] "in him," which Jervell calls "difficult to understand."[126] The difficulty lies in this, that, on the one hand, one may not conceive of this "in him" in an instrumental sense, whereby Christ himself would be the Creator; and that, on the other, one must guard against an interpretation by which Christ, too, is the object of God's creative act. The pronouncement forms an exact parallel, however, to what is elsewhere said of the church, namely, that it is God's workmanship, created in Christ for good works, etc. (Eph. 2:10); so also 1 Corinthians 1:30, where, likewise of the church, Paul declares that it is of God in Christ Jesus. From the analogy of the creation of the church in Christ we can more clearly understand the meaning of Colossians 1:16a. It is a matter of such a creation as places all things, just as the church, under the dominion and at the disposal of Christ with a view to the object appointed by God.[127] Likewise the creation of all things in the heavens and on earth "through him" and "unto him" has its analogy in the fact that the church is "through him" (1 Cor. 8:6), and that the church is directed toward him in the whole of its existence (cf. Rom. 14:8; 2 Cor. 5:15). All these expressions speak not so much of the mediation of Christ in the creation event,[128] as of his abiding, central place and all-embracing significance with respect to all that is in heaven and on earth. The same parallel with

---

124. See also N. A. Dahl, "Christ, Creation and the Church," in *The Background of the New Testament*, pp. 432ff.

125. See my *Col.*, pp. 139ff.

126. Jervell, *Imago Dei*, p. 226.

127. Cf. Eph. 2:10: *ktisthentes en Christō . . . epi ergois . . . hois proētoimasen ho Theos. . . .* For this use of *en* see further my *Col.*, p. 140.

128. *Di' autou ektistai* in v. 16b, a perfect in distinction from *ektisthē* in v. 16a, also speaks of the result.

Christ as the second Adam is to be found in the phrase "before all things," which does not express merely an abstract priority, but an absolute dominion of Christ over all creation,[129] entirely in accordance with his position as the Beginning, the Inaugurator of the new creation, as is evident from the words of verse 18b: that in all things he might be the First. Finally, we may view in this light the pronouncement, which when taken by itself is difficult to understand, that all things have their existence together in him (*ta panta en autō synestēken;* v. 17b). Here, too, the analogy with the existing of the church together in Christ is evident (cf. Rom. 12:5; cf. 1 Cor. 12:12; Eph. 4:16). From hence a clear light is also cast on the remarkable and difficult expression in Ephesians 1:10, where mention is made of the divine redemptive plan in order "to give existence to all things, those which are in heaven as well as those upon earth, by summing them up anew in Christ" (*anakephalaiōsasthai*).

The word *anakephalaiōsasthai* must be derived from *kephalaion,* summary, *summa* (not from *kephalē,* head). What is expressed is thus not simply that Christ will receive dominion over all things in heaven and on earth,[130] but also that everything exists together in him as in a summary, exactly the same therefore as *synēsteken en autō* (Col. 1:17). The *anakephalaiōsasthai* of Ephesians 1:10, which is the object of God's redemptive counsel (*eudokia*) "with regard to the dispensation of the fulness of the times," can thus be termed the eschatological counterpart of the *synestēken* of Colossians 1:17, which starts from the creation. For this reason one will certainly have to honor the *ana-*[131] and consequently must understand it as their having their existence *anew* in him. This "anew" is materially expressed in Colossians 1:20 in the words that God through Christ has reconciled, that is to say, pacified, all things to himself.

This analogous relationship between the church and all things as both having been created and existing together in Christ, is corroborated still further by the fact that Christ is the Head both of his church and of all things. That Christ is the Head of the church is repeatedly enunciated in Ephesians and Colossians (cf. Eph. 4:15; 5:23; Col. 1:18; 2:19). In Ephesians 1:22, however, he is also called the Head over all things (cf. Col. 2:10).[132] This description of Christ as Head is not merely a general title of majesty or honor. It stands, as we have already seen, in the closest connection with the qualification Image of God and thus with the position of the first Adam. The difference lies in this, that while in Colossians and Ephesians the church is again and again

---

129. Cf., e.g., B. Reicke, *TDNT,* VI, pp. 687f., *s.v. pro.*

130. The translation of the Dutch Bible Society has: "to sum up under one head," and thus combines the thought of *kephalē* and *kephalaion;* cf. Schlier, *TDNT,* III, p. 682. Materially this is certainly correct (cf. Eph. 1:22; moreover, see the text), although, in my view, it is not certain that *anakephalaiōsasthai* has this connotation.

131. The translation of the Dutch Bible Society (and the RSV) omits this.

132. According to Käsemann and others the addition *tēs ekklēsias* in Col. 1:18 is not original and thus the expression that Christ is the Head of the body would have a "cosmic" significance. But this is a consequence of the whole of Käsemann's view of Col. 1:15 (see above, pp. 78f.) and in itself not at all evident. For nowhere else is the all called the body of Christ, in contradistinction to the church.

termed the body of Christ, the same is not said of "all things." The Head-body relationship does not, as far as we can see, apply to them. At least it does not find expression in the available texts. But this does not alter the fact that there is an obvious parallel between the Headship of Christ over his church and that over all things. And we have to do here again with a category of creation, inasmuch as this "headship" is elsewhere applied by Paul to man (the husband) as the Image of God (1 Cor. 11:3, 7; Eph. 5:23).

In summary we can say therefore that Christ's original position of authority with respect to "all things" in Colossians 1:15 is described entirely according to an analogy with Christ's relationship to the church, as that is elsewhere given expression in Paul's epistles. In other words, from Christ's significance as second Adam all the categories are derived which further define his significance as the Firstborn of every creature. This analogy, which is discernible not only in the parallel of the two "strophes" of Colossians 1:15-20 but in the whole of Paul's preaching of Christ as the second Adam, makes it improbable indeed that in Colossians 1:15 we have to do with a passage that may be said to have had an entirely different origin, or that two "christological schemata" have been combined here which in essence do not belong together:[133] (a) the Pauline representation of Christ as eschatological last Adam, and (b) the gnostic representation of Christ as the divine *anthropos* antecedent to all things. The former is supposed then to be found in verses 18bff., the latter in verses 15-18a.

Undoubtedly what is said in Colossians 1:15ff. concerning Christ as the Image of God, Firstborn, and so forth, does not simply spring from Paul's conception of Christ as the second Adam in 1 Corinthians 15 and Romans 5. One can even say that a distinct difference exists between the two. Whereas in 1 Corinthians 15 and Romans 5 Christ is the second or last Adam, who follows after the first in the order of redemptive history, in Colossians 1:15 as the Firstborn, the Image of God, etc., he is antecedent to the first, and in this respect the first Adam cannot be regarded as his "type," as is the case in Romans 5 and 1 Corinthians 15. Even if one were able on this ground to speak of a twofold representation of Christ as Adam, on the other hand the place of Christ in the first creation is so plainly described in Colossians 1:15 on analogy with Christ's significance as the second Adam in the new

---

133. See Jervell, *Imago Dei*, p. 224. Jeremias points to the two different representations of Adam in Philo: (a) the ideal man (the Logos) created after the image of God, who is said to have been created first (Gen. 1:27), and whom one can also call the heavenly man; (b) the earthly man created from the earth (Gen. 2:7). With respect to Paul he puts the matter as follows: "In similar fashion [to Philo] Paul finds in Christ the divine image (Col. 1:15; cf. Gen. 1:27), while he refers 2:7, like Philo, to the creation of Adam. He also agrees with Philo as to the priority of the heavenly man (Col. 1:15: *prōtotokos pasēs ktiseōs*)." Paul is said, however, to distinguish himself from Philo by the fact that he ascribes to the firstborn heavenly man in addition an eschatological role and calls him, in contradistinction to the earthly Adam (Gen. 2:7), the *eschatos Adam* (*TDNT*, I, p. 143). What also distinguishes Paul from Philo, however, is that in addition to applying the name image of God to Christ as the *prōtotokos*, he applies it to the first Adam (1 Cor. 11:7). And with that the agreement with the schema of Philo has in principle been broken.

creation that a much closer and more essential connection must exist between the two than is obvious at first glance. On further reflection there is in Paul's preaching a highly organic and structural relationship between Christ's place in the *Endgeschichte* and in the *Urgeschichte*.[134] And this relationship is not only to be observed in that in Colossians 1 Paul describes Christ's "original" cosmic significance on the analogy of his significance as the second Adam in the re-creation, but conversely that he can denote Christ's exaltation as the last Adam with the words of Psalm 8, words in which the position of glory occupied by the original man is expressed (1 Cor. 15:25; Eph. 1:22). A reciprocal agreement and mutual interdependence are to be noted here, therefore, which make it impossible to extrapolate the Christology of Colossians 1:15-18a (still less that of 1:15-20) as an ill-fitting, alien, or added motif in the Pauline conception of Christ as the second Adam.

What we meet with in this "double" Adamitic significance of Christ (as the Firstborn of every creature and as the last Adam) is not the conjoining of two interpretations of Genesis 1-3 that do not go together, but rather Paul's vision of the all-encompassing significance of the salvation that has appeared in Christ. One is disposed to think here of the describing of ever greater circles around one center and starting point. This latter is situated in the all-controlling fact of Christ's death and resurrection. It is there that the new creation comes to light, Christ appears as the Firstborn from the dead and the Inaugurator of the new humanity. It is from thence that the redemptive significance of Christ's advent and work is made transparent, first in his human existence before and after the resurrection (flesh and Spirit); then even in his pre-existence as the Son of God sent for this task of second man; and finally in his significance as encompassing the whole of creation and history. The ultimate objective of God's redemptive work brings us back to the Beginning.[135] What was lost in the first Adam is regained in the second in a much more glorious way. For the second Adam is the Son of God. And the glory that Adam as the Image of God and Firstborn of every creature was permitted to possess was only a reflection of Christ's being in the form of God. Thus Christ's exaltation as the second Adam refers back to the beginning of all things, makes him known as the one who from the very outset, in a much more glorious sense than the first Adam, was the Image of God and the Firstborn of every creature. So the fundamental structures and implications of Paul's eschatological preaching of Christ are exposed to view. The new creation that has broken through with Christ's resurrection takes the place of the first creation of which Adam was the representative. It is, however, as much more glorious than the first as the second man, both in virtue of his origin and of his destiny, was superior to

---

134. On this point see also in detail N. A. Dahl, "Christ, Creation and the Church," in *The Background of the New Testament*, pp. 432ff.

135. Cf. Dahl, *ibid.*, p. 429: "The main idea, which is common to the different forms of combining the last things with that which was at the beginning, is the idea that the end will bring the final realisation of what from the beginning was the will of God the Creator, who is himself the first and the last (Isa. 44:6, 48:12; Rev. 1:8, 21:6 etc.)."

the first. In the description of this superiority of the second man in the categories that have been derived from the significance of the first man Paul comes to the full explication of the salvation that has appeared in Christ. In that sense one could call Colossians 1:15-20 the keystone of Paul's Christology; with the explicit addition, however, that it was not theological speculation, but pastoral care for the church and the warding off of what was alleged against the all-embracing significance of the salvation that has been manifested in Christ, that brought the apostle to this confession.

That which is enunciated in Colossians 1:15ff. is what in the context of the prayer of Ephesians 3:18 is called "the breadth and length and height and depth" and what he terms in Colossians 2:2, 3, likewise in the context of a very urgent paraenesis, "the riches of the fulness of knowledge, the understanding of the mystery of God, Christ, in whom are hidden all the treasures of wisdom and knowledge."

SECTION 14. CHRIST THE EXALTED AND COMING KYRIOS

After all that has been said in the preceding sections concerning the redemptive-historical character of Paul's preaching of Christ, one important facet still remains to be considered from this point of view, namely, that which follows on Christ's resurrection: his ascension to heaven, his sitting at the right hand of God, and his coming parousia.

As was already apparent to us in the Introduction,[136] some have supposed, in particular on the ground of his pronouncements concerning Christ as the *Kyrios* exalted in heaven, that they were able to ascertain in Paul a transition from the eschatological Son-of-Man Christology of the primitive church to a mystical or cultic Christ-experience oriented to Hellenistic piety. For the center of gravity in Paul's Christology is said no longer to be situated in the expectation of the coming Son of Man or Messiah, but in communion with the pneumatic *Kyrios*.[137]

Undoubtedly, Christ's exaltation in heaven and the communion maintained from there between the exalted *Kyrios* and his church by the Holy Spirit occupy a very important place in Paul's preaching. We shall have to go into this much more extensively later on.[138] One can even say that the overwhelming riches of the salvation that has already been revealed in Christ, and which has reached a certain conclusion by his exaltation, sometimes appear to thrust the viewpoint of its provisional character into the background and to place the spiritual appropriation of the gifts of Christ in the center. Moreover, it is the Holy Spirit in particular who comes to the fore as the one in whose

---

136. See above, pp. 25ff.
137. For the problems with respect to this title, raised especially by Bousset, see, besides the Christologies, such as those of Sevenster and Cullmann, my *Paul and Jesus*, pp. 80ff.; and E. Schweizer, *Erniedrigung und Erhöhung*, pp. 93ff. (cf. *Lordship and Discipleship*, pp. 57ff.).
138. See below, Sections 38, 61ff.

gifts the church receives a share in the glory of its exalted Lord, indeed, who represents the presence of Christ himself within the church. The pronouncements are particularly to be mentioned here in which Christ and the Spirit are placed in a certain relationship of identity with each other:

> Now the Lord is the Spirit (2 Cor. 3:17).
> There are diversities of gifts, but the same Spirit; and there are diversities of ministrations, but the same Lord (1 Cor. 12:4, 5).
> One body, and one Spirit ... one Lord, one faith, ... (Eph. 4:4, 5).

In these passages, which may be supplemented with others,[139] it is clearly apparent how much the Spirit is the one in whom the exalted Christ maintains communion with the church and that the church shares in no other way than through the Spirit in the gifts of its Lord (cf., e.g., 1 Cor. 12:3; Rom. 8:9; Eph. 3:16). It is accordingly no wonder that, precisely for the dispensation that has become effective with Christ's resurrection and ascension to heaven in which the church now has its existence, the apostle again and again points to the Spirit as the one in and out from whose communion the church is to live (Gal. 5:16, 25; Rom. 8:4, 13ff.).

Yet it is an absolute misconception to suppose that one is compelled to subtract this "pneumatic" from the redemptive-historical and eschatological character of Paul's preaching and that the characteristic significance of Christ is that of the *Kyrios* present in the cultus.[140] We must recall here what has already been said in Section 11, that for Paul, just as for the whole of the primitive Christian church, the Holy Spirit is pre-eminently the eschatological gift, the revelation of the great time of salvation, in accordance with Old Testament prophecy. For the church in the present there is in this without question an inexhaustible source of power, and Paul does not fail to point that out to the church again and again. But at the same time he constantly emphasizes that this dispensation of the Spirit is the dispensation of the Interim. One can even say that in Paul, more than occurs anywhere else, the accent is placed on this provisional character. This is surely the significance of the expression so typical of him, that the Spirit is "the first gift" (Rom. 8:23), "the earnest" of that which God is yet to give (2 Cor. 1:22; 5:5), indeed "the earnest of the inheritance" (Eph. 1:14), by whom believers are sealed unto the final redemption (2 Cor. 1:22; Eph. 1:13; 4:30), and who awakens and keeps alive in them the believing longing and watching for the full revelation of the children of God (Rom. 8:16, 23, 26). It is therefore out of the question that under the influence of the Hellenistic church Paul's pronouncements concerning the exalted Lord would no longer be supported by the historical-eschatological consciousness and that the redemptive-historical *post* would have passed over into a pneumatic *trans*. Not only would this break in two the whole structure of Paul's proclamation of redemption but it is also in conflict with his pronouncements on the Spirit

---

139. Cf. Hamilton, *The Holy Spirit and Eschatology in Paul*, pp. 3ff.
140. Thus Bultmann, too, *History and Eschatology*, p. 52.

himself, from which it is clearly evident that his preaching of the Spirit is governed by the expectation of Christ as the coming Lord.[141]

It is from this direction also that the close relationship that Paul establishes between Christ and the Holy Spirit must be approached. The Spirit can be identified with Christ in all sorts of ways because it is in Christ's advent and work that the work of the Spirit manifests itself, fulfilling and propelling toward the consummation. We have more than once cited to this effect the pronouncement in 1 Corinthians 15:45, in which Christ as the Inaugurator of the new humanity is termed the life-giving Spirit. And this relationship applies no less to the well-known words of 2 Corinthians 3:17: the Lord is the Spirit. We do not have to do here with a definition of the being of Christ as the exalted *Kyrios,* as though the person of Christ were entirely identified with the Spirit or perhaps even wholly dissolved in him.[142] Rather, in 2 Corinthians 3:17 Paul gives a summarizing statement of an argument in which the redemptive-historical contrast predominates.[143] Over against the ministration of death and of the letter of the Old Covenant, he places that of the righteousness and the liberty that are given by the Spirit. In that train of thought he can now call the Lord the Spirit, because in the Lord the life-giving and liberating work of the Spirit is carried into effect, the New Covenant is fulfilled, and the new creation takes place. Whatever deep mystery the relationship between Christ and the Spirit places before us as soon as we attempt to express this in ontological categories, it is unmistakable that the significance of Christ and of the Spirit in Paul's preaching define each other further in a redemptive-historical sense.[144] As Christ in the present and future power of his redemptive work can be known only from the all-embracing renewal and consummation of the Spirit of God, so on the other hand the promise of the Spirit and of his life-giving power receives its fulfillment, its form, and its prospect only in the person of Christ as the exalted and coming Lord. In this sense alone — that is, in the framework of the basic redemptive-historical structure of Paul's gospel — can the specific significance of this close linking of Christ and the Spirit be understood.

For the rest, the significance of Christ's exaltation is not described only in pneumatic categories, nor is it regarded only from the viewpoint of his relationship to the church. Along with this, Christ's central position with respect to all creation comes no less to the fore. For this

---

141. Cf. Hamilton, *The Holy Spirit and Eschatology in Paul,* pp. 17ff.; H. Berkhof, *The Doctrine of the Holy Spirit,* 1964, pp. 104ff.

142. For these conceptions see further Hermann, *Kyrios und Pneuma,* p. 123.

143. For the train of thought of 2 Cor. 3 see further below, pp. 218ff.

144. Ingo Hermann correctly argues, in his rich study *Kyrios und Pneuma,* that one must not wish to explain "the understanding of the relationship of the Spirit to the Lord in Paul's sense," as that reaches its zenith in the identification pronouncement of 2 Cor. 3:17a, on the basis of the doctrine of the Trinity (cf., e.g., p. 123; cf. also Hamilton, *The Holy Spirit and Eschatology in Paul,* p. 3). When Hermann attempts to prove, however (otherwise than Hamilton), that one can attribute to the Spirit no separate, personal existence, to be distinguished from that of Christ, in the sense of the doctrine of the Trinity (cf. pp. 132ff.), his argumentation requires further testing.

Paul draws from an arsenal of ideas and concepts that we also meet in part elsewhere in the New Testament. This holds even for the term "exalt" (Phil. 2:9), which is elsewhere used in connection with the Son of Man (John 3:14; 8:28; 12:34; cf. v. 32), as also for "sitting at the right hand of God" (Rom. 3:34; Eph. 1:20; Col. 3:1; cf. Acts 2:33; 5:31; 7:55ff.; Heb. 1:3; 8:1; 12:2; 10:2; 1 Pet. 3:22). This expression, drawn from Psalm 110:1, typifies the exalted *Kyrios* as the Messianic King. We also find Christ's exaltation expressed in Paul with the words of Psalm 8:6 (1 Cor. 15:27; Eph. 1:22; cf. Heb. 2:6-8). Here Christ is therefore the Man,[145] to whom God has subjected all things (cf. Phil. 3:21).

This whole position of authority in Paul's kerygma has particular reference to the cosmic spiritual powers (1 Cor. 15:24; Rom. 8:38ff.; cf. v. 34; Eph. 1:21ff.; Phil. 2:9; Col. 1:20; 2:10, 15; cf. also Eph. 4:8ff.); it is described at one time in its completion, at the parousia (1 Cor. 15:25ff.), then again as already having commenced with Christ's exaltation at the right hand of God (Eph. 1:21ff.; Phil. 2:9; Col. 1:20; 2:10, 15; cf. also Rom. 8:39). Hereby, particularly in Colossians, the analogy with Christ's original glory plays a part (cf. also Eph. 1:10),[146] just as elsewhere Christ's significance as the second Adam is determinative for the formation of Paul's expectation for the future (1 Cor. 15:27ff.; cf. v. 22; Eph. 1:22 — where, in addition to the expression derived from Ps. 8, the name Head over all things also occurs). The ideas are of various origins here, they are used promiscuously, and there is no question of a systematic terminology. Everything goes to show, however (particularly, to be sure, in Ephesians and Colossians, but also, for example, in the well-known christological "hymn" of 1 Tim. 3:16), what an important place the cosmic significance of Christ's exaltation occupies in the whole of Paul's train of thought, altogether in accordance with the fundamental eschatological structure of his preaching.

Bultmann has posited, in his work *History and Eschatology*, that Paul's picture of history and of eschatology is interpreted entirely on the basis of his anthropology. The result is said to be that history and the consummation of the world vanish from his sight, and that their place is taken by "the historicity of man," even though he retains the traditional representations along with it.[147] It is our conviction that there is here a reversal of the real and deepest structures of Paul's preaching. However much attention the apostle devotes in his preaching to the significance the divine activity in Christ has for human existence (as will appear from what follows), the decisive viewpoint, even of his expectation for the future, is nevertheless a different one, namely, that of the theocentric significance of the divine redemptive work manifested and coming to consummation in Christ.[148] The whole exaltation of

---

145. Cf. above, p. 84.

146. Cf. above, pp. 84f.

147. Pp. 43ff.; see also above, p. 50.

148. See W. Schrage, "Die Stellung zur Welt bei Paulus, Epiktet und in der Apokalyptik," *ZTK*, 1964, pp. 127ff.: "He [Paul] thought not only in anthropological categories but in dimensions that overlap human existence.... Just as Paul corrected apocalyptic on the basis of Christology, so he corrects, on the basis of apocalyptic, an exclusively individual- and personal-redemption-oriented—indeed, a purely anthro-

Christ in the present and in the future is directed toward this, that God shall be all in all (1 Cor. 15:28), and that at the name of Jesus every knee shall bow, of those in heaven and on earth and under the earth, and every tongue shall confess that Jesus Christ is Lord, to the glory of God the Father (Phil. 2:10; cf. Rom. 14:11).

This theocentric point of view is also inherent in Christ's all-embracing significance for the future of creation and humanity. In him, the Beginning and the Firstborn from the dead, the Fullness was pleased to dwell, in order through him to reconcile all things to himself (Col. 1:19, 20). And in him as the second Adam will the new humanity arise, be justified, and manifested (1 Cor. 15:22; Rom. 5:19, 21; Col. 3:4). We shall have to go further into the various facets of Paul's expectation for the future, particularly as these are expressly raised in 1 Thessalonians 4:13-18; 2 Thessalonians 2:1-12; and 1 Corinthians 15.[149] But this future expectation itself, of which Christ forms the central point, is the indispensable termination of the whole of his preaching; it functions there not as a traditional addition to a spiritualistic or existentialistic Christology, but stands in closest relationship with the center of his kerygma. The revelation of the mystery, the summary and the fundamental pattern of Paul's whole proclamation of Christ, will not be completed before Christ shall have been manifested in glory with all his own (Col. 3:4), the last mystery shall have been disclosed (1 Cor. 15:51; Rom. 11:25), and the creation now groaning and in travail shall have been redeemed from the bondage of corruption into the liberty of the glory of the children of God. It is for the revelation of that great day that the Spirit himself prays and groans and comes to the help of the church in its weakness (Rom. 8:21ff.).

---

pologically directed—soteriology (cf. Rom. 8:18ff.). What is at stake for Paul essentially is the eschatological dominion of God over all the world.... This dominion of God over the whole world is more than the new existence and hope of the individual. If Paul speaks of the *metaschēmatizein* of the *sōma* through the Lord, he immediately adds that the transformation *kata tēn energeian tou dynasthai auton kai hypotaxai autō ta panta* ensues (Phil. 3:21)."

149. See below, Chapter XII.

III
THE LIFE IN SIN

A. Sin as Mode of Existence

SECTION 15. THE PRESENT WORLD. AEON, COSMOS

The unfolding of the Pauline doctrine of salvation demands first of all a deeper insight into the manner in which man and the world have fallen into sin and have need of the redemption revealed in Christ. Further analysis demonstrates that here again the fundamental structure of Paul's preaching is of decisive significance, and that therefore, in approaching the Pauline doctrine of sin, we must not orient ourselves in the first place to the individual and personal, but to the redemptive-historical and collective points of view.

An obvious indication to this effect is given at the very outset in the manner in which Paul repeatedly speaks in summary fashion of the life-context before and outside Christ and of the human mode of existence in that life-context. This applies particularly to the idea "world" (cosmos) or "this world," as well as to "this [present] aeon," which essentially corresponds to it. Both ideas play a great part in Paul's redemptive-historical way of thinking, inasmuch as they — cosmos more in a spatial, aeon in a temporal sense — constitute the description of the totality of unredeemed life dominated by sin outside of Christ. This is the case, for example, when it is said in Galatians 1:4 that Christ give himself to deliver us "from the present evil aeon"; or likewise when in Ephesians 2:2, with the utilization of both terms, the former manner of life (the "once") of the church is described as walking according to "the aeon of this world," and this world-aeon is thereby denoted as the life-context dominated by sin and finding its determination in sin.

The apostle does not stop with these general qualifications, however, but he explains them further, especially in connection with "this world" and "this aeon," by speaking of the powers of evil, misery, and death that hold sway in this world. What he terms in Galatians 1:4 "this present evil aeon," elsewhere as "the power of darkness," is set over against the royal dominion of Christ (Col. 1:13); and in Ephesians 2:2 he further qualifies walking according to "this world-aeon" as following the course of "the prince of the power of the air, the spirit that now works in the sons of disobedience." The world is therefore in its unity and totality the domain of demonic powers, which he denotes as "angels," "principalities," "powers" (Rom. 8:38; 1 Cor. 15:24; Col. 2:14, et al.), "the world rulers of this darkness," "the evil spirits in heavenly places" (Eph. 6:12), of which Satan, as the "god of this aeon" (2 Cor. 4:4), is the head (cf. Rom. 16:20; 1 Cor. 5:5, et al.).

There is no doubt whatever that this subjection of the world to spiritual, demonic powers in Paul does not go back to an original dualism between God and the world, or between God and the powers. For it is true of all that is in heaven and on earth, and in particular of thrones, dominions, principalities, and powers, that they have been created in Christ (Col. 1:16), just as they have been conquered and reconciled (pacified) in him (Col. 2:15; 1:20); they belong to the creation of God (Rom. 8:39), and are, even in their activity of enmity against God and tyrannization of men, subject to God (2 Cor. 12:7). Similarly, these powers have no original control over the world, but the whole of the groaning creation has been subjected to vanity by God himself (Rom. 8:20). Nevertheless, it is the dominion of these powers that determines Paul's outlook on the present world. It is they who represent the "vanity," the worthlessness and senselessness to which the whole creation, groaning and looking with eager longing for redemption, has been subjected (cf. Rom. 8:19-23 and 8:38, 39). For not only sin, but also suffering, oppression, anxiety, and adversity belong to the dominion of Satan (1 Cor. 5:5; 2 Cor. 12:7; 1 Tim. 1:20; 1 Thess. 2:18). Elsewhere these demonic threats to human existence, such as oppression, persecution, hunger, want, danger, and sword, are themselves represented as personified powers that attempt still to separate the believer from the love of Christ (Rom. 8:35), just as death is his "last enemy" (1 Cor. 15:26), which employs sin as its instrument (1 Cor. 15:56; cf. Rom. 8:38f.).

In particular, however, it is the fact of its having fallen into the power of sin itself that determines the content of the concept "world." Although "cosmos" is also used in a more general sense[1] (as created world [Rom. 1:20], as human living space [Rom. 4:13; 1 Cor. 14:10]), it usually means the human situation qualified by sin, or mankind itself. Cosmos is the world turned away from God, rebellious and hostile toward him (cf. Rom. 3:16, 19; 2 Cor. 5:19), depraved mankind that is headed for judgment (Rom. 3:6; 1 Cor. 11:32). As such believers are redeemed from the present evil aeon (Gal. 1:4), the cosmos has been crucified for them and they for the cosmos (Gal. 6:14), they are considered as no longer "living in the cosmos" (Col. 2:20), and they must not let themselves be conformed to this aeon (Rom. 12:2). It is evident in these and many other pronouncements to what degree in Paul's thinking the "world" as a self-contained life-context stands over against God and his kingdom, and therefore can appear in a personified sense as the singular subject of human sin and depravity: the world does not acknowledge God (1 Cor. 1:21); it withstands him in its wisdom; it is without prospect in its sorrow (2 Cor. 7:10); indeed the "*pneuma* of the world" is even spoken of as a power determinative for all the thinking and doing of men, which places itself over against the Spirit who is of God (1 Cor. 2:12).

It is this conception of cosmos which in principle determines Paul's view of human nature outside Christ. A differentiation is made,

---

1. For what follows cf. the careful analysis of this idea by Bultmann, *Theology*, I, pp. 254ff.; further also Sasse, *TDNT*, III, pp. 892ff., and W. Gutbrod, *Die Paulinische Anthropologie*, 1934, pp. 140ff.

to be sure, in Romans 11:12, 15 between Israel and the world;[2] when it is said in Romans 3:19, however, that "the whole world" is deserving of punishment before God, all men are very explicitly included without distinction, Jews as well as gentiles. To belong to the world means to be a sinner, to participate in sin and to experience the judgment on sin (1 Cor. 11:32). For Paul, therefore, sin is not in the first place an individual act or condition to be considered by itself, but rather the supra-individual mode of existence in which one shares through the single fact that one shares in the human life-context[3] and from which one can only be redeemed by being taken up into the new life-context revealed in Christ (Col. 2:13).

SECTION 16. THE UNIVERSALITY OF SIN. FLESH, ADAM

With this conception of sin as coinciding with being in the world the universality of human sin results of itself. This fundamental notion concerning human nature finds expression in the epistles of Paul in all sorts of ways, directly and expressly, but also indirectly and by way of supposition. As regards the former, one may point in particular to the extensive indictment of Romans 1:18-3:20, by way of proof that outside Christ there is no salvation. To this end both Jews and gentiles stand indicted (Rom. 3:9): "For there is no distinction; for all have sinned, and fall short of the glory of God" (Rom. 3:22, 23). For proof of this universality of sin Paul appeals both to experience (in his sketch of depraved heathenism [Rom. 1:18ff.]), and to the assent of Judaism itself accused by him (Rom. 2:1, 21-24), and he concludes his telling indictment with an extensive appeal to the Scriptures: "None is righteous, no, not one; no one understands, no one seeks for God. All have turned aside, all together have become unprofitable..." (3:10-20; cf. 2:24).

A further explanation of this universality of sin is not given here. There is incidental expression here again that it is not the separate sins of men, but the paramount power of sin which is the predominating idea (Rom. 3:9;[4] cf. Gal. 3:22). But in this pericope Paul does not go further into the nature and origin of this solidarity in sin.

No less characteristic of this conception of sin as universal mode of human existence is the striking use, highly typical of Paul, of the qualification "flesh" (sarx). On the one hand, "flesh" has for him the significance of what is human in its weakness, dependence on God, and perishableness in itself; on the other hand, "flesh" is the pregnant and very specific description of man in his sin, and the coinciding of being human and being a sinner is therefore expressed in it.

Although it is exceedingly difficult and for our purposes un-

---

2. In accordance with the Jewish linguistic usage. Cf. Strack-Billerbeck, II, p. 191; cf. also Luke 12:30.

3. See Grundmann, *TDNT*, I, pp. 308ff., *s.v. hamartanō*.

4. *Pantas hyph' hamartian einai;* Gal. 3:22 even has the neuter *ta panta hypo hamartian.*

necessary to give an exhaustive treatment of this complicated usage in Paul, yet this twofold significance of flesh should be somewhat further elucidated.[5]

The basis for the former ("flesh" as mankind) is indeed the fact that "flesh," in the same sense as "body,"[6] can mean the concrete material corporeality of man, for example, when Paul speaks of "the circumcision of the flesh," in the outward, physical sense of the word (e.g., Rom. 2:28ff.), or of being present or absent "after the flesh" (Col. 2:1-5). In the same sense as "body," "flesh" can denote the whole man in his physical existence (cf., e.g., 2 Cor. 4:10, 11, where "body" and "flesh" are used synonymously; cf. also Gal. 4:13; 2 Cor. 12:7). Yet for Paul "flesh" has a much more inclusive meaning even in this first sense. Just as the Old Testament concept "flesh" (e.g., Isa. 31:3; Jer. 32:27; Job 10:4), or "flesh and blood," it denotes in Paul especially the human as such and taken by itself, as distinguished from and in contrast to the divine. There is not yet here *per se* an indication of human sinfulness, but only of human limitation and weakness; for example, when Paul says that he did not confer with flesh and blood (Gal. 1:16), that flesh and blood shall not inherit the kingdom of God (1 Cor. 15:50), that we do not have to wage war against flesh and blood (Eph. 6:12), or that no flesh may glory in the presence of God (1 Cor. 1:29). Regarding this meaning of "flesh" one is thus able to conclude with Gutbrod: "As the whole man, man is therefore *sarx*, absolutely distinct from God, i.e., he has nothing divine in him, which is not yet to say that he is evil, but simply that he is man, who is created, and not God, who created him."[7]

Now it is remarkable, and in a special sense characteristic[8] of Paul, that "flesh" can also be for him the description of man in his sin and depravity. One need compare only a few of the most distinctive pronouncements:

> For when we were in the flesh, the sinful passions ... were at work in our members ... (Rom. 7:5).
> ... I am carnal, sold under sin (Rom. 7:14).
> For the disposition of the flesh is death ... ; because the disposition of

---

5. For this cf. such monographs as those of C. H. Lindijer, *Het begrip sarx bij Paulus*, 1952, and the older and more recent studies discussed there (as those of De Witt Burton, Schauf, Käsemann, Davies, *et al.*); of Bultmann, *Theology*, I, pp. 232ff.; Gutbrod, *Die Paulinische Anthopologie*, pp. 40ff., 92ff., 145ff.; J. A. T. Robinson, *The Body*, 1952, pp. 18ff.; E. Schweizer, *TDNT*, VII, pp. 125ff., *s.v. sarx*.

6. See below on "body," pp. 115ff.

7. Gutbrod, *Die Paulinische Anthopologie*, p. 99.

8. Cf., e.g., Lindijer, who makes a comparative study of the Greek, Jewish, and Pauline use of "flesh," and comes to the conclusion that the use in Paul is not to be explained from Jewish and Greek usage even if it is much closer to the Jewish than to the Greek (*Het begrip sarx bij Paulus*, pp. 196ff.). The distinction between the Jewish and the Pauline use is precisely in the partial identification of sin and "flesh" in Paul (*ibid.*, pp. 216, 217). For comparison with the idea of "flesh" in the Qumran literature see the essay of K. G. Kuhn in *ZTK*, 1952, pp. 200-220: "[*Peirasmos-hamartia-sarx*] im Neuen Testament und die damit zusammenhängenden Vorstellungen"; H. Huppenbauer, "'Fleisch' in den Texten von Qumran," *TZ*, 1957, pp. 298ff.; J. P. Hyatt, "The View of Man in the Qumran 'Hodayot,'" *NTS*, 1955/56, pp. 276ff.

the flesh is enmity against God; for it does not submit to the law of God; indeed, it cannot; and they that are in the flesh cannot please God (Rom. 8:6ff.).

Now what the works of the flesh are is plain: fornication, uncleanness, ... (Gal. 5:19).

For he that sows upon [the field of] his flesh, shall of the flesh reap destruction (Gal. 6:8).

... among whom we also all once lived in the lusts of our flesh, acting according to the desires of the flesh ... and we were by nature children of wrath (Eph. 2:3).

In these pronouncements, however differently formulated, sin and the flesh are identified with each other: to be "in the flesh," to be "carnal," and the like mean to sin, indeed to be under the power of sin. This relationship of identity of sin and flesh is one of the most distinctive and radical data of Pauline anthropology. What is important for our present context is that there is here a new indication of the universality of sin, in that flesh on the one hand is a description of all that is man, and on the other of the sinful in man.

The pericope Romans 5:12-21 — which we have already cited frequently, and which deals with the Adam-Christ parallel — is of particular importance for insight into this universality of sin as mode of human existence in this world. To be sure, one cannot say of this pericope that it is intended to give an explanation either of the universality of sin or of the manner of its propagation. But we do receive a further insight here into the nature of the solidarity in sin as the apostle conceived of it. For the intention of Romans 5:12-21 is to point out that the connection that exists between the righteousness of Christ and the life of his people has its prefiguration or type in the connection between Adam's sin and the death of his descendants.[9]

In order to make this clear to his readers, Paul comes to the pronouncement so important for the whole structure of his doctrine of sin and redemption: "Therefore, as through one man sin entered into the world, and death through sin; and so death passed unto all men, for that all sinned ..." (Rom. 5:12).

---

9. For the (very differentiated) conceptions on the consequences of Adam's sin for all his posterity in Judaism see now, in addition to Strack-Billerbeck, III, p. 277, the extensive analyses of E. Brandenburger, *Adam und Christus. Exegetisch-religionsgeschichtliche Untersuchung zu Römer 5, 12:21 (1 Kor. 15)*, 1962. In the rabbis one finds in general the thought that on account of the sin of Adam death has come on all men. So far as the universality of sin is concerned, one meets frequently with the insight among them that God has also created the evil inclination in men (the *yēṣer hā-raʿ*), but that man can win the victory over it by keeping the law. The conception of the all-in-one, so characteristic for Paul, is not, however, to be derived from the rabbinic literature. Brandenburger is of the opinion that the basic ideas in it of the paralleling of Adam and Christ in 1 Cor. 15 and Rom. 5 become transparent against the background of "[Christian-]gnostic Adam-*anthropos* speculations" (*Adam und Christus*, p. 157). Notwithstanding the recognized material differences in principle (also acknowledged by Brandenburger), the whole problem of the historical relationship between Paul and the *gnosis* coming to expression in these later writings surfaces again.

The meaning of this much discussed pronouncement, if one takes into consideration the whole context of Romans 5, in our opinion[10] cannot be in doubt. One man has given sin access into the world; he has, as it were, opened the gate of the world to sin. So sin has entered in, here represented as a personified power (cf., e.g., v. 21); through and with sin death has come in as the inseparable follower and companion of sin. The words then follow: "and so [i.e., along this way opened by the one man] death passed unto all men, for the reason that all sinned." The final words give a further explanation as to how death, through one man, has passed and could pass unto all men. This happened because "all sinned," namely, on account of their connection with the one man; therefore Adam's sin was the sin of all, and in that sense it can hold for them that they all sinned. This union of all with and in the one is, as we have already seen,[11] the governing idea of this pericope, and it is in that idea that Paul indicates the typical significance of Adam with respect to the Coming One.

Many wish to understand the words, "for the reason that all have sinned," as referring to the later personal sins of all.[12] This is impossible, however, for more than one reason. First of all, even the words "and so death passed unto all" point to the entering in of and granting of passage to sin and death into the world through the one man. Were one to understand the concluding words of verse 12 of the personal sins of all, then this passage of death would rest once again on the sins of all, and "and so" would lose its exclusive reference to what precedes.[13] That this is not the meaning of the text appears from the following considerations:

(a) From the argumentation of verses 13 and 14, Paul appeals here to the period before the giving of the law, because the death of men then living cannot be explained from their "own," personal sin, but must have had its cause in the sin of Adam. There was sin then, too: "for until the law [came] there was sin in the world." The sanction of the law (death) did not as yet apply, however. For where there is no law, there is also no transgression (cf. 4:15), and "sin is not imputed when there is no law." Nevertheless, at that time also, death reigned over those who did not transgress in the same manner as Adam, that is, who were not confronted in the same manner as Adam with the divine command and the sanction on it. It is thus apparent that it was not their personal sin, but Adam's sin and their share in it, that was the cause of their death. The final words of verse 12b cannot thus be understood otherwise than in this corporate sense.[14]

---

10. For what follows see in greater detail my *Rom.*, pp. 111ff.

11. Cf. above, Section 10.

12. Of the later publications see, e.g., Bultmann, "Adam and Christ in Romans 5," in *The Old and New Man*, p. 62; Brandenburger, *Adam und Christus*, p. 175; E. Jüngel, "Das Gesetz zwischen Adam und Christus," *ZTK*, 1963, pp. 42-74.

13. Brandenburger recognizes that too. He says that Paul in v. 12d "brings a reservation to bear, a correction to the fatalism of the underlying schema [in the preceding]" and he adds to this that "because of this material divergence, the idea of an analogy (Adam-Christ) must immediately break down already in its implication." With this exegesis, understandably so!

14. It is no wonder that Bultmann, who wishes to understand v. 12b of per-

(b) That in the sin of all (v. 12) it is not a matter of the personal sins of Adam's descendants but of the one, fixed, first transgression that was the sin of all by virtue of their relation to the first Adam, is also unmistakably apparent in the sequel. Paul speaks here repeatedly of the one transgression or the transgression of the one, which resulted in death for all:

> . . . for if by the trespass of the one the many died (v. 15).
> . . . for the judgment led upon the ground of one [trespass] to condemnation (v. 16).
> . . . for if by the trespass of the one death came to reign (v. 17).
> . . . as by the trespass of one it came to condemnation for all men (v. 18).

To be sure, some wish to combine this concentration on the sin of the one with the personal sin of the many, by looking on the latter as a consequence of the former.[15] It is obvious, however, that in all these pronouncements the point of Paul's argument is not directed toward the designation of the connection between the one sin of Adam

---

sonal sins, calls vv. 13 and 14 "completely unintelligible" (*Theology*, I, p. 252). On his standpoint it remains inexplicable how Paul is able to say: "sin is not imputed when there is no law," while he says at the same time that death has reigned over all ("Adam und Christus," p. 154). Of the imputation of Adam's sin and the sinning of all with or in the one he takes no account, and then vv. 13 and 14 do remain entirely obscure. Others nevertheless have wanted to reconcile vv. 13 and 14 with the "personal" conception of sin in v. 12b. Thus, e.g., Brandenburger, who in a long-drawn-out and complicated argument (*Adam und Christus*, pp. 180-205) has thought to be able to explain the sense of vv. 13 and 14 approximately as follows: Paul is answering here to a possible objection from the Jewish side that his judgment pronounced in v. 12 (that all have sinned and thus deserve death) nevertheless could not simply apply to those who lived between Adam and Moses and therefore before the giving of the law. Paul is said then to contend in vv. 13 and 14 that this is indeed the case and that his pronouncement in v. 12b is in force for these people, too (cf. pp. 201ff.). But the course of the argument in vv. 13 and 14 gives no occasion to think that Paul by way of a parenthesis here refutes a Jewish objection. Moreover, his refutation of such an objection would hardly be convincing, inasmuch as this refutation would then consist only of affirmations of his own opinion, not of argumentation for its correctness; see also Jüngel, *ZTK*, 1963, pp. 53ff., whose interpretation of v. 13, however, is no more satisfying.

15. Thus, e.g., H. Bavinck, *Geref. Dogmatiek*, III, 4th ed., 1929, pp. 60ff. He is of the opinion that in v. 12b the implicit thought is not that all have sinned in Adam, but that here men's own personal sins are spoken of, which they commit as children of Adam. The sense of vv. 13 and 14 is also to be understood in this way, that although in the period between Adam and Moses men have not sinned as Adam because of want of the law, they nevertheless have died and thus were sinners, "not because each one personally transgressed a positive commandment as Adam and so each one for himself and by himself became a sinner, but because by the transgression of Adam sin had come into the world and reigned over all" (*ibid.*). But this exegesis is untenable; for in vv. 13 and 14 Paul intends to say that so long as one takes into consideration only the personal sins of those who lived before the law, their death as punishment on sin does not have a sufficient explanation. And this is not clarified by the fact that in that period already they sinned as children of Adam. Clarification comes only when one pays heed to their share in the one sin of Adam.

and the universal sinfulness of his descendants, but on the sentence (of death) that the one sin of Adam has brought on all men, because they are all included in the sin and in the death of the one (cf. 1 Cor. 15:21, 22).[16] In bringing judgment on all by his sin, Adam is also the type of the Coming One, as is evident in all the parallel statements mentioned above.

The recapitulation in verses 18 and 19 speaks to the same purpose, where the parallel broken off in verse 12 ("therefore, as...") is again picked up and completed: "So then as through one trespass [or: through the trespass of one] it came to condemnation for all men, even so through one act of righteousness [or: through the act of righteousness of one] to justification unto life for all; for as through the disobedience of the one man the many were made sinners, even so through the obedience of the one will the many be made righteous."

For that which occupies us in this section, the pronouncement that "the many were constituted sinners" is especially of importance. This is often translated: have become sinners. The objection to this is not that the verb used here could not be translated by "become" (although the striking expression employed here is not usual for it and therefore points in another direction[17]), but that the translation "become" of itself is suggestive of the moral and inner condition, the sinfulness of the many. In the context, however, something else is undoubtedly intended, namely, the reckoning of the many as sinners on the ground of Adam's sin and their share in it.[18] This is apparent not only from the parallel expression in verse 19b: "will be constituted righteous," which likewise has a forensic and not a moral significance, but also from the preceding pronouncements, which describe the share of all in Adam's sin again and again as a sentence extending to all and not as the transmission of moral deficiency.

On the other hand, this forensic conception of "were constituted sinners" does not signify, any more than "be constituted righteous," an abstraction of the actual situation of sin in which the world finds itself since sin was granted passage and entered in by the one. Paul does not speak of that any further in this context because in Romans 5:12ff. his object is a different one, namely, the involvement of the many in the one (Adam and Christ). But this does not, of course, alter the fact that by the entrance of sin into the world the situation has been profoundly changed. Sin has begun its calamitous regime. To be constituted sinners also means therefore to have been placed under the power of sin and

16. Cf. Greijdanus, *Rom.*, I, pp. 278ff. He writes that *eph' hō pantes hēmarton* in v. 12 does not serve to confirm the thought that all men are sinners. What is at issue in Rom. 5:12 is not original sin as inherited inner depravity, but the imputation of Adam's sin in the death of man (cf. 1 Cor. 15:21).

17. *Katestathēsan;* for the meaning "hold for, be reckoned as," see, e.g., Deuteronomy 25:6 (LXX), and Liddell-Scott, *Greek-English Lexicon*, 1953, p. 855: "to reckon as."

18. Cf. Greijdanus, *Rom.*, I, pp. 289ff. In v. 19 Paul does not speak of sin as inner impurity and depravity, but of "the position in which one is placed, of a quality which was received, and not in the first place of an inner property which was introduced." Cf. also E. E. Ellis, *Paul's Use of the Old Testament*, 2nd ed., 1960, p. 60.

death (cf. v. 21). Paul does not intend this in verse 19, however, as a personal and inner depravity, as the individual sinfulness of the many, but as having been subjected to the judgment that underlies this situation of death and sin.[19]

In summary it can thus be said with respect to Romans 5:12-21 that the universality of sin as moral depravity is not taught here in so many words; that the share of all men in the sin of Adam is indicated, however, and as its consequence they have been brought under the dominion of the power of sin and death. The presupposition of the whole chain of reasoning lies in the inclusion in the supra-individual situation of sin and death represented by Adam. Here again the basic structures of the Pauline theology are not individualizing, but redemptive-historical and corporate. It is a matter of two different modes of existence, that of the old and that of the new man, which are determined by two different aeons, and concerning which an all-embracing decision has been made in Adam and in Christ.

How this universal and collective character of sin is individualized in the life of all men is elucidated in a moving fashion particularly in those sections of Paul's epistles in which he deals with the inadequacy and impotence of the law.[20] Already in Romans 5:20 he speaks of the law coming in besides, by which the trespass that began with Adam only became more aggravated still. And in Romans 7:8-11 he goes expressly into this sin-provoking and sin-increasing significance of the law. In this confrontation of man with the law the situation of the first man in a certain sense returns, in the reviving of sinful desire and

---

19. G. C. Berkouwer also justly writes (*Sin*, p. 510) that in this pericope "Paul was not concerned about the *manner* in which the sin of one man is 'transferred' to another, or the *manner* in which the pollution of one generation 'becomes' that of another." Berkouwer, however, in 5:19 evidently attaches much value to the translation that many have *become* sinners (not "were regarded as" sinners), and he opposes an exclusively forensic conception of v. 19, according to which the many here are not judged according to what they "really" are. Now the debate over this "really" is misleading because in the forensic conception, too, it is naturally not a matter of a fiction or of a pretension, but of the reality of a share in Adam's sin by virtue of the principle of the all-in-one. That in Rom. 5:12ff. and in v. 19 Paul speaks of that and not also of the individual, personal, "actual" sins of the many seems to me difficult to refute with the argument that "when we utilize this term *forensic* in our explanation of Romans 5:19 we are suggesting a parallel to the doctrine of justification which can very easily lead us to confusions" (*ibid.*, p. 499), for the whole Adam-Christ pericope in Rom. 5:12-21 is full of parallels between the many being condemned in Adam and the doctrine of justification. The preceding v. (18) says in so many words that as through the one act of sin all men have come under condemnation, so through one act of righteousness all men have come to justification of life. It can hardly be said "more forensically" than with these concepts *katakrima* and *dikaiōsis*. This accordingly is the great objection to no longer choosing to understand v. 19 forensically. That this forensic factor does not mean an abstraction of being brought under the reign of sin and death is certainly correct, and I do not deny it. It applies to forensic righteousness, too, that it is a *dikaiōsis zōēs* (v. 18). But this does not mean that in v. 19 the individual acts of sin must already be taken into consideration, in order to escape the danger of "an 'as if'" instead of an "actuality" (*ibid.*, p. 498). It is only in v. 20 that account is taken of this personal sinfulness.

20. See below, Section 23.

in the "deceit" of sin (cf. Rom. 7:11); now, however, with this fundamental difference, that sin has already come into the world and has
dominion, so that sin can then manifest itself in all its force (Rom.
7:13). The sin of Adam thus becomes personal sin, from which it appears
as well that the universal and supra-individual character of sin involves
no reduction in the responsibility of Adam's descendants. However
little the connection between these two viewpoints forms a separate
point of discussion in the epistles of Paul that have been preserved to
us, it is certainly made clear in this way that sin is not a matter that may
be said to be foreign to man himself and for the dominion of which
he is able to excuse himself. Everyone will have to give an account of
himself to God (Rom. 14:12), and each man will bear his own load
(Gal. 6:5). The universality of sin is not, however, the sum total of
separate, individual sins, nor is the responsibility divided; rather, Paul
sees the latter — at least so far as his basic conception is concerned — as
a share of all in this universal sinfulness, the fleshliness of all that is
man. Sin itself, however, does not thereby become less sinful, i.e., it is
not deprived of its ethical character. This can also become clear to us
as we now go further into the essence of sin as described by Paul.

SECTION 17. THE ESSENCE OF SIN.
ANTHROPOLOGICAL OR THEOLOGICAL

Not infrequently, particularly on the ground of what has been said
above concerning the significance of cosmos and flesh as indications of
the sinful life-context and the sinful existence of man, a certain dualism
has been inferred in Paul's view of man. Some have even spoken of a
metaphysical, cosmic dualism that is said to underlie his anthropology
and by virtue of which the sin of man is said simply to consist in his
belonging to the material world as a reality in itself dark and hostile
toward God.[21] Representatives of the history of religions school have
associated themselves with this explanation and related it to the gnostic
mysticism of the Hellenistic mysteries, on which Paul is then said to
have been dependent.[22] Others have spoken of an anthropological
dualism in the sense of the Greek antithesis of the outward and inward
man, whereby the first would represent the lower, sensual and the second
the higher, God-related element of man, to which the significance was
ascribed of having to keep the first under control.[23] In all these conceptions sin bears a natural character, and its seat is sought in the
human as such, or in the sensual nature of man.

   These conceptions, though long propagated, no longer find much

---

21. Especially following the influential work of H. Lüdemann, *Die Anthropologie des Paulus und ihre Stellung innerhalb seiner Heilslehre*, 1872; cf. above,
pp. 17ff.
   22. So especially R. Reitzenstein, *Die hellenistischen Mysterienreligionen*, 3rd
ed., 1927, pp. 333ff.; cf. above, pp. 27ff.
   23. So, e.g., H. J. Holtzmann, *Lehrbuch der neutestamentlichen Theologie*,
2nd ed., II, 1911, p. 13.

favor, after having been amply and conclusively opposed from various
sides. Without going into all their facets and with a reference to that
which must yet be introduced in connection with other anthropological
ideas in Paul, it can be ascertained that the ideas world and flesh afford
no basis for such a conception of sin in Paul. It is unmistakable that
sin is not a cosmic but an ethical quantity, i.e., that it is not an original
principle standing independently over against God, to which the world
and man have fallen prey apart from their own will, but that it has
entered into the world through man (Rom. 5:12), and for the first man,
too, bore the character of transgression of the divine command and of
succumbing to temptation (1 Tim. 2:14). And so far as "flesh" is concerned, it appears from all the evidence that this idea for Paul (a) embraces much more than the sphere of the sensual, and (b) by no means
coincides with corporeality. With regard to the first, we need only point
out that "flesh" in Paul embraces all that is man, not only the body
(Col. 2:11), but also the inner man, the *nous* (Col. 2:18), and that the
sin of the flesh does not therefore consist only in the sensual, but no
less in the spiritual (Gal. 5:18ff.; 1 Cor. 3:1ff.). And with respect to the
second, that for Paul sin and corporeality do not coincide is evident
not only from his belief in the resurrection of the body, but also from
the explicit distinction he makes for himself as a believer between
"flesh" as temporal and as sinful mode of existence (2 Cor. 10:3; Gal.
2:20). The essence of sin is thus in no way to be inferred from such a
sensual conception of "flesh." We likewise read nothing in Paul of an
evil inclination created by God or placed in man, as this is spoken of
in Judaism.[24]

If sin is not thus to be inferred from humanness as such, it is another question how one is to approach and define the essence of sin
in the Pauline doctrine of sin. Of concern here are above all two
different kinds of conception, that of the anthropological and that of
the theological approach.

According to the first the Pauline conception of what sin is rests
in an anthropological prior understanding. This is supposed to admit
of being gathered from the anthropological conceptual materials of
which Paul makes use, and in this way to form the point of departure
for the right understanding of the whole of Paul's soteriology. This
method of approach is employed in particular by Bultmann. According
to him, underlying Paul's whole "theology" is a certain pre-theological
"understanding of Being" (in which he then finds a striking concurrence
with the view of man in the present-day philosophy of existence), which
one must first perceive if he wishes to grasp the purport of the whole
of his preaching.[25]

---

24. Cf. above, p. 95, n. 9.
25. For what follows, in addition to Bultmann's elaborate analysis of the
anthropological ideas in Paul in his *Theology of the New Testament*, I, pp. 187ff.
(esp. that of *sarx*, pp. 232ff.), see his summarizing views on the New Testament
"understanding of Being" (*Seinsverständnis*) in close connection with the Pauline
concept of *sarx*, in his fundamental essay "New Testament and Mythology," 1941, in
Kerygma and Myth, ET 1953, pp. 1-44; particularly pp. 17ff. On the hermeneutical

This pre-theological understanding of Being is said particularly to have found expression in Paul in the use he makes of the concept "flesh."

Bultmann repudiates the view that his idea denotes only the "sensual nature" of man or something of that sort. Rather, "flesh" typifies man's total mode of existence. In this understanding he proceeds from the significance of "flesh" as the designation of the sphere of the visible, the "available," that which one has at his "disposal" (the tangible) and as such the sphere of the transitory and temporal. Now sin, to be sure, does not consist in the "carnal," natural, transitory existence as such, but in permitting oneself to be determined by the "flesh" thus qualified. This takes place when man lives "after the flesh," that is to say, permits himself to be tempted into seeking his life, his happiness, his freedom in this sphere. Not only is the desire for material things involved, but also every striving to acquire for oneself a basis for life, advantage, merit, on the ground of what falls within the reach of human possibilities and which one has at his disposal. In particular the "works of the law" belong to this, on the ground of which man attempts to secure himself against judgment. This "living after the flesh" is the basic form and summary of human sin. It is at the same time man's misery. On the basis of this life after the flesh man can never come to him-"self," his destiny as man, his real "existence." He falls as a slave into that from which he thought himself able to derive safety (*securitas*). And over against that Paul places the life after the Spirit, the principle of the miraculous, divine power of life, that is, the sphere of that which does not lie within man's reach and which he does not have at his disposal, but which lies within the possibility of God. To decide (*entscheiden*) for this, to surrender oneself to this, is the life of faith of which the New Testament speaks. It is the trust to which the gospel summons man that just in this invisible reality, which he does not have at his disposal, life and liberty, his true existence, are situated.

The objection that we have against this view is not that it establishes a very close connection between the anthropological and the theological. That sin is also a perverting of true manhood and that, conversely, the salvation that has appeared in Christ restores man to his real destiny pertains, as we shall see still further, to the heart of Paul's preaching. Our objection is of another kind. It consists in the first place in that the idea of true manhood and thus the idea of the nature and the essence of sin as attack upon it, do not admit of being inferred (as a pre-theological *Daseinsverständnis*) from the significance that certain anthropological ideas, specifically the idea "flesh," have in Paul. And in the second place, closely connected with this, that the anthropological-theological relationship, as it functions in Paul's doctrine of sin and redemption, in this way undergoes a radical change.

So far as the first is concerned, it is no doubt true that the concept "flesh" is for Paul in the first place the denotation of the human in its weakness and transitoriness. But it is another matter whether the criteria can be derived from this significance for the Pauline idea of sin. It is our opinion that in this manner one entangles himself yet again

---

"prior understanding" (*Vorverständnis*) see "The Problem of Hermeneutics," in *Essays Philosophical and Theological*, pp. 234ff. For the whole question see my *Bultmann*, ET 1960.

in a certain, if very refined, dualism. For however true it may be that there are in Paul certain pronouncements in which sin admits of definition as the attaching of oneself to and permitting oneself to be determined by this human-in-itself[26] (which Bultmann then describes as the tangible, visible, etc.), this is not to say that the nature and essence of sin in Paul can be approached from the visible-invisible, tangible-intangible contrast. The criterion for what sin is does not lie especially in permitting oneself to be led and determined by the human-in-its-visibleness and limitedness, but in the human as existence perverted and turned away from God. What is deceptive in Bultmann's interpretation is that with the idea of sin as "flesh" he starts once again from the flesh as the humanly limited, etc., as though it were especially therein that the point of contact for sin lay;[27] whereas for Paul "flesh" denotes sin in the whole of its purport as turned away from and averse to God. Sin can be described, therefore, not only as "living after the flesh" (Rom. 8:5), but likewise as "being in the flesh" (Rom. 7:5; 8:8, 9). "Flesh" is thus a description of sin itself, in the most inclusive sense of the word (cf. Gal. 5:13ff.; Rom. 8:3ff.; Eph. 2:2, 3), and not only of that sin in which man makes his limitation and weakness the measure of all things. Rather, it can justly be said with Gutbrod that the sin of man consists in that he does not want to be flesh (in the sense of "man-in-weakness and transitoriness"), does not want so to be flesh as it has been given him to be, as the foundation of a life after the will of God.[28]

If one asks why in denoting this sinful human principle Paul so

---

26. So, e.g., in 2 Cor. 1:17, where "according to the flesh" denotes levity, that which is dependent on human happenstance or arbitrariness; also in 2 Cor. 10:2ff., where "according to the flesh" typifies the demeanor of someone who in false self-confidence asserts himself in a presumptuous way. Yet further Paul employs the expression "flesh" when he is rejecting confidence in circumcision, Jewish descent, blamelessness in the fulfillment of the law after the Jewish manner, etc. (Phil. 3:4ff.; cf. Col. 2:18, 23; Gal. 3:3). Acting "according to the flesh," trusting "in the flesh," etc., is to have confidence in that which is in and from man and which lies within the reach of man. Thus the "wise after the flesh" can also be spoken of, that is to say, those who in seeking after wisdom find their standard in their own human thoughts (1 Cor. 1:26; 3:1ff.).

27. Conversely, "living according to the Spirit" would consist in moving in another dimension, that of the Holy Spirit, which would have to do, not with man in his visibleness, not with the open, but with the hidden, not with man as flesh, but with his heart. Thus Bultmann, *Theology*, I, pp. 234f. For this further qualification of "flesh" he appeals incorrectly to Rom. 2:28ff. For "flesh" does not here stand over against Spirit as the "earthly-natural," but as the bodily over against the heart. The parallel contrast of "open-hidden" does not therefore give a characterization of what is in general "flesh" over against "Spirit," but of the corporeal (having been circumcised) as opposed to (having been circumcised in) the heart. For this reason, too, that which is hidden, not visible (heart), is not to be identified, as over against the flesh, as the sphere of God's Spirit. The invisible, the heart, the hidden, also pertains to the flesh (Col. 2:18; Eph. 2:2, 3); while conversely the visible and tangible belong to the reach of God's Spirit (2 Cor. 4:11). Bultmann's (very penetrating) analysis of the idea of *sarx* in Paul seems to me to be dominated by a dualistic conception of man, which in the final analysis is not ethical, but natural (the contrast between nature and spirit) and for which in the whole of his theology he wrongly appeals to Paul.

28. Gutbrod, *Die Paulinische Anthropologie*, p. 150.

much prefers to use the word "flesh," while a corresponding usage does not occur elsewhere, it should be pointed out that more than any other anthropological idea "flesh" was pre-eminently suited to form the redemptive-historical contrast to "new creation," the "life in [and after] the Spirit." For "flesh," more than all these other ideas, denotes man in his temporality and transitoriness. Involved here, as we shall see still further,[29] is the characteristic distinction between "flesh" and "body" in the Pauline usage. The body passes "over" into the new creation; the flesh does not. Flesh is man insofar as he belongs to the mode of existence of this world and perishes with it. Therefore, given the radical reversal Paul sees coming about in human existence, "flesh" is pre-eminently the concept that is able to denote the old existence, which has identified itself with sin. In the same way, on the other hand, "Spirit," as designation of the divine life, the creative and miraculous, again and again represents the new creation in Paul's epistles.[30] Flesh and Spirit thus constitute a dualism, yet not a metaphysical or a natural, but a redemptive-historical dualism that also embraces the ethical. For this reason flesh can describe the sinful-in-itself, without the Pauline doctrine of sin coming to rest fundamentally on an anthropological and not on a theological basis.

The principal objection against this anthropological approach to the Pauline doctrine of sin and redemption, however, is a different one still. It consists in the fact that in this way the real order of things is reversed. For it is not a pre-theological understanding of human existence that determines Paul's view of the nature and essence of sin; rather, his thoroughly theological concept of sin is decisive for correct insight into his "anthropology."

In order to demonstrate this we take our starting point in the well-known pronouncement in Romans 8:6ff.: "For the disposition of the flesh is death; but the disposition of the Spirit is life and peace; for the reason that the mind of the flesh is enmity against God; for it is not subject to the law of God, neither indeed can it be: and they that are in the flesh cannot please God."

According to this pronouncement the disposition and mind of the flesh is so reprehensible and fatal (for authentic manhood) because it means enmity against God. The point of departure for the thought does not lie thus in a certain conception of authentic manhood (man in his *Eigentlichkeit*), the corruption (death) of which would therefore be sin because in authentic manhood lies "at the same time" the good, that which was intended by God.[31] For then one is reversing the order. What signifies death for man is that he lives in enmity against God. Therein lies the destruction of manhood, and it is from thence that this must be understood in its anthropological implications. The theological (sin) does not arise *sub specie hominis,* but the anthropological (death) *sub specie Dei.*

---

29. Cf. below, pp. 115ff.
30. Cf. above, Section 11, and below, Section 78.
31. Bultmann, *Theology,* I, p. 232. That the law is "good" is also understood by him from this anthropological presupposition (*ibid.,* pp. 259ff., 212).

This determination, both of the essence of sin and of true manhood, finds its explanation in the fundamental fact that underlies all
the pronouncements on man, from whatever point of view they may be
given, namely, the creation of man by God. Even though little separate
attention is paid to this creation of man in Paul's epistles (cf., however,
1 Cor. 11:8-12; Eph. 3:9; Col. 1:16; 2 Cor. 4:6; 1 Tim. 2:13), this fact
is for Paul so fundamental and self-evident that any doubting of it
would make his whole gospel unintelligible (cf. 1 Cor. 8:6; Rom. 11:36).
It is also in harmony with this that Paul speaks of the man in Christ
as a "new creation" (kainē ktisis; 2 Cor. 5:17; Gal. 6:15; cf. Eph. 2:10,
15; 4:24; Col. 3:10), which in the nature of the case presupposes his
original creation by God.

One of the chief consequences of this creation of man by God
in Paul's epistles is the thought of human responsibility to God. Just
as all things are not only of and by, but also to God, so man as well
(Rom. 11:36). Out of knowledge of God as his Creator man is also to
glorify and give thanks to God (1 Cor. 10:13), and the corruption that
has entered in through sin consists just in the fact that this does not
take place (Rom. 1:21; 1 Cor. 1:21). These same fundamental ideas
govern the Pauline pronouncements on human life. It is not simply a
matter of the existence given by God to man, but above all of the
question for what, or, still better, for whom man lives and to whom he
dedicates his life. All this is not expressly and systematically expounded
in Paul's epistles, but the extent to which it underlies his whole view
of man can be inferred from the fact that he again and again designates
as the object of the salvation that has appeared in Christ that man
should no longer live for himself, but for God (Gal. 2:19; cf. 2 Cor.
5:15; Rom. 14:7, 8; 6:10, 11). The essence and the God-appointed nature
of human life lie in this directedness of man toward God, which is
most closely bound up with his creation by God. It is not only as creature that man has the ground of his being in God, but life in the
pregnant sense of the word for him also lies in having been directed
toward and dedicated to God (of which Paul speaks, for example, when
he says that the law was given us unto life [Rom. 7:10], and that the
just shall live by faith). If man turns aside from God, however, and
does not live for God, but for himself and sin (Rom. 6:10ff.), he thereby
abandons himself and falls into death. The anthropological pronouncements are thus founded in the theological: "Whereas God is the creator
of man and at the same time wishes to be his Lord, man has a life
which includes in it the possibility and the demand to be lived for him
as this God-given life."[32]

Now all this defines the essence of sin. Sin must be understood
out of the relationship in which God has placed man to himself as his
creature and in which he has given and held out the prospect of life
to him. For this reason sin in its essence is rebellion against God, refusal
to be subject to him (Rom. 8:7), enmity against God (Rom. 5:10; 8:7;
Col. 1:21), disobedience (Rom. 11:32; cf. Gal. 3:22; Eph. 2:2; 5:6, et al.).
One can define it as man's willing-to-have-command-of-himself, wanting-

---

32. W. Gutbrod, Die Paulinische Anthropologie, p. 26.

to-be-as-God.[33] It is on that account also the violation and corruption of true manhood. As such it can be defined as foolishness (Rom. 1:23; 1 Cor. 1:19), worthlessness, vanity, darkness, being alienated from the true life (Eph. 4:18), without God and therefore without hope (Eph. 2:12), being dead (Eph. 2:1, 5; Col. 2:13; Rom. 7:10). For as life and good lie in respect for the right relationship to God, so sin means turning manhood into death (Rom. 7:12ff.).

This enmity and disobedience toward God furthermore, just as the turning from true manhood, finds its expression and form in the transgression of the law. For the law is the norm appointed by God for man's relationship to God and for true manhood.

When Paul speaks of "law" in this sense — he is also able to use the word in the wider sense of norm, binding, and so forth (cf., e.g., Rom. 7:2ff., 22ff.), or to intend by it certain parts of the Pentateuch or of the rest of the Old Testament Scripture (cf., e.g., the play on words in Gal. 4:21, as well as the quotations from "the law," as in Rom. 3:10-19) — he means in general the law of Moses (cf. 1 Cor. 9:9; Rom. 10:5). He speaks of it in an undifferentiated sense, i.e., without expressly distinguishing between its various constituent parts, but in doing so he has the moral demands of the law especially in view, in particular those of the decalogue (cf. Rom. 13:8-10; Gal. 5:14; Rom. 2:17-22). It is the special privilege of Israel to have received this law, a matter to which Paul draws attention or alludes in a great many connections (cf. Rom. 2:17ff.; 9:4, *et al.*).

Yet the knowledge of the law is not confined to Israel. Very closely bound up with the view of man as creature of God is the fact that to the gentiles as well all knowledge of the law cannot be denied (Rom. 2:14ff.). Although they do not have the law as expressed in the form in which it was given to Israel, they do "by nature" *(physei)* that which is required by the law. This "natural" knowledge of the law has often been related to certain ideas from the Stoic ethic, according to which there is in every man a natural moral law, which corresponds to the rational, cosmic structure of law.[34] It can justly be pointed out, however, that for Paul "nature" was not, as for the Stoics, the real and highest norm, which then made itself felt in the law as its subjective reflection,[35] but that for him "by nature" has an entirely different background. He thereby speaks very definitely of the law and by that means qualitatively the same law as that which had been given to the Jews. To be sure, the gentiles do not have this law itself, but when in the course of time they nevertheless do what the law demands *(ta tou nomou)*, they show that the "work" required by the law has been written in their hearts; indeed, they are, by so doing, a law to themselves, namely, that one specific law (Rom. 2:14, 15).[36] These last words do

33. Cf. Grundmann, *TDNT*, I, p. 309, *s.v. hamartanō*.

34. Cf. Bultmann, *Theology*, I, pp. 71f.; and in connection with Rom. 2 above all the commentaries of Dodd, Lagrange, Althaus.

35. For this cf. M. Pohlenz, "Paulus und die Stoa," *ZNW*, 1949, pp. 75ff.; and also G. C. Berkouwer, *General Revelation*, ET 1955, p. 179.

36. Gutbrod justly writes: "If [*nomos*] without article implied here a gen-

not thus denote human arbitrariness or that man is his own law, but
rather the superior power of the will of God, from the knowledge of
which man cannot entirely fall away. Even in the absence of the written
law, he must inevitably set before himself the will of God himself
expressed in it. For this reason the passive voice of the words "the work
of the law [or, that the law requires] written in their hearts" is also to
be understood as: written by God. For not only is the writing of the
the law in general the work of God (Exod. 24:12, *et al.*), and not only
in particular is the writing of it in the hearts of men to be attributed
to no other (Jer. 31:33; 2 Cor. 3:2, 3), but it is true above all that the
law of which Paul speaks in this whole context is the law of God. God
declares himself thus to man, even though one does not belong to the
people of the law and the law is not known to him in that concrete
sense. The incidental[37] works of the law of the gentiles prove this,
despite all their ungodliness. How Paul intends this must surely be
understood in the light of Romans 1:19ff., 32, as fruit of continuing
divine revelation. God continues to reveal himself as God even to man
who is apostate and "alienated from the commonwealth of Israel." Being
"without God in the world" (Eph. 2:12) is therefore not to be understood apart from the connection with Romans 1:19. And it is this
revelation of God through which the sense of responsibility in man
cannot be lacking (Rom. 1:20), even though he suppresses it. It also
maintains in him, in spite of himself, the awareness of what death and
life mean for him (Rom. 1:32), awareness therefore also of true manhood. This is not detached from his awareness of God, however, but
springs precisely from it. The consciousness of manhood is implied in
the consciousness of God and of his law. Man is man in the relationship
in which God has placed him to himself and to his law.

No doubt all the questions that here arise have not been resolved
with these incidental pronouncements on the "natural" knowledge of
God and of the law. Not all sin is transgression of the law in an equally
conscious sense. Elsewhere Paul says, as we have seen, that sin is not
imputed where there is no law (Rom. 5:13; cf. 4:15), and by the law
he means the law of Moses. For this reason there is a difference of
responsibility in proportion to one's knowledge of the law (cf. Rom.
3:19), but this can detract nothing from the essence of sin (Rom. 2:12).
Sin is apostasy from God, refusal to be subject to him; it is also and
for this reason lawlessness, disobedience, violation of the divine order
of law. It is accordingly described as such by Paul in all sorts of ways.[38]
Sin is in its essence transgression of the law appointed by God for
man; it is on this account that sin is such a dreadful reality, bringing
disaster in its train. Its strength is the law, that is, what makes it so
fatal is that it is transgression of the law (1 Cor. 15:56).

---

eralization of the concept of law, the train of thought would be broken" (*TDNT*, IV,
p. 1070).

37. The plural *(ta tou nomou)* points to this.

38. *Anomia, parabasis, apeitheia, adikia.* That the qualification *paraptōma,*
often used by Paul as well, should represent a milder conception ("false step"),
appears incapable of being maintained in the light of further comparison of the
linguistic usage (cf. Michaelis, *TDNT*, VI, pp. 171ff.).

B. THE CONSEQUENCES OF SIN
SECTION 18. THE WRATH OF GOD

It holds furthermore for sin, its universality thus established and uncovered by the law in its dreadful character, that it does not remain
without consequences. Because sin is not a natural force or a condition
in which man participates against his will, the result of sin does not
bear the character of a fate to which man falls prey or simply of a
natural process of destruction in which he is included, but, on the
contrary, of a punishment that God decrees on him. As such the result
of sin is given expression by Paul under a great many aspects and with
the utilization of various terms.

The most inclusive and most radical idea for what is intended
here we find in the frequent expression "the wrath of God." On the
one hand, with this term the punishment of sin is denoted in its whole
extent; on the other hand, it is qualified in a pregnant manner as a
personal expression of God himself. In Paul's usage the former stands
in the foreground: the wrath of God there does not so much have the
significance of a divine emotion or of a movement within the divine
being as indeed of the active divine judgment going forth against sin
and the world. It is surely too one-sided to say[39] that the wrath of God
denotes nothing other than his judgment. "Wrath of God" not only
says something about what God does, but also about what he is in
doing it.[40] The word "indignation" (thymos) also points to this, a term
that is used in Romans 2:8 along with "wrath," and still more than the
latter denotes divine passion. This does not alter the fact that by the
wrath of God usually the working of the divine wrath is intended, as
may appear from the combinations "wrath to come" (Rom. 5:9; Eph.
5:6; Col. 3:6; 1 Thess. 1:10) and "day of [God's] wrath" (Rom. 2:5). It
is also clearly evident from the way in which in Romans 1 and 2 —
where Paul speaks at length of the wrath of God — mention is made
particularly of the effectuation of this wrath. "Tribulation and anguish"
stand in Romans 2:9 as synonyms of "wrath and indignation." In all these
pronouncements the idea of the working of God's wrath predominates
above that of the emotion.[41]

Further, it appears that every thought of an unbridled and norm-
less exercise of vengeance, such as is to be found in the heathen representations of the wrath of the gods, is entirely lacking here. Likewise,
it may not be inferred from the fact that "the wrath" is frequently
spoken of in an absolute sense (e.g., in Rom. 5:9; 12:19; 1 Thess. 2:16 —
in agreement with the usage of the Old Testament as well[42]), that the
wrath of God is a power operating independently, a personification of
an evil working of calamity no longer standing under God's control.[43]

---

39. So Bultmann, Theology, I, p. 288.
40. See also Stählin, TDNT, V, p. 425, s.v. orgē: "As in the OT, so in the
NT orgē is both God's displeasure at evil, His passionate resistance to every will
which is set against Him, and also His judicial attack thereon."
41. So Stählin, TDNT, V, p. 424.
42. Cf. Fichtner, TDNT, V, pp. 395ff., s.v. orgē.
43. G. H. C. Macgregor in his essay "The Wrath of God in the New Testa-

Rather, God's wrath is altogether determined by his righteousness and holiness. Again and again the apostle places both in the same context, for example, when God's wrath and "righteous judgment" *(dikaiokrisia),* or God's wrath and "righteousness" *(dikaiosynē)* are used as synonyms (Rom. 2:5; cf. vv. 2, 11; 3:5). The working of God's wrath is the realization of the curse he has attached as sanction to his holy law (Gal. 3:10). He can say as well, therefore, that it is the law that works God's wrath (Rom. 4:15), and he does his utmost in Romans 1:19ff. to show that the revelation of God's wrath does not fall on the gentiles apart from the knowledge of the true God, so that they are not to be excused.

Now this wrath of God is spoken of time and again as an eschatological reality.[44] This appears from the repeated reference to the coming wrath (Rom. 5:9; Eph. 5:6; Col. 3:6; 1 Thess. 1:10), which will be revealed on "the day of God's wrath" (Rom. 2:5). Then the righteous judgment, the divine sentence, is to be executed (Rom. 2:5; 5:16, 18; 8:1; cf. 8:33, 34; 2 Cor. 3:9). Description of this event is always exceedingly restrained. It does not serve to increase or satisfy knowledge about it, but to warn against the commencement of its reality. The possibility of averting the wrath of God lies just in its future character and in the preaching of it. In that sense one can say that the element of reserve is also implied in this future character of the divine wrath.[45] God still reserves to himself his definitive decision.

This does not mean, however, that the revelation of the wrath of God is posited as only a possibility. The most central pronouncements of Paul on the wrath of God point to its revelation as eschatological reality already in the present, together with the revelation of the righteousness by faith. This occurs in the first main division of Romans, in which, after the thematic definition of the gospel in 1:17, the alternative is set forth with great force: "For the wrath of God is revealed from heaven."

This pronouncement, which forms the starting point of an extensive delineation, must be understood in close connection with the revelation of the righteousness that is by faith, made central in verse 17.

---

ment," *NTS,* 1961, pp. 101ff., in some measure goes in this direction. He writes that we see a clear tendency in Paul "to depersonalize the wrath of God" (p. 104), and that "it would be fair to say that Paul does not think of God as being angry in quite the same immediate and personal sense as he thinks of him as actively loving." And he is of the opinion that "wrath" in Paul is the anthropological expression of the divine retribution, "not so much the personal attitude of God to man, but rather the inevitable process of cause and effect in a moral universe"...and "working (may we say?) relatively independently of God's immediate volition" (p. 105). But it must be regarded as questionable whether one may ascribe such ideas to Paul when he sometimes speaks of "the wrath" in an absolute sense. One may undoubtedly say that according to Paul, too, God does not will damnation for men in the same manner as salvation (1 Tim. 2:4; 4:10; Rom. 11:32); likewise that Paul does not attribute all the evil in the world in a direct sense to God (cf. 2 Cor. 12:7; 1 Cor. 5:5), but where he speaks in so many words of the wrath (of God) it is difficult to assume such a distance from "God's immediate volition."

44. Cf. the survey of Macgregor, *NTS,* 1961, pp. 103ff.
45. *Ibid.,* p. 104.

In both cases it is a matter of an eschatological reality,[46] which is "revealed," becomes visible, makes itself felt. That is not to say, so far as the wrath of God is concerned, that it would only now have become visible together with the righteousness that is by faith,[47] but indeed that in it the final judgment of God to be expected upon sin is in process of revealing itself and coming to execution; and that in an unmistakable way. For it reveals itself "from heaven," i.e., before the eyes of all, in such a way that everyone is able to see it[48] (cf. Acts 14:17; Luke 21:11; 17:24). This is further indicated in the manner in which God utterly abandons to error and sin those who turn away from him.

By linking this twofold revelation so closely together Paul wants to make his readers feel even more strongly the accent of the gospel. The eschatological reality thrusts itself forward in all respects — such is his intention — on the one hand as righteousness, acquittal, and on the other as wrath, the exercise of judgment. And the latter serves as proof[49] that it is only in the way of the righteousness proclaimed in the gospel that redemption and life are possible.

Already from this context it may appear with what earnestness Paul speaks of the wrath of God and how real this is for him; it is evident as well how incorrect it is to represent the situation as though behind this God preached by Paul, who is angry and saves, there nevertheless stands the hidden God, "the God of all mercy," who will ultimately save even the obdurate and reprobate;[50] equally, how arbitrary it is to posit with Ritschl that the idea of judgment in Paul may be said to have had validity only in his polemic with the Jews and was intended only dialectically.[51] Indeed, one can go further and say that

---

46. Cf. Oepke, *TDNT*, III, p. 583, *s.v. apokalyptō;* Bultmann, *Theology*, I, pp. 274f.; Nygren, *Romans*, pp. 99f.; Stählin, *TDNT*, V, pp. 431ff., *s.v. orgē.*

47. G. Bornkamm contends thus, in "The Revelation of God's Wrath," *Early Christian Experience*, ET 1969. He concludes (p. 64): "The revelation of this saving 'righteousness' of God is an eschatological event that is accomplished in the 'Now' of salvation history. To this same hour is bound the revelation of his wrath from heaven...." The nature of the operation of wrath, as Paul describes it, is not, however, bound to the time of salvation that has commenced with Christ. Nor is it only to be understood from the contrast with the revelation of the righteousness of God. For it is revealed "from heaven" in an unmistakable manner. See the text.

48. Cf. Schlatter, *Gottes Gerechtigkeit*, p. 48. The interpretation of Traub, *TDNT*, V, pp. 531f., *s.v. ouranos*, that these words may be said to be a denotation of the redemptive character of this revelation is without foundation and seems biased.

49. Lietzmann thinks incorrectly that in 1:18ff. the situation is portrayed as it existed before the advent of the gospel, so that the appeal to this operation of the wrath of God (as that is continued in Rom. 2) bears a hypothetical character ("so would God go on to judge if the gospel had not come") (*Rom.*, pp. 31, 40). Against this see especially Käthe Oltmanns, "Das Verhältnis von Röm 1,18-3,20 zu Röm 3,21ff," *Theol. Blätter*, 1929, cols. 110ff. Just as little can one construe the connection between Rom. 1:17 and 1:18 in such a way that "precisely because (*gar;* v. 18) God has to be wrathful against the whole world,... he gives righteousness [*ek pisteōs eis pistin*]" (so Stählin, *TDNT*, V, 426; cf. p. 431, *s.v. orgē*). The revelation of God's wrath (1:18) is not the motive for the giving of the righteousness by faith, but the proof that there is deliverance only in the way of this bestowed righteousness; see also my *Rom.*, pp. 40ff.

50. So Lietzmann, *Cor.*, p. 122.

51. Cited by Büchsel in *TDNT*, III, p. 938, *s.v. krinō.*

it is just the content of the gospel that opened Paul's eyes to the tremendous reality of the wrath of God. For as long as man stands on
legalistic ground, he is in many respects still living in the hope that
through his knowledge of the law and through the merit of the works
of the law he may be able to escape the wrath of God (Rom. 2:3); the
wrath of God is for him only a possibility. In the light of the advent
of Christ and of the significance of his death and resurrection, however,
the judgment of God on sin (Rom. 3:26), and along with that the
impossibility of achieving righteousness for oneself outside Christ on
the ground of one's own works of the law, have become completely
clear. The reference to the wrath of God constitutes, therefore, the
impressive accompaniment to the proclamation of the gospel. The
knowledge that "the Lord is to be feared" forms one of the most powerful and urgent reasons for Paul's apostolic zeal to persuade men to be
reconciled to God (2 Cor. 5:11ff.).

On the other hand, it may never be forgotten, and is evident even
from the foregoing, that it is always as a minister of the gospel that he
speaks of the wrath and of the condemnatory judgment of God. The
wrath and the enmity of God are not for a moment in contradiction
with God's reconciliatory will and love, and pointing to the wrath of
God has the constant intention of disclosing to man God's grace and
love in Christ. Indeed, the object even of the working of God's wrath
itself is to cause his plan of redemption to triumph. Here we must
examine a pronouncement into which it has often been thought necessary to read the impassive and arbitrary character of the wrath of God,
namely, Romans 9:22. With the utilization of the figure of the potter
the apostle speaks here of "the vessels of wrath, which were prepared
for destruction," and which "God, willing to show his wrath, and to
make his power known, endured with much longsuffering." However
much God's omnipotence is here placed in the forefront, two things
ought to be kept in view: first, that the phrase "the vessels [or objects]
of wrath,[52] prepared for destruction," refers to impenitent sinners, who
on account of their sin were[53] "prepared," ready, ripe for destruction
and as such were used by God in order to demonstrate the power of his
wrath in them; and second, that God did so in order[54] the better to
make known the riches of his glory on the objects of his mercy. To put
it concretely: Pharaoh's hardening is made to serve the more clearly to
elucidate God's redemptive work with respect to his people. Paul then

---

52. *Skeuē orgēs;* cf. Jer. 50:25 (LXX 27:25), where it is used in the sense
of instruments with which or by which God demonstrates his wrath. Here, in Rom.
9:22, the genitive does not have an instrumental, but a qualifying or objective
significance.

53. The passive participle does not say who the logical subject is. Greijdanus,
Rom., II, p. 443, sees in that, in our view rightly, an indication that the sinner himself
was active in this preparation, as was clearly evident with Pharaoh mentioned previously. This is not to deny that the logical subject, as in the parallel *ha proetoimasen* in
v. 23, is above all God; cf. Stählin, *TDNT,* V, p. 442: "they were prepared thereto by
God." But then surely in their sinful rebellion against him; for this whole pericope
cf. also below, Section 57.

54. This appears, too, from the connection of Rom. 9:22 and 23: for *kai*
here means "and that indeed" or "and that also."

employs this example to show how the hardening of the Jews, too, has been made subservient to the riches of the world (Rom. 11:12). God's wrath places itself in the service of his love. And that not only for the sake of the gentiles, but also of the Jews themselves, for whom the hardening need not signify a definitive judgment (Rom. 11:11), but who just in their hardening are still to be provoked to jealousy.

These pronouncements in Romans 9 and 11 show quite patently to what degree in Paul's preaching not only the killing power of the law, but also the working of God's wrath against sin that lies behind it are not detached from the divine redemptive work in Christ, but are rather seen cooperating closely with it. The dreadful reality of God's wrath is not thus robbed of its mysterious depth, nor is the place of God's wrath in the whole of God's work for man made transparent. But the certainty is explained with which Paul could write to the church of Thessalonica that God has not appointed us to wrath, but to the obtaining of salvation through our Lord Jesus Christ (1 Thess. 5:9).

If one inquires further as to the way in which this wrath of God is even now revealing itself and making itself known as an eschatological reality, here again the close connection between the theological and anthropological points of view is to be pointed out. The theological: for the revelation of God's wrath consists in the disturbance of the relationship in which God has placed man to himself. It is not merely a negative privation of God's communion; it consists in "alienation" (Col. 1:21; cf. Eph. 2:12; 4:18), "enmity," not only in the sense that human enmity raises itself against God (Rom. 8:7; Col. 1:21), but also that for man God has become an enemy (Rom. 5:10; 11:28). But likewise the anthropological: as communion and life with God imply true manhood, so alienation from God means the corruption, indeed the destruction of human existence. It is particularly from this viewpoint, too, that Paul points to the revelation of the wrath of God in the life of man under the power of sin.

Two ideas come to the fore here, summarizing the whole of the corruption of sin: in the first place death, the wages of sin in the most inclusive sense of the word (Rom. 6:23); in the second place the bondage of sin, moral impotence, in part to be characterized as inner discord.

Of these two descriptions of the punishment on sin, the first is naturally the most comprehensive and fundamental. Death is the fully developed fruit of sin. It is the just sentence of God (Rom. 5:12ff., 18), and at the same time the "natural" and inner consequence of sin; it is that at which sin, as it were, aims and in which it achieves its triumphs (Rom. 5:21); it is the fruit that one reaps when he sows to the flesh (sin) (Gal. 6:8; cf. Rom. 7:5). Death is therefore the end of sin (Rom. 6:21), not simply as conclusion, but as result, as that in which sin reaches its objective (Rom. 6:16).

Death is thereby not only a punishment that puts an end to life, but a condition in which the destiny of life outside Christ is turned into its opposite. This applies to death at the end of the earthly life. It is corruption (Gal. 6:8), destruction (Rom. 9:22; Phil. 3:19), in the

active sense of the word[55] (cf. Rom. 2:8ff.), the absolute antithesis of
the life intended by God and saved by Christ.

In addition to the future, however, sin brings forth death already
in this life. Thus Romans 7:25 speaks of deliverance from "the body
of this death" (possibly:[56] "this body of death"). However one chooses
to translate the expression, it is certain, as appears from the whole
context (cf. vv. 5, 10, 13), that Paul is speaking here of a condition of
death that has already set in. For by "body" he means not merely the
material organization of the body, but man in his present mode of
existence, that which he elsewhere calls the "body of sin" (Rom. 6:6),
or "of the flesh" (Col. 2:11).[57] Thus death works itself out in the sinful
life of man. Romans 7:9, 10 speaks of that in a very telling and explicit
manner: "when the commandment came, sin began to live, but I began
to die; and the commandment which is unto life, this I found to be
unto death." This "dying" is not to be taken as introspection, acquiring
an eye for guilt and punishment,[58] but the sin-ruled condition of his
existence,[59] which can be called dying because it is cut off from the
true life for God (Rom. 6:11ff.), because it is a life for death (Rom.
6:16). It is what Paul in this same context of Romans 7 calls "being
sold under sin." Sin brings death because it does not consist merely in
separate acts whereby man remains himself, but is a power that
corrupts him in his true manhood before God in such a way that
he can do nothing other than sin (Rom. 8:7), so that even the fear that
thereby arises within him (Rom. 8:15), and his sorrow concerning it,
cannot remove this condition, but is only the more productive of death
(2 Cor. 7:10). This has been correctly described in this way,[60] that the
insight of man into the hopelessness of his condition, into his "being
worthy of death" (cf. Rom. 1:32), in no respect whatever introduces
change into his existence, but rather must be reckoned a part of this
dying. Elsewhere Paul speaks to the same effect of being dead through
trespasses and sins (Eph. 2:1, 5; Col. 2:13), and he defines this condition
further as living in and doing sin in all sorts of ways, as being under
the wrath of God (Eph. 2:3). Conversely, the new life can be qualified
even in the present time as arising from the dead (Eph. 5:14), as being
"alive from the dead" (Rom. 6:13). In all this the reality of death is
apparent, as it even now works itself out through sin.

The second general denotation of the corruption of sin is that
of the bondage, the impotence, the imprisonment in which man finds

---

55. Cf., e.g., Oepke, *TDNT*, I, pp. 396f., *s.v. apollymi, apōleia*.

56. This depends on whether one takes *toutou* with *sōmatos* or with *thanatou*.

57. When Paul says in Rom. 8:10: "If Christ is in you, the body is dead
because of sin; but the Spirit is life because of righteousness," by this deadness of
the body he does not mean the same thing as in 7:24 (thus, e.g., Greijdanus), but
the subjection of the physical existence of believers to death; "through sin" does
not say that they must as yet pay for their sin with death, but that, as appears
from the judgment executed (in Christ) on sin, so far as their bodies are concerned,
they are obliged to go the way of Christ (cf. v. 11).

58. So Greijdanus, *Rom.*, I, p. 333.

59. Thus rightly Greijdanus on 7:24 (*ibid.*, I, p. 351).

60. Cf. Gutbrod, *Die Paulinische Anthropologie*, p. 130.

himself by and under sin. To be under sin, to be captive or shut up under sin, is the fate that the sinner brings on himself (Rom. 3:9; Gal. 3:22). Sin is represented again and again as a personal power, a lord, under whose mastery man has been sold as a slave and is henceforth required to live (Rom. 7:14). This idea is elaborated in a great variety of ways, particularly in Romans 6:12ff.: "Do you not know that him to whose service you present yourselves, you must also obey as slaves, whether of sin unto death, or of obedience . . . ?" (v. 16). The committing of sin therefore brings the slavery of sin along with it, in which one is obliged to place himself at the disposal of the demands of sin (vv. 13, 17, 19, 20; cf. Tit. 2:3; 3:3). Elsewhere Paul speaks of the debtor, prisoner of war, military conscript, one taken into custody of sin (Rom. 8:12; 7:23; Gal. 3:23), in short, the punishment of sin works itself out as a deprivation of human liberty, and so also of the conditions of true manhood: that one not direct oneself to sin as one's lord, but to God (Rom. 6:11).

The explication of these general descriptions is one of the most characteristic features of Paul's doctrine of sin. The following section deals with it.

SECTION 19. THE CORRUPTION OF MAN

The corruption of sin that is described in its universality as death and bondage has its effects furthermore in the various aspects of human existence. We come into contact here with the peculiar anthropological concepts and ideas that Paul employs. So far as the death and bondage brought about in man by sin are concerned, one can distinguish two different ideas in particular: first of all, the corruption of sin in the "inward man," the *nous,* the "heart," which from there extends itself in the (sinful acts of the) "outward man," in his "body," and in his "members." With the second idea the reverse sequence is in the foreground: the external man, the body, the members, appear to have been brought under the control of sin in such a way that the inner man, too (the *nous,* the heart, the will), is unable to offer resistance to the superior power of sin in the body. In the first case one could speak of the corruption of sin, which asserts itself from within over the whole of human existence; in the second case, of the bondage of sin, which, operating through "the body," holds the inward man in its grasp as a prisoner. The first idea is to be demonstrated particularly from the description of the corruption of sin in such passages as Romans 1 and Ephesians 4; the second dominates the well-known delineation of the power of sin in Romans 7:14ff.

Before going into this further (see below, p. 121), it is not superfluous to catch a sharper glimpse of at least the most prominent of these anthropological ideas.[61]

---

61. The literature on this Pauline "anthropology" is very extensive. Summarizing treatments are to be found (in addition to the older writing of H. Lüdemann,

Outward and inward man

We can start here from the distinction occurring a few times in Paul between "the outward man" and "the inward man"[62] (Rom. 7:22; 2 Cor. 4:16; Eph. 3:16). Although the pronouncements given in these places are highly important for our subject,[63] the distinction itself is of a very general and formal significance, describing the outward, visible, physical, and the inward, invisible, spiritual side of human existence. The latter is also denoted in Romans 7:22, 23 by "mind" (nous), and mentioned in contradistinction to "body" and "members." Similarly, "inward man" in Ephesians 3:16 is in many respects equivalent to "heart" mentioned in the same context. No general anthropological conclusions are to be drawn from this, however, e.g., of a dualistic man consisting of two "parts," or of a more or less "real" or "essential" part of man. Rather, the complete description—outward and inward "man"—points in another direction; man does not only "have" an outward and inward side, but is as man both "outward" and "inward," exists both in the one way and in the other. The relationship between this outward and inward man is indeed of especial importance in the definition of the corruption of sin. All this is to be perceived in its specific significance, however, only when we have first formed a clearer idea of such differentiated concepts as "body," "mind" (nous), "heart," et al. The expression "outward and inward man" is to be taken only as a general, "coarse" distinction.[64]

Body

For correct insight into the anthropological implications of the Pauline doctrine of sin, the role that is ascribed to the body (sōma) is of special importance. "Body" in Paul has a very comprehensive significance. One can take his point of departure here in the general popular usage by which "body" denotes the tangible and visible organism in which various "members" are to be distinguished. In that sense Paul speaks, e.g., of bearing the marks of Jesus in his body (Gal. 6:17; cf. 2 Cor. 4:10), of giving up the body to be burned (1 Cor. 13:3), of the seat of the sexual life in the body (Rom. 4:19; 1 Cor. 7:4; Rom. 1:24), concerning the body as personal, physical presence (2 Cor. 10:10). In this sense "body" is frequently synonymous with "flesh," insofar as flesh sometimes also denotes only the material corporeality of man (cf., e.g., Rom. 2:28—circumcision "in the flesh"; Col. 2:1, 5—being present or absent "after the flesh").

Die Anthropologie des Paulus und ihre Stellung innerhalb seiner Heilslehre, 1872, which starts from a certain metaphysical dualism; cf. above, p. 100) especially in the very valuable book of W. Gutbrod, Die Paulinische Anthropologie; in the detailed analyses of Bultmann, Theology, I, pp. 191-269; W. G. Kümmel, Man in the New Testament, ET 1963, pp. 38-71; see also C. H. Dodd, P. J. Bratsiotis, R. Bultmann, H. Clavier, Man in God's Design, 1952. Monographs on specific ideas, e.g., of W. Schauf, Sarx, Der Begriff "Fleisch" beim Apostel Paulus, etc., 1924; C. H. Lindijer, Het begrip sarx bij Paulus; J. A. T. Robinson, The Body; N. A. Waaning, Onderzoek naar het gebruik van [pneuma] bij Paulus, 1939; see also the relevant treatises in TDNT and the literature cited there.

62. Ho exō anthrōpos; ho esō anthrōpos.

63. See below, pp. 124ff.

64. Behm, e.g., justly writes (TDNT, II, p. 699, s.v. esō) that what Paul terms the inward man is essentially nothing new as against the Old Testament "heart" and that which Jesus means when says: "from within, out of the heart of man proceed..." (Mark 7:21), and in Luke 11:39: "your inward part is full of extortion and wickedness."

Closer inspection teaches, however, that "body" and "flesh" (in this restricted sense of the word) are not thought of as the external "constituent part" of man, as the material casing of the real, inner man, but rather denote the man himself according to a certain mode of his existence. This is evident from the manner in which Paul frequently speaks of the body as of the concrete mode of existence, co-extensive with man himself (cf. Rom. 12:1: "present your bodies a living sacrifice"; cf. also Eph. 5:28, where "himself" and "his body" are used promiscuously; similarly Rom. 6:12, where there is mention first of "the body" and in conjunction with it of "your members" and immediately following that, as a synonym, of "yourselves"; cf. also 1 Cor. 6:15 with 12:27: "do you not know that your bodies are members of Christ?" and "you are the body of Christ, and each for his part [his] members"). In the one instance the subject of the being members-of-Christ is "your bodies"; in the other, without a difference of meaning, it is the personal pronoun "you."[65] One finds the same comprehensive use of body in those places where body means approximately the earthly human life with the inclusion of death; so, e.g., when Paul says (2 Cor. 4:10) that he at all times bears about in his body the dying of Jesus, that the life also of Jesus may be manifested in his body; or when in Philippians 1:20 he expresses the earnest hope that Christ will be magnified in his body, and adds to this: whether by my life, or by my death (cf. also Col. 1:22). When Paul, moreover, speaks repeatedly of the human "members" (melē), the same thing is expressed. But the members point still more concretely to the different possibilities of acting, obeying, sinning, which man possesses in his bodily existence, for which reason, e.g., the "putting to death of the members which are upon the earth" can be spoken of (Col. 3:5), whereby one is not to think of some form or other of self-mutilation, but of the struggle man has to carry on in and with himself against sin. In this personal sense, too, "flesh" can sometimes be used as the equivalent of "body" or "members" (e.g., in 2 Cor. 4:10, 11, where "body" and "flesh" are used synonymously in describing the whole man in his temporal bodily existence).

With this equating of "body" and "flesh,"[66] however, one should not lose sight of the different points of view from which both descriptions regard man in his earthly mode of existence. "Flesh," even when it does not have the pregnant significance of human sinfulness, always has man in his weakness, transitoriness, especially in view; "body," on the contrary, represents the image of man as he was created by God, was intended for God, and will therefore be saved from death by God. When in 1 Corinthians 15 Paul speaks of the resurrection, he lays all the emphasis on the one hand on the fact that flesh and blood cannot inherit the kingdom of God, and on the other, that man will be raised according to his physical existence. Not as though the human body, as it now is, were not to die and perish. This body belongs to the transitory, to the flesh. It is, however, another, a spiritual body, that will be raised. Flesh is not spoken of in the same sense, i.e., that there will be a spiritual flesh. "Resurrection of the flesh" not only does not occur in Paul, but for him is a scarcely conceivable terminology (1 Cor. 15:50). "Flesh" in Paul is distinctive of the temporal and earthly character of human existence; "body" can also denote the future and heavenly.[67]

---

65. Cf. Bultmann, *Theology*, I, p. 194; for this changing of the significance of body from the visible and tangible "exterior" of man to "the man himself," see Bultmann's penetrating analysis of 1 Cor. 6:13-20 (*loc. cit.*).

66. For "flesh" see also above, pp. 93ff.

67. See also below, Section 78, pp. 548f.

It is evident from all this, on the one hand, how much man in the whole of his existence is "body," insofar, that is, as he cannot manifest himself in any other way than as a physical being, and experiences therein his responsibility as a man. It is also clear on the other hand, however, that there is a *Gegenüber* of the "I," the inward man, the *nous* (see below) on the one side, and his "body" on the other. The body is even then not only the physical and tangible, but man in his self-realization, which must receive its determination from "within." This relation which man has to his body (himself) finds expression, for example, in the pronouncement that believers are not to yield their bodies (their members) to sin (Rom. 6:12ff., 19); that they must put to death their "members upon the earth" (Col. 3:5); must present their bodies to God as a sacrifice (Rom. 12:1f.), etc. In the same sense (namely, as equivalent of the reflexive) the body can be described as the organ or means in which and by which man is to experience his responsibility before God. Thus Paul says (e.g., in 2 Cor. 5:10) that each one will receive that which he has done "through his body" *(dia tou sōmatos)*, whether good or evil. Similarly, in 1 Corinthians 6:13, that the body is not for fornication, but for the Lord. Likewise he prays in 1 Thessalonians 5:23 that the spirit, the soul, and the body of his readers may be kept blameless at the parousia of Christ, which of course does not refer to their bodily well-being or their health, but to that which they have done and will prove themselves to be in and through their bodily existence. In all these passages "body" is on the one hand not to be thought of detached from man himself, as though it were only the material-sensual organization: man not only "has" a body, but is a body. On the other hand, it is in this being a body that there is the possibility of the distinction between man and himself, between the "I" and its self-realization in thoughts and acts. In Paul's mode of expression this last can assume the form of a body that occupies a position of independence toward the "I," which has its own "lusts" and its own "practices," which the "I" is to put to death (Rom. 6:12; 8:13; Col. 3:5). It is in the harmony of the "I" and "the body" that the unity of human existence ("outward" and "inward") is disclosed, in the good as well as in the evil; on the other hand, it is in this distinction between the "I" and "the body" that there is also the possibility of inner discord in human existence, as this is portrayed for us with vivid colors, particularly in Romans 7:14ff.

Nous

Furthermore, we meet with a whole series of concepts in Paul that specifically describe and further define the "inward man" as "understanding" *(nous)*, "heart" *(kardia)*, "will" *(thelēma)*, "soul" *(psychē)*, "spirit" *(pneuma)*, "conscience" *(syneidēsis)*. Here the concepts *nous* ("understanding") and heart—again and again employed by Paul and closely connected with each other—occupy far and away the most important place.

In English there is really no equivalent for *nous*. It can sometimes simply be translated by "understanding," e.g., when speaking with the *nous* is placed over against "speaking in tongues" (1 Cor. 14:14ff., 19), i.e., speaking in such a way that man comprehends the sense and purport of it with his "sober" understanding (cf. 2 Cor. 5:13).[68] Thus it can be said (Phil. 4:7) that

---

68. The contrast in these verses of "my spirit" and "my understanding" is difficult. Some choose to understand by "my spirit" not the human spirit, but the divine *pneuma* bestowed upon man (so, e.g., Bultmann, *Theology*, I, p. 207; Wendland, *Cor.*, p. 84); others are of the opinion that the contrast "my spirit" and "my understanding" contradicts this (e.g., Grosheide, *1 Cor.*, p. 363). In our opinion,

the peace of God transcends all *nous,* i.e., the divine peace bestows that which man with all his reflection cannot give himself[69] (or: which surpasses all that the human understanding comprehends or is able to comprehend).[70] In a similar sense *nous* can mean level-headedness or intelligent judgment (cf. 2 Thess. 2:2).

Nous frequently has a more inclusive and pregnant significance, however, which does not correspond with our "understanding," or does so only partially. This is the case in those passages which especially relate *nous* with the knowing of God, for example, Romans 12:2, where the renewing of the *nous* is spoken of so as to discern what the will of God is. Still more directly involved with the knowledge of God is Paul's pronouncement concerning the gentiles, that the invisible things of God are known from his works through the *nous (nooumena;* Rom. 1:20). The *nous* here is not the seat of a natural or innate knowledge of God, is still less the divine light in man or something of that sort, but denotes the capacity, the susceptibility of man to take in the revelation of God that comes to him from without. This is not to say, however, that the *nous* knows merely in a receptive way. It is at the same time man in his inner self-determination; speaking religiously, it is both the capacity for being addressed and the responsibility with respect to the revelation that comes to him. The *nous* is therefore not merely a theoretical capacity, but also the point of departure, the determinative "center" of his acting.[71] Paul speaks to that effect, e.g., in Romans 14:5: "every man must be fully convinced in his own *nous*" (judgment, self-determination). Romans 7:23 is also typical of this meaning: "but I see in my members another law which is at war with the law of my *nous.*" Thus there is mention here of a law (to be understood in a more general sense as commanding power, constraint)[72] to which the *nous* as starting point for moral action has been subjected. The *nous* here represents that which man knows and wills with respect to the good according to his deepest self-determination (cf. the context).[73] Because not only the individual decisions are thought of here, but the continuous moral posture of man, *nous* can mean more generally: disposition, mind (cf., e.g., 1 Cor. 1:10; Col. 2:18ff., *et al.*).

This important place in human responsibility which is ascribed to the *nous* is also reflected in the ideas compounded with *nous* or derived from it, as, e.g., "thought" *(noēma;* 2 Cor. 3:14; 4:4; 2 Cor. 10:5; 11:3), in which the "moment of thought" is very closely connected with the "moment of disposition" that reveals itself in the willing and acting. Likewise the word "conversion," occurring only very seldom in Paul[74] *(metanoia, metanoein),* denotes a reversal of the *nous,* i.e., a radical turning about of man in all his thinking, willing, and acting (cf. 2 Tim. 2:25; 2 Cor. 12:21), the secret of which lies in turning to God with contrition (2 Cor. 7:9ff.), and which manifests itself in

---

in view of the whole context in which the concern is with *ta pneumatika,* one will certainly have to think of that which transcends the human spirit; cf. v. 2 as well and the synonymous use of *tō pneumati* and *en glōssē* (vv. 15, 18). It is difficult to say what is intended by "my spirit" if this is said simply of the human spirit. Besides, we have to do here with a very striking linguistic usage.

69. Cf., e.g., Behm, *TDNT,* IV, p. 959, *s.v. nous.*

70. Thus, e.g., in different variations Bultmann, *Theology,* I, p. 211.

71. Cf. Greijdanus on Rom. 1:28: "[*Nous*] is here disposition, way of thinking with regard to ethical questions, as appears from what follows" (*Rom.,* I, p. 121; see also Gutbrod, *Die Paulinische Anthropologie,* p. 52).

72. Cf., e.g., Bultmann, *Theology,* I, p. 259; Greijdanus, *Rom.,* I, p. 347.

73. For Rom. 7:14ff., see below, Section 20.

74. On this see Behm, *TDNT,* IV, pp. 1004f., *s.v. metanoeō.*

turning away from sin. Other ideas of the same kind, in which the "thinking" of man is very closely linked with his moral self-determination and his whole religious-moral attitude to life, could also be pointed out.[75]

For our purpose it is sufficient to ascertain that from the viewpoint of a theological anthropology the concept *nous* has great significance in Paul, in that *nous* on the one hand denotes the organ, the possibility, in which man is addressed as a thinking and responsible being by the revelation of God, and on the other hand constitutes as well the description of that by which he is most deeply determined in his thinking and acting.

Heart

The significance of the concept "heart" *(kardia)* is most closely connected with this. Just as in the whole of the New Testament,[76] so in Paul as well, heart is the concept that preeminently denotes the human ego in its thinking, affections, aspirations, decisions, both in man's relationship to God and to the world surrounding him. Theologically speaking, therefore, "heart" denotes man in his religious-moral quality. To what degree "understanding" and "heart" from this point of view belong together may appear from those passages where they are found in a parallel meaning (as Phil. 4:7; 2 Cor. 3:14ff.). Conversion, the reversal of the *nous,* is a matter of the heart (Rom. 2:5). Although an exactly delimited usage is not present, one can perhaps say that the heart is still more inclusive than the *nous,* in that the *nous* speaks of the human ego from the viewpoint of thinking — though this, as we have seen, is not in the least conceived of only as an intellectual faculty—whereas the affections, aspirations, passions, desires dwell in the heart and spring forth from it.[77]

It is of particular importance for our subject that the heart, just as the understanding, is expressly connected with God; again not as though the heart were that in man which is most akin to God—in his "heart," too, man does not transcend his humanness in any respect whatever—but in the sense that God declares himself through his revelation in or to the human heart as the center of human existence. Thus it is said of the gentiles in Romans 2:14ff. that, though they do not have the law, they nevertheless give evidence of the work of the law as written in their hearts. This certainly does not mean that even without the revelation of God's law, of his own accord, by virtue of an inward illumination residing in the heart, man bears knowledge of God's will, so that the heart is yet again to be viewed as the higher or divine in man; rather, just as was apparent with respect to the *nous,* the heart is here spoken of as the place where God declares himself to man, by virtue of his revelation in all his works.[78] Conversely, it is said of Israel that a covering lies on its heart until it turn to the Lord (2 Cor. 3:15ff.). That covering on the heart takes away the true knowledge of God, just as the shining of God's revelation in Christ in the heart again makes possible the true knowledge of the glory of God (2 Cor. 4:6). And as God by his revelation declares himself to the heart of man as the real center of his being, so this heart is the subject of the answer that man gives to this revelation, whether it be positive or negative; which thereupon is searched, proved, made manifest

---

75. For that see, e.g., the explanations of Gutbrod, *Die Paulinische Anthropologie,* pp. 54, 55; Bultmann, *Theology,* I, pp. 211ff.

76. Cf. Behm, *TDNT,* III, pp. 611ff., *s.v. kardia.*

77. For the proof passages, see Behm, *loc. cit.;* Bultmann, *Theology,* I, pp. 222f.

78. Cf. above, p. 118.

by God (Rom. 8:27; I Thess. 2:4; 1 Cor. 4:5). With the heart one believes
(Rom. 10:10), one lusts (Rom. 1:24), one obeys (Rom. 6:17), one does the will
of God (Eph. 6:6), etc. The personal pronoun could stand in all these expressions,
for what man *is* is determined by the quality of his heart. But in all this frequent use of the word heart, in the most decisive pronouncements that can be
given concerning man, it is brought out that man is led and governed ultimately
from one point, that he therein exhibits his real manhood, both in his susceptibility to the revelation of God and in his responsibility for his thinking, willing,
and acting.

Soul and spirit

Of much less importance for what occupies us is the use of the concept soul
(*psychē*) in Paul. *Psyche* in Paul is neither, after the Greek-Hellenistic fashion,
the immortal in man as distinct from the *sōma,* nor does it denote the spiritual
as distinct from the material. *Psyche* stands in general for the natural life
of man (cf. Rom. 11:3; 16:4; 1 Thess. 2:8—to give his "soul," that is, his life
for someone—*et al.*). This is most clearly evident in the well-known pronouncements in 1 Corinthians 15:44ff., where Paul places the first man Adam as
"living soul" over against Christ as "life-giving Spirit" and speaks of the
"psychical body" (*sōma psychikon*) sown in weakness and perishableness as distinguished from the spiritual body that is to be raised. *Psyche* and psychical
here plainly mean the natural and earthly life, which has no subsistence in
itself but is subject to death and destruction; it is here used all but synonymously with "flesh and blood" in verse 50, that which has been taken from
the earth (v. 47). In conformity with this Paul speaks as well of the "psychical
man," who cannot understand the things of the Spirit of God (1 Cor. 2:14),
and whom he places over against the spiritual, pneumatic man.[79] In 1 Corinthians 3:1 he equates psychical with sarkic, carnal. It is evident, therefore, that
psychical in this context denotes the limited-human that in itself is incapable
of grasping or understanding the divine wisdom, of which Paul has said in
the preceding chapter that it is the object of God's special announcement.
Psychic and sarkic thus approximate each other very closely here, in that they
both denote man in his limitedness and humanity over against the divine
possibilities and realities. Otherwise psychical and *psyche* is not in itself a
disqualification. Other than *sarx* it does not have the special pregnant significance of the natural man in his having turned-away-from-God, in his sin. Even
when it is not set over against the *pneuma* given by God it describes man in
his natural life, especially according to his inner existence, as may appear
in particular from the combinations "of one soul"[80] (= of one mind; Phil.
2:2), "of like soul"[81] (= of one spirit; Phil. 2:20), "well of soul"[82] (= cheerful;
Phil. 2:19, *et al.*).[83]
    Paul speaks of *pneuma* in much the same sense as of *psyche,* at least
so long as he intends the human spirit and not the Spirit of God given to
believers (as is usually the case when he speaks of *pneuma*). Just as *psyche,*

---

79. A contrast that is to be understood, according to Bultmann, neither from
the Greek usage nor from that of the Old Testament, but only from the gnostic anthropology (*Theology*, I, p. 168); however, see J. Dupont, *Gnosis. La connaissance
religieuse dans les épitres de Saint Paul,* 1949, pp. 178ff.
    80. *Sympsychos.*
    81. *Isopsychos.*
    82. *Eupsychein.*
    83. Cf. the expression *ek psychēs* (Eph. 6:6; Col. 3:22: "from the heart"),
by way of denoting that which man does with full inner assent.

pneuma denotes man in his natural existence, approached from within. The clearest evidence for this is surely the parallel use of *pneuma* in 2 Corinthians 2:13 (I had no rest for my *pneuma*) and of *sarx* in 2 Corinthians 7:5 (our *sarx* had no rest). Both times it is a matter simply of man in his natural condition, which can be denoted by spirit as well as by flesh. Here again there is no trace of the spirit as a supersensual divine principle inherent in man. Accordingly when Paul says elsewhere: the grace of Christ be with "your spirit" (Gal. 6:18; Phil. 4:23; Phlm. 25), this means the same thing as "with you" (Rom. 16:20; Eph. 6:24, *et al.*). In the same sense as "one of soul," etc., the apostle speaks of "in one spirit" (Phil. 1:27), "fellowship of the spirit" (Phil. 2:1, *et al.*). Nothing else is denoted by all this than man in his natural, inner existence. Accordingly when it is said in 1 Thessalonians 5:23: "may your spirit and soul and body be preserved entire, without blame at the coming of our Lord...," in all probability one is not to think here of a trichotomistic representation, in which three parts are to be exactly distinguished from each other in man, and in which the *pneuma* denotes a separate, higher area of life, distinct from the *psyche*. Rather, we have to do here with a (perhaps traditional) plerophoric mode of expression in which the inner life of man is denoted in two different ways, but to which no particular psychological or anthropological significance can be ascribed.[84] Paul speaks of the inner man in more ways than one. He uses the word "soul" as well as "spirit" for this without it always being possible to distinguish between them in a technical sense.[85]

As regards further the two different "directions" mentioned above (p. 114) in which the corruption of sin works itself out in human existence, we meet with the first representation especially in the description of the moral degeneration of the life of the gentiles in Romans 1 and Ephesians 4. As we have already seen, this delineation in Romans 1:18ff. serves to demonstrate from this radical corruption the already clearly visible manifestation of the divine wrath.

The specific nature of this corruption is that it quenches all better knowledge and volition in man, and so makes him commit sin with delight. For because these men, in spite of what they have received in their *nous* of the revelation of God and thus know of God, nevertheless do not glorify God and give thanks, they are abandoned to worth-

---

84. Cf. Gutbrod, *Die Paulinische Anthropologie*, pp. 90ff.; Kümmel, *Man in the New Testament*, pp. 44f.; Bultmann, *Theology*, I, pp. 205f.; M. Dibelius, *Th.*, p. 32; differently, A. Oepke, *Der Brief an die Thessalonicher*, 3rd ed., 1949, p. 143, who by "spirit" understands the "highest, God-related life-principle" and by "soul" the "natural life," and explains this formulation "from the coming together of oriental and Greek influences." Nowhere else in Paul, however, do we meet with such a tripartite view of man. J. A. C. van Leeuwen, *Paulus' zendbrieven aan ... Thessalonica*, 1926, understands "spirit" as the new principle of life by which the regenerated man is ruled in his soul and body (p. 395). Can one speak of this, however, as though it were a separate constituent part of man next to soul and body? For the interpretation we have followed also see H. Bavinck, *Geref. Dogmatiek*, 4th ed., II, 1928, p. 517.

85. Bultmann, in his profound analyses of the anthropological ideas in Paul, is of the opinion that "spirit" as distinguished from "psyche" appears to denote the self "as conscious or aware" and so approaches the modern idea of self-consciousness; and he appeals for that to such passages as Rom. 8:16; 1 Cor. 2:11 (*Theology*, I, p. 207). However, man as psychical being is also spoken of as knowing and understanding (1 Cor. 2:14; cf. Gutbrod, *Die Paulinische Anthropologie*, p. 79).

lessness in their reasonings and their foolish heart becomes darkened (1:20, 21). In this worthlessness of the inner man, this abandonment of the *nous* as the possibility for knowing God, and in this darkening of the heart, the wrath of God is being revealed. God gives him up to the evil lusts of his heart (v. 24), to a "reprehensible *nous*" *(eis adokimon noun)*, to do that which is not fitting (v. 28). For not only is the inward man given up to darkness and ignorance in his relationship to God, but he is also perverted and inclined to all unrestraint and reprehensible activity in his moral self-determination. In this way the corruption bursts through to the outside of his physical existence (v. 24). The corruption of the heart and of the *nous* is carried on in the outward man, in a life that is shameful and censurable before God and men.

We find a description similar to that of Romans 1 in Ephesians 4:17ff., where believers are urged not to walk as the gentiles walk, "in the vanity of their *nous*, being darkened in their understanding, alienated from the life of God, because of the ignorance that is in them, because of the hardening of their heart; who being past feeling have given themselves up to licentiousness." In all this they are alien to the life of God, the true life intended by God, directed to him, reaching its fulfillment in him. The cause is once again mentioned as ignorance *(dia agnoian)*, the lack of true knowledge, and the entrance in its place of the opposite, again connected with the worthlessness of the *nous;* and the hardening of their heart, which is the most central description of the human ego. The heart has now been hardened, has become unfeeling and insensitive on account of its having been turned away from God. And all this reveals itself in the walk of the gentiles. As in Romans 1 it is said again and again that God has given them up to all kinds of evil practices, so it is said of them here that they have abandoned themselves to these practices. That which is a judgment of God is at the same time an act of man.

These extensive delineations show that the corruption of sin resides in the human heart and understanding, just that from which, for the manifestation of his life, man ought to receive leadership and direction toward the good. These delineations of the darkened understanding and the depraved heart, as we have seen, apply especially to the gentiles in their deep moral decadence, and in general to the notorious sinners and enemies of the truth of God (cf. Col. 2:18; 1 Tim. 6:5; 2 Tim. 3:8; Tit. 1:15). This does not alter the fact that the apostle not only holds up this radical depravity in the gentiles and ungodly as a deterrent example, but by portraying it thus he wants to make those who have not yet fallen into it to feel the gravity of sin on account of the wrath of God even in their own life (Rom. 2:1ff.); as well, he wishes to make clear to believers from what a corruption they all have been delivered (cf. Eph. 2:1-3; Tit. 3:3). Hence, too, the renewing of the *nous* is a matter that is necessary not only for some, but for all, who will dedicate their bodies (i.e., themselves; see above) to God as a sacrifice well-pleasing to him (Rom. 12:2; Eph. 4:23); just as it is not only the doing but the willing of that which can serve to the salvation of man that is worked by God in believers for the sake of his good pleasure (Phil. 2:13).

On the other hand, it is necessary to guard against placing on a uniform level all that is said in the Pauline teaching on sin concerning the corruption of the inward man. Not everything that is said in this delineation of the radical depravity in the gentile world can apply simply as a verdict with respect to the total corruption of men taken individually. There is a difference even among the gentiles themselves. Not only does the apostle know men among the gentiles who are not guilty of these shameful sins, who rather in the civic sense have a right to the commendation and protection of the authorities because of their good works (Rom. 13:3ff.), and whose judgment and approbation the church, too, is to value (cf. Col. 4:5; 1 Tim. 3:7; 2 Cor. 8:21); but he also speaks explicitly of gentiles who give evidence (in their actions) that what the law requires has been written by God in their hearts, while their conscience also bears witness to their good and evil deeds (Rom. 2:15). This is not, as appears from the whole context of Romans 1:18-3:20, to say that these gentiles have no need of justification by faith and of the Spirit of Christ for their salvation; rather, in the imperfection of their works of the law they, too, with all others fall under the judgment of God on sin (Rom. 3:20, 23). Nonetheless, it may not elude us that in their deeds they are not only credited with a certain fulfillment of the law, but that they also have received in their hearts a notion from God of the requirement of the law and have put this into practice. And what applies to the gentiles also applies to Israel. To be sure, the whole of Paul's preaching is bent toward taking away from Israel their righteousness before God and uncovering their sin to them (Rom. 2:1ff.). But even so this does not alter the fact that he not only ascribes to Israel the knowledge of the will of God by virtue of the privilege of the law given to them (Rom. 3:2; 9:4), but also declares that they evince a zeal for God, a passionate desire to please him by their works of the law (Rom. 10:2). When the apostle adds to this: "but not in accordance with the right insight" (all' ou kat' epignōsin), he once again brings the *nous* into the picture. This time, however, not in the same sense as when he speaks of the darkening of the *nous* and of the abandonment to a pernicious *nous* that occurs among the gentiles. If this darkening of the *nous* leads the gentiles to all kinds of shameful sins, in Israel the want of the right insight works itself out in an entirely different way: in the attempt to make themselves acceptable to God by conduct as unimpeachable as possible (Rom. 10:3; cf. Phil. 3:6, 9). Accordingly when it is said elsewhere of the Israelites that they have become hardened in their *nous* (ta noēmata autōn epōrōthē; 2 Cor. 3:14), and that a covering has come to lie on their heart (v. 15), it is indeed, just as with the gentiles, a matter of a hardening and darkening of the heart and the *nous* (cf. also Rom. 11:7, 8), but nevertheless in an entirely different sense: it is not the desire for the reprehensible in a moral sense or the total lack of knowledge of the will of God that is here the consequence of the hardening and the inner corruption, but rather the attempt to be able with the exertion of all one's moral powers to be righteous before God. It is of importance for insight into the Pauline doctrine of sin to keep sharply in view this differentiated character of the corruption of the inner man outside Christ, and not to fall into a conception of the anthropological implications of this doctrine of sin that places everything on one level.

Particularly characteristic of these anthropological aspects of Paul's delineation of man in sin, however, is furthermore the "reverse direction" in which the corruption of sin works itself out, in other words, the direct connection that is placed between sin and the body. The bondage of sin to which man is subjected, his condition of death because of the divine wrath, is not only determined by the depravity of the inner man and its effect on "the body"; rather, one must say that the reverse is no less characteristic of Paul's anthropological conceptions: that sin, as it were, lays hold of the body "from without" and thus subjects the entire man to itself as a slave.

All sorts of expressions and pronouncements in Paul's epistles give evidence of this "direct" connection: sin-body. Thus, for example, in Romans 6:6 there is mention of the "sin-body" that must be done away with, so that "we" no longer serve sin. Here the body, in its being ruled by sin, is the impediment to the ego in ceasing to serve sin. Similarly, believers are warned no longer to permit sin to reign in their bodies that they should obey the lusts of that body (Rom. 6:12). Here again the direction is not from within toward the outside, but the reverse: sin wishes to take possession of the body, stirs up sinful desires in it, and thus bring the "I" under its dominion. Earlier we pointed to the expression: the (evil) practices of the body, which believers are to put to death by the Spirit (Rom. 8:13), and to the words: put to death your members on the earth (Col. 3:5), by which the same thing is intended. Here the body stands as the subject and bearer of sin in a certain relationship of independence over against the ego.

This connection between sin and body finds expression in its most pregnant form in the well-known pericope of Romans 7:14-27, where a distinction is made not merely between the influence of sin on the ego, the *nous,* the inward man, on the one hand, and on the body, the members, on the other, but where all the emphasis falls precisely on the discord between the two. The idea then is this, that through having in its power the body, the members, the flesh, sin makes the ego, the inward man, the *nous* powerless to do the good willed by him (the ego, etc.; Rom. 7:22-25). This opposition is so absolute that the apostle twice (vv. 17, 20) declares that it is no longer "he himself" but sin dwelling in him (i.e., in the flesh, his body, his members) that does the evil. However, this power of sin in his members is so great that he knows himself to be a prisoner by the law (power) of sin in his members, indeed calls himself carnal, sold under sin, a wretched man, who cries out asking who will deliver him from this body of death (vv. 14, 23, 24). In this whole representation the connection between sin and body is altogether in the foreground, and that as opposed to the will of the ego and of the *nous.* Sin, as it were, moves into the outward man, seats itself in him as in a fortress raised about the ego (the inward man, the *nous*), makes him thus its prisoner and prevents him from breaking out.

It is not surprising that some have seen in this representation a variant of the Greek idea that the body is the seat of sin and thus, as the lower, sensual principle, the prison of the higher, spiritual part of man, his soul. Yet on further reflection this conception cannot stand even momentarily. For, first of all, the body is not only a creation of God and thus not destined for sin, but for the Lord (1 Cor. 12:18, 24; 15:35ff.; 6:13, 15), but also in Paul's preaching the body is wholly included in the redeeming work of Christ. It shares in the resurrection of the dead (1 Cor. 15:35ff.), and even in its temporal-earthly existence is considered from the viewpoint of the keeping and renewing power of God (1 Cor. 12:9; 2 Cor. 4:7ff.; 12:7). Of an ethical antithesis, founded in the physical-sensual nature, between body and *nous*, outward and inward man, there can therefore be no question. But in the second place — so we have seen above — the body represents not merely a certain constituent part of man, but rather man himself in his concrete corporeal mode of existence. It is not only the body, but it is the man himself, who with his flesh (body) serves sin (Rom. 7:25), who himself is carnal, even though after the inner man he wants to do the good and he serves the law of God with his *nous* (Rom. 7:14, 22, 25). Consequently, we have to do in this representation in Romans 7 and elsewhere with something else, namely, with a particular anthropological construction of the ethical discord to which even the man who wants to do the good is subjected. Paul denotes that as the discord between the inward man and his body (flesh, members), whereby it is not said that the inward in itself represents the good and the outward by definition the evil in him, but that man has to wage war with himself, and in that struggle, without the power of the Holy Spirit, encounters an insurmountable resistance in himself. That Paul denotes the latter especially with "the body" does not involve any depreciation of the material with respect to the spiritual, but rests on the idea that man must come to self-realization in his physical existence, and in that existence is found accordingly the clear model of the bondage of sin. At the same time, we may be permitted to say that the importance of these pronouncements does not lie in the manner in which certain anthropological ideas are handled here, but rather in the thought expressed in them: although man is disposed and inclined to do the good, even then because he is flesh, because of his inclusion in the whole of the human solidarity in sin, he is nevertheless frustrated in a decisive manner in doing what is good.

Indeed, one can perhaps say that in this representation of the decisive impediment in the doing of the good that is situated in the body (the members, the flesh), the specific character of the Pauline doctrine of sin is reflected, as we have been able to observe it already in the first sections of our investigation. Paul regards sin not merely or in the first place from the individual and personal, but from the collective and supra-individual point of view. It is the fact of having been taken up into solidarity in sin, the fact that man is flesh, the fact of having been brought under the power of sin that surrounds him on every side and, as it were, occupies him, that governs the Pauline conception of sin. It is for this reason that such great emphasis can fall on the connection between sin and body (in the sense of concrete mode of existence subjected to sin). This conception of sin also makes itself felt in a decisive way in the representation of the inner discord of the ego in Romans 7 and finds its exactly corresponding counterpart in the structure of the Pauline doctrine of redemption.

SECTION 20. ROMANS 7 IN THE PAULINE "ANTHROPOLOGY"

Finally, as regards the much discussed difference of opinion — which to the present day has not been brought to a solution that is in some degree generally accepted — as to whether the discord delineated in Romans 7:14ff. is to be understood as pertaining to the remaining struggle against sin in the Christian life or whether Paul here intends to represent the impotence of the ego outside Christ and the power of his Spirit, we have elsewhere[86] chosen with conviction for the latter view on the ground of a detailed analysis of the context and the text of Romans 7 and wish to maintain that with undiminished force. It would be pointless, and would fall outside the context of the subject presently treated, to let all the arguments pro and con pass in review once again.[87] In part we must return to the purport of Romans 7:14-25 when in the following sections we shall have to treat further the inadequacy of the law and its powerlessness on account of the flesh — the real theme of Romans 7:7-25. What must yet occupy us here is the question as to how the discord thus understood between the inward man and the body, the *nous* and the flesh, is to be understood within the whole framework of the Pauline anthropology. In particular the objection must come up for discussion as to whether what is here said of the "inward man," the *nous,* the "I-myself" — if one chooses to understand this of man before or outside Christ — does not come into conflict with that which elsewhere is Paul's judgment of the total corruption of man outside Christ.

---

86. *Rom.,* pp. 153-171.

87. The question remains in discussion, even if in the exegetical literature the scale is more and more being turned in favor of the conception mentioned above; cf. the judgment of W. K. Grossouw: "... among modern exegetes an occasional one still takes up an exceptional position and understands Rom. 7:7 (14)-25 of the Christian existence" ("De verscheurde mens van Romeinen zeven," in *Vriendengave Bernardus Kardinaal Alfrink aangeboden,* 1964, p. 69). See also O. Kuss, *Der Römerbrief,* 2nd ed., 1963; S. Lyonnet, "L'histoire du salut selon le chapitre VII de l'Épitre aux Romains," in *Biblica,* 1962, pp. 117-151. The other view is still defended, with some variations, by J. M. E. Cruvellier, *L'exegese de Romains 7,* etc., 1961 (dissertation, Free University). A. F. N. Lekkerkerker, *De brief van Paulus aan de Romeinen,* I, 1962, attempts (in my view vainly) to break through the dilemma (p. 314). A mediating conception is defended by A. J. Bandstra, *The Law and the Elements of the World,* 1964, p. 142 (dissertation, Free University): "... Paul is describing his own experience and that of his fellow Jewish Christians at the point at which the message of grace in Christ 'had hit its mark' in them, or, if you will, their conversion experience."

It should first of all be established that the discord pictured in Romans 7 consists not merely in a certain temptation of the ego (the will to the good, the inward man), but in the absolute impotence of the I to break through the barrier of sin and the flesh in any degree at all. Undoubtedly it is said of the new man as well that he continues to be engaged in conflict with the flesh. Thus, for example, in Galatians 5:17 where it is said: "the flesh lusts against the Spirit, and the Spirit against the flesh; for these are opposed to each other, to prevent you from doing what you would." And similarly it is said to believers in Romans 6:12 that sin may not (continue to) reign in their mortal bodies, etc. All this points to enduring battle, struggle, resistance of the flesh against the Spirit. But the absolute distinction between these and similar pronouncements and the portrayal of Romans 7 is that the former are spoken within the possibility and certainty of victory (cf. Rom. 6:14: "for sin shall not have dominion over you; for you are not under law, but under grace"; Gal. 5:24: "but they that are of Christ have crucified the flesh with its passions and lusts"), while in Romans 7 everything is directed toward throwing light on man's situation of death, his having been sold under sin, his having been taken captive by the superior power of sin. The despairing "who will deliver me from this body of death?" is, to be sure, followed by the interjection of faith: "Thanks be to God! through Jesus Christ our Lord!" (vv. 24, 25). But this does not mean that the description of having been sold and made captive under sin and having been given over to the body of sin was not intended so absolutely as it is expressed. The power of Jesus Christ, the delivering might of the Spirit of life in Christ, which is spoken of in verse 25 and in Romans 8:2ff., are not in some way to be "accommodated" or otherwise discounted in the (description of the) death situation of Romans 7:14-25; rather, they put an end in principle to the absolute sovereignty of sin over the ego described in Romans 7. The elements placed over against each other in Romans 7 are consequently not (as in Gal. 5) the Spirit and the flesh, or (as in Rom. 6) grace and the law, but the human ego, the "I-myself" (v. 25!) and the flesh, the law of God and the law of sin. In the struggle between those parties the victory is to the flesh and sin, and the ego finds itself, despite all that it would will and desire, in absolute bondage and the situation of death. Other powers must enter the field, another than the "I-myself" must join the battle, if deliverance is to come. So far it is from any suggestion that since there is mention here of a *dis*-cord, this were able to furnish the proof that the struggle between the old and the new man is described here in the manner of Galatians 5:17.

For this reason those scholars are certainly right who point out that what is said "in favor" of the ego in the description of Romans 7 (vv. 15-17, 18b-22, 25) does not relativize the representation of having been sold and of bondage under sin, nor is it intended to apply a reduction to it, but precisely to place the superior power of sin in that much sharper a light.[88] The connecting links in the chain of the argument of Romans 7 corroborate this, as is easy to demonstrate in a de-

---

88. Cf., e.g., Kümmel, *Man in the New Testament*, pp. 54-61.

tailed analysis.[89] In spite of everything in the I, the inward man, etc., that may offer resistance to this power of evil it avails nothing. It can only make defeat the deeper, and the situation of death the more hopeless. However one therefore supposes himself constrained to judge of the resistance of the ego in the natural man, it can in no respect whatever have the significance of a less serious assessment of the human situation of death. The purport is precisely that as long as these weapons must be fought with, every chance of deliverance or victory is utterly lacking. This and no other is the effect of Paul's anthropological pronouncements of Romans 7.

The question arises finally as to whether what Paul says in Romans 7:14-25 "in favor" of the "I," the inward man, the *nous,* admits of being reconciled with the general picture with which we meet elsewhere in his epistles concerning the corruption of sin in man outside Christ. It is a question here in particular of those pronouncements in which the apostle says: "for I do not that which I will, but what I hate, that I do . . . so now it is not I that do it, but sin which dwells in me . . . , for I delight in the law of God after the inward man. . . . So then I of myself with my *nous,* indeed, serve the law of God; but with my flesh the law of sin." It is held that this is not to be reconciled with a pronouncement like that in Romans 12:2, where it is said so clearly that the *nous* must be renewed in order to discern what the good will of God is; and with Philippians 2:13, where not only the doing, but also the willing of the good is ascribed to God.

In our judgment too little account is taken in this way of what we have already observed above concerning the differentiated and shaded picture that the apostle gives of the bondage of sin and its corrupting operation in man. Romans 7 does not fall outside that, but brings it out in still fuller relief. The idea of and zeal for the good have not been quenched in the same way in all men, Jew and gentile, under the law and without the law. It is in harmony neither with the teaching of Jesus nor with that of Paul to deny zeal for the law or desire for the good to every man outside Christ, or to consider such impossible in him. It is likewise not in harmony with the reality to which Paul, without fear of being wrongly understood, appeals with a certain degree of self-evidentness (Rom. 2:14ff.). This takes away nothing from the necessity of total renewal. The *nous* and the will, even when they have not been depraved and darkened in the manner of the heathen life given up to debauchery, have need of total renewal, in that they have no alternative but to look for their point of departure and strength no longer in their own moral impulse, in the law, or in the light of nature, but in Christ and the government of his Spirit. This is nowhere more evident than in Romans 7, where it is just the utter bankruptcy of the strength of the will, of the better I, of the *nous* in its moral self-determination that is spoken of. The whole contrast here lies between the I-myself of verse 25 and the "through Jesus Christ our Lord" of verse 24. But thereby every knowledge, zeal, effort, recognition of the

---

89. Cf. my *Rom.,* pp. 155ff.

excellence of the demand of the law above the will of the flesh need
not yet be denied in man outside Christ.[90]

Involved here also, of course, is the style Paul employs in Romans
7, in this case the correct characterization of the ego that is speaking
here.[91] Some suppose that in Romans 7:14ff. Paul is no longer speaking
simply of the "ordinary" non-Christian, but of the one who stands "on
the highest plane attainable by pre-Christian man,"[92] that is to say, of
the man who gives himself to the law with all his strength, to whom
one cannot simply apply what is said of the heathen in Romans 1,
Ephesians 2 and 4, or Titus 3. In a similar sense others are of the
opinion that Romans 7:7ff. refers to the "inward state" of the Jew under
the law, who does not content himself with the half-heartednesses that
Paul scourges in Romans 2.[93] Still others hold the view that Paul here
does give the general picture of a man under the law, before and without Christ, but viewed with the eyes of a Christian.[94] Finally, the
opinion has also been defended that Paul here speaks of a kind of
transitional period in which the man finds himself who, although already confessing Christ, still struggles to hold fast to the law;[95] but this
conception has found very little acceptance.

It is certainly no easy matter, if even possible, to typify this ego
of Romans 7:7-25 with a single word. It is unquestionably not to be
taken in a biographical sense as a description of Paul's personal experience before or at his conversion. Romans 7 and 8 are too much concerned with redemptive-historical contrasts and categories and not with
individual experiences for that to be the case. At the same time, it is
not simply a rhetorical-generalizing statement: so is it in general with

90. One should think here, too, of the manner in which in the Qumran
literature the struggle of man against sin under the law is spoken of; see below,
p. 133, and the literature cited there.
91. See also the article by Grossouw, referred to in n. 87.
92. So, e.g., Gutbrod, *Die Paulinische Anthropologie*, p. 53.
93. Thus E. Stauffer, *New Testament Theology*, ET 1955, p. 93. Of this
"Jew under the law" he writes further: "He is a 'zealot' in the sense of Gal. 1.13f.
and Rom. 10.2f. He means to take God's will revealed in the law utterly seriously.
But that involves him in a conflict of which the contented and the compromisers
have no inkling," etc. Stauffer speaks hereby of the redemptive-historical significance
of Rom. 7 and calls this chapter "a chapter about the Jewish man who fights under
the banner of the Torah, and therefore fights to the bitter end, because he is fighting
in a lost position" (*ibid.*, p. 275). Although according to Stauffer the autobiographical
interpretation of Rom. 7 (as, e.g., that is given by Deissmann, *St. Paul*, pp. 93ff.)
suffers shipwreck on Phil. 3:6 (where there is not the slightest indication of such
a pre-Christian despairing of Paul, but rather the reverse), yet he thinks that "the
characteristics of *homo sub lege* in Rom. 7 must logically include the pre-Christian
Paul" (*loc. cit.*).
94. So, e.g., Althaus, *Rom.*, p. 67: "Therefore it does not depend on how
far the actual situation of the person without Christ under the law becomes *clear* to
him. But Paul also does not rule out the possibility that it *can* become clear to him."
For this conception see also Kümmel, *Man in the New Testament*, p. 60; Bultmann,
Theology, I, pp. 264ff.; and also (somewhat less explicitly) Lindijer, *Het begrip sarx
bij Paulus*, p. 159.
95. For this see, e.g., in Lindijer, *Het begrip sarx*, p. 157, n. 3. Differently still
Bandstra, who judges that Paul is here describing his experience of conversion (see
above, the note on p. 126).

man under the law, seen now with the eyes of faith. Although it is surely more than personal, in that the redemptive-historical contrast is the real starting point of the drama sketched out in Romans 7, yet the personal setting is not to be characterized as merely rhetorical. It is especially the moral man shackled by the law with whom Paul can so easily identify because he was once so himself. That man is here described in his struggle and defeat, with the law as ally and sin and the flesh as adversaries, in his high aspirations and his complete failure. One must undoubtedly say that particularly in the recognition of total bankruptcy, as in verses 14ff. and 24, the natural man speaks the language of misery, as that can only be plumbed in its depth and understood out of the knowledge of redemption. For that reason at a given moment the spark, as it were, leaps over from "the other side": "Thanks be to God, through Jesus Christ, our Lord!" But this is not to say that this whole delineation therefore has no point of contact in man's own experience outside Christ, or could not mean for him, too, a disclosure of his actual situation. Paul draws so living and gripping a picture because he wishes to set before the eyes not only of the man in Christ, but also of the man under the law, the absolute necessity of another moral power than that of the I-myself, the *nous*, the inward man. And by relating the whole struggle to the ego, he lets it be felt on the one hand, as in solidarity with these wrestlers with and under the law, that he himself, once also under the law, is no stranger to this striving; on the other hand, how much for him the light has arisen on the prospectlessness of it. And, moreover, we may not forget that the picture can be so graphic and existential for the very reason that the struggle against the flesh never loses its actuality (Gal. 5:17), and that therefore the question as to how one is to be unvanquished in that struggle never becomes an obsolete (because resolved) theological problem, but remains a matter of faith, which falls continually under the threat of becoming a matter of the "I-myself."

Surveying all this, one cannot say that the portrayal of the corruption of sin in Romans 7 falls outside the general framework of the Pauline doctrine of man in sin. Rather, it forms in a certain sense its culminating point, in that it indicates that the corruption of sin in all its radicalness is not only to be sought in the blind heathen given up to all manner of perversity, but also in the man who lives under the strength of the law, who looks for his ideal and his moral strength in the law, and nevertheless must be brought to the recognition of having been sold under sin and of the "wretched man that I am, who will deliver me?"

C. SIN AND THE LAW
SECTION 21. THE ANTITHESIS WITH JUDAISM

It has already become clear in the above that the Pauline doctrine of the essence and universality of sin and of its outworking in human existence bears a very radical character and utterly excludes every possibility of redemption and renewal of life outside the salvation wrought by Christ. It still remains to us in this chapter, however, to treat what may perhaps be called the most drastic and most characteristic aspect of the whole of this doctrine of sin: the manner in which the law functions in this hopeless situation of sin and sin's corruption.

We touch here on one of the most striking and distinctive parts of Paul's preaching, one that has played a great role in the history of church and theology and which continues to be the object of all manner of inquiry in the exegetical literature.[96] In general it can be said that what Paul was seeking to do was to show that in the situation of death into which man has come by sin, the law can offer relief and help in no respect whatever, indeed that it — and here his view of the law receives its most critical and pregnant intensification — makes the man who would be saved by the law sink down still more deeply into the morass of sin and sin's corruption. It is this strong, negatively directed judgment of the significance of the law in the Pauline doctrine of sin and redemption that constantly attracts renewed attention, has given rise to all kinds of divergent views, and, particularly from the Jewish side, has not infrequently evoked radical, critical questions.[97]

It is in his confrontation with Judaism that Paul comes to this absolutely negative estimate of the law as means of salvation, and without some insight into the theological-soteriological conceptions of the old synagogue, the position he occupies toward the law is incapable of being understood. Although — as is more and more apparent — it is no simple matter to give a summary exposition of Judaism, itself in a spiritual and religious respect so richly variegated, on the subject of its conception of sin and redemption,[98] yet one will have to say that the deepest difference between Paul and the Judaism that he combatted did not lie so much in divergent notions concerning the origin and universality of sin. Although here too all kinds of differently shaded

96. The relevant literature, which consists in the views summarized in the New Testament "theologies" as well as in a large number of monographs on this subject, is difficult to survey. In addition to the older works listed under *nomos* in *TDNT*, IV, pp. 1022ff., see, e.g., the very extensive bibliography in A. J. Bandstra, *The Law and the Elements of the World*, pp. 193-207.

97. See, e.g., the highly critical chapter "Paul's Teaching About the Law," in the book by H. J. Schoeps, *Paul. The Theology of the Apostle in the Light of Jewish Religious History*, pp. 168-218.

98. On the doctrine of sin in Judaism in general see, e.g., Bousset-Gressmann, *Die Religion des Judentums*, 3rd ed., 1926, pp. 399ff.; G. F. Moore, *Judaism*, I, 1927, pp. 445ff.; Strack-Billerbeck, III, pp. 155ff.; further also E. Sjöberg, *Gott und die Sünder im palästinischen Judentum*, 1938; Stählin/Grundmann, *TDNT*, I, pp. 289ff., *s.v. hamartanō*. More especially, for the more radical streams including the Qumran community, e.g., H. Braun, "Spätjüdisch-häretischer und frühchristlicher Radikalismus," in *Beitr. z. hist. Theol.*, 1957, pp. 10ff., 41ff.; the same author, "Röm. 7,7-25 und das Selbstverständnis des Qumran-Frommen," in *ZTK*, 1959, pp. 1-18; J. P. Hyatt, "The View of Man in the Qumran 'Hodayot,'" in *NTS*, 1955, pp. 276ff. For the whole see also Schoeps, *Paul*, pp. 168ff.

conceptions are to be noted,[99] it can be said in general[100] that for the old synagogue universal sinfulness as a fact of experience was an incontrovertible matter. It concluded this from the universality of death. There is no death without sin. Therefore all who die must be sinners. To be sure, the reason for which every man must die is frequently sought in the disobedience and punishment of the first man, a punishment that has passed on to all men.[101] Yet there are other voices as well, which seek the origin of death, not in Adam's sin, but in personal, individual transgressions.[102] A doctrine of original sin in the sense of the hereditary transmission of a moral corruption caused by Adam is on the other hand not demonstrable (no more indeed than it is in Paul).

Particularly important for the Jewish doctrine of universal human sinfulness is the notion of the good and evil predisposition (yēṣer) in man. These are regarded as pertaining to human nature and therefore as created by God. Now, it is the moral vocation of every man by the strength of the inclination to good and with the help of the law to overcome the inclination to evil.[103] In the Manual of Discipline of the Qumran community one meets this doctrine in the idea of the two spirits, that of the light and that of the darkness, both created by God, between both of which man sees himself placed and compelled to choose (1QS III, 13ff.). Elsewhere there is mention of the evil germ or root, which must be overcome by the law.[104]

In all this a great deal is of course to be observed that differs from what we find in Paul. Nowhere does the apostle teach, for example, an innate evil predisposition created by God; on the other hand, the corporate idea of the all-in-one — as we have been able to point out above (Section 16) — is much clearer in him and much more important for the structure of his whole theology than is demonstrable in Judaism.

Yet, so far as the doctrine of sin is concerned, the real antithesis between Paul and the Judaism he controverts does not lie in the evaluation of these differences, but in the diametrically opposed judgment as to the strength and function of the law in this universal sin situation.

For Judaism the great counterpoise to the threat and power of sin is in the law given to Israel. The law is the unique means to acquire for oneself merit, reward, righteousness before God, and the instrument given by God to subjugate the evil impulse and to lead the good to victory. It can rightly be said, therefore, that for the Jews the law was the pre-eminent means of salvation, indeed the real "substance of life."[105]

---

99. On this see, e.g., the analyses of E. Brandenburger, *Adam und Christus,* pp. 15-67.

100. For the following see also Strack-Billerbeck, III, pp. 155ff.

101. Cf. Strack-Billerbeck, III, p. 227; Brandenburger, *Adam und Christus,* pp. 45ff.; see also the pronouncements quoted in Schoeps, *Paul,* p. 189.

102. Brandenburger, *Adam und Christus,* pp. 62ff.

103. On this teaching see in detail Strack-Billerbeck, IV, 1, pp. 466-483; Brandenburger, *Adam und Christus,* pp. 33ff.; see also the literature referred to in Hyatt, *NTS,* 1955, p. 280, n. 2.

104. For this notion of IV Ezra at length see Brandenburger, *Adam und Christus,* p. 33.

105. So W. Bousset, *Die Religion des Judentums,* 3rd ed., 1926, p. 119; Strack-Billerbeck, III, pp. 126ff.

Undoubtedly all kinds of differences are to be noted in the Jewish sources in their estimation of the gravity and strength of sin. The predominant tendency is the doctrine, not infrequently presented in a highly quantitative sense, of the meritoriousness of the works of the law, which eventually enable man to obtain eternal life. In the multiplicity of the commandments is the means for gaining much merit. Every fulfillment of the law, in the sense of an act in conformity with a concrete prescription of the law, contributes to the treasure of merit, just as, conversely, every concrete transgression brings the sufficiency of merit into jeopardy.[106] But next to this business-like and quantitative conception of sin much deeper tones are to be heard, in which expression is given to uncertainty and despair springing from a much more adequate consciousness of the power of sin.[107] Not infrequently the moral power of man and the preponderance of the evil inclination or impulse are spoken of very pessimistically. This occurs particularly in the pseudepigraphic and apocalyptic literature, as well as in some of the Qumran writings.[108] The conviction that man needs the divine mercy and help if he is not to fall prey to the power of sin finds expression in some pronouncements, for example, in the collection of songs of the Qumran community, in a manner that is frequently very moving.[109]

But all this does not alter one matter, namely, that Judaism knew no other way of salvation than that of the law, and that it saw even the mercy and the forgiving love of God as lying precisely in the fact that they enable the sinner once more to build for his eternal future on the ground of the law. The idea that man should have to renounce the law for the source of his moral strength and for his righteousness before God contradicts at its very core the Jewish doctrine concerning the object of the law and the inner connection between law and sin. Just this is the privilege of Israel above the gentiles, that in the law it has received the means of life. It possesses the Torah as "a protective and saving resource against the power of the evil impulse."[110] It is the law that is able to give man life, and the works of the law that by their greater number must drown out the accusation of sin. And even where in Judaism the greatest receptivity appears for the help of God, and a Spirit of God is spoken of who must purify and help man to make his way perfect, no other and better way of salvation is intended than that of the righteousness and perfection to be pursued in the way of the law.[111]

---

106. See further below, Section 29. Also Strack-Billerbeck, IV, 2, pp. 4ff.; Bousset, *Die Religion des Judentums*, pp. 392ff.; Hauck, *TDNT*, V, pp. 561f., *s.v. opheilō*.

107. See, e.g., Bousset, *Die Religion des Judentums*, pp. 388ff.; Gutbrod, *TDNT*, IV, p. 1058, *s.v. nomos;* Schoeps, *Paul*, pp. 184ff.

108. See the literature cited above, p. 131, n. 98.

109. Cf., e.g., Hyatt, *loc. cit.;* also P. Benoit, "Qumrân et le Nouveau Testament," in *NTS*, 1961, pp. 292ff.

110. Schoeps, *Paul*, p. 196.

111. Cf. for this at greater length Benoit, *NTS*, 1961, p. 294.

It is this redemptive significance that Judaism ascribed to the law against which the antithesis in Paul's doctrine of sin is directed, and he develops a doctrine of the law that is among the most distinctive aspects of his preaching.

If we attempt to analyze further this absolute rejection of the law as means of salvation, then it should be premised at once that in Paul this does not originate from a depreciation of the works of the law as such, nor from a certain discomfort about acting, nor from the (modern) contrast between the works of the law as something "external" and the disposition as the "true" obedience, any more than it does from criticism of the content of the law.[112] It has already become apparent from the foregoing that the apostle does not speak here out of any resentment against an undertaking in which he had once been unsuccessful.[113] Paul himself, as it were, expressly cuts off misapprehensions of this sort when in Romans 7:7 he poses the question: What then is the law? and replies in verse 12 that "the law is holy, and the commandment holy and just and good," and when in the same context he says explicitly that "the commandment is [intended] unto life" (v. 10) and that "the law is spiritual" (i.e., divine; cf. 1 Tim. 1:8). Similarly, he says in Galatians 3:21 that the law is not in conflict with the promise, and that if the law had the power to make men alive, righteousness would be of the law. As norm for the will of God and guide to life, the law is therefore unassailable and perfectly trustworthy. If one were to fulfill its requirements he would in fact live (Rom. 10:5; Gal. 3:12; cf. Rom. 2:7, 10). For this reason he does not deny the special privilege of the Jews, that they are the people to whom belongs the giving of the law (Rom. 9:4), that on that ground they "know the will and are able to discern the things that really matter" (Rom. 2:18), and in the law possess "the embodiment of knowledge and the truth" (Rom. 2:20). The situation of man under the law therefore, comfortless as it is, is not so on account of the law's giving to him, as an inferior revelation, only a limited or even a false knowledge of God.[114] The preaching of the gospel does not set over against the law a new concept of God, or a new view of the obligation in which man stands toward God. The apostle on this account continues to point even the believer, who no longer expects righteousness and life from the works of the law, to the judgment as the place where retribution takes place according to what has been done in the body, whether good or bad (2 Cor. 5:10; cf. 1 Cor. 1:8; 3:12-15; 4:4ff.; 1 Thess. 3:13; 5:23). So far is it from his mind that he should have to detract anything from the divine nature of the law itself or on the standpoint of faith set himself above it.

The true ground of Paul's absolute rejection of the law as means of salvation is accordingly an entirely different one. It is situated in the fact that in the light that has arisen in the death and resurrection of

---

112. Cf. against these various conceptions cropping up in the history of the investigation the detailed expositions of Schlatter, *Der Glaube im N.T.*, 4th ed., 1927, pp. 324-331; see also Bultmann, *Faith and Understanding*, I, pp. 226ff.; Gutbrod, *TDNT*, IV, pp. 1076ff.; A. A. van Ruler, *De vervulling van de wet*, 1947, pp. 367ff.

113. So rightly Nygren, *Commentary on Romans*, p. 13.

114. Cf. Bultmann, *Theology*, I, pp. 262f.

Christ, not merely has a better way of salvation come to view, placing the old in the shadow and making it superfluous, but *the absolute inadequacy of the law as means of salvation* has also fully emerged. For this reason Paul's antithesis with Judaism consists not only in the positive proclamation of the righteousness by faith without the works of the law, but also in the evidence, argued *per negationem*, of the insufficiency of the law to insure sinful man righteousness before God and life. It is this last point of view which lends to Paul's doctrine of sin its most characteristic features and structure and with which therefore we must occupy ourselves in a thorough fashion before going on to a discussion of the righteousness that is by faith.

SECTION 22. NO RIGHTEOUSNESS BY THE LAW. "BOAST" AND "SKANDALON"

The evidence of the insufficiency of the law as means of salvation is, in the main, adduced in two different ways. In so doing Paul follows the twofold redemptive function that Judaism (as we have already seen) ascribes to the law: as a means to be justified by the works of the law and as a weapon against the power of sin.

With regard to the first, his opposition is directed above all to Jewish boasting in the law and trusting in the possession of the law. This occurs particularly in the great indictment of Judaism in Romans 2:1-3:20. The possession of the law is of no avail, nor is circumcision. For not the hearers, but the doers of the law will be justified; and it is not the circumcision that takes place outwardly, in the body, that makes one a true Jew, but that which is hidden, which takes place in the heart, according to the Spirit and not according to the letter (Rom. 2:12-29). And because it is just this that is wrong with the Jews, they have no reason to exalt themselves above the gentiles and to glory in the law. For, even though they do not fall into all kinds of perverse sins dishonoring to God and man, in which the wrath of God is already manifestly revealing itself (Rom. 1:18-32), it is not as though they had nothing to do with these sins, but they share in them in a great many ways, as they themselves will be compelled to admit (Rom. 2:1ff., 17ff.). For this reason they deceive themselves in a fatal way. They misjudge the continuance of God's longsuffering toward them, which is intended to lead them, not to security of mind, but to conversion. Instead of acquiring a treasure of merit, as in their delusion they suppose, they are accumulating for themselves the wrath of God for the future on account of their recalcitrance and impenitent heart (Rom. 2:1-12).

It is evident already from this detailed and telling accusation that Paul starts from a completely different conception of sin and of the law from that of Judaism. Although the Judaic conception acknowledged universal sinfulness, and that of the Jews as well, and though it could thus concur with Paul in his indictment in a great many respects, yet for the Jews the ground for trusting in the law had not herewith been taken away. Rather, they were led by it to a quantitative conception of the law and of sin.[115] The judgment of God according to works was conceived as a weighing out of sins and works, the outcome of which is, to be sure, hidden on earth and a matter of uncertainty, but in the event of a final preponderance of good works will nevertheless turn out favorably. And over against those who, in Judaism, too, made a problem of the keeping of the whole law and all the commandments, the possibility of righteousness and life through the law was maintained in all sorts of ways even for the sinful man because no other avenue had been given than that of the law.[116]

Over against this we see in Paul a radicalization of the law both quantitatively and with respect to its content. When Paul in Romans 2:21ff. holds up to the Jews all kinds of individual sins, this is for him (otherwise than for the Jews) a decisive proof of the impossibility of being justified by the law. For the law requires, as he shows explicitly elsewhere, that it be fulfilled in its entirety (holos ho nomos; Gal. 5:3), and the Scripture pronounces its curse upon everyone who does not continue in all things that are written in the book of the law, to do them (Gal. 3:10; cf. Deut. 27:26).[117] Every quantitative reduction of the law is therefore pure willfulness and in conflict with the law itself; and every sin, however much man is inclined in his delusion to forgive it in himself or merely to subtract it from the works of the law that remain to him, makes him guilty of the law as a whole.

This quantitative radicalization of the law is accompanied by, or rather coincides with, a qualitative one. While the Jews ascribed to circumcision, to the ritual and ceremonial institutions and prescriptions in the law in general, a special significance for being a Jew and belonging to the chosen people of God, Paul locates the criterion for the true fulfillment of the law and righteousness in conversion to God, in the circumcision of the heart according to the Spirit, as opposed to conformity to the letter of the law (Rom. 2:4, 29). In all this Paul clearly stands in the tradition of prophetic criticism, as it is to be found in the Old Testament and especially in Jesus, of externalized, ritualistic-legalistic religiosity. To be sure, we do not find in Paul the express and detailed indication of the content of the law and of the true nature of the obedience it demands that we do, for example, in the Sermon on the Mount, and direct appeal to Jesus is missing, at least in Paul's epistles; but even so one can certainly say[118] that Paul's conception of the law is in complete agreement with that of Jesus. Paul, too, reduces

---

115. On this see, e.g., Strack-Billerbeck, III, pp. 160ff.; IV, 2, pp. 4ff.; Bertram, TDNT, II, pp. 645ff., s.v. ergon; Gutbrod, TDNT, IV, p. 1058, s.v. nomos.

116. See Schoeps on "this question of the 'fulfillability' of the Torah" in Judaism (Paul, pp. 177ff.).

117. In Deut. 27:26 the words pas and pasin are lacking. There can be no basis in this, however, for playing off Deut. 27:26 against Gal. 3:10, as Schoeps does to some extent (Paul, p. 176). Deut. 27:26 is undoubtedly intended positively, and the negative conclusion of Gal. 3:10 is not drawn there. But this does not entitle one to relativize the sense of Deut. 27:26 with respect to the pas and pasin of Gal. 3:10.

118. Cf., e.g., Bultmann, Faith and Understanding, I, p. 227; see also his essay "Jesus and Paul," in Existence and Faith.

the whole content of the law to love (Rom. 13:8-10; Gal. 5:14), just as in 1 Corinthians 13 he speaks in exalted terms of love as the way that is much more excellent than the highest gifts, and even calls it greater than faith and hope (1 Cor. 12:31; 13:13). In all this his qualitative idea of the law and its demand and, in conformity with this, also of sin is evident. He speaks of it chiefly in the singular, and not infrequently in personifications (Rom. 7). For this reason it can be ascertained without question that Paul was an apostle and disciple of Jesus in this sense, too, that his rejection of the law as means of salvation is[119] grounded in the same radical view of sin as that which occupies such a central place in Jesus' preaching and exposition of the law.

However important all this may be, the principal thing has not yet been said. Just as it can be said of Paul's whole doctrine of the world and man in sin that it is only to be perceived in the light of his insight into the all-important redemptive event in Christ, so too, and indeed in a special sense, the function the law occupies in Paul's proclamation must be seen in the light that for him has dawned in Christ on the law and its works. What makes Paul's pronouncements on the law so deeply moving and powerful, what causes him to attribute this peculiar, not infrequently paradoxical significance to the law, is not to be accounted for from polemical zeal against Judaism, nor from reading the Old Testament, nor even from the words of Jesus transmitted to him, but it is the light that has burst on him concerning Christ's death and resurrection, the absolutely new situation that has begun with them and which has regard to the relationship in which every man stands to God in the most existential sense of the word. Only then does the nature of man outside Christ become apparent, does his "own righteousness" on the ground of the works of the law emerge at once in all its wretchedness and self-conceit into the light of day, then too does the insufficiency of the law as means of salvation first become fully manifest.

It is not a matter here, as has been said by some interpreters, of the postulate of a dogmatic tenet, namely, that with the advent of the Messiah the law is no longer in force.[120] For without regard to the question as to whether such a rabbinistic theologoumenon in fact found general acceptance in Jewish theology, one might then expect that for his pronouncement that Christ is the end of the law (Rom. 10:4), Paul would surely have appealed in opposition to Judaism in one way or another to such a dogma and to its Old Testament foundation. The actual state of affairs, however, is an entirely different one. When in the light of Christ's death and resurrection Paul came to the conviction that the law cannot be the means of life and the ground of man's righteousness before God, this is not a dogmatical-theoretical premise or conclusion, but it rests on the redeeming significance of Christ's death and resurrection themselves, or, as Paul himself expresses it, on

---

119. See further Section 28.
120. Cf. Schoeps, *Paul*, p. 171: "The abolition of the law is a Messianological doctrine in Pauline theology"; however, see already A. Schweitzer, *The Mysticism of Paul the Apostle*, pp. 188-189.

the revelation of the righteousness of God in them, by faith and without the works of the law. Nowhere does this ground for Paul's radical rejection of the law as the means of salvation and of what man supposes himself able to acquire of righteousness and life in that way find clearer expression than in his personal statement in Philippians 3:4ff.:

> If any other man thinks he has reason for confidence in the flesh, I yet more: circumcised the eighth day..., as to the righteousness which is in the law blameless.
> But what things were gain to me, these have I counted loss for Christ's sake. Yes, truly, I count all things to be loss because of the surpassing worth of the knowledge of Christ Jesus my Lord. For his sake I have suffered the loss of all things,[121] and count them as refuse, in order that I may gain Christ and be found in him, not having a righteousness of my own, which is of the law, but that which is through faith in Christ, the righteousness which is from God upon the basis of faith....

This pronouncement is of importance because it gives us an insight into the way in which the apostle himself learned to know the absolute nullity of the works of the law as the basis for man's righteousness before God. It has often been represented as though already before his conversion he had reached a deadlock with his efforts to find his right-ousness before God in the works of the law, and that therefore at his conversion a heavy burden had fallen from his shoulders. The above-cited pronouncement points in an entirely different direction, however. He himself, too, had formerly attached the highest value to his law-works, he knew himself to be "blameless" in respect of the righteousness that is to be obtained in the performance of the law (v. 6). Indeed, he speaks of his past to the same effect in Galatians 1:13ff. The law and the works of the law before his conversion stood not for his spiritual bankruptcy, but for his "gain." He found it extremely difficult, as one so far advanced in the righteousness of the law, to relinquish all this at once and renounce it. Only "for Christ's sake," "because of the knowledge of Christ" his Lord, which surpassed all earlier attainments, he learned to count it as loss and suffered it all to be taken away. He expresses the same thing negatively when he says in Galatians 2:21: "if righteousness is through the law, then Christ died to no purpose." It is clearly evident here that Paul's repudiation of the law and its works as means of salvation in the Jewish sense of the word is neither a theoretical dogma, nor rests on subjective experience, but is grounded on that which God has revealed and bestowed of righteousness and life in the death and resurrection of Christ.

At the same time, however, it is therein that the deepest motives of Paul's rejection of righteousness by the law become evident and the correct light breaks in on the real situation of man and the world out-side Christ. Not only the transgressions of the law themselves, whether as flagrant sins or in a more refined form, make man guilty before God

---

121. *Ezēmiōthēn;* really: "I suffered loss"; "ich liess mich an dem allen schädigen" (Dibelius, *An die Philipper,* 3rd ed., 1937, p. 88); "I have experienced this comprehensive devaluation" (Stumpff, *TDNT,* II, p. 890, *s.v. zēmia*).

and prevent him from being righteous before God on the ground of the works of the law. The very attempt to maintain oneself before God and to gain life on the ground of one's "own" works and merit makes such a seeking of righteousness a vain and reprehensible undertaking before God. We touch here the most profound and real aspect of the antithesis. It does not bear only or primarily an ethical character. It is in the full sense of the word religious in kind. For in the relationship of man to the law what is most profoundly involved is his relationship to God. And where the latter is misjudged in its real character, there the relation of man to law is also denatured, whether because he breaks out into sin or because he attempts to gain confidence through the law over against God. Thus what seemed to be "gain" is basically nothing other than "loss" and "refuse." That is the knowledge that in the cross and resurrection of Christ has broken in as a light on Paul's own life and on the life of every man outside Christ.

Therefore the apostle views the question as to whether and how man is justified before God not only in the light of the law, as an ethical question, but in the broader light of the whole of God's revelation. When he describes the ungodliness of the gentiles in Romans 1:18ff., he states his reason for that by referring to God's self-revelation in his works, to which they pay no heed and by which they are not moved to the acknowledgment and glorification of God. And when he wishes to show why Israel, although it has not fallen into the flagrant sin of heathenism, yet cannot obtain righteousness and life from the works of the law, he points not only to Israel's transgression of the law (Rom. 2:12ff.), but, when he searches for the deepest cause, to Israel's misjudgment of the gracious character of its election as the people of God, through its having laid hold of the law to lean on it over against God and by fancied merits to place God under obligation to it (Rom. 9:11; 9:30-10:3; 10:16-21). The paradoxical phenomenon presents itself here that not merely in its transgression of the law, but also in its zeal for the law, Israel has not been able to obtain righteousness before God and life. Paul is able to indict the Jews on the one hand on account of their transgression of the law (Rom. 2), but on the other hand does not want to withhold from them the recognition of their zeal for the law (Rom. 10:2): "For I bear them witness that they have a zeal for God, but not according to knowledge."

This must not be taken, however, as though the law stood in the way of their gaining the favor of God. It is rather so that the manner in which Israel made of the law a means of salvation and relied on it for its righteousness before God prevented Israel from attaining the real object of the law and thus made it reprehensible before God. Paul gives expression of this as follows: "But Israel, although following after the law of righteousness, did not arrive at that law. Why not? Because it did not start from faith, but from supposed works" (Rom. 9:31ff.).

Zeal for the law can altogether alienate man from God, and has precisely the effect of making him a sinner. This occurs when faith is no longer the point of departure for the fulfilling of the law, but man addresses himself to what he takes for the work of the law. For the law then becomes detached from God, in the sense that man no longer trusts in God for his righteousness but in his works. And man in this way no longer arrives at the law, that is to say, no longer at the righteousness and at the life to which the law points him.[122] The apostle is therefore able to demonstrate the impossibility of acquiring righteousness and life in the way of works at one time to those who praise the law with their mouth but in reality grossly transgress it (Rom. 2:17ff.), at another to those who with all their zeal and irreproachableness likewise do not find what they are seeking (Rom. 9; Phil. 3). In both cases man with the law in hand is faced with his bankruptcy. And surely the second is less evident and easy to accept. But it is not on that account any less real, indeed it is in a certain sense still more drastic because it strikes man in his moral earnestness and exertion; because it not only confronts him with his deficiency, but also casts his "gain" into the balance and compels him not only to acknowledge his sin, but also to renounce his very virtues before God.

This brings us finally to a pair of concepts that occupy an important place in Paul's preaching and enable us to understand still better the depth of the antithesis with Judaism.

The first is the qualification "boast" and "boasting,"[123] which he frequently uses in describing the confidence of the Jewish nation in their special privileges as the people of God (Rom. 2:17), particularly in their possessing and knowing the law in that capacity (Rom. 2:18, 23),[124] and in the possibility inherent in that fact of gaining righteousness for themselves before God (Rom. 3:27), a boast the apostle also describes as finding rest in and relying on the law (Rom. 2:17). Although we need not think of this "boasting" as a defiant and haughty glorying in their own works, but above all of their priding themselves on the possession of the law as the people of God, it follows from all that has been said above concerning Paul's judgment of the works of the law that he utterly rejects such a boast. In fact the frequent use of the concept "boast" in Paul's epistles is, even when he speaks of it in a

---

122. *Eis nomon ouk ephthasen.* These words are taken differently. Some wish to understand by them that they have not arrived at the real content of the law, namely, Christ; cf., e.g., Greijdanus, *Rom.,* II, p. 444: "It [the law]...also exhibited the Lord Christ in silhouette and thus summoned to believe in Him for salvation"; and Michel, *Rom.,* p. 219: "...the actual meaning of the law lies outside of itself in Christ." In our view the law is in this way too little understood in its own original significance. One comes to the righteousness at which the law aims only when one approaches this out of faith and not out of one's own works of the law. It is a question therefore not only of that which lies outside the law or was shadow-like, being concealed in it, but of the law's own content and purport as law of God to man. What it foreshadows and demands is a matter of faith, not of meritorious works. Together with Rom. 7:10, 12 this passage comprises one of the most positive pronouncements of Paul on the significance of the law.

123. *Kauchēma, kauchēsis,* of which the former denotes the ground or possibility, the latter the act of boasting, although a rigid distinction is not to be maintained (cf. Bultmann, *TDNT,* III, pp. 645ff., *s.v. kauchaomai.* For the whole question see Bultmann, *Theology,* I, pp. 242ff.).

124. On the law as "Israel's glory and honor and jewel" see at length Strack-Billerbeck, III, pp. 115ff.; cf. pp. 97ff., 126ff.

positive sense, a great protest against the Jewish boasting in the law and the possibility of merit sought in it, and he aims at imparting thereby a contrary content to the idea of "boast."

The cause for this rejection of boasting in the law is here again not that he would not acknowledge the Jewish prerogative. In the midst of his polemic against the boasting of the Jews he explicitly recognizes those privileges (Rom. 3:1ff.). The cause is rather that what is most deeply at stake in the concept "boasting" is the question as to what it is in which man places his trust.[125] It is here that the real contrast lies. For boasting in the law and resting in it mean in practical terms boasting in the works of the law (Eph. 2:9), i.e., trusting in the work of man, that is to say, trusting in the flesh (Phil. 3:3), establishing "their own righteousness" (Rom. 10:3). Boasting in the law is thus so fatal because it passes by the real character of Israel's privilege, no longer relies on the grace of God himself and on the electing character of his covenant but on man's own activity, so as to fix all hope and trust in it. And with that the deepest cause for which every striving to gain righteousness and life in the way of the works of the law must fail has again been laid bare: in this manner man becomes confident and strong against God, the flesh boasts in itself instead of boasting in God (cf. 1 Cor. 1:29ff.). Boasting is therefore not a phenomenon restricted to the Jews. It is equally characteristic of the Greeks, who glory in their wisdom (1 Cor. 1:19-31). It is the natural impulse of every man, against which even the Christian must continue to be warned (Gal. 6:4; Rom. 11:17ff.).

To what degree, finally, the apostle has received from Christ, and the righteousness given in him, the correct insight for this essentially so haughty and pernicious striving of man emerges clearly in this frequent and pregnant use of "boast." When Paul has given in Romans 3:21-26 the great programmatic summary of his gospel, the first conclusion he draws from it is: "Where then is the boasting? It is excluded. By what manner of law? Of works? No, but by the law of faith" (v. 27).

That there is no place for boasting becomes quite clear only from the gospel, in which "the law of works" has given way to "the law of faith," that is, in which another order governs. From that other order, as it is evident already in Abraham's life and as it already for him excluded every boast (Rom. 4:2), the unfoundedness, indeed the mortal peril of every human boast as trusting in the flesh is manifest: "that no flesh should boast before God" (1 Cor. 1:29), and that but one possibility and one ground of boasting should remain: boasting in the Lord (1 Cor. 1:31; 2 Cor. 10:17), and in the cross of our Lord Jesus Christ (Gal. 6:14).

Closely related to the above and highly typical for what occupies us here is finally the repeated mention of offense *(skandalon)* and

125. Bultmann correctly writes that for Paul (as for the Old Testament and for Philo) "the element of trust contained in [*kauchasthai*] is primary" *(TDNT, loc. cit.);* cf. the synonymous use of *kauchasthai* and *pepoithenai* in Phil. 3:3ff.; 2 Cor. 10:7, 8, and cf. 2 Cor. 1:12 with 3:4.

stumbling *(proskomma)* as the cause for the vain striving of man to be able to stand before God on the ground of his own righteousness. When the apostle asks himself in Romans 9:31ff. why the Jews, despite all their zeal, have not obtained the righteousness of God, he answers (in addition to what has already been cited above, p. 139): "They have stumbled at the stone of stumbling; even as it is written: Behold, I lay in Zion a stone of stumbling and a rock of offense: and he that believes in him shall not be put to shame" (vv. 32ff.).

If one asks wherein this offense or stumbling consists, then, as appears from the whole context, it can mean nothing other than that Israel has not been willing to be deprived of its own righteousness and that it has stumbled at the fact that Zion is only built when it trusts solely in God and not in the work of man.[126] Not to have seen and understood that, to have stumbled at that, is the cause for the bankruptcy of the righteousness that is by the works of the law: it is for this reason that Israel has not obtained it, that God has given them a spirit of stupor, that their table has become a snare and a trap and a stumbling block and a retribution to them (Rom. 11:7ff.). Here too the apostle shows the deepest cause for the inadequacy of the works of the law: it consists in the offense taken by human pride at the absoluteness of divine grace, at the exclusion of all human pretension and merit.

The same idea is to be found in two other highly important *skandalon* pronouncements:

> ... Christ the crucified, to the Jews a *skandalon* (1 Cor. 1:23).
> ... if I still preach circumcision..., then the *skandalon* of the cross has been done away (Gal. 5:11).

Both pronouncements set the cross of Christ as the *skandalon* over against the Jewish doctrine of salvation by works. The real and deepest cause for the Jewish rejection of Christ the crucified lies in the fact that the cross deprives man of his own righteousness.[127] The *skandalon* of the cross therefore ought to be maintained, and one may not meet halfway the man who is offended at it by permitting him after all to provide in part for his righteousness (circumcision in Gal. 5:11).

On the basis of all this it may be determined that for Paul the striving of man to obtain his righteousness before God in the way of the works of the law is doomed to failure not only because man cannot come up to the fulfillment of the law as God requires it of him, but because it is already fundamentally sinful to wish to insure oneself righteousness and life; indeed, this is the human sin *par excellence*. This insight, which one may surely call the foundation of Paul's whole

---

126. The quotation in Rom. 9:33 is a combination of two texts from Isaiah, 28:16 and 8:14, of which the first speaks of the work of God as the foundation of Israel's salvation and the second of the offense that lay in that for self-willed Israel.

127. Undoubtedly there was also the more general "offense" for the Jews, that they could not conceive of the Messiah as a crucified one. For "they demand signs" (1 Cor. 1:22), demonstrations of divine glory. For these two motifs and their relationship to each other see also G. Stählin, *Skandalon*, 1930, pp. 205ff.

view of man outside Christ, can be characterized as a radically deepened concept of sin. It rests ultimately, however, not on an analysis of man, but on the revelation of God's work in Christ's cross and resurrection; in the light of that work the seeking of righteousness on the basis of the works of the law first fully manifests its essentially proud and carnal character: as an idle boast and taking offense at the sovereignty of God's grace.

SECTION 23. THE LAW IMPOTENT BECAUSE OF THE FLESH. THE BONDAGE OF THE LAW

To this first great point of view, from which he elucidates the insufficiency of the law as means of salvation, Paul, however, adds a second: not only can the law not give man the righteousness that makes him acceptable before God (Gal. 3:21); it is also incapable of breaking the power of sin and conquering "the flesh," so that sin might no longer reign in the "mortal body" (Rom. 6:12). That is the second great viewpoint from which the argument is conducted in the Epistle to the Romans against confidence in the law and life under the law. Paul arrives at that in 6:15, where he tells the church that in the struggle against the power of sin it may live not under the regime of the law, but under that of grace. In 7:1 he returns to this viewpoint, and after having first, positively, pointed to the death of Christ as the end of this regime of the law (the old dispensation of the letter; 7:6), he once again, negatively — but now from this new viewpoint! — establishes the bankruptcy of the one who in the conflict against sin chooses to seek his strength in the law (and not in the Spirit; 7:6; 8:2).

If this general purport of Romans 7 in the whole course of the argument of Romans 6-8 were kept more clearly in view there could, in our conviction, scarcely exist any fundamental difference of opinion concerning the question as to whether Paul here draws the picture of the man in Christ or outside Christ. It has indeed been said that already in Romans 1:18-4:25 accounts have been "settled" with the law and that therefore it is not to be supposed that the inadequacy of the law would be raised afresh in Romans 7. But this objection is based on an insufficiently exact analysis of the course of the argument in the Epistle to the Romans, and passes over the two different viewpoints from which the antithesis with Judaism must come up for discussion. What is undoubtedly set forth at length in Romans 1:18-4:25 is that man cannot be justified by the works of the law. Accordingly it is not that with which Romans 7 is once again concerned. What is under discussion in chapters 6, 7, and 8:1-13 is that the one justified by faith is no longer to live in sin (6:1ff.). What this means for the struggle against sin ("let not sin therefore reign in your mortal body," etc.; 6:12) is indicated in Romans 7:1ff. Its import is no other than that in that struggle believers are no longer to live under the vigor of the law, but of the Spirit (Rom. 7:6). It is this redemptive-historical contrast of the old and new (7:6) which governs everything and in the light of which one is to answer the anthropological questions (see above). If, on the other hand, one turns the matter about and takes his point of departure in the anthropological description of what is then conceived as the struggle between the old and the new man, it is no longer to be comprehended how one could still maintain the real, redemptive-historical theme of these chapters (the antithesis between law and Spirit) in an intelligible manner.

The remarkable thing about the evidence of the insufficiency of the law furnished here consists in that Paul now represents the law as a power that provokes and, as it were, calls forth sin (in the sinner). The law does not restrain sin, but causes it to awaken; it does not reduce sin, but rather makes it to increase (cf. Rom. 5:20). Already in the introduction of Romans 7 this is said indirectly when there is mention of "the sinful passions, which were [aroused] by the law." The meaning is that the sinful passions properly assert themselves only when they encounter the resistances of the law.

This idea is developed and elucidated in the sequel (Rom. 7:7-13) in a very telling and, one may surely say, dramatic fashion:

> What shall we say then? Is the law sin? By no means! Indeed, I should not have known sin, except through the law. For I should not have known desire, if the law had not said: Thou shalt not covet.
> Sin, however, taking its starting point in the commandment, called forth all kinds of desire in me: for apart from the law sin is dead. I was once alive apart from the law; but when the commandment came, sin began to live, but I died . . . for sin, taking its starting point in the commandment, deceived me. . . .

It is not the law itself, therefore, which is sin. But sin avails itself of the law as its starting point,[128] that is to say, sin — here thought of as a personified power — gets its opportunity through the law. For the law forbids sin. Consequently, when the law comes on man with its prohibition, sin springs into action and awakens in man the desire for what is forbidden by the commandment. In that sense it can be said that the desires are "by the law" (v. 5). Thus it can also be understood that sin is "dead" apart from the law, that is, sin asserts itself in man only when the law comes to him with its prohibitions. Then sin begins "to live" (v. 9), it stirs from its slumbering, its resistance awakens to the power that is bent on bridling it. What is written in 1 Corinthians 15:56 applies here as well: "the strength of sin is the law." Without the law sin would not have been able to make men rebellious and lawless. For this reason it can also be said that sin, starting from the law, deceives man. By holding up the commandment to man as the end of his liberty and by promising him life in the transgression of the commandment, sin draws man under its enchantment. It promises him just that which the law appears to take away, and leads him thus into death.

The depiction is strongly reminiscent of the story of the fall of the first man, without one being able to say, however, that the I=Adam.[129] Yet the imperfects and the aorists are not to be fixed in

---

128. *Aphormēn labousa* (vv. 8, 11); cf. Bertram, *TDNT,* V, p. 473.
129. Against this cf. above, pp. 99f.

the life of a specific individual. The I has a much more general significance.[130] With obvious allusions to the first fall into sin it says how sin
takes possession of man *not in spite of,* but just *by means of* the law and
that therefore victory over the dominion of sin can be gained, not by
the strength of the "thou shalt" of the law, but only under the operation
of grace, i.e., of the Spirit (Rom. 6:12-7:6).

It is frequently contended, however, that with the above, the
negative-preparatory significance of the law in its innermost core has
not yet been laid bare. For this is said to consist, in Paul's train of
thought, not only in the law's awakening transgression in the sinner
and thus bringing him under the judgment of the law, but no less in
the "pious" misuse of the man who takes hold of the law in order to
be able to establish his own righteousness before God.

Thus Bultmann, for example, writes that the redemptive-historical
significance of the law consists in that it leads man into sin, not, however, only because it stimulates his desire for transgression, but also
because it offers him the utmost possibility to live as a sinner, by con-
verting his resistance to the law into striving after a righteousness of
his own by means of the fulfillment of the commandment.[131] For this
conception Bultmann does not appeal to any pronouncement of Paul
on the law, but to what in his judgment is the essence of the Pauline
conception of sin: the high-handed striving of man to stand in his own
strength and to seek salvation in his own creaturely existence.[132]

Schlier writes to the same effect on Galatians 3:12 ("and the law
is not of faith, but rests upon the principle: he who does these things
shall live by them") that for Paul the curse apparently cleaves to the
"doing" itself, insofar as this is directed to the works of the law. Thus
not merely because the law is not fulfilled qualitatively, but even because the law by its character as commandment provokes man to the
performance of deeds, it brings curse along with it. To be sure, the
latter is not so evident as the former. Nevertheless, it is no less real.
For the desire of man for "himself," the passion "to gain control of
oneself and to be one's own master," is awakened and satisfied by
the law in sinful man.[133] However, this conception, which one also finds
in various elaborations in the dogmatic literature of the present day,[134]
is untenable as an exegesis of the negative effect of the law described
in Romans 7. It is no doubt true that Paul again and again denounces
the pursuit by man of a righteousness of his own as the great impediment to the understanding of the gospel, as the root of Israel's unbelief.

---

130. Cf. above on the significance of the ego in 7:14ff. (p. 129).

131. *Theology,* I, p. 267.

132. *Theology,* I, p. 264. This view is entirely in harmony with Bultmann's
existentialistic-anthropological view of sin and redemption (pointed out above, pp.
101ff.). For Bultmann the essence of sin does not lie in the transgression of the
demand of the law, but in the attempt with the help of the law to seek life in
that which is "available," "over which man disposes," etc.

133. Schlier, *Gal.,* pp. 91, 92.

134. E.g., in A. A. van Ruler, *De vervulling van de wet,* pp. 401ff. (with
an appeal to H. F. Kohlbrügge); K. Barth, "Gospel and Law," ET 1959, in *God, Grace,
and Gospel;* G. C. Berkouwer, *Sin,* pp. 173ff.

But it is another matter whether he alludes to it (i.e., to this striving after self-justification) when he says that sin takes its starting point in the commandment and in this way, that is to say, by means of this commandment, deceives man and puts him to death. It is our conviction that the purport of these words (and of the whole of Rom. 7) is under such an interpretation very drastically bent and shifted. When Paul here speaks of the sin that is provoked and stimulated by the law, what he means by that is the transgression of the requirement of the law and not the "sin against grace" that manifests itself in the attempt at self-justification. The whole terminology of Romans 7 and 8 admits of no doubt whatever in this respect. This is so when there is mention in 7:5 of "the sinful passions which are aroused by law." One cannot explain these "sinful passions" as the "wrestlings" or "laborings"[135] of man to establish his own righteousness, without employing what is surely a very artificial and arbitrary interpretation. Sinful passions (and not sinful "laborings") are here unquestionably to be understood in a moral sense. And the same applies to the sin of "coveting" evoked by the law, of which verse 7 speaks. Here again it is very decidedly not a matter of "passion for our own self-glory before the face of God,"[136] but of sinful desire in the sense of verse 5 (cf. "all" covetousness in v. 8). To recognize this one need only read the continuation of Romans 7 as well, where sin as it is evoked by the commandment is understood as plainly as possible in its moral operation and strength ruling in "the members," and certainly not as the sin of self-righteousness (cf. 8:2ff.). The whole of the sin-producing effect of the law, as that is specifically described in Romans 7, speaks of the evil, sinful desire and act of the transgression of the commandment (cf. Rom. 7:5, 6, 8 with Gal. 5:16ff., 24), not of the passion to establish a righteousness of one's own before God. Althaus accordingly is correct when he writes that in following this explanation one must give a new interpretation to all the essential ideas of Romans 7 "in clear contradiction" to the context and Pauline usage elsewhere.[137] For this reason "the deceit" of sin, too, of which there is mention in 7:11, does not consist in the fact that sin urges man to cleanse, to justify himself, and to think that he is too good for the grace of God, but, altogether in harmony with Genesis 3:13 (to which the expression "deceive" evidently alludes; cf. 2 Cor. 11:3), in the false delusion that for him liberty, happiness, etc., lie in the transgression of the commandment.

It is the absolutely negative effect of the law understood in this sense that now further determines Paul's speaking about the law and the condition of man under the law. For not only does the law provoke sin,

---

135. Thus, e.g., van Ruler attempts via the translation "laborings" to understand *pathēmata* of the efforts of the legalistic man (*De vervulling*, pp. 381ff.). But irrespective of the fact that *pathēmata* in itself can hardly mean such a laboring or wrestling, it is impossible to take the combination *pathēmata tōn hamartiōn* (literally, the passions proceeding from the sins) in this sense; see the commentaries.

136. Berkouwer, *Sin*, p. 177, with a quotation from Barth: "Eigenen Ruhmes vor Gott."

137. *Paulus und Luther über den Menschen*, 1938, p. 39.

but when sin has once gained control of man the law is no longer able
to deliver him from that control. For "the law is impotent on account
of the flesh" (Rom. 8:3), and does not make the condition of the man
who has been sold under sin any better, but rather still worse. Paul
gives expression to this in a variety of ways and with a great many
figures, especially once again in Romans 7, in verses 14-25. In so doing
he lays all the emphasis on the fact that, since through sin by means of
the law man has been put to death and brought into slavery, he himself
no longer[138] has command over his actions, but finds himself under the
law of sin. We have dealt with the anthropological implications of
Romans 7:14 above (cf. Section 20). But all that is depicted here has
no other purpose than to say that man cannot live from the strength of
the law, but has died and still dies. The law "is no match for sin"; it
becomes, not on account of its essence, or through its character as commandment, but because its demand is frustrated by the unwilling and
impotent flesh (Rom. 8:3, 7), a means of bringing those whom sin has
vanquished into the clutches of sin. The insufficiency of the law as
means to life and with that the antithesis between "religion of law"
and "religion of faith" is incapable of being more sharply and more
dramatically expressed than is done in Romans 7:7-25. In the struggle
for redemption of life the law does not stand on the side of life, but
on that of death. In place of being a champion for good the law has
become a paladin of evil.

The consequence of this monstrous alliance of sin and the law
is that all kinds of qualifications that describe the corruption and curse
of sin now also apply to the law. As sin means death for man, so also
the law (2 Cor. 3:6). The law that should have been unto life has become unto death (Rom. 7:10, 13). And as sin has made man a slave, so
now the law as well. The figures Paul borrows from prison life are
highly characteristic here. The law is at one time the prison, then again
the warden, the jailer himself. Thus it is said in Romans 7:6: "but now
we are discharged from the law ..., which held us captive" (en hō
kateichometha). This idea of the law as warden and of man as subject
or slave of the law stands out in more ways than one especially in the
Epistle to the Galatians. Because the law acquires this significance for
man on account of his sin, however, the law and sin are alternately
spoken of as warden and as slave-owner. Cf. Galatians 3:22 and 23:

> ... the Scripture has imprisoned all things under [the power of] sin [as
> jailer] (synekleisen hypo hamartian).
> ... but before faith came we were held under custody by the law,
> kept under restraint ... (hypo nomon ephrouroumetha synkleiomenoi).

It is not simply a matter of forensic categories; the imprisonment
in which man is fettered has reference to the whole of his existence.
One need only read the stirring passages of Romans 7:7ff. and 7:13ff.
to understand this. Only when viewed from the standpoint of Christ —

---

138. The ouketi in vv. 17 and 20 does not therefore speak of the situation
as that has commenced with Christ, but as it is with having been sold under sin.

this is the great presupposition — does the law rightly disclose who man is apart from the revelation of God's righteousness without the law, and apart from the government of the Spirit that has been given in Christ.

In Galatians 3:24 Paul speaks entirely to the same effect of the law as the pedagogue, under[139] which we found ourselves "before faith had come." With this figure, too, it is above everything else a matter of the lack of freedom. This is clearly evident from the continuation of the metaphor in Galatians 4:1ff., where those who stand under the pedagogue are further described as heirs who are still minors and who differ in nothing from slaves, even though they are heirs of all. For they remain under guardians and stewards until the time appointed by the father. To be "under the pedagogue" is thus not to be understood as "being still at school," receiving instruction, but as being unfree, finding oneself in the position of a slave,[140] having been placed under an alien power. The pedagogue is the guardian who holds those who are underage in a position of subjection, in which they "in nothing differ from slaves." The change that enters in when the time appointed by the father ("the fulness of the time"; v. 4) has come accordingly consists in the fact that liberty dawns for those who were under the pedagogue (the law), so that they are no longer slaves, but sons (Gal. 4:4).

This whole negative significance — described in all kinds of metaphors — which the law has for man and which makes him live in a condition of slavery, Paul expresses in the set phrase "to be under the law" (hypo nomon einai; Rom. 6:14, 15; 1 Cor. 9:20; Gal. 4:5, 21; 5:18).

Although this expression is used with nuances, it denotes in the passages that are characteristic for the present connection not merely that God has subjected man to the norm of the law, but rather that he lives, groans, has been put in chains as a prisoner, a slave, one who is underage, under the hostile, enslaving power of the law; a bondage from which only the regime of divine grace can deliver him (Rom. 7:14; 8:2; Gal. 4:5).

In this context one ought also to point out the remarkable expression Paul uses in Galatians 4:3 and 9 as a synonym for this bondage under the law and which recurs in Colossians 2:8 and 20, namely, subjection to "the first principles of the world" (ta stoicheia tou kosmou): "So we also, when we were minor children, were slaves under the first principles of the world" (v. 3); and verse 9: "how can you now turn back again to the weak and beggarly principles, to which you desire to be in bondage all over again?"; cf. Colossians 2:20: "if you died with Christ to the first principles of the world, why, as though living in the world, do you submit to all manner of commandments?"

---

139. Here, too, hypo (paidagōgon), just as hypo hamartian and hypo nomon.

140. Cf. the enlightening explanation of the pedagogue, with much classical material, in A. Oepke, Der Brief des Paulus an die Galater, 1937, pp. 66ff.: "Furthermore the paidagōgos is not to be mistaken for the pedagogue in the modern sense.... He is the house-slave, the one who superintends the boys everywhere from about the sixth year to the onset of manhood." He then points as well to the unpopularity of these figures in antiquity, in addition to the lasting appreciation sometimes accorded to them. His exposition of the paidagōgos seems to me more successful than that of Bertram, TDNT, V, pp. 620ff., in which the significance of the law as deprivation of liberty finds altogether too little expression.

This expression has often been translated by "world spirits," and what is intended then are spirit powers, having their abode on the stars, who by means of all sorts of commandments, etc., are said to have brought men under their jurisdiction. Others, in a more Jewish sense, think of angels as defenders of the law, who wish even after Christ to continue their rule. But all these conceptions — however ingenious — are to be firmly rejected.[141] In connection with "world" Paul does not think here of the cosmos as the universe in which the star-elements are found, but, as is abundantly evident from Colossians 2:20, of the sin-dominated world of men, in which believers are no longer to "live" (which can scarcely be said of the cosmos as universe); cf. also Colossians 2:8 where (the *stoicheia* of the) world is another expression for (the tradition of) men. Accordingly, with the *stoicheia* one must not think of star-elements or something of that sort, but of the meaning the word also has elsewhere in the New Testament: first principles, the ABC's, primitive teaching (cf. Heb. 5:12). Paul gathers up under them in a somewhat denigrating manner ("weak, beggarly" principles) the legalistic prescriptions to which heathen religion subjects its adherents and which he sees returning in the form of all kinds of ceremonial, ascetic, and other regulations of Judaistic and syncretistic heresy in the churches of Galatia and Colosse. These primitive principles of the world, too, brought men under their jurisdiction, could give them no deliverance, but rather carried them ever more deeply into spiritual bondage. For this reason Paul equates them in their effect with the rule and slavery in which the man finds himself who wishes to be justified by the works of the law.

SECTION 24. THE LAW AS DISCIPLINARIAN UNTO CHRIST

All this naturally gives rise to the question, a question Paul himself asks emphatically in Galatians 3:19: Why then the law? If the law cannot bring salvation, cannot grant man merit and righteousness, is unable to restrain the power of sin, what significance must still be ascribed to the law and, in connection with this, what purpose does it have in the great context of the ways of God with man and the world in sin? The answer to this question is very closely associated with what has been said in the preceding chapter. It is precisely in the negative operation of the law that its purpose lies: to bar to man the way to salvation and thus — and here the reverse side of Paul's gospel shows itself in this preaching of the law — to vindicate in a negative fashion the indispensability of the way of faith.

The reasoning that is followed in Galatians 3:14-25 is highly characteristic and illuminating for this train of thought. Paul here places the promise given to Abraham and the law given by God to Israel at a much later time over against each other. The object of the argument is to make it clear that salvation for Abraham and his seed lay in this promise and not in the law. To that end the unconditional

---

141. Here see the detailed account in my *Col.*, pp. 172-176. Further, A. W. Cramer, *Stoicheia tou kosmou, Interpretatie van een nieuwtestamentische term*, 1961; and especially the full and detailed investigation of A. J. Bandstra, *The Law and the Elements of the World*.

character of the divine promise, not dependent on human achievements, is first elucidated.[142] In consequence the fulfillment of the promise by God cannot be contingent on the fulfillment of the law (which was added later) by man. The law, which came with its demands 430 years afterward, can no more nullify or place in the balance the promise once given to Abraham. The question remains: For what purpose the law? The answer is given in verse 19: "... it was added for the sake of the transgressions" *(tōn parabaseōn charin prosetethē).*

One must not form too narrow an idea of the effect of these words. Interpreters have often chosen to understand the pronouncement in this way: that the law has been given by God in order to bring man noetically to the knowledge of his transgressions. Although this element of the knowledge of and insight into sin is, of course, not lacking, the real meaning has not thereby been laid bare. "For the sake of the transgressions" is intended to say not only: in order to make them known, but also and indeed in the first instance: in order to bring out, to "pro-duce" the transgressions. In addition to the context of Galatians 3, that this is the sense of the words is evident from the pronouncements of Romans, which are still more explicit. We have already referred to Romans 5:20, where it is said in so many words that the law came in to cause the trespass to increase *(nomos de pareisēlthen hina pleonasē to paraptōma).* Here, too, as in Galatians 3:19, the concern is with the secondary character of the law, not, however, as in Galatians 3, with the addition of the law to the promise, but with the additional effect of the law in the sin situation that was inaugurated by Adam. This effect of the law was to increase sin. And it served for that purpose. It had to bring sin, which already existed but was not yet committed under the law (cf. 5:13), to its utmost development in order to accentuate the more clearly the grace of Christ in its all-transcending significance (v. 21). In this train of thought, therefore, the law is necessary for placing sin and thereby grace over against each other, as it were, in their full measure and most extreme tension. For this reason "to cause the trespass to increase" is not only the consequence,[143] but positively also the purpose for the entrance of the law; and the law not only makes sin to become "evident,"[144] but it produces sin and so increases it. These pronouncements thus expressly posit as the object of the law what, as we saw in the preceding section, is designated and described

---

142. See also my *The Epistle of Paul to the Churches of Galatia* (NICNT), 1953, pp. 129ff.

143. So (alas) the translation of the Dutch Bible Society of Rom. 5:20: "... zodat de overtreding toenam," as opposed to most of the commentaries (as, e.g., those of Lietzmann, Kühl, Zahn, Greijdanus, Althaus, Dodd, Kuss, Schlatter, Nygren, Gaugler). Calvin upholds the final conception, but in the sense of an increase of the knowledge of sin, not of the sin itself. He does cite the opposite view of Augustine, however.

144. So the translation of the Dutch Bible Society of Gal. 3:19: "...om de overtreding te doen blijken"; cf. also the commentaries of Calvin, and De Witt Burton. Here too, however, most scholars advocate the above-mentioned interpretation, in our view the only acceptable one (e.g., Greijdanus, Schlier, Oepke, Dibelius, Schlatter, Zahn, *et al.*). [The English versions have "because of the transgressions," which is quite as inadequate as that of the DBS—tr. note.]

in Romans 7:5, 7ff. as its effect: the bringing forth of sin as sin, unlaw-fulness, transgression of the law, the stimulating of desire through its very prohibition, the awakening, reviving of evil, when it feels itself impeded by the law. We shall therefore have to take the well-known pronouncements of Romans 3:20 and 7:7 on the knowledge of sin through the law not only in a noetic, but in an experiential, existential sense (cf. 2 Cor. 5:21).[145]

All this, added to what has already been said in the preceding section on the negative effect of the law, can enable us to know clearly the purpose of the law within the framework of the Pauline doctrine of sin: it is twofold, negative as well as positive. The negative aspect lies in that it does not open the way of salvation to man in his sin and self-conceit, but rather bars it; does not restrain sin, but increases it; does not liberate and quicken the sinner, but puts him to death and casts him into prison. For Paul no picture is too somber and too radical to throw light on this negative effect of the law and the divine purpose behind it in all its ruinous strength. This is the awful sharpness of the antithesis between Paul's doctrine of the law and that of the synagogue.

But in this utter negation of the law as means of salvation lies at the same time the positive aspect, as the reverse side of the gospel. This positive side is found already in the fact that the law in its damn-ing and killing force does not fall out of the control of the God and Father of Jesus Christ whom Paul preaches. Nowhere in Paul's epistles does the law bear the character of an independent power of fate oper-ating apart from God or contrary to God's design, which together with other corrupting powers must, as it were, be subdued by Christ.[146] For it is just in this enslaving, killing operation that the law is subservient to God's saving purposes; indeed, it is wielded by God himself. On the one hand it is only in this way that the awful threat that the law contains within itself for man outside Christ correctly comes to light: God himself is engaged with man in the law. By the law he imprisons him in the dungeon of sin and of guilt. The law is so deadly only for this reason, because it is the rod in God's hand.[147] At the same time, however, one is able to understand in this way how the law in this its killing power is nevertheless of positive significance in the divine plan of salvation.

---

145. See also the commentaries, e.g., of Zahn, Althaus, Nygren, Gaugler, Schlatter, on Rom. 3:20; 7:7, as also Bultmann, *Theology*, I, p. 266. Otherwise Greij-danus, who, though at Rom. 3:20 he refers to 7:5, in 7:7 considers only a "theoretical knowing, intellectual insight...without the additional thought of knowing by experience" to be spoken of. Paul would otherwise be saying that no evil lusts were at work in him other than as reaction against the commandment, which according to Greijdanus cannot be correct (*Rom.*, I, pp. 326, 327). But this argument passes over what Paul himself says in v. 8: "for apart from the law sin is dead." Greijdanus comments (rightly): "[*Nekra*] does not deny that there was sin but says that it did not stir, did not reveal itself," etc. (*ibid.*, I, p. 329). It is in this sense, in our view, that one will have to understand v. 7, however.

146. The idea has all the same been very much propagated, in a variety of nuances.

147. Cf. the striking passage on this subject in van Ruler, *De vervulling*, p. 387.

This double point of view — that it is God who makes use of the law and that with it he works toward the revelation of his righteousness in Christ — finds expression in a number of pronouncements, in which time and again the positive significance is set forth as the object of the negative:

> God has shut up all under disobedience, that he might have mercy upon all (Rom. 11:32).
> The Scripture [i.e., God] shut up all things under sin, that the promise by faith in Jesus Christ might be given to them that believe (Gal. 3:22).
> ... we were kept in ward under the law, shut up unto the faith which should be revealed (v. 23).
> ... the law is become our disciplinarian unto Christ, that we might be justified by faith (v. 24).

This enslaving, killing operation of the law thus has a positive meaning in the divine economy of salvation because God in this way makes room for the promise, for faith, for Christ. In that sense the law is the disciplinarian unto Christ. In Paul's train of thought that does not mean that the law on account of its sacrifices, priests, prescriptions for purification, etc., gave a "sketch of Christ" and that he was to be known and expected from it because in it he was "symbolized as in a shadow."[148] The function of the law intended here is not that in a positive sense it gradually leads those who find themselves "under it" to Christ, but rather that in a negative sense, on account of its enslaving and killing operation, it prepares them for the redemption that has appeared in Christ as liberation from that bondage. Along with this one will have to think, not in the first place of the subjective experience of those who are under the law, but of the objective significance of the law, as one comes to know it on the basis of the salvation given in Christ.[149] Yet in the redemptive plan of God it nevertheless has this negative preparatory significance.[150]

---

148. So Greijdanus, *Gal.*, p. 246. Others seek the positive significance of the law as disciplinarian in the fact that it should for a time "regulate Israel's external mode of life, protect it from losing its way by straying, on paths it chose by itself, into unbridled heathendom and from becoming unfit to receive future, higher instruction and thus unfit for its essential calling" (thus Zahn, *Gal.*, p. 186). However true all this may be in itself, it is not under discussion in this context. What is at issue, likewise in connection with the representation of the pedagogue, is the contrast between slavery and freedom (cf. Gal. 4:1ff.).

149. Cf. Bultmann, *Theology*, I, pp. 266f.

150. This is—also in this negative sense—contested by others, e.g., Schlier, *Gal.*, pp. 125ff., who takes the words *eis Christon* in Gal. 3:24 to denote only the *terminus ad quem*. He holds that justification by faith, "which appears through the *hina*-clause as the meaning and goal of the operation of the law, is in no sense effected or prepared by the law" (*ibid.*, p. 126). But however much it is true that one must not here start exclusively from the subjective life under the law—which by no means always produces despair and consciousness of impotence, but frequently legalism and self-sufficiency—this does not alter the fact that in the final clauses repeated time and again (see above), just as in the *eis Christon*, there is surely more in view than a period of time. It lay in God's intention not only *after* the time of bondage-under-the-law to make the liberty in Christ to dawn, but also *over against* this killing and enslaving operation of the law to make grace to appear

Schlatter expresses this in striking words: "Until he [Christ] came there was placed over us a watchman in the form of the law, which held us confined in imprisonment. What makes the law similar to a prison is not that it forbids us to do evil and warns us of sin. From evil Christ separates us fully and completely. Under the law we were guarded because it shut us off from God like a wall. It did not allow us access to his love. The gates of the sanctuary remained closed; we had to wait. It was yet night within us and around us. From God we heard only the one thing—his commandment and its threat; there was not yet the sunlight of his knowledge, which is eternal life. But this wall is not meant to be our eternal prison. These bars are pushed back when faith is revealed. It was a revelation for the world. We cannot imagine it until it comes, nor find it ourselves until it is given us. It shines on us like a ray from above. The scales fall away, the eye finds Christ, catches his glory, looks at God's face in him, and then the soul rests in him as its firm foundation. Not until Christ does the revelation of faith arise; but the imprisonment with which the law surrounded us is the silent preparation for it."[151]

SECTION 25. PAUL, JUDAISM, AND THE OLD TESTAMENT

Finally, one can ask whether, by attributing such an exclusively negative-preparatory significance to the law in the doctrine of sin and indicating that as being not only the actual effect, but also the effect of the law intended by God, Paul does not far remove himself from the positive purpose that in fact is ascribed to the law within the framework of the making of the covenant and giving of the law in the Old Testament. When, for example, in Galatians 4:24ff. he terms the covenant that derives its character from Mt. Sinai a covenant that brings forth children of slavery, as Hagar, is he then giving an adequate interpretation of this covenant? And when in Galatians 3:12 and in Romans 10:5 he places the Mosaic word "he [the man] that does [these things] shall live by them" (cf. Deut. 9:4; 30:12ff.; Lev. 18:5), over against (the righteousness by) faith, does he not overlook the well-known fact that in the context in which it was spoken this word of Moses does not have an indirect, negative, but rather a real, positive significance?[152] In a word, can the redemptive-historical significance Paul ascribes to the law be thought to be in harmony with the foundation on which the law was given in the Old Testament (Exod. 20:2), and on which its demand is intended to function, as appears from the whole Old Testament revelation of God?

We are faced here with an exceedingly complex problem, which

---

the more gloriously in its indispensableness and its richness. In this sense one may certainly speak with Schlatter of the law as "the silent preparation for the revelation of faith"; see also C. de Beus, *Paulus Apostel der vrijheid*, 1952, pp. 124ff.

151. *Gal. (Erläuterungen)*, p. 94.

152. Cf. the criticism of H. J. Schoeps, according to whom Paul had not at all rightly understood the law as "the saving principle of the old covenant," but fell victim to "a characteristic distortion of vision" (*Paul,* p. 213).

cannot be given an exhaustive treatment in all its facets. We wish to summarize in a few points what is, in our view, the basic point.

(1) It should be maintained first that for Paul the advent of Christ does not mean the great redemptive-historical incision in the sense that it was only with Christ that the possibility of faith had come, and that prior to it righteousness by the law was the only way of salvation assigned to Israel. Although he sometimes can express himself in this manner (cf. Gal. 3:25: "but now that faith is come ..."), it is not open to contradiction or misunderstanding that the way of faith for Paul constituted the essence of the Old Testament economy of redemption as well. Not only is the whole of his preaching of the gospel determined and confirmed by the fact that it is witnessed to by the law and the prophets (Rom. 3:21; 16:26, *et al.*), but he also points out in all detail how even Abraham "our father" was justified not by works, but by faith (Rom. 4), and over against the rule of law of Moses (see above) he establishes the rule of faith with an appeal to other Old Testament pronouncements, among which are even those of Moses himself (Rom. 10:6ff.; Gal. 3:11). And when in Galatians 4 he reproaches the church that it permits itself once more to be brought "under the law," he asks why it will not listen to "the law" (Gal. 4:21), and for the rule of faith against the law he appeals to the very law itself (cf. Rom. 3:31). For Paul too, therefore, the heart and content of the Scriptures is not the righteousness that is by the law, but that which is by faith; and that on the authority of the law itself.

(2) We may certainly not overlook the fact that when he appeals to the law in this manner, he nevertheless means the law in the larger sense, and not the law "consisting in commandments and ordinances" (Eph. 2:15). Yet this does not alter the fact that the people of Israel, even under the dispensation of the law, had received a better and deeper principle by which to live than that of "the righteousness which is of the law," and that the "hardening of their thoughts" lay exactly in their failure to appreciate this, so that in the reading of the Old Testament there was a veil before them, which prevented them from seeing the glory of God as that has now been revealed in the gospel (2 Cor. 3:14ff.; 4:3ff.). Thus what remained to them was the law without Christ, and for this reason their zeal for God, which Paul does not deny to them, was nonetheless a zeal "without insight" (Rom. 10:2), because in pursuing the law of righteousness they did not start from faith, but from fancied works (Rom. 9:32). In that sense, therefore, for Paul the failure of Israel lay in this: that by failing to appreciate the true nature of God's election (Rom. 9-11), they have not been able to see the law in the proper light, but have viewed it as a means for setting up their own righteousness (Rom. 10:3).

(3) Now, it is from this law, as it functioned in the synagogue's doctrine of redemption opposed by him, that Paul again and again proceeds, the law as he saw it before him in the life of the Jews, the law as he himself had also lived from it (Phil. 3:6), that is, the law before Christ and the law without Christ. That he is able to see the function of the law in another way as well, in the light of grace and of

faith, as the rule for the new life, is apparent from the manner in which presently he will again connect the life that is from the Spirit with the law (Rom. 8:4, *et al.*).[153] But in the antithesis with Judaism this function of the law does not arise, but the ultimate consequence is drawn from what takes place when the sequence of salvation and law is reversed, and the law itself is made a means of salvation. One can say, therefore, that in combatting the Jewish doctrine of the law Paul starts from the Jewish standpoint and from thence makes plain what happens to the law and to man and what from God's side must happen when righteousness and life are anticipated from the law and not from the promise, from human volition and endeavor and not from the power of the Spirit. Then the law that was given unto life becomes unto death, then Christ, in order to be able to give the law its rightful place in the life of his own (Rom. 8:3; Gal. 5:14; Rom. 13:8-10; 1 Cor. 7:19), must first become the end of the law unto righteousness to everyone who believes (Rom. 10:4; Eph. 2:15), and those who are to belong to God and live for him must first die to the law in Christ and through his body (on the cross) (Rom. 7:4, 6; Gal. 2:18). Here a distinction must clearly be made, therefore, between law and law, between the law as it functions before and outside Christ and the law whose requirement is fulfilled in those who walk after the Spirit. In the antithesis with Judaism Paul clearly has to do with this "first" law, and he regards the whole Old Testament legal dispensation from this point of view. Hence, for example, his pronouncement that "the law is not of faith" but it is doing that advances (Gal. 3:12); that the promise is obtained "not by means of the law," but of the righteousness of faith (Rom. 4:13); indeed, that if those who live from the law were able to become heirs, faith is made void and the promise deprived of its power (Rom. 4:14). In all these pronouncements Paul thus detaches the law from faith, he speaks of the law not as the rule of the new life or of the relationship of election entered into by God with Israel, but of the law as it functioned in the hardening that has come upon Israel (2 Cor. 3:14; Rom. 11:7ff.).

(4) It has indeed been remarked against this interpretation that if in his conflict with Judaism Paul had started from the law as it functioned in Judaism, he would in essence have taken his point of departure in a false position. And is it then, for example, able to be reconciled with the fact that Paul in Romans 10:5 lets Moses himself appear as the chief witness for this conception ("the man who does [these things] shall live by them")? Would Paul, in other words, have cited Leviticus 18:5 in support of a false prophecy?[154] Thinking further in this direction, one can ask whether Paul, when he posits the negative effect of the law as the intention of the law and of the Lawgiver (Gal. 3:19; Rom. 5:20; see the preceding section), does not then base this intention on a wrong use of the law. In these questions we are faced with the heart of the matter. Two things are surely to be distinguished here.

(5) In the first place, the identification by Paul of the concept of law with that of the Jewish-synagogical nomism does not mean that

---

153. See below, Section 46.
154. Cf. A. J. Bandstra, *The Law and the Elements of the World*, p. 101.

Paul attributed this conception to Moses. Paul sometimes seems to appeal to Moses for this conception, for example, when he says, in Romans 10:5, that Moses defines the righteousness of the law thus: "the man who does [these things] shall live thereby" (cf. Gal. 3:12). But this is no more than appearance. For this cannot mean that Moses himself was the promoter of this righteousness by the law. Without regard to the places where Paul appeals for the opposite principle (the righteousness by faith) to "the law" (of Moses) — for which see above — such a view is contradicted by the verse that follows Romans 10:5, in which the righteousness that is by faith is defined with a pronouncement likewise derived from Moses. Now, some have wished to resolve this in such a way that Moses himself, as it were, is said to have posited two possibilities, of which the first (righteousness by the law) was intended by him as a way impossible for the sinner.[155] But not only is such certainly not the intention of Moses in Leviticus 18:5 — who after all sets "this do and thou shalt live" as the rule of the covenant — but it also does not appear from the context that Paul wishes here to attribute this conception to Moses (namely, that the law cannot be fulfilled by sinful man). What Paul means to say is this, that he who strives after the righteousness that is by the law is then bound to the word of Moses, that is, to do what the law demands. Likewise the wrong use of the law, to be zealous for the law without understanding, finds in the law itself the standard to which, if it is to have a chance of success, it must measure up. In that sense it can be said that Moses (or the law itself) "defines" the righteousness that is of the law. This is not an appeal to Moses in support of "a false position," but a binding of this position to its own point of departure: he who seeks righteousness in the law faces, as appears from the law itself, the requirement of doing (cf. Gal. 3:10, 12).[156]

(6) If one reaches no other conclusion than this, that when Paul speaks of "the law" and "the righteousness which is by the law" he is reasoning from the Jewish-synagogical nomism and not from the intention of Moses himself, it is another matter — and this in the second place — when, starting from this presupposition, Paul now designates the way of the works of the law as a way of death. For with regard to the latter Paul finds many points of contact in the Old Testament itself. For in the Old Testament the law is indeed not, as with the later Jews,

---

155. So Greijdanus, *Rom.*, II, pp. 453ff.

156. Bandstra himself in the interpretation of Rom. 10:5 goes altogether his own way in understanding by "the man who does [these things]" Christ and by taking the pronouncement of Rom. 10:4 in that sense as well, according to which Christ is the end of the law (*The Law*, p. 104). Yet in this way not only would Paul have ascribed an idea to Moses that lies entirely outside the sphere of thought of Lev. 18, but he would also have given expression to this (surely very startling) explanation of Lev. 18:5 in such an enshrouded fashion that hardly anyone up to the present time has been able to understand his meaning. Moreover, in this way what remains of the antithesis between righteousness by the law and righteousness by faith (which Paul evidently wishes to express here), if the first clause (v. 5) were intended in a positive sense, namely, of the righteousness of Christ; to say nothing then of the inapplicability of this interpretation to Gal. 3:12 (where the qualification *anthrōpos* is wanting)?

placed under the viewpoint of the righteousness to be established by man himself (Rom. 10:3), but under that of the divine covenant of grace. But this does not alter the fact that in the Old Testament not only was the promulgation of the law already encircled with a threat and curse, but also that, particularly in the prophetic books, the unbridgeable chasm between the demand of God and the actual conduct of Israel is pointed out with increasing sharpness; and over against that the New Covenant is then proclaimed in which the Spirit will come in place of the law of the tables of stone to write the law of God in the hearts of men (Jer. 31:31; cf. Ezek. 11:19ff.; Isa. 59:21). That the law thus has a condemning and killing significance, indeed that no other life is possible out of this death than through God's own life-giving work, is not for the first time put in this way by Paul, on the ground of the misuse of the law by later Judaism, but is the shadow that in the Old Testament accompanies the law from the very beginning, increasingly takes away the light of the Old Covenant, and only disappears in the announcement of the New Covenant.[157]

For this reason the objection that Paul based his negative preaching of the law on a one-sided, nomistic conception of the law and thereby became the victim of distorted perspective is to be rejected emphatically even on the ground of the Old Testament. Paul does indeed see the promulgation of the law from the outset under the viewpoint of the shadows that accompany the law (cf. Gal. 3:10). He does not deny, however, that the law has been given unto life, nor that it was attended with the splendor of the divine glory, a proof of Israel's election as the holy people of God (2 Cor. 3:7). But for Israel this glory was too strong. It could not come up to the holiness of the people of God and, in the hardening of its understanding, has no longer been able to discover that in order thus to have intercourse with God it must live from his grace and not by its own works (2 Cor. 3:12ff.; cf. 1 Cor. 10:1ff.). For this reason the administration of the law that took place under the radiance of the divine glory became an administration of death and condemnation. In all this Paul does not place himself outside the Old Testament, but he harks back again and again precisely to the Old Testament, and he stands entirely in the tradition of Old Testament historiography and prophecy. When later Judaism constantly appealed to the privilege that Israel as the people of God had received in the law, Paul does not contradict this, but rather confirms it in a variety of ways (Rom. 3:1ff.; 9:4). But his opposition is directed against the fact that this grace-privilege had come to function as a ground for carnal boasting and as a means for Israel to acquire righteousness before God for itself. It is against this that he marshals Israel's own history and prophecy in many different ways, so that he can declare that the law, instead of making alive, has become death for Israel, and

---

157. In more recent Old Testament studies on this subject this point is clearly elucidated. Cf., e.g., W. Zimmerli, "Das Gesetz im Alten Testament," *TLZ*, 1960, cols. 481ff.; G. Von Rad, *Theology of the Old Testament*, II, ET 1965, pp. 388ff. On this see also H. Berkhof, "Gesetz und Evangelium," in *Festschrift für Heinrich Vogel*, 1962, pp. 127ff.

thus in the whole of the economy of God with his people it has had to fulfill the function of the increase of sin and disciplinarian unto Christ. Only a superficial interpretation of the Pauline doctrine of the law and of the Old Testament can see an antithesis between these two. In taking into consideration the real and deepest motifs both of Paul's pronouncements on the law and of the Old Testament revelation of God, one will not be permitted to ascertain a contradiction here, but rather profound harmony; one will as well be able to understand that Paul knows himself to be altogether consistent with the law and the prophets when, in his antithesis with Judaism, he now comes to his great positive formulation of the gospel: that of the revelation of the righteousness of God by faith without the works of the law (Rom. 1:17; 3:21).

IV

THE REVELATION OF THE RIGHTEOUSNESS OF GOD

SECTION 26. INTRODUCTION

When we consider further the content of Paul's gospel according to its different facets, we come into contact with a multiplicity of viewpoints and motifs, the unity and mutual relationships of which are not clear at first glance.[1] Just as in the preceding chapter we encountered a complex mass of causes and manifestations of the state of man and the world fallen into sin and death, even so, though in a much more glorious and inclusive sense — for redemption is more than restoration from the misery brought about by sin — the unfolding of the redemptive significance of Christ's death and resurrection, the fundamental motif of Paul's gospel, is like a multi-colored spectrum. It enters into the lostness of man and the world in all its dimensions and levels. It has reference to man's guilt and punishability in the divine judgment; to his inner discord and impotence; to his being encircled by a world that is turned away and alienated from God, his being threatened by powers that are inimical to God. But it speaks as well of the liberation of this world itself, of the redemption of the whole of the groaning creation, of the reconciliation of all things in heaven and on earth, already now and in the great future. From the viewpoint of the fullness of Christ it shows the church its place and task in the world that surrounds it and in the continuation of history, and bends its eye toward the future by holding out to it the prospect of the coming of the Lord, the resurrection of the dead, and the renewal of all things. Henceforth everything is placed in the redeeming light of Christ's death and resurrection, and all the dimensions of salvation become known, the breadth and length and height and depth, which are to be comprehended with all the saints, a knowledge of the love of Christ that surpasses understanding (Eph. 3:18, 19; cf. Rom. 8:38, 39).

We take our point of departure in those ideas in the Pauline doctrine of redemption which define the new relationship in which God in Christ has placed man to himself; in connection with which one is to think above all of justification and reconciliation. In so doing we do not set out in the footprints of those who hold the view that the Pauline eschatology bears a basically anthropological character and is oriented to the individual relationship of man to God.[2] It is true, to be

---

1. See H. Hofer, *Die Rechtfertigungsverkündigung des Paulus nach der neueren Forschung*, 1940, pp. 17ff.
2. For this conception (of Bultmann, *et al.*) see above, pp. 50, 89ff.

sure, that Paul's gospel, just as that of the entire New Testament, comes to a head in the religious relationship of man to God and in that which results from it. The gospel exists, so we may say, for this purpose, to summon man to faith and conversion, not to a religious *gnosis* that informs him concerning the secrets of the universe and of the invisible world inaccessible to him. This does not alter the fact, however — and in this respect, too, Paul's gospel does not differ from that of Jesus and from the apostolic tradition emanating from him — that the whole of man's relationship to God, even in its most individual aspects, is to be understood within the framework of God's all-embracing redemptive work in Christ and derives from that its new and peculiar character. What is typical of Paul's preaching is not that he comes to interpret and translate the original eschatological message contained in such concepts as justification and reconciliation, but rather, conversely, that these concepts — which in themselves were not new — now receive their background and their new content out of the realization of the divine plan of redemption embracing man and the world, the revelation of the mystery. For this reason what is said now concerning the relationship of God and man is not to be understood without all these aspects being involved together in the summons of the gospel which teaches man to understand himself in a new way, with respect to God as well as to the world and history surrounding him. This means therefore that in all that will now have to occupy our attention, and in connection with the point of departure just mentioned, we shall have to keep constantly in view the basic eschatological and christological structures of Paul's preaching.

If in treating this new relationship to God proclaimed in the gospel we allow justification to take precedence, some explanation for this is not superfluous.[3] One can object that this order is in a certain sense arbitrary. It does indeed form the starting point and to a certain extent[4] the theme of the very important epistles to the Galatians and the Romans. But these epistles are governed by a definite interest and a definite antithesis, namely, by the relationship of the gospel and the Jewish-synagogical doctrine of redemption. In other epistles other points of view are dominant, and for that reason the one gospel of Christ has another point and application: in the epistles to the Corinthians it is confrontation with the Greek *gnosis*, in those to the Thessalonians questions concerning the future, in that to the Colossians speculation about the cosmic powers, while in Ephesians the place and significance of Christ as Head of the church and Head of the world are central. One can ask himself, therefore, whether the traditional order of treatment which begins with the doctrine of justification is not one-sided and does not involve even the danger of a certain narrowing of viewpoint.

A further question is whether, if one takes his point of departure in this new definition of man's relationship to God, he cannot better begin with reconciliation. This concept, as we shall see still further, is

---

3. See also the comprehensive work of H. D. Wendland, *Die Mitte der paulinischen Botschaft*, 1935.
4. On this point see my *Rom.*, pp. 32ff.

wider in scope than that of justification, for the reason that it is not restricted, as is justification, to the relationship of man to God, but draws the whole of creation, "all things," into its range of vision.

These objections are certainly not without significance. If we nevertheless follow the traditional order of treatment, we do so for more than one reason. First, already in Chapter II we attempted to indicate the broad fundamental structure of Paul's doctrine of salvation, so that the otherwise not illusory danger of a narrowing of viewpoint need no longer be feared. Second, the entire unfolding of the salvation that has appeared in Christ cannot be understood by those to whom the gospel is directed otherwise than by faith; that is to say, out of the new relationship in which God wills to place man to himself. This does not mean that the whole content of the gospel may be said to find its point of concentration in this relationship; it does mean that it can only be understood by the believer out of this relationship.

And third, so far as the relationship of justification and reconciliation is concerned, although this relationship is capable of being expressed in more than one way[5] and one certainly cannot speak here of a hierarchical priority of justification with respect to reconciliation, yet giving justification first place does have this not inconsiderable advantage, that in his most systematic epistle, that to the Romans, Paul himself takes his point of departure in "the revelation of the righteousness of God" for his exposition of the whole of the gospel; while at the same time we find here the best connection with the Pauline doctrine of sin as that has been discussed in the preceding chapter, which, as we have seen, is given its most radical and most characteristic development in the relation of sin and law.

SECTION 27. THE ESCHATOLOGICAL CHARACTER OF JUSTIFICATION

For the proper understanding of the great theme of justification by faith it is necessary above all to obtain an insight into the manner in which it is connected with the basic eschatological-christological structure of Paul's preaching pointed out in Chapter II and, as it were, how it issues forth organically from that preaching. Because this background has frequently been lost sight of, for a long time this theme was ascribed too predominating a significance in the whole of Paul's proclamation of salvation and everything else was subordinated to it; at a later period others have, leading to a still greater dislocation of the organic relationships in Paul's doctrine, thrust this theme entirely into the background, in the interest of what was then regarded as the mystical-ethical main line.[6] The inadequacy of the one as well as the other of these two ways of judging Paul's preaching can be recognized easily when we endeavor to understand Paul's doctrine of justification primarily in the light of the

---

5. See below, pp. 182ff.
6. See above, Section 3.

general redemptive-historical or eschatological character of his preaching.

There is a clear indication of this even in the manner in which this theme twice comes up for discussion in the Epistle to the Romans:

> For therein [namely, in the gospel] is revealed [the] righteousness of God from faith unto faith (Rom. 1:17).
> Now, however, apart from the law [the] righteousness of God has been revealed, of which the law and the prophets bear witness (Rom. 3:21).

Even the opening words of Romans 3:21 — "now, however" — speak of the time of salvation that has been inaugurated with Christ's advent. It is the "now" of the fulfillment and realization of what has been promised and foretold,[7] as is expressly indicated by the words: "of which the law and the prophets bear witness." What is most characteristic of these pronouncements, however, is the repeated mention of the revelation of the righteousness of God. Intended here is not only a new doctrine or a new experience, but the appearing of that which had been determined in the counsel of God with respect to the fullness of the time. We have to do here with a variation of the expression, so characteristic for the basic eschatological structure of Paul's preaching,[8] "the revelation of the mystery," or "the revelation of Christ." To that revelation, as eschatological event, the appearing, the gift of the righteousness of God, now also belongs.[9] To put it in another way: Paul's doctrine of justification is a definite interpretation and application of his eschatology.[10] Exactly the same thing is expressed in Galatians 3:23 with the words: "the revelation of faith." Faith, as is clearly apparent in Romans 1:17; 3:21, is most closely connected with righteousness, as the means by which righteousness is obtained. What is meant by this "revelation" of faith is not only a certain knowledge or doctrine concerning faith, but the dawning of the time of salvation, in which faith takes the place of the law, for which reason "the coming[11] of faith" is also spoken of in the context of Galatians 3:21.

Already through this presentation of the gospel of righteousness by faith as "the revelation" of the righteousness of God and "the revelation" of faith, it becomes very clear how much this theme participates in and forms a consequence of the redemptive-historical character of Paul's preaching. All this becomes still more evident when we consider more carefully the concept "righteousness of God."

---

7. For the redemptive-historical significance of *nyni de* in Rom. 3:21 see Stählin, *TDNT*, IV, pp. 1109f., n. 33, 1117, n. 70.

8. Cf. above, Section 7.

9. See, e.g., Oepke, *TDNT*, III, p. 583, *s.v. apokalyptō:* "The disclosure of this righteousness is also an eschatological event." The perfect *pephanerōtai*, used absolutely in 3:21, indicates this still more clearly; but "therein [i.e., in the gospel] is revealed" in 1:17 is to be understood in the same sense. The gospel is thereby not only the means by which this eschatological event is noetically communicated, but it shares in this eschatological character of "revelation"; see also J. T. Bakker, *Eschatologische Prediking bij Luther*, 1964.

10. Cf. Wendland, *Die Mitte der paulinischen Botschaft*, p. 25: "The doctrine of justification is the explanation and application of this Pauline eschatology to the status of man before God."

11. For this also see below, pp. 174, 198.

Unfortunately, there is a profound difference of opinion among the interpreters of Paul as to the significance of this combination, a difference that has continued up to the present time.[12] For by this righteousness of God some understand an attribute or an activity of God[13] and take the words, that the righteousness of God is now (or has been) revealed, in this way, that God has now revealed himself as the Righteous One, or in his (saving) righteousness. Others see in the righteousness of God the denotation of that which man must have in order to be able to stand in the divine judgment. The revelation of the righteousness of God then intends to say that the time of salvation that has dawned with Christ and the gospel for man brings along with it righteousness, understood in this sense, before God[14] (or from God[15]). We consider it established[16] that the words in Romans 1:17 and 3:21 are intended in this latter sense; that "righteousness" here is therefore not a divine but a human quality and that the righteousness "of God" further defines that quality as righteousness that can stand before God (cf. Rom. 2:13;[17] 3:20),[18] which is valid in his judgment, the righteousness that God attributes to man as opposed to his own righteousness (Rom. 10:3), as it is also called in Philippians 3:9: "not having my righteousness, which is of the law, but that which is through faith in Christ, the righteousness which is from God *(tēn ek Theou dikaiosynēn)*, upon the foundation of faith."

It is apparent from this[19] explanation that in the concept "righteousness of God" we have to do with a forensic category and indeed in the eschatological sense of the word: it is a matter of what man requires in order to go free in the divine judgment. "Righteousness" can for this reason be used as the antithesis of "condemnation" (2 Cor. 3:9). In the same sense the verb "to justify" is employed as the divine verdict that means the opposite of the divine condemnation in the judgment (Rom. 2:12, 13; cf. Rom. 5:16, 18) and "the just before [i.e., in the judgment of] God" can be spoken of (Rom. 2:13) in contrast with "sinners" (understood in a forensic sense; Rom. 5:19).

On the ground of all this the specific significance of the great Pauline theme of the revelation of the righteousness of God may become entirely clear to us: it says nothing less than that what man requires in order to go free in the judgment of God and to know himself discharged

---

12. See especially A. Oepke, "[*DIKAIOSYNĒ THEOU*] bei Paulus in neuer Beleuchtung," *TLZ*, May 1953, cols. 257ff.

13. The genitive *Theou* is then taken as a subjective or possessive genitive.

14. Genitive of relationship.

15. Genitive of source *(gen. auctoris)*.

16. See the detailed discussion of this question in my *Rom.*, pp. 35-38.

17. *Para tō Theō.*

18. *Enōpion autou.*

19. For the eschatological development of the interpretation that we have rejected, see especially C. H. Dodd, *Romans*, pp. 9ff., and his *The Bible and the Greeks*, 1936, pp. 57ff.; for the later discussion, E. Käsemann, "The Righteousness of God in Paul," in *New Testament Questions of Today*, pp. 168ff.; C. Müller, *Gottes Gerechtigkeit und Gottes Volk*, 1964; P. Stuhlmacher, *Gerechtigkeit Gottes bei Paulus*, 1965; *against*, Bultmann, "[*DIKAIOSYNĒ THEOU*]," *Journal of Biblical Literature*, LXXXIII, 1964, pp. 12-16.

from the divine sentence is not only a matter of the great future which is still to be awaited, but has been revealed with the advent of Christ and in the gospel; as a present reality and as a redemptive gift of God it has been given, attributed, communicated in the gospel to everyone who believes (cf. Phil. 3:9; Rom. 5:1; 9:30; 1 Cor. 6:11). And all this in contradistinction to "the revelation of the divine wrath," which even now is visible to every eye in those who reject the knowledge of God, and will fall on those who suppose themselves able in the way of the works of the law to obtain righteousness and eternal life (Rom. 1:18-3:29).[20]

In order to grasp still better the profoundly radical significance of the revelation of the righteousness thus proclaimed and to understand fully the peculiar pregnance of the words in which it is expressed,[21] it is necessary here again to point to the historical background from which it emerges in the epistles of Paul, that of the Jewish-synagogical scheme of redemption.

Terminologically the whole expression "revelation of the righteousness of God" is derived from Judaism, inasmuch as here, too, the concept "just" or "justice" was understood in close connection with the judicial pronouncement in the divine judgment.[22] It is typical of this Jewish background that as soon as the concept "to justify" comes into the hands of the Greek interpreters its forensic meaning is no longer perceived, and they manage to attach an exclusively ethical significance to it.[23] Materially, however, there is an absolute antithesis between the Pauline and the synagogical doctrine of justification. And this comes to a head precisely at this revelation of the righteousness of God. Whereas for Judaism it was an incontrovertible matter that this righteousness, as the crucial, decisive factor in the judicial declaration of God, was not to be spoken of other than in a future-eschatological sense, Paul proclaims this righteousness as a present reality already realized in Christ.

We have to do here with the same antithesis that Jesus' preaching of the gospel evokes when in the presence of the scribes he declares that the Son of Man has authority on earth, i.e., here and now, to forgive sins (Matt. 9:6 and the parallel passages).[24] For Judaism the essence of divine justification lay in that it would take place in the future and in the heavenly judgment; that the whole of life consisted precisely in preparation for this, and that therefore it would be blasphemy to wish to anticipate this judgment which belongs only to God (cf. Luke 7:48-50). Looked at from this point of view justification is a matter still hidden with God, about which no one can obtain certainty any earlier than in the great judgment of God itself. The lack of assurance of salvation can for this reason be termed a prominent characteristic of the Old Jewish religion.[25]

---

20. For this "revelation of the wrath of God," see above, Section 18.

21. See also above, Section 21.

22. Cf. Strack-Billerbeck, III, p. 163; Schrenk, *TDNT*, II, pp. 212ff.; Oepke, *TLZ*, cols. 257ff.

23. See, e.g., Dodd, *The Bible and the Greeks*, p. 58.

24. See my *The Coming of the Kingdom*, ET 1962, pp. 73, 211ff.

25. Cf., e.g., Strack-Billerbeck, III, pp. 218ff.; IV, 1, pp. 3-12; W. Bousset,

Over against this Paul now preaches the revelation of this acquitting verdict of God and of the impunity (righteousness) founded on it for everyone who believes; a righteousness which may be spoken of no longer in terms of waiting and uncertainty, but rather in terms of a matter that has been accomplished and in the certainty of faith (Rom. 5:1; 8:31-34, 38); which already contains within itself the certainty of the entire eschatological salvation (Rom. 5:6-11). Here the christological-eschatological fulfillment character of Paul's preaching is developed in such a reversal of the Jewish doctrine of redemption that one is able to say that a more fundamental antithesis is inconceivable. It cannot be urged against it that there are also voices to be heard in Judaism that based their hope for the future not only on their own merit, but also on God's forgiveness and mercy.[26] For whatever may further be said of that, the difference in principle consists not only in the fact that Paul directs the gaze of the man who knows himself to be a sinner to the possibility of forgiveness[27] and to the part of mercy in the coming judgment, but that he speaks of the judicial verdict itself as a matter that has already been settled, the proclamation of which in the gospel is a power of God for everyone who believes.[28]

It is not in conflict with this present (in principle) character of the righteousness proclaimed in the gospel that Paul continues to speak of it in a future sense. In any case[29] this occurs in such a passage as Galatians 5:5: "for through the Spirit, by faith, we wait for the hope of

---

Die Religion des Judentums im späthellenistischen Zeitalter, 3rd ed., 1926, p. 392; also Rengstorf, *TDNT,* II, pp. 523ff., *s.v. elpis;* Schniewind/Friedrich, *TDNT,* II, p. 579, *s.v. epangellō.*

26. See, e.g., E. Sjöberg, *Gott und die Sünder im palästinischen Judentum,* 1939, pp. 148ff.; and Schoeps, *Paul,* p. 206.

27. It has often been observed that in his epistles Paul makes very little use of the expression *aphesis tōn hamartiōn,* which plays such a great part elsewhere in the primitive Christian preaching. He speaks of it only in Rom. 4:7 (a quotation), and later in Eph. 1:7; Col. 1:14. That this description, at least where it is a matter of the antithesis with Judaism, is entirely hidden behind that of justification, righteousness, etc., is certainly to be explained by the fact that in these last words the character of the gospel as fulfillment is given so much more pregnant expression.

28. For the use of the concept righteousness in the Qumran literature and the difference between the element of the mercy of God that plays a role in it and Paul's doctrine of justification, see the careful analysis by P. Benoit, "Qumrân et le Nouveau Testament," *NTS,* 1961, pp. 292ff. He concludes, "For Paul the eschatological judgment has already occurred in Christ, and that changes everything.... He is already 'justified' by the past act of the cross and baptism (1 Cor. 6:11; Rom. 3:24; vv. 1, 9, etc.). But it is remarkable that the sinner never appears 'justified' in Qumran" (*ibid.,* p. 294).

29. The question as to the extent to which the future tenses of Rom. 3:20; 5:19, *et al.* are to be taken as real or as gnomic or logical future is variously judged. With regard to Rom. 5:19, too, there is doubt whether what is intended is not already the presence of salvation that has commenced with Christ's advent. On the other side the timeless presents, as in Gal. 2:16; 3:11; 5:4, can just as well be understood of the future as of the present. See the detailed exegesis of Bultmann, *Theology,* I, p. 274. Against that Wendland understands Rom. 3:20, 30; 5:19 in the future-eschatological sense (*Die Mitte der paulinischen Botschaft,* p. 25; cf. Schrenk, *TDNT,* II, p. 207). It is incontrovertible, however, that righteousness is spoken of both in a real present and in a real future sense.

righteousness."[30] The manner in which this future righteousness is here defined, namely, as the content of the hope awakened by the Spirit which is obtained by faith, makes it clear, however, that this future righteousness is not another than that which has already been revealed. It is the same thing, but one can speak of it both in a present and in a future sense. Just as the adoption of sons,[31] righteousness can be represented as a benefit already obtained as well as still to be expected. But nothing is hereby detracted from its character of fulfillment and from the assurance of salvation given in it. What is true of all that has been given in Christ thus applies to justification, that we are not dealing here with a matter that has been concluded, which has been settled, and which we should thus be able to leave "behind us." The revelation of the righteousness of God in the gospel is precisely a power of God unto salvation (Rom. 1:17), which accompanies the believer as a constantly fresh and relevant thing. It binds him to Christ and his communion and so makes him by the Spirit to wait for the hope of righteousness. With regard to the present as well as the future the situation is thus different in principle for the believer from what it is for the man who lives out of legalistic religiousness. And here is the connection, to be discussed still further,[32] between this certainty of salvation and the knowledge of the coming judgment, in which it is not the hearers but the doers of the law who are to be justified before God.

SECTION 28. THE RIGHTEOUSNESS OF GOD IN CHRIST

Just as it is true of the entire revelation of the mystery that it has Christ for its content, so also the revelation of the righteousness of God, as the ground for acquittal in the divine judgment, takes place in Christ. And just as the entire Pauline gospel has its center in the death and resurrection of Christ, so also the gospel of justification by faith.

This revelation of the righteousness of God is related to the death and resurrection of Christ in all sorts of ways. Romans 3:21-31, where once again the basic eschatological-christological structure of Paul's gospel comes clearly to the fore, is very central and very pointed in the further exposition of this theme. Verses 24ff. are especially important here:

> ... being justified by his [God's] grace through the redemption that is in Christ Jesus, whom God set forth as a means of propitiation, through faith in his blood, as a demonstration of his righteousness because he had passed over the sins which had been committed previously under the forbearance of God; for the showing of his righteousness in the present time, that he might himself be just, and might justify him who has faith in Jesus.

What is of particular importance for us in this context is that

---

30. *Elpida dikaiosynēs;* objective genitive or genitive of apposition.
31. See below, Section 35.
32. See below, Section 31.

justification is founded here on the death of Christ. Moreover, God's righteousness is spoken of in a differentiating sense. God has made Christ a means of propitiation in his death, and in this way manifested his justice in his death. By this nothing other can be understood than that God has shown the adjudicating power of his righteousness in Christ, by giving him for others as a means of propitiation in death. The idea is then joined to this that God till this moment had not meted out the punishment on the sins of men that was due them, but passed over them in his forbearance, i.e., in his withholding of the judgment. Now, "in the present time," God has abandoned this attitude of waiting, however, and shown his vindicating righteousness, in the death of Jesus. Here again the apostle clearly elucidates the redemptive-historical significance of Christ's death, in the sense that the divine judgment on the sins of the world has, as it were, been drawn together in Christ's death, and in this way the *eschaton* has become present time. Just as Christ's resurrection is the breaking through of the new creation (2 Cor. 5; see above, pp. 53ff.), so the final judgment of God has become manifest in his death. God has in this way justified himself toward the world in him and at the same time made known, revealed, the righteousness that is necessary in order that those who have faith in Jesus might stand in the judgment of God. For just as the abandonment of Christ in death took place because of our sins, so his resurrection occurred for the sake of our justification (Rom. 4:25). Just as Christ's death was a demonstration of God's righteous judgment on the sin of the world, visited on him as the means of propitiation, so his resurrection was the demonstration and proof of the acquitting righteousness of God, revelation thus of righteousness in the sense of Romans 1:17; 3:21.

That the expression "the righteousness of God" is used here (in 3:21ff.) in a twofold sense (first, in vv. 21, 22, as a forensic quality conferred on man by God, which makes him go free; then, in vv. 25, 26, as the vindicatory righteousness of God[33]) cannot obscure the unmistakable meaning of this passage. It is indeed elucidated and corroborated in various ways by other pronouncements. Thus, in 5:9, where there is mention of "being now justified by his [Christ's] blood," which is entirely in harmony with 3:25. No less in 5:18, 19, where Christ's one act of righteousness that led to justification issuing in life is set over against the one sin of Adam that led to condemnation, and the justifying obedience of Christ is set over against the disobedience of Adam that constituted men guilty. Here, too, with the "act of righteousness" and "obedience" of Christ we are concerned with his death (cf. 5:8, 9). But Christ's death is not considered here from the viewpoint of God's retributive righteousness, but from that of Christ's voluntary and perfect obedience. Furthermore, reference may be made to Galatians 2:21, where the same connection between Christ's death and justification by faith is indicated indirectly: "for if righteousness is from the law, then Christ died to no purpose." And how much the vindicatory and retributive righteousness of God is effected in Christ's death and how this can

---

33. See also Benoit, *NTS*, 1961, p. 295: "Paul combines these two aspects admirably."

therefore hold as the only ground for the righteousness that is by faith appears very clearly from Galatians 3:13, where it is said that Christ, by suffering himself to be crucified for us, has become a curse for us, so that the blessing of Abraham might be communicated to the gentiles by faith and not on the ground of works. We find the same thought in Romans 8:3, where it is said that God "has condemned sin in the flesh" of his Son. All this is summarized finally in such pronouncements as 2 Corinthians 5:21: God has made Christ, who knew no sin, to be sin for us, that we should become the righteousness of God in him. The forensic idea is certainly very pronounced here. God not only treats the sinless Christ as though he were a sinner, but he makes him (by delivering him up to the death on the cross) to be sin in the forensic sense of the word. And it is in that sense that those who are in Christ through faith become righteous, indeed, become "the righteousness of God," that is, may identify themselves with that which is acquitted in the judgment of God. It is this connection between Christ's death and the justifying, acquitting judgment of God on those who belong to Christ which Paul expresses in 1 Corinthians 1:30: "From God," that is to say, from the power of his saving activity, "are we in Christ Jesus, who was made unto us . . . righteousness."

The significance of this abundant testimony is unmistakable: In Christ's death God has sat in judgment, has judged sin, and in this way he has caused his eschatological judgment to be revealed in the present time. But for those who are in Christ, he has therefore become righteousness, and the content of the gospel of the death and resurrection of Christ can be defined as the revelation of the righteousness of God for everyone who believes.

The question quite naturally arises as to the way in which Christ's death and resurrection can have justifying, acquitting power for everyone who believes. We face here again[34] the relationship of the "Christ-for-us" and the "we-in-Christ," two conceptions that one cannot separate, although they represent two different thoughts. On the one hand, it is clear that Christ's death and resurrection are considered in their own "objective" significance, without his people as yet being identified with this death and resurrection. This is very clearly the case, for example, in Romans 3:25, where it is said that God has made Christ publicly[35] to be a means of propitiation in his blood. Thus the justifying power of Christ's death and resurrection is sought in the fact that Christ dies in behalf of and — one may in connection with the significance of the propitiatory sacrifice[36] also say — in the place of his own. It is not they who are delivered up. for their sins and raised for their justification, but Christ (Rom. 4:25). In the same way, in Christ's death it is not they, but he in their behalf who is made to be sin (2 Cor. 5:21), and he became a curse for them (Gal. 3:13). Here Christ's death is repeatedly considered "in itself," and those who are justified in Christ's death and

---

34. Cf. above, Section 10.

35. *Pro-etheto*. The *pro-* indicates the public character of it (cf. Gal. 3:1 and, for the thought, John 3:14).

36. On this see further below, Section 32.

resurrection are not involved as those who have jointly died and been raised in his death and resurrection, but as those in whose behalf and in whose stead this death and resurrection took place and thus signified justification for them.

On the other hand, the corporate idea is most closely bound up with this substitutionary one. Christ died for them not as an alien or as one who had been designated to that end from a larger circle, but as the Son of God who for that purpose had entered "in the flesh," that is, into their mode of existence qualified by the old aeon. In this way God condemned sin "in the flesh" (Rom. 8:3). In this justifying power of his death and resurrection Christ can therefore rank as the anti-type of the first Adam, and the one righteous act consisting in his obedient self-surrender in death was thus unto the justification of all who were comprehended in him as the second Adam (Rom. 5:18, 19). And therefore, in the same context in which he terms Christ's death the death of all, Paul is able to define the significance of Christ's having-been-made-sin for us in this way: that we should be the righteousness of God, i.e., in this corporate unity with him (2 Cor. 5:14, 21); and that Christ has become righteousness for those who from God are in him (1 Cor. 1:30).

All this can enable us in some measure to understand the meaning of these profound conceptions, "Christ-for-us" and "we-in-him," also in their relation to one another. Christ's death and resurrection, which occurred for our sins and unto our justification, could take place in our behalf and in our stead for the very reason that as the Son of God he entered into our mode of existence, and in that mode of existence God not only delivered him up "for us," but also made us to be "in him." It may perhaps be said that Paul, at least in the Epistle to the Romans, starts from the justifying power of Christ's death "for us" (Rom. 3:21-5:11), in order thereafter, beginning with 5:12ff., to ground still more deeply and to throw light on this redemptive significance in the corporate idea of we-in-him. In so doing, he does not pass "over" from the one "conception" to the other, as though for him the first represented merely the traditional and the second the real, the adequate, idea. Rather, both belong to the unbreakable subsistence of Paul's preaching, and for him they have become an indissoluble unity. It is also in this unity of the "Christ-for-us" and the "we-in-him" that the theme of the revelation of the righteousness of God by faith exhibits in a clear fashion the basic eschatological-christological structure of Paul's preaching. For Christ's death was the demonstration of the judging and justifying judgment of God in the eschatological sense of the word because the old aeon and the old man were judged in him, and justification unto life and the new creation came to light in him as the second Adam. And the justifying power of his death and resurrection could for this reason benefit his own, because he as the second Adam was their Representative and they were in him. In that sense the foundation for the doctrine of justification, too, lies in the corporate unity of Christ and his own.[37]

---

37. Cf. Calvin on this relationship in A. J. Venter, *Analities of Sinteties?*

SECTION 29. RIGHTEOUSNESS BY FAITH,
WITHOUT THE LAW

No less distinctive than the present-eschatological character of the righteousness of God proclaimed by Paul and its revelation in Christ is furthermore that it is brought into the closest connection with faith: "for therein [in the gospel] the righteousness of God is revealed from faith unto faith" (Rom. 1:17).

Here again the apostolic preaching stands in the sharpest contrast to the Jewish-synagogical doctrine of redemption, and without this background the great Pauline dictum "by faith, without the law" is not to be understood. This antithesis is no less far reaching than that already discussed in Section 27; it not only means that the manner in which the righteousness of God is received is totally different in the gospel than in the theology of Judaism; but it also has the consequence that in Paul this righteousness itself acquires a content altogether its own and entirely divergent from Judaism, a difference that finds expression above all in the word "to impute" and which in later theology — likewise rooted in Christianity, in which this antithesis is continued — is denoted with the distinction between synthetic and analytic justification.[38]

When the apostle says in Romans 3:21, 28: "but now is the righteousness of God revealed without the law," the contrast with the Jewish conception of the righteousness from the law (Rom. 10:5; Gal. 3:21; Phil. 3:9), or through the law (en nomō; Phil. 3:6), or by means of the law (dia nomou; Gal. 2:21), is clearly indicated. Similarly, he speaks on the one hand of those who are "of the law" (Rom. 4:16; Gal. 3:10), or "under the law" (Rom. 6:15; Gal. 4:21), and on the other hand of those who are "of faith" (Rom. 3:26; 4:16, etc.). This "without," "of," or "by the law," respectively, is an abbreviated denotation of what is elsewhere called without, of, or by "the works of the law," or simply without, of, or by "works" (Rom. 3:20, 28; 4:2, 6; 9:12, 32; 11:6; Gal. 2:16, etc.). Paul uses an expression here that has its equivalent in the rabbinic maʿaśê miṣwôth or, what was still more current, simply in miṣwôth. The first means literally "works of the commandments," while the second, "commandments," has the pregnant meaning of the work resulting from the fulfillment of the commandments. For the fulfillment of the commandment is in this sense not to be conceived of as something abstract, but in the concrete sense of the work resulting from it, the individual fulfillment of the law as act.[39] It is these miṣwôth, these concrete fulfillments of the law, which according to the synagogue doctrine of redemption constitute the righteousness of man before God. By these fulfillments of the law and the merit resident in them the Israelite is able to store up a treasure[40] for himself in the day of judgment, on the ground

---

'N Analise van die dilemma insake de werklikheid van die regverdiging, 1959, pp. 122, 123.

    38. Ibid.

    39. See also Bertram, TDNT, II, pp. 645ff., s.v. ergon; Strack-Billerbeck, III, pp. 160ff.

    40. Thēsaurizein (cf. Rom. 2:5; Matt. 6:19ff.).

of which he is acquitted by God.[41] In this possession of the law as means
to righteousness and eternal life lies the great privilege of Israel. The
law was for the Jew, therefore, the real "substance of life."[42] The law
guarantees the Jews their position before God: it is for them the divine
privilege, in the midst of the universal sinfulness of man, to gain merit,
reward, righteousness before God. On that account the multiplicity of
separate commandments is a powerful instrument of redemption. "God
willed to allow Israel to earn merits, and therefore he gave them much
Torah and commandments, as it is said: In order to give Israel merits,
it pleased Yahweh to make the Torah big and strong."[43] And from
Hillel the word is handed down: "where there is much flesh, there are
many worms, where there are many treasures, many cares, where there
are many women, much superstition . . . and where there is much law,
there is much life."[44] It is on account of this attachment of value to the
multitude of ordinances, etc., as the means of gaining many merits, that
Paul reflects again and again on this complex, detailed character of
the law, on its character as "ordinance" (Rom. 7:8ff.; Eph. 2:15; Col.
2:14, et al.).

It is clear that with this view of "righteousness by the law," the
concept righteousness has another content for the Jews than for Paul.
It does indeed direct one's thoughts to the judgment seat of God, it
does move to be sure in the forensic sphere, but it is not a righteousness
conferred on man by God, but rather one ascertained, recognized, by
him. Justification, acquittal, accordingly has an analytical character
here; it rests on what man has and is, not on what he receives as righteousness from God, and this righteousness Paul is consequently able
to set over against the righteousness of or from God, as a righteousness
of man's own that he has himself realized or acquired (Rom. 10:3;
Phil. 3:9; Rom. 3:17, 21).

It is against this background that one must understand the different ways in which Paul further defines the righteousness of God
revealed in the gospel, namely, as a righteousness by faith, a righteousness freely given by God's grace, an imputed righteousness, an imputation of faith for righteousness, a justification of the ungodly (Rom.
3:22-24; 4:4, 5, et al.).

We shall have to return to the Pauline concept of faith in the
course of our investigation.[45] In the context in which it occurs here, as
faith in Jesus Christ (Rom. 3:22, 26, et al.), it receives its specific definition from the contrast with the works of the law, in the sense of the
word described above. For in all the pronouncements in which faith is
spoken of in connection with righteousness, justification, etc., it has the
significance of the means, instrument, way, foundation, channel by

---

41. For the references see Strack-Billerbeck, I, pp. 429ff.
42. See above, p. 132.
43. Thus a pronouncement of Rabbi Chananiah ben Akashiah (c. 150),
quoted by Gutbrod, *TDNT*, IV, p. 1058, *s.v. nomos;* cf. Strack-Billerbeck, IV, 2,
pp. 6ff.
44. In Bousset, *Die Religion des Judentums*, p. 119.
45. See below, Sections 40, 41.

which, along which, or on which man participates in the righteousness of God.[46] This finds its most pregnant expression in the seemingly pleonastic phrase "from faith unto faith" in Romans 1:17, that is, from A to Z a matter of faith and nothing else, righteousness *sola fide*.[47] The purpose of all these expressions, which nowhere make faith itself the ground or cause of justification, but only ascribe to it a mediating or instrumental significance, is none other than to designate the object of faith as the ground of justification. Faith does not justify because of that which it is in itself, but because of that to which it is directed, in which it rests. For this reason the exclusive emphasis with which faith is here placed over against works has a negative significance insofar as it speaks of man and his share in justification. Man is justified not on the ground of what he is himself or has or achieves, but precisely on the ground of that which he does not possess and which he in himself does not have at his disposal, but which he must receive, obtain, by faith. Faith here stands over against works as that which is absolutely receptive and dependent,[48] over against that which is productive, which is able to assert itself. The "law" of faith stands over against that of works, because it represents the principle, the order, by virtue of which all human claim and boasting are excluded (Rom. 3:27).

For this principle of faith Paul appeals especially to Habakkuk 2:4: "the just shall live by faith"[49] (Rom. 1:17; Gal. 3:11; cf. Heb. 10:38), and to the faith of Israel's progenitor Abraham (Rom. 4:2ff.). He can rightly do so because, notwithstanding all the differentiation that is involved in the application of these Old Testament words to that for which Paul is contending here,[50] faith in these Old Testament examples also consists in renouncing all human possibilities and trusting in the redeeming intervention of God. Such is expressed very plainly in the further characterization of this faith in Romans 4:17ff., where it is first said of Abraham that he believed in that God who gives life to the dead and calls into existence that which is not; a faith that did not weaken even in the face of his (Abraham's) own impotence and the barrenness of Sarah's womb (vv. 19, 20); in the same way this faith is defined in its

---

46. *Dia pisteōs* (Rom. 3:21, 22); *ek pisteōs* (1:17); *pistei* (Rom. 3:28); *epi tē pistei* (Phil. 3:9).

47. Cf. my *Rom.*, pp. 35, 38.

48. The functional significance of faith as human act in justification is of course not thereby denied. For this reason it is incorrect to characterize faith as an act of divine grace whereby justification is manifested, as Wendland wishes to do in *Die Mitte der paulinischen Botschaft*, p. 43; cf. also W. Michaelis, *Rechtfertigung aus Glauben bei Paulus, Festgabe für A. Deissmann*, 1927, pp. 121, 123, 136 ("in no way does human conduct need to be meant by *pistis*"). This conception is in the line of Deissmann, *St. Paul*, p. 147, who termed faith "the experience of justification." Lohmeyer, too, conceives of faith in the construction *dikaiosynē dia pisteōs* as "an act of God on the individual" (*Die Briefe der Philipper*, Meyer's Commentary, IX, 8th ed., 1930, p. 137, n. 2). But the absolutely gracious character of justification does not abrogate faith as an act of man. Cf. G. C. Berkouwer, *Faith and Justification*, pp. 176ff.; see further below, pp. 237ff.

49. That one should be obliged to translate: "the righteous by faith shall live," as argued, for example, in the commentaries of E. Kühl, H. Lietzmann, and A. Nygren, is to be decisively rejected; see my *Rom.*, pp. 39ff.

50. See below, pp. 176f.

present form in which it has come with Christ, as faith in him who raised Jesus Christ our Lord from the dead (v. 24). The distinctive feature of faith is here again that it stands over against "works,"[51] that is, over against any trusting in its own strength or possibilities, and that it utterly entrusts itself to the divine work of redemption.

For this reason in the antithesis of faith and works the term "faith" can be replaced by "the grace of God," with which then the true ground of justification is designated as opposed to works. This is voiced in all its fullness in Romans 3:22-24 where righteousness is first defined as the "righteousness of God through faith in Jesus Christ for all who believe," and then as "being justified freely by his [God's] grace" (cf. Rom. 5:15, 17). But it is apparent elsewhere that the real antithesis here lies between the way of faith and that of works, for in the first instance the grace of God is the supporting ground of justification, and in the second the merit of men. "You are severed from Christ, you who would be justified by the law; you have fallen away from grace" (Gal. 5:4). "If righteousness is through the law, the grace of God is nullified" (Gal. 2:21). And if there is even at the present time a remnant of Israel according to the election of grace, then this is "not upon the ground of works, inasmuch as grace would then no longer be grace" (Rom. 11:5ff.). Faith and works thus stand over against each other as grace and law (Rom. 6:14), and "by faith" is synonymous with "according to grace" (Rom. 4:16). For this reason "the order of faith" (Rom. 3:27) means not only (negatively) the exclusion of human boasting, but also (positively) the glory of God. When Abraham, although he observed that his own body was as good as dead, did not doubt through unbelief, but against hope believed in hope, then he gave glory to God (Rom. 4:18-22; cf. 2 Cor. 1:20).

Likewise in this indissoluble connection between — one can almost say, in this equation of — "by faith" and "by the grace of God," for a correct understanding of the character of both we shall have to take full account of the redemptive-historical content of Paul's doctrine of justification as grounded in the death and resurrection of Christ. For by "grace" one is not to understand a timeless attribute of God, which is "discovered" by faith in the way of a consciousness of guilt and awareness of the insufficiency of one's own works. It consists rather in the redeeming activity of God;[52] it is the grace that manifests itself in the redemption in Christ, whom God has set forth as a means of propitiation. Accordingly the antithesis between faith and works is not in the

---

51. How much Paul's appeal to Hab. 2:4; Gen. 15:6, et al., proceeds from an entirely different concept of faith from that of the Jewish religion of law, in which "faith" is simply subsumed under "works," has anew become clearly apparent from the interpretation of Hab. 2 in the pesher on Hab. (IQpH VII, 18ff.) found at Qumran, where the words "but the just shall live by his faith" are applied to all the doers of the Torah in the house of Judah, whom God will save "out of the house of the judgment" on the ground of their work and of their faith in (or faithfulness to) the teacher of righteousness. There is no question here of a faith in this teacher in the sense of the gospel. The reverse is the case; cf. also A. S. van der Woude, Bijbelcommentaren en Bijbelse verhalen, 1958, p. 43.

52. Cf. the section "Grace as Event" in Bultmann, Theology, I, pp. 288ff.

first place of the nature of the order of salvation *(ordo salutis)*, in the
sense that faith breaks through in a religious-psychological way, re-
nounces works, and learns to understand the gracious disposition of God
as the only ground of salvation. The exclusive significance Paul ascribes
to faith and to the grace of God in the doctrine of justification has above
all a redemptive-historical background.[53]

Faith represents a new mode of existence that has been given
with Christ's advent; it "comes" with the coming of the fullness of the
time (Gal. 3:23; 4:4), and with the manifestation of the grace of God
in the death and resurrection of Christ. Then it is disclosed that Christ
is the end of the law unto justification for everyone who believes (Rom.
10:4); likewise the insufficiency, indeed the folly, of trusting in the law
is understood, the consciousness of one's own imperfection and guilt is
born (Phil. 3:4-8), and the Old Testament evidences are discovered. It
is this sequence, and not the reverse, which is able to give us the proper
insight into the true nature both of faith and of the grace of God in
connection with justification.[54]

SECTION 30. THE JUSTIFICATION OF THE UNGODLY. IMPUTATION

Understood in this way, the relationship between justification, faith,
and the grace of God, in its contrast with justification from works, can
now enable us to understand the pronouncements that are perhaps
most characteristic for Paul's doctrine of justification, namely, those in
Romans 4:5, where he speaks of the justification of the ungodly and of
the imputation of faith for righteousness.

The antithesis with the righteousness that is of the law is nowhere
given voice more sharply than in this first expression. It is also out of
the question that by "to justify" here anything other or more is intended than what it means for Paul over and over again: acquittal in
the judgment of God. That the apostle here arrives at this paradoxical
pronouncement is, in the light of all the foregoing, no longer to be
considered strange or obscure in its meaning. Just as God has appointed
Christ to be an atoning sacrifice and has made him, who had known

---

53. This comes out too little in Schlatter's otherwise profound treatment
of the significance in Paul of faith *(Der Glaube im N.T.*, 4th ed., 1926), e.g., when
he writes: "The renunciation with which Paul came to the faith was in consequence
exclusively the simple act of repentance..." (p. 331), and "Because faith for Paul
included repentance in it, he described the beneficial act of Jesus... as the offer
of justification. Thus is the divine grace related to the consciousness of guilt, which
is pacified by it" (p. 334). With that a particular conception in the *ordo salutis*
takes the place of that which in Paul bears a fully redemptive-historical character.
Bultmann writes correctly that already the fact that the concepts "forgiveness of
sins" and "repentance" seldom occur shows that "the movement of will contained
in 'faith' is not primarily remorse and repentance" *(Theology*, I, p. 317; cf. his
article on *pisteuō* in *TDNT*, VI, p. 217).

54. Cf. above, Section 22, pp. 138ff. See there the discussion of the characteristic ideas "boast" and *skandalon*, which likewise occupy us here.

no sin, to be sin for us (cf. above, pp. 166ff.), so in Christ's death and resurrection there is acquittal, righteousness, for those for whom he was made to be sin, and they are thus the righteousness of God in him (2 Cor. 5:21). Every attempt to make certain reductions from the absolutely unanalytical character of this justification of the ungodly, whether by understanding justification as an anticipatory pronouncement on the ground of the subsequent ethical transformation of the ungodly, or by looking on the judicial aspect of the work of God in justification in unity with the ethical aspect of the work of God in sanctification, indwelling, etc.,[55] must be rejected as a violation or obscuring of the specific significance of Paul's pronouncement.[56] In the justification of the ungodly it is a matter of man as a sinner and not yet of his future inner renewal; it is also a matter solely of the forensic aspect of the divine work of redemption. On the other hand, one may not speak here of an "as if," as though it were only a question of a fictional matter, or of an "alien righteousness" in the sense of a bare relational reality.[57] For we may not detach this pronouncement from the whole redemptive-historical context of Paul's doctrine of justification. The justification of the ungodly is a justification "in Christ," that is to say, not only on the ground of his atoning death and resurrection, but also by virtue of the corporate inclusion in him of his own. That this involves more than only justification appears clearly enough from the whole of Paul's preaching, but even so cannot alter the fact that as Christ died for the ungodly at the time appointed for it (Rom. 5:6, 8), so the object of God's justification, from whatever viewpoint one chooses to regard it, is not the righteous, but the ungodly.[58]

It is in harmony with this, finally, that the "imputation pro-

---

55. For these conceptions, such as those of K. Holl, *et al.*, and of H. Küng, see, e.g., A. Venter, *Analities of Sinteties?*, pp. 1ff., 75ff.

56. See also Bultmann, *Theology*, I, p. 276: "Christ is 'our righteousness and our consecration' (I Cor. 1:30); and side by side with 'you were rightwised' stands 'you were consecrated' (I Cor. 6:11). But that is not expressed by the term 'righteousness' itself, and the relation between 'righteousness' and 'consecration'... is for the present unclear." This holds as well against E. Tobac, *Le problème de la justification dans Saint Paul*, 1941, who wishes to distinguish between the objective justification in Christ and the subjective by faith. He writes: "We can conclude that if righteousness and justification, objectively considered as effects of the death of Christ, do not presuppose but demand interior sanctification and the Spirit, they are, viewed subjectively as the characteristic of the believer, on the contrary, a fruit of the Spirit. Righteousness then no longer appears as a simple non-imputation of sin, but as an interior renewal, and it is this righteousness, effected by the Spirit of God, which God recognizes in justifying man" (p. 208). This last definition of justification is in conflict with the specific nature of the Pauline concept.

57. On this cf. Venter, *Analities of Sinteties?*, pp. 131ff.

58. Tobac, *Le problème de la justification*, pp. 204, 205, writes that "rigorously speaking this ungodly one who is justified by God is already not an ungodly one any longer: he is a believer united with Christ, a righteous one... whom God no longer considers separately from Christ, but whom he envisages uniquely as a member of the body of Christ." But in this way the corporate conception is employed in a manner that means a recasting of the Pauline concept of justification. In Paul himself this conception does not function in such a way, as may appear from the fact that in his suffering and death Christ does not represent the new, but the old man (Rom. 6:6).

nouncements" of Romans 4:3ff. are to be understood. Paul in this context derives the word "to impute" in the first place from the words of Genesis 15:6, that Abraham believed in God and that it was reckoned to him for righteousness. Starting now from the concept impute (in the otherwise not altogether transparent course of the argument of vv. 4 and 5[59]) he places faith and works over against each other with respect to this divine imputation as well. If a man has "worked" then imputation can only be spoken of "according to merit" and not "according to grace." If, however, there is no question of such works — as with Abraham — and "imputing" is nevertheless spoken of, then this imputation must bear the character of "grace"; in other words, faith is then reckoned for righteousness, just as in Psalm 32 the man is said to be blessed to whom the Lord does not impute sin.

On the meaning of these pronouncements, too — however one interprets the course of the argument — there can be no reasonable doubt. If faith is reckoned for righteousness, the ground for this imputation cannot be situated in that which man himself works or is, but just in that which not he, but God is able to effect and in which man can only receive a share through faith, that is, by grace. If it is thus said of faith that it is reckoned for righteousness, then faith is here again considered as the means or the instrument by which man participates in the divine grace; for this reason this imputation can also be equated with "the forgiveness of sins." Finally, the reckoning of faith for righteousness, too, cannot find its ground and origin in faith itself, but only in the grace that is embraced in faith, that is (when it is a question, as here, of acquittal in the judgment of God), Christ, who has become righteousness for his own.

The course of the argument of Romans 4:3-5 is so difficult to paraphrase because it is not entirely clear where the real starting point of the reasoning lies: whether in the fact that faith is not a "work" (thus Greijdanus, *Rom.*, I, pp. 220, 221; Schlatter, *Gottes Gerechtigkeit*, 1952, p. 161; Schrenk, *TDNT*, II, p. 207), or in the forensic-imputative significance Paul ascribes to *logizomai* (thus, e.g., Althaus, *Rom.*, p. 25; Heidland, *TDNT*, IV, pp. 290ff.). Verse 4 argues for the first conception, verse 5 for the second.

The appeal to Genesis 15:6 and the manner in which this functions in the course of the argument of Romans 4:1-5 surely deserves further elucidation as well. In the original context of Genesis 15:6 the words "righteousness" and "to reckon for" do not have the forensic significance that Paul, in harmony with the later legalistic-Jewish climate of thought, here attributes to them. "Righteousness," "justice," means in Genesis 15:6 — just as elsewhere in the Old Testament where the righteousness of the godly is spoken of (cf., e.g., Gen. 6:9; Job 12:14ff.), and to which they not infrequently made appeal over against God (cf., e.g., Ps. 1:5, 6; 5:13, *et al.*)—approximately "pious," "upright before God," standing in a right relationship to God by fearing him, hoping in him, etc. It does not thus mean so much blamelessly measuring up to a certain moral standard, as indeed living in a right religious relationship to God and his commandments (cf., e.g., Quell, *TDNT*, II, pp. 174-178; also J. Ridderbos, *Abraham de Vriend Gods*, 1928, pp. 196-198). Accordingly, "to

---

59. See the discussion in the small type immediately below.

reckon for righteousness" in Genesis 15:6 means that God accounted it to Abraham for righteousness (piety, godliness), judged it as righteousness in him, appreciated, that he in faith received God's word of promise. (In our view G. C. Aalders loses sight of this difference in meaning when he interprets Gen. 15:6 altogether in a forensic sense; *Het Oude Testament van verklarende aantekeningen voorzien,* I, 1952, p. 23.)

When for the gospel of the righteousness by faith Paul appeals to Abraham and the pronouncement of Genesis 15:6, he gives a different shade of meaning to the words of Genesis 15:6. He "translates" them, as it were, into the judicial-legalistic way of thinking of later Judaism. Materially, however, he remains entirely in harmony with the tenor of the Old Testament pronouncement, which is dominated by the gracious character of God's inter-course with Abraham and not by the doctrine of merit of the later synagogue (see also my *Rom.,* p. 92). At the same time, one is indeed on the wrong track when he fails to appreciate this forensic interpretation of Genesis 15:6 in the context of Romans 4, and in interpreting Romans 4 chooses to start from the original sense of the words of Genesis 15. This is done, in our view, by H. J. Jager in his *Rechtvaardiging en zekerheid des geloofs,* 1939. Jager posits emphatically that in Romans 4 there is an equivalence between faith and righteousness, that Abraham's faith is his righteousness, and is recognized as such by God (p. 104). It is a matter here, so he goes on to say, of the subjective righteousness consisting in faith that, worked by the Holy Spirit, is acknowl-edged by God as pleasing to him. "That Abraham unconditionally believed God's promise, that is recognized by God as his righteousness" (*ibid.,* pp. 105ff.). This conception, however, does not take into account the forensic context in which Paul places Genesis 15:6. It falls into the reverse of the error made by Aalders, who interprets Genesis 15 in the sense of Romans 4 and whose exegesis of Genesis 15 Jager therefore rightly rejects. Just as little, however, can one by "righteousness" in Romans 4 understand something "subjective," an attitude or disposition well-pleasing to God (in this instance, faith). It is a question here, in accordance with the whole argument of Romans 3-5, of righteousness as impunity in the judgment attributed by God to man, which does not rest on an "analytic" judgment of identity (God recognizes man for what he is), but rather on the "synthetic" acquitting verdict of God, which simply gives expression to what God attributes and grants to man as right-eousness. If one takes it differently, then the ground for justification lies yet again in something that is present in man (however much granted him by God), whereas the distinctive characteristic of the divine act of justifica-tion in this same context is expressed just in this way, that God justifies (not the believer, but) the ungodly; against Jager (and Woelderink) cf. also G. C. Berkouwer, *Faith and Justification,* pp. 84f. Others have taken the locution that faith is reckoned for righteousness as an abbreviated mode of expression for the idea that God imputes his righteousness given in Christ to one by faith and on that ground acquits him; thus H. Bavinck, *Geref. Dogmatiek,* IV, 4th ed., 1930, p. 195; cf. also J. Brinkman, *De "gerechtigheid Gods" bij Paulus,* 1916, p. 166; Greijdanus, *Rom.,* I, p. 224. Materially this is entirely correct, inasmuch as the obedience and the atoning sacrifice of Christ are the ground for justification (cf. above, Section 28). Formally, however, a *locutio compendiaria* is not to be thought of here, since the expression is borrowed from Genesis 15, where the word "impute for righteousness" does not as yet have this forensic imputative sense. The words "and it was reckoned unto him for righteousness" (Rom. 4) do therefore speak of faith as the imputative ground of justification, but then in the instrumental sense; cf. Philippians 3:9, where justification is spoken of as *tēn dia pisteōs Christou, tēn ek Theou dikaiosynēn epi tē pistei.* Although the terminology is fluid and, taken by itself, could give occasion to misunderstanding (cf. *epi tē pistei*: "on the basis of faith" [Phil. 3:9; Acts 3:16]), the matter itself is perfectly clear.

Thus Paul's doctrine of justification in its various facets — the redemptive-historical/christological, the forensic, the imputative — is an imposing and carefully integrated whole. The righteousness of God as eschatological redemptive gift, as condition and access to peace with God and eternal life, has now been revealed. It is revealed in the great redemptive event of Christ's death and resurrection, in which God as Judge has manifested his righteousness, both judging and acquitting. And as the redemptive gift of God it is given to those who are in Christ by faith. It consists for them, therefore, in imputation by grace, as a free gift, and not in the accounting of man's own works as merit. In that sense it can be said that faith is reckoned for righteousness, namely, as the means, on the ground of the obedience and righteous act of the One, to come to justification unto life and to peace with God through our Lord Jesus Christ (Rom. 5:1, 18, 19).

SECTION 31. JUDGMENT ACCORDING TO WORKS

The question that remains is whether the impressive consistency with which, in his opposition to the Jewish-synagogical doctrine of redemption, Paul rejects every appeal to human works and elucidates the whole of justification as an act of God's grace is capable of being reconciled with other pronouncements of his in which great emphasis is placed precisely on the fact that man is judged according to his works. It has already been mentioned that righteousness is not only a matter that has already been revealed, but is also still to be awaited as a future gift of God (Gal. 5:5). It has not yet been taken into consideration, however, that in more places than one the future judgment of God is closely connected with what each will have done. Not the hearers, but the doers of the law will be justified (Rom. 2:13). God will render to every man according to his works, for there is no respect of persons with God (Rom. 2:6ff.). This whole passage of Romans 2:1-16 is governed to such an extent by this motif that some have taken it as only a hypothetical preparation for Paul's real message: justification by faith and not by works. Paul is said here to speak of double retribution only in a "dialectical" sense; he is supposed to have wished here in the way of an untenable hypothesis to take the idea of the righteousness from works *ad absurdum* and therefore to place himself here on the "pre-evangelical standpoint."[60] But, however true it may be in itself that in Romans 2 and 3:1-10 Paul is elucidating over against Judaism the impossibility of justification by faith as the only way of salvation, this does not mean

---

60. So Lietzmann, *Rom.*, pp. 39ff. For this whole question in more recent exegesis, see also H. Braun, *Gerichtsgedanke und Rechtfertigungslehre bei Paulus,* 1930, pp. 23ff.

that on this latter, "evangelical," standpoint the judgment to come has been abrogated for believers with the death and resurrection of Christ, nor either that in this judgment the criterion would lie only in the presence of faith and not also of works. For, in the first place, Paul speaks of the latter not only in such passages as Romans 2 and 3, which impress on the man who seeks his salvation in the law the unconditional requirement of God, but no less in his paraenesis to the church in which he exhorts believers to the life that is from the Spirit and to the exhibition of the fruit of the Spirit (cf. Gal. 6:7ff.); he points them there to the judgment seat of Christ, before which they must all appear (2 Cor. 5:10; cf. Rom. 14:10, 11; Eph. 6:8; Col. 3:22-4:1), and he places the emphasis on the inadequacy of human judgment or of man's own conscience (1 Cor. 4:1-5).

This reference, recurring again and again in Paul's epistles, to the coming judgment and to the verdict, which will then be concerned with works, is likewise not, as some in fact have thought, as a lingering Jewish element to be distinguished from the real, evangelical "main doctrine,"[61] nor is it to be judged as an inconsistency. For the idea of the final divine judgment is so fundamental in all of Scripture and Paul appeals to it in a great many connections so much as a matter of course (cf., e.g., Rom. 3:6), that it is inconceivable that by proclaiming the righteousness by faith as the content of the gospel he would consciously or unconsciously have deprived this fundamental religious notion of its force. Rather, one will have to see in this self-evidentness the proof that for Paul both these realities, on the one hand that of justification by faith, on the other hand that of God's judgment of every man according to his works without respect of persons, are in no respect whatever in contradiction with one another.[62]

It should be added to all this, in the second place, that the whole idea that Paul's concept of faith is in fundamental conflict with such a retribution according to works must be rejected. Not only will it yet appear in the subsequent course of our investigation that justification and sanctification, Christ's dying *for* the sins of his people and their dying in him *to* these sins, are inseparable in Paul's preaching, not merely as indicative and imperative, but in the first place as two redemptive realities coinciding in Christ's death and resurrection; but the contrast "faith" and "works," as we have met with it in such an absolute sense, is not to be understood in any other way than as a contrast between the grace of God on the one hand and human achievement as the ground for justification on the other. That faith and works, however, are mutually exclusive only in this sense, but for the rest, where meritoriousness is not in question, belong inseparably together, is evident from the whole of Paul's preaching. Not only is faith at work through love (Gal. 5:6), but the apostle speaks in so many words of "the work of faith," i.e., the activity that goes out from faith and which can be mentioned in one breath with the labor of love and the steadfastness of hope (1 Thess. 1:3; cf. 2 Thess. 1:3). When it is said therefore

---

61. For this and other theories see the survey in Braun, *ibid.*, pp. 14ff.
62. *Ibid.*, p. 96.

in Romans 4 that to the one who does not "work" but who believes in him that justifies the ungodly, his faith is reckoned for righteousness, this is not in any way to be brought to bear against the "working" character of faith itself and likewise not against the judgment of the believer according to his works. For just as absolutely as faith is involved in justification by the grace of God and by nothing else, even so work emanates from this same faith; as faith it cannot remain empty and work-less, but becomes known as faith precisely in works. Indeed, in the pronouncements on the justification of the ungodly and the imputation of faith for righteousness and those concerning the just judgment of God according to every man's work, we have to do with the two poles of the same matter. For the first expresses as pregnantly as possible that the ground or cause of divine justification does not lie in human work as merit, but only in the grace of God. And in the second all the emphasis is placed on the work of faith, in the sense of its indispensable fruit. Yet this does not mean that justification by faith may be said to be the initial judicial act of God, which takes place in the present, and which is then to be followed in the final judgment by a justification on the ground of works. For it is true of the latter as well that it is a justification of the ungodly, an imputation of faith for righteousness, so long as what is at issue is the ground for justification. This does not lie in works, likewise not in that of faith, but in the revelation of God's grace in Christ embraced by faith. To be sure, works are indispensable as the demonstration of the true nature of faith and as the evidence of having died and been raised together with Christ. In that sense one could also speak of the reckoning of works for righteousness, although the apostle does not so express himself. For works, too, only find their acceptableness before God in the fact that they are from Christ, wrought in the believer on account of his death and resurrection (cf., e.g., Eph. 2:8-10: "for by grace are you saved through faith ...not of works, lest any man should boast. For we are his creation, created in Christ Jesus for good works, which God prepared beforehand that we should walk in them").

Surely the unity of grace, faith, and works cannot be elucidated more clearly than here. That is not to say that in every pronouncement, whether on justification by faith or on judgment according to works, this whole indissoluble unity is always transparent. But in the whole framework of Paul's unfolding of salvation as redemption in Christ, all this constitutes an integral unity. Accordingly, as soon as one loses sight of this, the one as well as the other is deprived of its real character; the receptive character of faith is denatured, as though it were not communion with the fullness of Christ, and on the other hand the divine judgment according to every man's works becomes a renewed legalistic motif. It is only in the inseparability of the two that the Pauline doctrine of the justification of the ungodly and the justification of the doers and not merely of the hearers of the law can attain its full span and development.[63]

---

63. On this subject cf. G. C. Berkouwer, *Faith and Justification*, pp. 103-112, and Schrenk, *TDNT*, II, p. 208.

The revelation of the righteousness of God thus understood can finally be considered, therefore, as the essence of the whole gospel, because this righteousness is the condition for obtaining the whole of the salvation that has been given in Christ. Paul speaks of this righteousness in Romans 5:18 as "justification unto life,"[64] and by this he means that the way to life and the receiving of a share in the new creation 'has been opened by the revelation of the righteousness of God in Christ. Because we have been justified by faith we have peace with God, the entrance to this grace has been opened to us, we are given the prospect of the glory of God, the certainty of eternal life (Rom. 5:1-11). For those who have received "the gift of righteousness" will reign in eternal life through Jesus Christ (Rom. 5:17). For as sin has reigned by death, so grace will reign unto eternal life (Rom. 5:21; cf. 8:10). For whom God justifies, them he also glorifies (Rom. 8:30). Or, as it is said repeatedly in the words of Habakkuk 2:4: "the just shall live by faith" (Rom. 1:17; Gal. 3:11).

This righteousness, just because it constitutes the access to the whole of the salvation revealed in Christ and all the gifts granted in it, can therefore be implicitly the denotation of the entire content of the gospel. The gospel is a power of God unto salvation, because therein the righteousness of God is revealed (Rom. 1:16ff.). "Righteousness" and "salvation" appear as synonymous concepts (Rom. 10:10). While life under the law is a life under the administration of death and judgment, in the same way the gospel is an administration of righteousness and the Holy Spirit (2 Cor. 3:7ff.). It emerges time and again that it is just this revelation of the righteousness of God which constitutes the cornerstone of the whole building: on the one hand a stone of stumbling and a rock of offense for those who seek their own righteousness; on the other hand the firm foundation for everyone who trusts in it (Rom. 9:30-33).

In a certain sense one can say, therefore, that Paul's proclamation of redemption consists in the exposition of this righteousness. Yet it would be too schematic a plan now to bring everything else under this one denominator. There are also other concepts, ideas, trains of thought, all of which have the same point of departure — the saving activity of God in the death and resurrection of Christ — and all of which have their essential foundation in this revelation of the righteousness of God, but which nevertheless give expression to the content of the gospel in other ways. In the chapters that are to follow we shall be obliged to give a further account of them.

---

64. *Dikaiōsis zōēs, gen. finalis* (cf. Bl.-Debr., Par. 166, "genitive of direction and purpose [result]"); justification unto life, justification that brings along with it and contains within itself eternal life; cf. my *Rom.*, pp. 121, 122.

V

RECONCILIATION

SECTION 32. GOD'S RECONCILING ACTIVITY IN CHRIST. THE PEACE OF GOD

Along with the concept of justification, the new relationship to God accomplished in Christ's death and resurrection is expressed in another way. The concept of reconciliation also plays an important part in Paul's epistles. It appears in more than one place as the parallel and equivalent of justification. So, for example, in Romans 5:9, 10, where "justified by his [Christ's] blood" is paralleled by "reconciled by his death," just as in 2 Corinthians 3:9 and 5:18 the "ministration of righteousness" and the "ministration of reconciliation" are alternately spoken of. Likewise in 2 Corinthians 5:18ff. it is said in so many words that God's reconciling act with respect to the world consists in his "not imputing unto them their trespasses." Other pronouncements confirm this equation.[1]

There is no warrant for wishing to subordinate one of these two concepts to the other. One could perhaps say that reconciliation as peace with God is the consequence of justification (Rom. 5:1). But then one is speaking of the *condition* of reconciliation, which is the result of the reconciling activity of God. Conversely, one can just as well speak of righteousness as the new reconciled relationship with God that has been effected by the justifying act of God. Better than making excessively sharp delimitations is the insight that we are dealing here with two concepts from different spheres of thought and life. Whereas "to justify" is a religious-forensic concept that is highly typical of the basic eschatological structure of Paul's preaching, "reconciliation" (in the sense of *katallagē*) has a more general, less qualified meaning in theological parlance. It originates from the social-societal sphere (cf. 1 Cor. 7:11), and speaks in general of the restoration of the right relationship between two parties. In the pronouncements of Paul it is often placed over against "enmity," "alienation" (Rom. 5:10; Eph. 2:14ff.; Col. 1:22), just as in a positive sense it has the meaning of "peace" (cf. Rom. 5:1, 10; Eph. 2:15ff.; Col. 1:20ff.).

When we look more closely at these pronouncements relating to reconciliation, it can be ascertained that this reconciliation is qualified above all by the fact that God is its Author and Initiator. This is put very emphatically in the great "reconciliation pericope" of 2 Corinthians 5:18-21: "And all this is from God, who through Christ has reconciled us to himself and has given us the ministry of reconciliation; that is,[2]

---

1. Cf., e.g., Bultmann, *Theology*, I, pp. 285ff.
2. The translation of *hōs hoti*, however, is not established.

that God was in Christ reconciling the world to himself." Conversely, mention is made of the church's being reconciled (Rom. 5:10), and believers are admonished by the word of reconciliation to let themselves be reconciled to God; reconciliation can therefore stand over against "rejection" (by God) (Rom. 11:15), and to the apostles has been entrusted the ministry (dispensation, distribution) of reconciliation (diakonia tēs katallagēs). The pronouncements in Colossians and Ephesians say essentially the same thing.[3] There Christ appears as the Reconciler, who reconciles Jews and gentiles, indeed through whom God reconciles "all things" to himself (Eph. 2:16; Col. 1:20, 22). In all this, entirely in harmony with the great fundamental motif of Paul's preaching, reconciliation is the work of redemption going out from God in Christ to the world,[4] for the removal of "enmity," for the restoration of "peace."

In the second place, for insight into the Pauline idea of reconciliation it is again of paramount importance to take full account of the eschatological character of Paul's preaching. As restoration of the right relationship between God and the world reconciliation of course also has reference to the disposition of man. Yet neither the point of departure nor the real thrust of the Pauline pronouncements on reconciliation is situated here. With reconciliation, being reconciled, peace, it is primarily a matter of removing that which stands in the way of the right relationship between God and (in the most comprehensive sense of the word) the world; in other words, of the eschatological restoration of all things. This is clearly evident from the context of the reconciliation pronouncements in 2 Corinthians 5. Reconciliation constitutes the foundation of the new creation, of the fact that the old has passed away, that the new has come (2 Cor. 5:17, 18), of the "now" of the day of salvation and of the acceptable time (2 Cor. 6:2). This objective-eschatological character of reconciliation may be still more sharply distinguished in the pronouncement of Colossians 1:20, where it is said that God through Christ reconciles all things to himself, having made peace through the blood of his cross. In connection with "all things," as appears from the context, one is to think of all that is in heaven and on earth, in particular of the power that the spirit world has obtained over the world of men fallen away from God and the bad relationship into which the world has thereby come to stand over against God. When it is said here that God through Christ has again reconciled "all things" to himself, what is meant is not the restoration of the right disposition[5] (e.g., among the apostate spirits), but rather of the divine

3. In Eph. 2:16 as well as in Col. 1:20, 22 the double prepositional compound apokatallassō is used, in distinction from all other Pauline passages where katallassō is employed. Percy has demonstrated clearly that there is no essential difference of meaning or instance arguing against the genuineness of Eph. and Col. (Die Probleme der Kolosser- und Epheserbriefe, 1946, pp. 17ff., 86ff.).

4. This in contrast with the word usage outside the New Testament. In Greek-speaking Judaism it is precisely God who becomes reconciled through the prayers, etc., of men. The equivalents of katallassein, too, have this meaning in the rabbinic usage. Cf. Büchsel, TDNT, I, p. 254; Strack-Billerbeck, III, p. 519.

5. As W. Michaelis in particular has argued in his Versöhnung des Alls, 1950, pp. 27ff., as the ground of his universalistic interpretations; see further my Col., p. 148.

government over all, through the fact, among other things, that the
authority of the powers that have set themselves against God has been
taken away and through Christ they have been subjected to God. With
reconciliation it is a question here, therefore, of the eschatological
pacification, which is also expressed by the words that follow in Colossians 1:20, that God has thus made peace through the blood of Christ's
cross. To be sure, some[6] have held the view that this "objective" conception of "reconcile" must be frustrated precisely by this element of
peace-making. But the idea of peace, which for Paul repeatedly denotes
the result of reconciliation, is not in conflict with such a conception of
reconciliation, but rather forms its confirmation. For in Paul (as in the
whole of the Scripture) "peace" refers not only or in the first place to
disposition, but is the denotation of the all-embracing gift of salvation,
the condition of *shalom*, which God will again bring to unrestricted
dominion. It is the peace that is to reign when "the God of peace will
soon crush Satan under the feet" of his people (Rom. 16:20). It consists
therefore as much in the pacification of the powers hostile to God as
in the restoration of peace between Jews and gentiles, the peace of the
Messianic kingdom, which is represented by Christ ("He is our peace")
because he has reconciled the enmity between the two through his cross
(Eph. 2:14ff.), and which stands in contrast to the wrath, indignation,
tribulation, and anguish of the eschatological divine judgment (Rom.
2:9, 10).

Now it is against this eschatological background that we have to understand all in the reconciliation pronouncements that has bearing on
the right relationship between God and the world of men, in the personal sense of the word. So the inadequacy of the conception that has
long been in vogue in the dogmatic and exegetical literature can immediately become clear to us, that the divine act of reconciliation
consists only in man's being exhorted to abandon his wrong and hostile
disposition toward God.[7] Over against this stands not only the whole
Pauline conception of the work of redemption, as this has already
become evident in his doctrine of justification, but also the clear testimony of the pronouncements on reconciliation themselves. Undoubtedly
reconciliation also has in view the removal of the enmity of unredeemed
man toward God of which, for example, there is mention in Romans
8:8: "the mind of the flesh is enmity against God." It also occurs in
this sense in the reconciliation pronouncements themselves when, for
example, it is said of Christ: "And you, who once were estranged and
hostile in mind[8] [toward him] . . . he has now reconciled" (Col. 1:21, 22).
    It is clear in addition, however, that the reconciling activity of
God does not merely have reference to human disposition, but embraces

---

6. Michaelis, *ibid.*, pp. 29, 30; also Büchsel, *TDNT*, I, p. 259.

7. For this (Ritschlian) conception of reconciliation see, e.g., E. Kühl, *Der
Brief des Paulus an die Römer*, 1913, p. 169; materially still in C. H. Dodd as well
(*The Epistle of Paul to the Romans*, 1947, pp. 20ff., 74ff.).

8. *Echthrous tē dianoia*, dative of relation: inimically disposed; *en tois ergois
tois ponērois* then says wherein this disposition reveals itself: as appears from your
evil works.

much more.[9] Man in his sin is an "enemy of God" not only in the active but also in the passive sense of the word. The apostle speaks very clearly to that effect, for example, in Romans 11:28, where the Jews are successively called "enemies [of God] for your sake" and "beloved [of God] for the fathers' sake." From the parallel it follows that "enemies of God" must here have a passive meaning. And the same thing undoubtedly applies to the "reconciliation" pronouncement in Romans 5:10: "for if, while we were enemies, we were reconciled to God...." Even if one chooses to assume that "enemies" here describes a reciprocal relationship,[10] the context clearly indicates that the abrogation of this enmity through reconciliation is the same as being delivered from God's wrath, being acquitted of sin and guilt, and thus describes not only the relation in which man stands toward God,[11] but also that in which God stands toward man.[12]

What Paul means by reconciliation, when he speaks of the restoration of the relationship between God and (the world of) men, can best be understood by starting from justification, of which, as we have seen, it appears as the parallel. In this reconciliation it is a matter first of all of the abrogation of man's relationship of guilt before God, of his sin not being imputed to him (2 Cor. 5:19). In that sense reconciliation is above all a gift that man "receives" by grace (Rom. 5:11), the ground for which, in the same manner as that of his justification, is in Christ — in his death (Rom. 5:10), in his cross (Eph. 2:16), in the body of his flesh through death (Col. 1:22). So far is Paul from any such suggestion as that reconciliation consists only in the removal of man's enmity toward God. Precisely as an act of God in Christ's death it is antecedent to all human *Umstimmung*, it took place without us and for us "when we were yet enemies" (Rom. 5:10), it consists above all in the effecting of peace as the fruit of justification (Rom. 5:1), and thus prepares the way to receiving a share in the new creation, the new things, peace as the all-embracing condition of salvation.

All the rest results from this. The reconciliation of which Paul speaks also consists, just as justification and in a still more explicit sense, in what is realized in the life of men from this restoration of fellowship. The "word of reconciliation" goes out to them that they should "let" themselves be reconciled to God (2 Cor. 5:20), that is, that from their side, too, they should enter into that reconciled relationship; and thus instead of living as unreconciled and enemies under the wrath of God, should accept the peace and love of God as a gift

9. So also Foerster, *TDNT*, II, pp. 183ff., and P. Feine, *Theologie des N.T.*, 7th ed., 1936, p. 235, versus the interpretation of Ritschl.

10. So Althaus, *Rom.*, p. 42; Sanday and Headlam, *The Epistle to the Romans*, 1950, pp. 129, 130; cf. also Greijdanus, *Rom.*, I, p. 270; Büchsel, *TDNT*, I, pp. 257ff., *s.v. katallassō;* the same writer, *Theologie des N.T.*, 1937, p. 197.

11. So Dodd, *The Epistle of Paul to the Romans*, p. 77; Kühl, *Der Brief des Paulus an die Römer*, p. 168, cf. p. 394; Foerster, *TDNT*, II, p. 814; Zahn, *Rom.*, p. 258; and Schlatter, *Gottes Gerechtigkeit*, p. 183.

12. So rightly Lietzmann, *Rom.*, p. 60; Feine, *Theologie des N.T.*, p. 235; Greijdanus, *Rom.*, I, p. 270; Nygren, *Commentary on Romans*, p. 203; Bultmann, *Theology*, I, p. 286, who for the connection between the active and the passive significance of *echthroi* rightly refers to Rom. 8:7ff.

and power, and be encompassed, governed, and led by them. Here again it is "peace" that fills up and explains the Pauline concept of reconciliation. For this peace is not only a denotation of the new relationship in which those who are justified and reconciled may stand toward God (Rom. 5:1), but also of the inner peace of the heart that pervades the whole man in all his doings (Rom. 15:13), and, surpassing all understanding, keeps and restrains the hearts and minds of believers (Phil. 4:7), and as arbiter gives judgment in their hearts when they find themselves in uncertainty or inner discord (Col. 3:15; cf. 2 Thess. 3:16).

Thus reconciliation empties itself into the whole of the Christian life, is its foundation and summation, just as the "ministration of reconciliation" coincides on the one hand with the "ministration of righteousness," and on the other with the "ministration of the Spirit" (2 Cor. 5:18; 3:8, 9).

SECTION 33. CHRIST'S DEATH AS ATONEMENT. KATALLAGĒ AND HILASMOS

As justification by faith is grounded in the death of Christ, so too in the pronouncements on reconciliation the death of Christ is brought up again and again as the foundation on which or the way in which this reconciliation takes place. Thus it is said in Romans 5:10 that when we were (yet) enemies, we were reconciled through the death of God's Son. And in Ephesians and Colossians we meet with a whole series of expressions that establish the connection between Christ's death and the peace and reconciliation wrought by him: "In Christ Jesus you who once were far off have been brought near by the blood of Christ" (Eph. 2:13); "for he is our peace, . . . having abolished in [or through] his flesh the enmity" (v. 14), ". . . that he might reconcile them both in one body unto God through the cross, having slain the enmity thereon [therein]." And in Colossians 1:20 it is said that God through Christ has reconciled all things, "making peace through the blood of his cross." . . . "And you . . . he has now reconciled in the body of his flesh through death" (v. 22). All this places before us the question as to what significance must be ascribed to the suffering and death of Christ in the whole of the reconciling activity of God.

In our discussion of the significance of Christ's death as the ground for justification[13] we confined ourselves to pointing out the general forensic meaning of Christ's death: in Christ God shows his vindicatory righteousness in the present time and thus justifies those who have faith in Jesus (Rom. 3:25, 26). The apostle also says in that context, however, that "God made him openly to be a means of propitiation in his blood" (Rom. 3:25), just as in Romans 5:9, as a parallel of "reconciled by his death" cited above, there is mention of being "justified by his blood." It is clear that this terminology, however closely connected it is with the forensic doctrine of justification, does

---

13. Cf. above, Section 28.

not simply flow out of it, and, as appears from the foregoing, is likewise bound up with the concept of reconciliation. Thus, in discussing the doctrine of reconciliation, that is, of the restoration taken in a wider sense of the broken relationship between God and the world, there is reason to go further into the complex of pronouncements that make this restoration rest on the passion and death of Christ. Moreover, at the same time the question can be discussed — a question that has frequently been raised in the history of Pauline studies[14] — as to what connection is made in his proclamation between the reconciliation that goes forth from God to the world and the necessity of the death of Christ.

What is meant in Romans 5:9, 10 by "justified by his blood" and "reconciled by the death of his Son" can best be elucidated by the pronouncement in Romans 3:25, with which these expressions are linked, that God "made [Christ] openly to be a means of propitiation in his blood." For here the significance of the words "in" or "by" his blood is explained by the combination with the idea *hilastērion*, means of propitiation.[15] The idea employed here ("to propitiate" — and the group of words[16] to which it belongs), in contrast to the concept *katallagē*[17] that has been dealt with so far, occurs only once in Paul and has its background in a complex of ideas wholly its own. While the concept *katallagē* (reconciliation) originates in the social-societal sphere, *hilastērion* (means of propitiation) is derived from the cultus, particularly from the propitiatory sacrifice that took place there. Thus, Christ's death is qualified by the designation "means of propitiation" as a propitiatory sacrifice, and the accompanying phrase "[consisting] in his blood" has materially the meaning of "propitiatory blood." The related expressions in Romans 5:9 are to be understood in the same sense and say that justification has been accomplished by his propitiatory blood and reconciliation by his propitiatory death.

That the concept "to propitiate," in the form of "means of propitiation," occurs only once in Paul does not mean that the thought it expresses is absent elsewhere in his epistles. Apart from what has already been said with respect to Romans 5:9 and 10, a few other pronouncements are to be pointed out here as well, which, although in another context than the present one, speak of Christ's death as a sacrificial death. Thus in 1 Corinthians 5:7, where in reference to Old Testament passages it is said: "for our paschal lamb has also been slaughtered

14. In post-war Dutch theology a lively discussion has developed on this point in the dogmatic literature, especially as a consequence of the views of F. W. A. Korff, *Christologie*, II, 1941, pp. 152-215. See, e.g., M. H. Bolkestein, *De Verzoening*, 1946; H. van Oyen, "Liefde, gerechtigheid en recht," *Ned. Theol. Tijdschrift*, 1946, pp. 27-41; A. F. N. Lekkerkerker, *Gesprek over de verzoening*, 1949, pp. 39-174; L. van der Zanden, *De spits der verzoening*, 1950; G. C. Berkouwer, *The Work of Christ*, ET 1965, pp. 254ff.

15. Others wish to translate by "mercy seat." For the arguments pro and con see, e.g., J. H. Stelma, *Christus' offer bij Paulus vergeleken met de offeropvattingen van Philo*, 1938, pp. 11ff., and G. Sevenster, *Christologie van het N.T.*, 1946, pp. 173, 174. In our opinion the translation "means of propitiation" decidedly deserves preference; cf. my *Rom.*, pp. 85ff.

16. *Hilaskomai, hilasmos, hilastērion (expiatio, Sühnung).*

17. *Reconciliatio, Versöhnung.*

(etythē), even Christ." The same holds for the words of the Lord's Supper quoted by Paul in 1 Corinthians 11:25: "This cup is the New Covenant in my blood." Finally, in Ephesians 5:2 where, likewise referring to traditional expressions, it is said that "Christ gave himself up for us as an offering and a sacrifice (prosphoran kai thysian) for a fragrant odor to God." In all these places not only is sacrificial terminology employed, but materially there is mention of Christ's death as a propitiatory death. This after all was the significance both of the Passover sacrifice and of the covenant sacrifice, which is spoken of in 1 Corinthians 11:25 (cf. Exod. 12:7, 13; 24:6-8). The words of Ephesians 5:2, as appears from the "for us," also point to the element of atonement.[18] To these then are still to be added those passages in which there is mention of Christ's blood in the sense of propitiatory blood. Besides those places (Rom. 3:25; 5:9) already discussed, 1 Corinthians 10:16; 11:25ff. are to be mentioned as such (in direct connection with the words of the Lord's Supper[19]). But the pronouncements on reconciliation in Ephesians 2 and Colossians 1 are also to be cited to this end, at least so far as mention is there made of peace, and reconciliation "through the blood of Christ" and "through the blood of his cross" (Eph. 2:13; Col. 1:20). Finally, the idea of the propitiatory sacrifice underlies those pronouncements in which Jesus is denoted as the one who died "for us" or "for our sins" (cf. Rom. 5:6, 8; 14:15; 1 Cor. 15:3; 2 Cor. 5:14; 1 Thess. 5:10, et al.).[20]

Now, it has often been supposed that in Paul's doctrine of justification and reconciliation the idea of Christ's death as a propitiatory sacrifice is not in the literal sense under discussion. The literal sense consists surely in the fact that the propitiatory sacrifice enters in substitutionally between the holy God and sinful man, because the life given up in the sacrifice through the attendant shedding of blood covers sin before the face of God and in this way atones.[21] A "metaphorical

---

18. That there is "no talk of the expiation of sins" in Eph. 5:2 and mention only of Christ's Self-surrender to God (Dibelius, Col., p. 89) is even for this reason untenable. But the Old Testament background of the sacrificial terminology employed here (cf. Exod. 29:18) clearly includes the idea of atonement. For although the words used in Eph. 5:2 do indeed denote the burnt offering and not the sin or guilt offering, the former is also attended with the sprinkling of blood, as means of atonement for sins (cf., e.g., W. H. Gispen, Bijbelsch Handboek, I, 1935, p. 281).

19. That we have to do with sacrificial terminology here has been clearly shown by J. Jeremias, The Eucharistic Words of Jesus, 2nd ed., ET 1955, p. 144 (cf. 3rd ed., ET 1966, p. 222); cf. also V. Taylor, Jesus and His Sacrifice, 1948, p. 261; my The Coming of the Kingdom, ET 1962, pp. 424ff. It is therefore incomprehensible how Behm, TDNT, III, p. 184, is able to write that "in 1 Cor. 10:11 there is not the least basis for the conjecture that 'the celebration of the Eucharist is for Paul a sacred sacrificial meal' [quoting Brinktrine]." See further below, Section 66, under (a).

20. See also Bultmann, Theology, I, p. 296.

21. For the idea of the propitiatory sacrifice, cf., e.g., W. H. Gispen in the Bijbelsch Handboek, I, p. 281: "As appears from Lev. 17:11, the soul of the animal whose blood was sprinkled upon the altar atoned for, covered, the sinner before the wrath of God." See also Gispen, Het boek Leviticus, 1950, p. 257: "And the blood can be used as such (that is to say, as means of atonement) . . . because the soul, that is, the life of the flesh, is in the blood . . . . The life of the animal comes in place of the life of the man" (p. 258); cf. also Herrmann, TDNT, III, pp. 302ff.

garment" has been spoken of here, with which no cultic ideas are said to have been connected,[22] and it has been posited that Paul spoke only in a figurative, metaphorical sense of Christ's death as sacrifice — among other things, because he makes equally straightforward and "free" use of the sacrificial figures when he speaks of his own death.[23] Similarly, it has frequently been contended that in Paul the substitutionary character of Christ's death stands entirely in the background[24] or is even entirely missing.[25] In the same line is the assertion of others that the reconciling passion and death of Christ are proclaimed only as divine activity, not as an "accomplishment of Christ" over against God, and that the necessity or possibility of this activity is not reflected on.[26]

But with impartial exegesis there can be no doubt that in the most literal sense of the word Paul speaks of Christ's death as a propitiatory death. What is decisive here, to be sure, is not that he uses the word "sacrifice," which in itself admits of all sorts of meanings, but the sense he attaches to it. And as to that there remains no uncertainty whatever, particularly in the light of Romans 3:25, 26. Christ is the means of propitiation appointed by God to the manifestation of his deferred righteousness. In Christ's death the righteousness of God thus reveals itself in the demanding and vindicatory sense of the word. His blood as atoning blood covers the sin which God until now had passed over, when as yet he kept back the judgment. All that men wish to detract from the real character of Christ's propitiatory death signifies a devaluation of the language of Romans 3:25 and 26, which is unmistakable in its clarity.

But the passages where in so many words Jesus is called the sacrificial lamb and his blood the blood of the covenant also contradict the assertion that sacrifice is here spoken of only in a figurative sense. "Our passover [lamb] has been sacrificed, even Christ" (1 Cor. 5:7) does not have in view only the voluntariness of Christ's death. Rather, the objective and passive stand in the foreground here. Christ's death is the necessary condition for the life of his own. In that sense he is also "our" paschal lamb. Similarly, his blood is the condition of the New Covenant (1 Cor. 11:25). The whole description of the cup in the Lord's Supper as "the New Covenant in my blood" is robbed of its deepest meaning when the idea of sacrifice is not taken here in its proper sense, that is,

---

22. So, e.g., Behm, *TDNT*, III, p. 184, *s.v. thyō*, and *TDNT*, I, p. 175, *s.v. haima*.

23. Cf., e.g., G. Aulén, *Christus Victor*, ET 1931, p. 88, i.a., with an appeal to O. Schmitz, *Die Opferanschauung des späteren Judentums und die Opferaussagen des Neuen Testaments*, 1910, pp. 213ff.

24. See, e.g., V. Taylor, *The Atonement in New Testament Teaching*, 2nd ed., 1945, pp. 84ff.

25. So, e.g., A. M. Brouwer, *Verzoening*, 1947, pp. 115ff.

26. So, e.g., Kümmel on 2 Cor. 5:21 (Lietzmann, *Cor.*, p. 205), by way of mitigating Lietzmann's here less biased exegesis. The latter also writes in *Rom.*, p. 50: "God appointed the crucified Jesus to be the means of expiation for humanity, for through his bloody death it was ransomed from the fate that threatened it on account of the guilt of its sin (i.e., Paul appraises the death of Jesus as a vicarious sacrifice, and the seeds of Anselm's doctrine of satisfaction are as a matter of fact present here)."

when the blood is not understood as the means by which the reconciliation between God and his people is accomplished and which is necessary for the forgiveness of sins and the new fellowship (Jer. 31:31ff.).[27]

Entirely in harmony with this is the idea of the substitutionary character of Christ's death on the cross, as that recurs time and again in Paul's epistles, when it is said that Christ "died for our sins" (1 Cor. 15:3; 2 Cor. 5:14); or "died for us" and "gave himself up for our sins" (Rom. 5:6, 8; 14:15; 1 Thess. 5:10; Rom. 4:25; 8:32; Gal. 1:4; 2:20). To be sure, the expression "for us" in itself does not yet signify "in our place"; it indicates that the death of Christ has taken place "in our favor." Nevertheless, the substitutionary significance of these expressions cannot be doubted. And it is corroborated by such expressions as that in 2 Corinthians 5:21: God made him who knew no sin to be sin for us; cf. Romans 8:3 and Galatians 3:13, where it is said that Christ has become a curse for us. In these passages the thought of the substitutionary (atoning) sacrifice is unmistakable, a thought that is enunciated in almost so many words when the phrase "One died for all" is explained by the words, "so then all have died" (2 Cor. 5:14). Even if one could give certain passages taken by themselves another sense, the whole complex of the pronouncements mentioned above can allow no doubt to remain as to the "atoning," substitutionary character of Jesus' death,[28] and every effort to detract from it readily does wrong to the most fundamental segments of Paul's gospel. Likewise the fact that reconciliation as the restoration of the broken relationship between God and the world has been brought about by God and that he therefore is the Author and Initiator of reconciliation is in no respect whatever in conflict with the idea of the propitiatory sacrifice that must cover and atone for sin before God. Not only does God turn in Christ to the world in order to effect reconciliation (katallagē), but Christ also stands in the place of men to offer himself up to God, to expiate (hilasmos) the sin of his people. In his death Christ represents God with men, but in it he also represents men with God (1 Tim. 2:5). God demonstrates his love toward us in the death of Christ (Rom. 5:8); he has delivered him up for us all (Rom. 8:32). But at the same time Christ's obedience is unto death on the cross (Phil. 2:8), the act of the one man, through whom the many are justified (Rom. 5:18, 19). The line not only runs from above downward, but in Christ it turns back to God. Here there is indeed a double movement to be spoken of in the reconciling work of Christ, in which is implicit the mystery of reconciliation.

This is not to be taken, however, in such a way that we have to do here with an unsolvable dialectic. For there is a clear connection between the reconciliation going forth from God and Christ's giving up of himself as a means of propitiation in order to cover the sin of the

---

27. Korff places all the emphasis on the covering, eradicating character of *hilasmos* (*Christologie*, I, pp. 171ff.). Rightly. But to the fact that sin must be covered before God through the death and the blood of Christ he is unable, in my opinion, to give any meaning. Here again, therefore, the *retributive* righteousness cannot be eliminated, as Korff wishes to do (pp. 173, 195).

28. Cf., e.g., Bultmann, *Theology*, I, p. 296.

people before God. But the latter is subordinate to the former, and not the reverse. For the same God with whom the restoration of the broken fellowship originates and who has summoned men to be reconciled to him (*katallagē;* 2 Cor. 5:18ff.) is also the one who has instituted the order of "propitiation" (*hilasmos*) by the death of Christ. By sending his own Son — and that for the sake of sin (namely, in order to cause it to be atoned for) — he condemned sin in the (that is, in Christ's) flesh (Rom. 8:3). And it is he himself who on the cross, before the eyes of all,[29] has made and designated Christ to be a means of propitiation (Rom. 3:25). Therefore every representation as though an *Umstimmung* were brought about in God by the propitiatory sacrifice of Christ and as though his wrath were only to be "appeased" in the sacrifice of Christ, is completely contrary to the Pauline gospel. It is divine love that evidences itself in the death of Christ and which to that end did not spare his own Son (Rom. 5:8; 8:32), but delivered him up for us all. But the depth of this love only becomes manifest in all its grandeur when, in the holy order of the justice appointed by God, Christ is made to be sin and delivers himself up as the atoning sacrifice to cover the sin of the world before the face of God.[30]

Finally, one can still ask the question as to the manner in which the idea of the substitutionary, atoning character of Christ's death is

---

29. The *pro* in *pro-etheto* denotes the public character; cf. *kath' ophthalmous pro-egraphē estaurōmenos* (Gal. 3:1): before the eyes of all has been made known as the crucified (not: "picture" before the eyes of all, in the sense of: to illustrate; to portray clearly).

30. The question that is frequently posed as to whether God is propitiated must find its answer in the light of the above. The answer must be unconditionally in the negative if what is intended is that God must be moved to change his mind, to another attitude. But even when this essentially heathen idea is left out of consideration, the expression is open to misunderstanding; it is nowhere employed by Paul, indeed, in the entire New Testament. This does not alter the fact that the word *hilaskomai* and its derivatives signify in the first instance "to cause to be graciously disposed," and thus have God for their object (cf. Bauer, *ad loc.*, and Büchsel, *TDNT*, III, p. 316). That in the New Testament God is nowhere the object of this propitiation is not, however, to say that "words which were originally used to denote man's action in relation to God cease to be used in this way in the NT and are used instead of God's action in relation to man," as Büchsel writes in summary (*TDNT*, III, p. 317). Heb. 2:17, in which there is mention of the high priest who for the people has to look after *ta pros ton Theon* and thus make propitiation for the sins of the people already proves the contrary. One can certainly say that the words *hilaskomai,* etc., in the New Testament (just as in the OT) have "sin" as their object (Heb. 2:17). But then surely not in the sense that the act that is necessary for this takes place through God. It occurs just (at the direction of God) through or in the name of sinful man, namely, in the propitiatory sacrifice. Hence also the phrase *hilaskomai peri tōn hamartiōn* (1 John 2:2; 4:10). The question that really matters in the discussion concerning the atonement and satisfaction is most profoundly not whether individual "hard" expressions, derived from the Old Testament or from the Reformation confessions, give expression in an adequate manner to the Pauline, New Testament, and, in general, biblical revelation of the atonement; through isolating these expressions one easily comes to a distortion of the biblical and Reformation idea of the atonement. The real point in question is the reality of the divine judgment on sin and the demand of God that sin be atoned for in the way of reconciliation appointed by him. In this respect Paul's doctrine of reconciliation is not susceptible to two kinds of interpretation.

integrated into the whole of Paul's eschatological preaching. Is there an intrinsic connection between this idea of reconciliation and the basic structures of Paul's preaching, as these have been pointed out in the foregoing? Some are of the opinion that the idea of Christ's death as propitiatory death does not represent the characteristic feature of Paul's view, and that in the formulations in question: died for our sins, etc., he follows the tradition (probably originating with the primitive church and in any case propagated in Hellenistic Christianity).[31]

In this conception there is certainly this truth, that, as we have seen, the idea "to propitiate" occurs only once in Paul, and that when he speaks elsewhere in an explicit sense of the sacrifice of Christ (1 Cor. 5:7; 11:25; Eph. 5:2) he apparently employs traditional formulations and expressions. Nor is one able to say that the doctrine of reconciliation in the sense of the propitiatory sacrifice is deliberately or expressly unfolded in his epistles, as is the case, for example, with the theme of justification and in part with that of reconciliation (in the sense of *katallagē*). This is not to say that for Paul the idea of propitiation does not occupy an important place. Materially it is found so frequently that one must consider it as pertaining to the central content of the Pauline kerygma.[32] But its significance is more often presupposed than expressly brought up for discussion. And in the few times the sacrifice of Christ is spoken of in so many words, the thought of propitiation still occurs indirectly, that is, in another context of thought (cf. 1 Cor. 5:7; 11:25; Eph. 5:2). It is in this circumstance, indeed, that one will have to look for the reason that certain theological currents, averse to this idea of reconciliation, have repeatedly supposed that it is to be met with in Paul merely in a figurative, symbolical sense. How much this last signifies a failure to appreciate the fundamental importance of reconciliation in Paul we have attempted to show above. But this does not alter the fact that it is more characteristic of the foundation than of the distinctive construction of Paul's gospel.

For insight into the relationship intended here the most important and conspicuous pronouncement is undoubtedly Romans 3:25. Here the idea of the propitiatory sacrifice is very directly linked with the doctrine of justification so characteristic of Paul's preaching. Here the absolutely unique eschatological significance of Christ's death as atoning death clearly emerges. At the great turning point of the times God grants righteousness to everyone who believes, by grace, as a free gift. But the revelation of this righteousness given by God also bears the hallmark of an eschatological judicial verdict, in that it is attended by a manifestation of God's vindicatory and demanding righteousness in the atoning death of Christ. That is also the significance of "to set forth publicly as a means of propitiation." It is this decisive, central act of propitiation, executed before the eyes of heaven and earth, in which God himself, passing over all the sacrifices that had formerly been offered, provides the means of propitiation and places it in the midst

31. So Bultmann, *Theology*, I, p. 296.
32. For the central significance of the sacrificial idea in Paul see also J. H. Stelma, *Het Offer van Jezus*, 1954, pp. 57ff.

of all. This is also the meaning of the "once" of the death of Christ, of which Romans 6:10 speaks; "once" is intended to say "once and for all," so as to distinguish it from all preceding sacrifices.[33] It is "the testimony in its own time" (1 Tim. 2:6), that is to say, the testimony that in the decisive moment goes forth from Christ's self-surrender to the world and mankind. In this sense, therefore, the idea of Christ's death as atoning death comprises one of the most essential definitions of God's work of redemption in the fullness of the time.

SECTION 34. RANSOM

Closely related to the idea of Christ's atoning death is that of ransom, which is denoted by various words[34] and repeatedly connected with Christ's death. Whereas, as we have seen, the idea of atonement pertains to the sacral, cultic sphere, that of ransom stems from the world of law.[35] To be sure, some hold that when Paul qualifies salvation in Christ as ransom he may thereby be said to think of the so-called sacral redemption of slaves, a familiar practice in the Hellenistic world. The slave was required to give to the priest the price that was necessary for his freedom. The latter gave him freedom in the name of the deity, while the money was put into the hands of the owner. This was a specific legal form, whereby the slave in fact redeemed himself, and the deity only appeared as the fictitious purchaser.[36] It is highly doubtful, however, whether such a connection may be made. Irrespective even of the material differences (with regard to the price, etc.), there is no formal similarity here. For in Paul's representation God does not appear as the Purchaser, nor does the priest standing in his service, but Christ, who through his death redeems his own. The price is not thus paid by God, but rather to God (see below). And with that the real point of resemblance has fallen away.

When we examine the texts more closely, those passages are first of all to be referred to in which the concept of ransom (payment) is specifically mentioned. So indeed very explicitly in 1 Timothy 2:5, 6, where there is mention of "the one Mediator between God and man, the man Christ Jesus, who gave himself a ransom (antilytron) for all." Closely akin to this is the pronouncement in Titus 2:14: "Christ Jesus, who gave himself for us, that he might redeem (lytrōsētai) us from all

---

33. Ephapax; cf. Sanday and Headlam, The Epistle to the Romans, 5th ed., 1950, p. 160.

34. Agorazō (1 Cor. 6:20; 7:23); exagorazō (Gal. 3:13; 4:5); lytroomai (Tit. 2:14); antilytron (1 Tim. 2:6); apolytrōsis (Rom. 3:24). Cf. the essay of Lyonnet, "[Exagorazein] bei Paulus," in Biblica, 1961, 42nd number.

35. To be sure, the concepts hilaskomai and lytron have their Old Testament background in words of the same stem, kipper and kōpher. While the former (to cover, to atone), however, usually has a sacral significance, the latter (ransom) lies in the terrain of civil law (cf. Procksch, TDNT, IV, pp. 329f., s.v. lyō, and Herrmann, TDNT, III, p. 303, s.v. hilaskomai. This applies to (ex)agorazō without qualification.

36. See A. Deissmann, Licht vom Osten, 4th ed., 1923, p. 274.

iniquity. . . ." These passages have rightly been viewed[37] as closely linked to the well-known words of Jesus himself in Mark 10:45 and Matthew 20:28, ". . . to give his soul as a ransom for many." The idea of Mediator that appears along with this (in 1 Tim. 2:6) designates Christ as the authorized representative both of God and of men. It is he who represents God with men and men with God.[38] In this latter function he offers the ransom payment. At the root of this idea is the old Jewish legal custom set out in the law, according to which a ransom could be given for the forfeited life (cf. Exod. 21:30).[39] According to this line of thought the object of the ransom is not the slave who receives his freedom, but the one condemned to death whose life is saved in this fashion.

This idea finds somewhat less clear-cut expression in those passages where the salvation of Christ is denoted with the general word "liberation" (apolytrōsis), a word that originally meant liberation-through-ransom, but is no longer always used in the strict sense (cf. Luke 21:28; Rom. 8:23). In our opinion it is undeniable that in certain places the ransom idea still obtains. Thus, for example, in Ephesians 1:7, where liberation (redemption) through his blood is spoken of,[40] and this liberation is then equated with the forgiveness of sins (cf. also Col. 1:14). The same applies to Romans 3:24, where the thought of setting at liberty is most closely connected with the reconciliation God has given through the blood of Christ. Here the thought of the sacral propitiatory death and the idea of redemption borrowed from legal life would then be coupled very closely together. Although it is not to be determined with certainty in each case to what extent the original significance of "redemption" plays a part in Paul's use of the word liberation, it cannot be denied that in his preaching in general the idea of redemption-by-ransom has no less clear a place than that of atoning death,[41] and where this liberation is related in particular to Christ's death one will have to take serious account of the possibility that in those passages (especially Eph. 1:7; cf. Col. 1:14 and Rom. 3:24) the apostle intended this liberation quite positively in the original pregnant sense of ransom.[42]

---

37. Cf. Büchsel, *TDNT*, IV, p. 349, *s.v. antilytron;* J. Jeremias, *Die Briefe an Timotheus und Titus,* 5th ed., 1949, p. 15.

38. Cf. Oepke, *TDNT*, IV, p. 619, *s.v. mesitēs.*

39. Cf. G. Dalman on Mark 10:45, in *Jesus Jeshua,* ET 1929, pp. 118f.

40. This is overlooked by Büchsel, when he writes: "Nowhere in all these passages [namely, where Paul uses the word *apolytrōsis*] is the death or blood of Jesus mentioned" (*TWNT*, IV, p. 357, *s.v. apolytrōsis.* This sentence is not translated in the English edition of the dictionary.)

41. It is accordingly incomprehensible why, as Büchsel supposes (*loc. cit.*), next to the (sacral) idea of *hilastērion* there is no longer any place for the conception—derived from legal life—of ransom in Rom. 3:24, especially because elsewhere, too, *apolytrōsis* is connected with the death of Christ.

42. Procksch—otherwise than Büchsel—in the same article in *TDNT* simply assumes this (cf. IV, p. 335); so also Arndt-Gingrich-Bauer, *Greek-English Lexicon,* p. 95, *s.v. apolytrōsis;* cf. also Dibelius on Eph. 1:7 (*Col.,* p. 60); and on Rom. 3:24 Greijdanus, *Rom.,* I, p. 194; Lietzmann, *Rom.,* p. 49; Sanday and Headlam, *The Epistle to the Romans,* p. 86; Althaus, *Rom.,* p. 28; otherwise Zahn, *Rom.,* p. 181; Schlatter, *Gottes Gerechtigkeit,* 2nd ed., 1952, p. 143; Dodd, *The Epistle of Paul to the Romans,* pp. 51, 52; Sevenster, *Christologie van het N.T.,* p. 171.

How explicitly Paul speaks of "to ransom," "to redeem," may appear finally from a quartet of other passages where in the Greek the ordinary word for "to purchase" as a business term (agorazō, exagorazō) is employed, namely, 1 Corinthians 6:20 and 7:23, where it is said: "You were bought and paid for,"[43] and Galatians 3:13; 4:5, where it is said that "Christ redeemed us from the curse of the law, having become a curse for us," and again, that he was born under the law "that he might redeem them that were under the law." All these passages relate the salvation thus described once again with Christ's death on the cross. When Büchsel writes: "Intentionally it is not said ... at what cost [the Christians were bought],"[44] this can be accepted only if it is definitely established that this price was the death of Christ[45] (cf. 1 Pet. 1:19). No other price or payment had in any case been spoken of. That we must so understand these passages — which have a paraenetic purpose and do not expressly describe the redemptive work of Christ — is clearly evident from Galatians 3:14; 4:5. There Christ's curse-death on the cross is designated as the manner in which he has bought us. This is also the significance of Christ's being "under the law" in Galatians 4:5.

Finally, the question arises here again as to the sense in which one will have to understand this representation of the salvation accomplished by Christ as redemption. Time and again scholars of every sort have laid stress on the fact that it is nowhere said to whom the price is paid. The main consideration here for most of them is the idea, correct in itself, that one must not think of a kind of business transaction between Christ and God, of which believers would then be the stake. To this extent one can consider it significant that it is not said that Christ paid the price to God.[46] Yet on the other side, one should take no less care to see that the objective character of what is here called "to redeem," "ransom," etc., is not compromised. One runs this risk, in our view, when it is posited that there is "no question here in fact of a case at law with God,"[47] or that Paul gives no answer to questions as to the significance of the necessity and the possibility of such a legal case with God and that, for Paul, in the cross of Christ God is not the

---

43. *Ēgorasthēte timēs:* you were bought for cash; cf. Lietzmann-Kümmel, *Cor.,* p. 29.

44. *TDNT,* I, p. 125, *s.v. agorazō.* Sevenster correctly writes that by *timēs* it is surely indicated that this liberation was anything but a simple matter, but that only because a price was really paid could this deliverance become reality (*Christologie van het N.T.,* p. 167, cf. p. 169).

45. Cf. Schlatter, *Erläuterungen,* VI, 3rd ed., 1920, p. 55; Grosheide, *1 Cor.,* p. 177; Lietzmann, on 1 Cor. 6:20 (*Cor.,* p. 28), who refers to Gal. 3:13, being contradicted by Kümmel (p. 176); Sanday and Headlam, *The Epistle to the Romans,* p. 86, who also understand *timē* of the death of Christ and observe that "the emphasis is on the *cost* of man's redemption."

46. Cf., e.g., Büchsel, *TDNT,* I, pp. 125, 126; Sevenster, *Christologie,* p. 169; Grosheide, on 1 Cor. 6:20: "Paul does not say from whom (viz., you are bought), nor should one want to ask that question" (p. 177); Oepke, *Gal.,* p. 58: "To whom the price is paid remains undecided."

47. Sevenster, *Christologie,* p. 169; he adds to this, however, that it surely does sound throughout the whole figure that in this ransoming the justice of God's law has been satisfied (*loc. cit.*).

Recipient but the One who is acting.[48] Altogether objectionable is the notion that Paul did not consider Christ as in reality burdened with the curse of God, but speaks in Galatians 3:13 from the legalistic standpoint that he himself had rejected; in Christ it would then (on this viewpoint) appear that the curse of the law is not the curse of God and in this way the idea that God deals with men on a legalistic basis would be carried *ad absurdum*. The deliverance from the curse of the law would then mean only "a release from a false conception of God's attitude."[49]

However much we have to guard against a pedestrian notion of "buy," "price," "pay," as though the salvation Christ has accomplished were a matter of a business transaction, this does not alter the fact that the whole thought of redemption and ransom rests on the awful reality of the curse of the law (Gal. 3:13; 4:5), a curse that one may not understand as an independent, blind force detached from God, but as the fulfillment of the divine threat against sin (Gal. 3:14). There is here in fact, however inadequate human words may be, a case at law between God and men, both Jews and gentiles.[50] In this Christ makes his appearance as the Mediator, who gives the ransom for all (1 Tim. 2:6). His death is the costly price in this case. Here again the great presupposition is that God himself has sent and given his own Son to that end (Gal. 4:4, 5). Just as in the passages that speak of Christ's atoning death (see above), this is the great secret that has now been revealed, the content of the gospel. In it Christ represents God with men (1 Tim. 2:6). As the one sent of God, he takes the curse upon himself and he dies, burdened with it, in place of men on the cross. He pays the price for them, he therein unites in himself God's saving will toward the world and his wrath against the sin of the world. In the complex of ideas concerning redemption the thought of substitution is here perhaps still clearer than it was in the concept of Christ's atoning death. It constitutes the fixed content of the ransom concept.[51] For this reason the expression "became a curse for us" not only means "in our behalf," but "in our place"[52] as well (cf. 1 Tim. 2:6; Tit. 2:14). Although it is not thus said that Christ redeems his own from God, yet God is the one whose holy curse is executed on Christ in their place. Justice is not thrust aside, but justice is satisfied. Although we meet with no word for "satisfaction" in Paul, the idea of substitutionary satisfaction is materially present here. Salvation consists in the possibility, given by God and realized by Christ, that justice is victorious in love and love

---

48. Büchsel, *TDNT*, I, p. 127. Büchsel is obliged, however—apparently *à contre coeur!*—to admit that "obviously action and the . . . receiving of effects cannot be absolutely separated" (n. 3).

49. So E. De Witt Burton, *A Critical and Exegetical Commentary on the Epistle to the Galatians*, 1948 (1921), p. 168. Oepke rightly speaks of this and similar explanations as "rationalizing interpretations" (*Gal.*, p. 57). Cf. Greijdanus, *De brief van den Apostel Paulus aan de Gemeenten in Galatië*, 1936, pp. 215ff.

50. Thus Schlier, e.g., correctly interprets *hēmas* in Gal. 3:13 (*Gal.*, pp. 93ff.).

51. Cf. Procksch, *TDNT*, IV, p. 329, *s.v. lyō;* cf. also Herrmann, *TDNT*, III, pp. 303ff., *s.v. hilaskomai.*

52. Oepke (*Gal.*, p. 57) points to the papyri for this use of *hyper (egrapsa hyper autou agrammatou*—the formula with which letters, etc., were signed in the stead of an illiterate).

in justice. And all this one should view not in the first place as the substance of Paul's personal experience or as the consequence of a severe, juridically conceived scheme of salvation, but as the apostolic unfolding of the meaning of the event, crossing all human expectations and calculations, of the death of Jesus Christ the Son of God. It is this eschatological fact of redemption which — in conjunction with the kerygma of the primitive church and in the light of the Old Testament, only now rightly understood — forms for Paul the propelling force for all his thoughts and causes him — not only as theologian, but as witness of revelation legitimated by Christ himself — to trace on all sides the salvation of the Lord realized in it.

SECTION 35. THE ADOPTION OF SONS. THE INHERITANCE

The new relationship between God and men, at the root of which lies justification, which can be considered as reconciliation and is effected by Christ's substitutionary work as Mediator (atonement, ransom), finally finds expression in the important concept adoption of sons (huiothesia). The close connection of all these definitions of the salvation that has appeared in Christ may be seen, for example, from the pronouncement in Galatians 4:4ff., that "when the fulness of the time was come, [God] sent forth his Son, born of a woman, born under the law, to redeem them that were under the law, that we might receive the adoption of sons." The adoption of sons is here described, therefore, as the object of the great eschatological redemptive event and as the direct result of redemption, just as that is said elsewhere of justification (Rom. 3:25, 26; 4:25) and of reconciliation (2 Cor. 5:18, 19). And as elsewhere God's grace and love are designated as the principle of justification and of reconciliation, so the apostle says in Ephesians 1:5 that God in his love destined us beforehand to the adoption of sons.

Scholars have accordingly been able to say of these various central concepts with a certain degree of justice[53] that they are only different figures for the same thing and are related to each other as concentric circles. However, this does not alter the fact, evident already from the preceding, that each one of these descriptions has its own specific significance and that only by means of the determination of that significance can the rich content of the gospel be illuminated. This applies as well to the concept adoption of sons.

The term stems from the Hellenistic world of law;[54] its content, however, must not be inferred from the various Roman or Greek legal systems,[55] nor from the adoption ritual of the Hellenistic mystery

53. Cf. J. L. De Villiers, Die betekenis van [HUIOTHESIA] in die briewe van Paulus, 1950, p. 3.

54. It does not occur in the LXX (Arndt-Gingrich-Bauer, Greek-English Lexicon, p. 841, s.v. huiothesia; W. Twisselmann, Die Gotteskindschaft der Christen nach dem N.T., 1939, p. 58; De Villiers, ibid., p. 69). For the Hellenistic use, especially in the papyri, see A. Deissmann, Neue Bibelstudien, 1897, pp. 66ff.

55. See the detailed discussion in De Villiers, Die betekenis, pp. 48ff. He is

cults,[56] but must rather be considered against the Old Testament, redemptive-historical background of the adoption of Israel as son of God.

Of special importance for this last point is the pronouncement in Romans 9:4, where Paul lists the "adoption of sons" as one of the privileges of Israel. To the same effect he applies to the New Testament church, with some modification in wording, the theocratic promise of God to David in 2 Samuel 7:14: "I will be to you a Father, and you shall be to me sons and daughters" (2 Cor. 6:18; cf. Rom. 9:26). From this original significance of sonship as the special covenant relationship between God and Israel it is also to be explained that Paul alternately and in very much the same sense speaks of "children of God" and "children" or "seed of Abraham" (Rom. 9:7, 8; Gal. 3:26, 29; 4:6, 7, 28, 29). It is this peculiar privilege of Israel as nation that, in conformity with the Old Testament promises of redemption (cf. 2 Cor. 6:16-18), passes over to the church of the New Testament and there receives a new, deepened significance. In Jesus' preaching, too, this redemptive-historical meaning forms the background of his repeated speaking of the sonship of God.[57]

When we consider in greater detail the passages where Paul expressly speaks of the sonship of believers and of their adoption as sons, it becomes clear at once that he is again thinking in redemptive-historical, eschatological categories. Sonship is not to be approached from the subjective experience of the new condition of salvation, but rather from the divine economy of salvation, as God foreordained it in his eternal love (Eph. 1:5), and realized it in principle in the election of Israel as his people. It took effect "when faith came" (Gal. 3:25, 26), that is to say, when the new order and dispensation of salvation became effective.[58] Or, as it is said still more explicitly in Galatians 4:4ff., "when the fulness of the time came, God sent forth his Son . . . , that we might receive the adoption of sons." Sonship is therefore a gift of the great time of redemption that has dawned with Christ. It is the fulfillment

---

of the opinion, in our view on good grounds, that Paul's usage of this legal term has reference only very generally to the practice of adoption frequently occurring at that time, without his having thought of the juridical details of the official Roman or Greek administration of justice. De Villiers, in the footsteps of L. Mitteis, does draw attention to the later legal usage of the *adoptio minus plena*, which served only to assure the right of inheritance to the adopted son and did not involve a full *patria potestas*. The only effect of such an adoption was the inalienable right of inheritance. The earlier Roman legislation did not know this form of adoption. In view of the close connection that Paul, too, places between sonship and heirship (see below) this form of adoption could have been in his mind. An objection is that the evidences for this practice of adoption only stem from a much later period, namely, from the fourth century A.D. See also Foerster, *TDNT*, III, pp. 768ff., *s.v. klēronomos.*

56. Cf., e.g., Bousset on Gal. 3:27 in *Die Schriften des N.T.*, II, 1917, p. 58. In these mystery liturgies, however, there is no question of an adoption as sons. It is a matter here of participating in the deity, an idea that is entirely lacking in the Pauline adoption concept.

57. Cf. my *The Coming of the Kingdom*, pp. 236ff.

58. Cf. above, p. 174.

of the promise that was given of old to the true people of God (Rom. 9:26; 2 Cor. 6:18).

The sonship of believers is furthermore closely bound up with the fact that Christ is the Son of God. When God reveals his Son, the adoption of sons also takes effect (Gal. 4:4), and it is the Spirit of God's Son whom God has sent forth into our hearts, who cries: "Abba, Father!" (v. 6). It is sonship "in Christ Jesus" (Gal. 3:26), that is to say, it is given with him in his advent; as the eschatological Bringer of salvation, he is the one in whom, for those who are included in him, this new redemptive state has been given.

Just as reconciliation, the adoption of sons signifies more than a purely forensic description of the salvation given with Christ. The term drawn from Hellenistic legal life *(huiothesia)* must not lead us astray here. Undoubtedly the adoption of sons can be put on a level and mentioned in one breath with justification (Gal. 3:23-26), insofar as it, too, is obtained only "through faith," and is set in an exclusive sense over against that which is sought in the way of works, as appears from the context in which Paul, in the Epistle to the Galatians, places sonship over against bondage under the law. It consists above all in a gift of God, given at the time appointed by him (Gal. 4:2), as a new status that means the end of being-under-the-law (Gal. 4:1-5). But at the same time[59] it denotes the new relationship to God in a more comprehensive sense: it is the fruit, the consequence of the reconciling, redeeming appearance of Christ (Gal. 4:5), it is the reconciliation accomplished by God himself, it is its realization.

This is also evident from the fact that the sonship of believers is related in particular to the work of the Holy Spirit. There is in the Pauline pronouncements a peculiar relationship of reciprocity between the adoption of sons and the gift of the Spirit, which has given occasion in the exegetical literature to all kinds of confused discussions.[60] At one time, in Galatians 4:6ff., it seems that sonship precedes the gift of the Spirit: "And because[61] you are sons, God sent forth the Spirit of his Son into our hearts, crying, Abba, Father!"

Then again, in Romans 8:14-16, sonship seems to be the result of the gift of the Spirit: "For as many as are led by the Spirit of God, these are the sons of God. For you have not received the spirit of

---

59. Some wish to distinguish still further between the "adoption" as sons as a forensic declaration of will and the relation of sonship itself.

60. Cf. on this at length De Villiers, *Die betekenis,* pp. 165ff. and the literature cited there.

61. This is at least the most obvious translation. In order, however, to escape the apparent discrepancy with Rom. 8:14, another translation has been proposed here: "And that you are sons—God has sent forth his Spirit into our hearts," etc. See, e.g., the translation of the Dutch Bible Society and furthermore the commentaries on Galatians, such as those of Zahn, Lietzmann, Lagrange, etc. Oepke says of it: "Paul cannot be held responsible for this monstrosity of a sentence" *(Gal.,* p. 74). One need not go so far in order to reject this translation as altogether too biased and with the great majority of interpreters, e.g., Calvin, Bengel, Schlatter, De Witt Burton, Greijdanus, Schlier, to choose for the translation of *hoti de este huioi* as giving the reason; cf. also De Villiers, *Die betekenis,* pp. 98ff.; see further below, in the text.

bondage again unto fear; but you have received the Spirit of the adoption of sons, through whom we cry, Abba, Father! The Spirit himself bears witness with our spirit, that we are the children of God."

Yet the unity of these pronouncements is not difficult to grasp if one pays heed to the place and significance that the work of the Holy Spirit occupies in the great eschatological *ordo salutis*. Precisely in connection with the adoption of sons the apostle speaks of the Holy Spirit as "firstfruits" (Rom. 8:23), in the same sense that he elsewhere terms the Spirit the "earnest" of the salvation of the great future[62] (2 Cor. 1:22; 2 Cor. 5:5; Eph. 1:14). Over against that the adoption of sons embraces more; it spans the present as well as the great future. Now the whole creation, subjected to vanity, still waits with earnest expectation for the revealing of the sons of God, when it will be delivered from the bondage of corruption into the liberty of the glory of the children of God (Rom. 8:19-21). And likewise believers themselves, however much they have already received the Spirit as firstfruits, groan within themselves in the expectation of the adoption of sons, when their body, too, will be redeemed (v. 23). Over against the provisional and temporary character of this gift of the Spirit stands thus the adoption of sons, which has, to be sure, taken effect with the appearance of Christ, but has a future and definitive significance. It is not to be viewed in such a way that the sonship of believers is a secondary gift that proceeds from the primary gift of the Spirit. It is rather that the adoption of sons represents the new state of salvation that has come with Christ[63] in its all-embracing and eternal destination, and that the Holy Spirit in the meantime as gift of the interim "helps us in our weakness" (v. 26). Where salvation cannot yet break through in its perfection, where the sonship of believers awaits revelation in its all-embracing significance affecting the whole cosmos, there the Spirit enters in as firstfruits, to keep alive in the hearts of believers the consciousness, the certainty, the liberty of sonship. The Spirit as Substitute and Intercessor of the church cries and teaches to pray: "Abba, Father!" and thus maintains the connection between what is and what is yet to take place (cf. Rev. 22:17).[64]

---

62. See also Section 14, pp. 87ff.

63. Cf. Greijdanus, *Gal.*, p. 262: "It is not the reception of the Spirit which is objectively the cause of being set free from the law, but Christ's advent and work of reconciliation is its objective ground. And the reception of the Spirit is the outworking and mark of that objective being set at liberty. . . ."

64. The significance of the "crying" of the Spirit (*krazō*) is variously understood. Some wish to understand it with a view to ecstatic speaking, glossolalia, in the church. So, e.g., Oepke, *Gal.*, p. 75. Wrongly, in our opinion. It is a question here in the first place of that which the Spirit says, who has been sent forth into the hearts of believers (Gal. 4:6). And in Rom. 8:16 it is said that this Spirit witnesses with our spirit, which in no respect whatever leads one to think of ecstatic glossolalia; cf. also Grundmann, *TDNT*, III, p. 903, *s.v. krazō*. Others see here a token of the boldness (Greijdanus), the joy (Schlatter), the desire, the trust, the steadfastness (Bengel) with which the Spirit teaches to pronounce the name "Father!" All this may contain truth, although the word "to cry" does not in itself evoke these associations. In our view one must simply think here of the Greek equivalent

In this light it is clear that no reason whatever exists to mistrust the translation of Galatians 4:6: "because you are sons, God sent forth his Spirit into our hearts," etc. It exactly reproduces the meaning of the apostle. The Spirit comes in order to "maintain" sonship. Romans 8:14ff. is in no way in conflict with this. The stress does not lie on the first part of verse 14, but on the second. The principal train of thought is this: he who by the Spirit puts to death the old man will live (v. 13). For those who do that (permit themselves to be led by the Spirit) are sons of God (v. 14). And for God's children the eternal inheritance has been prepared (v. 17). Verses 15 and 16, moreover, have a certain parenthetical significance. They say that the Spirit through whom the children of God are led to the putting to death of the deeds of the body is also the Spirit who works and keeps alive in them the consciousness and certainty of sonship by bearing witness "with their spirit" that they are children of God.

The further question now is what this adoption of sons in Christ by the Holy Spirit involves. We have already pointed out that sonship or the sonship of God is of old a collective aspect or privilege of the people of God. It should also be understood as such in Paul's epistles. This is evident even from the alternate use of "children of God" and "children [seed] of Abraham" (see above). The liberty of the children of God (Gal. 4:7) is none other than of those who have received as their mother the Jerusalem that is above, as the new center of life given over against the earthly Jerusalem (Gal. 4:26). It is belonging to the new people of God, whereby the gentiles, too, may be called "sons of the living God" (Rom. 9:26). The evidence of sonship accordingly lies in that one has by baptism put on Christ and thus belongs to this new unity in Christ, in which no distinction is made (Gal. 3:26, 27). This "congregational" aspect of the adoption as sons, however little it is further expressly unfolded in Paul's epistles, forms — one may say — the self-evident and dominating point of departure for all that is said about the sonship of believers.

This does not alter the fact, however, that it is just in these sonship pronouncements that the personal and intimate character of the reconciled relationship with God finds expression. God sends his Spirit into the hearts of his children to witness with their spirit (Gal. 4:6; Rom. 8:16). Conversely, this adoption of sons must make believers live in the true relation of sonship. They must put aside the slavish fear of God (Rom. 8:15), and ever and again[65] may call on him as their Father in the communion of the Spirit (Rom. 8:15; Gal. 4:6). How personally and — in a certain sense — in how deeply human a manner the apostle understands this exercise of communion, and the extent to which he knows human timidity and weakness in it, find their most beautiful expression precisely in these passages on the Spirit and sonship. The Spirit is not only the one who teaches us to stand in this childlike relationship to God and to pronounce steadfastly the name Father in spite of all that still raises itself against this relationship; he is also the

of the "crying" to God frequently employed in the Psalms, as the denotation of prayer; cf. further my *Rom.*, pp. 182, 183.

65. *Krazomen* (Rom. 8:15) and *krazon* (Gal. 4:6), both present forms.

one who maintains this living communion. He comes from God to awaken in the hearts of God's people the true consciousness of children, but he also mounts up, as it were, from the hearts of the children to God, because in their inability to find the right words in prayer he enters in for them with unutterable groanings; and God, the great searcher of hearts, will judge them according to this holy intention of the Spirit which is acceptable to God (Rom. 8:26ff.). Thus the work of the "Spirit-of-sonship" (Rom. 8:15) forms the indispensable and unbreakable link in the whole of God's plan of redemption. For to them who love God as their Father, all things must work together for blessing. For whom God knew beforehand as his son and has drawn to himself, these will he bring to the appointed goal: to bear the glorious image of his Son. To this end he calls them out of the world as his own, to this end he justifies them and leads them to glory (Rom. 8:28ff.). In these profound and moving words of Romans 8 Paul delineates the unshakable firmness and the intimacy of the relationship in which God draws and keeps his own to himself. Therefore as God's beloved children, in imitation[66] of their Father, they are to walk in love, even as Christ loved them (Eph. 5:1), as blameless children of God in the midst of a perverse generation (Phil. 2:15), as children of God who are at the same time the children of the light and of the day (Eph. 5:8; 1 Thess. 5:5).

It appears from all this how difficult it is to come to a meaningful delimitation of what must be considered the specific character of the sonship of believers.[67] In the context of the epistles to the Romans and to the Galatians sonship represents in a special sense the principle of liberty. This liberty, however, is likewise a very comprehensive concept. It consists in freedom from the law, and therefore, in harmony with what has been said about justification and redemption, has a forensic significance (Gal. 3:23-25). At the same time, however, as the liberty that is worked and maintained by the Spirit, it has a much more inclusive sense, particularly in the last chapters of Galatians, where liberty is described as the power and the principle of the whole Christian life and stands in contrast to the discord and impotence of the life that is under the law (Rom. 7:14ff.); while this liberty finally has reference as well to the future glory of the children of God (Rom. 8:21). This is not the place to go further into this liberty through the Spirit and in general into the working out of sonship in the life of believers. We must return to that in the following chapter when we shall treat still further the life by the Spirit as the subjective side of the salvation that has appeared in Christ.[68]

We still have to refer separately in this context to one important aspect

---

66. For this aspect of sonship see also W. P. De Boer, *The Imitation of Paul*, 1962, pp. 75ff.

67. See also the valuable development of the concept in De Villiers, *Die betekenis*, pp. 149-200: "Die wese van die [*huiothesia*]." One can also observe in that, however, how difficult it is to come to a valid delimitation of what "the essence" of *huiothesia* is.

68. Cf. below, Section 38ff.

of sonship, namely, to the close connection that Paul makes both in Romans and in Galatians between the adoption of sons and the place of believers as heirs. For this connection, too, the redemptive-historical viewpoint is of special significance. For however much the idea of being heirs, etc., has its motive in the Greek juridical term "adoption as sons,"[69] on the other side the concept "portion," "heir," etc., is in the Old Testament no less closely bound up with that of "people of God" and "seed of Abraham." We see therefore how in Galatians and Romans these three ideas — sons of God, seed of Abraham, heirs — run through each other: "For you are all sons of God, through faith in Christ Jesus. . . . And if you are Christ's, then you are Abraham's seed, and heirs according to the promise" (Gal. 3:26, 29).

Taken formally, heirship is therefore not derived from the sonship of God, but from belonging to Abraham's seed. Elsewhere, however, there is a direct connection between the first two:

> So you are no longer a slave, but a son; and if a son, then an heir through God (Gal. 4:7).
> And if children, then heirs; heirs of God and joint heirs with Christ (Rom. 8:17).

From this last phrase, "joint heirs with Christ," it is evident, just as with the adoption as sons, that Christ as the Son of God is the one in communion with whom the inheritance is received. He is also, however, the Seed of Abraham, to whom the promise of the inheritance had reference (Gal. 3:16, 18). The whole thought complex of inheritance, to inherit, etc., in Paul's epistles does not thus rest on an incidental figure of speech, nor only on an association of ideas in connection with "adoption as sons." It represents much more the primal promise given of old to Abraham and his seed (cf. Rom. 4:13; Gal. 3:8); it recurs in many different ways in the history of the people of God and acquires therein an ever clearer eschatological content.[70]

For this reason one is able to qualify this inheritance as "consummation of the sonship."[71] Paul's epistles, too, describe it ever and again as future glory, together with Christ (Rom. 8:17; cf. Eph. 1:18), as the (coming) kingdom of God (1 Cor. 6:9ff.; 15:50a; Gal. 5:21), as imperishableness (1 Cor. 15:50b), as eternal life (Tit. 3:7). The "inheritance" is the regular denotation of that which in the future is to be the portion of the true people of God (Eph. 1:14, 18; 5:5; Col. 3:24; cf. 1:12). However much, therefore, sonship contains heirship within itself and the latter is thus not merely a matter of the future, but very definitely of the present as well (as comes to the fore particularly in Galatians), this does not alter the fact that the gift that springs from heirship and which

---

69. Above all when one understands this as *terminus technicus* in the sense of *adoptio minus plena* (cf. above, p. 198). According to Foerster on the other hand the link between sonship and heirship in the theological usage was almost entirely lacking in the Old Testament and later Judaism (*TDNT*, III, pp. 781f.).

70. Cf. also Foerster, *loc. cit.*

71. So De Villiers, *Die betekenis*, p. 188.

likewise will only bring sonship to (full) "revelation" (Rom. 8:19) is still a matter of hope and expectation.[72]

From this side, too, the all-embracing significance of the sonship of believers given in Christ comes to light. It admits of expression neither only in juridical nor in ethical categories. It is the privilege of the church as the true people of God, but at the same time it affects the individual believer in the deepest motives of his existence. It has bearing not only on his inner, but also on his physical life; indeed, it brings with it the redemption of the whole cosmos. The present and the future are therefore spanned by it. The whole love of the Father, the whole redeeming work of Christ, the whole renewing power of the Holy Spirit, are reflected in it. At the conclusion of our discussion of reconciliation it is evident that the redeeming activity of God commencing with the justification of the sinner communicates itself in ever wider spheres.

---

72. It is accordingly difficult to understand how some are able to doubt that in general *klēronomia* does indeed have an eschatological content (in Foerster, *TDNT*, III, p. 783, n. 30).

VI
THE NEW LIFE

SECTION 36. THE GENERAL POINT OF VIEW

In the preceding chapters we have become acquainted with Paul's preaching of the salvation that has appeared in Christ, specifically according to its forensic and "objective" aspects, as the restoration of the right relationship to God in justification, reconciliation, the adoption of sons. It has thereby been evident again and again that the salvation thus described does not consist only in a new relationship, but that a restoration of the whole of life in the most inclusive sense of the word results from it and has been given with it. The righteousness of God that has been revealed in Christ is a "righteousness unto life" (Rom. 5:18), reconciliation accomplishes peace in the renewing of the world and man, the adoption of sons becomes manifest in the operation of the Spirit in the hearts of believers, etc. It is this taking effect of salvation in the existence of the world and man, this new mode of existence given with Christ's advent and work, to which our attention must now further be directed.

What is involved here, of course, is that which nullifies the operation of sin in man. The new life, the work of the Holy Spirit, faith as the new mode of existence, liberty, all these must come up for discussion here; in short, the entire reverse side of that which could be ascertained in Chapter III with respect to the outworking of sin in the death and bondage of man. It is of decisive importance for the understanding of this part of the Pauline preaching, however, that in accordance with its fundamental structures here also we keep in view the great eschatological, redemptive-historical line. Not only justification from the guilt of sin, but also deliverance from the power of sin, renewal, sanctification, faith, are for Paul above all "eschatological" realities, which demand to be understood as revelation of the new aeon that has appeared with Christ's advent and work. The work of the Holy Spirit, too, stands entirely under this sign. The Spirit as the Spirit of Christ is the Spirit of the new aeon, and all that he renews, re-creates, changes, is new and different because it pertains to this eschatological "newness." Undoubtedly all this works itself out and finds its application in the individual man, and the significance of the new manhood is explained further in all sorts of anthropological concepts and categories. Yet it holds here as well, and perhaps to a still greater degree than in the doctrine of sin, that the great *Vorverständnis* of all Paul's preaching is not of an anthropological but of a redemptive-historical, eschatological, that is to say, of a christological and pneumatological nature. The anthropological significance of salvation not only has its ground in

Christ, but in its various facets has also been designated out of that which has taken place in and with Christ. The result is that in Paul's preaching there is no such thing as a systematic development of the *ordo salutis,* a detailed doctrine of the anthropological application of salvation. The cause for this is not only that the character of Paul's doctrine is not "systematic" in the scientific sense of the word, but above all that his viewpoint is a different one.

To put it succinctly, Paul's doctrine of the new life does not find its determinative point of departure in the new "creature" but in the new "creation," as it is expressed in 2 Corinthians 5:17: "If any man is in Christ, he is [he belongs to the] new creation. The old things have passed away, behold! new things have come."

As we have already been able to ascertain (Section 10), all this does not speak in the first place of personal, individual regeneration, the individual past and the personal renewal. It is a matter here of redemptive-historical categories of old and new. Undoubtedly this does not mean a de-personalizing of salvation. The new man, as we shall see still further, is not merely a collective or supra-individual quantity. But as in the doctrine of sin, where the individual's inclusion in the great corporate relationship of solidarity in sin was the dominating point of view, so also in the doctrine of renewal, what predominates is the inclusion and participation in the new creation that has taken effect with Christ and is represented by him. What this means for the various facets of the new life and what anthropological implications all this has will have to appear further in the continuation of our inquiry.

SECTION 37. DEATH AND RESURRECTION WITH CHRIST

The extent to which the new life of believers receives its specific character in what "once" took place with Christ is perhaps most clear from the manner in which in the Epistle to the Romans — after first having spoken of the revelation of the righteousness of God in chapters 3-5 — Paul, in the opening words of chapter 6, raises the question of the new life and then answers: "Shall we continue in sin, that grace may abound? By no means! We who died to sin, how shall we any longer live therein?" (Rom. 6:1, 2).

The importance of this pronouncement lies first of all in that it is not an ethical or mystical reality that is denoted by the words "we who have died to [or for] sin." As is apparent from the whole context, it is not a question of dying to sin in a metaphorical sense (conversion or something like it[1]), but of the participation of the church in the death and burial of Christ in the one-time, redemptive-historical sense of the word.

That this is the meaning is evident from all that follows. It

---

1. Thus, e.g., Greijdanus, who with *apethanomen* wishes to think of coming to faith in Christ (*Rom.,* I, p. 293).

appears first of all from Paul's appeal to baptism to make his point. For the pronouncement that the church has died to sin is followed by the words: "Or do you not know that all we who have been baptized into Christ Jesus were baptized into his death? We were buried therefore with him through baptism into death. . . ."

This is not the place to go at length into the significance of baptism in Paul's doctrine of salvation. With a reference to that which is yet to be said about it,[2] it may here be already established, however, that the appeal to baptism has its ground in the significance of baptism as the incorporation into and the putting on of Christ (1 Cor. 12:13; Gal. 3:27, et al.), and in thus receiving a share in his redemptive work. The corporate idea is dominant here again. By their being baptized into Christ and thus belonging to Christ, that which once took place in him is also valid for his own, indeed it can be said of them that they with him have been buried and have died to sin. This is not only a sacramental occurrence, but denotes the participation of believers (by means of the sacrament of baptism) in the redemptive event at Golgotha and in the garden of the resurrection. Accordingly Paul can say simply (that is, without special reference to baptism) that if one died for all, then all have died (2 Cor. 5:14),[3] or similarly, that we "through the body of Christ" (that is to say, in the way of the bodily death of Christ on the cross) have been made dead to the law (Rom. 7:4). Here the church is directly involved in the redemptive-historical event: when Christ died, they died, and his death was their own. But this redemptive-historical event is appropriated sacramentally to believers, and Paul can therefore appeal for the former to the latter.

How we are to understand this function of baptism and this fact that Christ's death and resurrection have validity for the church is explained still further in the profound pronouncement of verse 5: "For if we have become incorporated into the likeness of his death, we shall be also in the likeness of his resurrection."

"Have become incorporated" (symphytoi gegonamen) harks back to baptism, which is herewith expressly termed the incorporation into the life-context represented by Christ as the last Adam. Now, when this last is defined as "the likeness of his death [and resurrection],"[4] this is to denote the agreement as well as the distinction between what Christ's death and resurrection signify on the one hand for himself, and on the other for his own. One cannot speak here of an identity. For Christ came (and died) indeed "in the likeness of sinful flesh" (Rom. 8:3), yet without himself being sinful. His dying to sin is therefore not the same as the church's having died to sin. Similarly his "being raised from the dead through the glory of the Father" is not simply to be equated with the church's "walking in the new state of life" (v. 4). For this reason one can speak of its incorporation into the likeness of his death (and resurrection); it participates suo modo in Christ's death and resurrection.

---

2. See below, Sections 64, 65.
3. Nygren speaks of 2 Cor. 5:17 as "the best conceivable commentary on the point under discussion" (Rom. 6:2-6; Commentary on Romans, p. 235).
4. Homoiōma tou thanatou (tēs anastaseōs) autou.

On the other hand, this likeness is not only a symbolic or noetic conformity, but a redemptive-historical likeness by virtue of its oneness
with Christ.[5] It is of this partnership in Christ's death and resurrection
that the church must now be conscious, not only with a view to justification, but also with respect to the dominion that sin is bent on exer-
cising on its life. It has (once with Christ) "died to sin" (Rom. 6:2), or,
as it is expressed in verse 6: the church must know "that our old man
was crucified with him, that the body of sin might be done away, so
that we should no longer be in bondage to sin." Here again it is a
question of that which has been enacted in Christ's death. Then was
"our old man" crucified with him; and "old man" intended here not as
the individual past of particular believers in their unconverted state,
but as the supra-individual sinful mode of existence (entirely in harmony with the manner in which Paul again and again speaks of sin;
cf. Section 15ff.). And this can be said in this way because Christ has
suffered "in the body" — as human mode of existence — indeed, "in the
likeness of sinful flesh" (cf. Rom. 7:4; 8:3; Col. 1:22), and because God
thus has judged sin "in the flesh," namely, of Christ (Rom. 8:3; Eph.
2:14). In this way our old man has been crucified, judged, with him,
"in order that the body of sin should be rendered powerless."[6] Likewise,
what is intended by this body of sin is, as we have already been able
to determine in another context (cf. pp. 124ff.), the present human mode
of existence ruled by sin. Of this bondage to sin the cross and the death
of Christ have made an end. Paul expresses this in a peculiar way,
with the aid of the old rule of law: he who has died is according to the
law free from sin,[7] he has paid sin its toll, sin no longer has any claim
upon him. This applies in the first place to Christ, as it is put into
words yet again in verse 10, by way of conclusion: "For the death that
he died, he died for [to] sin once for all; but the life that he lives, he
lives to God."

Here again the thought is not that Christ died once "for the
sake of" or "for the atonement of" sin (in the sense of justification or
of reconciliation), but that he once died to[8] sin (considered as an authority that exercises power, asserts its claims), freed himself from it
and escaped it by his death, just as now by having risen he lives for
God, at his command and for his service.

It is in this sense that it can also hold for the church that it has

---

5. For this exegesis see, e.g., E. Percy, *Der Leib Christi*, 1942, p. 27; Greijdanus, *Rom.*, I, pp. 297ff. For the discussion of other opinions (i.a., of those who
understand *homoiōma tou thanatou autou* to mean baptism) see my *Rom.*, pp. 127-
129. A clear survey of the divergent views may be found in Schneider, *TDNT*, V,
pp. 192-195, *s.v. homoiōma*.

6. *Katargēthē:* render inoperative, make ineffective, an expression frequently
occurring in Paul to denote that which has been done away with in Christ's advent; cf. Delling, *TDNT*, I, pp. 453f.

7. *Dedikaiōtai apo tēs hamartias.* For this idea that death sets one free
from all claims, cf. the rabbinic formulations cited in Strack-Billerbeck, III, pp.
232, 234. Thus it is a matter here of another *dikaioun* than in the sense of Rom.
3:21ff.

8. The dative *tē hamartia apethanen* is to be taken as a *dativus incommodi:*
to the detriment of.

died to sin, namely, because it was crucified and buried with him. And it is the validity of this redemptive-historical and sacramental reality that in Romans 6 the apostle wishes to set before the church and on the ground of which in the second part of this chapter he stirs it up to serve sin no longer. What he wants to teach it, over against the reality of sin, is beyond anything else a new basis for self-judgment in its belonging to Christ and having died and been raised with him. As he says in 2 Corinthians 5, that henceforth (that is to say, on the ground of the resurrection of Christ) he will know no man "after the flesh," but will understand him as participating in the new aeon and the new creation, so the church also, if it is truly no longer to live in sin, must learn to understand itself by faith: "So you also must judge[9] yourselves [in the faith] as dead to sin and as alive to God in Christ Jesus" (v. 11).

In these last words the whole argument of Romans 6:1-10 is gathered together. Having died once with Christ may, so far as the present is concerned, be understood and laid hold on as being dead[10] to sin (that is, no longer subject to its power), just as being "incorporated in the likeness of his resurrection" may be known and must be experienced as being alive to God and as having-been-brought-under-his-dominion. What has taken place "once" in Christ must thus be actualized in a new way of life. "As[11] alive from the dead" believers are no longer to place themselves at the disposal of sin, but of God. They must fight their battle in the certainty that their enemy has been overcome. For they no longer live under the rule of the law, but under that of grace (Rom. 6:12ff.).

In recapitulating we can thus establish on the ground of this "locus classicus" concerning the fact of having died and been raised with Christ that the dying and rising of the church: (1) is comprehended in the redemptive-historical reality of Christ's death and resurrection; (2) is appropriated to believers in baptism as the sacramental incorporation into Christ; (3) forms the content of the church's actual assessment of faith concerning itself; (4) must have its effect in the manifestation of its life as obedient to God.

How characteristic of Paul's doctrine of redemption this view of the significance of Christ's death is, appears from a great number of other pronouncements. This same reality is expressed not only as the church's having died, having been crucified, to sin — but also "to the

---

9. *Logizesthai*, the typical denotation of the judgment of faith on the ground of the redemptive event in Christ (cf. Rom. 8:18; 14:14; Phil. 3:12; see also Heidland, *TDNT*, IV, p. 290).

10. *Einai nekrous tē hamartia zōntas de tō Theō.*

11. *Hōsei ek nekrōn zōntas.* Some take *hōsei* as a comparison ("as it were"; so, e.g., Bl.-Debr., Par. 425,3; Arndt-Gingrich-Bauer, p. 907, *s.v.*; Zahn, *Gal.*, pp. 313ff.), others as a motivation ("because you are"; e.g., the commentaries of Kühl, Greijdanus, Dodd; also Bultmann, *TDNT*, III, p. 19; *TDNT*, IV, p. 894). Paul certainly does not here speak only comparatively or figuratively. Yet *ek nekrōn zōntas* is not simply in apposition to *heautous*. The *hōsei* speaks again of the judgment of faith. Faith is permitted so to see this, and one must act out of the power of this judgment of faith.

world," "to the law," "to the first principles of the world." Thus, for
example, when it is said of the church in Romans 7:4ff.: "So that, my
brethren, you also have died to the law through the body of Christ, in
order to be [the possession] of another . . . ; we are discharged from the
law,[12] having died to that which held us captive." Here again it is a
matter of having once died with Christ, as is certainly very clear from
the addition of "through the body of Christ." The law is here the
menacing, fettering power. For that which lends sin its power is the
law in its sanctions. As therefore "to be under the law" and "to be
under sin" are synonymous denotations[13] of the state of death and
slavery of life outside Christ, so the dying of Christ for the church signifies having died for or to the law, having escaped from its killing
power. Paul is able to say elsewhere as well, therefore, that he "through
the law died to the law," in order to live for God. For "I have been
crucified with Christ" (Gal. 2:19). Here again "to the law" and "for
God" are placed over against each other to indicate to whom it is that
one belongs and is subject. The law is again thought of as the power
that is hostile to (sinful) man, which brings him under its jurisdiction, which obstructs the way to life. To this law Paul has now died
"through the law." The words "through the law" look to the sanctions
of the law that fell on Christ when he gave himself up for his own
(v. 20), in particular to his death on the cross. But in that dying through
the law there took place at the same time the escape from, the dying
to the law, for Christ as well as for those who are included in him.

One should also mention the pronouncement of Colossians 2:20,
where the church is asked how, if it has "died with Christ to the first
principles of the world,"[14] it can any longer permit all manner of ordinances to be imposed on it as though it were living in the world. The
"first principles of the world" are once again legalistic principles, in
Galatians 4:9 called "weak and beggarly rudiments," because they cannot save man (cf. Rom. 8:3), but are not on this account any less tyrannical and hold man in bondage (Gal. 4:3). To these, however, believers
have now died with Christ, because Christ has prepared another way
whereby one can be saved.

Somewhat different, with essentially the same meaning, is the
formulation of Galatians 6:14, where Paul declares that he wants only
to boast in the cross of Christ, through which "the world has been
crucified to me, and I to the world." The expression "the world" here
represents everything in which a man would wish to "boast,"[15] that is
to say, on which in a religious sense he would suppose himself able to
depend, as, for example, the law and circumcision (cf. v. 13). It is
denoted as "world" — just as "first principles of the world" — because it
pertains to the life-context of the present aeon, the life before and outside Christ. All this has for Paul once and for all (the perfect is employed here) been crucified through the cross of Christ.[16] When Christ

12. Here again *katērgēthēmen* (see above).
13. Cf. above, Section 23.
14. Cf. above, pp. 148f.
15. See above, pp. 140ff.
16. See Oepke, *Gal.*, pp. 122ff.: "One ought not to reduce the meaning [of

was crucified, all this was seen to be inadequate as a vain ground for boasting, indeed as a power threatening man. On the other hand, Paul is able to say that he has been "crucified to the world." When Christ was crucified his own were also snatched away from the world as a power dominating and fascinating them. "Through" (the cross) here stands in place of "with" or "in" (Christ); the thought is essentially the same, the corporate idea is somewhat less prominent; in the middle is the cross, which once snatched away the church from the world and by which the world has become worthless for the church, indeed entirely reprehensible (cf. Phil. 3:8).

All these expressions — died (crucified) to sin, the law, the world — denote what is fundamentally the same reality. They are the powers of the old aeon, and it is this old, all-embracing life-context from under whose control the church has been delivered in the death of Christ. A few times Paul also speaks of it in an absolute sense, for example, when in Colossians 3:3 he says to the church: "for you have died...." Here again he means, as appears from the whole context of Colossians 3:1-4, dying with Christ, through which what is on the earth must no longer hold their attention, but what is in heaven. These "earthly things" consist not in the earthly and temporal in general, but in what binds man and keeps him a prisoner in them (cf. v. 5). The appeal to "for you have died" is therefore not an appeal to their conversion or to their ethical or mystical experience, but to their belonging to Christ when he died. Then they escaped from the snare and power of "earthly things."

The reverse side of all this is that just as the church has once died with Christ, it also has been raised with him. Here again the aorists denote the redemptive-historical moment, that of Christ's rising. The thought is thereby that as in Christ's death on the cross the church has died to the powers of sin, world, and law, in the resurrection of Christ it has been set at liberty for Another, in order to live for him, under his government, for Christ himself (Rom. 7:4; 2 Cor. 5:15); or for God (Gal. 2:19). From these passages, too, which speak of having been raised with Christ, it is evident how much the new life of the church not only has been grounded — as something that has taken place for them and outside them — but also has been given and has begun in the resurrection of Christ. This finds clear expression, for example, in Ephesians 2:4ff.: "God ... for his great love wherewith he loved us, even when we were dead through our trespasses, made us alive together with Christ — by grace have you been saved — and raised us up together, and made us to sit together in heaven in Christ Jesus...."

From the final words it appears unmistakably that Paul again thinks christologically and redemptive-historically and not in terms of anthropology and the *ordo salutis*. When Christ was raised from the dead all his own were in their death-state with him. By this "being dead" one is likewise not only to understand a moral condition, but the whole death-situation of the man outside Christ, also as being under

estaurōtai] to psychological experiences that Paul has had under the impress of the cross. He means what he says first of all objectively. But he embraces joyfully the turning which God gave."

the wrath of God, subject to the curse of the law. And the change that ensued can be called a "being made alive together with him", because, as it is said in the corresponding context of Colossians 2:13-15, God in this great redemptive act[17] with Christ forgave us our sins, nailed the law to the cross, and in him triumphed over the powers.

Finally, so far as resurrection with Christ is concerned, reference should be made as well to Colossians 3:1ff. One can call this passage, together with Romans 6, the *locus classicus* for the "objective," redemptive-historical significance of having died and been raised with Christ. The new life of believers is that which comes forth with Christ out of the grave, has gone to heaven with him, is there hidden ("your life is hid with Christ in God"), and will once more appear from there with the parousia ("when Christ, who is your life, shall appear, then you also will appear with him"). What has taken place and will take place with Christ, from dying to coming (again) in glory, has also happened to the church and will happen to it by virtue of its corporate unity with him.

Likewise the sacramental and existential significance of having died and been raised with Christ, as we met with it in Romans 6, recurs time and again. Closely related to Romans 6, for example, is the train of thought in Colossians 2:11ff. Here, too, having been buried with Christ "through baptism" forms the ground for the new self-judgment, that is, that the church need not be circumcised anew, but in Christ has already been circumcised, in "the putting off of the body of the flesh." What is meant is again that by being included in baptism in Christ's death and burial the church has escaped from sin's mode of existence.

The words "in the putting off of the body of flesh" state clearly once more what in Romans 6 is called having been incorporated in the likeness of his death. For through Christ's having been buried in the flesh, the church may in baptism know its "body of the flesh" to have been put off, buried, because baptism incorporates it into Christ and his burial. This circumcision, which takes place without hands, can therefore be termed "the circumcision of Christ," not only as a general description, but in view of what was implied in Christ's death and resurrection with respect to the church's old mode of existence.

We are in the same sphere of thought when we come to those pronouncements which found the church's manner of life on the fact that it has put off the old man and put on the new man, which has been created after God (Eph. 4:24; Col. 3:9, 10). On the one hand, as appears from the active verbal forms, something other is intended here than what in Romans 6 is called the old man's having been crucified together (with Christ). On the other hand, one is here again not to think in the first place of personal conversion or regeneration. It is having put off the old and having put on the new man in baptism to which the apostle here appeals in order to lend greater force to his moral imperatives. For it is in baptism that the believer has put on

---

17. The participles in vv. 14 and 15 indicate the manner in which this quickening from the situation of death took place and the manner in which God once realized it in Christ; cf. Oepke, *TDNT*, I, pp. 541f.

Christ (Gal. 3:27), and thus participates in the nullification in Christ of the old mode of existence and in the new creation of God revealed in him.

The redemptive-historical and the sacramental here, too, are very closely intertwined. This does not mean a sacramentalizing of salvation in the sense of a repetition or contemporizing of the unique redemptive fact in "the mystery" of baptism.[18] For Paul what once took place in Christ has also taken place with the church. The "in Christ" has its validity back into Christ's pre-existence (Eph. 1:4), and reaches out to his parousia (Col. 3:4). But so far as the church is concerned, through baptism the "once" becomes a "here and now." Through baptism what took place in him for it and with it is appropriated to it as an actual reality, in terms of which it may judge itself in faith.

For this reason Paul is able to say in Colossians 2:12 that the church has been raised with Christ "through faith in the power of God." Here, too, the redemptive-historical is not relinquished or transposed into an event of faith; what is expressed with these words is that the redemptive-historical occurrence is transmitted and appropriated to the church in the sacrament of baptism by means of faith. Baptism and faith here (and in Rom. 6!) repeatedly go together, for baptism takes place upon faith. Together they form the way or the means by which the redemptive-historical reality becomes an existential reality of faith. The new creation in Christ is communicated in baptism by faith, the new aeon becomes personal regeneration and new life (Tit. 3:5). The sacramental and existential aspects of the new life have their own independent place and significance. But they continue to be determined and qualified by the redemptive-historical, and only from thence can they be understood and comprehended in the overall context of the Pauline doctrine of salvation.

Finally, what Paul means when he says that the new life comes about through the gospel must also be understood from this point of view. So it is said in 2 Timothy 1:10 that Christ has vanquished death and brought life and incorruptibility to light "through the gospel" (cf. Tit. 1:2). And elsewhere the gospel is spoken of as "the word of life" (Phil. 2:16), a "fragrance of life unto life" (2 Cor. 2:16). The new life is communicated through the gospel; the re-creating, authoritative word of God is the shining of the gospel in the hearts of those who are saved (2 Cor. 4:4-6). Thereby the character of the new life of the church is again described as the appropriation wrought by God of that which once took place in Christ. For this is that of which the gospel speaks, and it is therefore the word of life, because it teaches us to understand what has taken place in Christ as an event that has taken place in him for and with his own.

On the ground of all the foregoing we are able to conclude that the new life of believers is not a matter that can be known or approached out of the inwardness of the spiritual life, but only out of what has

---

18. See below, pp. 406ff.

taken place in Christ's death and resurrection. Their life is Christ. And forasmuch as they have been included in Christ, they have a share in the life that has been brought to light through him. Baptism as the incorporation into Christ is for them, therefore, the demonstrable line of demarcation between the old and the new, and faith in the gospel means a new self-judgment, that of being dead to sin and alive to God.

On that account this new life is not a self-contained matter that has been given to believers once and for all and by which they are now automatically determined from within. Because Christ is their life, it has also gone with Christ to heaven (Eph. 2:6; Phil. 3:20), it is also hidden with Christ in God (Col. 3:3), and it waits for its revelation at the appearing of Christ from heaven (Col. 3:4). The church, so far as its life on earth is concerned, is determined, governed, nourished from heaven. The Jerusalem that is above is its mother, just as the earthly Jerusalem, as the point of concentration of life under the law, ruled her children in bondage (Gal. 4:26). For this reason to be a new creation is on the one hand to live in liberty, no longer to be a slave of sin, to be free for God, but consists on the other hand in a reaching out to the revelation of Christ, which is also the revelation of the children of God (Rom. 8:19; Col. 3:4). When he describes the new life in Philippians 3:10ff., Paul is able to speak of it as a "knowing of the power of his [Christ's] resurrection," a "fellowship with his sufferings," "becoming conformed to his death"; on the other hand, he also speaks of it as not yet having become perfect, not yet having obtained, but stretching out toward the future, "if by any means I may attain unto the resurrection of the dead." The new life of believers, just because it consists in participation in Christ's life, has on the one hand the character of having passed over into the world of the new creation; on the other hand, because this life is hidden and awaits its revelation, it has the character of life in the flesh by faith (Gal. 2:20), or as Paul in a way no less characteristic for the fundamental structure of his doctrine of salvation expresses it, of life in or through the Spirit. To go into the significance of this is now our task.

SECTION 38. LIFE THROUGH THE SPIRIT

As on the one hand Paul relates the new life as closely as possible to Christ's death and resurrection, so on the other the relationship between the new life and the Spirit is no less essential for his view. This finds very clear expression in the transition between these lines of thought in Romans 6-8. What in Romans 6 is called no longer being subservient to sin, on the ground of the resurrection of Christ, is termed in Romans 7:6 serving in the new state of the Spirit; similarly, being dead to sin and being alive to God in Romans 6 is synonymous with the pronouncement in Romans 8:9 that believers are no longer in the flesh, but in the Spirit.

We have already pointed out earlier[19] that the pneumatic and the redemptive-historical are not competitive motifs in Paul's doctrine of salvation; much less still do they come into conflict with each other. It is precisely the Spirit who is the great Inaugurator and the gift of the new aeon that has appeared with Christ; and consequently the contrast, so constitutive for Paul's preaching, between Spirit and flesh is not to be taken as a metaphysical or anthropological, but as a redemptive-historical contrast, namely, as the two dominating principles of the two aeons marked off by the appearance of Christ. Paul's speaking of the Spirit does not follow, therefore, in the footsteps of the Hellenistic "pneumatology," as though one were obliged to look there, more than in the Old Testament line, for the point of contact for the idea that the Spirit renews the whole existence of the church and is not only the Author of extraordinary signs, wonders, and powers.[20] For throughout the whole of the Old Testament the Spirit is spoken of as the creating and renewing power of God, the gift of the New Covenant, the possession of the coming Messiah, and the life principle of the congregation of the future. It is consequently in harmony with this that Paul links the Spirit with the advent and the person of Christ, and gives expression to the gift of the new life conferred in Christ not only in the categories of redemptive history (death and resurrection with Christ), but also in those of the *Pneuma*.

Highly illustrative for the redemptive-historical as well as for the pneumatic character of the church's new mode of existence is the manner in which Paul again and again elucidates the latter from the contrast between the Spirit and the law, so characteristic for his preaching, elsewhere qualified as the contrast between the promise and the law or between the Old and the New Covenant.

In our discussion of the inadequacy of the law as means of salvation,[21] we have already treated at length the negative side of this contrast in the light of the train of thought of the Epistle to the Romans. Man, so we have seen, is entirely dependent on the grace of God revealed in Christ not only for his justification (Rom. 3-5), but also for his deliverance from slavery under the power of sin (Rom. 6-8). The law is of no avail to him, either for the one or for the other. With a view to the latter — slavery under the power of sin — the pronouncement is then given, in Romans 6:14: "you are no longer under the law, but under grace." In Romans 7:1-6 Paul returns to this contrast and qualifies it now as (no longer) "serving in the old state of the letter, but in the new state of the Spirit." With that the great redemptive-historical contrast has been brought to its final, pneumatic denominator. The law (letter) and the Spirit thereby stand over against each other in the sense

---

19. Cf. above, Section 14.

20. In this sense, e.g., Schweizer, *TDNT*, VI, pp. 415, 416. According to this conception the Spirit in the Old Testament, as also in the whole of Judaism, would not be taken as "necessary to salvation but is a power for additional deeds" (p. 415). And on p. 416 he speaks of the Old Testament conception as "additional phenomenon," in contrast to the Hellenistic, in which the Spirit would much more be regarded as indispensable for everyone for the reception of the true life.

21. Above, Sections 22, 23.

that the Spirit enters in where the law has failed, in joining battle
against the power of sin and of the flesh and in vanquishing that power.
The impotence of the law to break through the power of the flesh is,
as we have seen (Section 23), painted with vivid colors in Romans 7.
Thus in Romans 7 the indispensability of the Spirit is demonstrated
per negationem, just as in Romans 1:18-3:20 *per negationem* the indispensability of righteousness by faith. And as in Romans 3:21 the
"but now!" of the revelation of the righteousness of God by faith is the
redeeming word in man's situation of death under the guilt of sin and
the condemning force of the law, so the "now therefore" of Romans
8:1ff. is the word of liberation for man under the power of sin and
under the impotent regime of the law which cannot conquer the flesh.
The antithesis between the law and the Spirit is thus not situated in
the fact that the Spirit places himself over against the content and
demand of the law. Rather, the object of the sending of Christ and of
the Spirit represented by him is that the just demand of the law should
be fulfilled, completed, finished, not only in Christ, but also in us
(Rom. 8:4). But law and Spirit stand over against each other, therefore,
as two regimes, on the one hand as a rule of curse and of death, on
the other of blessing and of life, because the law with its demand is
powerless on account of the flesh and hence exercises a rule of death,
while the Spirit overcomes the flesh and thus is the Spirit of life and
of liberty.

Elsewhere, in Galatians 3 and 4, we meet with the same line of
thought. In Galatians 3:1ff. Paul poses the question to the Galatians —
brought once again under the jurisdiction of the law — as to the manner
in which they have received the Spirit. Was it perhaps from the works
of the law or — as they could not deny — from the faithful hearing of
the gospel? And in what follows in this chapter he sets the Spirit and
the law over against each other anew by terming the promise given to
Abraham (according to which in Abraham all the families of the earth
should be blessed) "the promise of the Spirit" (v. 14), and then placing
this promise over against the law, promulgated 430 years later. Here,
too, the issue is the thought that the law, although in itself good and
not in conflict with God's promises (v. 21), cannot bring salvation because it is powerless (cf. Rom. 8:2!) to do that which God had promised
to Abraham: to make alive (v. 21), to give children to Abraham, to
bless all families in him. The law's ability to save is dependent on
fulfillment by men. It is "a matter of two parties," while the promise
as given by God is his responsibility alone (vv. 19, 20).[22] The promise
is the life-creating word of God himself that pledges to Abraham his
offspring. Therefore — while the law can only lead to bondage — sonship,
liberty, and the Spirit are to be found where life is lived from faith
and not from the works of the law (3:21-4:7). Here again the contrast
is between the impotence of the law and the omnipotence of the life-
creating Word of God, the promise, which has its power not in those

---

22. For this exegesis in more detail see my *The Epistle of Paul to the Churches
of Galatia (NICNT),* 1953, pp. 138ff.

who receive it, but in him who gives it, not on the ground of works, but by faith.

This train of thought is further illuminated and confirmed in a profound manner by the "allegory" of Hagar and Sarah (Gal. 4:21-31), in which, by way of a midrash, Paul demonstrates anew from the history of Abraham the contrast between what the law can do and what the Spirit can do. Already in the case of Abraham himself this twofold "principle" of law and Spirit is evident, which is then maintained throughout the whole of history. For it is said of Hagar and Sarah that they represent two covenants, the first that of the law and the bondage resulting from it, the second that of the Spirit and the liberty given by him (cf. 2 Cor. 3:6). The birth from Hagar represents the principle of the law, because it rested on the flesh, on Abraham's intervention, on human strength. Nor could it on this account produce the promised son, but only the child qualified by the slave woman Hagar. In this way Hagar represents the covenant of the law, Sinai, which is dependent on the power of man and therefore does not produce free men, but slaves. Isaac, however, was "born through the promise," and in that sense is the "child of the promise," that is to say, brought forth by the quickening power of God himself (4:23). For this reason he can be said to be "born after the Spirit" (v. 29), because it is the Spirit who gives the new, free life. In this way promise (Spirit) and law can here be placed over against each other: what the law was powerless to do ("to make alive"; 3:21) because it is dependent on the strength of the flesh, that the promise is able to do, because it is realized by the quickening Spirit of God. This is the other, the new covenant, and in it lies the secret of the new life of believers, because they, as Isaac, are children of the promise,[23] brought forth by the Spirit of God (4:28).

It is on the ground of this new principle of life, this sharing in and living under the power and the government of the Spirit, that Paul is now able in the Epistle to the Galatians to stir up believers to walk after the Spirit. This means on the one hand that they must not abandon again the freedom from the law given in Christ (5:1-12), and on the other that they must not continue to live in sin. For when they allow themselves to be led by the Spirit, they are not (any longer) under the law (5:18; cf. 6:14), that is to say, no longer powerless against sin as they were under the law, and the law likewise no longer turns against them as an accusing and killing power (5:23; cf. 1 Tim. 1:8, 9).

No less characteristic for what is intended by this contrast of Spirit and law is finally the terminology frequently employed by Paul: letter and Spirit. We find it in Romans already in 2:27-29, where a circumcision of two kinds is spoken of, namely, that which takes place in the visibleness of the flesh and that which occurs in the hiddenness of the heart. The first is qualified by the letter, that is to say, rests on that

---

23. *Epangelias tekna,* genitive of source. The expression therefore does not mean, as it has often been understood: children who have received the promise, but: children who have been begotten by the (power of the) promise of God, as Isaac. They are *hoi kata Pneuma gennēthentes* (v. 29). Promise and Spirit are here synonymous.

to which the ordinance expressed in letters can compel and lead man in his bodily situation; the second by the Spirit, that is to say, by the work of the Spirit in the heart of man. What a central significance the thought expressed in this terminology has may also appear from Romans 7:6, where the whole contrast between the old and the new life is expressed by the words "serve in the old state of the letter" and "in the new state of the Spirit." Here, too, it is the case that no disparagement of the content of the law is intended, as though that were an excessively precise and servile conception of the will of God (and in that sense leading to "letter-worship"), over against which the Spirit would then stand, as not binding to a letter, and so forth. Paul knows nothing of such a modern antithesis, and it can only divert us from what in reality is at stake here. What is at issue is once more two different regimes, the "old" and the "new," of which the first operates only in an external manner, approaches man with that which is couched in letters and therefore restricted in its sphere of operation to commandment, the prescription of "thou shalt" and "thou shalt not." Over against this old regime of the letter stands the government of the Spirit, which, in contrast with the letter which is powerless and therefore leads to slavery, has power over the heart of man and sets him free to serve God truly.

That we are to understand the contrast of letter and Spirit in this way and must take this old and new regime above all as a redemptive-historical antithesis is evident, finally, from the manner in which Paul expresses himself in the same terms, but with much greater fullness of detail, in 2 Corinthians 3, a chapter not easily interpreted[24] but very profound.

Against those who level criticism at the boldness and authority with which he asserts himself and in so doing attribute less becoming motives to him (2 Cor. 2:17; cf. 4:2), Paul maintains that he preaches the word of God in complete sincerity and without any reservation, because the result of his labor after all bears him out. For this he appeals to the church itself, which he describes as a letter (of recommendation) that has been written not with ink, but with the Spirit, not consisting in tables of stone, but in the tables of flesh in the heart (2 Cor. 3:1-3). Just as in Romans 2:29 and 7:6, all the stress lies on the contrast between the "outwardness" of the law ("ink," "tables of stone," "the visible"; Rom. 2:29) and the inner working of the Spirit. It is not said hereby that Paul equates the dispensation of the law with an "authority coming from without" and regards this as a "heteronomy" overcome by the Spirit.[25] That which makes the letter in its externality

---

24. Besides the commentaries, see the detailed discussion of Ingo Hermann, *Kyrios und Pneuma*, 1961, pp. 26ff.; further the penetrating article by W. C. van Unnik, "With Unveiled Face," in [*CHARIS KAI SOPHIA*] (Festschrift für K. H. Rengstorf), 1964, pp. 152-160. For the interpretation of 2 Cor. 3:13, see especially P. J. Du Plessis, [*TELEIOS*], *The Idea of Perfection in the N.T.*, 1959, pp. 138-141.

25. Cf. Wendland, *Cor.*, p. 117: "This pair of concepts 'letter/spirit' is often misinterpreted, since the contrast 'outward prescriptions and authority/inner freedom and attitude' or something similar is substituted for it. But such a contrast, which became so important with the Enlightenment and in contemporary philosophy, occupies Paul not in the least."

insufficient and by which it must give way to the Spirit is its restricted
sphere of operation. As a piece of writing and consisting in letters of
stone it cannot touch the heart. The Spirit stands over against it as
"the Spirit of the living God," who is mighty to give what he demands,
because he is capable of writing on the heart. Paul concurs very clearly
with the Old Testament prophecy concerning the gift of the Spirit in
the New Covenant (Ezek. 11:19; 36:26; Jer. 31:33), and terms himself
and his fellow-workers, in close connection with this, ". . . ministers of
a New Covenant, not of the letter, but of the Spirit; for the letter kills,
but the Spirit gives life" (v. 6).

In this contrast between letter and Spirit, between Old and New
Covenant, the glory of the new life from the Spirit is now further
demonstrated in the continuation of 2 Corinthians 3. Even the Old
Covenant, however much it was for sinful Israel an "administration of
death, carved in letters of stone" and destined to pass away,[26] took place
under the revelation of the divine glory: the children of Israel could
not so much as bear the glory that shone from Moses' face (cf. Exod.
34:30). How much more then must the New Covenant, the administration of the Spirit and of righteousness and destined to endure, be revealed in glory!

Here also, just as in Galatians 4:21-31, Paul elucidates this meaning with an "allegory" (cf. Gal. 4:24), or with a midrash-like explanation
of the datum already mentioned in verse 7, that the children of Israel
could not endure the glory that shone from Moses' face. Moses on this
account covered his face with a veil. Paul now demonstrates from this
the difference between the Old and the New Covenant, that is to say,
between Moses' appearance and his own. While Paul may appear without reservation, in complete boldness and without hiding anything, and
as a minister of the New Covenant need not mask the glory of God
that has now been revealed, Moses felt compelled to cover his face[27]
and to veil the full glory[28] of the Old Covenant, however much this as

---

26. See also Delling, *TDNT*, I, p. 454, for the redemptive-historical significance of *to katargoumenon*, repeatedly (vv. 7, 11, 13, 14) employed in 2 Cor. 3, in
contrast with *to menon* (v. 11; cf. 1 Cor. 13:13).

27. For the linguistic connection between *parrēsia* and covering the face or
the head, see van Unnik's study in "De semitische achtergrond van [*PARRĒSIA*] in
het N.T.," *Mededelingen Kon. Ned. Acad.*, 1962; as well as his "The Christian's Freedom of Speech in the N.T." (The Manson Memorial Lecture), 1962.

28. There is mention here of *to telos tou katargoumenou*. This has frequently been taken as the diminution and disappearance of the shining of Moses'
face (so also Delling, *TDNT*, VIII, p. 56: "The 'cessation' . . . of [*doxa*] on the face
of Moses"; apparently van Unnik as well — "With Unveiled Face," p. 161). But this
hardly makes good sense: Moses covered his face, not so that the Israelites should
not observe the diminishing of the glory on his face, but so that they should not
see the glory itself! That is the clear sense not only of Exod. 34, but also of the
whole argument of Paul. Moreover, *to katargoumenon* in this whole context signifies
the passing glory of the Old Covenant in general, not "the fading away" of the
shining on Moses' face. That was rather repeatedly visible. Finally "the end of that
which was passing away" is also richly tautological (cf. also Du Plessis, [*TELEIOS*],
p. 141). One will therefore have to understand *to katargoumenon* in v. 13 of the
Old Testament glory in general, just as in this whole context, and one can best
take *to telos* with Du Plessis as "summit," "full height" in much the same sense

yet bore only a transitory character. Moses did so (and had to do so) because this shining radiance, mirroring the glory of God, was incompatible with the position of Israel under the law, even though this glory had as yet only a transitory and no abiding significance.

And this situation in which the glory of God has been covered over and hidden continues — thus Paul — to the Israel of the present day. He appeals for this to the fact that "their minds were hardened" (v. 14),[29] in which there is also an operation that veils and obscures the truth. That appears to the present day when the Old Testament is read; the same veil that once hid from them the glory of God (in Moses) has remained; it lies now on their hardened heart which wishes to be saved by the law and not by faith, and in the reading of Moses prevents them from sharing in the glory of God. But as Moses when he turned again to God laid aside the veil, so now the covering which at the same time signifies slavery and the lack of freedom is taken away in Christ. And this is owing to the fact that the Lord is the Spirit, and that where the Spirit of the Lord is slavish fear gives way to the freedom and boldness in which one does not keep oneself at a distance from the glory of God as that has been revealed in Christ, but catches sight of and is transformed by it. This is Paul's meaning when he says that not only he himself in his ministry (cf. 4:1ff.) but "we all," with unveiled face, that is, in the liberty given by the Spirit, may reflect the redeeming radiance of the glory of God revealed in the gospel,[30] in order thus to be transformed according to the same image from (the now already manifested) glory to (the still to be expected) glory, even as that takes place from the Spirit of the Lord (vv. 17, 18).

With this last pronouncement, which explains the freedom of the Spirit from the fact that the Spirit is of the Lord and the Lord the Spirit, we have now returned to our starting point, and the important question arises as to how the communion in which the church stands with the Lord (being "in Christ") relates itself to that in which it stands with the Spirit (being "in the Spirit"). To put it in another way: What is the relationship between "having died and been raised with Christ" (discussed in the preceding section) on the one hand, and "life through the Spirit" or "being in the Spirit" on the other?

---

as glory *(doxa)* and not as "end" or "termination" (pp. 138-141). The intention is then clear and entirely in harmony with the purport of the whole pericope: Moses covers his face so that the Israelites should not observe the full splendor even of the passing glory of the Old Covenant (cf. Du Plessis: *"Telos* as the crown of glory"; p. 138).

29. *Alla* in v. 14 has, not an adversative, but a progressive significance: it adds a new point of view to the preceding (cf. van Unnik, "With Unveiled Face," p. 162; Du Plessis, [*TELEIOS*], p. 139).

30. It is not a matter here of "ein 'pneumatisches'... im Geiste geschehendes Schauen,... eine offene hüllenlose Erkenntnis des himmlischen Glanzes Christi" (so Wendland, *Cor.,* p. 120), but, as appears from the sequel in chapter 4, of the beholding of the radiance that shines forth from "the gospel of the glory of Christ" (2 Cor. 4:4). The question as to whether *katoptrizomenoi* in v. 18 must be translated by "reflecting" (Dutch Bible Society, Schlatter, Allo, Van Unnik, *et al.*) or by "looking at oneself in a mirror," "beholding in a mirror" (thus, e.g., Lietzmann, Kümmel, Grosheide), is not to be answered with certainty, although in our view most considerations argue for the former conception.

It is evident here again that the corporate viewpoint is decisive.[31] By virtue of having been included in Christ — so we saw — the church has a share in his death and resurrection, and it may in faith know itself as dead to sin and alive to God. But by virtue of this same union with Christ it participates in the Holy Spirit. For the Spirit is the Spirit of the Lord (Phil. 1:19; Gal. 4:6; 2 Cor. 3:18). To be of Christ, to belong to him, means therefore to "have" the Spirit, and if any man does not have the Spirit of Christ, "he is not of him," does not belong to him (Rom. 8:9). Being-in-the-Spirit is therefore not in the first place a personal, but an ecclesiological category: "You are in the Spirit, if so be that the Spirit of God dwells in you," namely, as the temple of God, as the new fellowship, as the body of Christ. Consequently he who is incorporated into Christ by baptism and is baptized into his body, is also baptized into the Spirit as the one who fills the body of Christ (1 Cor. 12:13). He who is joined to him (Christ) is thus one Spirit with him (1 Cor. 6:17), for there is one body and one Spirit (Eph. 4:4), that is to say, to belong to the one body of Christ signifies also to share in the one Spirit.

Here already[32] this corporate point of view makes plain the structural sequence of the Lord, the body, and the Spirit, as well as the manner in which the church participates in the Spirit. The thought is not that the Spirit first shows himself to individual believers, brings them together into one whole, and thus constitutes the body of Christ. For in this way participation in Christ would follow upon sharing in the Spirit, whereas the church has been given precisely with Christ as the second Adam. The sequence is accordingly the reverse: those who by virtue of the corporate bond have been united with Christ as the second Adam, have died and been buried with him, may know themselves to be dead to sin and alive to God, may also know themselves to be "in the Spirit." They are, because included in this new life-context, no longer in the flesh, but in the Spirit (Rom. 8:9).

This last contrast can now enable us to understand what is meant by this peculiar expression, "being in the Spirit." What is denoted is not a subjective state of consciousness, but an "objective" mode of being. The thought is that believers, who were formerly "in the flesh" and in their existence were determined by the flesh as sinful power, are now "in the Spirit," that is to say, have been brought under the government, the liberating rule of the Spirit, and are no longer liable to the service of the flesh, nor subject to the disposition of the flesh (Rom. 8:5-12). Or, as it is said in Romans 8:2: as before they lived under "the law [i.e., the power, the constraint] of sin and of death," so now they have been set free by "the law [the power, the dominion] of the Spirit of life in Christ Jesus." And as "to live in the flesh" signifies that one has been sold under the power of sin, has been made a prisoner of war and

---

31. For this cf. E. Percy, *Der Leib Christi*, 1942, pp. 9ff.; Schweizer, *TDNT*, VI, pp. 418f. See also above, Section 10.

32. See further below on the body of Christ, Chapter IX. Cf. H. Berkhof, *The Doctrine of the Holy Spirit*, pp. 42ff.

brought into slavery (Rom. 7), so "to live in the Spirit" signifies, according to Romans 8, that one has been brought under another, a liberating dominion. The contrast is therefore not approached from the vantage point of the individual, believing subject; it is much more a matter of placing over against each other two "worlds," the mode of being of the old and of the new aeon, of belonging to two spheres of power and influence (cf. Col. 1:13; Gal. 1:4).

For the rest, this expression "to be in the Spirit" occurs but a few times in Paul, and then as the antithesis of "to be in the flesh." Elsewhere the same thing is expressed by "to be after the Spirit" (Rom. 8:5), or "to live by the Spirit." Compare the following:

> . . . those who are after the Spirit (*hoi kata pneuma* [*ontes*]), mind the things of the Spirit (Rom. 8:5).
> . . . you are not in the flesh, but in the Spirit (*einai en pneumati;* Rom. 8:9).
> . . . if we live by the Spirit (*zēn pneumati*), let us also walk by the Spirit (Gal. 5:25).

It is clear, particularly from the distinction between to "live" by the Spirit and to "walk" by the Spirit in Galatians 5:25, that the first describes a specific condition, constituting the presupposition of the second, which signifies a walk, activity, manifestation of life that is commensurate with it. Similarly in Romans 8 a distinction is made between "to be after the Spirit" on the one hand and "to mind the things of the Spirit" on the other (vv. 5ff.); and further along this distinction is expressed by "to be in the Spirit" on the one hand and "to be led by the Spirit"[33] on the other (v. 14). In all these varied phrases the same thought is given expression again and again: that believers have been taken up into the new life-context of Christ, in which the Spirit rules, and that their new way of life must answer to its having been brought under this new redeeming sovereignty, a life that consists in being disposed toward, letting oneself be led by, and walking by the Spirit.

What this life by the Spirit involves further in its outworking and realization is expressed in Paul's epistles in a great many ways and in richly shaded terminology. In so doing he by no means restricts himself to the "objective" and supra-individual points of view, but shows us in various ways the nature of the pneumatic in the personal, individual life of believers. Very characteristic here is that the relationship between Christ and the church and between the Spirit and the church is not only described as being in Christ and being in or living by the Spirit, but also, conversely, as the being and dwelling of Christ and of the Spirit in believers. The Spirit is not only the one under whose dominion the church may live, but he also enters into the actual existence of believers. As the Spirit of the living God (2 Cor. 3:3) he makes

---

33. *Pneumati agesthai* will have to be understood reflexively. It is substituted for the active idea preceding in v. 13: *pneumati tas praxeis tou sōmatos thanatoun.* In Gal. 5:18, too, this meaning much deserves the preference.

alive, he gives eternal life (1 Cor. 15:45; 2 Cor. 3:6; Rom. 8:11; Gal. 6:6),
he is the Spirit of regeneration and inner renewal (Tit. 3:5; Rom. 7:6).
By the mediation of the Spirit the love of God that has been evidenced
in the dying of Christ works itself out in the hearts of his own (Rom.
5:5; cf. v. 8;[34] cf. Eph. 3:16). All the expressions of the new life of those
who belong to Christ can therefore be attributed to the Spirit. Paul
speaks of them as the disposition of the Spirit (Rom. 8:6), the love of
the Spirit (Rom. 15:30), the desiring of the Spirit (Gal. 5:17), the joy
of the Spirit (1 Thess. 1:6). He is not the Spirit of slavish fear, but of
childlike trust (Rom. 8:15); his fruit consists in love, peace, joy, etc.
(Gal. 5:22). He is also the principle and power of the new life in the
moral sense of the word, the Spirit of sanctification (2 Thess. 2:13).
The requirement of the law can only be fulfilled in those who walk
not after the flesh, but after the Spirit, i.e., in accordance with his
operation and intention (Rom. 8:4ff.; cf. Gal. 5:16, 25). The Spirit is
also the Spirit of knowledge and of revelation (Eph. 1:17), the Intermediary of the revelation of God in Jesus Christ, who cannot be known
through human wisdom, the Spirit who searches the deep things of God
and who has been given to the church in order to know what has been
given it by God (1 Cor. 2). He makes the church to be spiritual men
and women so as to be able to discern spiritual things; he is also the
author of extraordinary powers and gifts, which equip the church for
service (Rom. 12; 1 Cor. 12 and 14).

From all this it is clear how great the span of the work of the
Spirit is and how much Paul ascribes the whole of the new life, in its
origin as well as in its realization and consummation, to the Spirit, to
his operations, powers, and gifts.

SECTION 39. THE NEW MAN

For a right understanding of the renewing work of the Spirit the anthropological categories with which this renewal is defined are likewise
highly important. To have died with Christ also means that the old
man has been crucified with him, and to be in the Spirit also involves
putting on the new man or "the spiritual man" (1 Cor. 2:14ff.).

Now, in our investigation into the fundamental structures of
Paul's preaching we have already been able to ascertain[35] that the expression: the death of the old and the resurrection of the new man, has
a supra-individual significance and in Paul is not employed in the
sense of "the two segments" of one's personal conversion. Our old man
was once crucified with Christ on Golgotha. And likewise the active
"to have put off" the old and "to have put on" the new man (Col. 3:10;

---

34. *Hē agapē tou Theou* in v. 5 is to be understood, not as love for God,
but as the love of God — otherwise than as the tradition emanating from Augustine
conceives it (cf. Nygren on Rom. 5:5) — but then not merely as disposition, but as
the working out of the manner in which God has in fact demonstrated his love in
Christ's death (cf. Bultmann, *Theology*, I, p. 292).

35. Above, Section 10.

Eph. 4:24) refers above all to baptism as bidding farewell to the old mode of existence and becoming incorporated into the new being of the church, which Christ has created in himself unto "one new man" (Eph. 2:15). With "old and new man," too, therefore, the corporate point of view stands in the foreground. For this reason the church, in addition to being called "the new man," can be spoken of as the "perfect man" (*anēr teleios;* Eph. 4:13) and as the "one" man[36] in Christ Jesus (Gal. 3:28). This very striking and important idea — which is undoubtedly connected with the fact that Christ himself as "the second man" is placed over against "the first man" (1 Cor. 15:21ff.) — remains normative and directive in Paul for insight into the new life.

This does not alter the fact, however — and to this we must now direct all our attention — that this new man is brought about in the individual human existence and that other redemptive-historical and eschatological predicates, too, as for example new creation, regeneration, etc., are applicable to this concrete, historic humanity (cf., e.g., 2 Cor. 5:16; Gal. 6:15; Tit. 3:5). The putting off of the old man and the putting on of the new is therefore not only a choice of faith and a sacramental incorporation in baptism, but is also intended to be carried on as a continuous renewal, a repeated "putting on of the Lord Jesus Christ" in the concrete existence of believers (cf. Col. 3:10; Rom. 13:14). The new life consists not only in having once been raised with Christ and in having been placed under a new rule, but also in being renewed from day to day (2 Cor. 4:16).

If one traces the manner in which Paul describes this renewal also as new humanity, then a distinction is again to be made between descriptions that express the totality of this renewal and such as have specific aspects of it in view.

So far as the first is concerned, those expressions especially deserve further attention which describe the new life as new creation and then in particular as being created after the image of God or after the image of Christ and as regeneration.

It is implied in all these qualifications that the new life means a radical transformation, a passing over from a condition of death and slavery into one of life and liberty, which on this account is not to be explained from human effort and moral strength, but only from the creative command of God, no less mighty than the word with which he once called forth light out of darkness (2 Cor. 4:6). It is in these categories of creation, therefore, that the new man is spoken of again and again (Gal. 6:15; 2 Cor. 5:17; Eph. 2:10, 15; 3:9; 4:24; Col. 3:10; Tit. 3:5). The meaning of this is not only that the church has in Christ come to belong to the new aeon, the new order of things, and in that sense to the new creation, but likewise that this almighty and re-creating work of the Spirit enters into the existence of believers in a personal and individual way.

This is apparent particularly from those passages which speak of being created or renewed after God's image (Col. 3:10; Eph. 4:24). The new man is renewed after the image of him who created him, that is,

---

36. *Pantes gar hymeis heis este en Chr.*

of God (Col. 3:10). He has been created "after" (in conformity with) God (Eph. 4:24). Elsewhere Paul speaks of the image of Christ: as we have borne the image of the earthly, we shall also bear the image of the heavenly (1 Cor. 15:49; cf. Rom. 8:29: becoming conformed to the image of God's Son; 2 Cor. 3:18: being transformed after the image of Christ from glory to glory).

The background of both conceptions lies, of course, in Genesis 1:27. At the same time, however, the idea of Christ as the second Adam is predominant.[37] As such he is the image of God (2 Cor. 4:4; Col. 1:15), and, like the first Adam, he transmits his image to those who belong to him (1 Cor. 15:49), he takes on form in them (Gal. 4:19), just as it can be said elsewhere that they have been created in him (Eph. 2:10). The corporate point of view is here again in the forefront. What is called in Colossians 3:10f. having "put on the new man, which is being renewed unto knowledge in conformity with the image of his Creator, whereby Greek and Jew no longer matter ..., but Christ is all in all," is called in Galatians 3:27f. having "put on Christ, whereby Greek and Jew no longer matter ..., for you are all one [man] in Christ Jesus." Renewal after the image of God comes about therefore through the fact that the believer in baptism (Gal. 3:27) puts on Christ and thus the new man. It is the new existence of the body of Christ in which he in this way receives a share, which he henceforth is permitted to be. For this reason to be created after the image of God is the equivalent of bearing, reflecting, being transformed after the image of Christ. For Christ is all things in all those who have become new men in him.[38]

It is said at the same time that this creation after the image of God does not signify a return to the original image of God. Rather, as the heavenly and life-giving Spirit Christ represents an entirely different order and mode of existence from Adam as the earthly and living soul.[39] To be created or transformed into the image of Christ does indeed mean to share anew (just as the original man; 1 Cor. 11:7) in the glory of God, now described, however, as being transformed from glory to glory (2 Cor. 3:18). Elsewhere this reflection[40] of the glory of the Lord is described as being created after his image in true righteousness and holiness (Eph. 4:24), or as being renewed unto knowledge (Col. 3:10), being transformed by the renewing of the understanding (the *nous*; Rom. 12:2), or as Christ's taking on form in his own (Gal. 4:19).[41] Thus it is a matter here of the renewing of the inward man (2 Cor. 4:16), which assumes shape, however, in the renewing of the walk (Rom. 6:4). For the future, this being created after the image of God or being renewed after the image of Christ signifies the glorification of their whole existence, becoming conformed to "his glorious body" (Phil. 3:21; 1 Cor. 15:43ff.).

---

37. Cf. above, Sections 9, 12.
38. Cf. F. W. Eltester, *Eikon im Neuen Testament*, 1958, pp. 158ff.
39. Cf. below, Section 78.
40. Cf. above, p. 220.
41. Here, too, *morphē* and *eikōn* have a synonymous meaning (cf. above, p. 74).

It is entirely in the same sense as this creation after the image of God that regeneration (*palingenesia*) is to be understood, of which there is mention in Titus 3:5: "He saved us through the washing of regeneration and the renewing of the Holy Spirit." Here, too, just as with the image of God, a close connection is made with baptism as the sacramental incorporation into the body of Christ, the putting on of Christ and of the new man.

It has been argued, to be sure, that the idea of regeneration is incapable of being reconciled with the eschatological background of Paul's conception of the new life and is that much more evidence that the Epistle to Titus is not Pauline. "Regeneration," in the sense of a miraculous, inner transformation of the individual man, is supposed to stem from the Hellenistic mystical world of thought[42] and not to be in harmony with the dying and rising with Christ of which Paul repeatedly speaks.[43] But here again one is not to go by the sound of words. The word regeneration stems, it is true, not from the Jewish, but from the Greek world, even though it is also employed by Jewish writers such as Josephus and Philo in more senses than one. But in the Greek literature it has a very broad spectrum of metaphorical meanings: national renascence, individual, but also cosmic renewal.[44] That in the mystery religions it was a special "technical" denotation of certain mystical phenomena has in no sense been proved; much less still that the metaphorical use would there have its "Sitz im Leben." One will thus have to understand it against a broader background, and be compelled to interpret it in accordance with the context in which it occurs. Elsewhere in the New Testament it is employed in a future eschatological sense (Matt. 19:28). And here as well, in the context of Titus 3, it gives expression to the significance of God's coming (epiphany) in Christ (v. 4; cf. 2:11), which put an end to the "once" of the time before Christ (v. 3). The expression of the outpouring of the Holy Spirit in verse 6 is also typical eschatological terminology (cf. Acts 2:17; Joel 3:1; Rom. 5:5). Further, it is not correct that Paul may be said to speak of the new life only in terms of resurrection and not of (new) birth, as Schweitzer contends. In Galatians 4:21-31 his thoughts move entirely in the latter direction when, referring to the miraculous birth of Isaac, he terms believers children who are "begotten after the Spirit, not after the flesh" and calls the Jerusalem that is above their mother (v. 26). Even though the word does not otherwise occur in Paul, there is thus no obstacle whatever to assuming that what he elsewhere calls new creation he here denotes as new birth, without the eschatological background of his ideas thereby becoming eclipsed by the mystical. The expression "washing of regeneration," as also appears from the wholly Pauline addition and explication "renewing by the Holy Spirit," denotes no

---

42. Cf. Dibelius-Conzelmann, *A Commentary on the Pastoral Epistles*, pp. 148ff.

43. So especially A. Schweitzer, *The Mysticism of Paul the Apostle*, pp. 13-15; see also Oepke, *TDNT*, IV, p. 304, *s.v. louō*.

44. See, e.g., Büchsel, *TDNT*, I, pp. 686-688, as well as the comprehensive materials in J. Dey, [*PALINGENESIA*], *Ein Beitrag zur Klärung der religionsgeschichtlichen Bedeutung von Tit. III, 5,* 1937.

other reality than what is elsewhere called the new life effected by the Holy Spirit and appropriated to believers by baptism. And this, then, not only in its commencement or exclusively in its hidden existence, but in its totality as new creation, as total renewal wrought by the power of the Spirit.[45]

Along with this general and all-embracing definition of the new man, there are also the particular ones, whereby all those concepts recur which we have already attempted to analyze in treating the Pauline doctrine of sin (Section 19).

Here again a distinction is drawn between the inward and the outward man. As we have already been able to ascertain earlier, the "inward man" signifies in Paul nothing other than the inner spiritual character of man, as distinguished from the outward, that is to say, man in his bodily mode of existence turned toward the outside. To the former it now applies that with all the temptations, dangers, decay, to which the outward is exposed, he is renewed day by day (2 Cor. 4:16). What is intended is thus the actual continuous communion with Christ by faith, or as it is said in Ephesians 3:16: being strengthened with power through the Spirit in the inward man. And furthermore, there is the whole glorious language of faith of 2 Corinthians 4 to elucidate this being "renewed day by day."

In this renewal of the inward man, moreover, the significance of the heart and of the understanding (the *nous*) comes to the forefront. The conceptual material here, particularly when there is mention of the renewing of the heart, is very rich and varied. Christ "dwells" in the hearts of his own through faith (Eph. 3:17); God "sends" the Spirit of his Son into their hearts (Gal. 4:6) as the earnest and seal of their complete redemption (2 Cor. 1:22). He "pours" his love into their hearts through the Holy Spirit (Rom. 5:5; cf. Tit. 3:5); he "writes" his will in their hearts by the Spirit (2 Cor. 3:3); he "illumines" their hearts with the knowledge of Christ (2 Cor. 4:6); he enlightens "the eyes of their heart" through the Spirit of wisdom and of revelation (Eph. 1:18). The peace that has been accomplished by Christ "speaks the last word" in their hearts as an arbitrator again and again (Col. 3:15; cf. 1 Thess. 3:13), "guards" their hearts against wandering and temptation (Phil. 4:7), and directs their hearts in the right pathway in order that they may show love and be patient (2 Thess. 3:5). All this includes the outworking of the hidden work of the Spirit, who as the Spirit of the adoption of sons (and not — as that of the law — as the spirit of bondage) is also the Spirit of prayer and of boldness in speaking to God (Rom. 8:15; cf. 2 Tim. 1:7). Indeed, the Spirit is sometimes represented as himself in the hearts of believers praying to God (Rom. 8:26, 27;[46] Gal. 4:6). He unites himself with their prayer, so that their

45. That with regeneration "the renewal in principle of the life of man" is intended, which "begins in regeneration," as C. Bouma avers (*De brieven van de apostel Paulus aan Timotheus en Titus*, n.d., p. 441), at least cannot be derived from Tit. 3:5.

46. For this see also in detail E. Gaugler, "Der Geist und das Gebet der Gemeinde, Röm 8, 26-27," *Intern. Kirchl. Zeitschr.*, 1961, pp. 67-94; and above, pp. 201ff.

prayer becomes his prayer, and that which they cannot utter is judged by God, who searches the hearts, according to the intention of his Spirit (Rom. 8:27).

Nowhere does it appear more clearly than in these last pronouncements how intimate and how close the link is between the Spirit and the inward man of believers. Yet here as well the believing subject does not fall away and the human is not lost in the divine. In all these pronouncements we do not have to do with a mystical terminology in the technical sense of the word, but with a depiction and description, varied time and again, of the spiritual revolution that comes about in the heart of man when initially and repeatedly he is brought by the Spirit under the power of the gospel. For "the heart," as we have seen,[47] denotes man in his capacity for being addressed by, and in his susceptibility to, the divine revelation, as well as in his self-determination with respect to that revelation. Therefore, the heart is on the one hand the point of impact of the Holy Spirit, and it is there that the great decisions fall; but it is also clear that renewal by the Spirit does not confine itself to the heart of the inward man, but intends from thence to determine his entire humanity as well.

The renewal of the understanding (the *nous*) is closely bound up with that of the heart. It is effected in rightly knowing, discerning, what the will of God is (Rom. 12:2). It is described as being renewed "in the spirit of your thinking" (Eph. 4:23), that is to say, in its nature and definiteness. Elsewhere it is spoken of as "Christ-thinking" (*nous Christou;* 1 Cor. 2:16), that is to say, the mode of thinking governed and illumined by Christ in which the pneumatic man is distinguished from the physical; just as, conversely, it is said of those who deny the resurrection that they have "no knowledge of God" (*agnōsia Theou;* 1 Cor. 15:34). In all this it is not so much a matter of thinking in an intellectual sense, but of the new moral and religious consciousness, of the new insight into who God is and what his will is according to his revelation in Christ, and of permitting oneself to be determined thereby in the manifestation and circumstances of his life (life "in the body").

Therefore the argument does not hold that what is said in Romans 7 in favor of the inward man and of the *nous* must apply to the new man.[48] For in Romans 7 the inward man and the *nous* are spoken of insofar as these are willing to be led by the law, and it is precisely the renewing operation of the Spirit that is not taken into consideration. And it is this renewal alone in the believer that gives the power of divine love, which is necessary not only to enable him to understand the requirement of the law in all its depth, but even more to carry that into effect "in the body."

In this connection (with reference to the inward man) those passages are still to be pointed out where the human spirit and soul are mentioned as the seat and mode of manifestation of the new life (cf. Rom. 1:9; 8:16; Gal. 6:18; Eph. 6:18; Phil. 4:23; 1 Thess. 5:23; Eph. 6:6; Phil. 1:27, *et al.*). Insofar as *pneuma* and *psyche* do not simply represent

47. Above, pp. 119ff.
48. Cf. above, pp. 126f.

the personal pronoun, it holds here, too, that they specifically denote man according to his invisible and inner existence — however, not in the pregnant sense of "heart" and "nous." They are not so sharply delineated and simply form the profuse evidence that the new life is effected in the whole of man.

This renewal and illumination of the heart and of man evidence themselves further in their divine nature and power (and are at the same time distinguished from what is said in Romans 7 in favor of the *nous* and the inward man) in that they are carried through into the walk, the life-manifestation of believers. Paul speaks of that frequently, as we saw earlier, as "the body" and "the members."

Now so far as "the body" is concerned, a distinction is certainly to be made here. We have already seen that the body, as the concrete mode of existence of sinful man, can sometimes be identified with sin as the "body of sin" (Rom. 6:6), the "body of flesh" (Col. 2:11), the "body of death" (Rom. 7:24). Accordingly, the life from Christ by the Holy Spirit can be typified as a "doing away with the body of sin," "putting off of the body of the flesh," "putting to death of the earthly members," "deliverance from the body of this death" (Rom. 6:6; Col. 2:11; 3:5; Rom. 7:24). What is involved in all this is of course not the body as material organism, as though the new life could only reveal itself in man when he had laid aside, indeed had independently "put to death," his present corporeality. All[49] these expressions are obviously not intended of the body itself, but of the sinful mode of existence of man. This use of body is an exception, however. Elsewhere "body" (and sometimes "flesh"; see below) has a more neutral sense, namely, as the denotation of man as he appears toward the outside, as he reveals himself visibly. This body is also spoken of in terms of renewal: "Do you not know that your bodies are members of Christ..., a temple of the Holy Spirit, who dwells in you?" (1 Cor. 6:15, 19). It holds for the body as well that it "is for the Lord, and the Lord for the body" (1 Cor. 6:13). God must therefore be glorified in the body (1 Cor. 6:20), whether by life or by death (Phil. 1:20). Similarly, believers must present their bodies a living sacrifice, holy, well-pleasing to God (Rom. 12:1), they must present their members as weapons of righteousness (Rom. 6:13), and sin may no longer reign in their mortal bodies (Rom. 6:12). In all these pronouncements it is certainly not the corporeality of man that comes to the fore, nor is it always especially the struggle against sensual sin that is thought of, but what is intended is man as he translates his intentions into acts, as he becomes manifest before the eye of God and men.

Finally, those passages are to be pointed out in which body de-

---

49. This applies as well to the exclamation: "Who will deliver me from the body of this death?" (Rom. 7:24): "The apostle does not mean to die or to be rid of his body.... But the body, so far as it is dominated by sin, ... makes him long for deliverance, nevertheless not from the body as such, but insofar as it is the body of sin: it must be purified, renewed, sanctified" (Greijdanus, *Rom.*, I, p. 351). All this of course under the proviso of Rom. 8:23 where the future redemption of the whole earthly existence is intended by the words *apolytrōsis tou sōmatos.*

notes in particular the frailty and transitoriness of present human existence, just as this same idea can sometimes be described by "flesh." Of this frail and corruptible "body" or "flesh," too, it is now said that it can be the pattern of the new life. The pronouncements of 2 Corinthians 4:7, 10, 11, are characteristic:

> But we have this treasure in earthen vessels. . . .
> . . . Always bearing about in our body the dying of Jesus, that the life also of Jesus may be manifested in our body.
> For we who live are always delivered unto death for Jesus' sake, that the life also of Jesus may be manifested in our mortal flesh.

According to Schweitzer it would appear particularly from 2 Corinthians 4:11 that for Paul the new life in Christ is "an actual entity,"[50] from which it evidently must be inferred that the resurrection life of Christ also communicates itself to the corporeality of the present life of his own. Paul, however, clearly distinguishes between the new life and the flesh. For the flesh is here the human in its weakness and transitoriness. As such, that is, as flesh, it has no share in the new life. It holds for man as flesh that flesh and blood will not inherit the kingdom of God (1 Cor. 15:50).[51] Accordingly, when the manifestation of the new life in the flesh is spoken of (or as it is called in 2 Cor. 4:10 with the same meaning: in the body), a reality is intended that does not abrogate or in principle nullify the frailty and mortality of the present life, but rather manifests itself in spite of and in the midst of this weakness (cf. 2 Cor. 4:7ff.), and is only to be known and experienced by faith (Gal. 2:20).

With respect to the renewing of man this says two things: first, that the new manhood is realized even now in this present time. The eschatological gift of salvation takes effect not only in Christ, but also in believers in the flesh. In that renewing by the Spirit believers are therefore sealed even now; in it they receive the evidence and the seal of their perfect redemption (2 Cor. 1:20-22; cf. 5:5; Eph. 1:13, 14). In the second place, this manifestation of the new life in the flesh is a proof of its provisional character. For this reason one can speak of the hiddenness as well as the revelation of the new life in this time (Col. 3:3; cf. Rom. 8:19; Phil. 3:21).

These two aspects of life in the flesh also bring about the peculiar tension and polarity in the Christian life on earth to which Paul gives expression time and again in such a stirring manner, and which determine his own attitude toward life in such a distinctive way; at one time in the exalted language of faith, because of the Spirit, then again in deep and painful groanings, because of the flesh (cf. Rom. 5:3ff.; 8:22ff.; 2 Cor. 4:7ff.; 5:2ff.). For this reason he is able to describe the new life in this dispensation as knowing Christ and the power of his resurrection, participating in his suffering, and being conformed to his death; and on the other hand, as an eager longing for the resurrection of the

---

50. *The Mysticism of Paul the Apostle*, pp. 125ff., cf. pp. 17ff.
51. See further below, p. 549.

dead (Phil. 3:10, 11). For it is only this resurrection[52] which will bring
to manifestation the life of believers (Col. 3:4).

SECTION 40. FAITH AS THE MODE OF EXISTENCE OF THE NEW LIFE

Up to this point, with such general qualifications of the new life as
"dying and being raised with Christ," "life through the Spirit," "living
in the new state of the Spirit and no longer in the old state of the
letter," it has been the anthropological descriptions of this new life
that have especially received our attention. We come now to stand before
the question — which has already received a partial answer in the foregoing — as to the manner in which and the way along which this new
life by the Spirit is realized in man and makes him to be that new man
in all the facets that thus emerge.

In what has gone before we have already had to do with this,
insofar as in the pronouncements concerning dying and being raised
with Christ — in addition to the redemptive-historical "once" and the
sacramental point of view ("by baptism") — faith has been spoken of
repeatedly as the means and mode of the new life. For by faith the
church may know itself to be dead ("so you also must consider yourselves," etc.) to sin and alive to God (Rom. 6:11). By faith the church
has in baptism been buried and raised with Christ (Col. 2:12). Closer
inspection of the pronouncements that treat of the new life through
the Spirit enables us to see that here again it is faith by which (i.e., in
the way of which) the Spirit communicates himself to man in all his
operations and gifts and thus makes him share in the new life.

Here, too, the indissoluble bond between the Spirit and Christ is
of decisive significance. The Spirit does not work as an anonymous, incalculable, miraculous power, but as the Spirit of Christ. The relationship in which the church stands to the Spirit and the manner in which
it actually has a share in the Spirit is therefore determined by its relationship to Christ, that is, by faith in him. Paul prays that God may
grant that the church "be strengthened with power through his Spirit
in the inward man, that Christ may dwell in your hearts through faith"
(Eph. 3:16). The manner in which the power of Christ's death and resurrection is effected in the life of his own can thus be said to be that of
the Spirit as well as that of faith.

It can appear even from this how little ground there is for the
opinion, propounded in the earlier literature, that for Paul faith and
"mysticism," faith and pneumatic communion with Christ, represent
two different "lines," and stem from two different "worlds," on the one
hand from the Jewish, on the other from the Greek (mysticism).[53]

---

52. Furthermore, see below, Section 78.
53. Very representative here, e.g., is the writing of E. Wissmann, *Das
Verhältnis von [Pistis] und Christusfrömmigkeit bei Paulus*, 1926, which as a monograph on this subject is entirely dominated by this idea and with all the valuable
material it offers in detail is therefore not to be accepted in its general purport.

Especially striking in this connection is Galatians 2:20, the *locus classicus* for the "mystical" conception of the new life in Paul: "I have been crucified with Christ; and it is no longer I that live, but Christ lives in me; and insofar as I now [still] live in the flesh, I live by faith in the Son of God, who loved me and gave himself up for me." For more than one reason this pronouncement is of great importance for the right understanding of the new life in Paul. In the first place, the transition from "we with Christ" to "Christ-in-us" is very evident here. Having died once with Christ and knowing oneself dead to sin and alive to God (cf. Section 37) is linked with and grounded on pneumatic fellowship with Christ. But further, this passage affords clear insight into the character of this fellowship. Paul speaks of it as of a certain change of subject. The meaning is that for his life he is no longer cast on his own ego (the "I-myself" of Rom. 7:25b). For this "I" has been crucified with Christ. In its place Christ lives in him. It has then been said that this means a mystical depersonalization, an absorption of the human "I" of Paul into the pneumatic "I" of Christ. The concluding words say plainly, however, that Paul intends to be understood otherwise, and that "no longer I, but Christ in me" can be expressed thus, that he lives "in faith in the Son of God, who loved me and gave himself up for me."[54] By this faith — which is directed toward Christ in his loving Self-surrender — Christ dwells and rules in him and no longer his own, old "I." That the apostle writes all this in a context in which he vigorously upholds justification by faith (Gal. 2:16ff.) can only confirm that the life by faith and the life in communion with Christ through the Spirit do not represent two worlds of thought, but that faith is the manner in which one shares in the one as well as in the other. Here lies the fundamentally anti-spiritualistic and anti-gnostic character of Paul's "Pneumatology."

Other pronouncements are no less clear. In 2 Corinthians 13:5 Paul demands that the Corinthians prove themselves whether they are indeed in the faith. In order the more to impress on them the seriousness of this question, he follows it with a second question as to whether they (then) do not (any longer) know that Jesus Christ is in them. This paralleling is only understandable when "are in the faith" and "Christ is in you" denote essentially the same thing, and thus the pneumatic fellowship with Christ comes into being in the way of faith and is exercised by faith.

Now what is said explicitly and directly in these passages is no

---

54. The mystical interpretation chooses to take the words *en pistei zō* not as explanation, but as restriction. The first half of the verse would then, for example, according to Wissmann (who here borrows the words of Bousset), reflect "the keynote of Pauline Christianity." Next to that faith would then appear "at the moment the elated mystic realized that here and there he still finds himself in the base domain of *sarx*." Wissmann concludes: "It cannot be said any better how for Paul the present life in Christ is something completely different from the faith that looks at the facts of salvation of the past" (*ibid.*, p. 112). But it is precisely faith "looking at the facts of salvation of the past" (cf. v. 20b) that for the present enables him to experience the overwhelming power of Christ and of his love, as he declares in v. 20a; cf. also Mundle, *Der Glaubensbegriff des Paulus*, 1932, p. 156.

less evident indirectly from the manner in which Paul alternates the expressions "in Christ" and "in the Spirit" with "in the faith" or "by faith." That which at one time is called living, walking, standing in Christ (Rom. 6:11; Col. 2:6; Phil. 4:1; 1 Thess. 3:8), and elsewhere living, walking, in or by the Spirit (Gal. 5:25; Rom. 8:4), can also be called living, walking, standing in or by faith (Gal. 2:20; 2 Cor. 5:7; Rom. 11:20; 1 Cor. 16:13; 2 Cor. 1:24). In another place, to walk in Christ signifies the same thing as to be established in the faith (Col. 2:6, 7); the comfort of the apostle through the faith of the church finds its ground in the fact that they stand in the Lord (1 Thess. 3:7, 8).[55] One can conclude nothing other than that faith is the way in which, having died and risen with Christ, life through the Spirit, putting on the new man, being renewed after the image of Christ, regeneration, in short, the new creation of God, is realized and individualized. For this reason what is in one place called "new creation" can elsewhere be termed "faith" (cf. Gal. 5:6; 6:15). Faith represents in its manner the fullness of the time (cf. Gal. 3:23, 25; 4:4). As the new mode of existence it has a redemptive-historical significance in the same way as death and resurrection with Christ and being in the Spirit.

This leads us naturally into the relationship of faith and the Spirit.

In general Paul first speaks of faith and then of the Spirit. And this cannot be wondered at. Not only does righteousness by faith constitute the foundation for the new life and the work of the Holy Spirit that is therein revealed, but also the gift of the Spirit is itself by or from faith. So it is asked in Galatians 3:2: "This only would I learn from you: did you receive the Spirit by the works of the law, or by the hearing of faith?" a question that is clearly answered by Paul himself when he says in verse 14 that we have received the promise of the Spirit (that is to say, the promised Spirit) through faith. In Galatians 4:6 this is still further elucidated by the statement that because we are sons (through faith; 3:26) God has poured out the Spirit of his Son into our hearts. To mention still another place: in Ephesians 1:13 it is said that by having believed we have been sealed with the Holy Spirit, who has been promised us. In this train of thought the Spirit is again and again the gift of the great time of redemption, the content of the ancient promise of redemption. And faith in Christ who has the Spirit at his disposal is the way or means of coming to share in this promise of the Spirit[56] (cf. also Acts 2:38).

This is by no means to say, however, that faith, not only as a new "possibility" but also as a human act itself, is not also part of the renewing work of the Spirit, as though it were a decision by which man would have to secure for himself his share in salvation. To be sure, the active character of faith is very much in the foreground. Nor, so far as we are able to see, does the apostle say in so many words that faith

55. Mundle, *ibid.*, p. 159; Bultmann, *TDNT*, VI, p. 218.
56. Schweizer wrongly seems to want to deny this sequence (cf. *TDNT*, VI, pp. 425ff.).

is a gift of God[57] or of the Spirit.[58] Yet there can be no doubt whatever that faith, however much it bears the character of obedience and submission to the divine redemptive will (see below), nevertheless does not rest on the assent of man himself (that is, man in sin and in the flesh), but on the renewing and re-creating power of divine grace. Were it otherwise, then the gospel would be a new law, and the whole problem of the impotence of the law would recur.

We need not stop with this general consideration, however. The extent to which faith rests on the divine work of redemption in man likewise appears from those pronouncements of the apostle in which he points out the origin of faith as situated in the preaching of the gospel. Thereby on the one hand the character (to be treated still further) of faith as response and obedience to the gospel comes to the fore. On the other hand, it is also apparent, just in this correlation between faith and the preaching of the gospel, how much the latter not only advances faith, but also works faith, and calls this forth by the power of God that reveals itself in the preaching. Faith is "from hearing" and hearing by the word of Christ (Rom. 10:17; cf. 1 Cor. 15:11). By the gospel and its ministers the church has come to faith, "and that indeed to each as the Lord gave to him" (1 Cor. 3:5). They have planted but God has given the increase, they are God's fellow-workers, the church

---

57. The passages to which appeal is often made for this, namely, Phil. 1:29 and Eph. 2:8, taken by themselves give no decisive answer in this matter. In Phil. 1:29 it is said: "for to you the grace has been given *(echaristhē)*, for Christ, not only to believe in him *(to eis auton pisteuein)*, but also to suffer for him." Strictly speaking grace is spoken of here in the objective, not in the subjective-internal sense (as *gratia interna*). Grace consists herein, that the church may believe in Christ because the gospel has been made known to it. This is also evident from the analogy of the final words ("also to suffer for him"). There is likewise mention here of the grace of suffering in an objective sense, namely, as evidence of belonging to Christ, not of the grace of strength or perseverance in suffering (so Calvin, in our opinion incorrectly). That the power to believe as well as to suffer is of God is, of course, not denied, but even so is not said here in so many words (so, e.g., Greijdanus: "It [faith] is the fruit of the operation of God's grace in the heart of His elect, as the apostle here clearly declares"; *De brief van den Apostel Paulus aan de gemeente te Philippi*, 1937, p. 166). The evidence, too, drawn from the well-known pronouncement in Eph. 2:8: "for by grace have you been saved, through faith; and that *(kai touto)* not of yourselves, it is the gift of God; not of works, that no man should boast," in our view is not established. The question is whether *kai touto* refers back to the whole of the preceding pronouncement or only to "through faith." Most choose for the former (so, e.g., Calvin: *"Not of yourselves;* that . . . they may acknowledge God alone as the Author of their salvation"; *Commentary* on Eph. 2:8). That the text reads *kai touto* and not *kai autē* is in itself no conclusive objection against the second conception. What is more important is that *ouk ex hymōn*, corresponding with *ouk ex ergōn*, will surely have to refer to the whole preceding sentence. It is also possible, however, not to make *ouk ex hymōn* correspond with *ouk ex ergōn*, but to connect the latter directly with *dia pisteōs*. The words "and that not of yourselves, it is the gift of God" then receive a parenthetical significance, and are indeed to be understood of faith. One who accepted this conception would, in our opinion, have to admit to at least some uncertainty.

58. Schweizer also recognizes that *(TDNT*, VI, p. 426; cf. Bultmann, *TDNT*, VI, p. 219). In 1 Cor. 12:9 "faith, by the same Spirit" is spoken of, but here *pistis* has the special meaning of *charisma*, whereby one is capable of extraordinary powers (cf. 1 Cor. 13:2).

is God's field, God's building (1 Cor. 3:6, 9). It is in that sense that
Paul, especially at the beginning of his epistles, again and again thanks
God for the faith of the church (cf. Rom. 1:8; Phil. 1:29; Col. 1:4;
1 Thess. 1:3; Philem. 5). In that sense also we shall have to understand
those pronouncements in which the word of the cross or of the gospel
is called a "power of God" (1 Cor. 1:18, 24; Rom. 1:16). This expression
undoubtedly has broad significance; the gospel is the means that carries
on God's work of redemption in Christ, and it does so in all kinds of
ways. It exercises that power, however, by working faith in man and
makes him live by it (1 Thess. 2:13). Faith does not rest on human
wisdom, but on[59] the power of God (1 Cor. 2:5), which is the power of
his Spirit (1 Thess. 1:5), just as, conversely, there is mention of the
energeia of error that they should believe the lie (2 Thess. 2:11). One
finds the same train of thought in the striking pronouncement of 2
Corinthians 4:4ff., where it is first said of unbelievers that the god of
this age has stricken their thoughts with blindness, so that they do not
perceive "the light of the gospel of the glory of Christ." To the church,
however, the words apply: "For it is that [same] God who said: Let light
shine out of darkness, who has made it to shine in our hearts, to give
the light of the knowledge of the glory of God. . . ."

Accordingly, when faith is elsewhere called a matter of the heart
(Rom. 10:9, 10), and it holds for the word of faith (the gospel) that it
is in the heart of man (Rom. 10:8), it is evident that the heart is moved
to this faith by the same creative word of God as that by which he
caused the light to shine on the darkness of the primeval time. Nothing
is therewith detracted from the nature of faith as submission and obedience. It is characterized, however, by the fact that it is an obedience
that most profoundly rests on being claimed by the overwhelming power
of the word of God; it is bearing witness to the light God has caused
to arise in the heart.

In this context something should be said about what Paul time and
again terms the divine call and the calling of the church.[60] This expression is connected with what is already a qualification of the people of God
in the Old Testament and which as a *terminus technicus*[61] Paul transfers
to the New Testament church, as the "called" or "called saints" (e.g.,
Rom. 1:6, 7; 1 Cor. 1:2; cf. v. 9). He gives this word a pregnant significance, however, by understanding it of the word of divine power by
which God calls into being the things that do not exist and by which
he works what he commands (Rom. 4:17; 9:11, 25; 1 Thess. 5:24). It is
this effectual, efficient divine calling which now takes place through the
gospel and by which God has called the church to faith itself as well
as to the whole of the new life by faith.

It is also this effectual calling by the gospel through which God's
electing[62] grace is realized, not on the ground of human works or merit,

---

59. For *einai en* ("rest on") in 1 Cor. 2:5, see, e.g., Grosheide, *1 Cor.*, p. 78.
60. Cf. Gutbrod, *Die paulinische Anthropologie*, pp. 184ff.
61. See below, Section 55.
62. Cf. K. L. Schmidt, *TDNT*, III, p. 492, *s.v. kaleō.*

but of his antecedent saving purpose (2 Thess. 2:13ff.; 2 Tim. 1:9; Rom. 8:29ff.; 9:12). For those who thus have been called according to the divine purpose (Rom. 8:28), the preaching of Christ the Crucified One is the power of God and the wisdom of God (1 Cor. 1:24). It is this "faith of God's elect" (Tit. 1:1) which forms the mode of existence of the new life through the Spirit.

This placing of emphasis on the electing and effectual character of calling by the gospel and this connection between calling and the saving purpose of God do not in any respect signify in Paul's preaching a reduction from faith as obedience. Nowhere is this more apparent than in the extensive discussion of Israel's unbelief, whereby he time and again brings God's omnipotence and election into the picture. This appeal does not serve to give an explanation in an anthropological sense of the fact that Israel has hardened itself in unbelief and the gentiles have received Christ in faith, but to throw light on the great soteriological theme of Paul's proclamation: "not upon the ground of works, but of this, that he called" (Rom. 9:11, 16). On the one hand he thereby declares the Jews to be in default, and all those who seek righteousness on the ground of their works (Rom. 9:30ff.) and who in disobedience and contradictoriness have resisted this gospel-without-the-works-of-the-law (10:19ff.); on the other hand, in "but upon this ground, that he called" it is implied that faith is not a "work" to which one can appeal or (over against the Jews) in which one can glory (cf. 11:18ff.), but the fruit of the effectual, divine call (9:24ff.) by the gospel, so that the content of the promise given by God to Abraham is communicated as a life-giving power (Gal. 3:16ff.; 4:23, 28ff.). The guilty character of unbelief as disobedience to the grace of God is not herewith taken away (Rom. 10:3). The divine calling does not eliminate man, but demands of him just this, that he obey the gospel. But all this functions in a greater context,[63] in which not man but God, as the one who elects and is glorified, is the First and the Last (Rom. 11:36).

---

63. On this see further below, Section 57. Bultmann is of the opinion that the passages in which faith is represented as a gift or is even related to the divine purpose, if one chooses to understand them literally, place us before an irresolvable contradiction: "for a faith brought about by God outside of man's decision would obviously not be genuine obedience." He wants to understand these pronouncements in this way, that "the decision of faith does not ... go back to this-worldly motives of any sort whatever," but that these last "lose all power of motivation in the presence of the encountered proclamation" (*Theology*, I, p. 330). Paul does not, however, know this problematic. For him election does not mean that faith is worked outside the decision of man, but just that the power of the gospel brings man to the decision of faith. Therefore election cannot be "interpreted" as a lack of "this-worldly motive" in the decision of man, but rather as the lack of such a "this-worldly" motive for the calling of sinful man by God. In this calling and election God takes "reasons from himself." That in this calling the sovereign power of God is manifested to be gracious and to have mercy on whom he will is attested to by Paul with great force (Rom. 9:11, 12, 15, 24), but does not make faith and unbelief illusory in their character of (dis)obedience (Rom. 9:25; 10:20, 21). There is a deep mystery here which, on account of the heterogeneity of divine and human freedom, does not, however, admit of being reduced causally to one of the two (cf. below, pp. 353ff.).

SECTION 41. THE NATURE OF FAITH

The all-embracing significance of faith as the mode of existence of the new man gives us occasion to go further still into the nature of faith.

In general, in Paul as in the whole of the New Testament, faith is the central concept used to denote the human correlate of the eschatological redemptive reality revealed in Christ. In that sense faith itself has become a redemptive-historical concept, as this is voiced particularly in the typical expression of Galatians 3:23. For the same reason the concepts "faith" and "gospel" define each other reciprocally. For at one time the gospel can be called the "word of faith"[64] (Rom. 10:8), then again faith is typified as "faith in the gospel" (Phil. 1:27), still further as the "hearing of faith," i.e., the believing hearing of the gospel (Gal. 3:2, 5).[65]

This fundamental involvement of faith with the gospel determines the nature of faith in more than one way. One can thereby start from the content of the gospel as the message of redemption and then typify faith first of all as the surrender and trust of faith, especially in contrast to trusting in the works of the law. One can also, more formally, take his point of departure in the gospel as the message of redemption, whereby faith comes to the fore as the obedience of faith. Both points of view are, of course, very closely connected, and are equally characteristic for Paul's concept of faith. We begin with the latter as the more general and comprehensive.

Faith as obedience is of central significance for Paul's conception and is repeatedly defined as such in his epistles. He says immediately at the beginning of the Epistle to the Romans that he has received his apostleship unto "obedience of faith"[66] among all the gentiles; at the conclusion of the epistle this is repeated (at least according to many mss.; 16:26). The same thought is present when the apostle speaks of being "subject to the righteousness of God" (Rom. 10:3). For this righteousness is the great content of the gospel (Rom. 1:17). Unbelief means therefore not being obedient, being disobedient to the gospel (Rom. 10:16; cf. 11:30; 2 Thess. 1:18). Faith and obedience belong together and can be employed as interchangeable ideas (cf. Rom. 1:8 and 16:19; 1 Thess. 1:8 and Rom. 15:18), as can unbelief and disobedience (cf. Rom. 2:8; Eph. 2:2; 5:6). From all this the involvement of faith with the gospel as the authoritative communication of salvation is apparent. And the nature of faith is thereby determined in its initial intention.

This structure of faith as obedience is, of course — so we may say — not to be detached for a moment from the content of the gospel. It is no formal obedience that is to prepare the way for faith in the content

---

64. *Rhēma tēs pisteōs*, genitive of apposition in the sense of: the word that is intended for faith, is received in faith, or something similar; cf., e.g., Greijdanus, *Rom.*, II, p. 461.

65. *Akoē pisteōs*. For the explanation of this expression (and the various conceptions) see my *The Epistle of Paul to the Churches of Galatia*, 1953, p. 113.

66. *Hypakoē pisteōs;* the genitive is to be taken as a genitive of apposition or an epexegetical genitive: "obedience consisting of faith," or as a genitive of quality: "faith's obedience" (cf. Greijdanus, *Rom.*, I, pp. 67ff.).

of the gospel, but it is, in the first instance, just obedience to the content of the gospel itself, "subjecting oneself to the righteousness of God," being willing to be "subordinate" *(hypakoē)* to this righteousness as the way of salvation of grace revealed and ordained by God. Faith can (and must!) as such be called obedience, however, because the gospel does not come to man as a communication or offer that leaves him free, but asks of him the decision and the act to enter into that way of salvation ordained of God and to abandon every other means of salvation than that which is proclaimed to him in the gospel. It is the response and obedience to God's grace that is intended here, and faith must be qualified in this way because it cannot otherwise participate in the gift of grace than by responding to and following the gospel.

In close connection with this character of faith as obedience is the aspect of confession mentioned time and again in one breath with faith; so, for example, in Romans 10:9, 10: "If you confess with your mouth Jesus as Lord, and believe with your heart that God raised him from the dead, you will be saved. For with the heart man believes unto righteousness; and with the mouth confession is made unto salvation."

The connection is so close because "confessing" *(homologein* and *homologia)* originally meant "saying the same thing," "speaking to-gether," and hence contains the element of letting oneself be engaged for something or someone, being willing to declare oneself for some-thing in the presence of others, considering oneself answerable for something.[67] On the one hand, that which is typical of "confession" thus lies in the fact that it is the self-accountability of faith toward the outside. In that sense it has a certain forensic significance, whereby "the forum" or "the witnesses" may be thought of as the worldly tribunal or men in general, but also as the church or its representatives, before whom one professes his faith and commits himself to the content of the faith (1 Tim. 6:12ff.).[68] On the other hand, "confession" as *homologia* expresses that faith has a norm (in the gospel), and that adhering to this norm and knowing oneself to be responsible for this proceeds from the essence of faith. The spontaneity of faith in expressing itself (2 Cor. 4:13) and the obedience of faith as assent to the gospel go hand in hand in confession. In that sense "one confesses with the mouth unto salva-tion," that is, through giving expression to one's belonging to Christ by faith, and Paul speaks of it as the "obedient confession of the gospel of Christ" (2 Cor. 9:13). It is this binding of confession to the gospel by which on the one hand it is safeguarded against all false tradition-alism and intellectualism, and on the other against being dissolved in mysticism and idealism.[69]

This determination of faith by the gospel and this structure of faith

---

67. Cf. Michel, *TDNT*, V, pp. 207ff. He defines *homologia* in Paul as "re-sponse to the Gospel of Christ, obedience to its message, acceptance of its claim and expression of commitment" (p. 215).

68. For this passage and the various conceptions of the "many witnesses," see, e.g., C. K. Barrett, *The Pastoral Epistles*, 1963, p. 86.

69. Cf. Michel, *TDNT*, V, p. 212.

as obedience to the gospel are able also to give us an insight into the relationship in which faith stands to Christ.

For Paul speaks not only of "faith in the gospel," but very frequently of "faith in Christ" as well, and he employs various formulations for this.[70] On the basis of the formula "faith in (en) Christ" some have wanted indeed to make their point of departure a mystical concept of faith in Paul, in the sense of "something which is effected in the vital union with the spiritual Christ."[71]

In particular on this point of view the connection with the genitive (*pistis Iēsou Christou*, etc.) is not to be taken as an objective genitive, but as a genitive of communion or a mystical genitive,[72] whereby "Christ" is not the object of faith, but qualifies the communion that faith has with Christ: "Christ-faith."[73] It has rightly been urged as an objection against this, however, that one would likewise have to take the combination *pisteuein eis Iēsoun Christon* in that sense — which Deissmann does — but that with this conception the Pauline usage becomes entirely isolated from that which is followed elsewhere in the New Testament; furthermore, that *pistis* plus the genitive can mean being directed toward an object and in Paul does in fact mean this (cf. Phil. 1:27 — *pistis tou euangeliou*), just as Paul speaks of *pistis pros ton Kyrion*, whereby there is obviously no question of such a mystical union.[74]

But the whole manner in which for Paul faith functions as obedience to the gospel points in another direction. That is not to say that faith in Christ does not denote a personal relationship to Christ (cf., e.g., Gal. 2:20 and Rom. 10:9, 12, where, in close connection with believing and confessing, calling on Christ is spoken of). But this relationship is defined by faith in the gospel and is in a certain sense identical with it. For as little as faith in the gospel is directed merely toward a thing, a word, a Scripture, but in this word is directed toward the person who is its great content, so little is faith in Christ to be described simply as a personal relationship, but as a relationship to the person of Christ as he is known and comes to us in the gospel. It is faith in that Christ who means for the believer what is announced of him in the gospel; who has come into the world, who has suffered, died, risen, and who lives in heaven. Thus is he proclaimed, and thus have those who believe in him learned to believe (1 Cor. 15:11). For this reason faith, even when it is termed faith in Christ, is in its essence always defined by this

---

70. *Pistis, pisteuein* plus the genitive *Iēsou Christou, Christou Iēsou*, etc. (cf. Rom. 3:22, 26; Gal. 2:16, 20; 3:22; Phil. 3:9; Eph. 3:12); *pistis, pisteuein eis Christon*, etc. (cf. Gal. 2:16; Col. 2:5); *pistis en Christō*, etc. (cf. Gal. 3:26; Col. 1:4; Eph. 1:15; 1 Tim. 3:13; 2 Tim. 3:15); *pisteuein ep' autō* (1 Tim. 1:16); with a single dative (2 Tim. 1:2); *pistis pros ton Kyrion* (Philem. 5).

71. So Deissmann, *St. Paul*, p. 140.

72. *Ibid.*, pp. 140f.

73. So, e.g., also O. Schmitz, *Die Christus-Gemeinschaft des Paulus im Lichte seines Genitivgebrauchs*, 1924, pp. 21ff., who wishes to understand this genitive "in the sense of a completely general qualification of this faith" as "Christ-faith," "Christ-Jesus-faith," "Jesus-faith," "without finding expressed any trace of a concrete verbal relationship between the two nouns through the genitive as such, be it in the manner of the objective or subjective genitive" (*ibid.*, p. 132).

74. Cf., e.g., Lietzmann, *Rom.*, p. 48.

element of being bound to the gospel in its concrete redemptive content.

This last point can enable us to understand the close connection Paul again and again makes between faith in Christ and the tradition the church has received from him and the doctrine in which it has been instructed. Both concepts play a great role in the Pauline epistles. One will moreover, especially with "tradition," have to relinquish every thought of a collective, anonymous origin (as that notion is involved in our idea of tradition), as well as the conception that what is alluded to in general by this is the faith of the church as the bearer of this tradition. The idea that Paul employs, as has been convincingly demonstrated in recent years,[75] is oriented rather to Judaism and denotes the gospel as a clearly delimited authoritative tradition, of which certain qualified persons are the authorized bearers and conveyers. It is in this sense that Paul in particular utilizes the concept of tradition, the content of which is above all the redemptive event that took place in Christ and the bearers of which are the apostles called and authorized by him to this authoritative tradition (cf. 1 Cor. 11:2, 23; 15:1, 3; Gal. 1:12).[76] The expressions "to deliver" and "receive" (as tradition), of which Paul makes abundant use (cf. also Gal. 1:9; Phil. 4:9; 1 Thess. 2:13; 4:1; 2 Thess. 3:6), are to be understood in this sense, and one can only deplore the fact that in our translations, because of a lack of equivalent concepts, the pregnant significance of these expressions is in many respects lost.

Through the connection with tradition and doctrine understood in this way, faith in the gospel and faith in Christ are further qualified in terms of content and structure, and the obedience of faith is likewise characterized; as, for example, when there is mention in Romans 6:17 of having "become obedient from the heart to that form of teaching which you have received as [authoritative apostolic] tradition,"[77] and when faith in Christ is denoted as "having received Christ by tradition" (Col. 2:6; cf. Eph. 4:20) and the church is exhorted thus to hold fast to him.

In this manner a close connection is made between the faith of the church and apostolic authority, and the character of faith as obedience is determined by this apostolic authorization.[78] One need only glance at Paul's epistles to know how he wishes to have this obedience of faith understood. He does not come to the church only with logical argumentation, he does not only appeal to the conscience or to the manner in which the gospel makes provision for human need and lostness, but his words are supported above all by the authorization he has received as apostle of Jesus Christ and with which, when he sees the content of the gospel threatened or falsified in one way or another, he

---

75. See, e.g., Cullmann, "The Tradition," in *The Early Church*, 1956, pp. 63ff.; B. Gerhardsson, *Memory and Manuscript*, 1961, pp. 288ff., and the literature cited there.

76. See also my *The Authority of the New Testament Scriptures*, pp. 17ff.

77. Bultmann thinks that in this expression we have to do with an interpolation (*TLZ*, 1947, pp. 193ff.). But there are no sufficient grounds for this conception, and it is rather to be assumed, therefore, that the Pauline idea of doctrine and tradition here emerge in a pregnant, if striking, manner; cf. also Michel, *Rom.*, p. 136.

78. Cf. Mundle, *Der Glaubensbegriff des Paulus*, pp. 32ff.

lays down his authoritative word, brooking no contradiction: "I here-with make known unto you (gnōrizō; 1 Cor. 15:1; Gal. 1:11).

Here again the "formal" and the "material" aspects of the authority of the gospel and of the corresponding character of faith as obedience remain inseparably bound together. Paul does not first ask obedient recognition of his authorization and thereafter of the content of his message: his commission and authorization consist in the proclamation of the revelation of the mystery, and the nature of his apostolic authority is to be inferred from that (cf. Eph. 3:2ff.). On the other hand, it lies in the nature of the gospel as tidings of salvation of what God has done in Christ and what has taken place in Christ's death and resurrection, that the authority of the gospel does not rest only on the inner hold it lays on the heart and will of man, but first of all on the reality of that which has once taken place. The gospel therefore can be no gospel, faith no faith, and the obedience of faith to the gospel no obedience, if the tradition of the redemptive event was not trust-worthy and faith could not appeal for the latter to the former, and could not submit itself to it (1 Cor. 15:14ff.; cf. vv. 1ff.). For this unity Paul refers ever anew to his calling as an apostle of Jesus Christ, that is to say, to the preaching and tradition of the gospel warranted and authorized by the exalted Christ himself. Consequently faith in this tradition is not grounded ultimately in the trustworthiness of human eyewitnesses and bearers of the tradition, but in the manner in which the living Lord has appointed his apostles as the foundation of the church and demands its obedience to what they proclaim with authority in his name and power (cf. Rom. 15:18ff.; 2 Cor. 12:12; 1 Thess. 1:5; 2:13; Eph. 2:20).

From this the calling of the church to safeguard against corruption and error the faith thus directed toward Christ now proceeds of itself. As believers have "received Christ by [apostolic] tradition," so they are to walk in him, to be established in "the faith, as you were taught," and to take heed that the deceitful wisdom after "the tradition of men" and the "first principles of the world" does not make prey of them (Col. 2:6ff.). For the word that they have received by tradition is in truth God's word, which works in them that believe (1 Thess. 2:13). "To stand fast in the faith" means accordingly to hold fast to the tradition (2 Thess. 2:14, 15; cf. 3:6), as also the renewing of life and the putting off of the old man stand in the closest relationship with the knowledge of Christ thus received and must continually be subjected to that norm.

It is accordingly incomprehensible that when the Pastoral Epistles speak of "sound doctrine" and "sound faith" (1 Tim. 1:10; Tit. 1:13; 2:3), and time and again emphasis is placed on guarding the deposit[79] that has been entrusted to the minister of the gospel and to the church (1 Tim. 6:20; 2 Tim. 1:4), this is allegedly no longer compatible with the genuine Pauline conception of faith.[80] However much a (natural!)

---

79. *Parathēkē*. For this idea (closely bound up with *paradosis*) see C. Spicq, *Les Épitres Pastorales*, 3rd ed., 1947, pp. 327-335.

80. As, e.g., Kümmel thinks ("Der Glaube im N.T., seine katholische und

development is perceptible here, and the antithesis between the Christian faith and human tradition and wisdom has in the process of time assumed a more clearly delimited form, this does not alter the fact that this conformity with the tradition pertains to the essence of the Pauline idea of faith, that this faith therefore from the outset stands over against the wisdom of the heathen (1 Cor. 1:20ff.), and contains within itself the inner necessity of being guarded and defended against error and corruption (cf. also Rom. 16:17).

Furthermore, the important place that the element of knowledge occupies in the Pauline idea of faith proceeds of itself from this. Faith cannot be approached from the sphere of feeling, e.g., in the sense of heathen mysticism; neither can it be defined as an act of surrender or *Entscheidung*, without a clear awareness as to that to which it surrenders itself or for which it decides, but faith presupposes a knowing, on which it rests and from which it ever and anew derives its strength.

To be sure, the relationship of faith and knowledge, *pistis* and *gnosis*, just as that of faith and works, is ambivalent. On the one hand knowledge stands in faith's way, that is, when, just as good works for the Jews, it represents the human will to self-redemption. As this antithesis is developed in Galatians and Romans with respect to works, this threat to the Christian faith from the side of *gnosis* is elucidated especially in 1 Corinthians (cf., e.g., 1 Cor. 1:26-29). And this danger exists not merely from the side of what Paul calls "the wisdom of this world" (1 Cor. 1:21), but also from a certain kind of Christian *gnosis*. Paul does recognize that *gnosis* in itself: we know that we all have knowledge (1 Cor. 8:1). But he immediately adds to this: knowledge puffs up, love builds up. What is at issue here is a wrongly employed Christian *gnosis*, which elevates itself above one's neighbor, the weak; a knowledge that is indeed in the service of one's own individual freedom, but not of the edification of the church. This *gnosis* only promotes proud individualism and stands over against love. In that sense *gnosis*, even as works, can come to stand over against love; as such it is injurious and without profit (1 Cor. 13:2, 3).[81]

These are the negative pronouncements on *gnosis*. But just as faith stands over against "works" as the means to self-redemption and the ground for man's own boasting, but is nevertheless not without works, but brings these along with it, so it is with knowledge and wisdom *(sophia)*. God destroys the wisdom of the world, but Christ has become to us wisdom from God (1 Cor. 1:30). For this reason faith in Christ, as the fruit of the proclamation of the gospel, is also knowledge and wisdom, and these concepts *pistis* and *gnosis* define each other reciprocally in the Pauline conception of faith.[82]

---

reformatorische Deutung," *Theol. Blätter*, 1937, col. 217). For the recognition of the original Pauline idea of faith in the Pastoral Epistles see the beautiful pages Schlatter devotes to "faith" in these epistles, which far surpass the assertions of Kümmel (A. Schlatter, *Der Glaube im N.T.*, 4th ed., 1927, pp. 406-418).

81. See below, pp. 295ff.
82. Cf. Bultmann, *TDNT*, VI, pp. 220ff.

This integral linking of faith and knowledge in Paul's epistles can be demonstrated on the basis of an abundance of evidence that will not be exhausted here. It is the all-surpassing knowledge of Christ Jesus, which led him to abandon all his earlier attainments and to seek righteousness only on the foundation of faith (Phil. 3:8ff.). In that sense he is able to qualify his proclamation of the gospel, "the word of faith," as the "manifestation of the fragrance of the knowledge of Christ" (2 Cor. 2:14). This knowledge, of course, has reference above all to the resurrection of Christ as the content and cognitive ground of faith (Rom. 4:24; 10:9; 1 Thess. 4:14; Col. 2:12), and can be defined in general as the "knowledge of the glory of God in the face of Jesus Christ" (2 Cor. 4:6). Yet in addition Paul speaks of knowing in all sorts of ways in close connection with faith, especially in the frequently occurring idiom "for we know that" (Rom. 5:3; 6:9; 1 Cor. 15:58; 2 Cor. 1:7; 4:14, et al.).[83] Knowledge appears, moreover, as the ground and motive or as the implication of faith, it itself bears the character of faith-knowledge (Rom. 6:9; 2 Cor. 4:14), and it qualifies faith as a conscious, directed, and therefore convinced and assured faith.

Just as in faith, there is certainly a distinction to be observed in knowledge in the church. It is also true of both that the church has not immediately come to full maturity in them. Time and again a "growing," "increase," "being filled," "abounding," in knowledge is spoken of (Phil. 1:9; Col. 1:9, 10; 1 Thess. 3:12; 2 Cor. 8:7). Frequently faith and knowledge make their appearance in this respect as ideas that complement and reciprocally define one another. It is "the faith and the knowledge" (the faith-knowledge) of the Son of God in which the church is more and more to find its unity (Eph. 4:13); and elsewhere there is mention of an "abounding in faith, in utterance, in knowledge" (2 Cor. 8:7).

The distinction between initial knowledge and the continuing, developed knowledge of faith is sometimes given expression in a very trenchant manner. Paul says in 1 Corinthians 2:6 that he speaks wisdom (sophia) among those that are perfect, and he complains against the Corinthians who thought so highly of their knowledge that he cannot speak of this wisdom among them because they still conduct themselves so much as children. He calls them therefore "babes in Christ," who because of their carnal disposition cannot tolerate "solid food" (1 Cor. 3:1ff.). It is not said hereby that he distinguishes two groups, the "immature" and the "perfect,"[84] but that it pertains to the wisdom given in Christ to proceed from immaturity to maturity. The church as a whole must be brought to "all riches of the fulness of insight," "to the knowledge of the mystery of God, Christ, in whom are all the treasures of wisdom and knowledge hidden." Then will it no longer be thrown off its stride by specious fallacies and tossed to and fro and carried

---

83. *Eidotes hoti;* cf. Mundle, *Glaubensbegriff*, pp. 17ff.

84. Against this conception of Reitzenstein and others who wish to explain the idea *teleioi* from the Hellenistic mysteries as the denotation of those who had come to "the full gnosis," see the still valuable writing of K. Deissner, *Paulus und die Mystik seiner Zeit*, 2nd ed., 1921, pp. 39ff.

about by every wind of doctrine in the vain trickery of men (Col. 2:2ff.; Eph. 4:13ff.).

Moreover, what is thought of as the content of this knowledge *(gnosis, epignosis)* and wisdom *(sophia)* is not unclear in view of Paul's own epistles. On the one hand this knowledge has reference to the increasingly better understanding of the will of God in the ethical sense of the word. This is spoken of, for example, in Colossians 1:9ff., where the apostle makes mention of his intercession that the church may be filled with "the knowledge of God's will, in all wisdom and spiritual understanding, to walk worthily of the Lord"; in Philippians 1:9 he terms this same thing "the insight and the discernment to distinguish the things that really matter," which is apparently also intended in an ethical sense[85] (cf. also Philem. 6; Rom. 15:4).

Yet it is clear that this knowledge of faith and increase in it are not in the first place ethical in nature. In the opening of the Epistle to the Ephesians there is likewise mention of the abundant grace God has shown to the church, "in all wisdom and understanding, making known to us the mystery of his will" (Eph. 1:8, 9). As appears from the whole context, however, what is to be understood here by the "mystery of God's will" is not in the first instance God's requirement, but his redemptive will, as this has been revealed in the advent and work of Christ. Accordingly the prayer of the apostle is directed toward this, that God may give the church "the Spirit of wisdom and revelation in order to know him aright; enlightened eyes of the heart in order to know what is the hope of his calling and how rich is the glory of his inheritance," etc. (Eph. 1:17; cf. 3:18, 19). Here the content of the knowledge of faith consists in a deeper and more extensive insight into that which God has given and will give in Christ. Elsewhere as well "the knowledge of the mystery of Christ" and "the treasures of wisdom and knowledge, which are hidden in Christ," will have to be understood in this way. Sometimes "the Spirit, who searches all things, even the depths of God . . . that we might know what has been given us by God in Christ," is spoken of in still stronger language (1 Cor. 2:10ff.). With all this one is not to think of a certain mysterious doctrine or of esoteric revelations, which would only have been intended for a small group of "perfect ones." Paul, as he says in the same context of 1 Corinthians, knows no other gospel than that of Jesus Christ and him crucified (1 Cor. 2:2). The "mystery of Christ," the "depths of God," is that which God has purposed to himself in Christ and has brought to revelation in the fullness of time. But the knowledge of this mystery and of these depths consists not only in the handing down of that which has taken place, but also in the all-embracing significance of it. Paul's epistles give an unmistakable picture of that knowledge and wisdom as he, who calls himself the "steward of the mysteries of God" (1 Cor. 4:1), unfolds the significance of Christ's death and resurrection on all sides: in his Christocentric interpretation of the Old Testament (Rom. 4; Gal. 3; 4:21-31; 1 Cor. 10:1-13; 2 Cor. 3:7-18, etc.), in the tremendous redemptive-historical exposition of Romans 9-11 concerning Israel, lead-

---

85. On this see below, pp. 287f.

ing to the adoration of what here again is called "the depths" of God
(Rom. 11:33); further, in his designation of Christ as the second Adam
(Rom. 5; 1 Cor. 15) and the light that sheds on the resurrection of the
dead (1 Cor. 15:35-49). This wisdom and knowledge reach still further
when, as in his resistance against the false doctrine at Colosse, he extends the significance of Christ to the whole of the created world, the
powers that are in heaven and on earth, history, and when he leads
the church to understand itself, in the light of the significance of Christ
in that world and history, as the body of Christ, filled with all the
fullness of him who fills all things (Col. 2; Eph. 1:23). To trace the
course of the revealed mystery in this way, to grasp its implications
for the great future and for the manner in which it is to take place
(1 Cor. 15:51; 1 Thess. 4:15, 17) — all this together discloses something
of the treasures of wisdom and knowledge that are hidden in Christ.
They may be known by those who "have the *nous* of Christ," by the
"spiritual man" who does not stick fast halfway along in immaturity
but, taught by the Spirit, learns to discern all things and relates together all that which "is of the Spirit" in order thus to know what has
been given us by God in grace (1 Cor. 2:6-16). For not only is Paul
himself a dispenser and steward of these mysteries of God and not only
in his reiterated prayer that God may grant the church this knowledge
(which prayer functions at the same time as the introduction to what
he himself is able to communicate to the church of it), but he also
wants to make the church itself active therein so that it may build up
and establish itself in the faith out of the root from which it lives —
Christ — (Col. 2:7) and with all the saints may know all the dimensions,
forward, backward, in the height and in the depth (Eph. 3:18), as endowed with the Spirit of the knowledge and of the revelation of God
in Christ (Eph. 1:17; Phil. 3:15).[86]

No doubt this knowledge and wisdom in all their extent and
explications do not simply coincide with faith; they are not gifts that,
as it were, are ready to hand; they must be discovered, traced, and
investigated with all the saints and all generations. For the treasures
of wisdom and of knowledge are more than can be comprehended by
one man, one church, and — we may add to this — one generation. There
is also a difference of gifts, and not every member of the church has a
share in every gift in the same measure and in the same sense. Therefore under the diversity of gifts[87] Paul mentions both "the word of
wisdom" and "the word of knowledge." But this does not alter the fact
that this knowledge and this wisdom have only been given for the
building up of the whole church, and that this knowledge, likewise in
the respect in which it is more than the fundamental recognition of the
love of God turned toward us in Christ, further qualifies faith according
to its nature and in this way pertains to the new mode of existence of
the church that has been given it by the Spirit (1 Cor. 2:15, 16).

---

86. See also O. Cullmann, "La nécessité de la Théologie pour l'Eglise selon
le Nouveau Testament," in the *Bulletin de la Faculté Libre de Théologie protestante
de Paris,* Dec., 1957.

87. See below, Section 71, p. 447.

If in the above the indissoluble relationship between faith and the message of redemption has become clear and if in its light one may understand that already in the Pauline usage faith can denote not only the *fides qua,* but also the *fides quae creditur,*[88] on the other hand this faith is in its essence defined by the fact that it is faith in salvation, and thus bears the character of trust, surrender, hope. Not for a moment may the idea be allowed to take form that faith, because it is so closely connected to tradition and consists in obedient submission to the apostolic doctrine of salvation, lies only or in the first place in the noetic sphere and does not from the outset affect man in the totality of his existence. Even the fact that Paul describes faith as a matter of the heart (Rom. 10:9), and repeatedly links knowledge with the *nous,* is sufficient proof of the contrary, inasmuch as it is precisely these concepts which, as we have seen,[89] denote the new man in his central self-determination.

To be sure, the element of trust in Paul's epistles (no more than in the whole of the New Testament) is not frequently mentioned explicitly,[90] much less so, for example, than in the Old Testament Psalms. This is related to the fact that in the New Testament faith has to do above all with the all-embracing eschatological salvation revealed in Christ; whereas, for example, in the Psalms it is much more a matter of the personal lot of the one who prays in his necessity, in view of which the godly man puts his trust in God.[91] But this does not mean that trust is not an essential element in the Pauline conception of faith. Trust makes its appearance in the form of faith in Christ and the gospel, and is taken up in that and itself conversely defines the nature of faith. Negatively Paul is able to characterize the new life through the Spirit as "no longer trusting in the flesh" (Phil. 3:3ff.). Similarly, when in Romans 4 he posits the faith of Abraham exemplarily, he interprets this faith as trusting in the promise of God and in his power to carry out this promise (Rom. 4:11, 17-21); just as elsewhere he typifies the issue of faith, in harmony with the Old Testament Scripture, as "not being put to shame" (Rom. 9:33; 10:11; cf. Isa. 28:16), and once again conceives of faith in the sense of trust. In its most characteristic form this trust of faith appears in Paul as the antithesis of the Jewish trust in the law.[92] In this respect it has both a negative and a positive significance. It consists on the one hand in a relinquishing of every human achievement, it is the exclusion of all "boasting" or moral self-confidence, leaning on the strength of the law as the means of salvation; on the other hand it is the absolute surrender to God's grace, whereby "in faith" and "in grace" can be parallel expressions (cf. 2 Cor. 13:5; 1 Cor. 16:13; 2 Cor. 1:24). It is the certainty of having received "access to God" (Rom. 5:2), "boldness and access with trust through faith"

---

88. For this transition in usage see, e.g., Bultmann, *TDNT,* VI, p. 213.
89. Cf. above, pp. 117, 119, 227ff.
90. On this see also Mundle, *Glaubensbegriff,* p. 37, and Bultmann, *Theology,* I, pp. 323f.; the same writer in *TDNT,* VI, p. 218, *s.v. pisteuō,* etc.
91. So Bultmann, *TDNT,* VI, p. 7, *s.v. peithō,* etc.
92. Cf. above, Section 22.

(Eph. 3:12), the opposite of the spirit of bondage again to fear, the consciousness of the sonship of God (Rom. 8:15).

This same element of trust as an entrusting of oneself to divine grace lies at the root of knowledge as well. Knowledge of God is not the result of human initiative, reflection, or inquiry, but of God's concerning himself with man. This is clear from the remarkable manner in which in connection with the knowing of God Paul repeatedly changes the subject and object of knowing, and denotes the knowing of God by man as the reverse side and consequence of the knowing of man by God. So in Galatians 4:9: "but now we know God, or rather: we are known by him"; and in 1 Corinthians 8:2: "if any man thinks that he has learned to know anything, then he does not yet know as he ought to know. If any man loves God, however, he is known by him." Knowledge of God thus presupposes the relationship in which God has willed to place himself to man and which he has willed to enter into with him. For this reason this knowledge is knowledge of salvation, knowledge to which one can abandon himself, depending on God and trusting in him, and faith consists always in the joining of one's own lot and life with that which is "believed."

At the same time the nature of this believing knowledge of God and of the trust that coincides with it is defined by the nature of this being known by God in Christ. Here, too, the redemptive-historical viewpoint is predominant. To be known by God is not in the first place of an individual or mystical nature, and faith is accordingly not a condition of the soul that corresponds with the awareness of becoming known in such an ultra-individualistic sense,[93] but it has its ground in the manner in which God has once known, sought, redeemed us in Christ and in which he will carry on this work in him. It consists therefore in the certainty of the reconciliation once accomplished and of having been adopted as children, but it also involves the whole of life in all its facets, joys, needs, anxieties, and expectations in what God has done and will yet do in Christ, and knows itself to be included in it. In that sense Paul can term all that is not of faith, that is to say, is kept outside this all-embracing relationship, "sin," and in this same context and with the same meaning he is able to say: "for if we live, it is for the Lord, and if we die, it is for the Lord" (Rom. 14:23, 8). Faith is therefore not a condition in which one can rest when he has once attained it; to stand in the faith (Rom. 11:20; 14:4; 1 Cor. 10:12; 15:1; cf. 1 Thess. 3:8) is at the same time an unremitting struggle (Phil. 3:12-14), in which one can show himself more or less strong, in which it is possible to be weak and to be strong, to increase and to fall behind (Rom. 14:1; 2 Cor. 10:15; 1 Thess. 3:10). But even so, as faith it is not qualified by weakness but by strength, not by stagnation but by progress, because it may share even now in the strength God has revealed in Christ.

This consciousness of being permitted to live and share in the power of God as communion with the living Lord also belongs to the

---

93. Cf. Bultmann on "The Pauline Concept of Faith in Contrast to Gnosticism," *TDNT*, VI, pp. 220ff.

distinctive character of the Pauline concept of faith. Thus he prays in Ephesians 1:19ff. that the church may know how overwhelmingly great the power of God is with respect to those who believe, according to the working of the strength of his might, which he has wrought by raising Christ from the dead and by giving him a place at his right hand in the heavenly places (cf. 1:20; Col. 1:11). The continual operation of the new life accordingly takes place through faith in the working of God, who raised Christ from the dead (Col. 2:12). Therefore the gospel of the great works of God is the power of God for everyone who believes (Rom. 1:16; 1 Cor. 1:18). And the dwelling of Christ in the hearts of his own by faith is accompanied by being strengthened with power through his Spirit in the inward man (Eph. 3:16). Therefore the new life consists not only in possessing righteousness by faith in Christ, but also in knowing him and the power of his resurrection (Phil. 3:10), and faith manifests itself in power (2 Thess. 1:11); the Spirit is also a Spirit of power, and believers have to fulfill their calling according to the power of God (2 Tim. 1:7, 8). And this certainty of sharing in the power of God is the more striking because it is accompanied with the consciousness of one's own weakness (2 Cor. 4:17), is made perfect in human weakness, indeed learns to take satisfaction in that, so that the power of Christ may be the more clearly manifest in it (2 Cor. 19:9ff.). Indeed, this weakness itself forms a proof of the fact that all of life is bound to Christ. For he too was crucified out of weakness, but he lives out of the power of God (2 Cor. 13:3ff.). It is this solidarity with Christ in which the believer learns to understand the present life in its deepest significance (2 Cor. 4:11; 6:9; Col. 1:24; 2 Tim. 2:10), which already in this life makes itself felt as a source of strength and constitutes the evidence of the coming glory.

For this reason hope is indissolubly bound up with faith, not only by virtue of the inner affinity of certain spiritual experiences or conditions, but by virtue of faith's focus on Christ: "If we have died with Christ, so we believe that we shall also live with him" (Rom. 6:8). Thus Christ himself can be called the hope of glory, and it may be understood that "hope" can signify alternately the act *(spes sperans)* and the object of hope *(spes sperata)*. In all sorts of ways the apostle speaks of hope, together with faith and with knowledge (e.g., Col. 1:4ff.; Tit. 1:1ff.; Rom. 15:13), and in particular with faith and love, as giving expression to the whole of the Christian life (1 Cor. 13:13; 1 Tim. 1:3; Col. 1:4, *et al.*). Thus hope rests on faith (Gal. 5:5); it is termed the hope of the gospel (Col. 1:23), the hope of the divine calling (Eph. 1:18), it stands on a level with the one Spirit, one body, one faith, one baptism as the "one hope of your calling" (Eph. 4:4), and thus represents the new life given in Christ and wrought by the Spirit.

Furthermore, this hope, so far as its function and operation are concerned, directs itself toward the invisible things of the future which are eternal (cf. Rom. 8:24ff.; 2 Cor. 4:18; 1 Cor. 15:9), and derives its strength from them. For as hope it is not a weaker form of believing and knowing, but precisely a source of confidence and strength (2 Cor.

1:9, 10; 3:12). It is the earnest expectation of being put to shame in
nothing (Phil. 1:20). In consequence it is able to furnish patience and
meekness, so long as that which is hoped for has not yet come (Rom.
8:25; 1 Thess. 1:3, *et al.*), and in that once again to exhibit the figure
of Abraham, who in hope believed against hope (Rom. 4:18). Hope
does not put to shame (Rom. 5:5), for however much salvation is still
a matter of hope, in that way we have (already) been saved (Rom. 8:24).

From all this it appears with abundant clarity what a power, what a
certainty, and what a victory Paul ascribes to the new life as a life by
faith and in hope; on the other hand, they both represent no less the
provisional revelation of the new life and of the new man, and it is
striking how much the apostle alternately places the emphasis on the
one and then the other. In this way there enters into the concept of
faith the strong tension and emotion that are so characteristic of the
manner in which Paul, often in the most personal passages in his epistles,
gives expression to his own experience of faith. This provisional character comes to the fore particularly when believing is placed over
against "beholding":

> . . . for we walk by faith, not by sight (2 Cor. 5:7).
> . . . for we know in part, and we prophesy in part (1 Cor. 13:9).
> . . . for now we see in a mirror, [94] in a riddle[95] . . . now I know in part
> (1 Cor. 13:12).

The kerygma of Christ's resurrection is foundational and indispensable for preaching (1 Cor. 15:3-8, 14ff.), and one cannot for this
reason seek the essence of the gospel in paradox.[96] But what has happened and been seen in Christ has not yet taken place in believers.
Their life is hid with Christ in God, in heaven, and will only be revealed when Christ is revealed (Col. 3:3, 4). The salvation that has
appeared and been beheld in Christ can therefore as yet be only the
object of faith because, as Paul expresses it, "while we have our abode
in the body, we are away from the Lord" (2 Cor. 5:6). Therefore "to
be in the faith" means to have a share "already" in the new life as the
eschatological existence and gift of salvation; on the other hand, faith

---

94. *Di' esoptrou*, by way of indicating indirect seeing; cf. Lietzmann-Kümmel,
Cor., p. 189, referring to Behm's essay "Das Bildwort vom Spiegel," in *Reinhold-
Seeberg-Festschrift*, I, 1929, pp. 314ff.; differently: Kittel, *TDNT*, I, pp. 178ff., according to whom "to see in a glass" signifies "to see prophetically" and does not
point to a lesser degree of clarity and perspicuity. This would only be expressed
by *en ainigmati* — in our view a dubious interpretation.

95. *En ainigmati:* indistinctly.

96. So, e.g., Stählin, *Skandalon*, 1930, pp. 274ff. Paradox in his view pertains
to the essence of the Pauline kerygma. He seeks its origin in the "lapping" of the
aiōn mellōn into *aiōn houtos*, in the character of veiled revelation. But in our
opinion this is correct only to a certain extent. However much the *skandalon* lies in
the cross of Christ, and the life of believers, on account of the provisional character
of the fulfillment, is a life in the "nevertheless," on the other side the *skandalon* has been overcome in Christ, namely, in his resurrection. Over against the
characterization of the gospel as the *skandalon* of the cross stands that of the
martyria, trustworthy witness concerning the resurrection (cf. also 1 Cor. 9:1).

as the provisional mode of existence of the new life implies that one "yet" finds himself in the present temporal reality, that he has not yet been made perfect, not yet laid hold upon that which is before (Phil. 3:12ff.).

The pronouncement of 1 Corinthians 13:13 seems to be in conflict with this description of faith as the provisional mode of existence of the new life: so then *abide* faith, hope, and love. For this "abide" stands over against that which "shall be done away" (v. 8). It is difficult to understand the pronouncement to the effect that faith also "after the final consummation" is the manner in which one shares in salvation (so, e.g., Lietzmann, *Cor.*, p. 66; cf. the annotation of Kümmel, p. 189, who rejects other conceptions of "abide"; cf. also 2 Cor. 5:7), especially because it is also said of hope that it abides (cf. on the other hand Rom. 8:24; 2 Cor. 4:18). We shall have to take into account the contrast that is made between faith, hope, and love on the one hand and the charismata on the other, and must seek the solution in this, that the former have to do with that which, otherwise than the charismata, does not perish.[97] Faith and hope constitute the essence of the new life, because in them lies in principle the human accompaniment of the great acts God has done and will yet do in Jesus Christ. It cannot therefore be said of these as of the charismata that they "cease," "are rendered inoperative." In faith and hope the bond with Christ is firmly fixed, which, even though this, too, will receive its modification in "the perfect" *pro mensura vitae aeternae*, yet remains the same as in the provisional earthly dispensation and does not pass away. All this does not apply to the charismata, which, however much they seem to surpass the "simplicity" of faith, hope, and love and for this reason were more highly valued by the Corinthian enthusiasm, yet have only a provisional and transitory significance and in "the perfect" will be done away.

Others are of the opinion that faith and hope are understood here in a wider sense; so, e.g., Calvin, who conceives faith as the "knowledge of God and His will" or "if you prefer it, faith understood in its fullness, and in its proper sense." Grosheide interprets faith here as the relation in which man stands to God. "He [man] believes that God is as He has revealed Himself. . . . That is not something of this dispensation" (*1 Cor.*, p. 351), a conception similar to that of Calvin. In our view it is a too general conception of faith, not very likely for Paul. The explanation remains difficult, however.

The faith of Abraham is once again exemplary for this character of faith. Although he observed[98] that his own body was as good as dead, because he was about a hundred years old, and that Sarah's womb was dead, he did not doubt the promise of God through unbelief, but against hope believed in hope in the God who gives life to the dead and calls the things that are not into existence (Rom. 4:17ff.). In this way faith became increasingly powerful. He was strongly gifted in

---

97. Cf. G. Bornkamm, "The More Excellent Way (1 Corinthians 13)," in *Early Christian Experience*, ET 1969, pp. 185ff.

98. The reading *katenoēsen* without *ou* is to be preferred. Thereby the peculiar character of faith comes still more strongly to the fore. This does not consist in the fact that it no longer sees or wishes to see the reality sharply, but has just this thoroughly in view. "Becoming strong" through faith accordingly consists alone in building on God. Because one's own possibilities become less and disappear faith does not become weaker, but stronger (cf. also Nygren, *Commentary on Romans*, pp. 180f.; Schlatter, *Der Glaube im N.T.*, pp. 345ff.

faith,[99] and gave God the glory, in the full certainty that he was able to perform what he had promised (vv. 20, 21).

In this double description of Abraham's faith as "in hope against hope" believing in him who gives life to the dead and as "being fully assured," the tension-filled character of faith emerges very distinctly indeed; and it is clear that the apostle ascribes to this character of Abraham's faith a no less exemplary significance for the faith of the church than he does to its function in the appropriation of justification as a free gift. On the one hand faith stands over against the not-yet-glorified reality of this world-dispensation, and it in no way misjudges or idealizes this reality; it observes the impotence, the death in its own body, in all earthly temptation (Rom. 4:19; 2 Cor. 5:6), it believes although there is, viewed from this side, nothing for which to hope ("against hope"; *par' elpida*). But because faith has to do with that God who gives life to the dead and who calls those things which are not as though they were, it is at the same time certainty (Rom. 4:21; 8:38), hope, glorying, approvedness, meekness, strength (Rom. 4:18; 5:2ff.; 8:18; 2 Cor. 12:9), victory (Rom. 8:37).

This twofold character of faith, in the whole tension-filled polarity of the "already" and the "not yet," finds expression in Paul's epistles in all sorts of ways. All the assaults in his own life as apostle, in labors, in imprisonment, in stripes, and in dangers of death (2 Cor. 11:23), have their say in this. But there is at the same time the deep comfort of God who comforts the lowly (2 Cor. 7:6), the glorying and taking pleasure in weaknesses, necessities, persecutions, distresses for Christ's sake: "for when I am weak, then am I strong" (2 Cor. 12:10). Or, in the words of 2 Corinthians 4:7: "But we have this treasure in earthen vessels, that the exceeding greatness of the power may be of God, and not from ourselves. We are pressed on every side, yet not straitened; perplexed, yet not unto despair; pursued, yet not forsaken; smitten down, yet not destroyed."

No less clearly does this twofold character of faith find description in the beautiful passage of Philippians 3:7-14, in which he points out the object of the righteousness on the ground of faith: to know Christ and the power of his resurrection and the fellowship of his sufferings. The latter is not in conflict with the former, but rather prepares the way for it: "...if I, by becoming conformed unto his death, may attain unto the resurrection from the dead" (v. 11).

Thus suffering, too, becomes a token of victory, because it leads one in the footprints of Christ. *Via lucis via crucis.* But this conjunction of death and life, of suffering and resurrection, is not only a pattern that is to be gathered from Christ's death and resurrection, a program that one could automatically follow; it is, with all the knowledge of Christ, a wrestling, a stretching out with every effort of the soul toward that which has not yet been attained: "Brethren, I count not myself to

---

99. *Enedynamōthē tē pistei*, dative of relationship; cf. Greijdanus, *Rom.*, I, p. 247; otherwise Zahn, *Röm.*, p. 237, who sees here an instrumental dative and considers that what is spoken of is a physical empowering through faith, namely, to the conceiving of a son; in our view wrongly.

have laid hold, but one thing I do: forgetting the things which are behind, and stretching forward to the things which are before, I press on toward the goal of the prize of the calling of God, which is from above in Christ Jesus."

The entire new life is a matter of training oneself in the *militia Christi!* That applies in particular to the new obedience, concerning which we must speak in the following chapter.

VII
THE NEW OBEDIENCE

SECTION 42. INDICATIVE AND IMPERATIVE

The preceding discussion has made clear how much the new life is a work of God. This life finds its origin in the death and resurrection of Christ, comes into being through the Holy Spirit, and in its realization in the individual man is new creation, regeneration, etc., that is to say, the fruit of the working of divine power. The farthest thing from the apostle's mind is the notion that this new life is to be explained on the basis of man himself, as an ethical transformation that is realized from the slumbering powers for good in him and which thus can be denoted as a new birth and can be related to the death and the resurrection of Christ by way of resemblance. On the other hand, it is evident that this new life is not to be understood as a transcendent stream of life that pours into man from the outside and which develops in him *eo ipso* and whereby there would no longer be any place for human responsibility and decision in the real sense of the word.[1] For Paul also describes the new life in all sorts of ways as the new humanity, the illumination of the *nous,* the renewal of the heart, and as the body and the members becoming subservient to the will of God. This nature of the new life has become clear to us in particular from the significance of faith in it, as the way in which the new creation of God is effected and communicated in the reality of this earthly life, and is to be characterized as new obedience. From this same point of view we shall now attempt to deal with the moral content of Paul's preaching.

Again it is primarily a matter of the inner relationships and structures of his preaching and doctrine. We face here specifically the phenomenon that in the more recent literature is customarily designated as the relation of the indicative and imperative. What is meant is that the new life in its moral manifestation is at one time proclaimed and posited as the fruit of the redemptive work of God in Christ through the Holy Spirit — the indicative; elsewhere, however, it is put with no less force as a categorical demand — the imperative. And the one as well as the other occurs with such force and consistency that some have indeed spoken of a "dialectical paradox" and of an "antinomy."[2]

This confluence of indicatives and imperatives is so general in

---

1. For a defense of both these conceptions in the history of interpretation (on the one side the "ethical," as, e.g., by Lipsius, on the other the *naturhaft,* as, e.g., by Wernle, Holtzmann, *et al.*), see Gutbrod, *Die Paulinische Anthropologie,* pp. 206ff.

2. Cf., e.g., Stauffer, *New Testament Theology,* p. 181.

the epistles of Paul (as in the whole of the New Testament[3]) that we may confine ourselves to a few characteristic examples. So far, first of all, as the relationship of Christ's death and resurrection is concerned, the indicative is here fundamental, that those who are in Christ have died to sin (Rom. 6:2). This whole pronouncement, however, is directed toward stimulating human responsibility and arousing to activity: "Let not sin therefore reign in your mortal body . . . and do not present your members any longer as weapons of unrighteousness in the service of sin . . ." (vv. 12, 13). The redemptive indicative of dying and rising with Christ is not to be separated from the imperative of the struggle against sin. No less striking in this respect is Colossians 3:3ff., where in response to: "For you have died, and your life is hid in God," the command at once resounds: "Put to death therefore your members which are upon the earth: fornication, uncleanness," etc. Having once died with Christ does not render superfluous putting to death the members that are on earth, but is precisely the great urgent reason for it. The same applies to the categorical pronouncements concerning life in and by the Spirit. On the one hand it can be said of that life in the manner of the indicative: "the law of the Spirit of life has made you free in Christ Jesus from the law of sin and of death" (Rom. 8:2, 9); on the other hand, in the manner of the imperative, which subsequently seems to make the first categorical redemptive pronouncement conditional: "so then, brethren, we are debtors, not to the flesh, to live after the flesh: for if you live after the flesh, you must die; but if by the Spirit you put to death the deeds of the body, you shall live" (vv. 12,13). The imperative thus is founded on the indicative ("therefore," v. 12). But the succession of the imperative is also a condition ("if," v. 13) for that which has first been categorically posited with the indicative. In the same way the pronouncements in Galatians 4 and 5 which in a categorical manner attest to the receiving of the Spirit (4:6ff.), being born after the Spirit (4:28ff.), living by the Spirit (5:25), are followed by the summons to walk after the Spirit (5:16, 25), and the warning not to go astray because God will not suffer himself to be mocked and what a man sows he will also reap, whether corruption from the flesh, or eternal life from the Spirit (6:7ff.). And finally, so far as the pronouncements are concerned that have reference to the new life as a creation of God, here again we find the same duality. At one time it is said of the new man that he has been created in Christ (Eph. 2:15; 4:24), and exists in him (Gal. 3:28); then again, that those who are in Christ "have" (active) put off the old man and "have" put on the new man (Eph. 4:21ff.; Col. 3:9ff.); and this "putting on" of the new man now signifies receiving a share in Christ sacramentally through baptism (Gal. 3:27); then again a mandate as the daily responsibility of the church: "But put on the Lord Jesus Christ" (Rom. 13:14).

Now as regards the relationship to each other of these two different ways of speaking, it is immediately clear that the imperative rests on the indicative and that this order is not reversible. For in each

---

3. For Jesus' preaching in the Synoptic Gospels see, e.g., my *The Coming of the Kingdom*, pp. 241ff.

case the imperative follows the indicative by way of conclusion (with "thus," "therefore"; Rom. 6:12ff.; 12:1; Col. 3:5, *et al.*). In each case following the calling of the new life is set forth as the object of the positive redemptive pronouncements ("so that," "in order to," etc.; cf. Rom. 7:4; 2 Cor. 5:15, *et al.*). The relationship intended here is surely given its clearest expression in Philippians 2:12f.: "Work out your own salvation with fear and trembling; for it is God who works in you both to will and to work for his good pleasure."

The word "for" in the second clause furnishes the ground for the appeal in the first. It is the same relationship and the same "for" that is met with in Romans 6:14: "sin will not have dominion over you; for you are not under the law, but under grace." God does not work and has not worked in his good pleasure because man has worked his salvation with fear and trembling. The contrary is true: because God works and has worked, therefore man must and can work. For God works in him what is necessary for his (human) working. The working of man, therefore, takes place "according to the working of Christ, which works in him in power" (Col. 1:29; Eph. 3:20), the good works they do have been prepared by God "that they should walk in them" (Eph. 2:10), and the good work that God has begun in them he will carry on (Phil. 1:6). What the new man manifests in new life, what he works or exhibits in fruit of the Spirit and good works, he works out of and by the strength of God, out of the power of the Spirit and by virtue of his belonging to Christ. There can be no doubt whatever concerning this relationship. Indicative and imperative thus do not represent a certain division of property in the sense that the indicative denotes the divine and the imperative the human share in the new life, or that the imperative arouses the believer to what God has done for him so that from his side, too, he not fail to give an answer. All this would set next to each other those elements in the gospel and in reality which lie in each other, and would thus lead to a new legalism. The imperative is grounded on the reality that has been given with the indicative, appeals to it, and is intended to bring it to full development.[4]

On the other hand, however, the following will have to be taken into consideration.

(a) When we say that the imperative rests on and appeals to the indicative this must not be taken to mean that the indicative vindicates a given situation that exists apart from the imperative and which only needs to be brought into action by the imperative. For the imperative not only has the function of bringing the new life denoted by the indicative to manifestation, but is also a constant touchstone for the latter. And that not only because it is the criterion for the right functioning and self-realization of the new life, but also because it repeatedly places the new life itself under the condition of the manifestation of life demanded by the imperative. Characteristic here is the use of the imperative as answering clause *(apodosis)* after a conditional first clause

---

4. Cf. Stauffer, *New Testament Theology*, p. 181.

(*protasis*); thus, for example, in Colossians 3:1: "if you then were raised together with Christ, seek the things that are above." "If" in the first clause is certainly not merely hypothetical. It is a supposition from which the imperative goes out as an accepted fact. But at the same time it emphasizes that if what is demanded in the imperative does not take place, that which is supposed in the first clause would no longer be admissible[5] (cf., e.g., Rom. 8:9; Col. 2:20; Gal. 5:25).

This making of the indicative conditional on the execution of the imperative (cf. Gal. 6:7ff.) does not reverse the order and is likewise not intended only to unmask hypocrites. It applies as well to believers themselves. In the new obedience the new life must become evident, and without the former the latter cannot exist. The explanation of this relationship lies in the fact that the reality described by the indicative, however much to be appreciated as the gift of God and the new creation, yet exists in the way of faith (cf. above, Section 40); while, conversely, the execution of the imperative is not in the power of man himself, but is no less a matter of faith. Indicative and imperative are both the object of faith, on the one hand in its receptivity, on the other in its activity. For this reason the connection between the two is so close and indissoluble. They represent two "sides" of the same matter, which cannot exist separated from each other.

(b) This is not to say, however, that the imperative is only another form of the indicative, because the indicative denotes nothing other than the possibility which by the observance of the imperative must repeatedly be realized anew. According to this actualistic conception the new life consists only in actual decisions of faith, and a distinction can no longer be made between "life by the Spirit" (denoted by the indicative) and "walking by the Spirit" (demanded by the imperative);[6] indeed, the Spirit himself would mean fundamentally[7] nothing other

---

5. For this use of *ei, eige, eiper* (the Latin *si* or *siquidem*) cf. Bl.-Debr., Par. 372,7; 439,2; 454,2.

6. Thus Bultmann's interpretation of Gal. 5:25. He calls this pronouncement a paradoxical sentence — "open to misunderstanding so far as it seems to imply that there could be a *zēn pneumati* without a *pneumati stoichein*" (*Theology*, I, p. 333). Cf. also his article on *zaō* (*TDNT*, II, p. 869): "The *zēn pneumati* is a *stoichein pneumati*." In this same article he writes that the presence of the new life implies "a presence of remission with all the possibilities thereby given to believers." Every emphasis must be placed here on "possibilities." The new life is not an alteration of the inner being of man: "The believer does not have *zōē* for himself alone in the inwardness of his spiritual life, but stands in the history established by the act of salvation, in which this *zōē* is for those who obey the will to save."

7. It appears elsewhere that Bultmann hereby wishes to give a "demythologized" idea of the Holy Spirit and his work. Modern man, so he writes, cannot see how a supernatural entity, the *pneuma*, would be able to penetrate into the closed unity of his natural capacities and be operative in him. Allegedly Paul also basically intends something other. He does conceive of the "Spirit" as a mysterious entity in man (Rom. 8:11). "Yet in the last resort he clearly means by 'Spirit' the possibility of a new life which is opened up in faith.... Hence St. Paul's paradoxical injunction: 'If we live by the Spirit, by the Spirit also let us walk' (Gal. 5:25).... Thus the concept 'Spirit' has been emancipated from mythology" ("New Testament and Mythology," in *Kerygma and Myth*, pp. 6, 22).

than the possibility of the new life unlocked by faith and would thus be described as "the power of futurity."[8]

But in this way the content of both the indicative and the imperative becomes denatured. The distinction between the two does not consist only in the fact that the former posits as a possibility that which is demanded in the latter. The indicative speaks of the new life also as an antecedent being; one is undoubtedly able to say (with Bultmann) that according to Paul this new life is genuine life precisely in the fact that it is active in the concrete possibilities of life,[9] but it is no less true that (likewise according to the nature of real life!) it is determined in its decisions and expressions from within and — as the new life — has received the actual possibility for the new "walk" just through this inner reversal. One is doubtless not to conceive of this "life by the Spirit" as a state of being that exists separate from faith, but rather as a life by the same faith as that through which walking by the Spirit must take place. But it nevertheless represents a continuity, not only of walking, but also of a renewed *nous* and of an enlightened heart, in short, of a renewed manhood (cf. above, Section 39). And it is likewise the building up of this continuity of the new life that is advanced and demanded by the continuing imperative. For the content of the imperative, too, does not consist merely of actual decisions and "acts," but is determined no less by the continuity and the progress of the new life as the upbuilding of the new manhood.

(c) By way of conclusion we may say that the imperative is grounded on the indicative to be accepted in faith once and for all and time and again anew. Because believers may know themselves as dead to sin and alive to God, they must present their body and their members to the service of righteousness. The imperative preaches rebellion against an enemy (sin), concerning which faith may know and must know again and again that it has been defeated. Thus, too, the relationship of the continual and the actual in the new life becomes clear. The new life is a life and not a succession of signs of life. Nevertheless it is not a dormant but a militant life, a life by faith. Where faith slackens, the situation of Romans 7 becomes actual once again. The imperative is only fulfilled when faith is vigilant, militant, sober (1 Cor. 16:13; 1 Thess. 5:6, 8ff.; Eph. 6:11ff.). To that extent every imperative is an actualizing of the indicative. Yet it is not lost in that: it seeks the fruit of faith and of the Holy Spirit in sanctification (Rom. 6:21, 22; Gal. 5:22); it is directed toward the "more and more," toward the increasing and abounding, toward the growth and progress of the new life (Rom. 5:3; 2 Cor. 8:7; 9:8ff.; 1 Tim. 4:15).

This relation of the indicative and imperative is altogether determined by the present redemptive-historical situation. The indicative represents the "already" as well as the "not yet." The imperative is likewise focused on the one as well as the other. On the ground of the "already" it can in a certain sense ask all things, is total in character, speaks not only of a small beginning, but of perfection in Christ. At

---

8. *Theology*, I, p. 335.
9. *TDNT*, II, pp. 868f.

the same time it has its basis in the provisional character of the "not yet." Its content, therefore, is not only positive, but also negative. The paraenesis must also forbid, warn, indeed threaten (Gal. 6:7ff.). At the same time there is in the "not yet" the necessity for increasing, pushing ahead on the way that has been unlocked by the "already." The whole character and content of the Pauline paraenesis and of the new obedience is contained *in nuce* in these different points of view.

SECTION 43. THE THEOCENTRIC POINT OF VIEW. SANCTIFICATION

Before going into the concrete content of the Pauline paraenesis it is of importance, in close connection with what has been discussed in the preceding section, first to attempt a general approach and typification of this new obedience. Of particular consequence here is the manner in which in Romans 6, the chapter so fundamental for this whole subject, the significance of the new life is characterized as a moral reversal. To that end the moral life pattern of the old and the new man are placed over against each other. While it is true of the old life that it is governed by "the reign of sin in your mortal body, that you should obey the lusts thereof" and in the placing of the members of this body at the disposal of sin "as weapons of unrighteousness" (vv. 12, 13), the new obedience consists in the fact that believers "must place themselves at the disposal of God, as men who have been brought to life from the dead" and who "present their members to God as weapons of righteousness." Similarly the old life of those who have now become believers consisted in this, that they "were slaves of sin, and were free of righteousness" (v. 20). Now, however, they are "made free from sin and become servants to God" (v. 22). The great antithesis between the "now" and the "once," between the "you were" and the "you are," thus does not lie in being free as such, for the old man had his freedom, in that he "was free of[10] righteousness" (v. 20). Likewise the distinguishing mark of the old did not lie in servitude as such, for the new life, too, is characterized by servitude, obedience, indeed by being at another's command as a slave and placing oneself at the disposal of God and righteousness. The difference thus lies in the nature of the freedom and in the new directedness of the servitude, or, in other words, in the theocentric character of the new obedience. It is in this fact that the new life manifests itself as "life from the dead" (vv. 11, 13), and it is therein that the redemptive-historical framework of the Pauline paraenesis, too, becomes visible. As Christ in his death died to sin and by his resurrection lives for God (Rom. 6:10), so the new life in its moral manifestation is to bear the stamp of having died and been raised with Christ, in that it breaks away from the jurisdiction of the old

---

10. *Eleutheroi ... tē dikaiosynē;* the datives are to be taken as dative of advantage or disadvantage *(dativus commodi vel incommodi)*. The dative "expresses ... the possessor" (Bl.-Debr., Par. 188,2*).

center (that of sin, the flesh, the old "I") and the centripetal powers ("the lusts") pertaining to it, to find the new meaning of its existence and center in God. It is this radical reversal of direction and orientation in which the new life must be distinguished in the most fundamental manner from the old, in its unity ("your body") as well as in its various concrete and individual aspects of life ("your members").

With this theocentric determination of the Pauline paraenesis the connection with the anthropological viewpoints has at once been given. It is only in this directedness toward God that the true manhood is able to come to development. Once again this finds expression in so many words in Romans 6. As the wages that sin gives are death, so servitude to God means life (vv. 22, 23). Likewise the liberty to which the church is called and in which it is to stand fast (Gal. 5:1) signifies a freedom from all that threatens and hinders life, the true manhood. For while the mind of the flesh is death and brings imprisonment along with it, the mind of the Spirit is life and peace (in the sense of "salvation"; Rom. 8:6, 8). And while the works of the flesh prevent man from inheriting the kingdom of God and thus the true life (Gal. 5:19-22), the fruit of the Spirit means joy and peace (Gal. 5:22; Rom. 14:17), and freedom from fear (Rom. 8:15). Time and again the church is accordingly admonished and awakened to this freedom, peace, and joy (Gal. 5:1; 1 Thess. 5:16; 2 Cor. 13:11; Phil. 3:1, et al.). In the doing of the will of God is the promise of this and of the future life (1 Tim. 4:8). And elsewhere Paul calls the object of the divine reproof, which he also describes as "training," that "the man of God" may come to completeness and be perfectly equipped (2 Tim. 3:17; cf. 1 Tim. 6:11).

However much one is thus able to say that in the Pauline paraenesis the anthropological point of view coincides with the theological and is comprehended in it, it is perfectly clear on the other hand that the former is subordinate to the latter and arises from it, and that one cannot reverse the order. Man's freedom is in subservience to God, and without this servitude freedom has no place in the Pauline paraenesis. This servitude to God likewise does not come into view only insofar as it is necessary to give man freedom, joy, and peace; on the contrary, "for God" and "to God" are the motive and ultimate object of this obedience, as of all things (cf. 1 Cor. 10:31; Col. 3:17).

To what degree this theocentric viewpoint predominates in the whole of the Pauline paraenesis, even in all its individual and concrete applications, is clear as well in the point of departure for the extensive paraenetic section of the Epistle to the Romans (Rom. 12-15), namely, in 12:1, 2. Here again appeal to the redeeming activity of God in Christ takes precedence: "I exhort you therefore, brethren, by[11] the mercies of God," an appeal in which the church is determined not merely by its moral obligation, but also by the origin and possibility of its obedience. Further, the life pattern of the old aeon ("becoming conformed to this world") is here again set over against that of the new life ("becoming transformed"), and the paraenesis is directed toward the new manhood

---

11. *Dia* with the genitive "idiomatically with urgent questions = 'by' (Attic *pros tinos*)" (Bl.-Debr., Par. 223,4).

("the renewing of your *nous*"). In summarizing the content of the whole of the following paraenesis, however, the words of Romans 6 are again employed: "put your bodies [yourselves] at the service of God," which is then further qualified as a "living, holy sacrifice acceptable to God, a spiritual service," just as the renewing of the *nous*, too, must have its object and result in the fact that the man thus transformed and withdrawn from the schema of the present world will be prepared and able to "prove what the will of God is, the good, well-pleasing to God, and perfect."

The theocentric point of view — so we may conclude — *constitutes the great point of departure of the Pauline paraenesis.* The content both of the separate commandments and of the general ideas in which this paraenesis taken together is defined is to be approached from it.

The first concept that may be mentioned as such is righteousness. In Romans 6 it occurs no less than five times as a general definition of the new obedience (in vv. 13, 16, 18, 19, 20), as the antithesis of sin, death, impurity, lawlessness. Even from the repeated contrast with "sin" the all-embracing character of the concept righteousness is evident, as also its primary content and specific nature as directed toward God. This is corroborated by further analysis of the righteousness intended here. It is entirely oriented to the Old Testament equivalent *ṣedāqâ*, as a denotation of that which is well-pleasing to God, the doing of his will, the keeping of his covenant; it can be qualified in general as piety, obedience, and faithfulness toward God.[12] It rests on the proclamation of the will of God to his people and on the moral character of the relationship between God and those to whom he has made himself known and whom he has placed on his side. It harks back thus to the deepest foundations of the Old Testament revelation and religion. As such this idea of righteousness can incontestably maintain its place in Paul's epistles alongside of and over against the much more pregnant ˙ forensic use of the concept.[13] Moreover, it can exhibit still other nuances, at one time in a more general sense denoting conformity with the will of God (Rom. 6:13ff.; 14:17; 2 Cor. 6:7; Eph. 4:24; 6:14; Phil. 1:11; 2 Tim. 3:16; 4:8); then again, in addition to other more specific virtues, acting as a separate manifestation of the new life in the more restricted sense of: to do the right (Eph. 5:9; 1 Tim. 6:11; 2 Tim. 2:22), sometimes even in the special sense of charity (2 Cor. 9:10; cf., e.g., Matt. 6:1, *et al.*).

Of no less importance for insight into the theocentric character of this new obedience is the central and repeatedly recurring concept of sancti-

---

12. Cf. Quell, *TDNT*, II, pp. 174ff., *s.v. dikē*, etc.

13. It is therefore not correct to maintain that the idea of forensic righteousness here passes over into that of righteousness as life-power that overcomes sin, as Schrenk wishes to do (*TDNT*, II, p. 213, *s.v. dikaiosynē*). The idea of righteousness employed here (Rom. 6:12ff.) as religious-ethical qualification did not proceed from the forensic meaning, but has its own and broader background in the Old Testament *ṣedāqâ*.

fication. In Romans 6:12ff. it is also employed again and again to denote the object and the fruit of the new obedience.

> For as you have placed your members at the service of impurity and of lawlessness unto lawlessness, even so now place your members at the service of righteousness unto sanctification (v. 19).
> But now being made free from sin and become servants to God, you have your fruit unto sanctification (v. 22).

For a correct insight into the specific significance of the idea holy (*hagios*), which appears in Paul under various denominatives (*hagiasmos, hagiotēs, hagiōsynē*), it is necessary to recognize that it does not in the first instance have a moral content. It is rather, as is evident in particular against the Old Testament background, a general qualification of the people of God, also employed originally in close connection with the cultus. As chosen by God out of all the peoples and placed on his side, Israel is holy (Exod. 19:5, 6). Paul, too, starts from this holiness (Rom. 11:16), and transfers it to the New Testament church. Its holiness is situated above all in that it has been sanctified in Christ. He has, as a man his wife, appropriated the church to himself, made it his possession (1 Cor. 1:2; 6:11). For this reason it can be said that Christ has become to us wisdom, justification, sanctification, and redemption (1 Cor. 1:30); in this context one must by sanctification understand in the first place being appropriated and dedicated to God.[14] In the same sense there is mention of "called saints" (Rom. 1:7; 1 Cor. 1:2 — the "holy assembly" of the Old Testament [Exod. 12:16; Lev. 23:2, *et al.*[15]]; cf. 2 Tim. 1:9), "holy and beloved" (Col. 3:12 — in which also, as appears from the preceding "elect of God," the chief emphasis lies on having been appropriated by God and placed on his side), in general, too, the expression the "church of the saints" (1 Cor. 14:33, *et al.*), or simply "the saints" (Rom. 15:25, 26, *et al.*) as a description of the church.

It holds in a special sense for the idea of holiness understood in this way, however, that it not only points toward the privilege of the church of being permitted to be the people of God — the redemptive-indicative, therefore — but that it denotes no less the moral condition that answers to this state of holiness, according to the rule "be ye holy, for I am holy." Along with this, Christ enters the picture by the Spirit as the author of sanctification. He has reconciled the church through his death, to present it "holy and without blemish and irreproachable" before him (Col. 1:22; cf. Eph. 5:26, 27). In this combination "holy" clearly has the significance of moral perfection. This holiness comes about through the Holy Spirit. God has chosen the church to himself from the heathen, as beloved by the Lord and sanctified by the Spirit (2 Thess. 2:13). But this sanctification then involves active dedication to God by the church itself, the condition of moral holiness that cor-

---

14. Some indeed think that the four ideas of redemption in 1 Cor. 1:30 were formulated in contrast with the preceding *mōra, asthenē, agenē,* and *mē onta* (so J. Bohatec, "Inhalt und Reihenfolge der 'Schlagworte der Erlösungsreligion' in 1 Kor. 1,26-31," *TZ*, 1948, pp. 252ff.).

15. Cf. Procksch, *TDNT*, I, p. 107n., *s.v. hagios.*

responds with its calling and election. This last element of "answering to" the grace of having been appropriated to God the apostle likes to express with the concept "worthy": "to walk worthy of the calling wherewith you were called" (Eph. 4:1), or "worthy of the gospel" (Phil. 1:27), or "worthy of the Lord" (Col. 1:10), or "worthy of God, who has called you," etc. (1 Thess. 2:12), just as, conversely, one can speak of acting (eating and drinking) in a manner unworthy of this holiness (1 Cor. 11:27, 29). "Worthy" in Paul's train of thought of course has nothing to do with meritoriousness, but the motive lying in it is entirely derived from the gracious activity of God, by which he sanctified the church to himself and thus made it worthy of his calling (2 Thess. 1:11).

In the unfolding of this principle of moral holiness the cultic motif comes very markedly to the fore as well — understood now in a spiritual sense. As the holy people of God the church is the "holy temple" of God (1 Cor. 3:16, 17; Eph. 2:21). Believers are therefore to present their bodies[16] as a living, holy sacrifice, well-pleasing to God — their spiritual[17] service (Rom. 12:1; cf. 15:16). That which is dedicated and sanctified to God must be pure and without defect. Holy can for this reason also act as a synonym of spotless, blameless, undefiled (cf. Col. 1:22). Christ has sanctified the church (appropriated it to himself) that he might present it before him without spot or wrinkle or any such thing, that it might be holy and without blemish (Eph. 5:26). This is clearly sacrificial terminology (cf. 1 Pet. 1:19), in which the moral holiness of the people of God is given expression (cf. Eph. 1:4).

In the same sense as between "without blemish"[18] and "holy" there is an original (cultic) connection between "holy" and "pure."[19] This whole complex of ideas is expressed very clearly, for example, in 2 Corinthians 6:14ff., where as the (holy) temple of God the church is warned against contaminating association with unbelievers and idolaters. There is then reference to the appropriation of the church by the Lord and to his commandment that it is to be separate from the world (vv. 16ff.). To this the apostle links the admonition in 2 Corinthians 7:1: let us then "cleanse" ourselves from all defilement of the flesh and the spirit and perfect our sanctification in the fear of God. This cleansing from the flesh, etc., is here intended spiritually, of course (cf. Rom. 12:1), but terminologically it has its origin in cultic purification, in order thus to be "holy." We meet with the same combination in Ephesians 5:26, which we have already cited in this connection, where the cleansing resulting from sanctification (as appropriation) and necessary for holiness (as moral condition) is related to baptism (cf. also Phil. 2:14). Similarly, in a somewhat different train of thought but once again

16. Cf. above, pp. 229ff.

17. *Logikos* here has the meaning of *pneumatikos*, in order to denote the difference from the worship consisting in material sacrifices (cf. 1 Pet. 2:5).

18. This holds especially for *amōmos* — unblemished, in which no fault is to be found (cf. Exod. 29:1; Lev. 1:3, *et al.*); see also Hauck, *TDNT*, IV, pp. 835, 836, *s.v. mōmos* — blame, fault — and *amōmos*. It is different with *amemptos*, which also means blameless and occurs in connection with "holy" (1 Thess. 3:13), but does not have this (clear) cultic background.

19. *Katharos* and derivatives.

in close connection with the cultic, there is mention in 1 Corinthians 5:7 of the "purging out of the old leaven." Likewise in Romans 6:19 (im-)purity stands in close connection with sanctification. Further usage then gives it a more general meaning of moral-religious purity (1 Tim. 1:5; 3:9; 2 Tim. 2:21, et al.). Accordingly one is able to ascertain that the categories of holiness in Paul refer more to the new moral condition than to moral activity itself.[20] The latter is especially defined as cleansing, as cultic "cleansing" once provided priests and people with holiness before God. In the well-known passages of Romans 6 sanctification is consequently spoken of as the fruit and object of having been made free from sin (vv. 19, 22).

The various words we find for the concept holy (holiness) in Paul naturally bring this out in a shaded fashion. Paul speaks of *hagiasmos* (sanctification), *hagiotēs* and *hagiōsynē* (holiness). The latter denote the condition of holiness but occur only a few times in Paul (2 Cor. 1:12;[21] 7:1; 1 Thess. 3:14; in Rom. 1:4 *hagiōsynē* does not have the holiness of the church in view). Moreover, *hagiōsynē* in both instances has the nuance of the glorious, blameless aspect of holiness as the condition in which the church has to be before God and with a view to his coming.

The action noun *(nomen actionis) hagiasmos* (sanctification) occurs more often. In the most comprehensive sense of appropriation and moral renewal it occurs in 1 Corinthians 1:30: "Christ has become to us ... from God ... sanctification. ..." Frequently *hagiasmos* also signifies the object of active sanctification by the Spirit, and thus denotes the condition of holiness (as *hagiōsynē*). So, for example, in Romans 6:19, 22; in a more active sense in 1 Thessalonians 4:3, 4, 7; 2 Thessalonians 2:13; 1 Timothy 2:15. The meanings of sanctification and holiness are very close, however, and it is difficult in translation always to choose the right word. The subject of *hagiasmos* is Christ (1 Cor. 1:30), the Holy Spirit (2 Thess. 2:13), implicitly also the church itself (1 Thess. 4:3ff.), although the verb *hagiazein* always has God, Christ, or the Spirit as its subject, but nowhere in Paul's epistles the church or individual believers. With the concept sanctification it is of course a matter of moral holiness, but in a specific sense and from a very definite point of view, namely, of the moral condition answering to the fact of having been appropriated to the Lord. It is moral renewal *sub specie electionis* and *sub specie ecclesiae*.

A special use of *hagiazein* is to be met with in 1 Corinthians 7:14: "for the unbelieving husband is sanctified in [or by] the wife, and the unbelieving wife is sanctified in [or by] the brother. Otherwise your children would be unclean *(akatharta)*, but now they are holy" *(hagia)*. Holiness here, just as the holiness given by Christ himself to the church, has a strongly "objective" character. Because it is a question in this context of unbelievers, one will not be

---

20. Cf. Procksch, *TDNT*, I, p. 109: "... the reference of holiness is always to the static morality of innocence rather than to ethical action.... For this reason we should never translate [*hagiotēs*] or [*hagios*] as morality or moral, since this is to lose the element of the *religiosum*." In our view the first part of this pronouncement is too strong (cf., e.g., 1 Thess. 4:3).

21. The only place where *hagiotēs* occurs; here, too, the reading is not established. Some mss. have *haplotēti* instead of *hagiotēti*. The genitive *tou Theou* is somewhat strange (cf. Procksch, *TDNT*, I, p. 114). Yet it can be for just this reason that *haplotēti* was put in place of *hagiotēti*. In our opinion *en hagiotēti ... tou Theou* can be understood as: holiness ... which is in conformity with God.

able to think of appropriation by Christ and inner renewal by the Holy Spirit, but of such a state of holiness whereby the marriage no longer lies in the sphere of the life of the world apostate from God and abandoned to the power of darkness. The unbelieving party is to that extent comprehended in the believing party and must be judged by him (or her) and not the reverse. For that the apostle also appeals to the fact that "your" children are not "unclean" but "holy." Although not everything is plain here — who are "your" children here? are baptized or unbaptized children thought of, and are they then incorporated into the church or not?[22] — even so we shall have to proceed from the cultic-theocratic background of the concepts "unclean" and "holy." "Unclean" then means to be "in the world" and to lie under the jurisdiction of the powers ruling there; "clean" means to be under the claims and sphere of influence of the divine appropriation. In 1 Corinthians 7:14 the natural relationships of life constitute the medium for such a sanctification, a sanctification that by its very nature can be considered of broader purport than that of marriage and family but also has reference to other life relationships. The question as to whether Paul will have the sanctification of the children of believers regarded exclusively from the viewpoint of this natural life relationship (in the same manner, thus, as the sanctification of the unbelieving partner in the marriage) is bound up with the question as to whether or not the children were baptized and incorporated into the church, a question that cannot be answered in the light of 1 Corinthians 7:14 alone.[23]

In addition to *hagios* and its derivatives, *hagnos, hagnotēs, hagneia* (not *hagnizō* and *hagnismos*), and *hosios* and *hosiotēs* also occur in Paul, in the sense of holy and holiness. This terminology plays a much smaller part, however (in harmony with the usage of the LXX). Although the original background of *hagnos* in many respects coincides with that of *hagios*, in Paul it simply has the significance of morally clean, pure, innocent, chaste (cf. Phil. 4:8; 1 Tim. 5:22; Tit. 2:5; 1 Tim. 4:12; 5:2; 2 Cor. 6:6; 2 Cor. 7:11 [innocent]; 11:2 [chaste]; Phil. 1:17 [with pure intentions]). Still narrower is the significance of the use of *hosios* in Paul (and in the New Testament generally). The cultic significance scarcely has any part here (1 Tim. 2:8?); the word is employed in the general sense of clean, pure (cf. 1 Thess. 2:10), and is closely connected with the general term "just" (Eph. 4:24; Tit. 1:8). From this it may appear that, from a redemptive-historical point of view, of this complex of ideas *hagios* with its derivatives has by far the greatest significance.[24]

The specific significance of the concept sanctification as the comprehensive objective of the Pauline imperative is therefore unmistakable: the whole new life is qualified by it as the answer in purity to the

---

22. For the very divergent judgment of these questions see, e.g., the survey in G. de Ru, *De kinderdoop en het Nieuwe Testament*, 1964, pp. 160ff.

23. Cf. below, pp. 412ff.

24. For the general relationship of *hagios, hagnos* and *hosios*, cf. R. C. Trench, *Synonyms of the New Testament*, 11th ed., 1890, p. 327. He arrives finally at this delimitation that *hagios* represents the thought of being separated from the world, *hosios* that of the observance of the precepts given by God in his covenant, and *hagnos* that of actual purity. That this general delimitation does not hold good for the Pauline usage is apparent from the above. The various aspects of holiness are here (in Paul) in large measure "incorporated" in the usage of *hagios*. For this idea see further Savo Djukanovic, *Heiligkeit und Heiligung bei Paulus*, 1939; and my article "De Heiligheid van de gemeente volgens het Nieuwe Testament," *Vox Theologica*, 1948, pp. 187-194.

gracious election of God, as the dedication of oneself to God in blamelessness as a holy sacrifice. The religious, theocentric character of the new obedience surely finds its most pregnant expression in the concept of sanctification; just as, conversely, the ground and origin of this obedience is designated nowhere more clearly than here in the free, electing grace of God.

SECTION 44. THE TOTALITARIAN POINT OF VIEW. PERFECTION

A no less important general aspect of his paraenesis, closely connected to the fundamental structure of Paul's proclamation of redemption, is the totalitarian character of the new obedience demanded in it. Yet again one can approach this in more than one way. First there is the totalitarian character of the relationship in which the church is placed by Christ's work of redemption to all things[25] and by which the paraenesis, too, is determined in its compass. We shall go into this in still more detail in treating "life in the world."[26] In addition, however, there is the viewpoint that the whole man is involved in the saving activity of God in Christ. Because everything has been given in Christ, everything can also be asked in him, quantitatively and extensively as well as qualitatively and intensively. Next to the theocentric this totalitarian point of view pertains to the most essential and characteristic feature of the Pauline paraenesis.[27]

Here again Romans 6-8, 12, so important for our subject, are of decisive significance. As sin is a totalitarian regime that claims the whole man for itself (Rom. 6:12, 13; 7:14), so the new man must place his body (himself) and all his members (all his actions and potentialities) at the disposal of God. As having come to life from the dead (Rom. 6:11, 13), he is to be obedient to God with all his heart (6:17), and with a renewed *nous* to ask himself what is pleasing to God (Rom. 12:2). The willing as well as the doing, the body as well as the soul and spirit, are involved in God's gift and therefore in his demand (Phil. 2:13; 2 Cor. 8:10ff.; 1 Thess. 5:23). And as God has made those who are in Christ rich in all things (1 Cor. 1:5; 2 Cor. 9:11), so God will be served by them in all things. All things ought to take place to the glory of God (1 Cor. 10:31; Col. 3:17; cf. Phil. 2:14); in all things they are obedient (2 Cor. 2:9); all things should be done in love (1 Cor. 16:14). Filled with all wisdom and spiritual knowledge, believers must walk worthy of God, to please him in all things, bearing fruit in every good work, strengthened with all power unto all patience and longsuffering (Col. 1:9-11). The Pauline paraenesis is full of the words "every" and "all," and is in this way rendered in a totalitarian and uncompromising style, in a difficult to reproduce but highly distinctive manner.

---

25. On this see below, Section 62.
26. See Section 49.
27. For this cf., e.g., Wolfgang Schrage, *Die konkreten Einzelgebote in der paulinischen Paränese,* 1961, pp. 49ff.

In this connection the question arises as to how we have to conceive of the working out of this totalitarian imperative and the possibility of its realization in this life, in other words, the question of moral perfection. There is occasion to treat this question particularly in relation to the idea of sanctification discussed in the previous section. For we have seen that this sanctification for Paul denotes a condition of moral blamelessness that comes about in the way of purification.[28] As such it is defined further as that which is "blameless," "without spot or wrinkle," "in which no fault is to be found." This holiness and blamelessness are often spoken of in a final sense (Rom. 6:19; Eph. 1:4; 5:27; Col. 1:22), and what is thought of here is especially the future revelation of the saints at the appearing of Christ (1 Thess. 3:13; 1 Cor. 1:8). Yet the present historical character of this sanctification and blamelessness is in no sense relinquished. It is precisely the intention that the church may rise in this life to such a position of holiness that at the appearing of Christ it may go to meet its Lord without blame. For this reason Paul says that God will confirm the church to the end, that it may be without blame in the day of our Lord Jesus Christ, and in 1 Thessalonians 5:23 he prays that "the God of peace may sanctify them in every way[29] and that their spirit, soul, and body may be kept without fault and blameless at the coming of Christ."[30] The reference is thus to the object and result of its present sanctification.

On the basis of this and similar pronouncements some have come to the view that in Paul's conviction every truly baptized person, every real possessor of the *Pneuma*, every truly redeemed person, is free from sin, has crucified the passions and lusts, is a new man who has once again become obedient and under the prompting of the Spirit no longer falls into sin. This applies to Christians in general, at least insofar as they have truly been baptized, etc.; in particular this sinlessness is supposed to have been maintained as incontestable by the apostle on the ground of his own life from and with Christ.[31] Others place all the emphasis on the summons to perfection and fighting against sin joined to these indicatives of holiness, but are still of the opinion that Paul holds out the prospect of blamelessness in sanctification not only as a goal to be pursued, but also to be attained; indeed, that, certainly for himself in the first place, but surely also for every Christian, he describes perfection

---

28. Cf. E. Gaugler, *Die Heiligung im Zeugnis der Schrift*, 1948, p. 39.

29. *Hagiasai hymas holoteleis.* The adjective is used adverbially and means approximately "totally," "in all respects."

30. *Holoklēron hymōn to pneuma ... amemptōs ... tērēthein. Holoklēros* does not differ very much from *holotelēs.* One will have to connect it with *eirēnē* as the totality of salvation. It then denotes a condition of perfect integrity. The pronouncement exhibits a certain exuberance and is not easy to translate. Another (in my opinion not in every respect convincing) translation whereby the caesura falls after *pneuma* has been suggested by P. A. van Stempvoort, "Eine stilistische Lösung einer alten Schwierigkeit in 1 Thess. V. 23," *NTS*, 1961, pp. 262ff.

31. So H. Windisch, *Paulus und Christus*, 1934, p. 258; cf. his earlier work, *Taufe und Sünde im ältesten Christentum bis auf Origenes*, 1908, pp. 98-224, and P. Wernle, *Der Christ und die Sünde bei Paulus*, 1897.

as a victory in the struggle against sin, in which one in fact leaves sin behind him.[32]

One thing at least is indisputable: however much the apostle may speak in positive indicatives of being set free from the power of sin and of death, this does not mean that believers therefore *eo ipso* have left sin behind them as ground already conquered. If this were so, the constant admonition, continually renewed, would be incomprehensible. He describes the life of believers time and again from the double viewpoint of battling on the basis of victory and of gaining the victory on the basis of the battle.

The first viewpoint proceeds from the victory of Christ. Because Christ has died to sin, they are to live out of the consideration of faith that they too are dead to sin (as ruler), but live for God in Christ Jesus (Rom. 6:11). This living for God in Christ Jesus is now repeatedly described, however, in the terminology of a battle,[33] which not only starts from the victory that lies behind (in Christ), but also extends toward the victory that lies before (in the life of believers). It is in this way that the apostle speaks of his own service. Although this consists most profoundly in the proclamation of the victory of Christ (cf. 1 Cor. 15:54, 57), which is still more graphically described as being led by Christ in his triumphal procession[34] (2 Cor. 2:14), it is at the same time itself a military service, a going to war (2 Cor. 10:3, 4; cf. 1 Cor. 9:7), under the leadership of Christ as general (2 Tim. 2:3). And Paul sometimes speaks of this service, in which he knows himself to be armed from head to foot (2 Cor. 6:7), in a highly warlike manner: in this campaign it is a matter of demolishing strongholds and entrenchments and making prisoners of war for Christ (2 Cor. 10:3ff.). The life of those who have been made free by Christ now bears this same character of military service. It is indeed *militia Christi*.[35] It also occurs as such in the context of Romans 6: do not place your members as "weapons of unrighteousness"[36] at the command of sin, but of God as "weapons of righteousness" (v. 13). And the same thought is to be found in Romans 13:12, where there is mention of putting on "the weapons of the light." Here in the first place it is the moral struggle that should be thought of, as is evident from the context of Romans 6 and from the parallel

---

32. Cf., e.g., P. Althaus, *Paulus und Luther über den Menschen*, 2nd ed., 1951, pp. 68-74, 77ff., and the older literature cited there; especially T. Schlatter, "Für Gott lebendig in Christi Kraft" and "Tot für die Sünde, lebendig für Gott," two essays in the *Jahrbuch der Theol. Schule Bethel*, 1930, pp. 116-144; 1932, pp. 19-58.

33. It is remarkable that the proper words for battle, *machē* and *machomai*, are not only not employed by Paul — but nowhere else in the New Testament either — in a positive sense for the battle of the Christian life. Cf. Bauernfeind, *TDNT*, IV, p. 528, *s.v.*

34. To translate *thriambeuō* by "to cause to triumph" has little support in the linguistic usage. It is a matter here of being taken along in the triumphal procession of Christ, whereby one can still differ on the question as to whether one is to think here of a captive (so, e.g., Delling, *TDNT*, III, p. 160, *s.v.*) or of a sharer in the victory (cf., e.g., Lietzmann-Kümmel, *Cor.*, p. 198).

35. Cf. G. C. Berkouwer, *Faith and Sanctification*, ET 1952, pp. 47ff.

36. The genitive in *hopla adikias* and *dikaiosynēs* is a qualitative genitive: (un)righteous weapons in the service of (un)righteousness.

"works of darkness" — "weapons of the light" in Romans 13. That battle must be fought by believers placing their "members," that is to say, their whole manifestation of life,[37] at the service of God. There is thus no question of having already left the "stage of sin" behind. In the strength of Christ's victory sin is precisely to be combatted.

With what earnestness this exhortation is given and in what context this battle is to be viewed may appear still further from the familiar "armor"-pericope (Eph. 6:11ff.), where twice there is mention of the "whole armor of God" *(panoplia tou Theou)*, which is then distinguished in all sorts of particular items of armor (cf. 1 Thess. 5:8). Here again the concern is, if in a more inclusive sense, with the struggle against falsehood and unrighteousness, as appears from the designation of the parts of the armor (cf. 1 Thess. 5:6ff.), and in general with perseverance in the faith and the life springing from it (cf. vv. 6, 18ff.).[38] This struggle stands in a much wider context, however: it is waged not against "blood and flesh, but against the principalities, the powers, the world rulers of this darkness, against the evil spirits in the heavenly places" (v. 12). Thereby the believers' conflict of faith, in its moral aspects as well, is related to the continuing eschatological antithesis between the powers of darkness and the kingship of Christ (Col. 1:13). This is also the effect of what is said in Romans 13 concerning the passing of the night, the proximity of the day, and in this connection the changing of armor ("the weapons of the light"). Whereas elsewhere it is declared of these powers that Christ has subdued them and, as it were, has harnessed them to his triumphal chariot (Col. 2:15),[39] and delivered his own from their power (Col. 1:13), in Ephesians 6 the point of view of the "not yet," at least of the "not yet fully," finds expression (just as in the formulation of provisionality in Rom. 13:12: "the night is far spent, the day is at hand"). Thus the redemptive-historical point of view also has its moral implications.

The same thing becomes perceptible in Paul's warnings against the danger of "temptation" and, in close connection with this, against Satan. That Satan is thought of as the author of temptation is evident from such passages as 1 Thessalonians 3:5; 1 Corinthians 7:5; 2 Corinthians 2:11; 1 Timothy 3:7. While on the one hand Satan and his whole power have been subjected to the power of Christ, and the church is comforted with the knowledge that God will shortly crush Satan under its feet (Rom. 16:20), on the other hand his power and influence

---

37. Cf. above, pp. 116, 229.

38. In Hebrew manuscripts recently found in Palestine there is also mention of the battle that "the sons of the light" carry on. This terminology is reminiscent of that of Paul, both with reference to the "battle situation" in which these sons of the light have been placed and with regard to the great part the "armor" plays in it. A single glance at the character of this struggle of the sons of the light, in which national and apocalyptic points of view are sometimes difficult to distinguish, can enable us to see, however, in what a different world of thought we find ourselves here; cf. for the materials, e.g., the article by K. G. Kuhn, "Die in Palästina gefundenen hebräischen Texte und das N.T.," in *ZTK*, 1950, pp. 202ff.; see also Kuhn in *TDNT*, V, pp. 295ff., *s.v. panoplia.*

39. Here too *thriambeuō;* cf. p. 267, n. 34.

continue in the temptation of men, also believers (1 Cor. 7:5; 2 Cor. 2:11; 11:14; 1 Thess. 3:5). In this light we shall also have to understand the other warnings against temptations leading to sin, even though in these Satan is not expressly mentioned (1 Cor. 10:13; Gal. 6:4 [4:14]; 1 Tim. 6:9). The apostle, moreover, comforts the church that God is faithful and will not suffer it to be tempted beyond its capacity, and that accordingly no temptation beyond the human has overtaken it.[40] Nevertheless he points to the example of ancient Israel, and he voices the warning: "let anyone who thinks that he stands take heed lest he fall" (1 Cor. 10:12). All these references to temptation are thus determined by the same point of view we met with above: in a moral respect, too, believers are still in a threatened position. The victory of Christ does not remove the necessity for vigilance and soberness.

We shall have to consider from the same redemptive-historical point of view the pronouncements that speak of the continuing lust of the flesh in believers. Of primary importance here are the words of Galatians 5:17: "For the flesh lusts against the Spirit, and the Spirit against the flesh; for these are contrary the one to the other, that you may not do the things that you would."

Elsewhere Paul says concerning this rule of flesh and Spirit: "but you are not in the flesh but in the Spirit" (Rom. 8:9). This ascertainment is not nullified by Galatians 5:17. For first of all being "in the Spirit" does not mean that the Spirit takes hold of the human ego to such an extent that it is no longer exposed to the power of the flesh. Rather the pronouncement of Romans 8, too, is intended as a stimulus and basis for not living after the flesh, but allowing oneself to be led by the Spirit and thus no longer to be liable to the service of the flesh (cf. vv. 12ff.). With that, however, what is said in so many words in Galatians 5:17 is also presupposed, that believers have not yet been taken out of the arena in which Spirit and flesh contend with each other for power. Galatians 5 adds to this train of thought that the power of the flesh still asserts itself in them to the extent that "they do not the things that they would."[41] This "would" can scarcely mean anything other in this context than that which believers desire to perform in conformity with God's will[42] (cf. Phil. 2:13). Because of the continuing influence of the flesh, specifically of its "lusting," this willing is no unchallenged affair, but it is hampered at the point of its execution. This is not to say that, because believers do not act in conformity with what they will and as often as they will, they continue in one way or another in slavery

---

40. For the exposing of oneself to the demons, see 1 Cor. 10:21 (below, pp. 303f.).

41. Cf. R. Bultmann, "Christ the End of the Law," in *Essays Philosophical and Theological*, pp. 61f.

42. The question is how one must translate *hina* in Gal. 5:17, as final or consecutive. The difficulty when it is taken as final is that one cannot designate clearly by whom this purpose is postulated. The sentence construction does not allow us to think only of the Spirit or of the flesh, while it is also not acceptable to conceive of the clause introduced by *hina* as the object of both. Therefore *hina* has what amounts to a consecutive significance; cf., e.g., A. Oepke, *Gal.*, pp. 103ff., and my *Epistle of Paul to the Churches of Galatia*, 1953, pp. 203ff. The words *ha ean thelēte* mean "as often as."

after the flesh. That would be to revive the situation delineated in
Romans 7:14ff. of having been sold and being dead under sin. In Galatians 5:17 the apostle employs the still continuing influence of the
flesh, however, as an argument ("For. . . .") for allowing oneself to be led
by the Spirit and as a warning not to fulfill the lusts of the flesh. He
also says that when they do this, they no longer find themselves in the
moral impotence that marks the situation under the law. The great
difference between Romans 7:14ff. and Galatians 5:17 is thus that the
former is written out of the situation of the flesh; the latter on the
other hand takes the standpoint of the Spirit.[43] From the manner in
which the influence of the flesh and not doing what one wills are spoken
of in Galatians 5, too, it is evident, however, that the situation of
Romans 7 recurs, if not in principle, then incidentally,[44] when believers
do not live by faith and thus not from the liberty given them by the
Spirit. Inner discord is not thereby declared to be of the essence of the
Christian existence, but the situation of believers is designated as a
situation of conflict, also in a moral sense, in which unremitting watchfulness is necessary and which leads to victory only when they place
themselves time and again under the leading of the Spirit. It may
therefore be posited on the one hand that believers have left behind
them the mode of existence of the flesh and life under the law because
in Christ and by faith in him they have once died to them; on the
other hand, it may also be said, *e mente Pauli,* that the with and over
against each other of the old and new are for believers a continuing
reality, because and insofar as they remain exposed to the lusts and
temptations of the flesh. The liberty given in Christ in the Spirit may
and must regard sin as a conquered power, but not as an enemy who
can suffer no further defeat in the sense of moral perfectionism. It is a
liberty that calls men to battle just because this is no longer a hopeless
affair (Rom. 7), or exhibits the character of an uncertain struggle, but
one which, because the issue has been settled in Christ, may be fought
and won in the Spirit and the power going forth from him.

It is in close connection with this that we are to understand the pronouncements that speak of the "perfection" and "blamelessness" of the
life set at liberty by the Spirit. In so doing, as regards the concept
"perfect,"[45] one must be very much on his guard against an exclusively
moral interpretation and in general against the idea of a quantitative
state of moral perfection flawless in all its parts. The perfection of
believers refers above all to the totalitarian character of the fullness
of the redemption in Christ. Here again, however, there is a clear correspondence of the usage of indicative and imperative.[46] One meets with
the former in those passages in which participation in the fullness of

---

43. Cf. above, p. 127.
44. Cf. Schrage, *Die konkreten Einzelgebote in der paulinischen Paränese,*
p. 194.
45. On this see in particular P. J. Du Plessis, [*TELEIOS*], *The Idea of Perfection in the New Testament,* 1959.
46. Cf. *ibid.,* pp. 204ff., 242ff.

Christ is the prominent idea of "perfect" and "perfection" (cf., e.g., 1 Cor. 2:6; Phil. 3:15; Col. 1:28; 4:12). To this idea then is joined the thought of the maturity and adulthood of the Christian life as the full working through and unfolding of the salvation given in Christ, with respect to the provisional and temporal (1 Cor. 14:20; Eph. 4:13) as well as to the definitive and eternal (1 Cor. 13:10; Phil. 3:15).

The thought of the full unfolding and appropriation of what has been given in Christ and thereby of adulthood and maturity emerges very clearly in Ephesians 4:13, where there is mention of the building up of the church.[47] Here "perfect," in the sense of full-grown, having come to full development, stands over against children yet underage. One may observe this same contrast between 1 Corinthians 2:6ff. and 3:1ff., and in 1 Corinthians 14:20. And Colossians 1:28 will have to be interpreted in the same manner. Thus he is "perfect" who inwardly and in the manifestation of his life has appropriated the content of the Christian faith in the right way.[48] As such "perfect" also has an ethical significance, of course, although this does not come to the fore in Paul (cf. Eph. 4:14ff.; 1 Cor. 2:6ff.). Love in particular is related to perfection as "the bond of perfectness" (Col. 3:14; cf. Eph. 4:16 and 1 Cor. 13:8-13, where the perfect is also placed over against the childish). One must not so conceive of this bond, however, as though love itself were perfection; it is rather the means or the sphere by which and in which the church comes to this spiritual maturity.

In the well-known passage of Philippians 3:9-15 Paul speaks in a still more inclusive sense of being perfect. Although on the one hand he describes himself and the church as "perfect" (v. 15), namely, come to maturity in their judgment, just before, in verse 12, he has said: "not that I have already obtained it, or am already become perfect...." Here again it is a question of more than moral perfection; it is one of the appropriation of the full salvation in Christ, ultimately of nothing less than being glorified with Christ (v. 11), "the perfect" of 1 Corinthians 13:10.

If there is thus a clear distinction to be pointed out between this concept of perfection and that of ethical perfectionism and if one cannot simply appeal to the former for the latter, it is evident from this idea of adulthood and maturity that the new life knows growth, advance toward perfection. And this is also true in a moral sense, of course. To be sure, in Ephesians 4 these pronouncements are applied in the first place to the church as such.[49] But it may not be inferred from this that Paul does not[50] intend to summon every individual Christian to be a perfect, mature believer. From the sequel to Ephesians 4:13 it is sufficiently clear that this last is also the case. Therefore the frequent mention of increase of faith (2 Cor. 10:15), of "the harvest of

47. On this see further below, Sections 68ff.
48. So Percy, *Probleme*, p. 323; cf. Bultmann: "Paul had ... meant by [*teleios*] not 'perfection' but 'adulthood' " (*Theology*, II, p. 225).
49. On this point of view Gaugler, e.g., places all the emphasis (*Die Heiligung*, p. 51).
50. So, e.g., A. Wikenhauser, *Die Kirche als der mystische Leib Christi nach dem Apostel Paulus*, 1940, p. 182.

righteousness" (2 Cor. 9:10), of growing into a holy temple (Eph. 2:21; cf. 4:15; Col. 2:19), of bearing fruit in every good work and increasing in the right knowledge of God (Col. 1:10), of abounding more and more in thanksgiving (2 Cor. 4:15), joy (2 Cor. 8:2), the work of love (2 Cor. 8:7), in every good work (2 Cor. 9:8), etc., is also a clear indication of the character of the Christian life and of moral freedom. There is an ascent to be perceived in it (cf. Rom. 5:3ff.), not an ascent that is a matter of course and automatic, but in the exercise of faith. On this account Paul can urge on to the perfecting of holiness in the fear of God (2 Cor. 7:1), and he can make blamelessness the holy goal of those who have been made free in Christ (Eph. 5:27; Phil. 1:10; 2:15). He speaks of that particularly in relation to the appearance of Christ to be expected, as a gift that God is to give to the church (1 Cor. 1:8), and which he therefore asks of God for the church (1 Thess. 3:13; 5:23), but for which it must also prepare itself in its scrupulous distinguishing and doing of what God asks of it (Phil. 1:10).

We may say in summary that the dominant viewpoint from which Paul considers the Christian life is not the remaining temptation of the flesh, but the power of the Spirit conquering all sin. The idea that the believer must remain stuck fast in a small beginning is certainly not in harmony with his indicative and imperative pronouncements of per-fection. But he thereby always points toward the future and nowhere proceeds from the idea that the church has already reached a state of sinlessness or were able to rest in it. He speaks of a *posse non peccare,* not of a *non peccare,* and much less still of a *non posse peccare* as the picture of the Christian life. It is faith in the power and faithfulness of God (1 Thess. 5:24), not the moral result reached in the church, that makes him hold up blamelessness and spotlessness before the church as mandate and final goal, in the midst of all the present temptations and imperfections.

SECTION 45. UNITY AND MULTIPLICITY. THE CONCRETENESS OF THE PARAENESIS

If we now go further into the content of the Pauline paraenesis, we are faced with what is at first glance a confusing multiplicity of concepts, motives, and viewpoints, with the help of which Paul gives expression to the ethical effect of the gospel. An exhaustive treatment of this material demands a separate study,[51] and would go far beyond the boundaries of a general description of the content of Paul's preach-ing. We wish therefore to characterize the content of this paraenesis somewhat further by providing a summary from several points of view.

The first thing that can be of service here is the distinction of

---

51. There is a wide literature on the Pauline "ethic," both of a summarizing and of a more specialized nature. A very extensive list of the older and more recent writings is to be found, for example, in Schrage, *Die konkreten Einzelgebote in der paulinischen Paränese,* pp. 279-301.

the unity and the multiplicity in this paraenesis. Under the unity, then, are to be understood all the summarizing pronouncements and concepts in which the whole of the new obedience is qualified, for example, when there is mention of having been made subservient to righteousness, or of presenting oneself to God as a sacrifice (Romans 6, 12); and under the multiplicity the many separate commandments and prescriptions in which the content of the new obedience and righteousness is given more concrete form.

It is of importance to place all emphasis on both the unity and the multiplicity. So far as the unity is concerned, it is unmistakable that the content of the obedience demanded by Paul is primarily an indivisible matter, at bottom to be reduced to a unity. He speaks of it in the singular as "each man's work" (1 Cor. 3:13-15; Gal. 6:4), the "good work" (Phil. 1:6), "the work of faith" (1 Thess. 1:3; 2 Thess. 1:11); similarly "the fruit of the Spirit" (Gal. 5:22; cf. Rom. 6:22), the "fruit of righteousness" (Phil. 1:11; cf. 4:17). Galatians 5:22 is of special importance here because this "fruit" of the Spirit is further differentiated in a multiplicity of Christian virtues. It admits of being summarized in one word, love. "Let all that you do be done in love" (1 Cor. 16:14); "love is the fulfilling of the law" (Rom. 13:10; cf. Gal. 5:14). In Christ nothing other is of any avail than "faith working through love" (Gal. 5:6), just as it can be said elsewhere that "whatsoever is not of faith is sin" (Rom. 14:23).

Emphasis has rightly been placed on the fact that in this conception of the unity and indivisibility of the new obedience there comes to light on the one hand the agreement of Paul with Jesus, and on the other the great distinction between the Pauline and the rabbinic ethic. So far as the latter is concerned, it is well known that the rabbis, even though among them attempts are not lacking to reach unity from multiplicity, still sought their strength especially in elaborating the will of God as much as possible and in carrying on a casuistry that extended like a net over all of life. Although, so far as we are able to see, Paul does not in so many words broach the antithesis with the old synagogue in his epistles, it is clear that his paraenesis bears a totally different character and has received the clear stamp of the righteousness and fulfillment of the law maintained by Jesus over against the Pharisees and Scribes.

On the other hand one cannot close his eyes to the highly varied and in part very detailed character of the Pauline paraenesis. His epistles contain a multiplicity of individual admonitions, commandments, and advice, in which he holds before the churches their Christian calling not only as a unity but also in all its concrete multiformity, and he himself frequently expresses his paraenesis in the plural (cf. 1 Thess. 4:2; 2 Thess. 2:15; 1 Cor. 11:2, et al.). However distinctive his characterization of the new obedience in the singular as "the good work" may be, he speaks with equal positiveness of "good works" in the plural (Eph. 2:10; 1 Tim. 5:25; 6:18; Tit. 2:7, 14; 3:8, 14; cf. 2 Cor. 9:8; Col. 1:10; 2 Thess. 2:17). In this respect the nomenclature of the paraenesis entirely corresponds with the anthropological distinction favored by

Paul between "the body" (the unity of the human mode of existence coming to outward expression) and "the members" (individual, concrete acts; cf. Rom. 6:12ff.; 12:1; Col. 3:5, et al.).

The opinion has frequently been held, to be sure, that the multiplicity of the separate commandments stands in a certain relationship of tension with the essence of the new life as living in and walking by the Spirit, standing in liberty, etc. Some have wished indeed to conclude from this that the new obedience does not permit itself to be dictated to in individual commandments on pain of once again lapsing into legalism. With regard to the unmistakable multiplicity of the individual prescriptions and commandments in Paul's epistles scholars have come to all kinds of theories: to the degree that the eschatological consciousness in Paul himself and in the church grew weaker, he is said to have been compelled to take a stand on all kinds of concrete questions of practical life; or the original moral enthusiasm of the new ideal of life is said to have received a more and more necessary corrective in the pedagogical precepts of the apostle. Others have taken precisely the reverse position and have wished to see in the concrete individual commandments a still necessary (but in the long run superfluous) transitional situation of the Christian churches not immediately ripe for moral freedom, while still others do not want to conceive of these individual commandments as abiding and binding precepts, but as a current particularizing, with reference to certain concrete situations, of the one commandment of love and liberty.[52]

In the following section we shall still have to deal separately with the function of the law in the new life. Here we wish to confine ourselves to rejecting the view that the Pauline conception of the new life does not really admit of being reconciled with the laying down of individual precepts and commandments, and that their occurrence in the epistles of Paul would require further explanation. We have to do here with a conception of liberty and "Christian" autonomy that stems more from the world of the Enlightenment and Kantian philosophy than from that of Paul. The whole idea that these individual precepts, were one compelled to grant a binding character to them, would signify the way back to the Jewish legalism so forcefully opposed by him, is obviously alien to Paul's own world of thought. We have already seen how much as a matter of course, after having first emphatically rejected man's own righteousness before God as a dead-end street, he nevertheless qualifies the whole of the new life as servitude to "righteousness," in the religious-ethical sense of the word. And the same thing applies to the concept of "work" and "good works." That man is justified without the works of the law does not for a moment prevent him from vigorously demanding good works as the fruit of the new life and giving all kinds of prescriptions, commandments, advice, for these good works. If the nature of the new life and the new obedience demanded on the basis of it is in conflict with being subjected to new precepts and commandments, then Paul's epistles from first to last are no longer

---

52. For these various conceptions see *ibid.*, pp. 13-48.

comprehensible; for they are full of them. That the continuing practical concerns of the church and all kinds of concrete situations in which the young Christian church required guidance and direction gave the apostle occasion time and again to provide all sorts of precepts and commandments is surely self-evident and constitutes an important viewpoint in judging all these concrete prescriptions. But nowhere does he so represent the situation as though his interference with the practical moral life of the church were really a concession to practice and an evidence of the weakness of its spiritual life. Rather, he appeals for this to his special commission as an apostle of Christ. He writes to the Romans, for example, that although he is persuaded that they themselves, too, are full of goodness, filled with all knowledge, and able also to admonish one another, he has nevertheless by way of a reminder written somewhat boldly to them. And this, so he adds, in virtue of the grace of God given to him (of his apostleship), to be a minister of Christ Jesus for the gentiles in the holy priestly service of the gospel, so that the offering of the gentiles might be acceptable to God, sanctified by the Holy Spirit (Rom. 15:15ff.). Here Paul qualifies his apostolic office as that of the priest who is to exercise supervision over that which is offered in the sanctuary, and it is in virtue of this ministry which has been charged to him that, although convinced of their good intentions, knowledge, etc., he has nevertheless given clear instructions for their moral conduct and their relationships to one another. And, to mention yet another passage, in Colossians 1:26ff. Paul appeals likewise to the discharging of the office given to him, in virtue of which his proclamation of Christ consists in "admonishing every man, and teaching every man in all wisdom, that he may present every man perfect in Christ to God." Here again it is evident from the repeated "every man" how much the apostle counted it his duty not merely to proclaim Christ "in general," but also in a pastoral and pedagogical sense to see to the guidance and instruction of the church in its particular questions and needs. Undoubtedly in the process questions arise that are connected with the interim character of the time before Christ's parousia (1 Cor. 7; 1, 2 Thess.). But the express treatment of them is even so only a certain aspect in his preaching, and it would be a complete misjudgment of the nature of the Pauline paraenesis were one to choose to posit that its effect would be none other than to give the church a little practical guidance in view of the unexpected failure of the parousia to arrive. Here again the principal viewpoint of all Paul's proclamation does not lie in the absence as yet of the parousia of the Lord, but in the revelation of his death and resurrection that have already taken place. And it is accordingly in this that the individual commandments and precepts appear again and again to have their root and deepest motive (cf., e.g., Rom. 14:15; 1 Cor. 5:6-8; 2 Cor. 8:8, 9; Phil. 2:5, et al.). In all these passages it is clear that it is not the fact that Christ has not yet appeared that compels the apostle to concern himself with the progress of the life of the church, but that he is constantly intent, by all manner of moral precepts, on bringing to manifestation and development that which it has already received in Christ.

In view of this last point one will have to guard against seeing the concreteness of Paul's paraenesis exclusively as a current particularization, referring to the present situation, of the one great commandment and not as the giving of general rules. No doubt the apostle does not give a system of ethical rules and precepts. His precepts often have reference to specific situations in the churches, give answers to questions that have reached him. Thus the paraenesis on "the strong and the weak" in Romans 14 and 15 and in 1 Corinthians 8ff.; on the disputes in Corinth (1 Cor. 3), on the lack of discipline, going to law before unbelievers, abuses in the Lord's Supper, order in the congregation, in 1 Corinthians 5, 6, 11, 14, etc. This is by no means to say, however, that these precepts consist only in a current application of the commandment of love, which may indeed be important and instructive, but yet not of universal validity. For two things are to be borne in mind here.

In the first place, the apostle, even when he goes into all sorts of current questions concerning the life of the Christian church of the time, does not restrict himself to the giving of specific solutions or prescriptions that were of importance for specific occasions, but rather he teaches the church to approach and to answer these questions and situations from general points of view. One need only think, for example, of the broad pastoral treatment both in Romans and 1 Corinthians of the problem that was apparently such a burning issue in the church of the gentile Christians of the eating of meat that had been sacrificed to idols. This treatment is not confined to a few concrete instructions, but it teaches the church to judge these questions from a muliplicity of viewpoints. It upholds the liberty of eating and drinking in view of the redeeming work of Christ as well as from the consideration that the earth and all that is in it has been created by God and is therefore not to be rejected. It is no less forcefully brought to the forefront on the other hand that love for one's brother and the good of the church must in everything be the standard and rule of conduct. Furthermore the apostle warns against the rash and proud use of liberty, an occasion of falling also for those who think that they stand. The concrete situation repeatedly leads to general moral viewpoints and rules of life. The examples here lie ready to hand: in Colossians, where Paul wages war against a syncretistic tendency, he goes far beyond the actual situation in his admonitions and gives precepts that, besides being for the church of Colosse, are of very general purport (cf., e.g., 2:20; 3:1ff.). The same holds for such paraenetic pronouncements as those in 1 Corinthians 6:12ff.; 10:23ff.; 2 Corinthians 9:7; and 1 Timothy 4:5ff.

In the second place, however, it must be posited no less emphatically that, along with this paraenesis which has reference to specific situations, Paul also gives a great many prescriptions and commandments of which this last cannot be said, or at least does not appear to be the case. This holds not only for the admonitions that are kept very general, as, for example, in Romans 6:12ff., but in many instances also for all sorts of special and concrete prescriptions. Thus, for example, in Romans 12:3-21; 13, chapters in which a great number of concrete commandments are given without it being possible to determine

with any certainty that a specific occasion for them existed in the church
at Rome. And the same thing applies to most of the paraenetic closing
chapters in the Pauline epistles. One may conclude from this how much
the apostle felt the need to give the churches guidance in a moral and
pastoral respect, too, not only in current problems that cropped up
among them, but also in a more general sense. And one may gather at
the same time how far removed he was from the standpoint of many of
his later interpreters, with their assumption that the new life and
being-in-the-Spirit has no need of such concrete precepts and that anyone who lives by the Spirit will on that account know how he is to
walk by the Spirit. Even more than from his giving answers to and
entering into concrete questions or situations it is evident from these
more generally intended precepts how comprehensive Paul's paraenesis
is, from how many points of view he regards life and how many situations his commandments cover. It has been repeated endlessly that Paul
gives no systematic ethic, and this is indeed beyond discussion. But this
does not mean that in his paraenesis there is no line or "system" and
that his precepts consist only in disconnected admonitions without interrelationship. This is perhaps most apparent in the so-called *Haustafeln*
(schedules of household duties) in which various groups of persons are
successively addressed. But elsewhere, too, this "systematic" aspect is to
be observed. In 1 Corinthians 7 the apostle deals extensively with all
sorts of questions concerning marriage. In Romans 12:3-20 the concern
is with the manner in which believers are to live from the new disposition both among themselves and in their associations with unbelievers.
Elsewhere we meet with precepts for ecclesiastical life in the more
institutional sense of the word, and one is able to speak of the beginning of a liturgical and ecclesiastical order (1 Cor. 14; 1 Tim. 2, 3, and
5). From all this it is evident that though there is no question here of
a finished structure of precepts and commandments, and though an
"ethic" of motives rather than of cases is to be spoken of, yet Paul is in
no way averse to concrete guidance and precepts, on the one hand, and
to obedience closely conforming to them on the other. That with this
he did not wish to render inoperative the moral activity and independent judgment of the church itself, but by his example and determination of position intended just to stimulate it, is said in so many
words in more than one place and will have our attention still further.
The main thing in all this, however, is not what was most to be respected: his apostolic authority or the moral activity of the church; the
chief thing for him was that the church both in obedience to his precepts and by its own insight and sensitiveness for the things that really
matter should exhibit the image of the new life no longer subjected to
sin, but dedicated to God.

　　That — finally — in his paraenesis the apostle did not create something completely new, but in a great many ways, both in a material and
in a more formal sense, associated himself with what had been said
before him and with what for his purpose was fundamental or useful
goes without saying. An exhaustive treatment of the moral, conceptual,
and motivational materials in Paul's epistles would have to demonstrate

this in detail. In general it can be established that on the one hand
there is to be found in them a clear connection with Old Testament
definitions; on the other hand it is evident especially in the emphasis
that Paul, too, places on the commandment of love and in the manner
in which he interprets this in how profound a manner the preaching of
Jesus entered into the apostolic paraenesis. Elsewhere he defines the
moral vocation of believers in terms and schemata that appear in many
ways to have their parallels throughout the entire contemporary intellectual world of the apostle; the specifically Christian purport of these
does not so much lie in the terminology as in the general context in
which they have been taken up into the Christian preaching.[53]

SECTION 46. TERTIUS USUS LEGIS

After all that has been said in the foregoing on the theocentric and
totalitarian character of the new obedience as well as on the unity and
diversity that are to be observed in the paraenesis to this obedience,
the question now arises as to whether and in what way the norm of
the new life thus described is to be determined. To be sure, important
directives are already implied in the characterizations mentioned above;
for they speak of the character of the new obedience as directed toward
God, led by the Spirit, unconditional, and all-embracing. In Paul's concrete commandments in particular various points of view may be pointed
out that are of the greatest importance for defining the content of what
he denotes in general as righteousness, sanctification of life, good works.
The question remains, however, as to where it is that the apostle himself in his precepts and commandments derived the norms for the new
obedience required by him, as well as to the manner in which in its
moral judgment of itself and in its own activity the church is able to
receive correct insight into the will of God to be accomplished by it.
In particular it should come up for discussion here whether and, if so,
in what sense the law continues to function in the Pauline paraenesis
as the source of the knowledge of the will of God and as the standard
for the new life.

We are faced here with a much discussed question. After all that
has been said above on the "incidental" significance of the law,[54] as
well as on freedom from the law as means of salvation — which the
apostle declares with such great vigor[55] — it is not strange that many

---

53. Cf., e.g., the elaborate study of M. S. Enslin, *The Ethics of Paul*, 1930;
for the occurrence of specific schemata, the investigation of A. Vögtle, *Die Tugend und
Lasterkataloge im Neuen Testament*, 1936; K. Weidinger, *Die Haustafeln, Ein Stück
urchristliche Paränese*, 1928; S. Wibbing, *Die Tugend und Lasterkataloge im Neuen
Testament*, 1959; D. Schroeder, *Die Haustafeln des Neuen Testaments*, 1959. For the
"codification" of the extensive conceptual materials, e.g., Lindsay Dewar, *An Outline
of New Testament Ethics*, pp. 139-155.
54. Cf. above, Section 24.
55. See above, pp. 215ff.

have arrived at the idea that the norm for the new life can no longer be derived from the law.

The Lutheran Bishop Anders Nygren, for example, takes a very radical stand on this in his commentary on the Epistle to the Romans. According to him, Paul's pronouncements on having been released from the law, on Christ as the end of the law, etc., must be taken as absolutely having done with the law, and one may not attempt to grant entrance to the law in another way.

Thus Nygren writes, for example, with respect to the words of Romans 7:6, ". . . but now we have been discharged from the law," that Paul describes the role of the law in the Christian life "in a way that has often disturbed his theological interpreters." One had perhaps expected — so he writes — that the law no longer acts in that life as a power of destruction, but as an assisting agency that gives us instructions as to how the Christian life is to take shape ("the third use of the law"). Paul says the opposite, however. For him the law pertains entirely to the old aeon and is one of the powers of destruction under which we were held prisoner; therefore the new life is characterized by the fact that we have been made free from the law.[56] Similarly, he writes on Romans 10:3: "With full confidence Paul can tell how through Christ there is really an end to the law." For the law had as its purpose (a) to stop every mouth; (b) to insist on righteousness. This has now become reality in Christ. "The day of the law is past. Christ is the end of the law, the terminus of the law, the law's [telos]."[57]

However much such a conclusion seems at first glance to lie in the line of Paul's absolute rejection of the law as the means to righteousness, on more careful inspection it appears that it does not do justice to the whole of his pronouncements concerning the law. For whatever the great emphasis with which he speaks of having been discharged from the law and calls Christ the end of the law, in other places, as it were self-evidently, he time and again harks back to the law, namely, when he wishes to define the content of the new obedience and the express will of God for the new life. The principal pronouncements to be considered here are the following:

> For what the law could not do, in that it was weak through the flesh, God [has done]. . . , that the requirement of the law might be fulfilled in us, who walk not after the flesh, but after the Spirit (Rom. 8:3, 4).
>
> Owe no man anything, save to love one another: for he who loves the other has fulfilled the law. For the commandments . . . are summed up in this word: thou shalt love thy neighbor as thyself . . . ; love therefore is the fulfilling of the law (Rom. 13:8-10).
>
> Circumcision is nothing, and uncircumcision is nothing; but the keeping of the commandments of God (1 Cor. 7:19).
>
> . . . to them that are without law, I became as without law — although not without the law of God, for I stand under the law of Christ (1 Cor. 9:21).
>
> Serve one another through love. For the whole law is fulfilled in one word, in this: thou shalt love thy neighbor as thyself (Gal. 5:14).
>
> Bear one another's burdens, and so fulfill the law of Christ (Gal. 6:2).

56. Nygren, Commentary on Romans, pp. 275f.
57. Ibid., p. 380.

Now the attempt has been made so to interpret these pronouncements that on the one hand the positive significance of the law is recognized, but that on the other there would be no question in these passages of a *tertius usus legis* for believers. When it is said in Romans 8:4
that the requirement of the law is fulfilled in us, Nygren, for example,
acknowledges that there is mention here of the positive "purpose" of
the law, as well as of the fulfilling of the law, but in his opinion this
may not be understood of a fulfilling of the law by believers of which
they would then be capable by the power of the Spirit, but only of
fulfillment by Christ "and by the fact that we 'are in Him.' "[58] It is our
conviction, however, that a false antithesis is made here. For the words
"in us" are followed by "who walk not after the flesh, but after the
Spirit." And this is what is intended by "the fulfilling of the requirement of the law."

How great the difficulties are with which one is faced when he chooses to
couple these positive pronouncements on the law with an absolute rejection
of the continuing normative significance of the law appears most clearly from
Nygren's explanation of Romans 13:8-10. In his opinion there is no conflict with
the absolute interpretation of Romans 10:4. And he endeavors to make this
plausible as follows: Since the law is negatively directed against sin, Christ, who
is righteousness, signifies the end of the law. And the same applies to love. Where
love is, nothing occurs that the law forbids. Therefore the words "Christ, the
end of the law" and "love, the fulfilling of the law," would be expressions for
the same thing.[59]

It is evident, however, that this explanation could hold only if Paul
called love "the end" or "the making superfluous" of the law. He speaks of
the fulfilling of the law, however, as something that is required of believers
(v. 8) and which presupposes a continuing significance of the law. For that
matter, it is very difficult to maintain as the general characteristic of the essence
of the law that it is only negatively against sin and not positively for righteousness and requires this.

Most interpreters, even those who suppose that Paul speaks very un-
equivocally of the end of the Mosaic law, are therefore of the opinion
(on the ground of these unmistakable positive pronouncements) that
in one way or another he also retains the law. Thus Bultmann speaks
of two sorts of appreciation of the law in Paul, indeed really of two
sorts of law, on the one hand of the law as the eternal and abiding will
of God, on the other of the law that with Christ has been done away.
This latter is then said to appear in Paul especially as the "law of
Moses," and as the "incidental" law really does not go back to God,
but to angelic powers (Gal. 3:19ff.).[60] Others speak of a distinction in
Paul between the immanent will of the law itself and the will of God,
which has made itself known in the giving of the law. Of this Romans
8:4 and Romans 13:8-10 are supposed to speak; it is that which the Spirit
brings about in the life of Christians. But it may not be concluded from

---

58. *Ibid.*, p. 319.
59. *Ibid.*, pp. 434f.
60. *Theology*, I, p. 268.

this that Paul still ascribed to the law itself and to its legal demands a positive normative role for the moral life in the sense of the *tertius usus legis*.[61] Still others speak of Paul's "unschematic manner" of speaking. When in Romans 8:4 and 13:8-10 Paul speaks without prejudice of the "fulfilling of the law" he means that the Christian really attains to the Judaistic ideal by the operation of love. However: "the ideal is the same in name only, but in fact is something other: on the one hand faithfulness to the law working casuistically; on the other the operation of the divine Spirit without looking back at the 'dead' law."[62] And to mention still another distinction: G. Bornkamm writes, in connection with Galatians 5:14, that "the point of the passage is not the question of the setting aside of the law, but rather its fulfilment through the deed. [*Peplērōtai*] (gnomic perfect) thus refers to more than the obvious summarization of the law in the love-commandment, namely its complete fulfillment in love."[63]

If we survey the whole, so far as the positive significance of the law is concerned, the following may be noted by way of summary.

(1) However much, speaking out of the Jewish conception of the law as the means of salvation, Paul emphatically places the negative significance of the law in the foreground, on the other side the so-called "third use" of the law is also unmistakable in his epistles. After all that has been said on "having died to the law," Christ as "the end of the law," etc., the abiding significance of the law as the expression of the will of God is maintained with a certain self-evidentness.[64] Nor is there materially the slightest opposition between the one and the other. One can perhaps wonder at the fact that it all takes place so "silently" and that the apostle, at least in the epistles that have been preserved to us, apparently felt no need to go further into this relationship. But the same thing applies to the very positive manner in which he speaks of "good works" and "righteousness" as well. This involves the fact that it is absolutely impossible, without having recourse to arbitrariness and artificiality, to deny this double significance of the law, namely, both as pedagogue to Christ and as rule for the new life, either on the one side or the other, or to distinguish both aspects even terminologically from each other.[65] One will therefore not be able to maintain that love or

61. Cf. E. Kühl, *Der Brief an de Römer*, pp. 258-269, 438-440 (excursus on Rom. 8:1-4; 13:8-10).

62. So Lietzmann, *Rom.*, p. 113.

63. G. Bornkamm, *Das Ende des Gesetzes*, 1952, p. 135. This interpretation of *peplērōtai*, however, is difficult to maintain precisely with reference to Gal. 5:14. For here there is mention of the law being fulfilled *en heni logō*, which points not to the deed, but precisely to the "obvious summarization" of the law, the same as what is called in Rom. 13:9 *anakephalaioutai*: finds its summary expression; see also my *The Epistle of Paul to the Churches of Galatia*, p. 201, n. 4.

64. Cf. Bultmann, *Theology*, I, p. 341: "It is clear that Christ is the end of the law so far as it is claimed to be the way to salvation or was understood by man as the means of establishing his own righteousness, for so far as it contains God's demand, it retains its validity."

65. Cf. H. Berkhof, "Gesetz und Evangelium," in *Von Herrengeheimnis der*

the Spirit or even Christ is the norm and the rule of conduct of the new life, at least if this would mean a substitution for the law.

The pronouncements on love in Romans 13:8-10 and Galatians 5:14 are unmistakable in this respect. Love functions here not as a new Christian ideal or as a new norm, which comes in the place of the law or makes it superfluous. It is precisely required here as the summary of the law (*anakephalaioutai;* Rom. 13:9). In other words, the law does not find its criterion in love, but just the reverse, the requirement of love is so imperative because in it lies the summary of the law. This detracts nothing from the great significance of love as the summary of the law and thus the criterion for the fulfilling of the law: in this respect Paul's canticle of love, no less than Jesus' radical commandments in the Sermon on the Mount, is a matchless unfolding of the deep and unmistakable content of the law, an unfolding that can be such a radical and previously unattained pinnacle because it forms the reverse side of the preaching of God's unimaginably great revelation of love in Jesus Christ (cf. Phil. 2:5ff.; Rom. 12:1; Eph. 3:18, 19). But this detracts nothing from the significance of the law as the expression of this love and as source for knowledge of the will of God. Every antithesis men would make here between the binding character of love and the not-binding character of the law is to be rejected in the light of Paul's clear pronouncements.

The situation is no different with respect to the appeal to the Spirit. When the Spirit is repeatedly spoken of in connection with liberty and obedience, he undoubtedly acts not only as the possibility, but also as the norm of the new life. The Spirit is not only the power that subdues the dominion of the flesh; everyone who permits himself to be led by the Spirit is thereby led in a definite direction. The expression "to walk according to" the Spirit (*kata Pneuma peripatein;* Gal. 5:25) also speaks of a standard: Spirit and flesh not only represent two different powers, but also two different ethical principles. They both have their own "purpose," are both, in a contrary sense, bent on something.[66] The Spirit stands over against "the lusting" of the flesh (Gal. 5:17).

This does not mean, however — and in this context all the emphasis must lie here — that the Spirit as the standard and norm of the new life sets himself over against or in the place of the law and that he who walks after the Spirit or is led by the Spirit no longer has any need of commandment or law. However much this conception has been propagated in all sorts of literature on Paul,[67] it is in flagrant conflict

---

Wahrheit (Vogel festschrift), 1961, pp. 141ff. He points there to "the tendency of many Lutherans to separate the two aspects of the law terminologically as well, and to circumscribe the *usus normativus* as 'commandment' or 'paraenesis' and thus to place it over against the 'law.'... That runs contrary to the New Testament proclamation, which covers both aspects with the word *nomos.*"

66. Thus we shall have to understand *phronēma* in Rom. 8:6.

67. A well-known example is the pronouncement of Lietzmann on Rom. 6:6-23: "It would have been obvious to Paul, particularly because the struggle about circumcision was threatening, to pronounce the ceremonial law alone to be done away with — thus, in essence, the later church has solved it — and that would have eased

with the explicit pronouncements of the apostle. We must not here permit ourselves to be misled by the sound of some words. When in Galatians 5:18 Paul says "If you allow yourselves to be led by the Spirit, you are not under the law," it can appear as though for believers the knowledge and validity of the will of God were no longer situated in the law, but in the Spirit. Here again,[68] however, what is meant by "under the law" is the condition of impotence and condemnation to which man is subjected outside faith and the life-giving power of the Spirit. A moment later, in verse 23, it can accordingly be said that the law is not against such (i.e., those who allow themselves to be led by the Spirit). That the dispensation of the Spirit does not abrogate the validity and the requirement of the law, but precisely confirms this and brings it to fulfillment is not to be denied. The work of the Spirit consists precisely in the working out of the law in the life of believers (Rom. 8:4: "that the requirement of the law might be fulfilled in us, who walk not according to the flesh, but according to the Spirit"). The difference between the "mind of the flesh" and the "mind of the Spirit" lies precisely in this, that the flesh does not submit itself to the law of God, nor can it do so (Rom. 8:7). Nowhere in Paul's epistles do we find anything of a spiritualism that with regard to the content of God's will makes an antithesis between the law and the Spirit, the decree coming from without and the inner disposition.[69] The law itself is holy and spiritual (Rom. 7:14), and thus cannot be placed over against the Spirit; it is not made superfluous by the Spirit, but rather established. "Letting oneself be led by the Spirit" consists also in learning anew to discern and prove the good and well-pleasing and perfect will of God (Rom. 12:2), qualifications that with a little variation are elsewhere applied to the law (Rom. 7:12).

(2) Yet with the above everything has not of course been said. This is evident in particular from those pronouncements which have a bearing on the relationship of Christ and the law. Even though one understands the pronouncement of Romans 10:4 that "Christ is the end of the law" of the pedagogical significance of the law[70] and nothing has as yet been prejudiced with respect to the continuing normative purport of the law, nevertheless with the advent of Christ the validity of the law in its historical form has not remained the same. Of impor-

---

the battle for him. But Paul is no man of halfway measures. Thus he holds immovably to the antinomian point of view: where life moves in the Spirit, no kind of law has a place any longer. God nevermore approaches the one whom he has given his *pneuma* from outside with the casuistic demands of the law. He who walks in the Spirit does by himself what God's commandment would require, because the Spirit points him on the way. Christian morality is a spontaneous matter of course" (*Rom.*, p. 71).

68. Cf. pp. 147ff.

69. This, in our view, is also valid against the summary view of Brunner with respect to the law in Paul, in which he writes, i.a.: "God's will no longer confronts him as an alien law, for the believer is, as one reconciled to God, united with him; he no longer requires the Law, because God's Spirit has become the leader in him, showing him God's will" (*The Letter to the Romans*, ET 1959, p. 141).

70. Cf. above, Section 24.

tance in this context is the pronouncement in 1 Corinthians 9:21,[71] where Paul amplifies his declaration that to those that are without law he became as without law with the words: "although not without the law of God, but bound by the law of Christ." This passage contains three elements in which the relationship of Christ and the law in its continuing significance is clearly expressed:

(a) The law no longer has an unrestricted and undifferentiated validity for the church of Christ. In a certain sense the church can be qualified as "without the law."

(b) The law of God is not thereby abrogated.

(c) This continuing significance of the law can be qualified as "being bound to the law of Christ" (ennomos Christou). All three elements can be further elucidated from all the epistles of Paul.

As to (a), that the law of Moses in its particularistic significance as making a division between Jews and gentiles is no longer in force constitutes the foundation of Paul's apostolate among the gentiles. He speaks of it as "the law of commandments, consisting in ordinances" and as "the middle wall of partition." It holds for the law functioning in this way that it has been pulled down and rendered inoperative (Eph. 2:14ff.; cf. Gal. 2:14; 4:10; 5:2ff.; 6:12; Col. 2:16ff.; 3:11; also Rom. 2:26ff.; 3:30; 4 passim; 1 Cor. 7:18, 19). This holds above all for circumcision, but in general for "living as a Jew" (Ioudaizein, Ioudaikōs zēn; Gal. 2:14), as a description of those regulations which had the effect of maintaining the line of demarcation between Israel and the gentiles in a ritual-cultic and social respect. To be sure, in the epistles that have been preserved to us nowhere is a distinction made explicitly between the moral and the ceremonial, particularistic parts of the law, but materially Paul, certainly continuing to build on the antecedent missionary preaching (cf. Col. 2:6ff.), nevertheless starts from such a distinction. In Colossians 2:16ff., with regard to the keeping of dietary regulations, feasts, new moons, or sabbath days, we find the typical expression: "which are a shadow of the things to come, but the body is Christ's."[72] In comparison with the administration of redemption that has commenced with Christ, all these prescriptions are but provisional and unreal, as a shadow exhibits only the dim contours of the body itself.[73] Herein is the important viewpoint that with Christ's advent the law, also as far as its content is concerned, has been brought under a new norm of judgment and that failure to appreciate this new situation is a denial of Christ (Gal. 5:2).

In regard to (b), however great the significance of all this is for correct insight into the continuing requirement of the law, one cannot

---

71. See also C. H. Dodd, "[ENNOMOS CHRISTOU]," in Studia Paulina, 1953, pp. 96-110.

72. See A. J. Bandstra, The Law and the Elements of the World, pp. 90ff.

73. On the significance of sōma in this connection there is some difference of opinion. In our view one will have to think of a simple figure of speech. The contrast is not timeless-metaphysical (Urbild-Abbild, etc.), but redemptive-historical (skia tōn mellontōn); cf. Schulz, TDNT, VII, p. 398. That by to sōma Christ's resurrection body (Benoit) or the church (Masson, Schlatter) is intended here, seems to us difficult to reconcile with the context; see my Col., pp. 190, 191.

say that with Christ another law has come or that for Paul "the law of Christ," or simply "the law," may be said to mean the eternal and abiding law of God and that he spoke of it in conscious contrast with or distinction from the law of Moses. Some, to be sure, are of the opinion that one must not translate Romans 13:8 by "he who loves the other has fulfilled the law," but by "he who loves has fulfilled the other law," whereby the law of Christ as "the other law" would have been set in the place of or alongside the law of Moses.[74] But this translation is a labored evasion of the obvious, and the unmistakable intention of the text, viewed also in the light of Galatians 5:14, is otherwise. So far as the law of Moses is concerned, when Paul gives expression to the continuing demand of the law, he cites the decalogue specifically.[75] One can hardly make contrasts here between "Moses" and "Christ," nor between "the law" and "the law of Moses." And this holds, too, for the qualification "the commandments." However true it is that Christ has abolished "the law of commandments, consisting in ordinances" (Eph. 2:15; Col. 2:14), this does not alter the fact that it is said elsewhere that what really matters is the keeping of God's commandments (entolōn; 1 Cor. 7:19), and that in concrete cases an explicit appeal can be made to an individual "ordinance" in the law of Moses (Eph. 6:2; 1 Cor. 9:9ff.). Also the contrast between the unity (of the law of Christ) and the multiplicity (of the law of Moses), however meaningful this distinction may be in a specific context (cf. Mark 12:32ff.), must be rejected as false, if it is intended[76] to oppose the continuing significance of Moses.

As for (c), if one asks himself what the material content is of the expression "bound to the law of Christ" (1 Cor. 9:21), the answer will lie in the fact that Christ *suo modo* represents the law of God and thus the law of Moses. Not only does Christ by his Spirit bring about a new bond to the law in the hearts of believers,[77] whereby the law retains its force as the expression of the will of God in the New Covenant (Jer. 31:33; cf. 2 Cor. 3:3), but Christ also represents the new standard of judgment as to what "has had its day" in the law and what has abiding validity (Col. 2:17). Finally, one should point out the interpretation of the law given by Christ, to which Paul appeals in more than one place (cf. 1 Cor. 7:10ff.), which determines the expression of Galatians 6:2 as well, namely, that he who helps to bear the sin of his brother "fulfills the law of Christ."[78] There can thus be no doubt whatever that the category of the law has not been abrogated with Christ's advent, but rather has been maintained and interpreted in its radical sense ("fulfilled"; Matt. 5:17); on the other hand, that the church no longer has to do with the law in any other way than in Christ and thus is *ennomos Christou.*

---

74. So Gutbrod, *TDNT*, IV, p. 1071, *s.v. nomos.*
75. Cf. above, pp. 106ff.
76. Cf., e.g., E. Percy, *Probleme*, p. 356.
77. I doubt whether one can express this with the concept "immediate knowledge," as Bandstra wishes to do (*The Law and the Elements of the World*, p. 187).
78. On this also see Bandstra, *ibid.*, pp. 111-114.

(3) Finally, how much Christ, the law, the Spirit, and love constitute a unity may appear from a comparison of the following parallel pronouncements:

> For neither is circumcision anything, nor uncircumcision, but being a new creature. And as many as shall walk by this rule [canon], peace upon them, . . . (Gal. 6:15, 16).
> For in Christ Jesus neither does circumcision avail anything, nor uncircumcision; but faith, working through love (Gal. 5:6).
> Circumcision is nothing, and uncircumcision is nothing; but the keeping of God's commandments [is what really matters] (1 Cor. 7:19).

The new creation brings a new canon, a new standard of judgment, along with it. This is above all redemptive-historical in nature. It does not mean exemption from the law, or "Christian autonomy," but life in accordance with the rule of the new and no longer of the old. This can also be called faith that is active through love; or the keeping of God's commandments; or, as it is said in a similar pronouncement in Philippians 3:3, serving God by the Spirit. The combination of these pronouncements is so interesting because the canon given with the new creation (Gal. 6:16) appears to represent the category of the law (1 Cor. 7:19) as well as those of love (Gal. 5:6) and of the Spirit (Phil. 3:3). There is thus present a reciprocal definition and delimiting of motives. It can appear on the one hand that the law once given is no longer all-important. The content of the will of God is also determined from Christ as the Inaugurator of the new creation. Therefore to serve God by the Spirit means not only a new possibility of performing the law, but also a new view of the law, that of faith in the fulfilling work of Christ. For this reason the Christian life can be qualified as a "spiritual service" (logikē latreia), in which the sacrificial service no longer consists (as in the law) in the offering of sacrificial animals, but of the living self-sacrifice of believers (Rom. 12:1, 2), and holiness and blemishlessness no longer consist in that which is external and in the flesh, but in what is inward and in the Spirit (Phil. 3:3; Rom. 1:9), and in the liturgy of faith (Phil. 2:17). On the other hand, this "spiritualness" is nothing other than the work of love and the keeping of the commandments and ordinances of God.

That it does not come here to a precise delimitation of what is new and old, of what has been done away and what retains its validity, is surely characteristic of the new situation. This also puts an end to the "legalistic" view of life in the sense that the law would cover all "cases" of the Christian life and the right use of the law would consist only in a logical particularizing of the individual pronouncements of the law. Over against this, however, stands the fact that the whole of the law and the whole of life must be understood in the light of the salvation revealed with Christ, and that insight into the will of God for concrete life situations is no less dependent on faith in Christ, being led by the Spirit, and the inner renewal of man than on the knowledge of the law. As little as one may not divorce the former from the latter (see above), so little may the reverse take place.

That — finally — the apostle does not give the transient and the abiding, the special and the general aspects of the law in more detail, will have to be explained from the fact that he wanted to make the church understand its own responsibility and spiritual activity in these things and that in the new situation in which the young gentile churches found themselves he not only wished to be helpful to them in terms of spiritual counsel and instruction, but also endeavored to bring them to moral and spiritual independence. Those pronouncements point to this, for example, which insist on "proving" the will of God, "distinguishing" those things which "matter," etc.:

> ...and be not conformed to this world, but be transformed by the renewing of your mind, that you may discern what the will of God is, that which is good and well-pleasing and perfect (Rom. 12:2).
> And this I pray, that your love may abound yet more and more in insight and all perception, in order to discern the things that really matter (Phil. 1:9, 10).
> For this cause we...do not cease to pray...for you, that you may be filled with the knowledge of his will in all wisdom and spiritual insight (Col. 1:9).
> Therefore do not be foolish, but understand what the will of the Lord is (Eph. 5:17).

From these pronouncements, which can be augmented with others, it is evident that for knowledge of the will of God the right inner disposition must be present. These pronouncements, which speak of inner renewal, perception, etc., to be asked of God in order to distinguish the things that really "matter" (ta diapheronta) and what the will of God is, etc., are a remarkable parallel to what is said in Romans 2 of Judaism, which boasted in the possession of the law, not only as the means of salvation but also as the source of knowledge for the will of God, and which is addressed by Paul as follows: "You know the Will and are able to distinguish the things that really matter, because you are instructed in the law; you are confident that you are a guide of the blind, a light for those who are in darkness, a corrector of the foolish, an instructor of children, having in the law the embodiment of the knowledge of the truth."

Over against this proud consciousness of having the law, knowing "the Will," and being able to distinguish the things that really matter, the purport of Paul's exhortations to the church is unmistakable. And that not only because these churches as yet stood only at the beginning and had not yet reached maturity in the knowledge of the will of God (cf. Col. 4:12); likewise not only because for them the law no longer applied to the same extent as for the Jews and they therefore could not appeal in the same measure to the written word of God for knowledge of the will of God; but above all because for this knowledge of the will of God that inner renewal and illumination is necessary of which Paul speaks again and again with such great emphasis. This does not mean that the "givenness" of the will of God in the law is repudiated or set aside, but the right application of what may count as "God's commandments" is made dependent on an inner condition that is conformable to the content of the commandment of God. In that sense it must certainly be said that being led by the Spirit, that prayer and faith are no less necessary for the knowledge of the will of God than exact attention to the commandments and ordinances of the law of God as the holy and spiritual expression of his will.

SECTION 47. LIBERTY AND CONSCIENCE

The question should be answered in this connection as to how the conscience functions in the life set at liberty by Christ and what significance must be ascribed to it for knowing the will of God.

"Conscience" in general has for Paul the meaning of "knowing one's self," in the sense of moral self-judgment. Thus, for example, in Romans 2:15, where it is first said of the gentiles that "the work [i.e., the requirement][79] of the law is written in their hearts," which is then amplified with the words: "while their conscience also bears witness and their thoughts accuse or else excuse one another among themselves."

The last words are in our view to be understood of the inner man;[80] at the same time they give an elucidation of the function of the conscience: to accuse or to acquit. In 1 Corinthians 4:4; Romans 9:1; 2 Corinthians 1:12 the apostle also speaks of his conscience as an agency that exonerates him, and elsewhere in a less characteristic but more conventional sense of a "good" or "pure" conscience (1 Tim. 1:5, 19; 3:9; 2 Tim. 1:3, et al.).

This conscience is such an influential "witness" in man because it makes him understand that the requirement by which he is bound is a transcendent agency. Thus Paul says in Romans 13:5 that we must be subject to the governing authorities "for conscience' sake," which, as appears from the whole context, is motivated by the fact that the authorities represent a divine ordinance. As a result conscience is approximately the consciousness in man that in his moral activity he is bound to a divine standard of judgment standing above him, by which he has to measure himself.

It is clear that the freedom given in Christ, both in its significance as acquitting and as leading to new obedience, also has its reflec-

---

79. Cf. my Rom., p. 61.

80. Others are of the opinion that it is a matter here of the moral judgment of the community; so, e.g., Greijdanus, Rom., I, p. 145; Gutbrod, Die paulinische Anthropologie, p. 56; Schlatter, Gottes Gerechtigkeit, p. 93. Against this view see Zahn, Römer, p. 126; Lietzmann, Rom., p. 41; Bultmann, Theology, I, p. 217. A very special notion is defended by B. Reicke, TZ, 1956, pp. 157-161. One must here think of the arguments Paul adduces in his missionary preaching against the gentiles. One would take the preceding syneidēseōs as "feeling for," and the whole would then run: "what their feeling — even among one another — for the accusing or also for the excusing thoughts confirms" (ibid., p. 160), in our view (already because of the absolute, not further specified use one must attribute to tōn logismōn and the hereby certainly very strange interpolation: kai metaxu allēlōn) a not very satisfying explanation.

tion in the conscience. Thus Paul speaks in Romans 9:1 of the testimony of his conscience "in the Holy Spirit"; that is to say, in the inner self-judgment of his conscience he knows himself to be led and governed by the Holy Spirit. And elsewhere he places conscience in close relationship to faith, when in one breath he speaks of "a pure heart, a good conscience, and an unfeigned faith" (1 Tim. 1:5), of waging the good warfare "with faith and a good conscience" (1 Tim. 1:19), and of keeping "the mystery of the faith in a pure conscience" (1 Tim. 3:9). Liberty in Christ by the Spirit thus consists in the liberation of the conscience, in that it takes away the consciousness of guilt and gives the believer the awareness of being led in his speech and actions by the Holy Spirit. The conscience thus liberated then stands as "good" and "pure" over against the "accusing" and "defiled" conscience of those who have not escaped the guilt and power of sin (cf. Tit. 1:15; Rom. 2:15). For this reason the good conscience, just as the entire freedom of the new life in Christ, can occur under the viewpoint of the indicative, the gift of redemption, as well as under that of the imperative, the obligation it implies (cf. 2 Cor. 1:12; 1 Tim. 1:5, 19; 3:9).

Of particular importance for this point is what is said about the conscience in 1 Corinthians, in connection with the objection of some Christians against the eating of sacrificial food, and to a similar effect, if without mention of the word "conscience,"[81] in Romans 14. It is declared of these Christians in 1 Corinthians 8:7: "but some, because being hitherto accustomed to the idol,[82] eat [the meat] as meat offered to an idol; and their conscience, being weak, is defiled." The same mention of "the weak conscience" or "the conscience of the weak" is repeated in verses 10-12. This "weakness" of the conscience consists in the fact that it is easily "defiled," that is to say, quickly calls forth the consciousness of having sinned. Those who are thus "weak" are in danger of stumbling over all kinds of stones of offense that could be placed in their way.[83] It is said, therefore, that the "strong" who by their example incite the weak (v. 10) to do that in which these do not feel themselves at liberty make themselves guilty of becoming a "stumbling block" (v. 9), "wound" the conscience of the weak, and cause them "to stumble" (vv. 12, 13). The consequence could be that the weak "perish" (v. 11), by giving themselves up to that which their conscience condemns as

---

81. For this different usage in Rom. 14 and 1 Cor. 8 see, e.g., J. Dupont, *Gnosis. La connaissance religieuse dan les Épitres de Saint Paul*, pp. 279ff.

82. The text is not certain. Some read with D and some old Latin and Syriac texts *syneidēsei* (see also Nestle and the Dutch Bible Society); so, e.g., L. Batelaan, *De sterken en zwakken in de kerk van Korinthe*, 1942, pp. 21ff. In our opinion the preference is to be given to the reading *synētheia;* so most of the more recent scholars; see for the arguments, e.g., Lietzmann-Kümmel, Grosheide, J. Héring, *The First Epistle of St. Paul to the Corinthians*, ET 1962, p. 72. For the translation see Arndt-Gingrich-Bauer, p. 797, *s.v. synētheia.*

83. On the concept "weak" in detail see Dupont, *Gnosis*, pp. 272-282. He compares the Hellenistic-Greek notion of "weakness" (in connection with conscience) with the biblical, and concludes that Paul's usage must be understood in connection with the latter. "Weak" here has the connotation of sin, otherwise than in Greek thought where it points to a lack of strength of character or philosophical insight.

sin (v. 10). The passage concerning the strong and the weak in 1 Corinthians 10:23-33 also starts from these presuppositions.

The train of thought of 1 Corinthians 10:27-30 especially is not entirely transparent. It is clear that Paul does not find it necessary for conscience' sake to inquire after the nature of the meat that one has set before him even though it is an unbeliever who invites him to dinner (v. 27). Likewise, that the matter is different when someone— probably a "weak" brother is intended here[84] — says: this is meat offered to idols. Then one will refrain from eating for the sake of the one who informed him and for the sake of conscience (v. 28). Verse 29 gives a clarification: I do not mean your own conscience, but that of the other. It then follows, however: "for why should my liberty be judged by another man's conscience?" Must this question (possibly with that of v. 30?) be taken as an objection of one who is at liberty?[85] Others are of the opinion that these words are rather explanatory of the preceding words: "I do not now mean my own conscience."[86] The "for" in verse 29 seems to commend this view. Verse 30 is also understood variously: either as the continuation of the question of the objector, or as the continuation of Paul's explanation in verse 29 that he does not intend his own conscience; or also as an answer of Paul to the question of verse 29, taken as an objection (the train of thought is then: why — so someone will say — must I abandon my liberty for another? Paul's counter-question is: why should I give someone else occasion to speak evil of me in a matter that I myself enjoy with thanksgiving?).[87] The last conception seems unacceptable to us because in this way justice is not done to the "eating with thanksgiving" expressed with such emphasis. The most probable appears to be that in both verses Paul is continuing to speak in order to make clear that yielding to the "weak" brother does not imply relinquishing one's own liberty. If on the other hand one chooses to take both verses as an objection of a third party, then the concluding verse 31 can follow directly upon them only with difficulty.[88] At the same time the interpretation of this train of thought is not decisive for the correct conception of what Paul understands by conscience.

How much this judgment of conscience in the believer is bound up with his new mode of existence as a believer is evident as well from the paraenesis in Romans 14, which is occupied with problems of the same sort. Here "the weak" are expressly termed "the weak in faith" (v. 1; cf. v. 15). In this context the apostle also says that everyone must so act that he "is fully convinced in his own mind *(nous)*."[89] What is denoted in 1 Corinthians 8 and 10 with "conscience" is here called

84. Cf., e.g., Robertson-Plummer, *A Critical and Exegetical Commentary on the First Epistle of St. Paul to the Corinthians*, 2nd ed., 1929, p. 221; Gutbrod, *Anthropologie*, p. 65; Grosheide, *1 Cor.*, p. 282. Others understand by it the heathen host (e.g., Bultmann, *Theology*, I, p. 219), or a heathen partaker of the meal (e.g., Wendland, *Cor.*, p. 161; Lietzmann-Kümmel, *Cor.*, p. 51).

85. So Lietzmann-Kümmel, *ibid.*, p. 52; Wendland, *ibid.*, p. 61.

86. So Grosheide, *1 Cor.*, pp. 283ff.; Bultmann, *Theology*, I, p. 219.

87. So Gutbrod, *Anthropologie*, p. 65.

88. Lietzmann-Kümmel must agree to this: "To the pointed question we expect a searching answer; but it fails to appear..." *(loc. cit.)*. Has the question then been correctly interpreted, however?

89. *Hekastos en tō idiō noi plērophoreisthō.*

"faith" and "mind" *(nous)*.[90] Therefore no one may put a stumbling block in his brother's way (v. 13), even though that to which he would incite him is not in itself wrong (vv. 14, 15). For even the clean is wrong for him who eats "with offense"[91] (v. 20). The words "with offense" therefore are as much as to say "with a bad conscience,"[92] in the consciousness of "not being blameless before God." And at the conclusion of Romans 14 the expression "faith" is employed once again for this knowing oneself to be free (v. 22).

To this acting with a free conscience Paul finally joins a beatitude. The meaning is not that everyone is blessed who acts only without inner self-accusation and with a conscience that acquits him, but that in such cases as are here under discussion only those may be assured of the favor of God who do not act against their conscience.[93] For here too, without the word being employed, the conscience is intended. Accordingly it follows in verse 23 that he who doubts when he eats *(ho de diakrinomenos),* namely, whether he does indeed do well to eat,[94] is (therein already) condemned. For he is not acting from faith, and all that is not of faith is sin (v. 23). Here not-doubting and not-accusing-oneself (in other words, the good conscience) is again denoted as faith (cf. vv. 1, 2, 22); this is not to say that "faith" and "conscience" mean the same thing and that all who do not believe act with a bad conscience. The meaning is that for a Christian not a single decision and action can be good which he does not think he can justify on the ground of his Christian conviction and his liberty before God in Christ (cf. 1 Cor. 10:29).[95]

In summary, freedom in Christ is mirrored in the conscience insofar as the believer knows himself to have been cleansed from sin and in what he does receives the assurance of being blameless before God. This liberty makes him independent of the judgment of men (cf. 1 Cor. 10:29) and consists positively in inner certainty (Rom. 14:5), in not condemning oneself, not doubting, in the faith in which his moral decisions and actions take place (Rom. 14:22, 23). In the "con-

---

90. For *nous* see above, pp. 117ff.

91. *Dia proskommatos. Dia* indicates the attendant circumstance (cf. Bl.-Debr., Par. 223,3). The translation of the RSV (and the Dutch Bible Society): "it is wrong for anyone to make others fall by what he eats," seems to me less correct.

92. Cf. the translation of Lietzmann, *Rom., in loc.*

93. Others are of the opinion that *ho mē krinōn heauton* does not speak of a good conscience but, more objectively, of not holding oneself guilty: "he who has nothing to reproach himself for in his decisions" (so, e.g., Michel, with an appeal to Lietzmann, *et al.*). These words, however, correspond in our view with *ho de diakrinomenos;* see below.

94. "The *diakrinomenos* is the one who has no certainty as regards either his judgment or his action, who does with a bad conscience what he cannot refrain from doing, who is inwardly at odds with himself" (Büchsel, *TDNT*, III, pp. 947f., *s.v. diakrinō*).

95. Cf. Greijdanus: "faith ... according to its effect is a firm conviction .. with regard to that which is lawful in God's name ..." (*Rom.,* II, p. 615); also Bultmann, *TDNT*, VI, pp. 218f., *s.v. pisteuō:* "in the Christian *pisteuein* works itself out in knowledge of what he has to do in a given situation.... Though all believers stand in the one *pistis*, judgment may differ as to what they should do or not do, since *pisteuein* has to be worked out in individual life." See also Dupont, *Gnosis*, p. 370.

science" (respectively "faith") the believer knows himself bound to God, and he shares in the consciousness of the liberty obtained by Christ and given by the Spirit before God. This explains the great emphasis on not defiling one's own or another's conscience. For thereby communion with Christ is threatened, and the salvation of the believer is at stake (Rom. 14:15; 1 Cor. 8:11).

In this paraenesis it is not therefore a matter in the first place of knowing the will of God, but of the consciousness of being blameless before God.[96] The scope of Romans 14 and 1 Corinthians 8 is not so much ethical as religious. Paul clearly distinguishes between the requirement of God and the verdict of conscience (Rom. 14:14; 1 Cor. 8:8; 10:26). He who acts against his conscience sins, because in his decision and action he lets go of Christ. But this is not reversible, as though the good conscience were now able morally to sanction the actions of man. It is a question of respecting "the weak conscience" in a pastoral-religious sense, not of legitimating the conscience in an ethical sense. Rather those who are convinced, the "strong" in conscience, are warned not to be mistaken in that which in their view is permitted to them (1 Cor. 6:12ff.; 10:23ff.). The conscience is thus not the instance that enables the believer to know the will of God in his moral decisions, but which in these decisions reminds him of the judgment of God and of the necessity in them of preserving inviolate before the judgment of God the liberty wrought by Christ.

In this context, finally, an observation should be made on 1 Corinthians 4:1-4. Paul there declares that the judgment men pass on the conduct of his ministry affects him very little. Indeed, he does not pass judgment on himself. For even though he is himself conscious of no wrong (ouden emautō synoida), he is not thereby justified. He who judges him is the Lord.

In distinction from the older exegesis in the Reformation tradition, according to which the apostle is said to speak here of the inadequacy of the judgment of conscience, most of the new commentaries hold the view that the point of the argument is somewhat differently directed. It is not one's own pure conscience but the coming judgment of God, not the servant himself but the Lord, who will give judgment and distribute the palm of honor.[97]

In our view this latter exegesis is correct. Paul does not here speak so much of the inadequacy as indeed of the incompetence of his own conscience to justify him before men as the servant of the Lord. The words "But I am not thereby justified" therefore point away toward the judgment of the Lord as the only authority competent to justify Paul, also before men. One may indeed ask himself whether still another idea is

---

96. Bultmann, *Theology*, I, p. 219, interprets this to mean that it is only in the decision of conscience in the presence of a transcendental power standing over him that man truly becomes man, his ego "constitutes" itself, and he therefore reaches freedom precisely in the conscience. But this is to introduce an existentialistic concept of man and liberty entirely foreign to the text.

97. On the exegesis of this passage cf. in detail P. Althaus, *Paulus und Luther über den Menschen,* 2nd ed., 1951, pp. 96ff.

not also involved,[98] namely, that the conscience of man, though it is not conscious of any wrong, is never able to be the basis on which one can justify himself before others and himself, because the divine judgment goes much deeper and alone is infallible. In this case it would emerge the more clearly that the judgment of conscience can never be the end of all dispute. The liberty given in Christ therefore is mirrored in the conscience not as liberty from moral decision, but as freedom from guilt before God. That which is characteristic of Christian liberty of conscience does not lie in the sphere of the forming of moral judgments, but in that of the religious relationship to God.

SECTION 48. LOVE

The content of the new obedience, in the epistles of Paul too, finds its most central and fundamental expression in love. Nowhere is it more apparent than here how much Paul is not only the proclaimer of the death and resurrection of Christ, but also the one who continues Jesus' own preaching.[99]

This central significance of love in Paul's preaching of the new life can be shown in various ways. Just as faith can be called the mode of existence of the new life,[100] so also can love. Faith works itself out in love (Gal. 5:6). "To be rooted in Christ" can also be described as "to be rooted in love" (cf. Col. 2:7 and Eph. 3:17). "To belong to the new creation" can also be expressed as "faith working itself out in love" (cf. Gal. 6:15 and 5:6). Love is mentioned together with faith and hope as the real heart and content of the Christian life (1 Cor. 13:13; 1 Thess. 1:3; Col 1:4; Gal. 5:5ff.; cf. 1 Tim. 6:11; 2 Tim. 3:10; Tit. 2:2). Love is the first fruit of the Spirit (Gal. 5:22; cf. Rom. 15:30; Col. 1:8). Love therefore explains what it means to be in Christ, to be in the Spirit, to be in the faith. In it is realized the freedom from sin, to which believers have been called in Christ (Gal. 5:13); in it the demand of the law is fulfilled, which has become possible by the Spirit (Rom. 13:10; cf. Rom. 8:4); it is the content of the law of Christ (Gal. 6:2). In a word, the new life is realized in love, it is in its way the life of the re-creation, the eschatological mode of existence,[101] the pattern of believers in the time of redemption that has appeared with Christ (Rom. 13:10ff.; cf. Gal. 6:10).

In the first place this love derives its central significance from the fact that it is the reflection of the love of God in Jesus Christ. This becomes clear not only in those pronouncements in which, with an appeal to the love of God or of Christ, believers are stirred up to love

---

98. On this see also the citations from the commentaries of P. Bachmann, Schlatter in Althaus, *ibid.*, pp. 100, 101.

99. Cf., e.g., C. A. A. Scott, *New Testament Ethics*, 1948, pp. 76ff.

100. See above, Section 40.

101. Cf., e.g., Stauffer, *TDNT*, I, pp. 50ff., *s.v. agapaō*; Bultmann, *Theology*, I, p. 344; G. Bornkamm, *Early Christian Experience*, p. 188; C. Spicq, "l'Agapè de I Cor. XIII," *Ephemerides Theologicae Lovanienses*, p. 368.

one another as well (cf., e.g., Phil. 2:1, 2, 5ff.; Eph. 5:2, 25; Rom. 12:1, 9ff.), but also where love serves as the evidence of having been known by God in love. It is in that sense surely that we will have to take the pronouncement of 1 Corinthians 8:3: "If any man loves God, he is known by him."

"Being known by God" refers to the gracious and loving electing act of God; "to be known" by him in this way means the same as to have been chosen by him and loved by him (cf. Gal. 4:9; 1 Cor. 13:12; Eph. 1:6).[102] This divine love works itself out in the love of those known by him. Therefore the love of the church is a gift of God (1 Thess. 3:12; 2 Thess. 3:5). Here the link between love and sanctification also becomes visible. As it is the divine love by which he sanctified and appropriated the church to himself in Christ, so love is the sanctification with which the church is to dedicate itself to God, its spiritual service (Rom. 12:1, 9-21). The love of God revealed in Christ's self-surrender and working itself out by the Holy Spirit in the love of the church is the real secret and the clearest expression of its holiness; just as, conversely, in the expression of this love the church exhibits the evidence of having been chosen by God and placed on his side.

In the second place this love constitutes the vital element of the church. It is in love that the body, of which Christ is the Head, is built up (Eph. 4:15, 16), in which believers together are rooted and grounded (Eph. 3:17). For this reason love can be called the bond of perfection (Col. 3:14); indeed in its own way it forms the unity of the church (Col. 2:2). The application of the commandment of love consequently has in Paul the clear effect of stirring up the strong awareness in the church of mutual responsibility, of together forming a unity, and thus of pressing love into the service of the building up of the church. The church is to be a brotherhood and to live out of the consciousness of being a unique fellowship. Here again there is the clear relationship between love and sanctification. As a fellowship sanctified and appropriated by God to himself, the church is bound together and set apart by love. This structure of the Pauline idea of love admits of being demonstrated positively as well as negatively in many ways.

To be sure, we find the description "love of the brethren" (philadelphia) only a few times in Paul (Rom. 12:10; 1 Thess. 4:9); but when he writes concerning love he appears almost always to allude to this reciprocal, mutually edifying love of believers.[103] The liberty in Christ must show itself especially in this, that believers are to be servants one of another through love (Gal. 5:13). They are to owe one another nothing except love (Rom. 13:8). In all things they are to inquire after that which can serve to mutual edification and benefit (1 Cor. 14:26; 1 Thess. 5:11; Rom. 14:19). If any appeal may be made to them in Christ, if there is any fellowship of the Spirit, this is to appear in their unanimity, their oneness in demonstration of love, in oneness of soul and oneness of purpose, in not only attending to their own interests,

102. Cf., e.g., Bultmann, *TDNT*, I, pp. 709ff., *s.v. ginōskō;* G. Bornkamm, *Early Christian Experience*, pp. 185f.; J. Dupont, *Gnosis*, p. 53.
103. Cf. Enslin, *The Ethics of Paul*, pp. 241ff.

but also to those of others (Phil. 2:1ff.). Faith in Christ must go together with love toward all the saints (Col. 1:4), in being knit together in love (Col. 2:2).

For this reason the apostle time and again takes the field against every form of spiritual individualism; and that not only as this shows itself in coarse and unvarnished egoism, in the animosity and hatred of one man toward another, as, for example, this manifests itself among the gentiles (Rom. 1:29ff.), and which he describes under all kinds of specifications as "the works of the flesh" (Gal. 5:19, 20); he fears the continuation of that, too, in the church (2 Cor. 12:20), and he warns against it repeatedly in the so-called "catalogues of vices" (cf., e.g., Eph. 4:31; Col. 3:5ff.). In particular, however, he points to the more refined forms of individualism and self-direction as these crop up, for example, in certain spiritualistic phenomena in the church. We have some striking illustrations of these especially in the First Epistle to the Corinthians, but also in the Epistle to the Romans.

The first has reference to the individualistic experiencing of Christian liberty. The apostle sets over against this in general the fact that liberty in Christ must manifest itself in mutual Christian service through love (Gal. 5:13). In the familiar passages on "the strong" and "the weak" in 1 Corinthians 8-10 and Romans 14, he now gives an application of that principle which is highly characteristic of his conception of liberty and love. For although he recognizes the freedom of Christians on the one hand, also in the use of meat and drink, etc., with an appeal to love he warns against every individualistic and spiritualistic application of this liberty, namely, whenever this might give the weak in faith an occasion to sin. If in that case "the strong" would not wish to impose restrictions on themselves, they would be sinning against love, that is to say, against that which is to be subservient to the building up, the spiritual unity of the church. Here love stands over against the "knowledge" out of which the strong live:

> Knowledge puffs up, but love builds up (1 Cor. 8:2).
> All things are lawful, but not all things build up. Let no man seek his own, but that which is the other's (1 Cor. 10:23, 24).
> For if your brother is grieved by what you eat, you are no longer walking according to the requirement of love (Rom. 14:15).

The second example is in the same line and directs itself likewise against spiritual individualism. It has bearing on the relationship of love and the special *charismata* revealing themselves in the church. On the one hand there is mention here of what the church has received in its several members by way of spiritual gifts; on the other hand of the danger that the principle of self-direction and individualism is strengthened in this diversity of *charismata*. Paul now deals firmly with this, especially in 1 Corinthians 12 and 13. Nowhere does love emerge more clearly than here in its character as binding together and involving the church. We have Paul's struggle against spiritual individualism in the Christian church to thank for the celebrated chapters, 1 Corinthians 12 and 13.

In 1 Corinthians 12 he draws his argument from the unity of the body; as its members each for its part and in its own place together form one body, so believers in their various gifts and abilities form the unity of the body of Christ; they also must be conscious of this mutual fellowship and conduct themselves accordingly. This does not take away their individuality, and every one of them may aspire to the highest *charismata* (v. 31). Yet having reached this point of his admonition, he points beyond all these *charismata* and shows a way that is still more excellent,[104] and leads higher still than the zeal for all manner of *charismata*, that is, the way of love (1 Cor. 13).

Against this love even the most excellent *charismata* count for nothing — not speaking in tongues, not insight into the divine mysteries or *gnosis*, not faith to do miracles or utterly to abandon all that one has and is. Without love even one who possessed all these gifts would have to say of himself:

> . . . I am become sounding brass or a clanging cymbal.
> . . . I am nothing.
> . . . it profits me nothing.

Just because love, even as faith and hope, is the mode of existence of the Christian church, it must reveal itself in this bond to the brethren, in placing itself at the service of this upbuilding; therefore Christian love is not individualistic, proudly separative, but always above everything else concerned with the body and not the individual. For this reason to lack this love means to be nothing, with whatever brilliant *charismata* one may be endowed. For without love there is no communion with the body, in which alone a share in Christ is to be found.

Finally, it holds for love, in distinction from the *charismata*, that it never perishes. For it is not in the *charismata* that the church is rooted and grounded, but in love. And the *charismata* do not constitute the vital element of the body of Christ, the power that binds it together, but love. The breakthrough of the reality that has dawned in Christ also manifests itself in the *charismata*, and as such they constitute a possibility of entrance[105] to that which will one day be the portion of believers in perfection. However, they are again to be rendered inoperative[106] and disappear (vv. 8-10). They represent the period of immaturity, they do not lead to a real and adequate knowledge of what is to come and are as temporary possibilities doomed to pass away (vv. 11ff.). But it is not so with love. With faith and hope it has an abiding[107] significance, indeed it is the greatest of these three. For love consists

---

104. With most scholars *eti kath' hyperbolēn* will have to be taken as predicate with *hodon* and not in apposition to *deiknymi*, as Schlatter wishes; cf. for the reading and translation of this by no means easy passage Lietzmann-Kümmel, *Cor.*, p. 65 and esp. p. 188; Michaelis, *TDNT*, V, p. 85, *s.v. hodos.*

105. Cf. Michaelis, *TDNT*, V, p. 85, n. 153.

106. *Katargeō* (four times in 1 Cor. 13:8-11!) by way of indicating what will remain and what will perish with the mode of existence of this aeon; cf. Delling, *TDNT*, I, p. 453, *s.v.*

107. See also above, p. 250.

not only in the relationship to the salvation of the Lord (as faith and hope), but in it salvation is already realized[108] as the re-creation of human life in the communion of the body of Christ. For this reason love, although not possible without faith and hope, is nevertheless the greatest. And it is that not only in its individual appearance, but, as is evident from the whole context of 1 Corinthians 12 and 13, above all on account of the unity manifesting itself in it of the church appropriated to himself by God, the body of Christ, the temple of the Holy Spirit.

The particularizing of this love constitutes a large part of the content of the Pauline paraenesis. The one love unfolds itself in a great many "forms of love,"[109] especially in 1 Corinthians 13:4-7 and in Romans 12:9-21, but in a series of separate exhortations as well. In addition to love, Paul speaks, for example, of peace *(eirēnē)*, steadfastness *(makrothymia)*, kindness *(chrēstotēs)*, goodness *(agathōsynē)*, faithfulness *(pistis)*, gentleness *(prautēs)*, compassion *(oiktirmos)*, humility *(tapeinophrosynē)*, forbearing *(anachesthai)*, forgiving *(charizesthai)*, thinking about that which is true *(alēthē)*, just *(dikaia)*, honorable *(semna)*, pure *(hagna)*, lovely *(prosphilē)*, sweet-sounding *(euphēma)*, obligingness *(epieikeia)* (cf., e.g., Gal. 5:22, 23; Phil. 4:8; Col. 3:12-15; Phil. 4:5, *et al.*). Of all these concepts and descriptions some are more, others less "specifically Christian." These virtues, however, even though they occur in the same terms in the non-Christian Greek ethic, in Paul's epistles are always brought under the viewpoint of brotherly communion and the upbuilding of the church, and not, as in the Greek ethic, under that of character formation;[110] they are always understood therefore as the fulfillment of the requirement of love and thus approached from the liberty and obedience in Christ.

The concept humility *(tapeinophrosynē)*, for example, has a specifically Christian content (Phil. 2:3; Col. 3:12; cf. Rom. 12:16; 2 Cor. 7:6). This word, which occurs only sporadically outside the New Testament and then *in sensu malo*,[111] has its roots in the Old Testament, but is closely related by Paul to the self-humiliating love of Christ (cf. Phil. 2:3 and 8), and is further defined as "counting each other better than oneself" (Phil. 2:3), "not reaching out toward high things, but associating with the lowly" (Rom. 12:16), "in honor giving one another precedence"[112] (Rom. 12:10). In this humility it is a matter, therefore, not of one's relationship to God (as, for example, in 2 Cor. 7:6),[113] but of a certain manifestation, inspired by the example and self-surrender of Christ and therefore specifically Christian, of mutual love in the church. The antithesis is pride *(hypsēla phronein;* Rom. 11:20), self-conceit *(kenodoxia)*, and selfishness

---

108. Cf. Bultmann, *Theology*, I, p. 344.

109. Cf. G. Brillenburg Wurth, *Gestalten der Liefde*, 1953.

110. Cf., e.g., Bultmann, *Theology*, II, p. 225.

111. Cf. Arndt-Gingrich-Bauer, p. 812, *s.v.*; Enslin, *The Ethics of Paul*, p. 259.

112. *Tē timē proēgeisthai allēlous.* The translation is otherwise not settled; cf. in addition to the commentaries, e.g., Arndt-Gingrich-Bauer, pp. 712f., *s.v. proēgeomai;* Bl.-Debr., Par. 150*.

113. Where, however, there is mention not of *tapeinophrosynē*, but of *tapeinos:* lowly.

(*eritheia;* Phil. 2:3), imagining oneself to be something while he is nothing. Instead one must pay heed to himself and test his own works (Gal. 6:3).

Closely connected with humility is meekness. This manifestation of mutual love, too, is related to the example of Christ (2 Cor. 10:1). It is repeatedly mentioned in close association with "humility" (Eph. 4:2; Col. 3:12), as also with "gentleness" (*epieikeia;* 2 Cor. 10:1; Tit. 3:2). Its typical Christian form is found as well in Galatians 6:1ff., where the reclaiming without pride of those who have fallen into sin is termed a proof of a spiritual disposition and of the spirit of meekness. It consists in the bearing of one another's difficulties (in the sense of sins, difficult qualities with which one has to wrestle) and is in this way the fulfilling of the law of Christ. This meekness — the being "poor in spirit" of the Gospels — is not borne by a feeling of superiority in which one is able to bow down, but by the consciousness of being able in no respect whatever to raise oneself above another. It is the meekness of humility and shows therein the Christian character.[114]

Although a further analysis of Paul's paraenesis to mutual love could produce still more points of view, in our opinion the most distinctive of them have already been pointed out in what has been said above. The willingness to place oneself at the service of another, not raising oneself above him, in all things being mindful of the building up of the church, repeatedly come to the fore. This character of Christian love finds its most eloquent expression in the central section of 1 Corinthians 13:

> Love suffers long, it is kind.
> Love is not jealous, love does not vaunt itself.
> It is not puffed up, it does not behave itself unseemly,
> it does not seek its own, it does not become embittered,
> it does not take account of evil.
> It does not rejoice in unrighteousness, but rejoices in the truth.
> It covers all things, it believes all things,
> it hopes all things, it endures all things....

We have to do here, not with a current or traditional schema, but with an individual, deeply penetrating formulation of the commandment of love by Paul himself. On the one hand a great "humanity" and a matured psychological insight become manifest, whereby the concrete significance of what love is is not expressed in lofty generalities, but pointed out in the concrete relationships of man to man. On the other hand, it is clear from this giving of concrete form to the commandment of love that the apostle not only intends and sees before him individual men, but that his canticle of love is inspired by the new reality of the church as the body of Christ and the temple of the Holy Spirit.

With the above the question has in substance already been answered as to the object of the Christian manifestation of love. Paul speaks of

---

114. On the various virtues see still further Enslin, *The Ethics of Paul*, pp. 265ff.

it almost always from the viewpoint of relationships within the Christian church and of the building up of this congregational brotherhood as the body of Christ.

Only seldom does he speak explicitly of love for God, although this is not entirely lacking (Rom. 8:28; 1 Cor. 2:9; 8:3; Eph. 6:24 [love for Christ]). In a certain sense this can be called accidental since for Paul, too, love for God was the fundamental principle of true religion (cf. Deut. 6:4, 5; Matt. 22:38; Mark 12:29); and reconciliation to God, the restoration of the relationship of love, the great content of his gospel (Rom. 5:10ff.; 2 Cor. 5:20; cf. Rom. 8:7, 8). Nevertheless, it is remarkable[115] that even when he speaks of love as the fulfilling of the law, he only has love for one's neighbor in view (Rom. 13:8-10; Gal. 5:14), and that 1 Corinthians 13, too, seems to have to be understood specifically of love for one's neighbor. The cause will surely have to be sought in that, just as love for one's neighbor springs altogether from the new relationship of love between God and believers in Christ and cannot for a moment be considered as an independent "love of neighbor" or "philanthropy," so also, conversely, love for God shows itself in particular in love for one's neighbor. There is here a double command-ment, but no double love. That which in love for God transcends love for one's neighbor, however, finds its expression in a number of other descriptions. In this connection, for example, the numerous doxologies should be pointed out with which the apostle time and again interrupts or concludes his argument (cf., e.g., Rom. 7:25; 9:5; 11:33, et al.), as also the large place he ascribes to prayer, and specifically to thanks-giving in the Christian life.[116] That he says comparatively little con-cerning love for God certainly does not rest on a material disproportion in this respect. At most, one can say that the terminology of love is to be understood in particular of love for one's neighbor.

Of no less importance, finally, is the question as to the manner in which love for one's neighbor is applied specifically to one's non-Christian neighbor ("those who are without" [hoi exō]; 1 Cor. 5:12, 13; Col. 4:5; 1 Thess. 4:12). Two things are to be pointed out here. In the first place it is evident in various ways that Paul extends the command-ment of love as widely as possible and that every suggestion that this commandment holds only for Christians among themselves is entirely foreign to him. In 1 Thessalonians 3:12 he prays that the Lord may make believers "to increase and abound in love one toward another, and toward all men." And in the same epistle he charges them "always to follow after that which is good, one toward another, and toward all" (5:15). By "following after the good" materially nothing other is in-tended than love (cf. v. 15a; Rom. 13:10; 1 Cor. 14:1). And when twice he speaks of "all," he undoubtedly means by this those who stand out-side the church and come into contact with believers in their daily life (cf. Phil. 4:5). Accordingly he exhorts them to repay no one evil for evil (1 Thess. 5:15a), to aim at what is considered honorable by all men, and, insofar as it is possible and depends on them, to be at peace

115. Cf. Lindsay Dewar, An Outline of New Testament Ethics, pp. 128ff.
116. See also G. Harder, Paulus und das Gebet, 1936.

with all men (Rom. 12:17, 18). The whole pericope of Romans 12:9-21, so important for giving concrete form to the commandment of love, is evidence of the extent to which, in harmony with the commandment of Christ, love is not only to be directed toward the brethren but also toward those who are without, even though these are hostile and perpetrate violence and injustice (vv. 14, 17, 19ff.; cf. 1 Cor. 4:12).

This universality of love comes markedly to the fore notably in the Pastoral Epistles, and in more than one place is linked there with the center of the Christian faith in a very fundamental and impressive way. Prayers, intercessions, and thanksgiving must be made (when the church comes together) "for all men" (1 Tim. 2:1). For that is good and acceptable before God our Savior, who would have all men to be saved and come to a knowledge of the truth (v. 4; cf. 4:10). Likewise the person and work of Christ is the evidence and pattern of this universal love. For as the man Christ Jesus he was the Mediator between God and men, and he gave himself as a ransom for all (1 Tim. 2:5, 6). Similarly the church in the manifestation of its life "in the present world" is always to be conscious of the fact that "the grace of God bringing salvation has appeared to all men" (Tit. 2:11, 12), and therefore is to be gentle and to show meekness "toward all men" (Tit. 3:2). The church is also to be mindful, moreover, that it was "once" without understanding, disobedient, and malicious, and that it was solely the appearing of the kindness and love of God toward men that saved it (Tit. 3:3-5). Even in this striking terminology,[117] which is more associated with the Hellenistic court style than with the usage of the Bible,[118] there is expression of what an all-embracing significance the love of God revealed in Christ and the church's demonstration of love determined by it have in the midst of the surrounding world.

In all this the extent to which the basic motives of Paul's gospel govern all of his preaching, even his paraenesis, comes clearly to light. At the same time it is implied, however, that a fundamental distinction exists between the fellowship of believers among themselves and that with unbelievers. 1 Thessalonians 5:15 speaks of "one toward another, and toward all"; Galatians 6:10 of "toward all men, but especially (malista) toward those who are of the household of faith." This distinction does not point to a first and second "rank" of love — for the former less, for the latter more — but to a differentiation in fellowship and therefore also in the character of showing love. Love for one another in the church is the upbuilding and functioning of the body of Christ, the bond that joins the church sanctified to God together as those who belong to the same family (of God). Love for others is denoted as directed toward those "who are without" (Col. 4:5; 1 Thess. 4:12). This distinction is not removed even when for this showing of love the church is addressed on the basis of the love of God toward men.[119] And even though the church is thereby reminded of its own "once," the thought is never that the same solidarity exists between believers and unbelievers

117. Hē philanthrōpia epephanē tou sōtēros hēmōn Theou.
118. See the commentaries on Tit. 3:4.
119. Cf. Enslin, The Ethics of Paul, pp. 202ff., 237ff.

as between believers and other believers. For the love that is of God cannot attain its end outside fellowship in and love for Christ (1 Cor. 16:22). For this reason the church, even when love of neighbor is demanded of it in its full scope, is always addressed on the ground of what is peculiar to it and not what it has in common with those "who are without"; and for the church the real purpose of the demonstration of wisdom, humanity, love toward others must always be that these may be won for Christ and that the name of God may be praised (cf. 1 Cor. 10:32; 11:1; Phil. 2:15, 16; Col. 4:5, 6; Tit. 2:5, 8, 10).

SECTION 49. LIFE IN THE WORLD

In conjunction with the foregoing those pronouncements of the Pauline paraenesis deserve special attention which have reference in a broader sense to the participation of believers in life in the world. Here again the twofold aspect under which the life of the church is considered in general is of paramount importance. On the one hand, in virtue of their communion with Christ believers belong to the new creation, they have been redeemed from the present aeon and have gone over into the kingdom of Christ (2 Cor. 5:17; Gal. 1:4; Col. 1:13); on the other, they are still in the flesh, and consequently with all their present mode of existence they belong to the present world (Gal. 2:20; 1 Cor. 5:10). It goes without saying that this twofold relationship of the church to the world in which it lives must also determine its ethical conduct. The young Christian churches were thereby faced with all kinds of problems, and in his pastoral admonitions the apostle devoted minute attention to this.

Entirely in harmony with what has already been raised for discussion above, we can observe that these questions, too, are on the one hand viewed from the standpoint of the liberty in Christ, which appears to be of great significance likewise with respect to the life of the church in the world; on the other hand from that of sanctification, in the positive sense of the dedication of life to God, as well as in the negative significance of cleansing from all contamination of sin.

For the first the chapters are again of importance in which "the strong" and "the weak" are spoken of (Rom. 14; 1 Cor. 8-10), as also, though in a somewhat different manner, Paul's fight against the legalistic and ascetic tendencies in the church at Colosse (cf. Col. 2:16ff.), and against the false doctrine intended in the Pastoral Epistles (cf. 1 Tim. 4:3ff.).

Characteristic for the standpoint of those who took a free position on the ground of their Christian faith with respect to participating in life in the world and the enjoyment of earthly goods ("the strong") is the expression "all things are permitted me" (*panta moi exestin;* 1 Cor. 6:12; 10:23), as well as the word employed in that sense — "liberty" (1 Cor. 8:9 [*exousia*]; cf. 9:4-6, 12, 18; 10:29 [*eleutheria*]). Although Paul brings the consciousness of liberty thus expressed under more than one critical point of view (see below), in principle he is in agreement with it: "I know, and am persuaded in the Lord Jesus, that nothing is un-clean of itself" (Rom. 14:14).

From these words it can appear how much the liberty described in them is a matter of faith, proceeding from the knowledge of the Lord Jesus. In 1 Corinthians it is related to the knowledge emphatically thrust into the foreground by the Corinthians (cf. 1 Cor. 8:1ff., 7, 10, 11). However one is to judge of the origin of this terminology,[120] Paul recognizes this knowledge as the foundation for liberty, for by virtue of this knowledge we know that there is but one God and that, whatever mention there may still be of "gods" and "lords," for the church there is but one God the Father and but one Lord Jesus Christ, and that there is therefore liberty to eat everything that is sold in the market-halls, for the earth is the Lord's, and the fullness thereof (1 Cor. 10:23-26).

This same principle of faith, in much sharper language, is opposed to the heresy intended in Colossians, 1 Timothy, and Titus, which led to all sorts of timorousness and superstition in the matter of eating and drinking. In Colosse this heresy was connected with the fear of supernatural "powers" and the "worship of angels," which was then apparently attended with a legalistic-ascetic manner of life. Paul vigor-ously repudiates these prohibitive regulations and slavish prescriptions. He points to Christ as the head of all powers, even of the angels, out-side the area of whose power nothing is situated, not even food and drink. For this reason he qualifies all this scrupulousness and timidity — which easily degenerate into spiritual pride (2:18, 23) — as "worldly" and the invention of men, and he points the church to the death of Christ in which it has been redeemed from this worldly fear and wisdom. It must not "as though still living in the world" (that is to say, as though it had not yet been brought under the dominion of Christ; cf. 1:13) permit all manner of regulations to be imposed on it. And because it no longer lives under this bondage of the world, "handle not and taste not," etc., do not apply to it. The church has been redeemed from this bondage in Christ (2:20, 21).

He brings the same motives to the fore in 1 Timothy 4 and Titus 1, against legalistic-ascetic currents of the same sort. Those who believe and have right knowledge of the truth (cf. 1 Cor. 8:1ff.) look to God as the Creator of what the false teachers forbid use. This holds for eating and drinking and marrying. What in faith and with thanksgiving is received from the hand of God is not to be rejected. It gets its holi-ness through the Word of God that speaks of the redemption of the whole of life, and through prayer in which it is received believingly (1 Tim. 4:1ff.). A clearer rejection of all ascetic, legalistic, and spiri-tualistic motives is not possible than on the ground of these central ideas of the gospel. This is consequently to be seen as the background of the word in Titus 1:15 that to the pure all things are pure, that is, that to him who lives by faith in Christ no gift or food is wrong in itself. For Christ is the Lord of the world, and nothing has been with-drawn from his sovereignty (Col. 1:15ff.; 2:9ff.; 1 Cor. 8:6). This Chris-tian liberty finds its most fundamental and impressive interpretation in

---

120. Cf. above, p. 36.

the words of 1 Corinthians 3:22, 23: "For all things are yours . . . whether the world, or life, or death, or things present, or things to come, all are yours; but you are Christ's; and Christ is God's."

The liberty thus defined also occurs in Paul's epistles, however, under other points of view. We have already seen[121] that especially in 1 Corinthians 8-10 and Romans 14 all this liberty is placed under the discipline of Christian love as the building up of the church of Christ. Next to this stands yet another no less important consideration, namely, that of the holiness of the church and of the obligation to safeguard oneself in this liberty against the contamination of the world. For not only "the weak," but also "the strong" themselves are able to stumble in this liberty. As licentiousness it can become a new power over them. For this reason Paul can say in 1 Corinthians 6:12: "All things are lawful for me, but not all things are profitable. All things are lawful for me, but I will not be enslaved by anything."[122]

One must therefore be careful with this liberty. Paul warns in this connection against extramarital sexual intercourse. Even though it may be true that food and the stomach that ingests the food have no moral significance and only a temporary service, this is not to say that the resultant liberty to eat and to drink is also applicable to the body in general, that is, to surrender it to fornication. Such a conception of liberty, which in essence would mean a new enslavement, is also in conflict with the destiny of the body, namely, both now and in the great future to be for the Lord as a temple of his Spirit (1 Cor. 6:12-20). Elsewhere he says of the eating of (just as of the abstaining from) certain foods that it takes place, as appears from the thanksgiving pronounced in conjunction with it, in the presence and with the acknowledgment of the Lord[123] (Rom. 14:6); indeed, that whether one eats, or drinks, or whatever he does, he is to do all to the glory of God (1 Cor. 10:31). Here, as always, liberty is qualified by submission to the Lord, and must show itself as such. The expression "but not all things are profitable" (*sympherei*; 1 Cor. 6:12) is not therefore to be taken in a narrow, opportunistic sense, but it makes all things conditional on that which it yields to the Lord and his service.

The same thing applies in a still stronger degree when one enters on a terrain where other gods are served. Here, too, one could reason that if an idol is nothing, there is no objection to sitting down to a heathen sacrificial meal, for example, out of social considerations. Paul, however, will have nothing to do with Christian liberty here. He draws a singular distinction between the nothingness of idols and the nevertheless demonic character of the service of idols. Even in general no one is presumptuously to trust to his steadfastness; the example of ancient Israel in the wilderness can serve for a warning (1 Cor. 10:1-11). On this account the ordinary daily association of the church among the

---

121. Cf. above, p. 295.
122. The play on the words in the Greek — *exestin . . . exousiasthēsomai* — gives the thought exactly: the liberty can become a new tyranny.
123. The dative *Kyriō* is not so easy to render precisely; cf. Michel, *Rom.*, p. 302.

heathen must also compel it to caution. Yet this is only a temptation from the side of men, in which believers may rely on the assistance of God (v. 13). It is otherwise, however, if, on the ground of their "knowledge," they participate in the heathen sacrificial meals. For even though an idol is nothing, that does not mean that the demonic powers who incite men to the service of idols may be said to be imaginary. Rather, those who have communion with the worship of idols enter into communion with the demons to whom the heathen sacrifice, whether they know it or not.[124] Here one is faced with an ineluctable dilemma: either the table of Lord, or that of demons. Here every man who appeals to his "knowledge" or to the fact that he is "strong" must ask himself whether he thinks he is "stronger" than God himself, that is,, by willing and doing what God does not will (v. 22).[125]

From these examples the fundamental standpoint with respect to the sharing of the church in the gifts and goods of the world becomes clear on two sides. While one is able to say, on the one hand, that all things without exception are the possession of the church, it is no less true that through Christ and his cross the world has been crucified for believers, and they for the world (Gal. 6:14). This does not mean that Paul has become blind and deaf to all the goods and joys of the world; every ascetic element that seeks sin in the natural and created, or which attempts to further the avoidance of sin by the avoidance of the natural use of things, is alien to him. But it does imply that for him the world in its self-sufficiency, likewise in its legalistic self-righteousness, has received its judgment and has been done away in the cross of Christ, and that he himself therefore no longer is or lives for the world, insofar as he must love or accept it outside Christ.

Attention should still be devoted in this context to the association of believers with "those who are without." In discussing the requirement of love we have already seen[126] that this requirement extends to unbelievers; at the same time that the line of demarcation between believers and unbelievers has not hereby been obliterated. This last emerges forcefully in the warnings against allying oneself with unbelieving and sinful men (2 Cor. 6:14; Eph. 5:7ff.). This, too, cannot mean that believers in general may have no association with such; for then — according to Paul's own word — one would have to go out of the world (1 Cor. 5:10). They may have no fellowship with their sinful works, however (Eph. 5:11), nor, as it is said in 2 Corinthians 6:14 with a singular figure, permit themselves to be unequally yoked with them.[127] The presupposition is that believers and unbelievers bear a different yoke. The figure is also so striking because in Judaism "yoke"

---

124. For the question as to what "to sacrifice to the demons" must mean cf. Batelaan, *De sterken en zwakken in de kerk van Korinthe*, p. 77. Whether the "weak" in 8:7 were Jewish-Christians who were seized with a notion taken along from Judaism (cf. Batelaan, *ibid.*, pp. 23ff.) seems to me dubious indeed.

125. Cf. Lietzmann, with an appeal to Severianus: *mē thele, ha mē thelei ho Kyrios, hōs ischyroteros autou;* see also K. Staab, *Pauluskommentare*, p. 259.

126. Cf. above, pp. 299ff.

127. *Heterozygeō, hapax leg.;* cf. Lev. 19:19 (LXX). The thought is of two animals who, because they are unlike, bear unequal yokes.

is the symbolic expression of moral and religious obligations.[128] Because
of this fundamentally different approach to life in believers and unbelievers and this different rule of life they cannot go together, cannot
form one team. The thought is therefore not only that believers are
not to permit themselves — with a repudiation of their own "yoke" — to
be brought under one common "yoke" with unbelievers, but also that
with the maintaining of their own "yoke" they must not go together
with them. In this context Paul, with the quotation of prophetic pronouncements, also speaks of "coming out from among them" and "being
separate."[129] That this is not intended in an absolute sense is evident
from 1 Corinthians 5:9ff., where association[130] with people living in sin
is not forbidden. It is a matter of such joining together as that by
which the "yoke," the life principle and the rule of life of believers and
unbelievers, is at stake. Here an uncompromising posture is fitting, not
merely in spite of, but just on account of the responsibility the church
has in and for the world (cf. Phil. 2:15), and one may not in one way
or another endeavor to combine that which is from Christ and that
which runs counter to his rule (cf. 2 Cor. 6:14-16).[131]

In addition to the motive of holiness, finally, the motive of time plays
a special part in the Pauline paraenesis with regard to the acceptance
of life and intercourse in the world. This comes up for discussion in
particular in certain questions on marriage. In that connection Paul
writes the radical words of 1 Corinthians 7:29ff., among others:[132]

> I mean this, brethren: the time is short.
> Finally,[133] let those who have wives live as though they had none;
> and those who weep, as though they wept not;
> and those who rejoice, as though they rejoiced not;
> and those that buy, as though they kept nothing;
> and those that make use of the world, as though they used it not.
> For the form of this world is passing away....

128. Cf., e.g., Strack-Billerbeck on Matt. 11:29 (I, pp. 608ff.).
129. That expressly or especially the marriage relationship is intended here,
as D. van Swigchem holds (Het missionair karakter van de Christelijke gemeente, 1955,
pp. 84, 85), appears improbable already in view of these quotations.
130. Synanamignysthai. For its character cf. the expositions of van Swigchem,
ibid., pp. 65ff., 84ff.
131. Cf. F. J. Pop, De tweede brief van Paulus aan de Corinthiërs, 2nd ed.,
1962, p. 208: "Though it may be that according to a phenomenological standard the
one appears in a great many forms and shapes to correspond with the other, according to the standard of the gospel they are even in their similarities separated by an
abyss. The believer must be conscious of that. He may not play down or neutralize
the difference. He must see it, recognize it, and permit it to function in his life.
He will not enter into a marriage with an unbeliever, and he will also avoid all
kinds of forms of real fellowship. The antithesis holds and is effective."
132. See also the extensive article by W. Schrage, "Die Stellung zur Welt
bei Paulus, Epiktet und in der Apokalyptik. Ein Beitrag zu Kor. 7,29-31," ZTK, 1964,
pp. 125-154.
133. To loipon. The expression here perhaps amounts to "therefore," "consequently"; cf. Kümmel (following Fridrichsen) in Lietzmann, Cor., p. 178. Otherwise
Schrage, ibid., p. 132, n. 17.

The reservation here regarding all participation in the temporal life, its gifts, vicissitudes, structures, is so full of tension because in the broad context of Paul's paraenesis it does not mean avoidance of or abstinence from the gifts and possibilities of the temporal life, but rather acceptance of them and unavoidable involvement in them ("who weep . . . ," etc.). Moreover, resignation or pessimism has no part here. Everything is rather placed under the viewpoint of the passing away of "this world" toward that which is to come and of the shortness of the time that precedes it. Undoubtedly the question as to how short the time is plays a not unimportant role in this connection, and the consciousness of it in Paul's pronouncements is not always expressed in the same manner and does not always determine his pronouncements with respect to the practical life in the same fashion.[134] This distinction is not one of principle, however. For with all the tension that (as in the whole of his preaching) is to be observed in his paraenesis between the "already" and the "not yet," as well as within this "not yet" between the progress and the shortness of time, the expectation of the salvation not yet revealed remains of absolute significance. It is this expectation which on the one hand gives acceptance of the present life its deepest meaning (1 Cor. 15:19) and on the other places it as well under the continuing reservation of the disappearance of the form of this world and of the shortness of the time, though this reservation is felt with varying intensity. The way in which all this takes on concrete form is to be seen still further when, on the basis of several particular pronouncements, we go somewhat more deeply into a few of the facets of life in the world.

SECTION 50. MARRIAGE

The various aspects of Christian liberty and of the life of the Christian in the world are linked in a singular way in Paul's pronouncements on marriage.

Here again the motive of the creation and institution of marriage by God and of the liberty to accept marriage as such in Christ is fundamental. The apostle speaks of the institution of marriage by God and the regulation of marriage given with this institution, for example, in 1 Corinthians 6:16 and in Ephesians 5:31, as well as in 1 Timothy 4:4. He orients himself to this institution when in more than one place he describes the relationship of husband and wife to each other, and ascribes the first place in marriage to the husband (1 Cor. 11:3, 7-9; 1 Tim. 2:11ff.; cf. 1 Cor. 14:34; Eph. 5:22; Col. 3:18; Tit. 2:5). This motive of creation and the ordinance of marriage involved in it he then links most closely with that of Christian liberty and the marriage directives lying in it. This occurs in a very deliberate and explicit manner in the anti-ascetic pronouncements already cited above in 1 Timothy 4:4, 5, where it is said of marriage that, just as everything God has

---

134. Cf. below, p. 310; in general also Section 74.

created, it is good and not to be rejected, if it is received with thanks-giving; for it is sanctified by the Word of God and by prayer.

This general motive of sanctification, however, now finds a spe-cial application for marriage in other pronouncements. Thus, for exam-ple, in 1 Corinthians 7:39, where the demand is made of believers not to marry otherwise than "in the Lord," that is to say, with a believer; but also in 1 Corinthians 7:14, where the continuation of the marriage of a husband and wife, one of whom has become a believer, is moti-vated by the sanctification of the unbelieving partner in the marriage in or through the believing partner. The Christian motive especially has bearing on the mutual relations of husband and wife. Thus in 1 Corinthians 11 the husband's position of priority in marriage is fur-ther defined by the pronouncement that in the Lord the wife is no more without the husband than the husband is without the wife; for as the woman is of the man, so also is the man by the woman; all things, however, are of God (vv. 11, 12). It is not said here that "in the Lord" marriage has received another destiny than it had by virtue of crea-tion;[135] it is said, however, that in the Lord the principle of reciprocity, mutual dependence and service to one another in love, applies and comes into effect in a new way. For in Christ the husband does not have an advantage over the wife (Gal. 3:28). The distinction that exists between them by virtue of creation is not abolished, any more than that between Jews and Greeks; to be in Christ does not therefore mean natural equality. But all, both male and female *(arsen kai thēly)*, are one in Christ, that is to say, they together constitute one body (cf. 1 Cor. 12:13). And this must govern natural relationships as well, so that in marriage it is not one's own concern or asserting one's own superi-ority, but love in Christ, that must determine the relationship. Be-longing to Christ and belonging to one another as man and wife in marriage are therefore not separated, but the former is intended to work itself out in the latter. For this reason fornication is incompatible with belonging to Christ (1 Cor. 6:12-20). For the body of the believer be-longs to the Lord (v. 13), and it shares in the resurrection. Therefore the bodies of believers as members belong to the body of Christ, and a believing man cannot at the same time be one body and one flesh with a prostitute. The destiny of the body is therefore determined by Christ and by the Holy Spirit. This is also decisive for mutual relationships in marriage.

Nowhere does the apostle give stronger expression to this than in Ephesians 5:22-33, where in his paraenesis concerning the marriage relationship he not only goes out from the fact that every believer belongs to the body of Christ, but looks at the entire relationship of man and wife to each other in the light of the relationship of Christ and the church, which he then describes as a marriage relationship.

---

135. Cf. the pronouncement from the Talmud quoted by Strack-Billerbeck, III, p. 440: "...not a man without a woman and not a woman without a man and not the two of them without the Shekinah" (= God). Schlatter holds, therefore, that we have to do in v. 11 with a proverb, with which opinion Kümmel associates himself. See Lietzmann-Kümmel, *Cor.*, p. 184.

For the wife this implies the obligation to recognize the leading place of the husband,[136] for the husband the obligation of love. On the one hand the unity of Christ and the church therefore receives its explanation from the mysterious unity of husband and wife in marriage (5:32); conversely, the unity of Christ and the church throws light on the true experience of the unity of marriage.[137] Natural relationships serve in 1 Corinthians 6 and in Ephesians 5 as a depiction of the salvation given in Christ. But it is only therein that they, too, are identified in their true sense and requirement. This does not signify a spiritualization of natural marriage; rather a return and restoration of the natural out of Christ and the Holy Spirit. This is accordingly the deep meaning of the statement that what God has created, including marriage in particular, is sanctified by the Word of God and prayer.

The general purport of Paul's pronouncements with respect to marriage is therefore positive and fundamentally anti-ascetic. They comprise a Christian paraenesis in behalf of and not in opposition to marriage. It is this positive view which obliges believers to refrain from fornication and in general every man to acquire his own wife[138] in sanctification and honor (1 Thess. 4:4); likewise, in accordance with the commandment of Christ, the wife may not leave her husband, and the husband may not repudiate his wife (1 Cor. 7:10, 11). This commandment also applies to mixed marriages, as long as the unbelieving partner in the marriage does not wish to put an end to the marital union (1 Cor. 7:12ff.); if this last is indeed the case, then the believing partner in the marriage is no longer bound (v. 15).[139] This positive appraisal of mar-

---

136. *Hypotassesthai* speaks primarily of the recognition of a specific order. Cf. Schrage, in *ZTK*, 1964, p. 221.

137. For this passage at length see below, pp. 379ff.

138. *To heautou skeuos ktasthai.* For a long time past opinions have been divided as to whether *skeuos* must be taken as wife or as body (cf., e.g., Arndt-Gingrich-Bauer, pp. 761f., *s.v.*). The proof passages cited on either side give no definitive answer, although in our view it is difficult to rob of all their force the evidence cited for the conception that *skeuos* = wife and, e.g., in 1 Pet. 3:7 to take *skeuos* in the sense of instrument and not as *terminus technicus* for wife, as, e.g., Dibelius chooses to do (*Th.*, p. 21). In our opinion *heautou* (in contrast with the preceding *porneia*) and *ktasthai* (originally: "to acquire") argue more for the conception that by *skeuos* wife is intended; see also the argumentation of J. E. Frame, *A Critical and Exegetical Commentary on the Epistles of St. Paul to the Thessalonians*, 2nd ed., 1946, pp. 149, 150.

139. The question then is how one is to understand what follows: (but) "God has called us to peace." Ordinarily this is taken as the motive for not wanting to preserve a marriage with the unwilling unbelieving party, because this leads to discord. And the argument that in the marriage one would be able to lead such a person to conversion rests on an uncertain basis (v. 16: "for how do you know, wife, whether you will save your husband?" etc.). Cf. for this train of thought the commentaries of Lietzmann, Héring, Grosheide, *et al.* On the other hand, Jeremias wishes to view v. 15c as an express limitation of the permission given in 15a and b: "God has called us, however, to peace (with one another)." And this will to peace must be maintained especially in a mixed marriage, for the sake of the missionary obligation that this peace places on Christian husbands and wives. The words *ti gar oidas* in v. 16 he wants then, with an appeal to similar usage elsewhere, to take as "perhaps," "it may be" ("Die missionarische Aufgabe in der Mischehe," in *Neutestamentliche Studien für Rudolf Bultmann*, 1954, pp. 258ff.). In our opinion the objection to this

riage is also determined by natural considerations. Precisely to prevent fornication every man is to have his own wife, and every woman her own husband (1 Cor. 7:2), and they are not permanently to withhold themselves from marital co-habitation, in order even as married persons not to fall into temptation (vv. 3ff.). For this reason, too, the advice is given to unmarried persons and widows to marry, if they cannot control themselves. For it is better to marry than to burn (vv. 8, 9). And elsewhere it is said to the young widows that, rather than to go about idly and to be reduced to loquacious good-for-nothings, they are to marry, bear children, and be actively at work in their own households (1 Tim. 5:13ff.), as it is said in general of the (believing) married woman that she will be saved "through bearing children," that is to say, will participate in the way of believing and dedicated motherhood[140] not only in temporal but also in eternal life (1 Tim. 2:15).

At the same time Paul's epistles present another aspect. We have already dealt with this, or rather with its reverse side, in the advice cited above from 1 Corinthians 7 regarding the contracting of marriage and marital intercourse on the ground of a lack of self-control and of the motive that it is better to marry than to burn. Clearly this is not a motive for marriage that arises from Christian liberty, but rather an "accommodation" (cf. 1 Cor. 7:6) to the natural impulse to sexual relations, which may indeed be acted on, but even so only because a lack of self-control has become evident. The motive for marriage employed here consequently cannot be placed as secondary alongside that of Christian liberty. Rather it occurs in 1 Corinthians 7 as a limitation of the principal advice, namely, not to marry and therefore not to make use of one's liberty. For, thus Paul writes in answer to the questions put

interesting conception lies in v. 15c, of which the interpretation given by Jeremias certainly is not evident. The question is also difficult whether *ou dedoulōtai* in v. 15 means that the wife is entirely free (possibly even to marry another man) or is no longer obligated to seek restoration of the broken relationship with the unbelieving husband, without having the liberty, however, to enter into a new marriage. The expression *(ou)dedoulōtai* argues for the former, a binding the dissolution of which also means the complete freedom of the wife (Rom. 7:2); cf. the significance of *eleuthera* in v. 39 (which there denotes the complete freedom of the wife) and which in Rom. 7 forms the opposite of *dedetai*. Reference is also to be made to v. 10 where a case of *chōristhēnai* is mentioned, in which the wife, if she has deserted the husband (wilfully), is pointed simply to her obligations to be reconciled or otherwise to remain single. There is nothing of that in v. 15, but there the emphasis is placed on no longer being bound. All this seems to point to the fact that the apostle here gives a supplement to the command of Christ, of which he speaks in v. 10. It would, however, be incorrect on this basis to accept in general so-called wilful desertion as ground for divorce. This is precisely contradicted in the prohibition given by Christ (cf. Matt. 5:32); and the apostle obviously starts from the same train of thought in v. 11 over against a wife who has separated from her husband. In v. 15, however, if our exegesis is correct, we have to do with an exceptional case characteristic of the "missionary situation."

140. *Dia tēs teknogonias* speaks of motherhood not as a means to salvation, but as the way in which this salvation takes place. The thought is not so strange as could be gathered from the multifarious interpretations that have been given of this expression (see the commentaries). It is determined by what immediately precedes (the reminder of Gen. 3). Hence also the *sōthēsetai* (in relation to the preceding *en parabasei gegonen*).

to him by the Corinthians: "it is good for a man not to touch a woman." And though marriage remains lawful in view of the danger of fornication and in marriage husband and wife are not to withhold themselves from each other, this is true "by way of concession, not by way of command." For Paul would wish indeed that all men were as he himself, i.e., unmarried. Yet not everyone has received a *charisma* from God in this respect, in other words, the ability to deny himself marriage (v. 7). For this reason the unmarried and the widows are counseled to remain in their unmarried state, at least if they are able to control themselves.

Now it is of great importance to distinguish clearly the motives of Paul's preference for the single state in 1 Corinthians 7:1-7. The apostle speaks of that explicitly when in verse 25 he once again deals expressly with "virgins." He has no definite commandment of Christ handed down to him for them, but he gives his "advice,"[141] as one who has been permitted by the mercy of the Lord to be faithful (others translate[142] by: authorized to this end, qualified; v. 25; cf. v. 40). He does not therefore relativize his apostolic authority over against that of the Lord,[143] but he does wish (as appears from the expression "my advice"[144]) that this authority not be fully asserted here, but only that his opinion be made known by way of counsel.[145] He lets it be known, moreover, that his urging people to remain unmarried has its basis in "the present[146] distress" (v. 26). What is intended is specifically the distress in which believers find themselves in a world hostile to them, with which Paul himself had had and would yet have such an abundant acquaintance (cf. 2 Cor. 6:4; 12:10; 1 Thess. 3:7). What follows relates this[147] with the fact that "the time is short" (v. 29) and "the form of this world is passing away" (v. 31). This alludes to the end of things,

141. *Gnōmē*. For the usage see, e.g., Bultmann, *TDNT*, I, pp. 717, 718.

142. Cf. Lietzmann-Kümmel, *Cor.*, p. 33 and the evidence produced there. The translation is attractive.

143. For this frequently discussed question see my *The Authority of the New Testament Scriptures*, pp. 23f.

144. See also 2 Cor. 8:8, 10, where *gnōmē* is explicitly distinguished from speaking *kat' epitagēn*.

145. The following *nomizō...kalon hyparchein* lies in the same relative sphere of authority; cf. Grosheide, *1 Cor.*, p. 202. For the question of the element of authority in these pronouncements see also the valuable study by T. Delleman, *Het huwelijksvraagstuk in 1 Cor. VII*, 1939, pp. 9ff.

146. *Enestōs* is taken by some as "impending" (so the *Staten Vertaling*; the RSV; Lietzmann: "bevorstehende"; Héring: "[*Enestōs*] refers to an imminent future which is already in a certain way operative in the present"). Yet there is sufficient ground neither linguistically nor materially for deviating from the prevalent meaning in Paul (cf. Rom. 8:38; 1 Cor. 3:22; Gal. 1:4). It is accordingly taken as "present" by most scholars.

147. Grosheide, *1 Cor.*, p. 202, denies any connection between "the distress" and the end, and speaks of the distress through sin as long as the world exists (p. 256). This making the distress timeless seems to us not only in conflict with the context (vv. 29, 31!), but also with Paul's advice not to marry. This would then apply for all generations and under all circumstances and allow no place for marriage at all other than to prevent fornication. Grundmann, *TDNT*, I, p. 346, speaks in our opinion more correctly of "afflictions which derive from the tension between the new creation in Christ and the old cosmos" (*s.v. anangkē*). Cf. Delleman, *Het huwelijksvraagstuk*, pp. 15ff., and especially Schrage in the article cited on p. 305, n. 132.

which is at hand. The "distress" need not yet be understood therefore in the special sense of the last great tribulation, the "Messianic woes" (cf. Luke 21:23). But suffering in and because of the present world that has not yet been redeemed in its mode of existence, as the counter force of the redemption given in Christ (cf., e.g., Rev. 12:12), is indeed characteristic of the temporal life of believers; and even though they do not always feel this in their own persons it must restrain them from becoming attached to the gifts and pleasure of this world as though their life consisted in them (vv. 29ff.). And because of this distress, Paul fears more "tribulation in the flesh" for those who are married (v. 28) than for the unmarried, whereas he would spare them these anxieties (v. 32). At the same time this involves the religious motive that those who are married become more attached to the present life, are more divided in their attention, and will devote themselves more to their husband or wife and to earthly affairs and less to the cause of the Lord than the unmarried. For this reason he counsels the unmarried not to marry, and that indeed to their own advantage, not to cast a noose on them, not to hamper them in their own liberty, but so that (on the one hand[148]) what is seemly might be done *(pros to euschēmon)* and (on the other hand[149]) they might become entirely attached to the Lord without permitting themselves to be drawn away from him *(aperispastōs;* v. 35).

This "on the one hand and on the other" the apostle applies yet once more by discussing the question as to what one must do with his marriageable "virgin." Whether what is posed here is the problem of the betrothed and by "any man" the young man is intended,[150] or whether it is the problem of a father who has a marriageable daughter,[151] may be left undecided as not crucial for our discussion.[152] If the pressure for marriage becomes too great and things must take their course, he is to do as he wishes: he does not sin — let them marry. But he who is steadfast in his heart and does not feel this necessity, who has power over his own will and has come to the determination within to keep his virgin untouched, acts well. Thus he who marries (or gives her in marriage) does well, but he who does not marry her (or give her in marriage) does better (v. 38). This also applies, *mutatis mutandis,* to the widow (vv. 39, 40).

---

148. For this exegesis, cf., e.g., J. Héring, *The First Epistle of St. Paul to the Corinthians,* pp. 61ff.

149. *(Pros to) euparedron tō Kyriō.* The word occurs only here and means approximately "constant," "persevering."

150. This is argued at length, e.g., by Kümmel, "Verlobung und Heirat bei Paulus," in *Neutest. Studien für R. Bultmann,* 1954, pp. 275ff. See also the very extensive bibliography there.

151. The traditional conception, which has once again found forceful defense, among others, in A. Oepke, "Irrwege in der neuren Paulusforschung," *TLZ,* 1952, cols. 449-452.

152. In any case the hypothesis must be rejected that Paul here alludes to the "spiritual betrothals," familiar from a later period *("Syneisaktentum,"* "virgines subintroductae"), as is assumed among the more recent writers, e.g., by Lietzmann and Héring in their commentaries; Delling, *TDNT,* V, p. 836; Arndt-Gingrich-Bauer, p. 150, *s.v. gamizō;* Stauffer, *TDNT,* I, p. 652, n. 24. See what is in our opinion a conclusive controverting of this conception by Oepke and Kümmel.

If we summarize, the following can be established with respect to Paul's attitude toward marriage.

First, there is no basis for the opinion that on ascetic-dualistic grounds Paul considered sexual intercourse itself sinful,[153] or would have judged marriage on the basis of ascetic-dualistic motives.[154] The contrary is rather the case. Paul values marriage as an institution of God, protected by the express commandment of Christ, to be accepted and experienced in Christian liberty. Even in 1 Corinthians 7, the chapter to which appeal is made for an opposite opinion, in our view no ascetic-dualistic motives are to be discovered with reference to marriage.

Second, on the ground of all the data that have been preserved to us, just as little can it be maintained that for Paul marriage was a necessary evil, and that with him there is no question of a higher estimation of marriage.[155] In order to reach such an opinion one must not only deny to him such a pronouncement as that in 1 Timothy 4:4ff., but also leave out of consideration what he says concerning marriage and its relation to the unity between Christ and the church (Eph. 5:22ff.; cf. 2 Cor. 11:2), concerning the love with which married persons must give themselves to each other (cf. Col. 3:19), concerning the sanctification of marital relations even in a mixed marriage (1 Cor. 7:14). Likewise when in 1 Corinthians 7 the apostle gives his verdict in general against entering into new marriages, he does not do so on the ground of a fundamentally negative judgment of marriage, but of a special situation (v. 26). For this one can refer to a similar pronouncement of Jesus in Matthew 19:12c. Marriage is not hereby deprived of its intrinsic value, nor degraded to a necessary evil for incontinent, non-charismatic people; as gift and mandate for temporal life it is relativized in the face of the nearness of the coming kingdom and the new estimation of earthly life coupled with it.[156] However much Paul primarily values the Christian life in the world on the ground of the salvation that has already dawned in Christ, this does not alter the fact that again and again he speaks with great force of the coming kingdom of God as the end of the mode of existence ("the schema") of the present world. And this of course applies not only to marriage, but to all the facets of temporal life (1 Cor. 7:29-31).

The advice thus understood, however, sets us before the by no means simple question as to its binding significance for the Christian church. Although Paul himself surrounds it with all kinds of restrictive

153. Cf. G. Delling, *Die Stellung des Paulus zu Frau und Ehe*, 1931, pp. 62ff.

154. So also Bultmann, *Theology*, I, p. 202.

155. So Lietzmann-Kümmel, *Cor.*, p. 29, cf. p. 176; see also H. Preisker, *Das Ethos des Urchristentums*, 2nd ed., 1949, pp. 177ff.; E. Fascher, "Zur Witwerschaft des Paulus und der Auslegung von 1 Cor. 7," *ZNW*, 1929, pp. 62-69.

156. Cf. Schrage, "Die Stellung zur Welt bei Paulus," *ZTK*, 1964, p. 152: "Here, too, there is continuity only in discontinuity. Certainly the *kainē diathēkē* is also a *diathēkē*; certainly the *sōma pneumatikon* is also a *sōma*; certainly the *kainē ktisis* is also a *ktisis*. But decisive in all these stress-laden formulations is not the connection with the 'old,' not the identity, continuity, or even restitution; but what is decisive is the new, the break, the antithesis, the incommensurability, the totally other."

considerations (the danger of fornication, the charismatic character of abstinence from marriage, the continuing marital obligations of those who are married), his preference for the unmarried state in the situation in which he sees the church (see above) remains unmistakable. In our view one will have to take into consideration, moreover, that Paul in 1 Corinthians 7 is addressing himself to a church in which the idea prevailed that the future had already been realized and the resurrection had already taken place.[157] Against this, according to the nature of the prophetic-eschatological consciousness,[158] he thrusts into the forefront here the relativity of temporal life and the danger that devoting oneself to it involves more distinctly than he does elsewhere, where he places more emphasis on the institution of marriage by God and its sanctification by Christ. This absolute point of view also makes him estimate his own renunciation of marriage and that of others as a *charisma*.[159]

On the one hand the apostolic advice to the Corinthians to be explained from this fact signifies for the coming church, too, an abiding stimulus to be conscious of the provisional character of earthly life, in the face of the imperishable gift and the calling arising from it of the coming kingdom, even though this would mean *in concreto* the giving up of marriage. In this respect the apostolic advice in its pointing away toward the ultimate decisions that apply to man remains of absolute significance, particularly so if the contracting of a marriage would restrain or hinder believers from devoting themselves to that to which they could be called for "the affairs of the Lord" (v. 32). Accordingly, being able to abstain may be estimated as a special divine *charisma* and the pastoral suggestion of 1 Corinthians 7 against the excessive strain of voluntary celibacy remain in force as well.

On the other hand there is an indication, not only in the continuation of the earthly dispensation, but also in the whole of the apostolic instruction, that marriage — and the entire earthly life — will have to be estimated not only from the special viewpoint of 1 Corinthians 7. For however striking the agreement of 1 Corinthians 7:29-31 with similar pronouncements in the Jewish apocalyptic may be in certain respects, the great distinction lies in the fact that for Paul "eschatology" bears a christological character, that is to say, is determined not only by the consciousness of the speedy end of this world, but by the unity of the salvation that is expected and which has already appeared in Christ. Even now the believer belongs to Christ as his Lord, in life and in death, both in the present world and in the world to come; and that

---

157. Cf. further below, p. 539.

158. See also the striking (material) parallels of 1 Cor. 7:29-31 in 4 Ezra, cap. 14 (also denoted as 6 Ezra) in Schrage, *ZTK*, 1964, p. 141.

159. In this joining of the eschatological and charismatic viewpoint I go a somewhat different way from Delleman. It seems to me that he makes the *charisma* of abstaining too timeless and thereby places the gift of marriage and the gift of abstaining on the same level next to each other, indeed in general even places the unmarried state of those who have the *charisma* of abstaining higher than the married state (*Het huwelijksvraagstuk*, pp. 23ff., and esp. p. 28). In this way of thinking the viewpoint of Gen. 2:18 cannot function fully, and the special character of the apostolic advice comes too much in the shadow.

with all that he is and has and does (cf. Rom. 14:8). Therein lies his
liberty to eat and to drink, to marry and to be given in marriage, and
the fundamental boundary separating him from a contempt for or
shunning of earthly life resulting from the expectation of the end of
the world. But — and this should be expressly maintained in view of
1 Corinthians 7 — always in such a way that the repeatedly arising distress that has accompanied the church in its course throughout history
will have to remain for it the sign that liberty in Christ springs no less
'rom what it has to expect, than in what the church is already permitted
.o possess in faith; that is also to say, consists no less in abstaining from
marriage than in giving oneself to it.

SECTION 51. SOCIAL RELATIONSHIPS

Paul's admonitions relating to the life of work and the social relationships it involves are also characteristic of his general attitude with
respect to the life of the church in the world.

We meet with admonitions on the subject of work especially in
the Epistles to the Thessalonians. Already in 1 Thessalonians 4:11f. the
apostle exhorts believers that they consider it an honor to lead a quiet
life, to look after their own affairs, and to work with their hands, as he
has charged them, so that they conduct themselves becomingly in the
presence of those that are without and be dependent on no man's help.
And in 1 Thessalonians 5:14 he gives still another special warning that
those who live disorderly — among whom we have certainly to understand those who shirk regular work — are to be admonished. In 2 Thessalonians 3:6-12 there is even a separate pericope devoted to this "dis-
orderliness," in which he has people in view who no longer worked,
but instead troubled themselves with unnecessary things.[160] Just how
we are to conceive of this is not altogether clear. Usually spiritualistic
or eschatological tendencies are thought of (cf. 2 Thess. 2:1ff.), through
which some had been caught up in a certain agitation, had lapsed
into a disorderly life, and thereby not only caused their fellow Christians annoyance, but also endangered the good name of the church
with those standing on the outside (cf. 1 Thess. 4:12). However one is
precisely to view this idleness, Paul lets it be known that in no sense
whatever does this square with the content of the gospel. In 1 Thessalonians 4:11 as well as in 2 Thessalonians 3:6 and 10 he appeals to what
he taught them previously on this matter. In so doing he points to his
own example of industry (2 Thess. 3:7ff.; cf. 1 Thess. 2:9). How reprehensible he considered idleness is certainly evident from the pronouncement
in 2 Thessalonians 3:6, where with full apostolic authority he commands
believers to withdraw themselves from every member of the church
who conducted himself in this way. And he commands these people in

---

160. Paul uses a play on words — *mēden ergazomenous alla periergazomenous* —
which also occurs elsewhere and which scholars have attempted in all sorts of ways
to convey in translation; cf. J. E. Frame, *A Critical and Exegetical Commentary on
the Epistles of St. Paul to the Thessalonians*, p. 306.

the name of the Lord Jesus Christ to keep quietly to their work, and to earn their own bread (2 Thess. 3:12). From all this it is evident that the apostle wished to dissociate himself as sharply and clearly as possible from these practices, as though they had anything whatever to do with the gospel and the expectation given in it. Instead of falling into such an anti-social and agitated condition believers are to find honor precisely in quietness (1 Thess. 4:11; 2 Thess. 3:12), in an orderly and regular civil life, without being dependent on the assistance of others.

No special "Christian" standards for the life of work are to be derived from this paraenesis.[161] Paul appeals rather to generally recognized standards of order, tranquillity, and propriety (1 Thess. 4:11), and even summarizes his earlier instructions in the down-to-earth rule: "if any will not work, let him not eat" (2 Thess. 3:10). It appears here with great clarity that faith in Christ on the one hand, and application with diligence and order to one's daily work that one may thus earn his own bread and be an example to others on the other hand, are not two things that have nothing to do with each another or of which the first would even stand in the way of the second, but that it is precisely obedience and faith in Christ that constitute a most powerful and unmistakable incentive for an industrious life. That Paul may be said to renounce every other ordering than that of the coming kingdom, the ordering of love, in which work, too, is a matter of course and work-shyness a sin against the will of God,[162] seems to us in view of the passages that have been handled here an unproven thesis. Rather, the order[163] that is spoken of again and again and which is held before the church with the authority of Christ has reference to the will of God with respect to the natural life, an order that he not only infers from the Christian commandment of love, but without defining or analyzing it further designates as valid for work and which in connection with the authorities he denotes as *diatagē tou Theou* (Rom. 13:2).[164] It is to this effect that Paul also, in rejecting all manner of ascetic and spiritualistic heresy, writes to Timothy that godliness is profitable for all things, having promise for life for the present as well as for the future (1 Tim. 4:8). The revelation of Christ does not abrogate the order of the natural and present life, but makes it recognized and practiced, from the viewpoint of Christ, exactly in its divine significance.

In this sense Paul also speaks of social relationships. Of importance in this respect is 1 Corinthians 7:17-24, where in his paraenesis on questions concerning marriage it is said by way of general elucidation that each man is to remain in the particular situation in which he has come to faith and is to walk therein according to the requirement of

---

161. That that orderly work is also "the mark of the person determined by the *telos*, by the kingdom of God" — which is how H. Preisker, *Das Ethos des Urchristentums*, 1949, pp. 115, 116, interprets these passages, with a rejection of all kinds of other motives — is in our view not to be derived from the text.

162. So Preisker, *ibid.*, pp. 115, 116.

163. *Tous ataktous* (1 Thess. 5:14); *ataktōs peripatein* (2 Thess. 3:6, 11); *atakteō* (2 Thess. 3:7).

164. Cf. 1 Pet. 2:13, where there is mention of *pasē anthrōpinē ktisis*, to which one is to be subjected for the Lord's sake.

God. This, so he writes to the Corinthians, is the rule of conduct he lays down for all the churches. For this reason the wife who in her marriage with an unbelieving husband has come to conversion need not separate from him. For this reason neither circumcision nor uncircumcision stands in anyone's way in serving God. Let everyone, so he repeats in verse 20, remain in the calling in which — when he came to faith — he was called by God. The intention, as appears from what follows, is that one is not to run away from the "situation of his calling."[165] Therefore, in view of this calling, no one is to trouble himself if he was called as a slave. This does not stand in the way of his faith and of his service to the Lord. For, so he goes on,[166] the slave who was called in the Lord is one who has been ransomed by the Lord and thus bound to him[167] (v. 22), just as on the other hand he who was called as a free man is a slave to Christ. Both have been bought and paid for by him, and have only to guard against becoming the slaves of men, namely, by taking notice of their social prejudices as though there were a distinction with respect to Christ in anyone's social position.

One cannot say that in these verses Paul deals with social relationships as such. The intention is rather to throw light on the relative significance of the social position in which one finds himself in view of being a Christian (cf. Gal. 3:28; Col. 3:11). Two things are of great importance, however.

In the first place, the apostle apparently does not wish to see any premature encroachment on the existing social order. The announcement that he thus gives regulations to all the churches also seems to point to this. What he says in 1 Corinthians 7 on remaining in the situation of one's calling is therefore no incidental pronouncement, but a general rule of conduct laid down by him. The gospel does not make its appearance in the form of a new social program, and still less does

---

165. Some indeed wish to give the difficult *klēsis* a social significance: "occupation," "position." But the word does not elsewhere have this meaning. We shall have to understand it in close connection with the religious *eklēthē*, namely, the condition or situation in which one has been called of God to the faith (cf. v. 24; see also Lietzmann-Kümmel, *Cor.*, pp. 32 and 176; K. L. Schmidt, *TDNT*, III, p. 491, n. 1).

166. The significance of the intervening verse is uncertain. Paul says here to the one who has been called as a slave: "but if you can become free, *mallon chrēsai.*" The question is whether one is to take these last words as (1) rather make use (of that freedom) (Schlatter, Robertson-Plummer; Rengstorf, *TDNT*, II, p. 272), or (2) rather make use (of your position as a slave) (e.g., Lietzmann-Kümmel, Wendland; Liechtenhan, *Gottes Gebot im N.T.*, 1942, p. 104), or also (3) make that much more use (of your calling), that is, as free (Grosheide). It counts against (1) and (3) that Paul here urges precisely remaining in the "calling." V. 22 also seems to connect better when one takes v. 21 according to (2). However, v. 23 would again be able to connect with (1) and (3). The *alla* with which v. 21b begins counts against (2). If one takes the whole according to (2), then such a contrast (*alla*) appears not to be present. In general it is not to be understood why the apostle would rather see anyone remain a slave who in a legitimate way was to become free. In our opinion it is impossible to decide here with any certainty, although we incline to (1) or (3). V. 21 is then to be taken as a concessive intercalation in the argument.

167. With *apeleutheros Kyriou* one will best be able to think of the condition of the *libertus*, who was bound to the master that had set him at liberty as to his *patronus;* cf. Lietzmann-Kümmel, *Cor.*, p. 178, in dependence on W. Elert.

it overthrow the existing order by force. Rather, it enters into the existing structure of society in order to permeate it with a new spirit, that of Christ. Yet the apostle also recognizes in the social order something more than human arbitrariness or the abuse of the power of one over another. It is rather an order in which a higher divine ordinance is effecting itself, whereby the world is maintained and which requires recognition as such above everything else. Thus and not otherwise the repeatedly recurring admonitions addressed to slaves and masters are to be understood (Eph. 6:5ff.; Col. 3:22ff.; see also below).

This does not imply that Paul identifies the existing social order, especially slavery, with the divine order, or regards it as unalterable. To be sure, nowhere has a pronouncement been preserved in which he criticizes the institution of slavery and declares it to be contrary to the gospel. On the other hand, nowhere does he take it back to a divine ordinance, as, for example, in the case of the subjection of the wife to the husband. The context in which he speaks in 1 Corinthians 7 of remaining in the situation of one's calling is also of importance. Paul here places being a slave and being free on a level with being or not being circumcised. With respect to the latter, too, he desires no instantaneous or revolutionary alterations (vv. 17, 18). Yet he was plainly aware of the revolution that his preaching of the gospel must mean for the whole institution of circumcision.

Essentially — and this is the second thing to be observed with reference to 1 Corinthians 7:20ff. — his motivation for remaining in the situation of one's calling meant a revolution for the institution of slavery. For this does not consist in a spiritualistic or eschatological indifference to social relationships, but in a new appreciation of man out of Christ, whereby a renewal of social relationships must become possible and necessary from within. In 1 Corinthians 7 this last point is not the real focus of the paraenesis. This does not alter the fact that the apostle here too judges slaves and free men together out of their relationship to Christ, and in verse 23 warns them (both!) not to be slaves of men, that is to say, in their consciousness of calling by God not to be guided by human judgment basing itself on their social position. However much his paraenesis again refrains from drawing social conclusions, indeed places the emphasis precisely on the acceptance of the existing social order, it is not to be disputed that just this motivation for remaining in the "situation of one's calling" must be of deep and sweeping significance for mutual human relationships.[168] It was certainly not that here the dynamite was placed that must eventually lead the slaves to revolt — the argument rather opposes that — but it was the salt or, if one will, the leaven of the kingdom of God (Matt. 5:13; 13:33), which for those who would not draw back from the force of Paul's words must also be of deep and radical social significance.

The Epistle to Philemon provides a highly illustrative corroboration of all this, and may serve in many respects as the criterion of what

---

168. We cannot therefore admit that "in any case nothing can be deduced of permanent significance for Christian ethics from this passage" (Lindsay Dewar, *An Outline of New Testament Ethics*, 1949, p. 166).

can be said on other counts concerning Paul's attitude regarding slavery. To begin with, Paul sends the runaway slave Onesimus back to his master Philemon.[169] Furthermore, he acknowledges in the whole epistle the right of the master to his slave (cf. vv. 12, 14, 18). Likewise it is not demonstrable that Paul at this time directly or indirectly asked for the manumission of Onesimus. Even if one holds the view, in company with various interpreters,[170] that in verses 13, 14, 20ff. Paul requests the return of Onesimus, this is not to be identified with a formal manumission. The juridical side of the matter is not treated.[171] On the other hand, the manner in which Paul now announces Onesimus to his master is such that the old master-slave relationship is entirely broken through, or at least altogether overshadowed by another. He calls Onesimus "formerly a good-for-nothing," but "now of much profit both to you and to me," "him, that is my whole heart" (vv. 11, 12); and he says that perhaps for this reason he was parted from his master for a time, that he should have him back again forever, no longer as a slave, but as much more than a slave: as a beloved brother. He, Onesimus, is altogether that for Paul even now; how much more then for his master, to whom he now belongs both as a slave and as a brother. On this account Paul asks as well that his master, if he feels bound to the apostle, receive Onesimus as he would Paul, etc. (vv. 15-17). Accordingly, whatever Paul may precisely have wished of Philemon, he leaves the decision to him, namely, on the foundation of the wholly new relationship in which he now stands to his slave. And it is this re-forming and re-orientation "from within" which one can qualify as the heart and purport of Paul's "social-ethical" paraenesis.[172]

---

169. At least following the traditional view. J. Knox, in *Philemon among the Letters of Paul*, 1935, has attempted to make plausible that it was not Philemon, but Archippus, who was the master of Onesimus, and has connected Col. 4:17 with what Paul asks in Philemon of the master of Onesimus. Philemon in Laodicea would then have to appear before Archippus in Colosse as the advocate of Onesimus and our Epistle to Philemon would then be the letter intended in Col. 4:16; cf. Dibelius, *Col.*, pp. 101, 102. A decision on this hypothesis is not necessary for our purpose.

170. Cf., e.g., P. Ewald, *Die Brief des Paulus an die Epheser, Kolosser und Philemon*, 2nd ed., 1910, p. 278; E. Lohmeyer, *Die Briefe an die Philipper, an die Kolosser und an Philemon*, 1930, p. 188.

171. Cf. Dibelius-Greeven, *Col.*, p. 107; Liechtenhan, *Gottes Gebot im N.T.*, p. 105.

172. For Paul's whole handling of this case see also the detailed and penetrating essay by P. J. Verdam, "St. Paul et un serf fugitif," in *Symbolae van Oven*, 1946, pp. 211-230. Verdam treats first the Mosaic, and then the Roman law regarding runaway slaves. He is of the opinion that Paul, without mentioning the Roman law with a single word, permitted himself in the returning of Onesimus practically to be guided by the operative law (pp. 227-230). At the same time, however, by the manner in which he approaches Philemon he is said to undermine the foundation of the Roman law in the matter of slavery (consisting in the absolute right of disposal of the master over his slave), if not in a juridical fashion. Verdam concludes (p. 230): "It is clear that by accepting the juridical order and attacking slavery in an absolute sense, these two characteristics in the attitude of St. Paul and in his letter to Philemon are the same as in the Mosaic code." Essentially this last point is certainly correct. Because Paul, however, derived his motivation from the new relationship in Christ, he attacked not only the absolute right of disposal of the master over his slave, but also the root of slavery as such, even if indirectly and

Under this twofold point of view, finally, Paul's express admonitions to slaves and masters in the so-called *Haustafeln* are to be understood (Eph. 6:5-9; Col. 3:22-4:1; cf. 1 Tim. 6:1, 2; Tit. 2:9, 10). On the one hand a very strong emphasis is there placed on the subjection of slaves to their masters, and serving wholeheartedly in this relationship (not slavery itself!) is pointed out as the will of the Lord (Eph. 6:5-8; Col. 3:22-24). Moreover, especially in the Pastoral Epistles, the motive that Christian doctrine may not be blasphemed through rebellious disturbances plays an important part (1 Tim. 6:1; Tit. 2:10). The slaves are also warned not to conduct themselves in a self-conceited manner toward their believing masters because these are brethren, but rather to be all the better slaves for them (1 Tim. 6:2). It is surely apparent here that Paul did not think of an abolition of slavery as a social institution on Christian grounds. On the other hand, in the *Haustafeln*, too, the slave-master relationship, and its reverse, is completely elucidated and judged out of the newness of the individual and collective relationship to Christ. What a revolution this meant can be gathered even from the single fact that Paul successively addresses slaves and masters as equal members of the church, and describes their relationships to one another as two sides of the same responsibility. In no way whatever could this be reconciled with the position of the slave in the world of that day, nor with that in Judaism.[173] But in addition, slaves are not to serve their masters in the way of eyeservice as men-pleasers (Eph. 6:6; Col. 3:22), but in the fear of the Lord and as bondservants of Christ, a motive that involves not only a rejection of the character-corrupting and inhuman practices of the household slavery of the time, but above all the secret of true independence and of a new self-judgment. Conversely, the same is impressed on masters when they, too, are pointed to their Lord in heaven (Eph. 6:9; Col. 4:1). Paul does not speak — so we can summarize — "concerning slavery," but he speaks to Christian slaves and Christian masters, and he exhorts them to see and experience their position in society out of Christ.[174] That at the same time an enormous tension was introduced into slavery as a social system cannot be denied, but even so it must be viewed, as far as we are able to see, more as the consequence than as the deliberate object of Paul's admonitions. However, because he approaches the problem of social relationships in this way, that is, from the religious-ethical side, his admonitions retain for every social relationship, however much modernized, an abiding and unmistakable significance. Accordingly, one can ask himself whether the Christian relationship between masters and servants within the boundaries of slavery sketched by the apostle cannot also serve as a humiliating example to modern society with so many relationships destitute of all personal ties.[175]

---

perhaps not deliberately, more deeply than was the case in the mitigating prescriptions of the Mosaic laws.

173. Cf., e.g., Strack-Billerbeck, IV, pp. 719ff.

174. "The issue is not the word 'slavery' but its content" (Verdam, *Symbolae van Oven*, p. 229).

175. Further see Rengstorf, *TDNT*, II, pp. 270ff., *s.v. doulos;* G. Brillenburg Wurth, *Het Christelijk leven in de maatschappij*, 1951, pp. 187ff.; and for a com-

SECTION 52. SUBJECTION TO CIVIL AUTHORITY

Of particular importance, finally, is what Paul writes on the attitude of Christians toward the civil authorities. In this connection three passages especially come up for discussion — Romans 13:1-7; 1 Timothy 2:1-4; Titus 3:1. Of these Romans 13:1ff. is certainly the most important.

The significance in the whole of Paul's preaching of the positive attitude toward civil authority that is taken here has given occasion to all sorts of speculation. In particular the need has been felt for a more christological approach than is explicitly the case in Romans 13 itself. This leads first of all to the question as to whether the context in which Romans 13:1-7 arises more or less unexpectedly and abruptly is able to yield a further motivation for the content of this paraenesis.

Some are of the opinion that Paul here wishes to prevent the misunderstanding that those liberated by Christ are no longer under the rule of the powers of this aeon; thus he is said to warn against any anticipatory, eschatological-anarchistic posture in the world.[176] Moreover, one can consider whether perhaps such tendencies were cropping up in the church at Rome.[177] There is no evidence for this, however. Others accordingly choose to seek the occasion more generally in the circumstance that the question naturally occurred to Christians (especially in Rome!) as to what their relationship must be to the authorities, and that Paul, also in view of the revolutionary attitude of many Jews, set great store by elucidating his loyalty toward the government.[178] Some also point to the fact that the occasion for speaking of the authorities can have lain in the immediately preceding passage. In 12:19 Paul rejects personal vengeance, and speaks of the vengeance God himself will execute. In this way he would have come to speak of government as one of the means of God's retribution.[179] Others, in view of the foregoing commandment of love and the reference that follows in Romans 13:11ff. to the coming end of things, think that the whole of Romans 13:1-7 must be read from the viewpoint of the "nevertheless." It is certainly no longer self-evident that the Christian must conform in this ordinance, "nevertheless," in view of the provisional character of the present dispensation of redemption, he must still do this.[180]

One can indeed make a meaningful connection between Romans 13:1-7 and the preceding rejection of the urge to personal retaliation. It is also clear that the position of the church in the world in Romans 13:1-7 is not for a moment detached from its expectation for the future (cf. Rom. 13:11, 12). Yet it is not to be denied that the admonition to the church to be subject to the constituted authorities is based neither on

---

parison of this problem with the conceptions of the Stoics: H. Greeven, *Das Hauptproblem der Sozialethik in der neueren Stoa und im Urchristentum*, 1935; H. D. Wendland, *Botschaft an die Soziale Welt*, 1959 (*Studien zur Ev. Sozialtheologie und Sozialethik*, V), pp. 104-114, cf. pp. 58-64.

176. Cf., e.g., Nygren, *Commentary on Romans*, pp. 426-431.

177. Cf. Althaus, *Rom.*, p. 112.

178. Cf., e.g., Schlatter, *Gottes Gerechtigkeit*, p. 350; see also Greijdanus on Rom. 13:1-7 (*Rom.*, II, p. 563); Sanday and Headlam, *Romans*, pp. 369ff.

179. Cf. Sanday and Headlam, *Romans*, p. 366; Lagrange, *Saint Paul Épitre aux Romains*, 1931, p. 310; see also Michel, *Rom.*, p. 281.

180. Cf. O. Cullmann, *The State in the New Testament*, 1956, pp. 57f.

the one nor on the other, but only on the God-ordained character of government and on the protection one enjoys from it if he does that which is good. Consequently one seeks in vain in Romans 13:1-7 for an immediate connection between the basic redemptive-historical, eschatological structure of Paul's preaching and his paraenesis concerning government.[181] On the other hand, it may not be forgotten that Romans 13:1-7 forms a subdivision of the paraenetic part of the epistle that begins with 12:1, and is therefore characterized by the qualification given there of the Christian life as "liturgy," the service of God in everyday life. Viewed in this context Paul's intention becomes more transparent: obedience to earthly authorities is also involved in what Romans 12:1ff. calls the spiritual sacrificial service, the placing of one-self at the service of God in virtue of the mercy of God shown to the church.[182] This obedience is a submitting of oneself to the order appointed by God.[183] Included in the paraenesis beginning and in principle based in Romans 12:1ff., Romans 13:1ff. says therefore that the divine ordinances for the natural life, in particular those which involve the institution of the authority of government, retain their validity for the church, indeed that it is precisely the church, called and destined to God's service by his demonstration of mercy in Christ, that has to respect this ordinance. To this is then added the motive of its welfare, the possibility of being able as church to exist in the world (vv. 3, 4). This last point is also met with very clearly in 1 Timothy 2:2: "that we may lead a tranquil and quiet life, in all godliness and gravity." At the same time the church represents the divine redemptive will with respect to all (sorts of) men (1 Tim. 2:2, 3). By its intercession for the civil authorities and its example (cf. 1 Pet. 2:15) it is also in civil life to subserve the well-being of all and to give evidence of that which the church itself has received in Christ. It is in this way clearly evident that obedience to the authorities is not merely a minor and incidental matter, a temporary conformity of the church to an order that is fundamentally no longer its own, but constitutes an integral part of the new obedience of the church of Christ; this appears also from the choice of words in Titus 3:1: "Remind them to be in subjection to rulers and authorities, to be obedient, to be ready unto good work...."

The great positiveness and emphasis with which Paul speaks of the divine economy in Romans 13 in connection with the (heathen) government remain striking: "... for there is no government[184] but of God; and those that be are ordained by God. So that he who resists the government withstands the ordinance of God ... for it is in God's service for your good ... for they are ministers of God." Therefore dis-

---

181. For the so-called "christological" interpretation of "the powers" see below, pp. 325f.

182. On this see, i.a., the important essay by Käsemann, "Principles of the Interpretation of Romans 13," *New Testament Questions of Today*, p. 199.

183. *Hypotassesthō, tetagmenai* (Rom. 13:1); *antitassomenos, diatagē* (v. 2; cf. v. 5).

184. *Exousia* seems especially, just as in the corresponding rabbinic usage, to mean "the government" (plural: "the authorities"); cf. Foerster, *TDNT*, II, p. 562.

obedience to the government exposes one to the (divine) judgment[185] (v. 2), as for one who does evil the civil authority in general is an avenger in the service of (divine) wrath[186] (v. 4); it is necessary to be subject to him not only because of the wrath of God that one otherwise brings on himself — from fear, thus — but also "for the sake of conscience." In these last words, too, it is implied that in this submission to civil authority it is a question of an obligation appointed by God.[187] In addition, there is the surely very positive judgment Paul gives concerning the effect of the power of government: it is not the good, but the evil who have to be afraid of it. "Would you have no fear of him who is in authority? then do what is good, and you will receive his approval" (vv. 3ff.).

In explanation of this certainly very positive attitude some have pointed to the favorable experience of Paul with the Roman government.[188] Others have even said that he would not have written these words if he had foreseen the coming persecution under Nero, etc.[189] But in the first place such a conception attributes to Paul a naively optimistic evaluation of the existing political order that bears no relationship to what he himself had already experienced and to what since the death of Jesus had repeatedly been the experience of the Christian church. In the second place, it is completely in conflict with the fundamental definition of his position, which is not founded in the first instance on what is to be expected from the civil authorities, but what one owes them for God's sake. That this last is posited with so much force proves rather that Paul does not have a specific government or prevailing order in mind, but that he speaks from a deeply rooted conviction, one that is not assailed by the misdeeds of a specific government. For this one can refer to the Old Testament and the late-Jewish tradition (cf. Prov. 8:14, 16; Deut. 1:17; Ps. 72:1ff.; Ps. 82:1, 6; Wisdom 6:3; Apoc. of Bar. 82:9; Enoch 46:5).[190] But more than a conformity with what was the general Jewish conviction or the well-understood self-interest of the Judaism of the Diaspora, there emerges here the faith of the apostle that the world is the creation of God, has not been abandoned by him, and has therefore been placed under his ordinances. That the authorities themselves can abandon entirely the distinction to be maintained by them between good and evil and place themselves at the service of evil (cf. 1 Cor. 2:7, 8) does not prevent him from continuing to elucidate God's purpose with government, nor from giving expression to his faith that God upholds his purpose, continues to

---

185. *Krima lēmpsontai:* will receive punishment. It is not eternal punishment that is intended, but the punishment of the government executed in God's name (cf. v. 2a).

186. *Ekdikos eis orgēn:* it executes the vindicatory justice whereby God's wrath (judgment) is realized.

187. Cf. above, p. 288.

188. G. Kittel, "Das Urteil des N.T. über den Staat," *ZST*, 1937, p. 663.

189. So, e.g., Kühl: "In the latter part of the Neronian dominion such unlimited appreciative judgments about the governing circles could no longer have passed his lips" (*Der Brief des Paulus an die Römer*, 1913, p. 435).

190. Cf. Strack-Billerbeck, III, pp. 303, 304.

establish justice on earth through government, and thus continues to press it into the service[191] of the well-being of the world.[192] This last point is expressed so generally that from the connection he here makes between civil authority and the punishment and wrath of God one will not be permitted to conclude that only sin explains and justifies the origin and existence of government.[193] Even though this general well-being is advanced by the fact that government because of the wickedness of men is authorized and obligated to bear the sword — and that not merely as an ornament[194] — that is in no respect to say that government is to be accepted and respected by the Christian church only as a necessary evil; rather in its office lies the proof that by its service God maintains and wills to see maintained his justice and his goodness in the world created by him (cf. 1 Tim. 2:2).

That Paul expresses all this with such great emphasis must find its cause in the fact that the church was particularly in need of such a paraenesis with this motivation. We see repeatedly that Paul continues to bind it to the divine ordinances for the natural life. The earnestness with which he does this is difficult to explain otherwise than that because of a wrong notion of the dispensation of redemption that has gone into effect with Christ's advent the church ran the danger of viewing the ordinances that till now had obtained for it as a point of view superseded in Christ. This danger could arise in particular with regard to the significance of government. Was there not in the fact that Christ was the church's Lord the possibility of dissociating itself from every "worldly" bond, the more so as not only good but also evil was frequently to be feared from it? In this danger of anticipation and spiritualism more than in any other consideration the explanation will have to be sought for Paul's very emphatic paraenesis to submission to civil authority. That which with so much stress is put first — "every man . . ." — one will thus be permitted to paraphrase: "everyone, even the believer in Christ."[195] The reassuring "for rulers are not a terror to those who do good, but to him who does evil" points in the same direction. The meaning of the pericope is therefore not to be taken concessively — having to conform to the order of government in spite of its provisionality[196] — but positively to preclude every proleptic or spiritualistic understanding.

Although there is no mention here of the political calling of believers as sharers in the task of government, this very deliberate desig-

---

191. *Leitourgoi* (v. 6) meant originally: to perform a service for the people. The alternation of *diakonos* (v. 4) and *leitourgoi* has no particular significance. The latter word is more solemn and has the touch of the official.

192. *Soi* (which is missing in a few mss.) *eis to agathon* has a general significance (not only applicable to believers).

193. So, e.g., E. Brunner, *The Letter to the Romans*, p. 109: "The possessors of political power are instruments of the divine rule of wrath. . . . That is the dignity, that is also the limit of the State."

194. *Eikē* is usually translated "in vain." The expression denotes not only the threat that lies in the sword of government, but also the duty of the government to exercise its power where necessary.

195. Cf. E. Gaugler, *Der Brief an die Römer*, II, 1952, p. 273.

196. As Cullmann supposes (*The State in the New Testament*, pp. 57f.).

nation of government as the continuing instrument in the hand of God is of great significance for the whole understanding of the life of the church. However much its "life" and its "citizenship" are in heaven (Col. 3:3; Phil. 3:20), its place and calling lie in the ordinances of the present world. And this is the more striking on account of the expectation for the future that emerges so clearly in this context (vv. 11ff.). This expectation does not act as a relativizing factor for what concerns life in the order appointed by God, but holds the church just that much more responsible in it. It is of particular importance, moreover, that Paul adduces no other ground for this obedience to the civil authority than that the civil authority is ordained by God. Out of opposition to a "natural theology" some have repeatedly sought for a deeper "christological foundation" of Romans 13:1-7. But Paul evidently has no need of that in this context, because for him there is no antithesis here; his reference to the divine ordinance does not rest on the conception of a natural order standing by itself or to be gathered from experience, but is a consequence of his "Israelitic" faith in God nurtured from the whole Old Testament revelation of God, who just because he is the Creator of the world is also its Redeemer, and who in the work of redemption upholds the order of this world even in its fallen state. Also for this reason it is altogether important to him that the church should not withdraw itself prematurely from this order appointed by God and the shield provided for it in that order, and he is not engaged as much as possible in relativizing this order on the ground of his faith in Christ, but rather in buttressing it as strongly as possible.

All this means — in the nature of the case — not that the church is here summoned to a "blind" obedience to government and that Paul declares every existing governmental power inviolable and sacrosanct. Although in the words he employs there are no further criteria as to how far this obligation to obedience extends and whether in the existing order modifications or revolutions are permissible — questions of which the former certainly was and the latter probably was not relevant for his readers of that day — government, precisely as a divine ordinance, both so far as its own functioning and so far as the duty to obedience are concerned, has not been withdrawn from, but rather subjected to the criticism of those who see in submission to its authority the service of God, Christian "liturgy" in everyday life (Rom. 12:1, 2). Where the boundaries lie cannot be foreseen or determined *a priori* in every detail. That for Paul "to obey God rather than men" was no less valid than for the other apostles, in keeping with the word of the Lord himself (Acts 4:19; 5:29; cf. Matt. 22:21), may be accepted as incontestable without additional proof. What interests him here, however, is not to point the church to these boundaries on the basis of its being Christian, but to make it clear to the church that it has to give effect to its obedience and service to Christ, not without, but within the boundaries set for it by the civil authorities.[197]

---

197. Cf. Käsemann, *New Testament Questions of Today*, pp. 211f.: "Paul sets himself ... passionately against the separation of creation and new age. The new age is not suspended in midair: it takes root on this our earth to which Christ

Over against this appraisal of the authorities in Romans 13:1 stands another, not different in principle, in 1 Corinthians 6:1ff. and 1 Corinthians 2:8. To be sure, in 1 Corinthians 6:1 believers are rebuked that for their trivial disputes they go to law before "the unrighteous, and not before the saints." By this, however, the *vitium* of "injustice" is not imprinted on the heathen government or administration of justice as such[198] — "unrighteous" is as much as to say "heathen," in distinction from the "saints" in Christ — but it is held out to Christians as their duty that they resolve their disputes among themselves. The general effect of this word is therefore not that Christians wherever they are able to bypass the state without thereby threatening it in its existence must do this,[199] but rather that the Christian church is to know its own calling. By instituting legal proceedings before the worldly judge — how-ever much this in itself can be an appeal to the justice appointed by God (cf. Luke 18:1ff.) — it gives evidence, and at that in the presence of non-Christians, of having forgotten its high calling and destiny (vv. 3ff.).

And, finally, as concerns 1 Corinthians 2:8, the apostle certainly speaks in a very reprehensible sense of "the rulers of this world" as the earthly, human (and not the demonic![200]) authorities who have nailed Jesus to the cross. Nevertheless, there is here in no sense a counter-instance contrary to Romans 13, as though the latter rested on the assumption that the persons in authority are always in the service of the right and never of the wrong. Such a "naive" explanation of Romans 13 we have already rejected above.

No mention has been made above of the interpretation that chooses to think of the "powers" in Romans 13:1ff. as angelic powers. The idea is then that the state is the executive organ of the invisible angelic powers, of which Paul frequently speaks elsewhere. Interpreters then speak indeed of a "demonistic" or — as the advocates of this view prefer! — "christological" conception of the state. For they proceed from the thought often occurring elsewhere in Paul that Christ has subdued the powers and has placed them under his dominion. In this (provisional)

---

came down. It does not create for itself there an island of the blessed; . . . it creates the possibility of the kind of service which can no longer be universal and alive if it is not carried out in the midst of the old, passing world, thus . . . preserving the world as divine creation."

198. So Schrenk, *TDNT*, I, p. 151: "the Gentiles are described in this way because as despisers of the divine law they cannot be expected to do justice."

199. So Cullmann, *The State in the New Testament*, p. 61, who in our opinion wrongly finds in 1 Cor. 6:1 and 2:8 a point of view opposite to that of Rom. 13. To the same effect Brunner, *The Letter to the Romans*, p. 110.

200. At present many think here of "spirit-powers" and then connect to this the gnostic myth according to which these spirits are said to have recognized the Redeemer descended from heaven because of his human form and by nailing him to the cross permitted themselves to be taken off guard; cf., e.g., Lietzmann-Kümmel, *Cor.*, pp. 12, 13, 170 and the literature mentioned there; also Bultmann, *Theology*, I, p. 175. Others hold the view that Paul here speaks both of the human and of the demonic powers that stand behind them and use them as tools (Cullmann, *The State in the New Testament*, pp. 63, 100). Against this whole conception, how-ever, see the in our view conclusive argumentation of J. Schniewind, "Die Archonten dieses Äons," in *Nachgelassene Reden und Aufsätze*, 1952, pp. 104ff.

binding they would accordingly do service in the divine economy of the life of the state. At the same time the possibility exists, however, that they attempt again to break away from God. Against this background Romans 13 would then have to be understood. Christians are to submit themselves to the civil authorities as a provisional institution willed by God and administered by the "powers." At the same time they are to be mindful, however, of a possible demonizing of this power of the state, etc.[201]

This conception, which has been the subject of much discussion for a considerable time and still is in part, has nevertheless gained but little approval,[202] however ably it has been defended by some. The great objection against it is that Paul nowhere with so much as a single word relates angelic powers and (human) authorities to each other, and that one must rely therefore on the fact that he employs the same word for both — *exousiai* (and on the connection made in 1 Cor. 2:8, in our view incorrectly — see above — between angelic powers and worldly rulers; as well as on the manner in which angels are introduced in 1 Cor. 6:3). Likewise it is nowhere to be demonstrated from the New Testament that the powers conquered by Christ have been pressed into his service "provisionally," as would then be presupposed in Romans 13:1. However much one attempts with this conception therefore to establish a closer bond between the central christological character of Paul's preaching and his paraenesis concerning civil authority in Romans 13, the grounds that are adduced for this are completely inadequate to justify such a radical reinterpretation of Romans 13.

---

201. In this form this conception has been propounded anew and maintained against criticism by Cullmann, *The State in the New Testament,* pp. 65ff., 95-114 (the latter first appeared in *TZ,* 1954, pp. 321-336). In the same or somewhat different form it was defended earlier, i.a., by H. Schlier, "Mächte und Gewalten im N.T.," in *Theol. Blätter,* 1930, cols. 289ff.; G. Dehn, "Engel und Obrigkeit," in *Theol. Aufsätze für K. Barth,* 1936, pp. 90ff.; K. L. Schmidt, "Das Gegenüber von Kirche und Staat in der Gemeinde des N.T.," in *Theol. Blätter,* 1937, cols. 1-16; K. Barth, *Church and State,* ET 1939; W. Schweitzer, *Die Herrschaft Christi und der Staat im N.T.* Less clearly also in H. Berkhof, *Christ and the Powers,* ET 1962, p. 58, n. 5, who recognizes that the connection between the powers and the life of the state is not to be demonstrated from Rom. 13:1, but appeals for this connection to 1 Cor. 2:8 (see above).

202. In particular it has been contested by G. Kittel, *Christus und Imperator,* 1939, pp. 48ff.; H. von Campenhausen, "Zur Auslegung von Röm 13," in *Festschrift für A. Bertholet,* 1950, pp. 97ff.; E. Käsemann, "Römer 13, 1-7 in unserer Generation," in *ZTK,* 1959, pp. 351ff. See also the highly balanced and conclusive refutation in Gaugler, *Die Heiligung im Zeugnis der Schrift,* II, pp. 275-279, and the summary of all these objections in eleven points in Schrage, *Die konkreten Einzelgebote,* p. 223. In the commentaries on Romans this conception has almost nowhere found agreement (cf., e.g., Michel, on Rom. 13).

VIII

THE CHURCH
AS THE PEOPLE OF GOD

SECTION 53. TWO PRINCIPAL ASPECTS

The church also belongs to the central content of Paul's preaching. In all that has been said of the redemptive work of God in Jesus Christ, the church has continually been included. From a redemptive-historical point of view it has a fixed place in that work. It does not first come into view as a gathering of individual believers who have come to participate in the gift of Christ and the Holy Spirit, Rather, it has an *a priori* significance, namely, as the people that in his saving activity God has placed on his side and which he intends to be the exemplification of his grace and redemption. Consequently all that has been said in the foregoing about the salvation given in Christ has special reference to the church and to the individual believer because he belongs to the church. In treating the various facets of salvation this has frequently been evident.

This central and integral significance which Paul ascribes to the church in all his proclamation of redemption appears especially from the two principal points of view from which he considers the church: in the first place, the church is the continuation and fulfillment of the historical people of God that in Abraham God chose to himself from all peoples and to which he bound himself by making the covenant and the promises. In this Paul associates himself with the general view of the church as it is to be found in the whole of the New Testament, although in his epistles he provides his own thorough elaboration of it. In the second place, he gives his own form of expression to the real being and character of the church when he speaks of it as the body of Christ.

Both ways of viewing the church are indissolubly connected to each other, as we shall see still further, and together they constitute a unity. In the first the redemptive-historical aspect of the church predominates, and in the second the christological. In both, however, the salvation given in Christ bears a corporate character, and is given and received only in the fellowship of the people chosen and called by God to himself and of the one body of Christ. We wish now under both of these principal aspects to examine more closely Paul's pronouncements on the church in their diversity and unity. Because of the volume of material we shall distribute it over various chapters, and devote the first of them exclusively to a discussion of the church as the redemptive-historical people of God.

SECTION 54. EKKLESIA

The redemptive-historical significance of the New Testament church as the people of God already finds clear expression in its most prevalent name *ekklesia*. Without going again into all the questions connected with the early Christian use of *ekklesia*,[1] with which Paul associates himself, it may be taken as established that the Christian church is thereby ascribed the title of the Old Testament people of God as the *Q*e*hal-Yahweh*.[2] The frequent use by Paul of the qualification "church of God" can also point to this,[3] the equivalent of *Q*e*hal-Yahweh* in Deuteronomy. At the same time the use of this name for the early Christian church must not be taken as a simple repristination. Rather, in it the consciousness was voiced that in its existence as the Christian church the true people of God, the Messianic congregation of the great end time (cf. Matt. 16:18ff.), had been revealed, and that the privileges and qualities attributed to ancient Israel in the making of the covenant in the wilderness had found their God-intended application in this church. Paul associates himself with this usage and the thought contained in it,[4] when for him too *ekklesia* constitutes the customary description of the communion of those who believe in Christ and have been baptized into him.

Just as elsewhere so (and especially) in Paul *ekklesia* is at one time the description of the church in its totality, irrespective of its being scattered over various localities, then again of the local church or even of the so-called house-churches (for this last use see Rom. 16:5; 1 Cor. 16:19; Col. 4:15; Philem. 2). As a description of the church as a whole the use of *ekklesia* in Ephesians and Colossians is particularly to be pointed out (cf. Eph. 1:22; 3:10, 21; 5:23-32; Col. 1:18, 24, although it is there also used of the local church and house-church [Col. 4:16, 15]). In the remaining epistles *ekklesia* usually means the local church. As a rule it is then called simply "church," although sometimes also plerophorically "the church of God" (cf. 1 Thess. 2:14; 2 Thess. 1:4; 1 Tim. 3:5 [and 1 Cor. 1:2 and 2 Cor. 1:1 (?); see below]). There are then outside Ephesians and Colossians passages of which it is usually judged that Paul speaks of the *ekklesia* as a whole, whether as the "church of God" (1 Cor. 10:32; 11:22; 15:9; Gal. 1:13; 1 Tim. 3:15), or simply as the "church" (1 Cor. 12:28; Phil. 3:6).[5]

---

1. See also my *The Coming of the Kingdom*, pp. 344ff.

2. In the LXX *ekklēsia* is in this sense regularly the translation of *qāhāl*. Among the rabbis *qāhāl* is used only infrequently as a designation of collective Israel or of great parts of it (cf. Strack-Billerbeck, I, pp. 733, 734). In the Greek Jewish writings, too (Sirach, Psalms of Solomon, Philo), *ekklēsia* serves as the denotation of Israel as the people of God; cf., e.g., Bultmann, *Theology*, I, pp. 38f.; K. L. Schmidt, *TDNT*, III, pp. 527ff.

3. Cf. L. Rost, *Die Vorstufen von Kirche und Synagoge im Alten Testament*, 1938, p. 154.

4. See also the clear and complete explanation of A. Wikenhauser, *Die Kirche als der Mystische Leib Christi nach dem Apostel Paulus*, 2nd ed., 1940, pp. 4-33.

5. Starting from this usage it is then assumed that the address in 1 Cor. 1:2 (*tē ekklēsia tou Theou tē ousē en Korinthō;* cf. 2 Cor. 1:1) likewise does not speak of the local church at Corinth, but of the church of God insofar as it is found

To be sure, the attempt has been made to understand the passages mentioned above (apart from Colossians and Ephesians) of the local church. Thus Cerfaux, for example, has wished to make it plausible that *ekklēsia tou Theou* originally had reference to the church at Jerusalem and that when Paul speaks in 1 Corinthians 15:9, Galatians 1:13, and Philippians 3:6 of his persecution of the church (of God) he is not thinking of the church in general, but of the church at Jerusalem.[6] And so far as 1 Corinthians 10:32 and 11:22 are concerned, it is said that there is no reason to think of the church in general; rather, the gathered local church is again intended. Paul would then have transferred the title that originally pertained to the church at Jerusalem specifically to the church at Corinth in order to set its obligations clearly before it. In this sense 1 Corinthians 1:2 and 2 Corinthians 1:1 are consequently to be assessed as a simple designation of the local church.[7]

Now in our view one may with good reason maintain that, in addition to the local and universal church, *ekklesia* in Paul can have the significance of a religious gathering (cf. 1 Cor. 11:18; 14:19, 28, 34, 35). This is especially clear in 1 Corinthians 14:34ff. where "in the churches" stands over against "at home," and therefore can be translated "in the church meetings." In this sense 1 Corinthians 11:22, too, can be understood, not of the church in general, but of the church meeting. Here again "house" stands over against *ekklēsia* as the place where one eats and drinks. One can also interpret 1 Corinthians 14:4 in this way. In other places, however, one can hardly deny the meaning of *Gesamt-gemeinde*, the church-in-general. Thus in 1 Corinthians 12:28 where apostles, prophets, etc., are spoken of as given by God "to the church." Here it is obviously a matter not only of that which applies to the individual local congregation, but to the church in general. Regarding 1 Corinthians 10:32 one may be doubtful because with *ekklēsia tou Theou* one can think both of participants in local church gatherings[8] and of the church in general.[9] In our view it is otherwise, however, with the three passages where Paul speaks of his persecution of "the church of God" (1 Cor. 15:9; Gal. 1:13; Phil. 3:6). Although this name certainly will have been applied in the first instance to the church at Jerusalem as the mother church and to the churches afterward established in Judea (1 Thess. 2:14), it is apparent even from this last passage that "church of God" was not employed by him as a *terminus technicus* for the church in Jerusalem or in Judea. In the plural form of 1 Thessalonians 2:14 the principle is already clear of the particularization and extension of this name. Paul's attacks, too, were not directed only or in the first place against the primitive church at Jerusalem, but also against the Christians in cities abroad (Acts 9:2; 22:5; 26:11; Gal. 1:17). For his object was the complete extirpation of the name of Christ

in Corinth (cf. the address in Ignatius' epistles to the Ephesians, Magnesians, Trallians, Philadelphians, in 1 Clement, and in Polycarp to the Philadelphians); thus, e.g., Schmidt, *TDNT*, III, *loc. cit.;* Bultmann, *Theology*, I, p. 94, *et al.*

6. L. Cerfaux, *The Church in the Theology of St. Paul*, ET 1959, pp. 109ff.
7. *Ibid.*, p. 113.
8. Thus, e.g., Cerfaux, *ibid.*, p. 112.
9. Cf., e.g., A. Wikenhauser, *Die Kirche*, p. 7.

(Acts 26:9; Gal. 1:13).[10] In the three places mentioned one is undoubtedly to think, therefore, of the church in general.

Furthermore, however one chooses to take 1 Corinthians 1:2 and 2 Corinthians 1:1, it is in our view incontrovertible that from the beginning Paul in his epistles ascribes more than one meaning to the title *ekklesia*: next to that of the local (house-)church and church meeting also that of the church in general, the church as a totality. The passages in Ephesians and Colossians (and 1 Tim. 3:15) are therefore not in conflict with the general usage of Paul, though it remains true that in Ephesians and Colossians *ekklesia* has the meaning almost exclusively of the church-in-general while elsewhere the majority of Paul's pronouncements concerning the *ekklesia* have reference to the local church or church gathering.

When one inquires after the relationship of both these meanings of *ekklesia,* the view that has frequently been advocated that the universal church is for Paul a secondary concept and is intended as the joining together or confederation of individual churches is to be repudiated even on the ground of the little that has so far been said about the *ekklesia*. For if the concept of the *ekklesia tou Theou* has above all a redemptive-historical content and speaks of the church as the true people of God, the manifestation of the (Messianic) congregation of the great future, then it is clear that for Paul, not only in Ephesians and Colossians but in all his preaching, the thought of the universal church is primary and the local church, the house-church, and the church gathering can be denoted as *ekklesia* because the universal *ekklesia* is revealed and represented in them. Consequently we see that for unity and peace in the local church Paul appeals to the unity of the church as the body-of-Christ (that is, as we shall see still further, to the unity of the church as a whole; 1 Cor. 12; Rom. 12). The fact that the usage of *ekklesia* outside Ephesians and Colossians to a preponderant degree denotes the local church is thus in no way decisive for the fundamental idea of the *ekklesia* in Paul's epistles. It proves only that in these pronouncements he is occupied with relationships in the local church — which in view of the concrete purpose of his epistles is not to be wondered at — and that he regards and addresses these local churches according to what they are as the manifestations and representations of the people of God in general.

SECTION 55. "SAINTS," "ELECT," "BELOVED," "CALLED"

Along with *ekklesia* we meet with several other frequently recurring expressions in Paul that function as customary designations of the church and in which the same self-consciousness of the Christian church and the same apostolic judgment find expression as in the name *ekklesia*. First of all, the description of the church as the "saints" (*hagioi*) is to be pointed out here. One finds it especially in the address at the be-

---

10. So rightly Wikenhauser, *ibid.,* p. 7.

ginning and in the greetings at the conclusion of various epistles (cf. Rom. 1:7; 1 Cor. 1:2; 2 Cor. 1:1; Eph. 1:1; Phil. 1:1; Col. 1:2; Rom. 16:15; 2 Cor. 13:12; Phil. 4:21, 22). In part this designation occurs next to that of *ekklesia* (1 Cor. 1:2). It is evident from this that one is not to make a specific distinction between the two (as though, for example, "church" were and "the saints" were not to denote a solidary relationship; we have to do here with synonymous expressions).[11] This expression "the saints" or "saints" occurs not only in these more or less formal passages, however, but also in the organic contexts of Paul's epistles where it denotes believers, whether thought of to a greater or lesser extent in a congregational relationship (cf. Rom. 8:27; 16:2; 1 Cor. 6:1; Eph. 1:15; 5:3; 6:18; Col. 3:12). Here, too, there is reason to suppose that this name was applied in the first instance to the primitive church at Jerusalem. In more than one place by "the saints" Paul means specifically the Jerusalem church (Rom. 15:25; 1 Cor. 16:1; 2 Cor. 8:4; 9:1, 12). It is clear here as well, however, that this name came into effect wherever Christian churches sprang up.[12] Furthermore, this name was not first employed by Paul. Just as in the case of *ekklesia* we have to do with a general early Christian usage (cf. Acts 9:13, 32, 41; 26:10; Heb. 3:1; 6:10; 13:24; Rev. 5:8; 8:3, 4, *et passim;* Jude 3). Likewise the consciousness that was expressed in this self-designation of the Christian church and which was strengthened through its use by the Apostle Paul was none other than that which underlay the use of *ekklesia*. With it there was a harking back to the naming of Israel as the holy people of God (Exod. 19:6; Lev. 11:44, 45, etc.), also expressed as a substantive: "(the) saints" (cf. Deut. 33:3; Num. 16:3; Ps. 16:3; 34:10; 89:6), partly also in conjunction with "the people" or the "congregation." From this qualification of empirical Israel we again see a special use developing, namely, the designation of the true people of God that is preserved and delivered by the Lord from the godlessness and judgment into which empirical Israel is becoming submerged, and to which in the great future he will fulfill his ancient promises (cf., e.g., Isa. 4:3; 6:13; Dan. 7:18, 21ff.). This special and eschatological use of "the saints" is also to be found in the later Jewish apocalyptic[13] and the sects,[14] as has appeared anew from the Qumran scrolls.[15]

From all this the significance of this designation of the Christian church in Paul can also be clearly seen: as the communion of the "saints" it is the true people of God, the eschatological Israel, which may apply to itself the promises of God because of the salvation that has appeared in Christ. On the one hand the church is in this way

---

11. Cf. *ibid.,* pp. 22ff., and the survey given there of the use of "saints" in Paul, the other writings of the New Testament, the apostolic fathers, the Old Testament, and Judaism.

12. Cf. W. G. Kümmel, *Kirchenbegriff und Geschichtsbewusstsein in der Urgemeinde und bei Jesus,* 1943, pp. 16, 17, and the literature discussed there.

13. Kümmel, *loc. cit.*

14. Cf. Wikenhauser, *Die Kirche,* pp. 27, 28.

15. Cf., e.g., K. G. Kuhn, "Die in Palästina gefundenen hebr. Texte und das N.T.," in *ZTK,* 1950, p. 199.

identified with Israel as the people of God; on the other hand, however, it is thereby distinguished from empirical Israel.

The same thing is true *mutatis mutandis* of the description closely linked with the qualification "the saints," namely, "the elect" *(hoi eklektoi)*, "beloved" *(ēgapēmenoi)*, and "called" *(klētoi)*. Paul speaks in more than one place of (the) "elect" of God as a variation of the "we" of the church (Rom. 8:33; cf. vv. 31, 32) and as a synonym for "saints" (v. 28; similarly in 2 Tim. 2:10, cf. vv. 11ff.), also as a title of the church (Col. 3:12: "God's elect, saints and beloved"); in Titus 1:1 he further defines his own apostolate as directed toward and having reference to the "faith of God's elect."[16] Here again "God's elect" is to be taken as a designation of the church, as "a self-designation of Christians."[17]

This usage, which has its traces in the whole of the New Testament (cf. Matt. 24:22, 24, 31 and the parallel passages in Mark 13; Luke 18:7; 1 Pet. 1:1; 2:9; 5:13; 2 John 1, 13), just as the qualifications already discussed, is to be traced back to the Old Testament designation of Israel as God's chosen people (cf., e.g., Deut. 7:6, 7; 14:2, *et passim;* 1 Kings 3:8; 1 Chron. 16:13; Ps. 105:6, etc.). In a special sense God's people of the future are denoted in this way (Isa. 14:1; 43:20), that is to say, those whom the Lord will cause to remain out of the ruin and judgment that is to come upon sinful Israel (Isa. 65:8, 9), in distinction from those who have forsaken him (Isa. 65:15, 22). It is frequently employed in this sense in the later eschatological and apocalyptic literature.[18]

"Beloved" is used synonymously with "elect" by Paul as a designation of the church (cf. Rom. 1:7; 1 Thess. 1:4; 2 Thess. 2:13; Col. 3:12). This name, too, goes back to the peculiar relationship between God and Israel, qualified as a love-relationship especially in Hosea, but also elsewhere[19] (cf. Rom. 11:28, where the still unbelieving Jews are called "beloved for the fathers' sake"); and it is employed in this sense in the later Jewish literature as well.[20]

Finally, the qualification of the church frequently employed by Paul as "the called" is still to be mentioned here (cf. Rom. 1:6, 7; 8:28; 1 Cor. 1:2, 24). This expression is closely connected with the preceding, as appears, for example, from the combination *klētoi hagioi* in Romans 1:7 and 1 Corinthians 1:2, as well as from the relationship the apostle establishes between the church's having been called and chosen (cf. Rom. 8:28; 9:11, 12; 2 Thess. 2:13, 14). This designation of the "called" will also have to be understood with reference to the historical calling of Israel by the Lord (cf. Isa. 41:9 [in close connection with election]; 42:6; 43:1; 45:3; 48:12; 51:2). The expression *klētē hagia* in Exodus

---

16. *Kata pistin eklektōn Theou; kata* is somewhat difficult to translate here; one may take it finally or relationally; cf. C. Bouma, *De brieven van den apostel Paulus aan Timotheüs en Titus,* 1942, pp. 374ff.

17. Dibelius-Conzelmann, *A Commentary on the Pastoral Epistles,* p. 131, n. 1.

18. Cf. Schrenk, *TDNT,* IV, pp. 183ff., *s.v. eklektos.* The Qumran sect also applied this name to itself (cf., e.g., 1QS 11; 1QH 14, 15; 15, 23).

19. For the proof passages see, e.g., Quell, *TDNT,* I, pp. 31ff., *s.v. agapaō.*

20. Cf., e.g., Strack-Billerbeck, III, p. 24.

12:16 and Leviticus 23:2ff. (LXX)[21] is also of importance for our subject. It is certainly very possible that this combination lies at the root of the singular expression in Paul in Romans 1:7 and 1 Corinthians 1:2 (cf. 2 Tim. 1:9).[22] One may accordingly consider whether *klētoi* is not to be taken as a substantive in this combination and therefore must be translated by "holy called ones."[23] It is certainly clear in any case how closely the notion "called" and that of *ekklesia* are connected with each other via the Old Testament.[24]

That these various designations of the church as "saints," "elect," "beloved," "called," so far, too, as their specific meaning is concerned, are closely related to one another and reciprocally supplement each other can easily be realized. The leading idea of them all is this, that God has chosen and called[25] a people to himself out of all peoples, as Abraham was called out of Ur, and believers have been called by the gospel of God's grace and to himself. As such they are his beloved, and they are holy, placed on God's side and separated from the world. Just as the name "church," these qualifications denote believers in Christ as the church of the great future, the continuation and manifestation of the true people of God in the redemptive-historical sense of the word. Paul's concept of the church is here in full agreement with what is said of the new fellowship elsewhere in the New Testament, beginning with the primitive church at Jerusalem. In Paul, moreover, it comes to the fore that it is not only the holy remnant of Israel that belongs to this holy people of God, but likewise those from among the gentiles whom God has chosen, has called to himself, and wills to consider as his beloved (cf. Rom. 9:25, *et al.*). This of itself leads us to the question of the relationship of ancient Israel and the Christian church.

SECTION 56. THE NEW COVENANT. UNIVERSAL AND PARTICULAR

The significance of the church — which has repeatedly come to light in the foregoing — as the continuation of Israel, as the elect, called, holy people of God, ought now to be defined further according to its content and essence. We have already seen in the analysis of these various designations that this "continuation" is no simple matter. On the one hand, in a positive sense it presupposes that the church springs from, is born out of Israel; on the other hand, the church takes the place of

---

21. The translation of *miqrā'-qōdesh* = holy assembly (convocation), in the LXX rendered as *concretum pro abstracto*.

22. Cf. Procksch, *TDNT*, I, p. 107, s.v. *hagios*; Cerfaux, *The Church in Paul*, pp. 118ff.; K. L. Schmidt, *TDNT*, III, p. 494, s.v. *klētos*.

23. Cf. Cerfaux, *ibid.*, p. 119, n. 30.

24. Whether Paul also made an etymological connection between *klētos*, *klēsis*, and *ekklēsia* is not to be said with certainty; cf. Schmidt, *TDNT*, III, pp. 530f., s.v. *ekklēsia*, and Cerfaux, *The Church in Paul*, pp. 184f.

25. For the relationship and delimitation between *klētoi* and *eklektoi*, cf. E. von Dobschütz, "Prädestination," in *Theologische Studien und Kritiken*, 1934, pp. 9ff.

Israel as the historical people of God. This means a new definition of the people of God, and likewise a new concept of Israel. The question is how one is to conceive of this redemptive-historical transition, on the one hand with regard to the historical Israel of the Old Testament that God has chosen to himself and to which he has given his promise, on the other hand with regard to the unbelieving Israel that has rejected Christ and thus placed itself outside the fulfillment of the divine promises to Abraham and his descendants.

Paul himself is occupied with this matter time and again and in various contexts in his epistles. Three different points of view admit of being clearly distinguished in them:

(a) In the foreground is the new — new, that is to say, as given with the revelation of Christ — definition of the essence of the people of God, which may be expressed as well in terms of the New Covenant.

(b) This new definition at the same time represents the real nature of Israel's election and the content of God's purpose with respect to his people.

(c) This new definition does not exclude continuing concern with historical Israel; the latter, even in spite of its unbelief, as the once chosen people of God remains involved in the fulfillment of his promises.

The new definition of the essence of the church as the people of God stands first. It is not the natural, national, or ceremonial prerequisites that are decisive here. What counts is to be of Christ, faith, sharing in the gifts of the Spirit.

In Paul's preaching this finds expression in a great many ways in the definition of "seed of Abraham": they who are "not only of the law, but also of the faith of Abraham" (Rom. 4:16); they who "are of Christ" are "Abraham's seed and heirs according to the promise" (Gal. 3:29). Similarly he is not a Jew who is one outwardly, and that may not be called circumcision which takes place externally in the flesh; but he is a Jew who is one in secret, and circumcision is that which takes place in the heart by the Spirit, not by the letter (Rom. 2:28, 29).

This last pronouncement in Romans 2 is also of importance for the reason that without directly mentioning the name of Christ it signifies a radicalizing of the concept Jew, and thereby of the definition of the essence of the people of God. We have already stated that such a renewing of the concept Israel, congregation of God, etc., is found not only in Paul and in the New Testament, but also in certain currents and movements within Judaism itself, particularly where men had in view the prophecies of the great end time and the people faithful to God, the holy remnant of Israel, revealing themselves in it. The great distinction between this contemporary Jewish radicalizing of the concept of Israel, people of God, etc., on the one hand, and the Pauline on the other, however, is that the former comes about altogether within the sphere of the law and of national Judaism, while for Paul, even when he speaks of being a Jew in the heart and the Spirit, faith in Christ and his gift of grace are all-important, and therefore natural descent from Abraham is no longer a determinative factor for belonging to the people of God.

This emerges very clearly in the differing conception of contemporary Judaism on the one hand and Paul on the other concerning the New Covenant which according to prophecy God would establish in the great future, and in which the Old Covenant made at Sinai would receive a new and better realization.[26] In addition to that which was already known, for example, from such writings as the Book of the Jubilees and from the publication of the Document of Damascus found at Cairo in 1909, it is particularly the scrolls of the Qumran sect discovered near the Dead Sea that have given us an insight into the way this idea of the New Covenant lived on in certain circles of later Judaism that regarded themselves as members and as the fellowship of this New Covenant, in distinction not only from the gentiles but also from those in Israel who had left the true service of God. The New Covenant thus conceived remained entirely restricted to the descendants of Abraham and in essence consisted in nothing other than in a stricter view of the law, the worship of the temple, the ceremonial regulations, etc., and remained therefore wholly particularistic and legalistic in nature.

On the other hand, for Paul the promise of the New Covenant is one of the great supports of his spiritual and universal definition of the church as the people of God and the new Israel. To be sure, he speaks only in a few places explicitly of the New Covenant, namely, in 1 Corinthians 11:25 and 2 Corinthians 3:6ff., but it has frequently been pointed out rightly that the idea of the New Covenant in Paul's conception of the New Testament church and the salvation given to it plays a much greater role than may be gathered from the sparing use of this datum of revelation and from the slight attention that has been paid to it in the history of interpretation.[27]

In this context the pronouncement of Romans 2:28, 29 just cited ought immediately to be pointed out. The apostle is reflecting here on such passages as Deuteronomy 10:16, 30:6, and Jeremiah 4:4, in which the spiritual circumcision of the heart (and not only that of the body) is promised to Israel as future redemptive gift and at the same time is laid down as a demand; and he draws from this the conclusion that the criterion for being a Jew and circumcised does not lie in distinctive external marks but in fulfilling the commandments of God (cf. vv. 26, 27). We meet with the same thought in the significant mention of the "so-called circumcision or uncircumcision" (Eph. 2:11), or when physical circumcision is ironically characterized as "mutilation" and the (true) circumcision is qualified as the worship of God by the Spirit (Phil. 3:2, 3). In these and similar pronouncements being a Jew and being circumcised acquires a purely spiritual significance, and the natural and empirical factors are not even taken into account any longer.

---

26. For the following see also W. C. van Unnik, "La conception paulinienne de la nouvelle alliance," in *Littérature et théologie pauliniennes (Recherches bibliques,* V), 1960, pp. 109-126 (repr. in *Sparsa Collecta,* 1973, pp. 174ff.); and, from the Jewish side, H. J. Schoeps, *Paul,* pp. 213ff.

27. Van Unnik, *ibid.,* pp. 98ff., 118.

This spiritual disposition now forms the real content of the New Covenant of which Paul calls himself the minister (2 Cor. 3:6), and which, as the administration of the Spirit and of the righteousness given in Christ, he sets as the privilege of the New Testament church over against the administration of death and of condemnation, under which the Israel not yet converted to God lives (2 Cor. 3:16; cf. Gal. 4:24, 25). It is nowhere more apparent than here what a central significance the notion of the New Covenant occupies in Paul's preaching in general and in his definition of the essence of the New Testament church in particular. This New Covenant is grounded in the blood shed by Christ on the cross, in which the congregation receives a share in the Lord's Supper (1 Cor. 11:25).[28] And the evidence that this New Covenant has taken effect and that the church of Christ may understand itself in terms of it is the spiritual renewal of the church itself, which he terms an epistle of Christ, prepared by his labor as a minister of the New Covenant, written not with ink, but by the Spirit of the living God, not on tables of stone, but on tables of flesh in the hearts (2 Cor. 3:3).[29] In all these qualifications the apostle is clearly reflecting on that which had been promised in prophecy concerning the New Covenant (Jer. 31:33; Ezek. 11:19; 36:26). It is on account of this fulfillment of the prophecy of the New Covenant in the Christian church that all the privileges of the Old Testament people of God in this spiritual sense pass over to the church. To it, as the church of Christ, the pre-eminent divine word of the covenant applies: "I will be their God, and they shall be my people.... I will receive you, and I will be to you a father, and you shall be to me sons and daughters" (2 Cor. 6:16ff.). Out of this fulfillment in Christ the whole nomenclature[30] of all the privileges Israel as God's people was permitted to possess recurs with renewed force and significance in the definition of the essence of

---

28. See below, Section 66.

29. Cf. above, pp. 218ff.

30. Paul does in general continue to reserve the names "Israel," "Jews," "Hebrews" for the national Jewish people (for the shaded significance of these designations cf. the relevant articles in *TDNT,* and K. L. Schmidt, *Die Judenfrage im Lichte der Kapittel 9-11 des Römerbriefs,* 2nd ed., pp. 7ff.). Yet in this, too, a certain movement is perceptible. Even the distinction Paul makes within national Judaism between who is and who is not a "Jew," between "Israel" and "those who are of Israel" (Rom. 2:28ff.; 9:6), tends to a usage that denotes the believing gentiles as well and therefore the Christian church as such as "Israel." In 1 Cor. 10:18 Paul is on the verge of such a way of speaking when he refers to "Israel after the flesh." For the words "after the flesh" do not here intend to introduce a distinction within national Israel, but speak of national Israel in distinction from another Israel, which is not explicitly mentioned, but by which evidently the church is meant as "spiritual Israel." At the same time, however, he does not yet come to such a use of Israel here. In our view this is certainly the case in Gal. 6:16: "And as many as shall walk by this rule, peace be upon them, and mercy, and upon the Israel of God." To be sure, others are of the opinion that here it is only the part of Israel believing in Christ that is intended. For this old point of contention see, e.g., the discussion between G. Schrenk and N. A. Dahl in *Judaica,* 1949, 1950. In our opinion, however, the arguments pro are decisive (cf. my "Israël in het Nieuwe Testament," *Exegetica,* II, 2, 1955, pp. 33ff., 71). To what extent Paul was accustomed to make use of such an expression is uncertain, however. In the epistles preserved to us Gal. 6:16 is the only example.

the Christian church: being sons of God (Rom. 8:14ff.; Eph. 1:5); being heirs according to the promise (Gal. 3:29; 4:7); sharing in the inheritance promised to Abraham (Rom. 8:17; cf. 4:13; Col. 1:2); being heirs of the kingdom of God (1 Cor. 6:9, 10; 15:50; Gal. 5:21). For this reason the church may rejoice in the hope of the glory of God (Rom. 5:2; 8:21; 2 Cor. 3:7ff., 18; Phil. 3:19), the splendor of the presence of God among his people, once the privilege of Israel (Rom. 9:4). Likewise the worship of God, at one time the prerogative of Israel (Rom. 9:4), is now the distinguishing mark of the Christian church as "spiritual worship" (Rom. 12:1), the service of God by the Spirit (Phil. 3:3), as Paul knows himself to be the *leitourgos* of Jesus Christ who in the priestly administration of the gospel has to see to the irreproachableness of the offerings of the gentiles (Rom. 15:16; cf. Phil. 2:17). In a word, all the richly variegated designations of Israel as the people of God are applied to the Christian church, but now in the new setting of the salvation that has appeared in Christ. Conversely, the wretchedness of the gentiles before their conversion to Christ can be described not only as being dead in sin, etc. (Eph. 2:1), but also as having been "excluded from the commonwealth of Israel and strangers to the covenants of promise" (Eph. 2:12), and their salvation can be characterized in the spiritually understood terminology of the covenant: no longer are they "strangers and sojourners," but "fellow citizens with the saints and members of the household of God" (Eph. 2:19). As Israel was once the peculiar possession of God (Exod. 19:5), so the church in all its parts, Jews and gentiles, is now the people of God's possession (Eph. 1:4; cf. Tit. 2:14). The more one views the Pauline epistles from this vantage point, the richer the materials prove to be that characterize the New Testament church in its continuity with ancient Israel on the one hand, and as the church of the New Covenant qualified by the forgiveness of sins and the gift of the Spirit on the other.

This new definition of the essence of what may be called the seed of Abraham and the people of God furthermore signifies a breaking through of the boundaries that obtained till now, a universalizing of salvation and with it of the church as the people of God. "There is no question of Jew or Greek, of slave or free, male or female" (Gal. 3:28; cf. Col. 3:11). It pertains to the essence of Paul's proclamation and of his overall significance in the history of redemption that with all pneumatic force, the adduction of evidence from the Scriptures, and theological argumentation, he placed beyond dispute this universal character of the Christian church as not bound to national, social, racial, or other anthropological prerequisites and embracing all sorts of men. This occurs notably in his running polemic with Judaism and Judaistic Christianity, in particular as that becomes evident in the epistles to the Galatians and to the Romans. But likewise where the antithesis element comes less markedly into the foreground, as, for example, in Ephesians and 1 Timothy, this universal character of the Christian church is central again and again, and the newness of the time of salvation that has dawned with Christ's advent is pointed out in the fact that the particularism of the old dispensation no longer obtains. This last perhaps occurs most emphatically in Ephesians 3:2ff., where Paul calls the participation of the gentiles in the promise the content of the mystery of Christ. Here he concentrates God's whole plan of redemption revealed in Christ with respect to the fullness of the times (cf. 1:9) in the universality of the people of God. Or, as he terms it in Ephesians 2:12ff.: those who once were far off have now been brought near by the blood of Christ, through his having broken down the wall of partition that made a division; thereby those who were alienated from the commonwealth of Israel and had no share in the covenants of the promise (v. 12) have become fellow citizens of the saints and members of the household of God (v. 19), and they have received a place in the building of God and are builded together into a dwelling place of God in the Spirit (v. 22); all these are descriptions of the privileges of the people of God that were once restricted to national Israel but are now without distinction the portion of those who belong to Christ.

Paul speaks of this insight and of his corresponding apostolic activity as the stewardship (oikonomia) of the divine grace given him with respect to the gentiles (Eph. 3:2), a mystery of redemption that in earlier generations was not made known to the children of men, but now has been revealed to God's apostles and prophets by the Spirit (v. 5). The universal character of the church pertains to the fullness of the time, constitutes as well the content of the mystery, and is evidence of the coming of the eschatological time of salvation. As such it also pertains to the gospel preaching of the new creation of God that has become effective with Christ (cf. Eph. 2:15).

In Paul's epistles this universalism is further explained in all sorts of ways. It proceeds from the grace-character of the righteousness of God revealed in Christ. Hence this righteousness is for all who believe, and there is no distinction (Rom. 3:22; 10:12). The gospel is a power of God unto salvation for everyone who believes, for the Jew first, but also for the Greek (Rom. 1:16). Hence God is not only the God of the Jews, but also of the gentiles (Rom. 3:29). And, to mention still another context of thought, in 1 Timothy 2 the apostle commands — certainly here again in view of the Judaistic heresy (cf. 1 Tim. 2:7) — that in its intercessions the church is to remember "all men"; for God will have all men to be saved and to come to the knowledge of the truth (vv. 2, 4), whereby under "all men" one is again to understand all sorts of men, not only Jews, but also gentiles (cf. v. 7).

It is remarkable, moreover, that Paul not only refers this universality, this lack of distinction in the proclamation of the gospel, back to the character as grace and faith of the salvation that has appeared in Christ, but time and again thrusts through more deeply and in so doing brings into the picture the whole of the knowledge of God given to Israel. In particular the confession of the unity of God held before Israel in the Shema (cf. Deut. 6:4), and reiterated by Judaism with never ceasing vigor, is for Paul — otherwise than for the Jews — the proof of the divine redemptive will. Compare the following:

Or is God the God of the Jews only? Is he not the God of the gentiles also? Yes! of the gentiles also, since God is One, who will judge the circumcised . . . and the uncircumcised . . . (Rom. 3:29, 30).

God will have all men to be saved. . . . For God is One; One also is the Mediator between God and men, the man Christ Jesus, who gave himself a ransom for all . . . (1 Tim. 2:4, 5, 6).

From the fact that God is one and that there is no other God than he who has revealed himself to his people Israel, it is therefore concluded that the God known and worshipped by Israel must also be the God of the gentiles. Precisely that which for the Jews was the ground for their particularism — apart from Israel's God there is no God — here becomes the ground for the universalism: all men have to do with one God in judgment and in grace. It is that God who judges without respect of persons and will render to every man according to his works (Rom. 2:6, 11), but who will validate the faith of the circumcised and uncircumcised equally (Rom. 3:30). As the one God he has to do, not with Jews only, but with all men (Rom. 2:9, 16; 3:28). Because God is one the knowledge of his grace is also a knowledge that concerns all men. As apart from him there is no Judge, so apart from him there is no Deliverer and Savior, and his salvation has to do with all men (1 Tim. 4:10; Tit. 2:11). For this reason there is one Mediator who is the Mediator between God and all men, and the Mediator is so very emphatically called the man Christ Jesus, who gave himself for all (all men, without social or national distinction, without distinction in kind). The revelation of the mystery of the righteousness of God by faith alone teaches us — so we may say — to discover the grace of God, but in that grace God himself in his universal redemptive will also teaches us to discover man anew in his never — not even in his deepest alienation from God ("without God in the world" [Eph. 2:12]!) — abrogated relationship to God. Without this universality both in his judgment and in his demonstration of grace God cannot be one, God cannot be God, and man cannot be man. That the divine election of Israel and of the church as people of God is not herewith nullified, but rather is maintained in its sovereign character as grace will be discussed further in what follows. It is of importance here to point out that for Paul the universality of the church is a reality that not only proceeds from the revelation of the mystery in the fullness of the time, but also has its ground in the fundamental revelation, antecedent to everything else, that had been given to Israel as the people of God, that God the Lord is one. Here on the one hand the Jewish synagogical particularism has been broken through, which indeed maintained that God is the God of all men, in that they were created by him and will stand before his judgment seat, but which further could not regard heathendom in any other way than as the *massa perditionis* that without hope of salvation had fallen into Gehenna and had no share with Israel in the future world.[31] At the same time the way was prepared for the new understanding of the prophecy that made mention of the future redemption

---

31. Cf. Strack-Billerbeck, III, pp. 139ff., p. 185, p. 81 sub 3.

of the gentiles together with Israel. In proof of the universal mercy of Christ for the gentiles as well as for the Jews Paul appealed, i.a., to the prophetic pronouncements in which the gentiles are exhorted to rejoice with God's people and to sing and to praise the Lord together and in which it is said of the root of Jesse raised up to rule over the gentiles that in him the gentiles shall hope (Rom. 15:9-12). Indeed, how much the universality of the salvation revealed in Christ governs the whole of his understanding of the Old Testament appears in a very striking manner when, for the pronouncement "not from the Jews only, but also from the gentiles" (Rom. 9:25, 26), he appeals to the words of the prophet Hosea, which in their original context have reference in the first place to the receiving again of the people Israel that had fallen away from God and was therefore first cast off by him: "I will call that my people, which was not-my-people; and her beloved, that was not-beloved. And it shall be, that in the place where it was said unto them, You are not my people, there shall they be called sons of the living God."

The not-my-people *(Lō'-'Ammi)* and the not-beloved *(Lō'-Ruhāmâ)* is therefore no longer restricted to the penitent members of the people Israel, but extended to the gentiles; a transition in interpretation that on the ground of the sovereignty (understood in a new way) of God's grace in Christ brings to full explication in its previously not under-stood inner dynamic and hidden import the qualitative content of the prophecy that speaks of this same grace.

For the rest, it should be borne in mind that in this new concept of the people of God given in the revelation of Christ a new restriction and in a certain sense a new particularism is implied. No one is ex-cluded, but neither does anyone belong to the people of God as a matter of course by virtue of birth, or by virtue of his humanity. They who are "of Christ" are the seed of Abraham and heirs of the promise (Gal. 3:29). These are those who have been called (Rom. 9:24), who are of the faith, who walk in the steps of the faith of Abraham (Rom. 4:12, 16ff.). This is the meaning of the joining together of the proclama-tions of redemption for the gentiles and the announcement of calamity on Israel, at the close of Romans 9, for instance. But this is also the meaning of the warning issued to believing gentiles, that is, against boasting in their privilege, lest God pluck out the wild twigs grafted into the olive tree, just as he has not spared the natural branches (cf. Rom. 11:17ff.). Even the most universal pronouncements of the apostle, therefore, in which he speaks of the redemptive will of God with respect to all men and of his own universal commission as apostle and teacher of the gentiles, are never to be detached from belonging to Christ and from the unconditional requirement of faith (cf. 1 Tim. 2:4, 7; 4:10; cf. v. 8). For this reason in the parallel between "the many," "all," and "all men" who through Adam have been constituted sinners and through Christ have been justified, etc. (cf. Rom. 5:15, 18, 19; 1 Cor. 15:22), it is not a question of equal numbers of persons, but first of "the many" (or "all") who by virtue of descent have been comprehended in Adam, then of "the many" ("all") who belong to Christ by faith.[32] For it is only in Christ, who by God has been made a stone of stumbling and a rock of offense, as well as a foundation by whom none shall be put to shame, that Jew and Greek, slave and free, male and female, have become the new unity, the one new man (Gal. 3:28; Eph. 2:15); in him the people of God, Israel, circumcision, promise, sonship, and heirship receive their new definition and content; therefore in him, too, is the only and utterly decisive criterion of what may be called by the name of Israel (cf. Rom. 9:33).

SECTION 57. THE NATURE OF ELECTION. GOD'S PURPOSE

If in the foregoing the new and spiritual concept of the church as the people of God clearly emerges, the second point of view indicated above (p. 334) deserves no less attention, namely, that of the unity and continuity of the divine work in the election and gathering in of his people.

However much, in harmony with the whole revelation of redemption in Christ, we may speak of a new definition of the essence of the congregation of God, this does not mean that it may be said to represent a radically new character, a reality supported by an entirely new root. One would form a wrong notion of Paul's idea were he to understand the New Testament church as a *novum quid* that has broken away from the fetters and scales of ancient Israel and in relation to the legalistic and particularistic character of the Old Testament people of God is a spiritual and universal communion. The ties here are much deeper than that.[33] The new definition of the essence of the church does stand in absolute contrast with the legalistic-synagogical concept of the New Covenant and the people of God, but not in contrast — and all the emphasis must now fall on this — with the intention God himself had from the beginning with the calling and formation of Israel as his people. And this holds not only for the blessed and universal future of this people, as that had already been foretold in Old Testament

---

32. Otherwise Jeremias, *TDNT*, VI, pp. 542f. He is of the opinion that *hoi polloi* in Rom. 5:15c and in 5:19 has "the greatest conceivable breadth," that is to say, must have reference "without distinction to all mankind." He appeals for this to Rom. 5:18 where there is mention of "all men" to the same effect, on the one hand in connection with Adam, on the other with Christ. And he concludes: "Christ's obedience affects mankind in the same way as does Adam's disobedience." But this is true only if one understands thereby the new humanity, in distinction from the old (in Adam); for in the whole of Paul's preaching it is unthinkable to refer justification to all men without distinction; cf. also Bultmann, who explains *hoi polloi* in Rom. 5:19b as "the members of the humanity founded by Christ" (*Theology*, I, p. 277). Likewise the *pantes* in 1 Cor. 15:22 cannot be understood otherwise than in a distinguishing, qualified sense, on the one hand as those who belong to Adam, on the other as those who belong to Christ, "all members of the range of persons belonging to them" (Kümmel, in Lietzmann-Kümmel, *Cor.*, p. 193 — against Lietzmann in the text, p. 80).

33. See also van Unnik, "La conception paulinienne," in *Littérature et théologie pauliniennes*, 1960, pp. 122ff.

prophecy, but no less for the manner in which God dealt with his people from the very beginning, for the nature of his election, for the distinction he made between Abraham's children, for his whole purpose with respect to his people and its effectuation.

We touch here the deepest foundations of the Pauline conception of the church. He is pressed to unfold them by his polemic with Judaism. Is he not a revolutionary and innovator in his spiritual and universal understanding of the people of God? Does he not nullify the law and trample on the privileges of the offspring of Abraham? Paul's answer is that he rather upholds and does justice to the law, that is, the book of God's great acts in the past (Rom. 3:31). And he endeavors to show this just by permitting the history of Abraham to speak in all sorts of ways. Abraham's calling and election is the secret of Israel. In God's promise to Abraham all the prerogatives and privileges of Israel are contained. But how has God dealt with Abraham and how has he spoken to him and given him his promises? To this history of Abraham Paul returns again and again to substantiate the soundness of his spiritual and universal conception of the people of God and the seed of Abraham.

First of all, one should point here to the extensive argument from Scripture in Romans 4, the chapter in which an answer is given to the question as to the way in which Abraham, "our father according to the flesh,"[34] became the recipient of God's promises and the great Testator of Israel (Rom. 4:1). What is at issue here is of course the appeal of the Jews to their natural descent from Abraham. Over against this Paul sets the fact that God's promises to Abraham and his seed applied, not to the circumcised, but to believing Abraham, so that his fatherhood is extended but also restricted to all who believe. The spiritual criterion for belonging to the seed of Abraham and to the people of God is not therefore a revolutionary breaking through of the boundaries that were appointed of old to the people of God, but rather answers completely to the manner in which God revealed himself already to Abraham.

Of no less importance is the argumentation in Galatians 3:15ff. Here, too, the question is under discussion as to who are to be understood by the seed of Abraham mentioned in the promise. Paul appeals here, very remarkably,[35] to the singular "and to thy seed," to which he gives the interpretation "which is Christ" (v. 16), and to which he then joins the conclusion that all who have been baptized into Christ and have put on Christ are the seed of Abraham and heirs according to the promise (v. 29). Then he expressly states that there is no longer any distinction between Jew and Greek, slave or free, male or female. For they all are one[36] in Christ Jesus. The thought of the one body is clearly present here, although the word is not mentioned. Because of this unity, however, the promise of the one seed can have reference

---

34. We take *kata sarka* here therefore as in apposition to *propatera*, not as the predicate to *eurēkenai*.

35. See further my *The Epistle of Paul to the Churches of Galatia*, 1953, pp. 132ff.

36. *Heis*, masculine.

without distinction to all who are in Christ. The christological deter-mination of the idea of what may count as the seed of Abraham, heirs of the promise, etc., is here inferred in a very pregnant manner from the way in which God himself spoke to Abraham of "thy seed."

It should be noted that this argumentation does not rest merely on the incidental seizing on a particular expression. In the Epistle to the Romans, which was written later, the background of this chain of reasoning becomes clear to us. Here the question as to the true nature of Abraham's seed and of God's election of his people comes up for discussion in a sharply defined manner when in Romans 9-11 Paul sees himself placed before the enigma of Israel unbelieving and therefore excluded from God's promises.

The point of departure for this profound argumentation in its en-tirety[37] is again that in order rightly to understand the address of the promise given to Abraham and to his seed one is not to start from natural descent from Abraham. From the very outset God himself made a distinction among the children of Abraham. He did not without more ado reckon all the seed of Abraham as the children in whom he would bless all the nations, but he eliminated Ishmael and designated Isaac. Paul qualifies this further as follows — and here the criterion of this discriminating activity of God also becomes visible — "... it is not the children of the flesh that are the children of God, but the children of the promise are reckoned for the seed" (Rom. 9:8).

It is a question, therefore, of the manner in which Ishmael and Isaac were conceived and born. Whereas Ishmael was a "child of the flesh," that is to say, was begotten and received by Abraham as a son in the natural way, Isaac was a "child of the promise." With these last words Isaac's origin is pointed out. He was not only the bearer, but in the first place the fruit of the promise.[38] For "the word of the promise is as follows: about this time I will come, and Sarah shall have a son" (v. 9). We have to do here with the same thought and with the same idea of the promise as in Galatians 4:28, where Isaac, and believers, are spoken of as children of promise, i.e., children who have been born out of the strength of the promise and not by virtue of natural procreation ("after the flesh"); for this reason the expression "according to the Spirit" can be employed as a synonym for "children of promise" (Gal. 4:29).

The distinction God made from the beginning in the election and formation of his people is therefore very plain. In the birth of Isaac and with the elimination of Ishmael he indicated clearly that the ground for his election of Israel in no respect lay in any human quality, in the potentialities of human "flesh," or in natural descent, but only in his own divine work, in the quickening strength of his promise, in the power of his Spirit.

Paul points to this same principle in the birth of Jacob and Esau,

---

37. For a further justification of the following see my *Rom.*, and the summary view given there of "God's omnipotence according to Romans 9" (pp. 227-231); also "Israel," 1955 (*Exegetica*, together with G. C. Aalders), pp. 43-70.

38. *Ta tekna tēs epangelias*, genitive of origin; cf. above, p. 217.

even if it manifests itself there in another way. Here a "natural" birth does take place, but God once more intervenes by designating, not the elder, Esau, but the younger, Jacob, contrary to all custom and expectation, as the continuation of the holy line[39] of the people of God. Here again, however, there is no arbitrariness, but God acts according to the same motive and pattern as with Isaac and Ishmael: ". . . that the electing purpose of God might continue [in force]: not upon the strength of works, but of him who called . . ." (Rom. 9:11).

That the seed of Abraham as the people of God would be carried on in Jacob and not in Esau was not because of Jacob's excellence above that of Esau. For when they had not yet been born and had not yet done anything either good or evil (v. 11), this decision was already announced to Rebekah. In setting the younger above the elder it became manifest anew in what way and according to what standard God has formed his people: to cause his electing purpose to continue in force.

It is of great importance to understand this expression (*hē kat' eklogēn prothesis*) correctly in its complexity. There is mention of God's "purpose," his method of dealing determined beforehand with respect to the formation of his people. Of this it is now said that it bore an "electing" character, or rather, that it took place "according to the nature of election." In "election" there is not of itself the thought of a decree[40] (although a decree or purpose can also be electing). "Election" was used originally[41] to describe the manner in which Israel became the people of God, that is, through God's having called it to himself out of all peoples, having placed it on his side in distinction from those others. In so doing the emphasis was constantly placed on the fact that this electing, distinguishing character of Israel's calling did not rest on Israel's excellence above that of others, but had its cause only in God's good pleasure (cf., e.g., Deut. 7:6ff.; 9:4, 5); "election" therefore denotes the sovereign, gracious character of God's calling of Israel, not motivated by the object of the election.

The purpose of God thus qualified now asserted itself in relation to the birth of Jacob and Esau. It was not Esau, the elder, but Jacob, the younger, who was destined to be the bearer of the promise. This election is accordingly described in the following words: "not upon the strength [or ground] of works [or qualities in man], but only upon this ground, that he called." The whole formation of the people of God and therefore also of belonging to this people — this is the conclusion — rests on nothing other than the sovereign, electing character of his grace.

In what follows (vv. 14ff.), the apostle upholds the freedom of this sovereign grace and the right of that freedom. God is free to have mercy on whom he will; on the other hand he is free to pass by others

---

39. That this is the point in question and not "election and reprobation" as the denotation of the eternal personal destiny of both is clearly apparent from the words of the divine statement: "the elder shall serve the younger." In v. 13, too, Jacob and Esau are spoken of as two peoples, in harmony with Mal. 1:2ff. See further my *Rom.*, pp. 213, 214.

40. This is correctly emphasized in the dissertation of H. Venema, *Uitverkiezen en Uitverkiezing in het N.T.*, 1965, *passim*.

41. Cf. above, Section 55.

with this mercy and even to harden them in their sin. Paul is not guided here by an abstract concept of divine freedom, but by the freedom of God's grace as this has revealed itself in the history of Israel. The apostle observes a clear divine intention in it. If God has mercy on whom he will and has compassion on whom he has (will have) compassion, Paul paraphrases this as follows: "it is not dependent upon whether anyone wills, or whether anyone runs, but upon God who has mercy." For God is free to maintain the validity, not of human effort or strength, but of his grace only. He is also free, therefore, to make the resistance of others, in this case of Pharaoh, subservient to the sovereignty of his grace and the glory of his name revealed therein by hardening them in this resistance.[42] When in vindicating that Paul reaches out for the familiar Old Testament figure of the potter, this occurs in order to throw light on the purposefulness of this might and freedom in addition to God's sovereign command over what he has made. If the potter is free to give the objects he makes of clay the destiny that seems best to him in the conduct of his work as a potter, would God then not be free, in order to show the power of his work and the riches of his glory on those whom he has destined to that end, not as yet to give up immediately to judgment those to whom his wrath goes forth (because of their sin) and who are therefore ripe for destruction, but first to demonstrate to them the power of his grace on his people?

The purport of Paul's argument is not to show that all that God does in history has been foreordained from eternity and therefore, so far as his mercy as well as his hardening is concerned, has an irresistible and inevitable issue. Rather, it is his intention to point out in the omnipotence of God's activity the real intention of his purpose. Everything is made subservient to the electing character of God's grace, not based on human merit or strength, and of the calling and formation of his people. So did God originally display it in Israel and to Israel, contrary to all human calculations, and contrary to all human resistance. And so does God maintain this sovereign electing character of his work of redemption over against Israel, when Israel misjudges this nature of its election as the people of God and has come to trust in its own righteousness, instead of in the righteousness of God (9:30ff.). Thus it can happen that Israel because of this misjudgment of its calling and election is placed next to Pharaoh as the exemplification of God's reprobation and hardening, and that what applied to Pharaoh holds for Israel as well, namely, that God by Israel's hardening and fall has chosen to make known the riches of his mercy (to the gentiles) (Rom. 11:7-10, 12, 15). At the same time, however, it is evident that one may not identify the omnipotence and sovereignty of God's grace thus upheld on the one hand and of his reprobation and hardening on the other with irrevocable "eternal" decrees, in which God would once and forever have predestined the salvation or ruin of man: for God has not

---

42. The words *eis auto touto exēgeira se* are to be taken in this way. They do not speak of Pharaoh's appearance as king or of his human origin, but of his recovery from the preceding plagues (Exod. 9:16; see furthermore my *Rom.*, in loc.).

only reprobated and hardened Israel in order to display his mercy to the gentiles, but no less to provoke Israel itself to repentance and "jealousy" (Rom. 11:11ff.). This concept of election denotes the omnipotence, not the deterministic character of God's work of grace and of the formation of his church. Election is an election of grace (eklogē charitos), that is to say: it does not take place on the ground of works (Rom. 11:5, 6). This contrast between grace and works dominates the whole argument of Romans 9-11 with respect to the calling and election of the people of God.

Meanwhile it has been apparent that in the course of his argument in Romans 9 the apostle also reaches back for the divine work of redemption in history to the purpose of God underlying it and says of that, too, that it bears an electing character (Rom. 9:11). Elsewhere there is still more extensive mention of this divine purpose with respect to the formation of the people of God, and it is appropriate here to go further into the nature of this purpose.

Paul speaks of this purpose in all sorts of places and in more than one way. In addition to purpose (prothesis, protithemai; Rom. 8:28; 9:11; Eph. 1:9, 11; 3:11; 2 Tim. 1:9), he makes mention of foreknowledge (proginōskō; Rom. 8:29; 11:2), foreordination (proorizō; Rom. 8:29, 30; 1 Cor. 2:7; Eph. 1:5, 11), to prepare beforehand (proetoimazō; Rom. 9:23; Eph. 2:10), but then further of God's good pleasure (eudokia; Eph. 1:5, 9; cf. Phil. 2:13), the counsel of his will (boulē tou thelēmatos autou; Eph. 1:11), his mystery (mystērion; 1 Cor. 2:7; Eph. 1:9; 3:9). As is evident from the places cited, this thought is especially prominent in the conclusion of Romans 8 and in the first chapters of Ephesians. The distinguishing feature of all these pronouncements is that they have reference to God's counsel with respect to his work of redemption in Christ in the fullness of the times. Especially typical of that is the redemptive-historical expression "mystery," which we have already discussed at length.[43] In 1 Corinthians 2:7 it is spoken of in a very explicit sense as "the wisdom of God consisting in the mystery which God foreordained before the ages with respect to our glory" (cf. Eph. 1:9; 3:9). The christocentric character of this purpose also finds clear expression in Ephesians 1:9, which speaks of God's good pleasure that he purposed in Christ with respect to the "economy" of the fullness of the times; and in Ephesians 3:11, where the apostle speaks of God's eternal purpose that he formed in Christ Jesus. The expression "purposed in Christ" is difficult to define adequately, but certainly makes it clear that Christ was the object and the center of this purpose and that its execution would take place in him and through him.

In this relation to Christ the church, too, has a place in this purpose of God and is its object. He has, so it is said in Ephesians 1:5, predestined us unto sonship through Jesus Christ in him.[44] Similarly Romans 8:29 says that God predestined us to be conformed to the image

---

43. Above, Section 7.

44. The words eis auton are difficult, but indicate again the nature of the predestination.

of his Son, and Ephesians 1:11, that we have received the heritage in
Christ, destined to that end according to the purpose of him who works
all things according to the counsel of his will. In all these passages it
is evident that the church was the object of God's predestination and
counsel in virtue of its belonging to Christ.

All this finds its most pregnant expression in that God even
"before the foundation of the world" chose the church to himself in
Christ (Eph. 1:4). Here again it is a matter, as always with election,
not simply of a decree of God that only later comes to realization, but
of the actual appropriation of the church to himself before the foundation of the world. How this is possible and how one is to conceive of
it are seen from the words "in Christ." Paul speaks here, too, of the
comprehension of the church in Christ. As it, although still on earth,
has in Christ received a place in heaven (Eph. 2:6), and thus in Christ
participates in the heavenly blessings (Eph. 1:3), so — Paul makes the
connection here expressly[45] — it was already united with the pre-existent
Christ and thus chosen by God in him. The inclusion of the church in
Christ, its corporate existence in him, Paul traces back to this pre-
existence. As its life is hid in God with the Exalted One (Col. 3:3), so
its election is in him before the foundation of the world. Even there
the church's being in Christ can be spoken of, and thus its election in
him in whom God purposed his good pleasure, indeed, who himself
can be called God's "Foreknown" before the foundation of the world
(1 Pet. 1:20).[46]

Of particular importance is the question as to what purport this

---

45. Cf. *kathōs* in Eph. 1:4.

46. H. Venema, who in his *Uitverkiezen en Uitverkiezing in het Nieuwe
Testament*, wishes to understand election exclusively as an action of God in
time and history and therefore entirely rejects the idea of an eternal election, takes
Eph. 1:4, too, as that which God does through Christ in human history (p. 56).
To that end he translates *en Christō* with "by Christ," explains *exelexato* as man's
being brought "under the saving working of Christ" in history (pp. 52, 53), while
pro kataboles kosmou would then "indicate that 'chosen in Christ' transcends earthly
measure. It is indeed an historical occurrence, but it is not historically limited. It
also transcends history." But it is plain that herewith not only is another category
introduced (*pro* is not spatial, "above," but temporal, "before"), but the whole
pronouncement becomes entirely unclear, which it is not in an unforced interpretation of *pro*. In addition *katabole tou kosmou* is a matter that coincides or at least
is connected with the beginning of history and not a designation of a supra-historical
dimension that would then have to accompany the continuing, historical election of
the church by Christ. There can here be no question of an election other than that
which takes place before history. And therefore the translation of *en Christō* with
"by Christ" cannot be maintained. Further along Venema does try to retain the
category of origin in some measure. "Christ was the eternal Son of God and shared
as such in the eternal love of God. Thus we now as believers who . . . are chosen in
time, have to do in our election with what is eternal with God," etc. (pp. 60, 61).
But one cannot proceed in this way to spread over eternity and history that which in
Paul has been fixed at one point (aorist!) *pro kataboles kosmou*. The same objection
must be urged against the attempt of Venema to divest the concepts *proorizein* and
prothesis tōn aiōnōn (pp. 65, 72ff.) of their pre-temporal significance. With every
(justified) defense against a deterministic conception (cf., e.g., in Venema, p. 62), the
evidence of the pre-temporal elements in the Pauline doctrine of election and predestination may not be denied.

reference to election before the foundation of the world has, or, in general, what function all these *pro*-concepts fulfill in the whole of the Pauline doctrine of salvation.

In general they must be understood within the framework of the basic biblical notion[47] that all things in heaven and on earth come to pass according to the antecedent counsel and intention of God. Thus, for example, Paul speaks in Ephesians 1:11 of the church as having been destined beforehand for the future glory, in accordance with the purpose of him (God) "who works all things after the counsel of his will" (cf. Gal. 1:4; Rom. 9:19). All that is said here of God's purpose with respect to the church stands in the great context of the counsel of God the Creator and Consummator of all things. With this the "depth-aspect" of the divine activity is pointed out, and this activity is seen to be "free from what we know in the world to be arbitrary and precarious" and our attention is directed "to what can be called the opposite of chance and contingence."[48] It is a question here of course, not of formal concepts that speak only of the existence of a plan of the divine counsel antecedent to everything else, but of the counsel and will of that God who in his saving acts has revealed himself to his people.[49] It is consequently on the ground of this counsel of God, realized in Christ and revealed in the gospel, that Paul extols and worships the unsearchableness of God's decrees and the inscrutableness of God's ways and at the same time rejects every human counsel or deliberation (Rom. 11:33, 34).

The frequent mention of God's purpose with respect to the church must also be understood in this light. Paul's intention is not to point to its "having once been thus determined," but rather to elucidate the meaning and significance of the salvation revealed in Christ in terms of the priority of God's counsel and plan. In particular this reference serves to throw light from still another side on the absolutely gratuitous character of the salvation given in Christ, on its not resting on human merits.

This emerges clearly in the expression of Romans 9:11 already discussed, where the significance of "the electing purpose of God" is explained by the words "not upon the strength of works, but of this, that he called." The appeal to the purpose of God functions here, therefore, as the proof that the formation of and belonging to the people of God rest only on the antecedent sovereign grace of God and not on human works. 2 Timothy 1:9 is also very clear in this respect, where it is said that God saved and called us "not according to our works, but according to his own purpose and according to the grace which was given us in Christ Jesus before times eternal."[50] Here too

---

47. Cf., e.g., Schrenk, *TDNT*, I, pp. 633ff., *s.v. boulē, boulēma*, and III, pp. 47, 54ff., *s.v. thelō, thelēma*.

48. Thus G. C. Berkouwer, *Divine Election*, ET 1960, p. 151.

49. Cf. K. L. Schmidt, *TDNT*, V, p. 456, n. 4, *s.v. proorizō*.

50. The words *pro chronōn aiōniōn*, in view also of Tit. 1:2, will have to be taken, not as the equivalent of *pro katabolēs kosmou*, but as "before inconceivably long periods of time"; cf. C. Bouma, *De brieven van den apostel Paulus aan Timotheüs en Titus*, p. 377.

God's purpose stands over against human works. It is a matter not of the activity of God alone over against human activity, but of antecedent divine grace over against human merit. The contrast is of a purely soteriological nature. "Purpose" and "grace" are here coordinated as a kind of hendiadys, at least as two concepts that further define each other reciprocally. In Titus 3:5 Paul expresses the same thought with the words: "not upon the ground of works of righteousness which we should have done, but according to his mercy." What in 2 Timothy 1:9 is called God's purpose and grace is here simply called his mercy. The reference to God's purpose has as its object, therefore, the placing of all the emphasis on the precedence and priority of divine grace and thus on the absolutely gratuitous character of God's saving work and of his calling to salvation. God has not thereby been guided by what might be found by way of meritoriousness or excellence in man, but in the full sense of the word has taken "reasons from himself."[51]

On closer examination of the passages in question this intention of the appeal to the divine purpose so clearly emerging in Romans 9:11 and 2 Timothy 1:9 (Tit. 3:5) appears time and again to form the meaning of the frequent mention of God's purpose, his foreordination, his counsel of redemption with respect to man's salvation. In handling this motif certain nuances and diversities are to be observed according to the extent to which these are involved in the train of thought. Thus in 1 Corinthians 2:7, where Paul has to do battle not with Jewish legalism but with the Greek *gnosis,* God's hidden wisdom consisting in the divine mystery that God foreordained before the aeons unto our glory is set over against the wisdom of this aeon. The appeal to the divine mystery, however, in this context has a significance analogous to that in the passages discussed above. Here again it is not intended to place the divine *arcanum decretum* over against human wisdom, by which all human counsel and knowledge come to stand under an absolute and hidden restriction, but rather to demonstrate that the wisdom and power of God revealed in Christ's cross have exposed human wisdom that in its foolishness and vanity sought to ignore God (1 Cor. 1:23; 2:6ff.), and thus have deprived human boasting of all ground (1 Cor. 1:31).

This character of God's work of redemption and of the formation of his people antecedent to all human wisdom and power also governs the pronouncements of God's purpose, predestination, foreknowledge in Ephesians 1 and 3.[52] To be sure, here — otherwise than in Romans 9 — this purpose is spoken of more in a positive than in an antithetical sense, but the whole of the opening of the epistle (Eph. 1:1-14) is especially intended to throw light on the universal character of salvation not restricted to Judaism.[53] And to set this universality of the grace of the redemption given in Christ in greater relief and to raise it above all doubt or uncertainty the apostle speaks here with a certain redun-

---

51. Cf. above, p. 236, n. 63.
52. Cf. Schrenk, *TDNT,* III, pp. 56f., *s.v. thelēma.*
53. See also J. H. Roberts, *Die Opbou van die Kerk volgens die Ephese-brief,* 1963, pp. 51ff.

dancy of concepts and phraseology of God's purpose, his foreordination, his counsel of redemption. This finds very explicit expression in the repeated mention of God's *eudokia,* a concept that embraces the element of God's kindness as well as his freedom. God's predestination is determined by this *eudokia* (Eph. 1:5), and it is in accordance with this same *eudokia* that the mystery of his will in Christ has come to revelation (v. 9), which is therefore to say that God's purpose was a free and saving purpose and was motivated by nothing other than by his own sovereign redemptive will. And that which finally settles everything is the christocentric character of this divine purpose formulated in all sorts of ways and with a rich variety of expression in the pronouncements we have already cited. It cannot be more clearly apparent than here — so we may conclude — that all these *pro*-concepts are intended as categories of redemption. What prompts Paul to hark back again and again to the divine purpose is not an abstract predestinarianism or reference back to God's decrees as the final cause in the chain of events, but the designation of sovereign, divine grace as the sole motive of his work of redemption in history.

This purpose is undoubtedly not confined to the manner in which this work of redemption is to be brought about, but has reference from the outset to those who will share in it. For Paul also speaks of the church as having been known and elect beforehand (Rom. 8:29; Eph. 1:4), of its having been predestined to sonship and the inheritance (Eph. 1:5, 11), of the preparation beforehand of the objects of mercy by God (Rom. 9:23), and of their good works in Christ (Eph. 2:10). One can raise the question as to whether after all the idea has not hereby been given of a predestined *numerus clausus* of the elect and whether with that — even though not said in so many words[54] — those who do not belong to this *numerus clausus* have not been excluded in virtue of this same purpose before the foundation of the world.

One can only say of these questions that they place Paul's pronouncements concerning the church as foreknown by God and elect in Christ under another point of view than that of Paul himself and thus abstract and extrapolate them from the context of the Pauline doctrine of salvation, an extrapolation that easily leads to conclusions Paul himself does not draw and which are entirely in conflict with the tenor of his preaching. When — as, for example, in the so-called *catena aurea* of Romans 8:29ff. — Paul joins God's purpose, predestination, calling, justification, and glorification in one indissoluble bond, this is not an abstract pronouncement concerning the immutability of the number of those predestined to salvation, but a pastoral encouragement for the persecuted and embattled church (cf. v. 36), based on the fixed and unassailable character of the divine work of redemption. This fixed character does not rest on the fact that the church belongs to a certain "number," but that it belongs to Christ, from before the foundation of the world. Fixity does not lie in a hidden *decretum,* therefore, but in the corporate

----

54. For Rom. 9:13, which is frequently taken in this sense, see above, p. 344, n. 39.

unity of the church with Christ, whom it has come to know in the gospel and has learned to embrace in faith. It is therefore a *metabasis eis allo genos,* a crossing over from the economy of redemption revealed and qualified in Christ to a causal predestinarianism abstracted from it, when one chooses to reduce the links of this golden chain fundamentally to one thing only, that only they will inherit glory who have been foreknown and predestined by God to that end. Likewise the expression "chosen in Christ" does not say that Christ is the means or the medium through whom or in whom an antecedent absolute decree would be effected[55] — for such a foreknowledge or election of the church abstracted from Christ there is no place within the framework of Paul's doctrine of salvation — but the intention is simply to make the church aware of its solidarity with Christ in all the wealth of the implications this relationship includes. On the one hand this solidarity with him means that the church was chosen in him even before the foundation of the world, predestined to be conformed to his image, that he might be the Firstborn among many brethren (Rom. 8:29). On the other hand, the nature and scope of this "chosen in Christ" are known and defined only by the realization of the divine purpose in history. The links of the *catena aurea* both actually and cognitively cannot be detached from one another; the predestinarian and the redemptive-historical "in Christ" define each another reciprocally. Those who have been chosen in Christ before the foundation of the world are also those who in the fullness of the time have died and been raised with him, who have been called through the gospel and have been incorporated into his body in the way of faith and baptism. This means, among other things, that one can speak of the number of those who have been foreknown by God and who have died and been raised with Christ (or: for whom Christ has died) only when he at the same time takes the event of preaching into consideration and respects this to the full according to its nature (that is to say, according to the nature of the divine call to faith and conversion). That is in no respect to say that, conversely, the center of gravity would have to be shifted from divine predestination to human freedom. For first of all with such a shift — and now from the human side — everything would be brought under another viewpoint than that from which Paul speaks. For him individual human freedom of will is not constitutive for the decision with which man is confronted by the preaching of the gospel.[56] Rather he repeatedly brings out that the contexts in which the preaching of the gospel takes place transcend the individual freedom of man. He says of the church that it is God's workmanship, created in Christ Jesus to do good works, which God prepared beforehand that we should walk in them (Eph. 2:10). This also refers to what follows the preaching. He describes the calling of believers accordingly, as we have already seen,[57] as a divine creative act, a *creatio ex nihilo* (cf. Rom. 4:17 with Gal. 4:28), or, as he writes of the preaching

---

55. On this conception see further G. C. Berkouwer, *Divine Election,* pp. 137ff.

56. So rightly C. Müller, *Gottes Gerechtigkeit,* p. 80, against Bultmann.

57. Above, pp. 235ff.

of the gospel in 2 Corinthians 4:6: "the God who said: Let light shine out of darkness, has made it to shine in our hearts." And, conversely, he speaks of those who do not follow this call as disobedient and unbelieving, whose thoughts have been stricken with blindness by the way in which this world thinks, by the god of this age, "so that they do not perceive the shining of the gospel of the glory of Christ" (2 Cor. 4:4). Nothing could be farther from the truth than that in the relationship of election and preaching Paul takes his point of departure in individual human freedom.

Yet the relation between the purpose of God, his election, and the preaching of the gospel remains of paramount importance in order to eliminate every notion of an automatic or deterministic election. Likewise nowhere in Paul's thought does the hidden decree of a *numerus clausus* function as the background or explanation of the separation that comes about by the preaching of the gospel, as though through this decree the same gospel were for those who are saved a fragrance of life unto life and for those who are lost an odor of death unto death (2 Cor. 2:16). Rather, we must ascertain that over against such a deterministic conception he maintains the liberty of God's grace and the religious and ethical character of the encounter of man with his Creator in the gospel (Rom. 9:19ff.). Just as little is divine calling only to be defined as the authoritative word that separates between light and darkness. God also places himself, as it were, in a relationship of dependence with respect to those whom he calls. He struggles with Israel to lead it to faith and conversion (Rom. 10:21); Paul terms himself an ambassador of God as though God through his mouth were issuing the invitation: Let yourselves be reconciled to God (2 Cor. 5:20); his whole effort is bent toward persuading men and moving them to faith (2 Cor. 5:11); and this he regards as the glory of his ministry that if possible he might provoke Israel to jealousy and save some of them (Rom. 11:14). Similarly, he declares elsewhere that the grace of God has appeared, bringing salvation for all men; he speaks of God's love toward man and of his redemptive will with respect to all men (Tit. 2:11; 3:4; 1 Tim. 2:4; 4:10). On the other hand he maintains fully the human responsibility of both believers and unbelievers with regard to the gospel; he qualifies faith as obedience and unbelief as contradiction and disobedience. And even when he speaks of unbelief as a blinding and qualifies it as a consequence of God's righteousness and hardening (cf. Rom. 11:8ff.), he does not do so in an abstract and timeless manner, but he points out precisely what the function of such a hardening is in the whole of redemptive history, and he makes it understood that this therefore "need" not bear a definitive character, but rather, as with the rejection and hardening of unbelieving Israel, presupposes a situation that is still "open."[58] Likewise when he comforts the church with the declaration that the Lord is faithful to establish and guard it (2 Thess. 3:3; 1 Cor. 1:9), that our unfaithfulness does not nullify his faithfulness (2 Tim.

---

58. The emphatic pronouncement of H. Venema, *Uitverkiezen*, p. 171, that "they who have been rejected by God in the sense that the Scripture speaks of it, are never again chosen by him," cannot be maintained in the light of Rom. 11:15.

2:13; 1 Cor. 10:13; cf. Rom. 3:2), and when he repeatedly points the church for this to its inclusion in Christ even before the foundation of the world (Rom. 8:29ff.; Eph. 1:4), this assurance nowhere acts as a logical deduction from the immutability of God's decree, but as faith in the trustworthiness of God's promises and in the unshakableness of his *eudokia* in Christ (cf., e.g., Tit. 1:2). Hence this comfort is attended with the admonition in faith to continue in the mercy of God, lest he execute the judgment of Israel on those who are now believers and break them off from the olive tree as unprofitable and dead branches (Rom. 11:18ff.); indeed, Paul is able to say of himself as well that he is always mindful lest he, having preached to others, should himself be rejected (1 Cor. 9:27). Of course, the certainty and comfort that lie in God's faithfulness and in election in Christ are not again placed in doubt or made contingent on human faithfulness and perseverance, but this certainty is placed and kept within the context where it alone applies and with which the church alone has to do, namely, that of the revelation of the gospel as a power of God for everyone who believes (Rom. 1:16), and thus of the electing character of God's grace, not resting on human power or wisdom, that he who boasts should boast in the Lord (1 Cor. 1:16ff.).

Seemingly these different "lines" cannot be reconciled with each other: on the one hand, God's creative word of omnipotence by which alone the light can shine in the heart, on the other, human responsibility for faith and conversion; on the one hand, blindness and spiritual impotence, on the other, struggling under commission from God to bring back to him those who have turned away; also on the one hand, the certainty of God's faithfulness and the irrevocableness of his election and calling, on the other, the warning against the danger of being broken off from the olive tree on account of pride and being rejected as a participant in salvation. There is indeed not only a lack of clarity here but an inner contradiction, if one conceives of the divine purpose and the number of the elect in a deterministic sense as an immutably established decree of the counsel of God; or if, on the other hand, one supposes that without the individual's power of decision human responsibility toward the gospel becomes a fiction.[59] Of the first it must be said that it is in conflict with the manner in which Paul, and the entire biblical revelation, speaks of God's acting in history. And so far as the second is concerned, there is nothing more contradictory of the Pauline doctrine of salvation than if man were to become God's workmanship and new creation in virtue of a decision of his own will. "If a person had this possibility, he would not be a creature but would stand on his own."[60] We are faced with the unmistakable fact that Paul does not found the responsibility of man with respect to his being saved or lost in the fact that man may be said to be free to decide concerning it, but that through the preaching of the gospel God calls and fits him

---

59. See the view of Bultmann cited above, p. 236. Cf. also his essay "Grace and Freedom," in *Essays Philosophical and Theological*, p. 168.
60. C. Müller, *Gottes Gerechtigkeit*, p. 80.

for this responsibility; and that, where freedom has been lost and has
become spiritual impotence and blindness, the responsibility of man as
the creature of God is nevertheless not taken away or abrogated. God
maintains his right as Creator even where man has been sold and
blinded under the power of sin. What remains is not a contradiction
resulting from false premises, therefore, but the sovereign manner in
which God calls man to faith and conversion and in Christ forms the
church for himself. For while, in order to maintain the free character
of his grace, not related to human merits or autonomy, he passes by,
blinds, and punishes man in his delusion, at the same time his all-
embracing love goes forth from the gospel which justifies the ungodly.
And while the power of his calling is so great that it calls forth light
out of darkness and living from the dead, his calling is an invitation,
a stretching forth his hands all the day long to a disobedient and
gainsaying people. Of this electing activity and of the purpose of God
revealed in it Paul speaks, one may perhaps say, in a dialectical manner,
in that he ever and again approaches the freedom of God's grace with
respect to sinful man from two sides. What prompts him in doing so,
however, is not the desire to find the transcending viewpoint from
which he might be able to grasp the divine and the human, as it were,
in a single glance, in order thus to arrive at a theodicy that would give
a justification of God's doings and an explanation of the being of man.
What moves him is something entirely different, namely, according to
the measure of the revelation of the mystery in history to reach an increasingly more basic explication of the absolute sovereignty of God's
grace. For this reason he relates the preaching of justification by faith
alone with God's election and purpose. Also in this election and purpose
the church of the New Covenant is to find the ground of its existence
as well as its unity with Israel once chosen out of all the nations. Finally,
this nature of election enables Paul to connect the meaning of Israel's
hardening and the nevertheless irrevocable character of God's calling
and gifts of grace with the formation of the New Testament church.
This leads us to the last of the three viewpoints mentioned at the beginning of the present chapter.[61]

SECTION 58. THE FUTURE OF ISRAEL

After all that has been said in the preceding sections on the Christian
church as the continuation of the people of God, on the New Covenant
and the nature of divine election, it can appear as though no "problem"
remains with respect to historical Israel: only insofar as it believes in
Christ may it lay claim to the name of Abraham's children and to the
promises given to Abraham and his seed. And insofar as it rejects Christ
and trusts in the possession of the law, circumcision, and its own righteousness, it can no longer assert its right to the name and privilege of
Israel in the redemptive-historical sense. The church, then, as the people

---

61. Above, p. 334.

of the New Covenant has taken the place of Israel, and national Israel is nothing other than the empty shell from which the pearl has been removed and which has lost its function in the history of redemption.[62]

The remarkable thing is that while Paul's pronouncements on faith and belonging to Christ as the only criterion of what in an enduring sense may count as the seed of Abraham seem to warrant this conclusion in every respect, he himself time and again feels the need to guard against the thought of such an exclusion of empirical and national Israel as the people of God and to deny it as not consistent with the historical election of Israel. Already at the beginning of Romans 3, after his telling indictment against Jewish confidence in the law and circumcision and after the radical declaration: "he is not a Jew who is one outwardly," the question follows that is to preclude misunderstanding: "What advantage then has the Jew? or what is the profit of circumcision?" And the answer is: "Much in every way!" (Rom. 3:1). As such a privilege he then mentions in the first instance: "this, that to them the words of God were entrusted," by which in this context those words of God are especially intended with which God pledged himself to them and whereby therefore God's faithfulness is at issue (Rom. 3:3). In the continuing argument of 3:3ff. he does indeed impress on his readers that these promises have their reverse side in God's threatenings and that they too remain in force, so that Israel is not to deceive itself in the possession of the words of God. But at the beginning of Romans 9, when in unremitting antithesis with the Jewish synagogical teaching he has shown that righteousness and life are not by the law, but only by faith and by the Spirit, and that therefore no salvation is possible apart from this righteousness revealed by God in Christ, he returns once more — and now in a much more concentrated and detailed manner — to this acknowledgment of Israel's privileges. For on the expression of his great sorrow at Israel's unbelief and his statement, reminiscent of Moses, that he could wish himself to be anathema from Christ for the sake of his brethren according to the flesh, he gives the following enumeration of their privileges: "who are Israelites, whose is the sonship [of God], and the glory, and the covenants, and the giving of the law, and the

---

62. The sharpest verdict to that effect in the epistles of Paul that have been preserved to us is certainly that of I Thess. 2:14ff., where he says of the Jews in Judea that they killed even the Lord Jesus and the prophets and persecuted him (Paul) to the utmost; that they do not please God and are the enemies of all men, because they try to prevent him from speaking to the gentiles that they may be saved, in order thus — so he goes on — at all times to fill up the measure of their sin. Therefore the wrath has come on them to the end (eis telos). Although this pronouncement has wrongly been associated with anti-semitic statements in antiquity (cf. Dibelius, Th., pp. 11ff.; E. Käsemann, "Paul and Israel," New Testament Questions of Today, p. 183), the sharpness of it is unmistakable. It is reminiscent of passages such as Matt. 23:32, et al., where there is also talk of a closing off, a maturation of the process of sin in Israel and of an inevitable judgment coming on it. This "full" judgment (eis telos is here to be taken in a modal sense) Paul now sees as having come on those whose crime he has described in the foregoing. Although no conclusions may be drawn from this for the Jewish people as a whole (see further below, the text), it comes out very clearly in this passage that Paul will have nothing to do with any special excuse for the Jews because they are the people of God.

worship, and the promises; whose are the fathers, and from whom is Christ, as concerning the flesh, who is God over all to be blessed for ever" (Rom. 9:4, 5). And then indeed, in order to avert every suggestion that God's Word is not trustworthy, he comes to his differentiated speaking (already discussed at length above) of the seed of Abraham and the distinction between Israel and Israel. Similarly, in chapter 10 he places beyond any question the fact that Israel did not lack knowledge of the gospel, but that it is just the mistaking of God's grace and of its own privilege that has put it outside the salvation given in Christ. But in Romans 11:1 the provocative question recurs whether God, contrary to the express witness of prophecy, has after all cast off Israel as his people. Consequently it is especially this chapter in which Paul endeavors to find the synthesis between Israel's rejection as the people of God on the one hand and its election on the other; an antithesis whose tension-filled unity is nowhere expressed more clearly than in Romans 11:28, 29, where he says of unbelieving Israel that as regards the gospel they are (God's) enemies[63] for the gentiles' sake, but as regards election, God's beloved for the fathers' sake. For — and this by way of explanation of the latter words — "the gifts of grace and the calling of God are irrevocable."

One cannot confine himself here to a certain stabilizing of both aspects, for example, by attributing to Paul a double conception of election: on the one hand a broader, historical, national election; on the other — or rather, within that — an election in the narrower, personal, soteric sense of the word. Although the differentiated application of the concept of election, now of believing Israelites, then again of the whole of Israel (cf. Rom. 11:28 and Rom. 11:5), may give occasion for this double conception, it is plain that in Romans 11 the apostle does not content himself with such a static "solution," but that he wishes to regard Israel, at present still unbelieving not only historically but also actually, from the viewpoint of the one electing, saving activity of God with his people. How he combines both points of view and how the problem of the meaning of Romans 11 is to be resolved, also with reference to the national renascence of the State of Israel long much under discussion,[64] will have to appear from careful and unbiased exegesis.[65]

Here again the argument begins with a forceful denial that God has cast off Israel as his people, contrary to the express witness of prophecy. The opposite is first of all inferred from the fact that in

---

63. *Echthroi*, in a passive sense, just as *agapētoi*.

64. For a clear inventory of the theological views on the State of Israel see, e.g., H. Berkhof, "De Staat Israël en de theologie," *In de Waagschaal*, June 4, 1955. Furthermore G. C. Berkouwer, *The Return of Christ*, pp. 354ff.

65. For the exegetical literature, in addition to the already cited writing of K. L. Schmidt, *Die Judenfrage*, etc., cf. G. Schrenk, *Die Weissagung über Israël im N.T.*, 1951; H. M. Matter, *De toekomst van Israël*, 1953; countless articles in *Judaïca* (i.a., on Gal. 6:16; see above); my "Israël in het Nieuwe Testament in het bijzonder volgens Rom. 9:11," *Exegetica*, II, 2, 1955; C. Müller, *Gottes Gerechtigkeit*.

spite of all unbelief and apostasy there is still, as in the days of Elijah, a remainder, a remnant *(leimma)*, which God has kept to himself and of which Paul himself also constitutes the proof. And that remnant is said to be "according to the election of grace," whereby once again the unique and abiding character of Israel's election as the people of God is maintained, but with which at the same time the antithesis is confirmed against those in Israel whose expectation is not of grace, but of their works. Therefore within Israel the distinction also applies between "the elect" *(hē eklogē)* who have obtained it on the one hand, and "the rest" who have been hardened on the other. There is thus no discrepancy between Romans 9 and Romans 11.[66] Already in Romans 9 Paul placed God's faithfulness beyond question, and here, in Romans 11, he maintains the line of separation within Israel to the full (v. 7). In so doing prophecy is cited at length to throw light on the rightfulness of the judgment of hardening (vv. 8ff.).

Yet this, too, cannot be the final word. Likewise with respect to this hardening Paul continues to take into account the special intent God has with Israel. They have now indeed stumbled and fallen (vv. 11, 22), but not because the real and final object of the divine judgment on them may be said to lie in this fall. To that end Paul points to the blessed result that (just as Pharaoh's hardening once had; 9:22, 23) their fall and rejection have had for others, namely, the gentiles. It is this blessing, which was implied for the gentiles in Israel's unbelief, that is pointed out in Romans 11:11-33 again and again (11:12, 15, 27, 30), and in which it is indicated that God's redemptive will also embraces Israel, which at present is still unbelieving. Moreover, he makes use of an *a minori ad maius* chain of reasoning: if their fall is the riches of the world, and their reduction[67] the riches of the gentiles, how much more, then, their full number *(plērōma)*? And further: if their rejection is the reconciliation of the world, what will their acceptance be (for the world) but life from the dead (vv. 12, 15)?

"Full number" and "acceptance" have clear eschatological significance.[68] Both concepts here define each other reciprocally. It is a question of such an acceptance that, just as from the gentiles (v. 25), so also from Israel, the "full number" will be saved. "Full number" stands over against Israel's present "reduction." In an antithetical sense it also corresponds with "remnant" *(plērōma* over against *leimma)* in verse 5. There is indeed in "remnant" the idea that Israel has not been entirely abandoned by God, but at the same time that by far the greater part of Israel is now excluded. The "remainder" represents the thought of

---

66. So rightly G. C. Berkouwer, *The Return of Christ,* p. 342; C. Müller, *Gottes Gerechtigkeit,* p. 38.

67. For this translation of *hēttēma* see my *Rom.,* p. 254. (Tr. note: the Dutch here is *achterstelling,* the German *nachstellen:* their being put back, reduced. Hence, I have translated "reduction." This is not, however, to be understood quantitatively, of being diminished in number, but qualitatively, of their being disadvantaged, reduced in the sense of being brought down, lowered, lessened, subordinated.)

68. Cf. Michel, *Rom.,* p. 241; *plērōma autōn* is "apokalyptische Vollzahl."

God's saving grace as well as that of his punishing judgment.[69] On the other hand "fulness" speaks of what is not kept back, of the full share of Israel in the coming redemption, no longer being held back but accepted. Paul's thoughts reach out in that direction when he realizes what the present reduction of Israel already means for the gentiles. How much greater must that blessing be when Israel itself is permitted to share abundantly in the salvation of the Lord. For — this is the underlying idea involved — salvation comes to the world from Israel. In Abraham's seed shall all the families of the earth be blessed. Therefore life from the dead, the great eschatological redemption and renewal, is also to be the fulfillment of the promise of redemption given to Israel.

The entire argument of Romans 11:15-32 is intended to throw light not only on the possibility, but also on the certainty of this "acceptance" and "fulness" of Israel. In so doing the apostle points to the interdependence of the gathering in of the gentiles and that of Israel. First the stream of grace has gone from (unbelieving) Israel to the gentiles; now it must turn back from the believing gentiles to unbelieving Israel. Jealousy of the gentiles must come to fill Israel (v. 11), and the preaching of the gospel to and by the gentiles must save Israel (v. 14) and move them not to persevere in their unbelief (v. 22), and by the mercy shown to the gentiles it will make them, too, in their turn, obtain mercy with God (v. 31). It is this expectation which possesses the apostle with respect to the majority of Israel still unbelieving, and which he communicates to his readers as a "mystery." One is not to think here of a special revelation he received, an esoteric secret, but of the insight he has into the realization of God's counsel now becoming visible with regard to the gathering in of the gentiles on the one hand, and Israel on the other. As God causes the salvation that has rebounded from the wall of Israel's unbelief to stream out to the gentiles, so it must be his hidden intention therewith that the gentiles become a cause of deliverance for Israel. That he would thereby have in mind a conversion of Israel at one point in the eschatological end time does not appear from Romans 11. There is no question of another conversion than that which results from the preaching of the gospel in history (cf. 10:14ff.; 11:11, 14, 22) and from the activity presently coming to them from the believing gentile world (11:31). Even the pronouncement in verses 25 and 26 constantly quoted to this effect does not speak of such a final conversion. It says that the hardening has come on a part of Israel until the full number of gentiles shall have come in (to salvation, to the kingdom), and that thus all Israel shall be saved, as it is written. It does not say that Israel then or thus will come to conversion,[70] but that thus the salvation of all Israel (in the above-described

---

69. Cf. C. Müller as well (Gottes Gerechtigkeit, p. 46). He points to the fact that later Judaism (Apocalyptic, Damascus Document, Qumran texts) also ascribed great significance to the idea of the "remnant," but for the great majority entertained little or no hope.

70. This continues to be my great objection to the view of Berkhof, et al., that they simply substitute "be converted" for the words "be saved" (cf. Berkhof, Christ the Meaning of History, ET 1966, pp. 145f.; C. Müller, ibid., pp. 43ff.) and thus at a decisive point in the argument introduce an apocalyptic miracle of con-

sense of "full number") shall become a fact, when the full number (*plērōma*) of the gentiles has also been brought in.[71] Israel as a nation will not again exhibit the image of the people of God before the gentiles, too, have brought their full portion into it. Till such time, that is to say, until this great hour of the consummation, Israel will in part exhibit the image of hardening, the evidence of the judgment of God. Only under the concurrent mark of God's judgment on the unbelief of a part of Israel will Israel come to its fullness and just then be redeemed from that judgment. The mystery (v. 25) is thus situated in the manner in which this fullness of Israel is to be saved: in the strange interdependence of the salvation of Israel and that of the gentiles. Israel, which was chosen from among the gentiles, must, contrary to every human expectation, first give way to the gentiles. But as Israel because of its disobedience has become a cause of salvation for the gentiles, so

---

version, of which the text speaks with not so much as a single word. "And so all Israel shall be saved" in the whole of Paul's reasoning acts as a prospect for the present preaching of the gospel to Israel (11:13-15), not as a kind of palliative in view of Israel's present hardening. The entire wrestling of the apostle for Israel's conversion, his pain, his effort to be permitted to save a few of his hardened brethren, his declaration that he is himself willing to be cut off from Christ, loses its tension when the real decision loses its present, historical character and is shifted to "post-history." "One can also make it unnecessarily difficult for oneself," Berkhof writes, and he explains that "the moment will come that even [*sic!*] the shrewdest exegete will feel some of Paul's joy, because . . . all Israel will be saved" (p. 146). One will want to be grateful for this encouragement, but with that may not lose sight of the fundamental division that according to the apostle also takes place in Israel. Paul's joy does not consist in the fact that for Israel, because of its historical election, there would be "broader perspectives" than for the gentiles (p. 144), but that despite the punishment of hardening that has come on part of Israel, its *pleroma* will be saved.

71. It seems to me that Berkouwer, in *The Return of Christ*, takes altogether too little account of the future element in Paul's pronouncements. "He does not . . . attempt a narrative account of future events. He is simply concerned with the Israel of his day" (p. 347). Paul speaks here — so Berkouwer — in a high pitch of expectation of the immediate coming of the Lord and is occupied with the maximal possibilities which, out of the evidence of the salvation on the gentiles, he sees *now, in his own time*, for Israel (pp. 347ff.). The "all Israel shall be saved" may not be understood as a foretelling of a future event or as an isolated mystery, but as the expression of "a praying, serving, active orientation toward Israel's return to the way that is now open to it" (p. 348). Only thus, that is, as a timely expectation of what is now possible and with which one is occupied, does Paul's pronouncement have abiding relevance, and not if we are obliged to see in it a prophecy of an event in the end time (pp. 349, 358). Nevertheless, with however much justice Berkouwer places the emphasis on the "now" of 11:30, this does not alter the fact that "all Israel will (only) be saved when the *pleroma* of the gentiles shall have come in." That speaks of the final event: *plērōma* here has a future-eschatological sense, just as in v. 12, and *pas Israēl* is synonymous with it (= *to plērōma autōn;* v. 12). This has nothing to do with the idea of a narrative, "reportorial" account (a notion which, in this context, seems to me to create false dilemmas); it does have to do with the as yet unfulfilled redemptive counsel of God. The manner in which Paul sees this fulfillment as being realized is the mystery, which does indeed open up before him "now." But neither in Paul's day nor in our own can one detach this from the still to be expected *plērōma* as a not yet fulfilled eschatological, or if one will, apocalyptic reality, whereby the question of whether more or less "near at hand" plays no special part.

now the gentiles must provoke Israel to jealousy. There is thus an interaction. God grants no mercy to Israel without the gentiles, but neither does he do so to the gentiles without Israel. As he first shut up all under disobedience, so will he have mercy on all. The whole argument of Romans 11:11-32 leads to the indication of this mutual relationship of dependence, of this undulatory movement of salvation (cf. vv. 30-32), and on this, too, the doxology of the depth of the riches, wisdom, and knowledge of God and of the inscrutableness of his ways is founded (vv. 33-36).

There is therefore no contradiction between the definition of the essence of the New Testament church as the people of God and holding to Israel as the object of God's irrevocable gift of grace and calling. By making faith the criterion of the children of Abraham (Gal. 3:26ff.) and giving believing gentiles a place among his posterity (Rom. 4:16), the election of historical Israel is not nullified or rendered inoperative in order to make room for the formation of the new people of God, the Christian church. Rather, Paul wishes to show that it is precisely in historical Israel that God has chosen the Christian church and called it to himself (Gal. 3:16); on the one hand this is to say that all who belong to Christ by faith also belong to this church, but on the other hand that the historical bond between God and Israel continues to be maintained in its real significance. That significance has always consisted in the fact that Israel's election is an election of grace and that for Israel, too, therefore, there is no other way than that of faith. Consequently the irrevocable character of God's gifts of grace and calling, which remain valid for Israel, consists in that he will restore Israel to this true sonship by the proclamation of the gospel and by provoking it to jealousy. But in that way he will not only preserve to himself a remnant according to the election of grace, but he will also lead the *pleroma* of Israel, Israel as people, all Israel, to salvation with the fullness of the gentiles.

On the one hand Israel is thus bound to the church of the gentiles; the stream of grace must return from them to Israel, after it has first passed Israel by because of its unbelief and come to the gentiles. But on the other hand, the church made up of the gentiles is bound to Israel. For the life from the dead, the great future, is not to dawn without the *pleroma* of Israel; all nations will be blessed with Abraham's seed. The holy root of Israel continues to support all, the holy leaven permeates all, and the gentiles are grafted into the olive tree of Israel (Rom. 11:24). There is re-creation, but there is also continuity,[72] because Israel has always been the product of God's life-creating grace; there is a New Covenant, but not without connection to, rather with the maintaining of what constituted the essential mystery of the Old Covenant. Thus, on the one hand Paul is able to see the church of the gentiles as endowed with all the privileges and blessings of Israel, and to see it occupy the place of unbelieving Israel, and yet on the other to uphold to the full the continuation of God's original redemptive intentions with

---

72. Against the actualistic interpretation of election in C. Müller, *Gottes Gerechtigkeit*, pp. 78ff.

Israel as the historical people of God. And all this because of the gracious character of God's election and because of Christ, who is the seed of Abraham as well as the second Adam: the one in whom the whole church, Jews and gentiles together, has become one body and one new man. This last observation leads us now to the second great Pauline conception of the church, that is, the church as the body of Christ.

IX
THE CHURCH
AS THE BODY OF CHRIST

SECTION 59. VARIOUS VIEWPOINTS AND PROBLEMS

The most typical description of the church in Paul is that of the body of Christ. Although the idea that underlies this designation certainly occurs elsewhere in the New Testament[1] — one need only think of the figure of the vine and the branches in John 15 — nevertheless the qualification "body of Christ" is typically Pauline. In general it gives a further explication of the significance of the church as the people of God. It describes the christological mode of existence of the church as the people of God; it speaks of the special bond with Christ that the church has as the people of God and the new Israel.

There is a bewildering number of conceptions concerning the significance of "body of Christ" as a designation of the church. At first glance it is even difficult to form a clear idea of all these conceptions and to give a useful classification of them. This holds in particular for the development of the investigation that has taken place in recent years both from the Protestant and especially from the Roman Catholic side, and in which scholars have attempted with a great deal of acumen and with the aid of all manner of materials from contemporary Judaism as well as from the Greek world to arrive at a revision, modification, or clarification of earlier insights. Although it is not possible within the framework of our inquiry to describe and assess the history and development of this investigation[2] at all completely, nevertheless for a correct insight into what is before us in this chapter it does seem indispensable to go somewhat more deeply into these developments.

Generally speaking, the qualification of the church as the body of Christ is a denotation of the special, close relationship and communion that exist between Christ and his church. To be sure, some have been of the opinion — as will appear still further in handling the relevant texts — that in this designation it is not so much a matter of the communion between Christ and the church as it is of the relationship of

---

1. Cf., e.g., E. Schweizer, "Die Kirche als Leib Christi in den paulinischen Homologoumena," *TLZ*, Vol. 86, 1961, cols. 168ff.
2. On this see, among others, J. J. Meuzelaar, *Der Leib des Messias*, 1961, pp. 1-19; J. Havet, "La doctrine Paulinienne du 'Corps du Christ,'" in *Littérature et Théologie Paulinienne (Recherches Bibliques*, V), 1960, pp. 185ff. For the developments in Roman Catholic theology (and exegesis) see the accurate and valuable surveys in W. D. Jonker, *Mistieke Liggaam en Kerk in die Nuwe Rooms-Katolieke Teologie*, 1955.

believers to one another.[3] Accordingly they have appealed for this to the manner in which in the Greek world, for example, communal life in the state and society was spoken of under the figure of the body. However, most scholars are of the opinion that Paul's meaning is by no means exhausted with this social or practical interpretation of the concept "body of Christ." It qualifies not only the fellowship of believers, but primarily the nature of the fellowship between the church and Christ himself. The questions that arise time and again are therefore these: in what sense is *this* fellowship qualified by this idea? how is one to take the word "body" here? and what leads Paul to make use of just the word body in denoting this relationship?

If one examines the answers that are given to these queries, in the main one may distinguish between two kinds of conceptions, namely, those which understand the qualification body of Christ in a figurative, collective sense and those which take it in a real, personal sense. In the working out of each of these two interpretations large and substantial differences again reveal themselves. Still, the distinction between (A) the metaphorical-collective and (B) the real-personal explanations of the words "body of Christ" seems the most serviceable for the exegetical approach to the whole problem.

(A) The view that takes the expression "body of Christ" in a metaphorical sense, at least in the first instance, is the more traditional, both in Roman Catholic and in Protestant exegesis. Its point of departure is that the qualification "body of Christ" is a figurative representation of the vital communion of the church with Christ. "Body" is therefore not the real, historical, or glorified body of Christ, but the church as fellowship. On the nature of the fellowship thus metaphorically described there are, also in regard to this figurative view of "body," again profound differences, in particular between (1) the Protestant and (2) the Roman Catholic interpretations.

(1) So far as the former is concerned, it is characteristic of the traditional conception that body of Christ is here exclusively understood of the pneumatic mode of existence of the church on the ground of its communion with the exalted Christ. It is the Spirit who constitutes this communion. The church is the body of Christ as the fellowship in which he dwells by his Spirit and which he by his Spirit enlivens and fills.[4] In this context the body of Christ is accordingly often spoken of as the invisible church and the mystical union between Christ and the church.[5]

---

3. For this "practical meaning of the Pauline concept," see Meuzelaar, *ibid.*, p. 16, who also holds this view (cf. pp. 168ff.). Among the Roman Catholic exegetes this conception has been defended by L. Deimel, *Leib Christi*, pp. 22, 42, *et al.* H. Schlier, *Christus und die Kirche im Epheserbrief*, 1930, defends it with regard to the statements in Romans and 1 Corinthians, as contrasted with those in Ephesians and Colossians; see further below in the text.

4. For this conception in the exegetical literature see the work of Traugott Schmidt, which appeared already in 1919 but continues to be influential, *Der Leib Christi* — in this connection, e.g., pp. 142ff.

5. For this conception in the classical (Augustine, Calvin) and in the present-day ("ecumenical") theology, see H. M. Matter, *De Kerk als Lichaam van Christus (Rome, Reformatie, Oecumene)*, 1962, pp. 7ff.

(2) In traditional Roman Catholic exegesis the church as the body of Christ is not thought of in the first place pneumatically, but as the fruit of the union of the church with the divine-human nature of Christ. Especially determinative for this is the manner in which, according to the Roman Catholic view, the church receives in the eucharist a share in the body of the Lord. All this has the effect that the church is spoken of as the body of Christ in a very "massive" fashion, and great emphasis is laid on the identity of Christ and his church-body. The church can be called the body of Christ because in the church, as it were, Christ receives an extension of his existence, so that this united mode of existence of Christ and his church can be denoted as the "mystical" or "collective Christ." Even so in the traditional conception the description of the church as body of Christ, notwithstanding this identity, continues as a description to bear a metaphorical character. The church is indeed united with the personal body of the Lord, understood in the literal sense (e.g., in the eucharist), yet it is itself not that body, but it is that body as the totality of those with whom Christ thus makes himself one.[6]

Therefore, however important the differences are in this traditional figurative view of "body of Christ," particularly between the Protestant and the Roman Catholic interpreters, it cannot be said that these go back to a fundamentally different interpretation of the terminology, i.e., of the word "body." For both start from the collective significance of the body as the designation of the organic whole of believers in their union with Christ. The difference lies in the manner in which the nature of this union is understood.

(B) In recent years serious criticism has been leveled against this traditional, metaphorical interpretation of the concept "body of Christ," from both the Protestant and the Roman Catholic sides. So far as the Protestant interpretation is concerned, this criticism is directed first of all toward the one-sided pneumatic character that was ascribed to the body of Christ. On the other hand, contemporary criticism of the traditional Roman Catholic view is especially opposed to the collective extension Christ's existence is supposed to have received in the church as his body. Recent Roman Catholic exegetes can discover nothing of this in Paul. It is remarkable, however, that this twofold criticism, however different in point of view and result, is one in that it has gone over from the figurative to the real, personal conception of "body of Christ," that is to say, body taken in the sense of the historical and glorified body of Christ. We want here also to go somewhat further into (1) the newer Protestant and (2) the Roman Catholic view.

(1) For the former it is especially E. Percy who has become representative in his frequently cited work *Der Leib Christi*.[7] The point of

---

6. So far as the exegetical literature is concerned, the clear expositions of A. Wikenhauser, *Die Kirche als der Mystische Leib Christi nach dem Apostel Paulus*, 2nd ed., 1940, are representative for this traditional conception set forth in all manner of variations; see also E. Mersch, *The Whole Christ*, ET 1938.

7. *Der Leib Christi* [Sōma Christou] *in den paulinischen Homologoumena und Antilegomena*, 1942.

departure for Percy's criticism lies in that the traditional conception explains the expression body of Christ on the analogy of an anthropology understood in a dichotomistic sense. The church is the body of Christ because Christ constitutes it by his Spirit and enlivens it by his indwelling. This is a representation of the relationship of body and soul (spirit) that in Percy's opinion is entirely foreign to Paul. For this reason neither can it hold as the principle of interpretation for the designation of the church as the body of Christ.

However, the material objection urged by Percy weighs no less heavily, that with this conception the communion between Christ and the church denoted by "body of Christ" is understood primarily or exclusively as a spiritual or "mystical" union constituted by the Spirit (as indwelling and enlivening force). It should be maintained against this "mystical" conception, however, that in Paul this unity, as also finds expression in the formulae "in Christ" and "with Christ," in the first place bears a redemptive-historical character in that the church ("the many") has been comprehended in Christ, and it is this "objective" solidarity which above all makes the church the body of Christ.[8] Thereby the spiritual indwelling of Christ in the church maintained by the Spirit has not been denied or become of less significance; but, as we have already been able to demonstrate in detail, the objective, redemptive-historical unity of the "all in One" lies at the root of this spiritual communion. And if, as Percy has shown, this unity also constitutes the point of departure for the qualification "body of Christ," it is clear that one cannot understand this on the analogy of the idea of the human body inhabited by the soul or animated by the spirit.

It is another question how with this view set forth by Percy the use of the designation "body of Christ" is then to be explained. Percy himself has here arrived at a very radical, in our view also very debatable, solution, namely, by no longer taking the term "body of Christ" in the metaphorical, but in the literal sense, as the designation of the historical body of Christ that died on the cross and rose on the third day. Proceeding on the idea that the church was comprehended in Christ's death and resurrection and thus may be regarded as incorporated into him, it would also coincide with Christ's bodily existence in which he suffered and died for it. And so Percy comes to the conclusion that this body of Christ identical with the church is fundamentally no other body than that which died on the cross and rose on the third day.[9] It is undeniable that both terminologically and materially a leap is made here. That Christ has suffered in his body for his own as their substitute and representative and that in him they have been included in that, have died and been buried with him and "through his body" have been put to death (Rom. 7:4), is not the same as that they themselves now *are* his body in

8. For this interpretation of "body of Christ" as the whole of those who have been included in Christ see also, e.g., S. Hanson, *The Unity of the Church in the New Testament*, 1946; for the connection with the "Adam theology" in Judaism, Schweizer, "Die Kirche als Leib Christi," *TLZ*, 1961, cols. 163ff.

9. *Der Leib Christi*, p. 44.

the literal and historical sense of the word. For not only is "have been included in" not the same as "identical with," but also the idea that in his body Christ represents his own is not reversible in the sense that his own would now likewise represent that body. Transitions take place here and conclusions are drawn that, however closely they sometimes seem to approach the Pauline usage, nevertheless are not found in Paul himself, and cannot be accepted as legitimate conclusions from what Paul in fact says.[10]

We may go on to note that the breakthrough from the figurative, collective to the literal, personal interpretation of the body of Christ is a frequently occurring phenomenon in the more recent literature.[11] One meets with it also, for example, in the work of J. A. T. Robinson, *The Body*. "The leap" is made here again, if in a way somewhat different from Percy. Robinson starts from the words of institution of the Lord's Supper, which also occur in Paul. When Jesus says "This is my body . . . my blood," he is said thereby to transmit himself ("his actual self, his life and personality") to his disciples. And Robinson's conclusion is: "Insofar then as the Christian Community feeds on this body and blood, it *becomes* the very life and personality of the risen Lord."[12] He acknowledges: "There is a jump here, from 'feeding on' to 'becoming,' which is not explained." And Paul is the only one who makes this jump. This "extraordinary leap from the Eucharist to the *Ecclesia* itself as the extension of Christ's human personality" Robinson thinks himself able to explain, however, with an appeal to Paul's experience on the road to Damascus. He saw there the risen Lord in his glorified body, who asked him, "Saul, Saul, why persecutest thou Me?" and to Paul's question: "Who art thou, Lord?" responded: "I am Jesus, whom thou persecutest." Paul's apostleship was therefore — thus Robinson — based on "the revelation of the resurrection body of Christ, not as an individual, but as the Christian Community."[13] One may seriously doubt, however, whether this can in fact hold as an explanation for "the leap" and as an answer to the question why — as Robinson puts it — "the Body of Christ inevitably meant for him [Paul] what it did." For the fact that in these pronouncements Jesus identifies himself with his church does not in the

---

10. See further below, pp. 373ff.

11. One can refer here already to the conception of Albert Schweitzer. According to his view, in Paul's thinking the church forms such a close unity with Christ that it even now shares in the resurrection-corporeality of Christ (cf. *The Mysticism of Paul the Apostle*, pp. 101ff.). From this idea via a meaningful simplification that of the body of Christ purportedly came into being. "The participation of the elect with Christ in the same corporeity becomes a being part of the body of Christ" (*ibid.*, p. 117). This conception, which is characteristic of Schweitzer's book, has not found acceptance because of its extremely realistic anticipation of the participation of believers in the resurrection-corporeality of Christ. Even so Schweitzer with his eschatological view of the unity of Christ and his own has here also had great influence (over against the pneumatic-mystical view) (cf. Percy, *Leib*, p. 32, n. 69). He should therefore certainly be mentioned in the context of the authors listed above.

12. *The Body*, p. 57.

13. *Ibid.*, p. 58.

least signify that therefore the church can be denoted as his (glorified) body. One would then have to reach the conclusion that on the road to Damascus in Jesus the church also appeared to Paul, and that not as an earthly, but as a heavenly reality. But with that we would unquestionably go beyond all the bounds of the sense of the words of Acts 26:14ff.; 9:4ff.; 22:7ff.[14]

(2) However little justification this "leap" of the identification of the church with the body of Christ taken in a literal sense may have, still this explanation given from the non-Catholic side has become a base for a whole series of newer Roman Catholic writings that — in divergence from the traditional Roman Catholic explanation — likewise have come to enter a plea for this literal and personal meaning. To be mentioned here in particular is the work,[15] which has given leadership in this respect, of the Louvain professor L. Cerfaux, who has been followed by such other Catholic authors as P. Benoit, W. Goossens, J. Havet, et al.[16]

According to Cerfaux a development has taken place in Paul with respect to the church as body of Christ. The point of departure is the comparison, borrowed from Greek thought, of the church with the body, the members of which stand in organic relation to each other (1 Cor. 12; Rom. 12). It was no more than natural, however, that under Paul's pen this formula "should grow more involved."[17] Because Paul infers the unity of the church from the eucharist, that is to say, from having a common share in the bread as the body of Christ (1 Cor. 10), at a given moment he combines this body of Christ with "the body" of the Greek simile, in order subsequently to substitute the former for the latter: the one body of the Hellenistic formula denotes the one body of Christ. And that body, as appears from the text of the Supper, is his "real and personal body." Consequently this body in the literal sense is the source and central point of unity in the Christian world: "Identified with this body, they are one. Among themselves, they are all 'one' by reference to the body of Christ."[18]

In the Prison Epistles this development in Paul's thinking is carried further. "It could be said that the word sōma fascinated Paul."[19] While in Romans and 1 Corinthians he bases the fact that the church is one body on communion with the crucified body of Christ in the eucharist, in the Prison Epistles the glorified Christ and the glorified body

---

14. Besides, one meets fairly frequently with the conception that the source of Paul's qualification of the church as the "body of Christ" is to be sought in this self-identification of Christ with his church. In addition to the literature mentioned in Meuzelaar, *Der Leib des Messias*, p. 13, see also L. Cerfaux, *The Church in the Theology of St. Paul*, p. 262, n. 1, according to which even Augustine held this view. Cerfaux himself rejects it.

15. See the previous note.

16. P. Benoit, "Corps, tête et plérôme dans les Épîtres de la captivité," *Revue Biblique*, 1956, pp. 5ff.; W. Goossens, *l'Église Corps du Christ*, 2nd ed., 1949; J. Havet, in the article cited above, in *Littérature et Théologie Paulinienne*, 1960; see furthermore the literature mentioned there on p. 187.

17. *The Church in the Theology of St. Paul*, p. 266.

18. *Ibid.*, p. 278.

19. *Ibid.*, p. 325.

of Christ define the essence of the church. It is the glorified Christ who fills the church with his presence, and it is he whose body the church is now called in so many words (Eph. 1:22ff.; Col. 1:24): "a new formula, one which is possible only on the level of the epistles of the captivity."[20] Accordingly it is here that the identification (Robinson's "leap"!) takes place. The glorified body of Christ in heaven is the dwelling place of the fullness of his Godhead. Because the church may identify itself with this body, it receives in turn the fullness of the divine life. "In the mystical order nothing is opposed to a true identification of the Church with the glorious body of Christ. The Church and Christ are the same body in virtue of a mystical identification of the church with the risen body."[21]

The difference between this newer Roman Catholic conception of the church as the body of Christ and the traditional is, that the "body of Christ" is no longer understood in a metaphorical and collective, but in a "real" and "personal" sense.[22] Undoubtedly in both Roman Catholic conceptions the unity expressed rests on the church's participation in the historical divine-human nature of Christ. Whereas in the traditional view, however, this unity is thought of as a union of Christ with the body (conceived of collectively) of the church, and Christ thus in his church receives an extension of his existence, which has indeed been denoted as the mystical or collective Christ, the newer view will know nothing of such a collective conception of the "body of Christ." According to it, in this qualification of the church it is precisely the point that the union is not of Christ with the *collectivum* of the church, but, conversely, of the church with the personal body of Christ. The special feature of this exegesis therefore lies in this, that it regards the identification of the church and the body of Christ from the viewpoint of the personal (historical and glorified) body of Christ, and not from that of the church as a collective body intended in the metaphorical sense.

Without going further into all the modifications[23] of this new conception and into the attempts in the Roman Catholic exegetical and dogmatic literature to combine it with the traditional conception (maintained in the encyclical *Mystici Corporis* of Pius XII, 1953!),[24] it can thus

---

20. *Ibid.*, p. 330.

21. *Ibid.*, p. 343.

22. To be sure Cerfaux writes: "the expression is always metaphorical," but he then defines this metaphorical quality thus: "The name of the mystically present cause (the risen body) is attributed to the effect (the Christians are the *pleroma* of Christ)" (p. 344). Apparently therefore no "ontic" identification takes place. The church-body of Christ can be regarded as "a reality distinct from the physical body" *(loc. cit.).* But even so the word "body" refers in both cases to the personal (glorified) body of Christ. The word "metaphorical" does indeed restrict the identification of church and body of Christ, but not the literal, nonmetaphorical sense in which "body of Christ" is spoken of.

23. For this see, e.g., W. D. Jonker, *Mistieke Liggaam,* and J. Havet, in *Littérature et Théologie Paulinienne,* 1960.

24. Interesting and characteristic for the manner in which the attempt is made to combine more recent exegesis and older church doctrine is the effort J. Havet

be determined in general that so far as the identification of the church with the body of Christ taken in the literal sense is concerned, it is in very close agreement with the exegesis of Percy and Robinson, even though the "leap" (of this identification) for all these authors certainly does not have the same dogmatic background and significance. It is not our purpose here, however, to give a further description of all these details, but rather to return to the exegesis of the Pauline texts. It is evident from the above that in so doing, among others, the following questions arise:

(a) Is the expression "body" as designation of the church in Paul's epistles (or a part of them) to be understood only as a comparison or metaphor that elucidates mutual relationships within the church?

(b) Is this expression, understood of the relationship between Christ and his church, to be taken in a literal or metaphorical sense?

(c) If one is to start from the metaphorical view, then what is to be understood by the unity of Christ and his church expressed thereby?

(d) Is it possible to point out or explain the origin of this Pauline mode of expression? This last question will at the same time bring us into contact with the gnostic and Jewish methods of interpretation, which one encounters in the more recent literature.

SECTION 60. "BODY" AND "BODY OF CHRIST" (ROMANS AND 1 CORINTHIANS)

It has rightly been observed in all the thorough discussions on the significance of "body of Christ" as definition of the essence of the church that Paul's pronouncements with respect to it, at least so far as Romans and 1 Corinthians are concerned, above all have a clear paraenetic purport.[25] In Romans 12:3ff. believers are admonished that everyone is to know his own place in the church as a whole, and this is elucidated with the figure of the body in which are many members, but in which every member does not have the same function. In this way the church, too, is to know itself: we as many are one body in Christ, but individually members one of another (v. 5). And what follows shows that believers must conduct themselves according to that rule by each being content with his own gift and useful in it. The still more elaborate "body-pericope" of 1 Corinthians 12:14ff. is to the same effect. There, too, it is a question of the many members (and functions) of the one body. The illustration then takes on the character of a parable: "if the foot said, 'because I am not the hand...,' and if the ear said," etc., whereupon the true nature of the body is expounded in its unity and diversity, with continuous indirect application to the church (vv. 15-27). In these pericopes it is therefore beyond question the mutual unity (and diver-

---

(ibid., pp. 213ff.) makes to remain in harmony with the collective view of the corpus Christi in the encyclical mentioned above.

25. Cf. especially Meuzelaar, Der Leib des Messias, pp. 16ff., 171ff.

sity) of the church that is elucidated and commended under the figure
of the human body. Paul's argumentation here is clearly reminiscent of
the corresponding figurative usage in other Hellenistic writers, among
whom some, likewise in parabolic form borrowed from the functions of
the body, throw light on the necessary mutual cooperation within a
specific community.[26]

There can thus be no doubt but that in applying the name "body
of Christ" to the church the organic unity of the church within itself
played a not unimportant part, and that this application also has an
exceedingly practical and paraenetic significance. On the other hand, it
is highly superficial to suppose that in some or in all of the epistles of
Paul this idea of the body is restricted to the mutual unity and diversity
of believers,[27] and that the addition "of Christ" is then to be taken only
as a qualifying genitive, in the sense of "belonging to Christ," "the
Christian" body, or something of that sort.[28] The real question may
even be said to be whether Paul's qualification of the church as the body
of Christ took its point of departure in such a general conception or
figurative usage with respect to certain parts of human society and only
from thence acquired deeper dimensions.[29] The concept "body" in Paul's
thinking occupies in various respects such an important place[30] that the
reverse is more natural, namely, that at the root of this metaphorical
language applied to mutual relationships in the church there is a deeper
concept of the church as body of Christ. This is not only a reasoning
from probability, but also appears from the structure of Paul's argumentation. For he does not rise from the relationships within the church

---

26. See the detailed surveys, e.g., in Wikenhauser, *Die Kirche*, pp. 130-143;
see also Meuzelaar, *ibid.*, pp. 149ff. The most familiar in this respect is surely the
fable, occurring in various forms, of Menenius Agrippa (on the function of the state
as "stomach" with respect to the other "parts of the body" of society). A question
that arises here is whether in this literature "body" already has the metaphorical
significance of "organism," community, etc. According to some this is not to be
shown of the Greek *sōma* (in contrast to the Latin *corpus*) (cf., e.g., Wikenhauser,
p. 225). In particular a Greek inscription at Cyrene has come into discussion in
this connection in which there is mention of *sōma*; see T. W. Manson, "A Parallel to
a N.T. Use of [*sōma*]," *Journal of Theol. Studies*, 1935, p. 385. Others, however, have
strongly disputed that here or elsewhere *sōma* has the significance of "community";
cf., e.g., Cerfaux, *The Church in St. Paul*, pp. 272ff.

27. As Schlier, e.g., supposed for Romans and 1 Corinthians, in contradistinction to the Prison Epistles, where an entirely different conception of the church
as body purportedly emerges (*Christus und die Kirche im Epheserbrief*, 1930, pp.
39ff.). On the other hand, Meuzelaar, e.g., wishes to understand the entire Pauline
usage (including Colossians and Ephesians) exclusively of these mutual relationships
of believers (*Der Leib des Messias*, pp. 168ff.).

28. Matter chooses to think of a genitive of origin or authorship (*originis* or
auctoris): as God has composed the human body in a certain way, so the church
is the creative work of Christ and thus his body (wrought by him). He also wishes
to understand the abridged expression in 1 Corinthians 12:12 — "so also Christ" —
in that sense, as: "so Christ does it also" (*De Kerk als Lichaam van Christus*, pp.
19-22).

29. As Cerfaux, e.g., also wishes (see above, p. 367).

30. To have clearly demonstrated this is the merit of the writing of Robinson, *The Body*, although there are objections to be urged against his exegesis.

(as body) to the relation of the church to Christ, but reasons just the other way around: because the church is the body *of Christ,* therefore it is to conduct itself within as "body," and the foot must not say: "because I am not the hand," etc.

This holds immediately for the familiar pronouncements in Romans 12 and 1 Corinthians 12. In Romans 12:4ff. it is said that as in one body we have many members, but all the members do not have the same function, so also as many we are one body in Christ, but individually members one of another. That the church is one body and is to conduct itself as such has its ground therefore in the fact that "the many" are one body "in Christ." Similarly it is said in 1 Corinthians 12:12ff. that as the body is one and has many members . . . so is (it) also (with) Christ *(houtōs kai ho Christos).* Although we have to do with an abridged mode of expression, it is certainly clear that Paul here again does not infer that the church is the body from its own existence as community, but precisely from Christ and from the bond that joins the church to him. The significance of this reference to Christ is none other than that which is expressed in the recapitulatory words of 1 Corinthians 12:27: "Now you are the body of Christ."

The central question, then, is what is intended by this expression "body of Christ." We concentrate first on the data from the "principal letters," not in order to introduce a division between these and the Prison Epistles or *a priori* to assume a development in Paul's ideas, but because the representation in Ephesians and Colossians is complicated by the fact that in them there is not only mention of the body of Christ, but also of Christ as the Head of the body.

There is a clear indication for the meaning of the apostle at the very outset in the words just cited from Romans 12:5: so we (as the) many are one body in Christ.[31] Both the characteristic expression "the many" and the definitive "in Christ" are borrowed from the familiar terminology that denotes the many as having been included in the one, the church as being represented by Christ. The distinguishing feature of the idea of "body," therefore, is that these many in virtue of this common belonging to Christ form in him a new unity with each other. They are not each one individually, but as a corporate unity, all together in him. The specific character of the qualification thus lies in placing in the forefront the new unity that "the many" form in Christ. But the constitutive factor of this unity is in the many having been included "in Christ." It is therefore on this idea, so fundamental for Paul's preaching,[32] that the conception of the church as the one body *in* Christ, or, as it is put in 1 Corinthians 12:27, as the body *of* Christ,[33] now rests.

31. The rendering *hoi polloi* stands over against *to de kath' heis.* The intention of *hoi polloi* is to give expression to the collective: all of us. It does not say, however, *hoi pantes,* which is indeed materially the same (cf. Gal. 3:28), but is circumscribed here with the characteristic expression *hoi polloi.* Further see the text.
32. Cf. Section 10.
33. This is shown very clearly in the writing of Percy, *Der Leib Christi.*

With this, then, the view has been refuted that the idea of the body of Christ rests on the pneumatic indwelling of Christ in his church. The church then, on the analogy of anthropological dichotomy, is thought of[34] as the organ that is "enlivened" by Christ and thus is joined into a unity and bound together. Yet notwithstanding the objection that Paul does not think dichotomistically and the term "body" does not for him denote only the external and material organization of man to be brought to life by the soul or the spirit, but man himself (including his "soul"),[35] it is unmistakably apparent from the above terminology that the one body is not conceived in the first instance as a pneumatic but (we may perhaps say) as a redemptive-historical, "objective" unity. As believers, by virtue of their being-of-Christ, belong to the one seed of Abraham (Gal. 3:29; cf. v. 16), so are they also, if of Christ, his members and together his one body. As we shall see still further, the pneumatic is undoubtedly of paramount importance in the further realization of this unity of the body. But as we have already been able to ascertain in another connection,[36] the sequence in this conception is nevertheless not: Christ $\longrightarrow$ the Spirit $\longrightarrow$ the body, but rather: Christ $\longrightarrow$ the body-in-Christ $\longrightarrow$ the Spirit.

The correct translation and exegesis of 1 Corinthians 12:13 are of particular importance for what engages us here: "for in one Spirit we were all baptized into one body, whether Jews or Greeks, whether slaves or free, and we were all made to drink with one Spirit." The pronouncement serves as a further confirmation of the preceding paraenetic exposition, that with all the diversity of gifts one is yet always to keep in view the unity of the Spirit. To that end the apostle now points in verses 12 and 13 to the unity lying "behind" this unity of the Spirit, the unity of the body, and he reminds the church of the moment of their baptism as the incorporation into the body of Christ ("baptized into one body"). The expression does not say that the unity of the body comes into being by baptism, in the sense of: "so that we are of one body,"[37] or: "in order together to form one body."[38] Rather, the term employed here — "to baptize into" *(baptizein eis)* — denotes that the one baptized is brought into relation with an already existing person or unity (cf. 1 Cor. 10:2; Gal. 3:27); this means therefore incorporation into an already existing[39] body, namely, the communion of those who have been comprehended in and baptized into Christ. Hence the Spirit, too, is not thought of here as the factor constituting the body (so

---

34. For this older idea (as held by H. J. Holtzmann, T. Schmidt, A. Wiken-hauser), see the detailed refutation by Percy, *Der Leib Christi*, pp. 10ff. (cf. also above, pp. 364ff.).

35. See above, Section 19.

36. Cf. above, Section 38.

37. So, e.g., Wikenhauser, *Die Kirche*, p. 102; also Lietzmann, *Cor.*, p. 63 (see, on the other hand, the rectifying annotation of Kümmel on p. 187).

38. So Matter, *De Kerk*, p. 20.

39. So rightly Percy, *Der Leib Christi*, p. 16.

that one would have to translate: "by one Spirit"[40]), but as the gift in which believers share in virtue of their incorporation into the body. For to be in Christ, to belong to his body, means to be in the Spirit (Rom. 8:9),[41] to have been brought under the rule of the Spirit. In this train of thought it is not the Spirit who incorporates into the body by means of baptism, but, just the reverse, incorporation by baptism means being baptized with the Spirit of Christ. This is also evident from the following expression in 1 Corinthians 12:13 (which removes all uncertainty with respect to the exegesis of this passage): "and we were all made to drink with one Spirit." Whether one still chooses to understand this being made to drink of baptism[42] or — in our view[43] with more reason — of the Lord's Supper,[44] it is clear that the Spirit is not intended here as the Author of the body, but as the gift in which all participate by virtue of their belonging to the one body of Christ.

The same thought underlies the remarkable and profound warning against fornication in 1 Corinthians 6:15ff.: one may not make the members of Christ the members of a prostitute. For he who is joined to a prostitute becomes one body (one flesh) with her. But he who is joined to the Lord is one Spirit with him. To be a member of Christ's body means to be one Spirit with him, to share in and be governed by his Spirit. As a member of Christ's body he must allow himself to be guided by the Spirit, and cannot at the same time be one body with a prostitute. Here again fellowship with the Spirit is inferred from that with the body, and not the reverse. If one asks what is the basis of being a member of Christ and the resultant being a "temple" of the Spirit, a clear answer is given in what follows: "And you are not your own, for you were bought with a price" (vv. 19, 20). To be of Christ, to be a member of his body, rests on the fact that he has once appropriated his own to himself. Therefore believers are also one Spirit with him, as belonging to him and as members of his body. For where the Lord is, and where his body is, there his Spirit is also (Rom. 8:9ff.; 2 Cor. 3:18).

This brings us finally to the passage that has played (and still plays) a special role in relation to this subject, and which can serve in a certain sense as a touchstone for the results we have reached so far, the familiar pronouncement on the Lord's Supper in 1 Corinthians 10:16ff.

As we have seen, in this pronouncement of 1 Corinthians 10:16, 17, various interpreters see the transition (or as Robinson terms it: the leap) to the identification of the church with the historical and glorified body of the Lord in the literal sense of the word. For as Paul first says that the bread is the communion with the body of Christ and a little

---

40. So, e.g., Wikenhauser, *Die Kirche*, pp. 101, 102, 116ff.; Grosheide, *1 Cor.*, p. 330; and (alas!) the translation of the Dutch Bible Society and the RSV.

41. Cf. above, Section 38.

42. So, e.g., Lietzmann-Kümmel, Grosheide ("not of baptism ..., but of the receiving of the Spirit at baptism"), Percy, Wikenhauser.

43. See further below, p. 420.

44. So, e.g., Schlatter, Käsemann, Wendland, Goppelt (in *TDNT*, VI, p. 160; cf. p. 147, n. 17, 18).

further along that the church because it partakes of the one bread is therefore one body, so — this is the conclusion or the leap — this body must be the same as the first mentioned, i.e., the body of Christ in the literal, historical, and glorified sense of the word.[45]

Yet it is our conviction that in this way one makes a tremendous mistake and so completely misinterprets Paul's ideas. For regardless of what has already been said about this leap (in thought), this conclusion also founders on the significance that (communion in) "the blood and the body of Christ" have here. It is not the (historical) body of Christ that is herewith described, which one can then identify with the glorified body,[46] that is to say, with Christ himself in his humiliation and exaltation or with his personality.[47] In this double connection — communion with the blood and communion with the body — it is precisely a question of a very specific significance and function of this historical blood and body of Christ. The words refer clearly to the institution of the Lord's Supper (as may also appear from a comparison with 1 Corinthians 11:23) and will therefore have to be understood in harmony with it. That is to say that body and blood here denote the body once surrendered in death and the blood of the Lord shed as atoning blood. "Blood" and "body" are not therefore a general description of Christ's person on earth or in heaven, but call to mind, as sacrificial terminology,[48] his voluntary self-surrender in death. Christ gives his own a share in that sacrifice when he gives them his body and blood to eat and to drink,[49] and it is this sharing in Christ's sacrifice that Paul — in view also of the whole context, which speaks of sacrificial meals, Greek as well as Jewish — intends to express by the words "communion in the blood and in the body of Christ" (cf. 1 Cor. 11:26).[50]

---

45. Cf. the statement of Robinson quoted above. Percy's conclusion, too, is to this effect (*Der Leib Christi*, p. 44). And especially the Roman Catholic exegetes (cf. Cerfaux, *The Church in St. Paul*, pp. 276ff., and above all Benoit, in *Revue Biblique*, 1956, p. 14). Benoit writes on 1 Cor. 10:16f: "The word *sōma* can only have the same meaning in verses 16 and 17. Now the inference from the first verse to the second is remarkable: by receiving in their body, through the sacramental rite, the body of Christ, they 'are' all together a sole body, that is to say, this body...."

46. So, e.g., Wikenhauser, *Die Kirche*, p. 109: "Body and blood mean the glorified body and glorified blood of the exalted Lord; that means, however, the heavenly Christ himself..., the body of the historical Christ, which of course is no longer body of flesh (Col. 1:22) but body of glory (Phil. 3:21)." Bultmann, too, writes (*Theology*, I, p. 147) that it would be wrong to inquire whether by body the crucified "fleshly body of Jesus" or the pneumatic body of the Glorified One is intended. "The *doxa*-body of the exalted Christ is identical with the body put to death on the cross."

47. So Robinson: Jesus' body and blood here mean Jesus' "actual self, His life and personality" (*The Body*, p. 57).

48. J. Jeremias, *The Eucharistic Words of Jesus*, 2nd ed., p. 144 (3rd ed., p. 222).

49. For this explanation see also, e.g., E. Gaugler, *Das Abendmahl im N.T.*, 1943, p. 52; E. P. Groenewald, [*KOINŌNIA*] (*Gemeenskap*) *by Paulus*, 1932, pp. 105-115; my *The Coming of the Kingdom*, p. 427. Very clearly Matter as well (*De Kerk*, p. 24).

50. On this at length see further Section 66 under a.

But from this follows the absolute impossibility in one way or another of identifying the church with this historical blood and body of Christ. Regardless still of the leap in thought from "communion in" the blood and body to "being" the body (and blood?) of Christ, one is faced with a completely absurd notion were he obliged to identify the church with the self-surrender and self-sacrifice of the Lord denoted in this way — by blood and body. When in verse 17 it is said of the church therefore: "because the bread is one, we [the] many are one body; for we all partake of the one bread," it is here — in precisely the same manner in which "the many" and "the one body" are spoken of in Romans 12:5 — the unity of the church that is denoted in virtue of its common share in the one bread and therein[51] in the sacrifice made for it by Christ. That there is mention here of "body" in a twofold sense is unmistakable, namely, first of the body with the blood of Christ surrendered in death and then of the church described as the one body.[52] It also makes a great deal of sense in this context because not only is there a warning given to the strong that they are to remain aware of the incompatibility of Christ's body and blood with the sacrifice of idols, but also that they are not to lose sight of the obligations they have toward the weak as fellow-members of Christ's church (cf. vv. 23, 33).

On the ground of all that has been said above we are now able to form a clear conception of the sense in which in Romans and 1 Corinthians Paul speaks of the church as the body of Christ, as that occurs in the most explicit sense in 1 Corinthians 12:27, where in conclusion he says: "Now you are the body of Christ and members each for his part." In so doing we can mark off our view with respect to the explanations we pointed out above. In summary, the following answer can already be given to the questions resulting from that survey of opinion.

(a) The designation of the church as the body of Christ does not intend in the first place to qualify its mutual unity and diversity, but to denote its unity in and with Christ.

(b) This unity of the church with Christ thus qualified has its real ground neither in the spiritual indwelling of Christ in the church, nor in the thought that the Spirit constitutes the communion between Christ and the church, but in the church's belonging to Christ in the redemptive-historical sense, in the inclusion of "the many" in the one.

(c) In virtue of this common belonging to and inclusion of "the many" in Christ, individual believers are qualified as members of Christ

---

51. That the unity of the body of the church is inferred from the one bread (and not from the one body) is of importance. According to the ancient eastern idea the rite of the breaking of bread establishes the fellowship of the table (cf. Jeremias, *The Eucharistic Words of Jesus*, 2nd ed., pp. 153f. [3rd ed., p. 232], and the literature mentioned there). It appears from all this that the course of Paul's reasoning is not determined by the identification idea.

52. Cf. E. Käsemann, "The Pauline Doctrine of the Lord's Supper," *Essays on New Testament Themes*, p. 110: "Paul for his part agrees with this conception [namely, that of the traditional significance of 'body'] but in v. 17 gives it a new turn."

and the church as his body. That the church should thereby be identified with the historical and glorified body of Christ is in no way evident in the passages we have examined. Insofar as the church as body is related to the communion with the blood and body of Christ exercised in the Lord's Supper, this rests on its common share in the sacrifice made for it by Christ and in no way on such a communion with the historical and glorified body of Christ as would make it this body. The qualification of the church as the "body of Christ," therefore, clearly has a figurative, metaphorical significance, however real and literal the unity and communion with Christ expressed thereby is.

(d) As the church's being appropriated by Christ and included in Christ is not restricted to the redemptive-historical aspect, but also works itself out sacramentally and pneumatically,[53] so the believer's incorporation into and belonging to the body of Christ is represented by baptism and the Lord's Supper; and so the church can only reveal itself as the one body of Christ in virtue of the gift of the Holy Spirit given by him to his body.

(e) The question as to why Paul denotes the unity of the church in Christ thus understood specifically with the name "body" has not yet been answered in the above discussion. It can already be ascertained that a reference to the current Hellenistic imagery in which certain social or political communities are compared with a body does not provide an adequate explanation. For believers do not together constitute one body because they are members of one another, but because they are members of Christ, and thus are one body in him (Rom. 12:5; 1 Cor. 6:15). Just as little can this mode of speech be explained on the analogy of an anthropology conceived in a dichotomistic sense. The question remains therefore whether and how *terminologically* one can further elucidate and "place" this metaphorical designation of the church as the one body comprehended in Christ and belonging to Christ. In order to answer this question we shall first have to examine the remainder of the materials.

SECTION 61. BODY AND HEAD
(EPHESIANS AND COLOSSIANS)

In the epistles to the Ephesians and Colossians the idea of the church as the body of Christ receives a still further unfolding and elaboration. It is evident especially in these epistles that this qualification of the church pertains to the fixed substance of Pauline ecclesiology. Furthermore, along with all the fundamental similarity with Romans and 1 Corinthians an important distinction also appears, namely, that here Christ is repeatedly called the Head of the church or the Head of the body, something that does not occur within the framework of the body pronouncements in Romans and 1 Corinthians.

What a fixed "technical" significance the qualification "body" has

---

53. Cf. above, Sections 37 and 38.

acquired here may be shown in a great many ways. Not only is the church again and again simply called the body of Christ (Eph. 1:23; 4:13), and believers his members (Eph. 5:30), but "body" as a designation of the church is also used here in an absolute sense, whether or not further explained with the words: (which is) "his church" (Col. 1:18, 24; Eph. 4:4; Col. 3:15; 2:19). The peculiar expression in Ephesians 3:6 is typical of this pattern, where it is said of the gentiles that they, in addition to being fellow heirs, are "fellow body" (*syssōma*) and sharers in the promise in Christ Jesus.

The basic thought in Ephesians and Colossians is therefore the same as that in Romans and 1 Corinthians: the church is the one body in virtue of what Christ has accomplished for it and in virtue of its having been comprehended in him when he once suffered and died for it. This finds clear expression in the well-known passage of Ephesians 2:14ff., where the corporate unity of Jews and gentiles is explained thus: "He [Christ] . . . has made both one[54] . . . by abolishing in his flesh the law of commandments . . . that he might create the two in himself into one new man[55] . . . and might reconcile both to God in [or into?] one body. . . ."[56] All these indications of unity elucidate the thought of the one body in Christ. The two parties have become a unity in Christ — when in his flesh, his human mode of existence, he suffered and died for both on the cross. He created them both in himself into one new man (cf. Gal. 3:28), a description equivalent to "one body in him." And this creation is not only intended of the spiritual communion between Jews and gentiles founded in Christ's death, but he already united both in himself on the cross, as the one new man(kind) represented by him. It is uncertain how one is to take the last expression, which speaks of the reconciling of both in one body. Is the one body understood here of Christ in the sense of "in his flesh" (v. 15), and is the reconciliation of both groups founded therefore in the fact that they have been reconciled to God in one body on the cross? Or by the one body is the church to be understood here, in the sense of the one new man who in this unity has by Christ been reconciled to God? It is difficult to decide between these two conceptions.[57] But this passage clearly shows wherein the unity of the church is founded and why it can be called his body or one body in him: because already in his suffering and death he represented it in all its parts and united it in himself into a new unity.[58]

---

54. *Poiēsas ta amphotera hen.*

55. *Hina tous duo ktisē eis hena kainon anthrōpon.*

56. *Apokatallaxē tous amphoterous en heni sōmati.*

57. *En heni sōmati,* e.g., is understood by Dibelius-Greeven of the church; cf. the Dutch Bible Society translation: "tot een lichaam verbonden." Percy understands it of the historical body of Christ on the cross and refers to Rom. 7:4; Col. 1:22 (*Der Leib Christi,* pp. 39, 42; *Probleme,* p. 109). In view of the parallel pronouncement in Col. 1:22 and of the words following in Eph. 2:16 ("*dia tou staurou*"), this view does indeed have more to be said for it.

58. One can observe how closely the thought of Christ's own historical body and that of the church as the body of Christ here approach each other. But it is also clear that one may not identify them with each other. For the one new man

The relationship of the body and the Spirit, too, is the same as that which is presupposed in 1 Corinthians 12:13.[59] This is clearly evident, for example, from the paraenetic pronouncements in Ephesians 4:3ff., and in Colossians 3:15. Both passages are concerned with keeping the peace in the church, in Ephesians 4:3 further defined as "the unity of the Spirit." In order to lend greater force to this admonition the apostle reminds believers of the fact that they are after all one body: ". . . one body and one Spirit, even as you were also called in one hope," etc. (Eph. 4:4). And in Colossians 3:15 the same thing is expressed in this way: ". . . to which peace you were also called in one body." Keeping the unity of the Spirit is therefore motivated by the unity of the body. One body and one Spirit. The sequence is not accidental. Because the body is one, there can only be talk of one Spirit, and the church is called to keep the unity of the Spirit. In principle the Spirit presupposes the body, and not the reverse. For it is Christ who intends now to fill those who are one body in him with the gifts of his one Spirit.

This spiritual aspect of the body of Christ emerges very clearly in Ephesians and Colossians — along with the redemptive-historical aspect. One can observe that thereby Christ's position of authority as the exalted Lord receives particular emphasis. In this context Christ again and again is termed the Head. As the one who has been invested by God with all power and who is the Head of all things, he has been given to the church as his body (Eph. 1:20-23). As such he also has all spiritual gifts at his disposal (Eph. 4:8ff.). The church as his body may have fellowship with him as the Head of all things, but especially as *its* Head (Col. 1:18; Eph. 4:15ff.; Col. 2:10, 19). And in that spiritual communion, from this being filled out of Christ as the Head (Eph. 1:23; Col. 2:9, 10), the church is to realize itself as the body of Christ, be built up as his body and build itself up (Eph. 4:12, 16). This spiritual upbuilding must bring it to adulthood ("unto a full-grown man," mature manhood), "to the measure of the stature of the fulness of Christ" (v. 13). Here again, as in Ephesians 2:15 and Galatians 3:28, the church is identified with a person, a new man, a (mature) man. But whereas in Galatians 3:28 and Ephesians 2:15 it is a matter of the givenness of the one person and the one body in Christ, here the spiritual and historical development, the maturation of the one man or the one body, receives all the emphasis. What the church is in Christ, it is more and more to become. This is then elucidated with all kinds of figures borrowed from the organic composition of the human body: the body, which is a closely fitting whole and held together by the service of all its joints, derives its growth from Christ in order to build itself up in love (Eph. 4:16); or, as it is said in similar words in Colossians 2:19: the body, supported and knit together by joints and ligaments, draws its divine growth from Christ, the Head. We have to do here in a certain sense with the same ideas as in

---

(the one body) is not identical with the historical body of Christ, but is "created" by him as a new unity.

59. Above, p. 372.

Romans 12 and 1 Corinthians 12: as the body of Christ the church is to reveal itself as a genuine body in unity and diversity. But here, more markedly than in Romans and 1 Corinthians, the spiritual connection emerges between the church and the glorified Christ, who is time and again called the Head not only of all things, but also of the church that is his body.

This same idea is developed in a somewhat different manner in the well-known pericope of Ephesians 5:22-33, in which the head-body relationship is spoken of as an analogy of the marriage relationship. We have already met with this analogy in 1 Corinthians 6:15ff., in the warning against fornication. However, whereas in 1 Corinthians 6 only the category of the "body" plays a part, in Ephesians 5 the relationship of husband and wife, Christ and the church, is described as that of head and body. Here, too, at least so far as Christ and the church are concerned, the origin of this relationship is sought in what Christ once did for the church: He is the Head of the church, being the Savior (*Sōtēr*) of the body (v. 23). To that is then joined, in continuous analogy with what the husband and wife owe each other in marriage, the spiritual character of this head-body relationship. For as the husband, if he loves his wife, loves his own body, himself, his own flesh, so also Christ nourishes and cherishes the church; for we are members of his body (vv. 28-30). In so doing Paul cites — just as in 1 Corinthians 6:16, but here much more fully — the words of Genesis 2:24. He applies the "great mystery" expressed there, that the two are one flesh, to the relationship of Christ and the church,[60] in order to demonstrate how deeply this unity is anchored and in what a close, spiritual communion it is realized.

All this naturally places us before the question as to how one is to conceive of this relationship of head and body, whereby the question we have already discussed recurs, as to how Paul came to make use of specifically this mode of expression for this relationship.

So far, first of all, as the head-body relationship is concerned, one can easily arrive at the idea that the naming of Christ as the "Head" of the church must be understood within the framework of the "body"

---

60. The meaning of vv. 31-33 is not entirely certain and is interpreted rather differently. In our view Paul quotes Gen. 2:24 in v. 31 in order to give expression with the words of Scripture to the idea of the one flesh, of which there has been frequent mention in the foregoing both with a view to marriage and to the unity of Christ. This being one flesh (one body) is a great mystery. Paul, however — regardless of how others speak of it, *egō de* — speaks of it with an eye to Christ and the church, and understands this unity in the light of *that* relationship, as he has done continuously in the foregoing. V. 32 thus gives no allegorical sense to Gen. 2:24 (as if the church were spoken of there), but points for the understanding of the mystery, that two parties can be one flesh, to the relationship of Christ and the church. For this engages the apostle in this whole pericope no less than the unity of marriage. The conclusion in v. 33 introduced with *plēn* ("but let each one of you also love his wife as himself...") then says that, however one chooses to view this further, believing husbands are to love their wives as themselves (for this use of *plēn* cf. Bl.-Debr., Par. 449, 2).

terminology already familiar to us from Romans and 1 Corinthians. A certain augmentation or complication of the figure would then take place,[61] in the sense that Christ functions as the Head of the church represented as the body, that is, as the most prominent part of the body. And one can all the more easily come to this idea because in particular two passages of Ephesians and Colossians seem to advance it; Ephesians 4:15ff. for one, where it is said that we (the church) in every way grow up into him who is the Head, Christ, from whom the whole body receives its growth. Here, at least at first glance, the Head appears to be thought of as a specific organ of the body, and the whole imagery seems to be borrowed from this organic functioning of the human body. One finds the same idea, then, in the pronouncement of Colossians 2:19, where there is also mention of "the Head, from whom the whole body[62] equipped and knit together by means of sinews and connecting organs receives its divine growth." This "organic" conception of the relationship of Christ as the Head and the church as the body has accordingly been long and frequently advocated.[63]

Closer examination, however, enables one to realize quickly the untenable nature of this explanation. First of all, the representation of a body nourished from the head and growing up toward the head, as one would then have to take Ephesians 4:15, 16 and Colossians 2:19, is physiologically difficult to imagine, and was certainly not current in antiquity.[64] For that matter Paul does not formulate: "the Head, from which," but "the Head, from whom," that is, from Christ (Col. 2:19; Eph. 4:15). More importantly, however, from Paul's own terminology clearly another idea emerges than that of such a composite metaphor. For the church is continually represented as the whole body (in Eph. 4:16 as well), and not merely as the remaining parts of the body belonging to the head, which the idea of a trunk would then imply. In 1 Corinthians 12:16 the functions of the head are likewise compared with those of the church (and not with those of Christ). And what entirely settles the matter is this: Christ cannot be thought of as a (subordinate) part of his own body, which is involved in the process of growth toward adulthood and which as part of the body must itself consequently be "in Christ." Even from these "organic" texts themselves it is evident that one arrives at all kinds of absurdities when one chooses to take "body" and "head" as one, composite metaphor. This is still more clearly the case when one takes into consideration the application of the head-body relationship to the marriage relationship, as this occurs in Ephesians 5:23ff. There the husband is called the head (of the wife) and the wife the body (of the

---

61. Cf., e.g., Percy, *Der Leib Christi,* pp. 52ff.

62. The view that by *pan to sōma,* not the church, but "the all" is intended is to be rejected with certainty; cf. further my *Col.,* p. 195.

63. For the literature see the full discussion of this question in J. H. Roberts, *Die Opbou van die Kerk volgens die Efese-brief,* 1963, pp. 94, 95.

64. Cf. I. J. Du Plessis, *Christus as Hoof van Kerk en Kosmos,* 1962, p. 81; Roberts, *ibid.,* p. 96. However, see also P. Benoit, *Revue Biblique,* 1956, p. 27, who for the opposite opinion refers to Plato, Hippocrates, and Galen. But whether Paul can be regarded as dependent on these very special ideas seems very dubious.

husband) (cf. vv. 23, 28). But it is unwarranted and absurd so to conceive of this as though the wife constituted the trunk of this unity of the two and the husband the head. The intention is obviously a different one. This is in consequence no less the case with the relationship of Christ as the Head of the church and of the church as his body. We have to do here not with one and the same metaphor but with two, each of which, although they are (can be) closely connected with each other, yet has an independent significance and an independent existence.[65]

That we are not mistaken in this conclusion is not only apparent from the fact that in Romans and 1 Corinthians only the church is spoken of as the body and not Christ as the Head, but, especially with respect to the concept "head," can easily be demonstrated from the Pauline texts available to us. Paul repeatedly speaks of the head in a metaphorical sense, without the thought being implied of a body belonging to it. God is the Head of Christ, Christ is the Head of every man, the husband is the head of the wife (1 Cor. 11:3). This is not to say that Christ therefore is the body of God, or every man the body of Christ. Husbands indeed are to love their wives, "as their own bodies" (Eph. 5:28), but, as has been said, it is just here that the combination of both ideas into one becomes impossible. Similarly, when in Ephesians 1:22 Christ is termed the Head over all things and in Colossians 2:10 the Head over all principalities and powers, this does not mean that "all things," all rule and power, are also his body or belong to his body. The qualification "head" has its own independent significance, regardless of whether the metaphorical mention of a "body" is joined with it.

The question as to what is meant by "head" in these contexts admits of being answered in particular from the pericope of Ephesians 5:22ff. already discussed. From the headship of the husband over the wife and of Christ over the church here first of all the subjection of the wife to the husband is inferred, just as the church is subject to Christ. Headship points therefore to a position of rulership and authority.[66] But this position of superiority and rulership of the head both for Christ and for the husband is not something that stands by itself, but arises from the very specific, unique character of this headship. As we have already seen, for Christ it is founded in the fact that he is also the Preserver or Savior of the body. It says with respect to the relationship between Christ and the church that the church has its origin in him and that it therefore is dependent on him as the one who has prepared the way for it and to whom it owes its existence. The headship of the husband will also have to be understood in this sense. In 1 Corinthians 11:3, 8, 12, it is related to the history of the origin of mankind, namely, that the woman is from the man, has her existence from him, and is therefore the "glory"

---

65. See Benoit, ibid., pp. 24ff.; see also the following note, however.

66. Benoit proceeds from this general significance of "head" (ibid., pp. 25ff.), with which he then attempts to combine the thought of the organic-physiological bond between body and head (p. 27). He calls this "a very felicitous adaptation," but thus arrives at a combination of two very different ideas of head, which are in our view very difficult to combine with each other, one from the Semitic and one from the Greek world (pp. 25 and 27). To the same effect J. Dupont, Gnosis, 1949, pp. 450ff.

of the man, just as the church is the "glory" of Christ (cf. Eph. 5:27). Head thus points not merely to superiority, control, rule, but first of all to a relationship of beginning, which is determinative for the whole of continuing existence. This same relationship exists between Christ and "all things," powers, principalities, etc. He is of them and in them "the First," because all things from the beginning have been comprehended and have their subsistence in him as the Firstborn of every creature.[67] "Head," "Pre-eminent"-ness, is therefore also in the closest connection with origin: it implies that Christ is the Beginning and the Firstborn, of all things in general as well as of the church in particular (cf. Col. 1:15-18).

All this may serve as evidence that with "head" we must not form physiological conceptions derived from the relationships within the human body, but that the concept rather must be understood from the structures and connections of the human community. We come into contact here again with the thought of the containment and representation of the one in and through the other, who by his position as first or by his unique and decisive action with regard to the other or the others occupies a determinative and dominant place. In this inclusive and representative sense Christ is the Head of the church, just as he is Head of all things, and he has thus obtained abiding control over the church and over all things.

In his relationship to the church, however, continuing communion in the pneumatic sense of the word is also joined with this headship. He who as the Head is the Savior of the body is also the one who cleanses the church by baptism in order to present it glorious to himself. And just as the husband as the head of the wife loves her, nourishes and cherishes her, so Christ as well (Eph. 5:25ff.). Here Paul can even refer to the mystery of the two being one flesh. As the Head Christ so much desires to unite himself by his Spirit with the church and to dwell in it, because it is from him and is one in him and with him.

If one may assume with certainty, therefore, that the concepts "head" and "body" each have their own independence and are not to be viewed as representations mutually dependent on each other, on the other hand it can also be seen from the above how these two qualifications can be so closely related to each other. The ground for this conjunction does not lie in that "head" and "body" in Paul's thought may be said gradually to have merged into one composite metaphor, but that both concepts, each in its own way and each from "its own side," materially give expression to the same idea, namely, that of the church's belonging to Christ, both in the redemptive-historical and corporate as well as in the pneumatic sense of the word. Thereby "head" in that relationship places all the emphasis on the initial position and the resultant redemptive significance of Christ with respect to the church; while "body" on the other hand regards the same relationship from the side of the church. It

---

67. Cf. above, Section 13.

expresses the entirely unique character of the church's belonging to Christ, just as the wife belongs to the husband as "his own" body (Eph. 5:28), and in distinction from "all things," of which Christ indeed is the Head, but which nevertheless do not together constitute his body. At the same time "body" serves to throw light on the mutual relationships within the church itself in its dependence on and in its pneumatic communion with Christ (Rom. 12; 1 Cor. 12; Eph. 4:16ff.; Col. 2:19).

The conjunction of both points of view, as we have already seen, is sometimes so close as to give the impression that both representations run over into each other, as in Ephesians 4:15ff. and Colossians 2:19. This is no more than appearance, however. A fading of the boundaries does not take place here, either in the representation or in the thing itself. "Head" and "body" form two separate figurative categories and retain this independence even when they are linked together. "Head" and "body" constitute — so we may conclude — each for itself, but especially in their connection with each other, the shaded expression of what, in accordance with the everywhere visible fundamental structures of his preaching, the Apostle Paul understands by the unity of Christ and the church. They are not its only expression and therefore do not occupy a monopolistic position in Paul's ecclesiology. But we may surely be permitted to say that they give expression to that unity in a fashion that in the richness of its possibilities for application is nowhere surpassed or even has its equal in all of Paul's preaching and in the whole of the New Testament.

The question remains as to whether something can be said still further by way of explanation on the origin and background of this remarkable dual terminology.

In more recent exegesis the attempt has been made particularly in two different ways to explain the Pauline head-body terminology in Colossians and Ephesians against a broader background. The first is the so-called gnostic interpretation, as that has been introduced notably by Schlier[68] and Käsemann[69] and has been favorably judged, for example, by the Roman Catholic exegete Wikenhauser.[70] The gist of this interpretation is that the influence of the gnostic myth of the Primal-Man Redeemer is to be perceived in Paul, according to which the souls of all men belong to one cosmic pneumatic body, which as Primal-Man is said to have ended up in matter; while the members of this body are said then to be gathered again into one body by the Redeemer and brought back to heaven. Moreover, in some of the gnostic texts the Redeemer makes his appearance as the cosmic pneumatic Head[71] and the redeemed as his body; in others there is mention only of the body and of the members of the Primal-Man Redeemer. These gnostic notions need not have been the immediate literary source for Paul, but would form the

---

68. Especially in his *Christus und die Kirche im Epheserbrief*, 1930.
69. *Leib und Leib Christi*, 1933.
70. *Die Kirche*, pp. 239, 240.
71. See also the article of Schlier, *TDNT*, III, pp. 673ff., *s.v. kephalē*.

conceptual materials of which he (or whoever else then the author of Colossians and Ephesians may have been) availed himself for his purpose.

This interpretation, which impressed many in the 1930s, has lost its attraction for most interpreters. Further investigation of the gnostic sources especially has[72] led to a much more sober judgment. Insofar as these sources exhibit a certain agreement with the idea of the body of Christ, as in the Manichaean writings, they are so late that they are not to be considered as a source for Paul. And as far as one is now able to form any conception of Gnosticism in its old form, also on the basis of newly made discoveries, every trace of the idea of the church as body of Christ is lacking in it.[73]

In addition, if one were to have to conceive of the Head-body relationship according to this late gnostic pattern, then the objection pointed out above against the "organic" view, which thinks of head and body as one whole and on this account does not admit of being connected with the Pauline idea, basically recurs with unabated force.[74] Everything points to the fact, therefore, that if there can be talk here of a mutual interdependence, it is rather to be sought in syncretistic post-Christian Gnosticism than in Paul. On these grounds accordingly this gnostic interpretation is finding fewer and fewer adherents in the more recent literature.[75]

Another interpretation has taken its place with increasing force. This attempts to explain the head-body terminology and the complex of ideas expressed by it from Paul's Jewish background. In so doing interpreters start from the concept of Christ as the second Adam and from the idea of representation given with it. Paul is said therewith to have elaborated and applied to Christ a motif well-known in Jewish theology. Continuing to build on this, they have then attempted to bring the termi-

---

72. For the so-called doctrine of "the redeemed Redeemer" see already above, pp. 28, 35ff.

73. Cf. especially H. M. Schenke, *Der Gott 'Mens' in der Gnosis, Ein religionsgeschichtlicher Beitrag zur Diskussion über die paulinische Anschauung von der Kirche als Leib Christi*, 1962. He has examined all of the materials afresh and concludes: "Thus it is necessary to take leave of the very interesting theory of Schlier and Käsemann" (p. 155).

74. Roberts also rightly points to this (*Die Opbou*, p. 96): "The gnostic interpretation [of Schlier] ... does not, however, lead to a much more conceivable picture of the thought, for here the ordinary human body and its relations is only exchanged for the cosmic Anthropos-form with its giant body.... This Anthropos is [still according to the interpretation of Schlier opposed by Roberts] really the complete body and at the same time (as Redeemer) distinguishable as the head who gathers to himself, for it is a matter here of the myth of the unity of God and the soul." Still without regard therefore to the fundamental irreconcilability of the gnostic myth and the Pauline kerygma, the former cannot serve in any respect whatever as the interpretative key of the Pauline idea. Others, as Schweizer, for example, deny that the concept body occurs at all in Gnosticism as a "giant-body" containing all redeemed souls within itself ("Die Kirche," *TLZ*, 1961, cols. 162ff.).

75. See already Percy, *Der Leib Christi*, pp. 39ff.; also his *Probleme*, p. 112; Hanson, *The Unity of the Church*, pp. 113ff.; Cerfaux, *The Church in St. Paul*, pp. 370ff.; Benoit, *Revue Biblique*, 1956, pp. 17ff.; Meuzelaar, *Der Leib des Messias*, pp. 8ff.; I. J. Du Plessis, *Christus as Hoof van Kerk en Kosmos*, pp. 7ff.; Schweizer, "Die Kirche," *TLZ*, 1961.

nological question both of (the church as) the body and of (Christ as) the Head of the church to a solution in the light of the Jewish usage.

The matter has been approached from more than one side.

On the one hand, W. D. Davies[76] has related the qualification of the church as the body of Christ to certain rabbinic speculations on the body of Adam, on the ground of which the rabbis endeavored to vindicate the unity of the human race. This one body of Adam was said to have been composed of the dust of the whole earth, so that east and west, north and south were brought together in it; it was also said to be "bisexual" so that in him both male and female were present. The body of Adam therefore embraced the whole of humanity. "Was it not natural, then [thus Davies], that Paul when he thought of the new humanity being incorporated 'in Christ' should have conceived of it as the 'body' of the second Adam, where there was neither Jew nor Greek, male nor female, bond nor free.... The purpose of God in Christ is ... the reconstitution of the essential oneness of mankind in Christ as a spiritual community, as it was one in Adam in a physical sense."[77]

Others have sought the terminological background especially in the Jewish use of the qualification "head." Whereas in the Greek parallels that have been instanced "head" is always understood as a physical organ of the body, in the Jewish world of thought head signifies the progenitor or the leader.[78] It would as such, just as in Colossians 1:15-18, exhibit close affinity with such concepts as "beginning" (arché), "firstborn" (prōtotokos), in which the first not only in temporal order but also in order of rank is denoted. In this way the concept "head" terminologically would express the idea of the personification and representation of the many-in-one.[79]

Now, in evaluating all this one will always need to distinguish carefully between the material and the terminological question. It is incontestable, in our opinion, that the idea of the all-in-one underlies Paul's speaking of the church as the body of Christ; likewise that the parallel with the first Adam plays a much more important part in Paul's ecclesiology than has frequently been supposed. It is another question whether the matter has hereby been made transparent terminologically.

One can hardly contend that this is so with regard to the explanation proposed by Davies. For not only is there in Paul's epistles no trace whatever that for the universal character of the church (in which "there is neither Jew nor Greek, there is neither slave nor free, there is neither male nor female," etc.)

76. *Paul and Rabbinic Judaism*, 1955.

77. *Ibid.*, p. 57.

78. Schweizer summarizes thus in his valuable article "Die Kirche als Leib Christi in den paulinischen Antilegomena," *TLZ*, 1961, col. 255.

79. Such publications as the following move in this direction — publications that otherwise provide a shaded interpretation of the Pauline use of the concept head: L. S. Thornton, "The Body of Christ in the New Testament," in *The Apostolic Ministry*, 3rd ed., 1957, to the point, pp. 68ff.; S. F. B. Bedale, "The Meaning of [kephalē] in the Pauline Epistles," in *Journal of Theol. Studies*, 1954, pp. 211ff.; Meuzelaar, *Der Leib des Messias*, pp. 117ff.; I. J. Du Plessis, *Christus as Hoof*, pp. 22ff.; Roberts, *Die Opbou*, pp. 96ff.

in one way or another he fastened onto the fantastic speculations of some rabbis concerning the composition of the body of Adam; but the whole suggestion that the "body" of Christ would answer to this body of Adam created from the dust of the earth also has no basis in all that Paul writes elsewhere on the first Adam (cf. 1 Cor. 15:45ff.; Eph. 5:31). To be sure, there are possibilities for explanation here. Paul says of the husband, too, that he is the head of the wife (because the woman is from the man) and that on that account he is to love her "as his own body"; and by analogy Adam could be called the head of all who are from him, and these many could also be called his body[80] as having sprung from him and as the unity of the many belonging to him. Ephesians 5:23-33 proves that such a conception is not far removed from Paul,[81] and it corresponds with what is in our view the basic idea both of *sōma* and of *kephalē*. But even though this collective and corporate way of thinking should find support in the notions to which Davies calls attention, yet terminologically this considerable difference remains, that *sōma* in Paul denotes "the many," whereas in the materials adduced by Davies it signifies Adam's own physical body. Furthermore, there is no question in them of Adam as head.

The greatest value ought, in our opinion, to be attached to the explanation which with an appeal to the Jewish world of thought chooses to see in the concept "head" an indication of the idea of representation. Here also the evidence is not overwhelming. Clear indications are lacking, for example, that Adam is termed the head of mankind in this representative sense.[82] Likewise the materials that have so far been introduced contain no convincing connection between the head thus conceived and a "body" answering to it, as in Paul. Some advocates of this interpretation of "head" are even of the opinion that the origin of the concept "body" must be entirely dissociated from it and sought somewhere else.[83] All this shows clearly that there can be no question of a somewhat current and generally equivalent usage in the Jewish sources, so far as our acquaintance with them presently extends. It can, however, be put to the credit of this new examination of the concept "head" that for the use, so characteristic of Paul, of this qualification it seeks a much more appropriate background than is the case when one attempts to trace this in the physiological relationship of head and body conceived in the manner of the Greeks.

We are able to determine in conclusion, therefore, that however

---

80. E. P. Groenewald also writes to this effect in "Die Ekklesia in die Nuwe Testament," in *Ned. Geref. Teologiese Tydskrif*, 1962, p. 393, i.a., with a reference to Rom. 7:24. That by *sōma tou thanatou* Paul means the body of which Adam is the head demands further semasiological proof, however.

81. That in the meantime the conception of the church as "Leib Christi" has its origin in that of "Weib Christi" and in the fact that the wife in Eph. 5 is equated with the body of the husband, as is argued by Dom Casel, seems to us too weak, motivated only on the ground of Eph. 5:28 (for this conception see Wikenhauser, *Die Kirche*, p. 231). Certainly this passage contains an important indication as to the direction in which and the background against which the solution of the terminological question must be sought.

82. Cf. the sparse materials in Schweizer, "Die Kirche," *TLZ*, 1961, col. 245, n. 14.

83. So Meuzelaar, *Der Leib des Messias*, p. 121.

much — particularly so far as the idea of "body" is concerned — the terminological question has not yet been completely resolved, there need be no doubt as to the essential meaning of the apostle with this double qualification. The basic idea of both lies in the conception, so typical for Paul's doctrine of salvation, of "the many in the One." While in Romans and in 1 Corinthians all attention is concentrated on the revelation of the church as one body, in Colossians and Ephesians the bond between Christ and his own itself comes into view, especially in its continuing pneumatic and all-embracing significance. Everything is here focused on making the privilege implied in this relationship for the church to be understood in all its fullness, specifically in view of Christ's position as the Head of all things. This last point still requires a separate discussion.

SECTION 62. CHRIST THE HEAD OF ALL THINGS. THE CHURCH AS PLEROMA

Already in examining the fundamental structures of Paul's preaching we were made aware[84] of the central significance Christ has not only with respect to the church, but also to all things. Both in virtue of creation and in virtue of the restoration of the lost coherence of all things in him he forms the great point of integration for all that is in heaven and on earth. It is especially in the epistles to the Ephesians and the Colossians that these profound ideas are given expression (cf. Eph. 1:10; Col. 1:16, 17); in the Epistle to the Colossians, which is perhaps first in terms of chronological order, in unremitting opposition to a heresy that apparently caused the church to live in slavish fear over against the spiritual powers surrounding it (cf. Col. 2:18ff.).[85]

What still requires our separate attention in this chapter is the connection Paul makes, precisely in these two epistles, between Christ's all-embracing significance as the Head of "all things" and his position as the Head of the church.[86]

Even a superficial inspection of the relevant statements teaches us that in the description of Christ's "cosmic"[87] significance Paul's repeated concern is just that relationship with the church. This is very clearly the case, for example, in Colossians 1:18, where after the extensive pronouncements on Christ's all-embracing significance it follows: and this (thus delineated Christ) is the Head of the body, that is, of the church. The intention of the argument is therefore not to broach this

---

84. Cf. above, Section 13.

85. For the heresy in Colosse see further my Excursus in *Col.*, pp. 198-202; cf. pp. 105ff.

86. For this subject see in particular F. Mussner, *Christus, das All und die Kirche*, 1955; I. J. Du Plessis, *Christus as Hoof van Kerk en Kosmos*. Further M. A. Wagenführer, *Die Bedeutung Christi für Welt und Kirche*, 1941; P. Benoit, "Corps, tête et plérôme dans les Épîtres de la captivité," *Revue Biblique*, 1956, pp. 5-44.

87. This terminology is not derived from Paul himself. For he does not speak in this connection of *kosmos*, but of *ta panta*: all things, the all or universe.

all-encompassing significance of Christ as a "separate subject," but, as is evident from the whole occasion for this Epistle to the Colossians, to bring home to the church its consequences for its own life.

If we now consider in what respect the church shares in the glory of Christ its Head, we ought to catch a still closer view of this glory itself. First of all, his superiority above all rule, authority, power, and dominion (Eph. 1:21; cf. Col. 1:16; 2:10), by which angelic powers are intended,[88] both in their subjection to and in their rebelliousness against God. This superiority, which has been conferred on Christ by God in his exaltation (Eph. 1:20), is closely bound up with the significance with respect to "all things" that he had already at the creation of the world (Col. 1:15ff.), and which, in accordance with the divine good pleasure regarding the fullness of the times, has taken effect anew (Eph. 1:9, 10). All this has its deepest ground in the fact that "the whole fulness was pleased to dwell in him" (Col. 1:19), or as it is said in Colossians 2:9: "in him dwells all the fulness of the Godhead bodily." In consequence Christ is the Head of all things (Eph. 1:22), or of all principalities and powers (Col. 2:10), and in virtue of this glory conferred on him he "fills all things" (Eph. 4:10; 1:23).

We are confronted here with a very extensive complex of expressions and ideas the interpretation of which presents us with great problems. In addition to the fact that Christ is here again called the Head and is represented as the one in whom, as the Image of God and the Firstborn of every creature, all things in heaven and on earth are summed up and have their integration point — expressions which, as we have seen,[89] seem to have been derived from the Adam theology — the words "fulness" (plērōma) and "fill" repeatedly come to the fore here, as a denotation of God himself and of Christ's all-embracing significance, words that are furthermore employed of the church in its relation to Christ. The frequent use of these words in Colossians and Ephesians is very striking, and it is difficult to give an explanation of them. It is clear indeed that with this "conception of fullness" Paul is pitting himself, at least in Colossians, against a religiosity[90] that was highly conditioned by belief in cosmic powers over against which man finds himself in a slavish position of subjection. Paul on the other hand speaks of God as "the whole fulness"[91] (Col. 1:19). Although this expression is very un-

88. For the significance of these "powers" see my *Col.*, pp. 141ff.; I. J. Du Plessis, *Christus as Hoof*, pp. 53ff.; W. Caird, *Principalities and Powers, A Study in Pauline Theology*, 1956; G. H. C. Macgregor, "Principalities and Powers," in *NTS*, 1956, pp. 19ff.

89. Cf. above, Section 13.

90. The question as to whether this also started from the concept "fullness" is difficult to answer. Despite all the speculations on the heresy at Colosse, we know too little about it. And just as uncertain is the connection that some have wished to make between this heresy and the *pleroma* ideas in later Gnosticism; see also the essay by G. Münderlein, "Die Erwählung durch das Pleroma," *NTS*, 1962, pp. 264ff.

91. At least if one is to take *pan to plērōma* as the subject of *eudokēsen* and *katoikēsai*, which is highly probable in view of the same combination of *plērōma* and *katoikei* in Col. 2:9; see further my *Col.*, p. 146. Others wish to understand *plērōma*

usual — that God actively fills all things is, even in biblical usage, much less unusual (cf., for example, Jer. 23:24) than that he himself should be the Fullness or the Filled One[92] — the thought is apparently this, that outside or above God nothing or no one has existence or power. In this expression therefore one will have to look not so much for a description of what God is "in himself," but of his relationship to the whole of creation:[93] he embraces all things and the existence of all rests in him. He is "all and in all" (1 Cor. 15:28). Accordingly when it is said that it pleased the whole fullness[94] to dwell in Christ, this is, as appears from the context of the sentence, in explanation of the preceding qualifications of Christ as Beginning, Firstborn, the First in all things (Col. 1:18). As little therefore as there is anything in heaven or on earth outside God and his reach, so little is there anything outside Christ. The whole fullness of the deity dwells in him bodily (Col. 2:9), that is, the whole might and glory of God with respect to all things becomes manifest in him, makes its appearance in him, and asserts itself in him.[95] For this reason the church is to hold to him and not to the wisdom of the world (Col. 2:8ff.).

---

in 1:19, not of God, but of the universe filled by God, which God has made to dwell in Christ; cf., e.g., the translation and explanation of Benoit in La Sainte Bible, 1949, pp. 55f. Some choose also to carry this translation through into Col. 2:9, where by *pan to plērōma tēs theotētos* is then understood that which is filled by divine virtue ("that which is filled with the divine virtue, the whole sphere where the divine virtue exercises itself, dwells in Christ"). That is, therefore, the universe. So J. Dupont, Gnosis, 1949, p. 475. But this leads to very labored translations and rests on the pantheistic stoic idea that the universe can be called the fullness, the *pleroma* of the deity, which is something other than the Old Testament idea that God fills the universe. We shall, therefore, as is most clearly apparent from Col. 2:9, with *pan to plērōma* first of all have to think of God's own fullness in the sense of the all-embracing character of God's relation to and power over the world. In 1:19 Münderlein wants to think of the Holy Spirit and understand the aorist *eudokēsen* of the baptism of Christ (in NTS, 1962, pp. 270, 272). In 2:9 Christ would then be defined as "incarnation of the Spirit of God . . . and indeed in his sovereign position" (p. 273). In our view it is indeed a question of a category of omnipotence, and therefore the reference to Christ's baptism does not seem in place.

92. The background of this expression has been sought in various directions: in the syncretistic literature, characterized as gnostic, of the Hellenistic *Umwelt* (Schlier, Dibelius), in the Stoa (Dupont, Benoit), then again in the rabbinic literature (Meuzelaar, Münderlein). The difficulty is that the literature in which *plērōma* does occur as a denotation of the deity (as in the Hermetic writings and the Odes of Solomon) is content-wise the farthest removed from Paul; that the Stoa did know the idea of the filling of all things by the deity, but did not speak of this in this absolute sense of the *Pleroma*. The same thing applies to the Old Testament and rabbinic writings, although there of course no pantheistic principle of life is understood by this filling of all things by God, as in the case of the Stoics. It is very difficult therefore to introduce anything that gives the exegesis of *plērōma* support (cf. Delling, TDNT, VI, pp. 302ff., s.v. *plērōma*). For all the materials see the detailed expositions of Dupont, Gnosis, pp. 419-493 ("Plenitude Cosmique").

93. Cf. Münderlein, NTS, 1962, p. 275: "This concept cannot mean the 'essence of that which constitutes God' . . . but it designates God . . . as active, almighty Lord over creation and history."

94. The words *en autō eudokēsen . . . katoikēsai* are apparently borrowed from Ps. 67:17 LXX. This also argues for the intransitive translation of *katoikēsai*.

95. The significance of *sōmatikōs* is very differently conceived. See the discussion of seven different interpretations in my Col., pp. 17ff.

We shall have to understand the statements relating to this matter in Ephesians to the same effect. In 4:10 it is said that Christ has ascended above all the heavens, "that he might fill all things." As it is said of God in the Old Testament that he fills heaven and earth (Jer. 23:24),[96] so this pronouncement of omnipotence can be transferred to Christ: the whole universe falls within the reach of his mighty presence. He is the one (Eph. 1:23) who in every respect fills the universe.[97] And to this effect one will have to understand the expression of 3:18ff., that the church will be in a position to understand "what is the breadth and length and height and depth." These absolutely employed dimensions are again a denotation of the all-embracing character of the "fulness of God" represented by Christ, controlled by him, and standing at his disposal[98] (3:19; cf. v. 15).

Now it is this glory of Christ as the Head of all things which determines his position as the Head of the church; the "fulness" terminology returns here.[99] The church is "his *pleroma*" (Eph. 1:23), that is to say, the (area or dominion) filled by him.[100] We meet with precisely the same thought in Colossians 2:10 where, after the words "in him the whole fulness of the deity dwells bodily," it is said of the church: "and you are filled in him who is the Head of all power," etc.; similarly in Ephesians 3:19 the object of the indwelling of Christ in the church is said to be: "that you may be filled unto all the fulness of God." Finally, Ephesians 4:7ff. is also to be mentioned in this connection, where it follows on the declaration of the fullness of the power of Christ that he has furnished his church with all manner of gifts (apostles, prophets, etc.), so that it will attain to mature manhood, to the measure of the stature of the fullness of Christ.

While it is said of Christ on the one hand, therefore, that he fills

---

96. LXX: *mē ouchi ton ouranon kai tēn gēn egō plērō? legei Kyrios.* Cf. Delling, *TDNT*, VI, p. 288, and above all Münderlein, *NTS*, 1962, pp. 266, 270.

97. *Ta panta en pasin plēroumenou.* We understand *ta panta*, then, in the sense in which it is used in 4:10 (also with *plēroō!*). *En pasin:* in all respects; what is meant is that Christ asserts the fullness of his power everywhere and in every respect, also in every creature. One can also take *en pasin* instrumentally (= *dia pantōn:* "With all the powers which go forth from Him Christ rules over and among all the forces which have become subject to Him"; Delling, *TDNT*, VI, p. 292). Others think that *ta panta en pasin* must be understood of the church and appeal to Col. 3:11: "filling all in all the members of the church" (Masson, *l'Epitre de Saint Paul aux Colossiens*, p. 156). But after *to plērōma*, which must also be understood of the church (see below), this sounds somewhat tautological.

98. On the "four dimensions" see the full discussion in Dupont, *Gnosis*, pp. 476-489.

99. Percy, *Probleme*, pp. 384ff., and Delling, *TDNT*, VI, p. 304, otherwise correctly emphasize that *plērōma* in Eph. and Col. is not used in entirely the same sense, but with considerable differentiation.

100. That *plērōma* is to be understood here as "completion" (in the sense that Christ would find a certain completion in the church as his body; so already ancient Greek interpreters; cf. K. Staab, *Pauluskommentare aus der griechischen Kirche*, 1933, p. 320; of the later writers, e.g., Dibelius, *Col.*, p. 65; P. Ewald, *Die Briefe des Paulus an die Epheser*, 2nd ed., 1910, p. 104) has been conclusively refuted by Percy, among others (*Der Leib Christi*, pp. 50ff.; *Probleme*, p. 384).

all things (with his mighty presence) (Eph. 1:23; 4:10), yet the church can be called his *pleroma* in a special sense, the domain filled and ever increasingly to be filled by him (Eph. 1:23; 3:19; 4:13; Col. 2:10). There is apparently a distinction here, therefore, between filling and filling that coincides with the difference between Christ's Headship over "all things" on the one hand and of the church on the other. If the first speaks especially of his power and of the containedness of all things in him, the second has reference primarily to the appropriation of the resultant benefits and gifts of Christ to and by the church. This is seen most clearly in Ephesians 4:7-16, where Christ's position of authority over all things is immediately joined with what Christ wishes to give the church for its spiritual growth and maturity. Accordingly Ephesians 5:18 mentions being filled with the Holy Spirit (cf. Eph. 3:16-19; Col. 1:19). It is without doubt a question therefore of a pneumatic reality, which must be understood, however, against the background and in the light of Christ's all-embracing power. The view of that power — and this is the effect of this continuous linking of the twofold Headship of Christ — is on the one hand to keep the church from being overawed by any other power, as though it did not possess in Christ everything necessary for its perfecting, and on the other hand to urge it on to seek its fullness in the fullness of its Head. This fullness and all-sufficiency of Christ are to bring it to adulthood, make it draw from him all that is necessary for its growth, so that in its faith and knowledge of Christ it will not bog down along the way, will not be moved and tossed to and fro by every wind of doctrine and by the craftiness of human error (Eph. 4:14; cf. Col. 2:18, 19), but will be firmly rooted and grounded (Eph. 3:17; Col. 2:7ff.).

Although this combination of the *pleroma* of the church (as gift as well as mandate and goal) with the *pleroma* possessed by Christ particularly in Colossians must be seen against the background of the heresy that hampered the church in its stability and growth, it is clear that broad perspectives for the life of the church in general are opened in it.[101] On the one hand, in this growing fullness of the church which is derived from Christ, the all-embracing and all-transcending power and grace of Christ reveal themselves (Eph. 2:7), an announcement (and challenge!) particularly to the principalities and powers in the heavenly places (Eph. 3:10). In that sense this fullness of the church is a prophecy and a representation of the redemptive work of Christ embracing heaven and earth. On the other hand, there is in this fullness of Christ in which the church is permitted to share an indication as to its own place and development in the world. In its own existence and in its relationship to the world it has to show itself as the church of him who is the Head over all things. It has, therefore, also so far as its own existence and conduct are concerned, to see all that is in heaven and on earth from the vantage point of the all-embracing sovereignty of its Head. It has to rid itself of the "elementary principles of the world" (Col. 2:8, 20),

---

101. See, e.g., H. Berkhof, *De katholiciteit der Kerk*, 1962, pp. 61ff.; I. J. Du Plessis, *Christus as Hoof*, pp. 116ff.

that is to say, the world view and the pattern of conduct that belong to the unredeemed world[102] and not to Christ and which bring those who live by them into a slavish position of subjection. In distinguishing and rejecting them lies the adulthood of the church, and in proportion as it lives more out of the fullness of Christ instead of according to these worldly principles will it increase in spiritual growth and fullness (Col. 2:7, 8, 20ff.; 3:1ff.; Eph. 4:13, 14).

When Paul views the existence of the church in the world surrounding it from the viewpoint of Christ's original position, confirmed in his death and resurrection, as the First in the universe, here again the principal motif of his whole doctrine of salvation remains in force, which can be expressed in the contrast of "already" and "not yet." That is also clear in Ephesians and Colossians.[103] On the one hand the victory of Christ over the powers is nowhere proclaimed more plainly and more triumphantly than here. God has disarmed them in Christ, made a public example of them, and harnessed them to his triumphal chariot (Col. 2:15; cf. Eph. 1:20ff.; 4:8ff.). Through him God has reconciled, pacified, subjected all things to himself[104] (Col. 1:20). On the other hand it continues to hold for the church as well that it has to wage war not against flesh and blood, but against the principalities, the powers, the world rulers of this darkness, the evil spirits in the heavenly places[105] (Eph. 6:12). The powers, however much already vanquished in Christ, have not yet become harmless. But in order to be able to contend against them suitably, the church has received an armor from God, so richly furnished that it is able to continue to stand (Eph. 6:13ff.). It is in that sense that the church even now may represent and exhibit the fullness of Christ; that both in its gift and in its mandate it shares as his body in the place and power of Christ its Head who fills all in every way (Eph. 1:23); and that in the believing exercise of this share it attains to its spiritual growth and upbuilding. The various facets of this upbuilding will have to be dealt with further in a separate chapter.

---

102. Cf. above, pp. 148f.

103. According to Bultmann a difference reveals itself here between Eph. and Col. and the epistles of Paul that he accepts as genuine. He describes this as follows: "Whereas according to Paul the victory of Christ over the cosmic powers is yet to be awaited as the event of the coming last time ... in the other view the victory is already gained" (*History and Eschatology*, p. 55). And accordingly the "historicizing" and "neutralizing" of eschatology in its progress demonstrates itself in these epistles. But in the (other) epistles of Paul, too, the starting point of the paraenesis lies in the victory Christ has already achieved over the powers (cf., e.g., Rom. 8:37, 38). How much the point of view of the "not yet" also plays a role in Eph. and Col. is evident from what follows (see above in the text).

104. For this exegesis of "reconcile" see my *Col.*, pp. 147ff., i.a., against the view of Michaelis, *Versöhnung des Alls*, 1950, pp. 27ff., who also wishes to think here of a restoration of peace with God in the personal sense of the word. Against that see Percy, *Probleme*, p. 95, and Benoit, *La Sainte Bible*, p. 31.

105. For this peculiar use of the expression *en tois epouraniois* in comparison with *ouranos*, see H. Odeberg, *The View of the Universe in the Epistle to the Ephesians*, pp. 4ff.

SECTION 63. THE CHURCH AS THE PEOPLE OF GOD AND AS THE BODY OF CHRIST

If we ask ourselves, finally, what the relationship is between the two great conceptions of the church that we find in Paul, namely, that of the people of God and that of the body of Christ, it can be said in general that the conception of the church as the body of Christ gives expression in a pregnant and special manner to the peculiar character and newness of the eschatological people of God revealing itself in the church.[106] In so doing the following points are to be distinguished.

(1) The essential idea of the qualification of the church as the body of Christ lies in that the people of God has its unity and common existence in Christ. This unity rests on the redemptive-historical conception of "the many" (or "all") as belonging to and being represented by or in the one. There is a close connection here between people of God and body of Christ, inasmuch as the people of God is included and represented in such fountainhead figures as Abraham, Isaac, and Jacob, as well as in the mediatorial figure[107] of Moses (cf. Rom. 4:1; 9:7ff.; 1 Cor. 10:2 ["all into Moses"]) and thus exhibits a clear prefiguration of the corporate unity of the church in Christ. Both conceptions approach each other most closely in Galatians 3:16, 27-29, where there is mention first of Christ as *the* seed of Abraham, and then it is said of all who are of Christ that they together form one (person, body). Although the idea of body is not mentioned here, it is certainly present materially.[108] Therefore, "body of Christ" gives expression to the unity of all who in Christ are the people of God and the true seed of Abraham. Paul gives a universal scope to this corporate unity of the people of God, not only by reckoning the believing gentiles, too, as of the seed of Abraham, but also by going back beyond Abraham to Adam, to qualify Christ as the second Adam and the church as the "new man" (humanity), "new creation" (Gal. 6:15; Eph. 2:15; 4:13). The corporate idea of the all-in-one is thereby the same, however. And it is in this train of thought that Christ as the Beginning, Firstborn, second Adam, *Sōtēr*, etc., can be called the Head of the church and thus the Head of the body.

(2) The common existence of believers in Christ as his body thus understood gives a sharper and richer picture of the church than can be drawn even on the ground of its significance as the eschatological people of God. If the latter speaks especially of the origin of the church, its election by God, its course through history, it is its mode of existence that is denoted as the body of Christ, its concrete being, its inner substance, both as concerns internal relationships and its relationship to Christ.

With respect to relationships within, the church can and must learn to understand its unity and diversity, its limits and its universality from the fact that it is the body of Christ. It is in that sense accordingly

---

106. Cf. C. Müller, *Gottes Gerechtigkeit und Gottes Volk*, pp. 102ff.
107. Cf. Gal. 3:19, 20.
108. So Müller, *Gottes Gerechtigkeit*, p. 103, and Schlier, *Gal.*, p. 130.

that the concept body of Christ functions especially in the Pauline paraenesis. Because all believers together are one body in Christ, the dividedness of Christ is in conflict with its being, for Christ is not divided (1 Cor. 1:13).

Nor can one restrict this unity to the sphere of what is invisible and hidden. Not only does the word "body" not denote an invisible but a visible mode of existence, but on the ground of being together in Christ Paul concludes the necessity of a visible, outward manifestation of unity as the body (cf. 1 Cor. 1:13; 12:12ff.; Rom. 12:4, 5; Eph. 4:15, 16, 25; Col. 3:14, 15). Diversity, breadth, difference in gifts, ability, and mandate have been given along with the existence as body. And Paul places no less emphasis on this diversity within and in virtue of the existence of the church as body over against all self-direction, sectarianism, and spiritual intolerance than he does on the unity. At the same time the universality and catholicity of the church are implied in its unity anchored in Christ; for in Christ there is neither Jew nor Greek, male nor female, slave nor free. For this reason they all together form one body, and within the body of Christ all discrimination is excluded; as on the other hand the boundary of the body of the church is situated in this unity in Christ. One cannot make the members of Christ the members of a prostitute (1 Cor. 6:16), one cannot at the same time participate in the body and blood of Christ and in that which is sacrificed to idols, for the one bread constitutes one body, inclusively and exclusively (1 Cor. 10:16-22), and there is no communion of light with darkness (2 Cor. 6:14ff.). In all sorts of ways and with a wealth of figures and turns of phrase Paul instructs the church with a view to internal relationships and its manifestation in the world to understand itself as the body of Christ, and every believer as a member of this body.

(3)   The real and supporting ground of the whole conception of the people of God as the body of Christ, however, lies in the unity of the church with Christ himself. This unity is, as has been sufficiently expounded, not merely or in the first place of a spiritual kind, but goes back beyond that. Nor can one say that the qualification body of Christ exclusively or especially expresses the pneumatic aspect of this unity. The church is the body of Christ not only in virtue of his spiritual indwelling, but already because Christ is the *Sōtēr* of the body, has purchased his church for himself, and it had always been included in him. One cannot rightly represent the matter in such a way, therefore, as though at bottom a certain spiritualism were attached to the *corpus Christi* idea and that the counterpoise for that were in the connection with the concrete historical conception of the people of God.[109] It is again evident indirectly how important it is whether one chooses to seek the background of the "body" (of Christ) in the Jewish or in the Hellenistic world.[110]

All this does not alter the fact that the qualification body of Christ

---

109. Müller, *ibid.*, p. 104. By what is here denoted "at bottom" Müller means "on the basis of its gnostic origin."
110. Cf. above, pp. 383ff.

(in the nature of the case) also has a pneumatic significance, insofar as it refers to the communion between the church and the exalted Christ. That communion is in question especially in the "body" pronouncements in Ephesians and Colossians, although there, too, the logical priority of "body" is apparent with respect to the Holy Spirit.[111] The same thing applies to the designation of Christ as the Head. At the same time —so we have seen — this Head-body conception makes the connection between the church and "all things," in that Christ as the Head of the church is also the Head of all things, and the church thus is the *pleroma,* the area of the power of him who fills and governs all things in all respects.[112]

Undoubtedly, therefore, the designation "body of Christ," as a further christological definition of the people of God, contains a wealth of new viewpoints and possibilities of expression for elucidating fully the place and significance of the church as the New Testament people of God. Yet one must be on his guard against incorrect distinctions or contrasts, for example, as though a certain transition were to take place here from redemptive-historical to pneumatic thinking, or something of that sort. The basic idea of the body of Christ is that all that the church is as the New Testament people of God it is *in Christ,* and that its historical mode of existence and manifestation in the world, too, must answer to that. "Body of Christ" is the christological concentration of "people of God," just as it is implied in the Headship of Christ that the redemptive-historical and pneumatic unity of the people of God is grounded in Christ and is effectuated in communion with him.

---

111. Cf. above, pp. 377ff.

112. Whether one chooses to include in the concept "catholicity" (of the church) this connection of the church with "all things" established in Christ, as Berkhof wishes to do (*De katholiciteit der Kerk,* p. 59), is in our view not a question of exegesis, but of dogma-historical usage. There can be no doubt about the matter itself.

X

BAPTISM AND THE LORD'S SUPPER

SECTION 64. DIFFERENT DEFINITIONS OF BAPTISM

In the preceding chapters we have been struck time and again by the great significance Paul ascribes to baptism (as well as, though less frequently, to the Lord's Supper) as medium in the appropriation of the salvation given to the church in Christ. This proved to be the case particularly in the chapter[1] on the new life as dying and rising with Christ and as life through the Spirit. Baptism came into the discussion repeatedly as the way in which and as the means by which the church participates in the redemptive event that took place once for all in Christ and receives a share in the gift of the Spirit. The same can be said of what became apparent in the preceding chapter concerning the significance of the body of Christ. It holds for that body, too, that incorporation into it and participation in the pneumatic communion with Christ come about by baptism,[2] just as this communion with Christ and the church's being one body together are renewed and confirmed by the Lord's Supper.[3]

This is the place to go somewhat more deeply and more deliberately into the significance of baptism and the Lord's Supper as means of salvation. In so doing we can make use of what has already been discovered and shall try to avoid repetitions as much as possible. Nevertheless, we cannot confine ourselves to what has already been dealt with because the significance of baptism and the Lord's Supper came out there only in an indirect and incomplete way. This is particularly the case with baptism because in the epistles of Paul it is ascribed a more varied meaning than has been apparent in the foregoing chapters. Moreover, in addition to the passages where Paul explicitly mentions baptism there are others where this is not the case, but where even so one has good reason to inquire whether he does not implicitly intend baptism. The situation is somewhat simpler with respect to the Lord's Supper because the passages that may be cited for it are pretty much restricted to the two well-known pericopes of 1 Corinthians 10 and 11. Methodologically, therefore, a discussion of the Supper offers much less difficulty. For that reason we shall first attempt to form a summary picture of the pronouncements that bear on baptism, in order thereafter on the basis of a further analysis of 1 Corinthians 10 and 11 to treat separately the significance of the Lord's Supper.

1. See above, Chapter VI, Section 37.
2. See above, p. 372.
3. See above, p. 374.

In considering Paul's statements on baptism we shall have to realize that the apostle nowhere gives a detailed "treatment" of the meaning of baptism, but rather repeatedly presupposes an understanding of it.[4] His pronouncements on baptism, therefore, frequently bear the character of an appeal to what the church knows, or ought to know, respecting it and a further explanation of what is to follow from baptism for the consciousness of its faith and conduct. Nevertheless, in these references to baptism a very important doctrinal element is also implied, and therefore the attempt has been made to arrive at a "Pauline" doctrine of baptism.[5]

When one examines the statements relating to it more closely, it becomes apparent that Paul denotes the redemptive significance of baptism in various ways, whereby, as we may suppose,[6] he now makes use of more traditional formulations and then again employs descriptions that are to be interpreted out of the fundamental structures characteristic of his preaching.

(a) To the more traditional definitions undoubtedly belongs, in the first place, the typification of baptism as a cleansing bath. One finds this most clearly in 1 Corinthians 6:11 and Ephesians 5:26:

> ... but you allowed yourselves to be washed, but you were sanctified, but you were justified in the name of the Lord Jesus Christ, and in the Spirit of our God (1 Cor. 6:11).
> ... having cleansed it [the church] by the bath of water with the word (Eph. 5:26).

That the expressions "to wash" and "bath of water" refer to baptism cannot be doubted. In both we find baptism, in harmony with the whole of the early Christian proclamation,[7] characterized as the symbol of and means of salvation for the washing away of and cleansing from sin, which is described in 1 Corinthians 6:11 both in the ethical and in the forensic sense. That the washing with water is attended with "the word" that comes from God to the one baptized is

---

4. Cf., e.g., the ē agnoeite in Rom. 6:3.

5. The literature is very extensive. Of the more recent special studies the following are to be mentioned: R. Schnackenburg, *Baptism in the Thought of St. Paul: A Study in Pauline Theology*, ET 1964; also his further reflections in the *Münchener Theologische Zeitschrift*, 1955; J. Schneider, *Baptism and Church in the New Testament*, ET 1957, pp. 30ff.; O. Kuss, "Zur paulinischen und nachpaulinischen Tauflehre," in *Theologie und Glauben*, 1952, pp. 401ff.; G. Bornkamm, "Baptism and New Life in Paul," in *Early Christian Experience*, pp. 71ff.; G. R. Beasley-Murray, *Baptism in the New Testament*, 1962, pp. 127ff.; E. Klaar, *Die Taufe nach paulinischen Verständnis*, 1961; M. Rissi, *Die Taufe für die Toten*, 1962; G. Wagner, *Pauline Baptism and the Pagan Mysteries*, ET 1967; G. Delling, *Die Taufe im Neuen Testament*, 1963, pp. 108ff.; E. Dinkler, "Die Taufterminologie in 2 Kor. 1,21f.," in *Festschrift für O. Cullmann*, 1962, pp. 173ff.; G. Braumann, *Vorpaulinische Christliche Tauflehre bei Paulus*, 1962; G. de Ru, *De kinderdoop en het Nieuwe Testament*, 1964, pp. 56-91.

6. Cf. for this especially Braumann, *Vorpaulinische Christliche Tauflehre*, pp. 1-13.

7. Cf. Schnackenburg, *Baptism in St. Paul*, pp. 3ff.; Delling, *Die Taufe*, pp. 96ff.; Bultmann, *Theology*, I, pp. 136ff.

expressly added in Ephesians 5:26 and pertains to the bases of Christian baptism. We shall have to return in what follows to the relationship of the two as well as that of baptism and faith. It may simply be assumed in the meantime that faith is presupposed in all this even on the ground of the middle voice: "you allowed yourselves to be washed," as well as of the indissoluble link between faith and justification.[8] The allusion in 1 Corinthians 6:11 to the baptismal formula is furthermore to be pointed out — "in the name of" (however difficult this may be to interpret[9]) — as well as the connection between baptism and the Holy Spirit (see below); and in Ephesians 5:26 the clear indication that Christ is the author of the cleansing that takes place in baptism and that baptism functions as the instrument.

In addition, baptism is mentioned as "bath of water" in Titus 3:5: "He [God] saved us, through the bath of regeneration and renewing of the Holy Spirit."

In this pronouncement baptism is once again qualified as a cleansing bath; but then as a cleansing that, as is evident from the immediately preceding words, is to be understood in the context of the saving, eschatological activity of God ("the appearing" of his mercy, etc.) and which represents the total renewal of the life of man resulting from it. In that sense here again the mention of the Holy Spirit[10] is to be understood: the washing with water of baptism represents the new birth[11] as the transition from the old mode of existence dominated and qualified by sin to that which derives its character from the Spirit as the eschatological gift of salvation.

(b) All this now leads us naturally, in the second place, to those pronouncements in which baptism is simply qualified as the baptism of the Spirit. Here again Paul concurs with the early Christian view of baptism (cf. Mark 1:8; Acts 2:38; John 3:5, *et al.*). In Paul's epistles this baptismal motif is directly mentioned in 1 Corinthians 12:13, where a baptism *in* or *with* (not *by*[12]) the Holy Spirit is spoken of. As has already been observed, in the whole framework of Pauline (and early Christian) proclamation one must ascribe an eschatological significance to this bestowal of the Holy Spirit. The Spirit of the promise (Eph. 1:13) is "poured out" by God in accordance with this promise concerning the last days (Joel 2:28; Acts 2:4, 17; Rom. 5:5; Tit. 3:6), and he therefore may be understood as "firstfruits" and as "earnest," namely, of the future inheritance (cf. Eph. 1:14; Tit. 3:6, 7; 2 Cor. 1:22; Rom. 8:16, 23). The connection between baptism and the Spirit thus does not consist specifically in an incidental outpouring of unusual gifts of the Spirit, but in the transition of the baptized to the new life that has been brought to

---

8. Cf. Beasley-Murray, *Baptism in the New Testament*, p. 166.

9. Cf., e.g., Bietenhard, *TDNT*, V, p. 273.

10. The words *pneumatos hagiou* are only to be taken with *anakainōseōs* and not also with *palingenesias*.

11. For this conception see the detailed discussion above, pp. 226ff.

12. See above, pp. 372f.

light by Christ, in which not only are the guilt and uncleanness of sin washed away, but in which, positively, the new government of the Holy Spirit also prevails. Baptism is, likewise according to Paul, not only a preparatory sacrament — as for John the Baptist — but a sacrament of fulfillment as well. This becomes evident particularly through the relationship between baptism and the Holy Spirit.

The question still remains — a question to which various answers have been given — as to whether Paul alludes to baptism in the passages in which he speaks of sealing with the Holy Spirit:

> Now he that establishes us with you in Christ ["in the Anointed"], and anointed us, is God; who also put his seal upon us, and gave us the earnest of the Spirit in our hearts (2 Cor. 1:21, 22).
>
> In whom [Christ] you also, having heard the word of the truth, the gospel of your salvation, in whom, having also believed, you were sealed with the Holy Spirit of promise, which is an earnest of our inheritance (Eph. 1:13, 14).
>
> And grieve not the Holy Spirit of God, in whom you were sealed unto the day of redemption (Eph. 4:30).

For many commentators it is definitely established that with this sealing by the Holy Spirit Paul intends baptism, just as very early in the Christian church (in conjunction with circumcision; Rom. 4:11?) this was explicitly qualified as a seal (cf. 2 Clem. 7, 6; 8, 6; Herm. Sim. VIII, 6, 13; IX, 16, 3ff.; 17, 4). They further couple this with the idea that is said to underlie the baptismal formula: "baptizing in(to) the name of . . . ," namely, that the one baptized is "stamped" by baptism as the property of Christ and placed under his protection. This sealing with the name (as sign of ownership and protection) would then coincide with the gift of the Spirit conferred in baptism.[13] And baptism would be understood by the qualification "sealing" as an eschatological act in which the baptized passes over to the ownership of him in whose name the baptismal act takes place. Through the giving of the Spirit as the earnest the judicial action understood in this way would be completed.[14] According to some, the expression "who anointed us" also has reference to baptism, whether what is intended by it is the anointing with the Holy Spirit, or an anointing that follows the baptismal act, as that is known to us from the ancient church.[15] Others, however, are much more reserved in their judgment and consider it at the very least uncertain that "sealing" and "anointing" directly allude to baptism.[16]

---

13. Cf. Bultmann, *Theology*, I, pp. 137ff. In an earlier period it was thought that the expression *sphragis* as a denotation of baptism stemmed from the mystery religions (cf. J. Leipoldt, *Die urchristliche Taufe im Lichte der Religionsgeschichte,* 1928, p. 67). But this view no longer has much support (cf. Wagner, *Pauline Baptism,* p. 271).

14. See especially E. Dinkler, "Die Taufterminologie in 2 Kor. 1,21f.," in *Festschrift für O. Cullmann;* cf. also the article "Taufe" by Dinkler in *RGG,* 3rd ed., 1962, col. 630.

15. Cf. Dinkler, *loc. cit.,* as well as Wendland, *Cor.,* p. 112.

16. Cf., e.g., Schnackenburg, *Baptism in St. Paul,* pp. 86ff.

To our mind one will with "anointing" have to think directly of the gift of the Holy Spirit (cf. Luke 4:18; Acts 10:38; 1 John 2:20, 27). And, as appears from Ephesians 1:13; 4:30, the same thing applies to "sealing." What is characterized here is not baptism in the first place, but the gift of the Spirit. The point of departure for the term "sealing" does not lie therefore in sacramental appropriation or "stamping" in behalf of Christ (because the one baptized is transferred to his name), but in the evidence that the gift of the Spirit itself produces in him who receives it. The latter is thereby furnished with the seal that he belongs to God, just as the gift of the Spirit may be accounted the firstfruits and earnest of the inheritance.

All this does not alter the fact that, given the connection between the Spirit and baptism, what applies to the Spirit can easily be transferred to baptism and that these Pauline statements on sealing by the Spirit can lie at the root of the later "technical" denotation of baptism as a "seal."[17] That these pronouncements themselves already betray such a denotation of baptism is, in our opinion, incapable of being substantiated. In any case, the term seal or sealing in Paul does not yet have the general significance that the later ecclesiastical and confessional usage attributed to baptism by it; for him it denotes especially the sealing power of the Spirit, whether or not understood within the framework of baptism.

(c) The descriptions of baptism most characteristic for Paul are not those, however, which have reference to cleansing from sin and the gift of the Spirit, but those which denote baptism as the entrance of the order of life represented by Christ and at the same time as the incorporation into his body. It is this conception of baptism which we have met time and again in the preceding chapters and which now calls for further discussion.

It is not only a matter here of the statements that speak of being "baptized into Christ's death," or of being "buried with him by baptism into death" (Rom. 6:3, 4; cf. Col. 2:11, 12). These expressions are rather to be viewed as a very characteristic, but special, application of a more general idea, i.e., that baptism binds one to Christ and the order of life represented by him. It is this union with Christ by baptism that Paul intends when in Galatians 3:27 he describes baptism as "putting on Christ": "For as many of you as were baptized into Christ have put on Christ. There is neither Jew nor Greek," etc. Closely related to this is the pronouncement in Colossians 3:9-11: ". . . seeing that you have put off the old man with his doings, and have put on the new man . . . , wherein there is not Greek and Jew," etc.

Here again there is undoubtedly an allusion to baptism. We have already been able to determine that with this old and new man

---

17. Cf. Bultmann, *Theology*, I, p. 137: "Even if Paul does not necessarily imply the actual use of the noun 'seal' [*sphragis*] for baptism, at any rate, behind the cognate verb used by him lies the idea that did lead to this terminology in later sources."

one is not to think in the first place of the conversion of individual believers, but of the common mode of existence of "the many" in Adam and in Christ respectively.[18] This "new man" is put on by baptism, and that can now be called "putting on" or "drawing on" Christ. Although the derivation of this expression and the idea of "putting on" to be judged by it are uncertain,[19] the essential meaning of these pronouncements is not open to question: baptism makes one participate in Christ as him who, as the one seed of Abraham and as the "second man," represents and contains within himself those belonging to him. In that same sense one can speak of being "baptized into his body."[20]

From this perspective the much discussed descriptions of baptism in Romans 6 and Colossians 2 may also be understood:

> Or do you not know that all of us who were baptized into Christ were baptized into his death? (Rom. 6:3).
> We were buried therefore with him through baptism into death (Rom. 6:4).
> ... in whom [i.e., Christ] you were also circumcised ... having been buried with him in baptism, wherein[21] you were also raised with him through faith (Col. 2:11, 12).

What interests us now in these pronouncements, which we have discussed earlier in another context,[22] is the peculiar connection Paul makes between baptism on the one hand, and dying, being buried and raised with Christ on the other, so that baptism can be qualified as a baptism into Christ's death, etc. That we should have to ascertain here the influence of the mystery religions[23] in which the initiates were brought into a specific relationship with the cultic deity who dies and comes to life again is, despite the lingering effects of this conception in some of the literature,[24] increasingly viewed as an undemonstrable and improbable thesis.[25] For regardless of what is to be said against this so-

---

18. Cf. above, pp. 62ff.

19. Some choose here again to think of certain actions in the mystery cults, especially in the worship of Isis (Leipoldt, *Die urchristliche Taufe*, p. 60). But against this see, e.g., Wagner, *Pauline Baptism*, p. 273, n. 62; and Oepke, *TDNT*, II, p. 320. Old Testament parallels are also brought forward (cf. Oepke, *loc. cit.*); but the comparative materials for the "putting on of a person" are in our view not very convincing (cf. Judg. 6:34; 1 Chron. 12:18). Some have also thought of the taking off and putting on of clothing in connection with immersion (cf., e.g., W. F. Flemington, *The New Testament Doctrine of Baptism*, 1948, pp. 57ff.); or of being clothed with a uniform on induction into the army (so Cullmann, *Baptism in the New Testament*, ET 1950, p. 36). The gnostic myth is also in vogue here: "the Redeemer encloses the redeemed as a garment" (cf. H. Schlier, *Gal.*, pp. 128ff.). There are also those who prefer to think of an independent coinage by Paul himself (cf. Wagner, *Pauline Baptism*, p. 273).

20. Cf. above, pp. 372ff.

21. *En hō* refers to baptism, not to Christ. See, e.g., the detailed argumentation of Beasley-Murray, *Baptism in the New Testament*, pp. 153ff.

22. Cf. above, pp. 206ff.

23. On this see what has already been said above, pp. 23ff.

24. E.g., in Bultmann's *Theology*, I, pp. 140ff.

25. See also Wagner, in *Pauline Baptism;* he has once again analyzed exhaustively all the materials and on this basis has come to an absolutely negative result.

called analogy itself, not a single piece of evidence can be adduced that in these heathen cultic acts such a co-dying and rising took place as would be comparable to Christian baptism. One must assume, then, that Paul himself (or the gentile Christian church, with which he supposedly associated himself) attached this significance to baptism, although it did not occur in the mystery religions. But that does not explain precisely what it was intended to explain, namely, how Paul arrived at this special conception of baptism.[26]

Entirely distinct from this is the symbolical interpretation given in many commentaries[27] of this connection between baptism on the one hand and the dying, being buried, and rising on the other.[28] This symbolism is said to lie in the going down of the one baptized into, and the emerging again out of, the water of baptism, which pictures dying on the one hand and resurrection on the other. But this whole symbolism — as we have already attempted to demonstrate at some length elsewhere[29] — appears to us to be a fiction. In Paul's statements themselves it has no support whatever.[30] So far as the water of baptism is concerned, its symbolical significance, as appears from the whole of the New Testament, is that it purifies, not that one can sink down into it and drown,[31] to say nothing of being buried in the water. There is likewise no basis for the notion that the posture of the one baptized would suggest such a symbolism. Were one able still to think of a dying at the moment of immersion ("the waters" closing over the head, etc.), the single time that Paul speaks of "being baptized into his death" cannot really offer sufficient evidence for this conception. To see this moment of immersion especially as a symbol of burial, however,[32] seems to us entirely absurd. For not only is one not buried in water, but it is also difficult to symbolize burial by immersing oneself for an instant under water. And so far as resurrection is concerned, if the only place where "being raised with him in baptism" is mentioned (Col. 2:12) were intended to denote coming up out of the water as a symbol of the resurrection, surely the preposition "out of" (ek) and not "in" (en) would have been used (as with dying and being buried with him in baptism). The more one goes

---

26. Cf. further my *Paul and Jesus,* pp. 6ff.

27. See the quotations (from Greijdanus, Dodd, Lagrange, *et al.*) in my *Rom.,* p. 132. Wagner, too, attempts to support this view (*Pauline Baptism,* pp. 288f.).

28. Undoubtedly as an *a posteriori* interpretation of baptism from the kerygma; cf., e.g., Beasley-Murray, *Baptism in the New Testament,* p. 133: "only because the kerygma gives this significance to baptism; its whole meaning is derived from Christ and His redemption — it is the kerygma *in action,*" etc.; cf. also Wagner, *ibid.,* pp. 286ff.

29. *Rom.,* pp. 132ff.

30. Dodd, e.g., also acknowledges that "Paul does not indeed draw out the suggestion of the symbolism," although he adds to this: "but it lies near the surface" (*Romans,* p. 87).

31. Lietzmann speaks explicitly of a symbolical death by drowning in baptism (*Rom.,* p. 65).

32. As Wagner puts it, speaking as though the matter were perfectly clear: "Baptism is the image of a burial"; cf. Beasley-Murray, *Baptism in the New Testament,* p. 133: "The symbolism of immersion as representing burial is striking." But what on earth would lead one to think of such a burial at the moment of immersion?

into the matter, the more he is compelled to the conclusion that the
symbolic connection thus made between baptism and the death, burial,
and resurrection of Christ, however frequently advanced, finds no
support whatever either in the texts[33] or in the thing itself.

We can all be the more decided in our rejection of this symbolic
view because there is no necessity whatever to explain in this way the
relationship between baptism on the one side and the death, etc., of
Christ on the other. Moreover, it contains within it the danger of divert-
ing attention from the specific significance Paul here ascribes to baptism.
For when he speaks of "being baptized into Christ" and describes this
further as "being baptized into his death," the fact that baptism unites
the one baptized with Christ as the second Adam is also at stake here, as
may appear from the immediately preceding Adam-Christ pericope; thus
that those who are baptized into him may now know that they are
included in Christ's death, burial, and resurrection, and that they ought
no longer to live in sin, as precisely that to which they have died in
him. It is with this last application that Paul is concerned in the context of Romans 6 (cf. vv. 1, 2). The function of baptism therefore consists
in this, that it incorporates or implants the one baptized into this corporate ("bodily") unity between Christ and his own (Rom. 6:5). For this
reason the expression "to be baptized into Christ" in Romans 6:3 and
Galatians 3:27 cannot simply be interpreted as an abbreviation of the
formula, to be "baptized in the name of Christ," as is often assumed.[34]
Rather, this compressed expression has a more pregnant significance,
in that it is the denotation of the union of the one baptized with Christ
in this corporate sense and thus with his death, burial, and resurrection.
It is this meaning of baptism as incorporation into Christ which is
denoted in verse 5 by the characteristic expression: "are implanted"
(symphytoi gegonamen). Believers are implanted or incorporated by
baptism into what has taken place with Christ, what is applicable therefore sui generis[35] to their own existence.

This last point can enable us at the same time to see that this
baptism into the death of Christ, as also burial and resurrection with
him in baptism, has for Paul a very comprehensive significance. The
death, burial, and resurrection of which there is mention here are undoubtedly the death, burial, and resurrection of Christ; to be buried
with him in baptism consequently means to participate by baptism in
that death and in that grave. To be buried with him in baptism is to
say that by baptism we are laid in Christ's grave, not that baptism
would be the grave in which we, just as Christ once died, now die as

---

33. The only thing that might be able to offer support could perhaps be
the conception that by homoiōma tou thanatou (tēs anastaseōs) autou in Rom. 6:5,
baptism is meant. But this view is to be regarded as incorrect, as we have already
discovered above (pp. 24f.); cf. the cogent arguments of Bornkamm against that (Early
Christian Experience, pp. 77f.); Wagner, Pauline Baptism, pp. 283ff.; Beasley-Murray,
ibid., pp. 134ff.; see also my Rom., p. 129, and the older literature mentioned there.

34. See also above, p. 207.

35. For this reason: symphytoi tō homoiōmati tou thanatou autou, etc.;
cf. above, p. 207.

well. This latter conception,[36] which looks on baptism therefore as spiritual death to and spiritual resurrection from sin, on the analogy and ground of Christ's death and resurrection, is to be firmly rejected. Baptism is not a grave and resurrection — there again the danger of the symbolical interpretation — but baptism incorporates us into, makes us participate in, Christ's death on Golgotha and resurrection in the garden. This does not alter the fact, however, that participation in that one death and that one grave has not only a once-for-all, *einmalig*, redemptive-historical, but also an actual significance, namely, that in this death of Christ the power of sin has been broken for those who belong to him, so that those who have once died to sin in him cannot and may not live any longer in it (Rom. 6:1, 2). And all this is appropriated to them by baptism into his death.

The same thing is meant, too, by putting off the old and putting on the new man in baptism. For the old man, too, has once been crucified with Christ (Rom. 6:6), and the laying aside of the old man in baptism signifies above all, therefore, participation in that unique event. At the same time it is not restricted to that, but this putting off in baptism also signifies an actual departure from this old mode of existence, a departure that goes on after baptism in the continuing "mortification of the members that are upon the earth" (Col. 3:5; cf. Gal. 5:24). And the same applies to putting on the new man. It can be linked with baptism (cf. Col. 3:10) because in baptism believers are raised together with Christ in the unique, redemptive-historical sense of the word (Col. 2:12). But this putting on is also a choice, an act, which is further carried on and realized throughout the whole life of the believer (cf. Eph. 4:24; Rom. 13:14). It is consequently to that continuing, actual condition of being dead to sin and alive to God that the whole admonition based on baptism in Romans 6:1-11 is directed (cf. v. 11). That is the comprehensive meaning of having been "baptized into the death of Christ." Baptism does not thereby become a parable of Christ's death and resurrection in the life of believers, a symbol of conversion. Baptism connects the believer with Christ's death and resurrection, and "to be crucified and raised with Christ in baptism" does not denote conversion. But the one is not without the other, for to have been baptized into Christ and to have been introduced into his body by baptism is also to have been baptized into his Spirit, and does not mean only to have died to sin, but also to live and serve in the new state of the Spirit (Rom. 6:12ff.; 7:4).

The whole of this conception of baptism lies at the root of the pronouncement of Colossians 2:11. Paul is engaged here in a polemic against those who wish to induce the congregation to submit to circumcision. This has become superfluous, however, for in believers the spiritual circumcision ("made without hands"), the circumcision of Christ, has been carried into effect.[37] For they participate by baptism[38]

---

36. For this conception, which is again presented in various ways, see, e.g., the survey in Beasley-Murray, *Baptism in the New Testament*, pp. 131ff.

37. For this exegesis see further my *Col.*, pp. 179f.

38. In a certain sense, therefore, baptism has come in the place of circum-

in the burial of Christ, and through it they have escaped the claim and power of sin. Here again, therefore, the connection between baptism and the burial of Christ: not as if baptism were a symbol of burial, nor either as if there were a specific relationship between baptism and the burial of Christ, but because both in Romans 6 and Colossians 2 the apostle wishes to bring home to his readers that they are no longer subject to the power of sin. In the burial of Christ "the body of the flesh," the old man, has been laid aside once and for all. To be baptized means also to participate in an actual sense in what once took place in Christ.

This whole significance of baptism intended under sub-section c, which admits of the briefest possible formulation in the words "to be baptized into Christ" (Rom. 6:3; Gal. 3:27), is finally given a very illuminating explanation in the remarkable analogy of baptism that Paul introduces in 1 Corinthians 10:2 in another context. For there he compares the New Testament church with ancient Israel — as he does so often — and says of the latter that "our fathers were all baptized into Moses in the cloud and in the sea."[39] This, too, has nothing to do with symbolism, as though cloud and sea were in one way or another to denote a bath of water. For the cloud was a shining cloud, and Israel went through the sea on dry ground. Cloud and sea represent rather the redemptive event by which Israel escaped the tyranny of Pharaoh and the life of slavery in Egypt. And in this redemptive event the fathers all shared because they "were baptized into Moses." There is here no question of a real baptism. The expression is fashioned on the analogy and as a type of Christian baptism (Moses is Christ; cf. v. 4: "that rock was Christ"), and denotes again the many as being brought under the one and the many as being saved in and through the one. For just as God has baptized and incorporated the church in Christ, so Israel's salvation lay in the fact that it had received Moses as leader and head and was contained in Moses. That for this, in the instance of Moses, too, Paul employs the expression "were baptized into" (although there was no question of an actual baptism) demonstrates to what an extent the idea of incorporation forms the dominating element of the expression "to be baptized into Christ (Moses)." As, however, to have been baptized into Christ means for the church baptism into Christ's death and resurrection as well, so also the fathers were all baptized into Moses in the cloud and in the sea, that is to say, they all participated in the discriminating and saving operation of the cloud and the sea that God accomplished for them by the ministry of Moses. The analogy is certainly very striking therefore, although the idea that underlies it in the context of 1 Corinthians 10ff. is developed in a somewhat different way from Romans 6 (cf. 1 Cor. 10:3 with 1 Cor. 12:13!). It is difficult to find a clearer and more authentic

cision, but nevertheless not in the sense that here the one sacramental act is set in the place of the other. Circumcision in the flesh has been replaced by circumcision of the heart. In that circumcision, in taking off the old mode of existence, baptism gives a share, because it gives a share in the burial of Christ.

39. *Eis ton Mōusēn ebaptisanto en tē nephelē kai en tē thalassē.*

explanation for what Paul means when, as in those pronouncements already discussed under "c," he wishes baptism to be understood as becoming incorporated into Christ and the divine redemptive event represented by him.

SECTION 65. BAPTISM AS MEANS OF SALVATION

The question remains as to what is meant when baptism is defined in various ways as the means by which, or as the way in which, salvation is appropriated to the one baptized, regardless now of whether this salvation is defined as cleansing from sin, communication of the Holy Spirit, or incorporation into Christ or into his body. With all these additional qualifications of baptism the same question is at issue, namely, that of baptism as means of salvation; or in other words: what happens in or by baptism?

This question can be put still more sharply when one attempts to delimit it further on two sides. In the first place, the relationship must be established between what happens to the one baptized in or by baptism and what has already preceded it. For we have previously been able to ascertain repeatedly that, in addition to sacramental incorporation into Christ, there is already a predestinarian (cf. Eph. 1:4), and above all a redemptive-historical relationship between Christ and his people. The question is, therefore, how the sacramental aspect relates itself (in particular) to the redemptive-historical aspect of the participation of the church in Christ (I).

In the second place, in determining the appropriating character of baptism the significance of faith must be discussed. For while baptism is ascribed the significance of mediating salvation, the same can be said of faith. This compels us to further reflection on the relationship of the operation of baptism and that of the believing acceptance of the gospel (II).

(I) As far as the first point is concerned, it should be observed that in the epistles of Paul that have come down to us this relationship of having been included in Christ in the redemptive-historical and predestinarian sense and sacramental incorporation into (the body of) Christ and thus into his death and resurrection, is not expressly treated or explained. We are left to conclusions, therefore, which we must draw ourselves, with all the difficulties and dangers of such a procedure. We shall have to be on our guard in so doing against all sorts of constructions that originate in specific a priori dogmatic or philosophical conceptions of baptism (and the Lord's Supper), but which have no support whatever in the epistles of Paul. This is particularly the case with all kinds of speculations on the connection between the baptism of believers and the death of Christ that take Romans 6 as their point of departure. In the more recent Roman Catholic theology the so-called mystery theology has especially occupied itself with this connection. Its representatives

speak thereby, in the footsteps of O. Casel, of Christ's death being made
present time in the sacrament, in which event the one baptized is then
said to be taken up and involved *in mysterio*. Moreover, while Casel
thought primarily of a connection with the Hellenistic mystery cults,
the present conception is that such a representation *(Vergegenwärtigung)*
of the divine creative or redemptive activity in the cultus extends much
further than the Hellenistic cultus, indeed, that it is a primitive phenomenon in the religious life of man and, in particular, formed the center
of Old Testament worship as well.[40] Such a making-present of the unique
redemptive event of Christ's death is now said to have been intended by
Paul in Romans 6. One is not to think here of a new redemptive act of
God or Christ in the sense of a repetition, but in baptism we have to
do with the sacramental form under which the historical crucifixion of
Christ appears present or becomes accessible to us, so that we "can co-
accomplish this death, even die it."[41] Although there is no intention of
detracting from the once-for-all and definitive nature of Christ's death
on the cross,[42] yet the idea is evidently this, that the event of Christ's
death (and not merely its redemptive significance) in one way or another extends to baptism, so that one can as yet die and be buried in it
with Christ himself. And this sacramental "form" of the once-for-all
death of Christ is then said to be denoted in Romans 6:5 by *homoiōma*.

But the fundamental error of this view is that baptism is not the
moment or the place[43] of dying together, etc., with Christ. If this were
so, Christ would continue to die, if not anew, yet *in mysterio,* for in the
event that the dying, etc., of believers together with Christ takes place
in baptism and does not have thereby, as Warnach (rightly) maintains, a

---

40. Cf. Warnach, "Taufe und Christusgeschehen nach Römer 6," in *Archiv.
für Liturgiewiss.*, 1954, pp. 329ff.

41. *Ibid.*, pp. 305, 306. This sacramental "form" of the once-for-all redemptive
event would then be denoted by the *homoiōma* of Rom. 6:5 (*ibid.*, p. 297), i.a., with
an appeal to Kuss and in continuing polemic with the (likewise Roman Catholic)
Schnackenburg, who will not hear of such a "cultic-mysterious representation of the
act of salvation" in Paul and is of the opinion that it seems "to be excluded by the
course of thought in Rom. 6" (*Münchener Theologische Zeitschrift*, 1955, p. 51; cf.
his *Baptism in the Thought of St. Paul: A Study in Pauline Theology*, p. 132). Kuss, in
Theologie und Glauben, pp. 310ff., thinks, on the other hand, that the thesis of
a sacramental *Gegenwärtigsetzung*, or representation, of the redemptive event in
baptism "can be denied only with great difficulty," although he cautiously adds to this
concerning the nature and manner of this *Gegenwärtigsetzung* that "in particular
the details are lacking and their determination if necessary must remain a task of
speculative theology" *(loc. cit.)*. Warnach, too, who defends this view with great
force, acknowledges that Paul has not shown "how the cultic presence is to be
explained more fully; but to my mind he has still, through the choice of the term
[*homoiōma*], which one of course may not press, pointed to the direction in which
the solution of the problem must be sought" (*ibid.*, p. 321). One can conclude even
from this how vague the boundaries are between exegesis and speculation. Against
this conception of *homoiōma*, which has been adopted among Protestants, e.g., by
J. Schneider, *Baptism and Church in the New Testament*, p. 32, see also Wagner,
Pauline Baptism, pp. 206f.; for a detailed discussion of the older relevant literature
also M. Barth, *Die Taufe ein Sakrament?*, 1951, pp. 187ff.

42. Cf. the formulations of Warnach, in *Archiv. für Liturgiewiss.*, 1954, p. 324.

43. The *"Ort"* (*ibid.*, p. 291).

metaphorical or pneumatic significance, Christ in consequence must die or continue to die in one way or another (sacramentally or in a mystery-like fashion) in baptism.[44] And it is out of the question that Paul would have intended this or "have pointed in that direction."[45] In baptism the death of Christ as an event is not made to be renewed in the present and represented as a death in which believers are to "die" with him, but believers are so involved in what took place once and for all that it can be said of his death that it is their death as well. To put it in more concise terms: the death of Christ is not prolonged in baptism and brought to believers, but believers are in baptism brought to Christ's death, that is to say, made to share in what has occurred once for all.

Another conception, in a certain sense opposite to the preceding one, is to be encountered in some Protestant exegetes and is described as the hypothesis of "contemporaneity."[46] According to this view the historical redemptive death of Christ is not (as with Casel, Warnach, and others) located in the present in baptism, but, conversely, the one baptized is made "contemporaneous" with Christ, so that the whole existence of the Christian is taken up into this redemptive event. The believer becomes "contemporaneous" with the cross and resurrection of Christ in the sense that he has a real share in this unique event with the elimination of all that separates him from this event spatially and temporally.

Although this conception certainly does greater justice to Paul's intent, insofar, that is, as it concentrates thinking entirely on the moment of Christ's death (on Golgotha) and resurrection, yet one can scarcely say that baptism fulfills the function of removing the temporal distance between Christ's death and the believer. One is obviously at work here with ideas that have been drawn from another theology than that of Paul.[47] The specific character of baptism into Christ's death is not that time falls away, or that the one baptized is made contemporaneous with Christ in his death, but that by baptism the believer becomes a sharer in what has taken place with Christ. Baptism does not make us die anew with Christ, but rather rests on the fact that he has died for us and we with him, because he is the second man, the last Adam, who when he died and rose substitutionally and representatively comprehended and united the many in himself. It is incorporation into this solidaric relationship, the "body" of the last Adam, which takes place in baptism and by which it becomes a baptism into his death.

We must conclude, therefore, that to have died and been buried

---

44. Cf. Beasley-Murray, *Baptism in the New Testament,* p. 132.

45. That *homoiōma* denotes this is entirely without foundation. It does not speak of some "form" or other in which Christ dies in baptism, but of believers receiving a share *sui generis* in the death and resurrection of Christ. See above, p. 208.

46. The idea of "contemporaneity" was introduced in particular by W. Traugott Hahn, *Das Mitsterben und Mitauferstehen mit Christus bei Paulus,* 1937. One frequently meets with this terminology elsewhere as well (making Christ's death "contemporaneous," "the removal of the temporal distance between Jesus' death and the baptism of believers") (cf., e.g., Percy, *Leib Christi,* p. 28; Wagner, *Pauline Baptism,* p. 292, and literature cited there).

47. Cf. Schnackenburg, *Baptism in St. Paul,* pp. 149ff.; G. C. Berkouwer, *The Sacraments,* ET 1969, pp. 118ff.

with Christ neither comes about in baptism in the sense of the mystery theology, nor becomes an actual occurrence in baptism in the sense of the doctrine of contemporaneity, but that dying with Christ has been given with incorporation into Christ, and is thus appropriated to the one baptized as a given reality by baptism as the rite of incorporation. That is to say, therefore, that to have died once with Christ on the cross and to be baptized into his death do not coincide, but form two points of view. Both do have reference to the same matter, that is, to participation in the unique redemptive event. But even so one cannot allow them to coincide, either by bringing the death of Christ to baptism in the manner of the mystery theology, or by making baptism contemporaneous with that death. There are clearly two foci here, and not one. According to the first, believers are regarded as "the many," who were already included in the death and resurrection of the one; according to the second, by baptism they become incorporated into this solidaric relationship with the one and thus into his death and resurrection. It is not easy to define the relationship between these two viewpoints in the right way. Undoubtedly baptism has the important noetic significance of a personal confirmation and assurance of what once took place in a corporate sense in Christ. Paul again and again appeals to baptism as the evidence and cognitive ground of the church's share in Christ. Because believers have been baptized they know, or at least they must and may know, that they have once died, been buried, and raised with Christ (Rom. 6:3;[48] Col. 2:12[49]). In that sense the later characterization of baptism as the seal of belonging to Christ — a qualification Paul uses for circumcision (Rom. 4:11) — is certainly not out of place.

On the other hand, the meaning of baptism is certainly not to be expressed exclusively in noetic categories. Baptism is also the means by which communion with the death and burial of Christ comes into being (dia tou baptismatos; Rom. 6:4), the place where this union is effected (en tō baptismati; Col. 2:12), the means by which Christ cleanses his church (katharisas tō loutrō; Eph. 5:26), and God has saved it (esōsen hēmas dia loutrou; Tit. 3:5), so that baptism itself can be called the washing of regeneration and of the renewing by the Holy Spirit (Tit. 3:5). All these formulations speak clearly of the significance of baptism in mediating redemption; they speak of what happens in and by baptism and not merely of what happened before baptism and of which baptism would only be the confirmation. On the other hand, it is plain from all his preaching that baptism, as means of salvation, does not have an exclusive significance. Thus what is here attributed to baptism can elsewhere be ascribed to faith (see below). And thus what is here represented as appropriated to believers by baptism can elsewhere be ascribed to them already in Christ's death as the proof of God's love and as the reconciliation with God accomplished in him (Rom. 5:8, 10). We can draw no other conclusion than that baptism accomplishes in its own way what already obtained in another way, and thus occupies its own

---

48. Ē agnoeite.
49. Syntaphentes autō en tō baptismati: causal.

place in the whole of the divine communication of redemption.

What that mode and that place are can only be viewed in the proper light when one does full justice to the various aspects of the divine appropriation of salvation. It is just as incorrect to say that the comprehension of the church in Christ takes place only by baptism, as it is that baptism merely symbolizes or confirms *a posteriori* what is already an accomplished fact. Nor can one say that in baptism there is a realization of the possibility that was already present in Christ's death and resurrection, or that baptism is to be termed the actualization of a more potential inclusion in Christ as the second Adam.[50] All such schemes detract from that which has already gained validity in Christ's death and resurrection, not merely as a possibility, but as an accomplished reality in Christ and on this account for the many comprehended in him. On the other side it is apparent — and here we approach the "Sitz im Leben" of baptism — that what in God's election and in the redemptive event in Christ has in a corporate sense already come to be reality is not effected apart from the preaching of the gospel and the individual choice of faith corresponding to it. It is in the framework of this individualizing application of what once happened in Christ that baptism has a place as the divine promise and appropriation of salvation, and as the believer allowing himself to be invested with it; but even so, always in such a way that this appropriation is the incorporation and entry into a solidaric relationship that is not first constituted by baptism, but is grounded in the antecedent good pleasure of God and forms the secret of the all-encompassing significance of Christ's death and resurrection.

(II) This understanding of baptism within the framework of the proclamation of the gospel and the faith corresponding to it can also make clear the relationship between baptism and faith. How close this connection is may appear already from the fact that everything ascribed to the members of the church in virtue of their baptism is represented no less clearly as the fruit of faith. That applies not only to the epistles of Paul, but to the whole of the New Testament.[51] So far as Paul is concerned, he speaks, for example, in Galatians 2:19ff.; 6:14, of having died together with Christ, etc., without any allusion to baptism, and in Colossians 2:12 it is expressly said that being raised together with Christ in baptism takes place "by means of faith." In Titus 3:5 baptism is the means by which God has saved us; in Ephesians 2:8 it is faith; and the same applies to the relationship between baptism and the Spirit on the one hand and that between faith and the Spirit on the other (cf. 1 Cor. 12:13 with Gal. 3:2). 1 Corinthians 6:11 says that we are justified by baptism, while nearly everywhere else in Paul justification

---

50. For similar formulations see, e.g., Warnach, who says that the "previous solidarity with Christ as the new Adam ... merely fashions the basic possibility of our taking part in Christ's work of salvation" (in *Archiv. für Liturgiewiss.*, 1954, p. 315, cf. p. 317); and in general all who think that baptism is the real place or the moment of dying and rising with Christ.

51. Cf. the extensive survey of the relevant pronouncements in Beasley-Murray, *Baptism in the New Testament*, pp. 272ff.

takes place by means of or on the ground of faith. There can consequently be no suggestion that in Paul baptism can in any sense whatever be detached from faith. Nor does faith have a merely preparatory significance with regard to baptism, in the sense that only baptism would bring us into full communion with Christ;[52] nor, conversely, can one view baptism only as a visible preaching or promise that must awaken faith in the one to be baptized or would presuppose merely a preparatory faith in him.[53] Baptism is the baptism of believers, and the apostle's often repeated reminder of the moment when his readers submitted themselves to baptism is at the same time an appeal to their choice of faith that attended and preceded it. In all these statements faith is the implicit presupposition of baptism, and for this reason faith can be spoken of apart from baptism and one can even ascertain in the New Testament "the relative unimportance of the action [of baptism] as such."[54]

This is not to say, however, that faith gives baptism its power, nor that baptism can be reduced to an act of faith or to a baptismal experience.[55] For however much baptism derives its character from the fact that it is administered to believers and that the baptismal act can be described in terms of believers "submitting themselves to baptism," the subject of baptism is not faith, but God. Not only do the passive pronouncements point to this, those in which believers are clearly the object of the baptismal act, but also the explicit "he [God] saved us through washing with water" (Tit. 3:5), and "he [Christ] cleansed it" (Eph. 5:26). Baptism is the means in God's hand, the place where he speaks and acts. On the other hand, this last excludes every suggestion as though baptism were anything in itself and imparted salvation *ex opere operato*.[56] It is God who gives baptism its power, on the faith of the one baptized. For this reason, too, the admonitory figure can be held up before the church of the fathers, who were, to be sure, all baptized into Moses in the cloud and in the sea and all ate the same spiritual food and drank the same spiritual drink, but with most of whom God was nevertheless not well pleased (1 Cor. 10:1ff.). Neither does this make the operation of baptism dependent on the condition of the recipient in the sense that only faith can make baptism effectual, but it says that baptism remains dependent on divine action, that God does not make himself dependent on baptism or surrender his control over baptism, but rather reserves this to himself and maintains the correlation between faith and baptism.

If the significance of faith for baptism admits of being clearly distinguished in this way, that is to say, from the point of view that God is the person who acts in baptism, it is from the same vantage point that the peculiar, independent significance of baptism with respect to faith

52. Cf. W. Mundle, *Der Glaubensbegriff bei Paulus*, 1932, pp. 123ff.

53. Cullmann appears to think along this line (*Baptism in the New Testament*, pp. 49ff.).

54. Oepke, *TDNT*, I, p. 540.

55. Cf. Bultmann, *Theology*, I, pp. 311f.

56. For the question of the (perhaps incorrectly so-called) "vicarious baptism" in 1 Cor. 15:29 see pp. 24f. above.

can be better recognized. Baptism can add nothing to the content of faith. Baptism and faith are both means to the appropriation of the content of the gospel. However, while faith according to its nature is an act of man, baptism according to its nature is an activity of God and on the part of God. That which the believer appropriates to himself on the proclamation of the gospel God promises and bestows on him in baptism. One can therefore speak of a sequential order only in part. For although baptism presupposes faith, the place of faith is not only prior to baptism, but in and after baptism as well. Baptism, however, according to its essence is once for all, because it marks the transition from the mode of existence of the old man to that of the new. Baptism is a rite of incorporation, and as such expresses the corporate communal character of the salvation given in Christ. For this reason faith is not without baptism, just as baptism is not without faith. For faith responds to the call of God through the gospel, and in baptism God takes the one thus called under his gracious rule and gives him a share in all the promises of the gospel. Therefore the pronouncements of 2 Corinthians 1:20ff., even though the formal denotation of baptism is uncertain here, can still apply to baptism materially. Because baptism is incorporation into Christ, God's promises that are yes in Christ are likewise yes in baptism, God establishes us in Christ by baptism, and baptism, in that it makes us participate in the sealing with the Spirit, itself has sealing power. This establishing and sealing and earnest-giving yes of God is the word that accompanies baptism as washing with water (Eph. 5:26). It is salvation by the washing of regeneration for everyone who with his mouth confesses Jesus as Lord and in his heart believes that God has raised him from the dead (Rom. 10:9;[57] Tit. 3:5).

A separate word ought still to be devoted in this context to the question as to whether the epistles of Paul offer support for *infant baptism*. In this connection very extensive discussions have long been carried on, but recently anew, as to the meaning of the somewhat obscure statement in 1 Corinthians 7:14. Here the unbelieving partner in a marriage is spoken of as sanctified in or by the believing partner. The question was whether, in a marriage in which one of the two partners had become a believer, the latter was obligated to leave the other, unbelieving, party. Paul denies this on the ground of the "sanctification" of the unbelieving through the believing party. The meaning is that the continuation of such a marriage is not objectionable as something taking place outside Christ. It is not the unbelief of the one, but the faith of the other that is determinative for the acceptability of the whole. "Sanctified" here implies being taken up into the relationship of life dedicated to God. Paul now appeals for this to the position of the children: "else were your children unclean; but now are they holy." All kinds of problems arise here: by "your children" is it the children of the mixed marriage who are intended, or the children who have gone over to Christianity

---

57. Cf. Bultmann, *Theology*, I, p. 312, according to whom it can hardly be open to question that Rom. 10:9 "is a reference to the confession made at baptism."

with their parents, or the children who were born after this conversion, or the children of believers in general? This last is usually adopted, although there are those who decide for one of the other possibilities. Can anything be inferred from "but now are they clean" with respect to baptism? It has been possible to ascertain that the concepts "unclean" and "holy" were also used for the children of proselytes born before and after the conversion of the parents to Judaism. The former were baptized as "unclean" (with the parents), the latter were not, as born in "holiness."[58] From correspondence with this usage some[59] have wished to conclude that in the earliest Christian church, too, children were only baptized on conversion of the parents, the children born afterwards were not.

But the question then arises as to what was done in the case of these children born later. Were they no longer required to be baptized at all? This, in view of the significance Paul attaches to baptism as means of salvation, is scarcely conceivable. But if they were baptized only later, after having made a confession of faith, were these children in the time between their birth and baptism (as adults) placed at a disadvantage as compared with the children born before conversion, a position that is most implausible? Although "unclean" and "holy" thus correspond to pre-Christian usage, one will hardly be able to draw conclusions from the pre-Christian baptismal practice (of proselytes). One may not forget that the baptism of proselytes was an additional ceremony (additional to circumcision), and thus not the real or only ritual of incorporation. The question remains whether one can conclude the baptism of all children from "but now are they holy." In view of the fact that in this same context it is also said of the unbelieving partner in the marriage that he is "sanctified," the qualification "holy" appears in itself too weak a basis for this conclusion. For the unbelieving marital partner was, though "sanctified," yet not baptized. In our opinion, it will have to be ascertained that in 1 Corinthians 7:14 baptism is not in view, and that solely on the ground of the terminology employed here one cannot reach conclusions that are at all dependable with respect to infant baptism. There is indeed an indication in the "holiness" of the children in 1 Corinthians 7:14, if one links this passage with the so-called "house" texts, from which it appears that on the conversion of believing parents their "household" was also baptized, that is to say, their family. From that it can be gathered that with children (otherwise than with the unbelieving husband or wife) this "holiness" also found expression in and in part rested on baptism. Paul speaks expressly of such a "household" baptism in 1 Corinthians 1:16 (cf. 16:15). This points clearly to infant baptism, therefore, and such can scarcely have remained confined to the children who were born while still "in heathenism" (see above). In accord with this Paul in his epistles addressed children as belonging to the church and to the Lord (Eph. 6:1; Col. 3:20). That the children "are holy" thus means that they, together with and belonging to their

---

58. See the materials in J. Jeremias, *Infant Baptism in the First Four Centuries,* ET 1960, p. 46.

59. Jeremias, *et al.*

parents, were incorporated into the church by baptism and in this way participated in the gifts of Christ and in the liberating rule of his Spirit. This does not of course mean that faith would for them be superfluous — such would presuppose a magical operation of baptism detached from God himself — but rather that the way of faith is more plainly opened for them and the obedience of faith more emphatically demanded of them. To be sure, the criterion or human "point of contact" for infant baptism, otherwise than in the case of adults, does not lie in the personal faith of the one baptized, but in the fact that the children belong to the parents and to the solidaric relationship represented by them. The "implantation"[60] takes place here on the ground of the bond that joins children to their parents, "natural" and "Christian," according to the rule of Romans 11:16. In view of the manner in which Paul and the whole of Scripture speak of this relationship between parents and children, one can quite rightly maintain[61] that the absence of an express mention of infant baptism in the New Testament is rather to be explained from its "self-evidentness" than from its not yet having come into existence. On the other hand, it is no less apparent that Paul's pronouncements on baptism presuppose faith confessed before baptism and do not start from a situation for which infant baptism is characteristic. This is not to say that they would no longer be applicable to such a situation; but that in order not to lose the correct view of the Pauline (and New Testament) doctrine of baptism one must maintain faith as a co-constituting factor of baptism.[62]

SECTION 66. THE REDEMPTIVE SIGNIFICANCE OF THE LORD'S SUPPER

Paul writes of the Lord's Supper in two passages in close proximity to each other, i.e., in 1 Corinthians 10:14-22 and 1 Corinthians 11:17-34. Both pericopes have a paraenetic significance and warn against abuses in Corinth. In 1 Corinthians 10 the Supper is introduced in connection with the freedom some permitted themselves of continuing to take part in heathen sacrificial meals. Paul declares this to be irreconcilable with the Lord's Supper and in so doing comes to a further explanation of what the Supper is. In 1 Corinthians 11 the occasion is even more direct: the Supper was celebrated with a shameful lack of a sense of Christian

---

60. The *symphytoi genesthai* of Rom. 6:5.
61. Cf. G. de Ru, *De kinderdoop*, pp. 258ff.
62. For the exegetical discussion on infant baptism, in addition to the literature mentioned above (n. 5), see the writings of O. Cullmann, *Baptism in the New Testament;* J. Jeremias, *Hat die Urkirche die Kindertaufe geübt?*, 2nd ed., 1949; P. H. Menoud, *Le baptême des enfants dans l'Église ancienne*, 1948; T. Preiss, "Die Kindertaufe und das Neue Testament," *TLZ*, 1948, pp. 651-660; J. Murray, *Christian Baptism*, 1952; J. Jeremias, *Infant Baptism in the First Four Centuries;* K. Aland, *Did the Early Church Baptize Infants?*, ET 1963; also the detailed discussion in Beasley-Murray, *Baptism in the New Testament*, pp. 306ff.; and now in particular G. de Ru, *De kinderdoop en het Nieuwe Testament*.

fellowship. Beforehand[63] (v. 21) everyone began to partake of his own meal, that is, of the food he had brought along himself, in the course of which the rich feasted on what they had with them and the less well supplied were left to look on. Whether this lack of solidarity was connected with a sacramentalistic conception, according to which all that mattered in the Supper was eating and drinking the elements, not the meal shared together,[64] can be left to the side. Paul calls these shameful abuses incompatible[65] with the Supper of the Lord and asks whether the Corinthians have no respect for the church. He then contrasts what took place in the congregation at Corinth with the Supper as it was intended and instituted by the Lord himself, as appears from the words of institution.

In view of the parallel train of thought in these two pericopes we wish to attempt to arrive at a synthetic treatment of the data presented in them. We take our point of departure in the words of institution recited by Paul in 1 Corinthians 11. The solemn traditional terminology he here employs not only indicates that he associates himself with an existing version of the words of institution, but also marks these words as authoritative apostolic tradition, and, as the words (received) "of the Lord" further deliberately accentuate, casts light on the revelational character[66] of this tradition. Likewise the words "in the night in which he was betrayed" are not to be taken as a mere historical reminiscence, but give to the content of the message the character of unimpeachable validity and sanctity.[67] The thus understood revelational character of the words of institution here recorded is confirmed by a comparison with the Synoptics. A detailed examination of the difference and agreement lies beyond the bounds of our design.[68] On the whole

---

63. Many think hereby of an *agape* meal accompanying the Supper proper, as is known from the post-apostolic period (Tertullian, *Apol.* 39). There is no unanimity here, however. On the relation of the *agape* meal and the Supper cf., e.g., B. Reicke, *Diakonie, Festfreude und Zelos*, 1951, pp. 32ff., 252ff.; see also *Bijbels Woordenboek* (Romen, Roermond, Maseik), 1954, *s.v. Agape*.

64. Cf. Schweizer, *RGG*, 3rd ed., I, 1957, col. 11, *s.v. Abendmahl*; G. Bornkamm, "Lord's Supper and Church in Paul," in *Early Christian Experience*, pp. 123ff.

65. *Ouk estin kyriakon deipnon phagein* (v. 20). Some translate: "it is not possible [in this way] to eat the supper of the Lord." Others: "[this] is not eating the supper of the Lord."

66. So Käsemann, too, "The Pauline Doctrine of the Lord's Supper," *Essays on New Testament Themes*, p. 120. For this terminology of the tradition (*parelabon* and *paredōka*) see also O. Cullmann, "The Tradition," in *The Early Church*, pp. 55-99, and my *The Authority of the New Testament Scriptures*, p. 19.

67. Cf. Käsemann, *ibid.*, p. 121.

68. The following elements we find only in the report transmitted by Paul: (a) the solemn introductory words: "the Lord Jesus in the night in which he was delivered up took bread," etc., to be taken not merely as chronological information, but (in view of the allusion to Isa. 53; cf. Rom. 4:25) as a liturgical expression of the redemptive significance of Christ's surrender; (b) the absolute: *to hyper hymōn* after *sōma;* the textual witnesses have added various participles (*klōmenon, thryptomenon, didomenon*) in order to escape the harsh construction — see, however, the version of Luke; (c) the word of the cup which, in place of "this is my blood" (of the covenant), runs: "this cup is the New Covenant in my blood"; (d) the double command to *anamnesis*. For comparative analyses of the reports of the

it can be determined that not only in the purport but also in the wording there is a great measure of agreement between Paul and the Synoptics, both so far as Mark (and Matthew) and particularly the longer text of Luke[69] are concerned. A closer examination of the contents leads us to the following viewpoints (whereby repeatedly 1 Corinthians 10:14ff. is also taken into consideration).

(a) The Lord's Supper as a sacrificial meal

In the detailed discussion that we have devoted elsewhere[70] to the words of institution in the Synoptics we reached the conclusion that the significance of these words and of the actions of Jesus accompanying them come to stand in the proper light only if one keeps clearly in view the peculiar character of the meal in the night in which Jesus was betrayed, that of a sacrificial meal. Not only does the whole ritual of the meal point to this, in which in many respects one can recognize that of the Passover meal, but it is in this way alone that the crucial words that speak of Jesus' body and blood can be understood in their proper significance. "Body" and "blood" do not speak generally of Jesus "himself" or of his "personality,"[71] but, as has been demonstrated in particular by Jeremias,[72] are to be taken as the terminology of sacrifice. They speak of the body of Christ given in death and of his blood shed sacrificially, as may appear from the fact that Christ's blood is related to the New Covenant, which recalls on the one hand the making of the covenant at Sinai, which was also accompanied with the shedding of sacrificial blood, and on the other hand the prophecy of the New Covenant in Jeremiah 31. In the framework of this sacrificial terminology the eating and drinking of Christ's body and blood now become perfectly clear. It is the eating and drinking of the sacrifice at the sacrificial meal. Christ does not appear at the Supper as the priest who offers his sacrifice to God, but as the Host who appropriates to his people the sacrifice that he would offer for them, or has offered for them. What is true in general of the sacrificial meal can thus be said in particular of the Supper: it cannot be viewed as a sacrificial act or as a continuation of the literal occurrence at the altar or sacrifice. Participation in the sacrificial meal is not an active participation in the sacrificial act, but the appropriation coming about through the meal of the sacrificial act by the eating and drinking of the *victima* (that which was sacrificed).[73]

That Paul intends the Supper to be understood to this effect is evident not only from the repetition of the words of institution and

---

Supper see the survey of E. Schweizer, *RGG*, 3rd ed., I, col. 12ff., and earlier in *TLZ*, 1954, col. 579ff.; cf. also H. Lessig, *Die Abendmahlsprobleme im Lichte der neutest. Forschung seit 1900*, 1953, pp. 52ff.

69. On this at greater length see my *The Coming of the Kingdom*, pp. 407ff.
70. *Ibid.*, pp. 406ff.
71. See also above, pp. 374ff.
72. J. Jeremias, *The Eucharistic Words of Jesus*, 3rd ed., pp. 222, 237.
73. So Sverre Aalen, "Das Abendmahl als Opfermahl im Neuen Testament," in [*CHARIS KAI SOPHIA*] (*Festschrift für K. H. Rengstorf*), 1964, pp. 128-152, especially p. 143.

the manner in which he does this (express reference to the night in which Jesus was "delivered up,"[74] the further modification of "this is my body" by the words "for you," and the direct connection he makes in vv. 26 and 27 between the bread and cup and "the death of the Lord"[75]), but also finds a very striking and convincing confirmation in the manner in which he appeals to the Supper in 1 Corinthians 10.[76] For here he sets the eating and drinking of the Supper over against participation in heathen sacrificial meals, and then, in verse 18, brings in by way of clarification the Jewish sacrificial meal as well ("behold Israel after the flesh," etc.). The fundamental idea is not only to show generally that one cannot at the same time have to do with idols or demons and with Christ, but very specifically this: that eating and drinking both at the one table and at the other is irreconcilable because they both are an eating of a sacrificial meal and thus signify fellowship with the demons and with the Lord, respectively.

Already in 10:6, where the apostle points to the warning example of Israel, specifically to their idolatry with the golden calf, he alludes particularly to the sacrificial meal held in connection with it: "the people sat down to eat and drink, and rose up to play." Already then the heathen sacrificial meal was the antithesis of eating and drinking the "spiritual food and the spiritual drink" (v. 4). The same thing is the case with the eating of what had been offered to idols in Corinth. Not as though an idol were anything. But certainly, because whoever sits down at an idolatrous sacrificial meal enters the domain of the demons. Paul terms this becoming (table) "companions of the demons" (koinōnous tōn daimoniōn ginesthei), just as in the same context he speaks of the "cup of demons" and "the table of demons" (provisioned with food from the altar) (vv. 20, 21). The meaning is that at the heathen sacrificial meal one sits at table with the demons, eats and drinks from the table where they are host,[77] and thus exposes himself to a more than human temptation.[78]

By way of elucidation Paul then points to the Jewish sacrificial meals: "Are not those who eat the sacrifices partners in the altar?"[79] The general idea here again is that he who partakes of the sacrificial meal

---

74. Cf. above, n. 68.

75. For this reason the idea that the terminological incongruence between the words of the bread and the cup involves a differing significance of bread and cup is to be rejected. According to some, that is, the first would give a share in the crucified, the second in the exalted Lord (so Käsemann, in Essays on New Testament Themes, pp. 130ff.); according to others (exactly the reverse!) the first ("this is my body") must be understood of the exalted ("this I am myself") and the second on the other hand has reference to the death of Christ (so Schweizer, RGG, 3rd ed., I, col. 14). All this is not only forced, but fails to appreciate the specific significance of the (sacrificial) terminology employed here.

76. The enduring merit of the article by Sverre Aalen is, in my opinion, to have demonstrated this with a profusion of comparative materials (especially from the Jewish world).

77. Cf. Aalen, [CHARIS KAI SOPHIA], p. 133.

78. Cf. above, pp. 303f.

79. The translation "altar" (thysiastērion, as the altar of the true God always in contrast with the heathen altar, bōmos) is established; cf., e.g., Behm, TDNT, III, p. 182.

enters into fellowship with God himself.[80] But the point here is the special way in which this takes place, namely, by eating that which has lain on the altar (cf. 1 Cor. 9:13; Matt. 23:19ff.), and in this way having fellowship with that which has occurred on the altar. The basis of the meal lies in the sacrifice; the sacrifice, because of its atoning character, opens the way for the eating and drinking with rejoicing of heart in the favor of God.[81] And this is represented by eating the offering of the altar.

In the light of all this no misunderstanding can remain with respect to the description of the Supper as "the communion in the blood and in the body of Christ." It is communion effected through the medium of the cup and bread with the sacrifice of Christ's body and blood given in death, just as those who in Israel ate the sacrifices had communion with the altar. It is eating and drinking, which presupposes this sacrifice, in the deliverance and joy Christ has obtained for his people. For this reason the Supper can be set over against the (table) "fellowship of the demons," and the "cup" and "table of the Lord" over against those of the demons. For at this table Christ is the Host who makes his people participants in his sacrifice. "Table of the Lord" unites both ideas, of sacrifice and of meal. The expression is reminiscent of Malachi 1:7, 12, where it has the meaning of altar. But here it denotes the place where one eats from the altar, that is to say, where participation in the redemptive significance of Christ's sacrifice of his life (body and blood) takes place.

In what has just been said an interpretation has been given in the most authentic fashion of the words of institution: "This is my body for you," and of the manner in which one is to conceive of the *praesentia realis* of Christ in the Supper. The "is" places the link with Christ's self-surrender in death in the bread and in the cup, connects the redemptive significance of his sacrifice to eating the bread and drinking from the cup. The reality of it is defined by the context in which bread and cup function here, namely, as the elements of the sacrificial meal, or, as Paul terms it in 1 Corinthians 10, of the table of the Lord. The gifts represent participation in the sacrifice, not in a magical operation detached from the Lord himself, but because he himself as the Lord of his table gives his table companions in the bread and wine a share in his body given up for them and in his blood shed for them. The bread and cup as communion in the body and blood of Christ are therefore not a means of salvation in the sense that they effect the presence of Christ, but, just the reverse, the presence of Christ as the Lord of his table, by means of bread and wine, effects communion with his body and blood, participation in his sacrifice. "Communion in the body and blood of Christ" means nothing other therefore than the participation of his people in Christ's death. Because this communion comes about at the table of the Lord, however, the Supper is not only a relation to what once has hap-

---

80. Cf., e.g., Groenewald: "in the sphere of divine power" ([KOINŌNIA] [Gemeenskap] by Paulus, 1932, pp. 115, 116); cf. also Hauck, TDNT, III, p. 805.
81. On this at length cf. Aalen, [CHARIS KAI SOPHIA], pp. 133-141.

pened and been accomplished for the church on the cross, but also an entering into communion with the living Lord. For this reason Paul warns those who would by taking part in the heathen sacrificial meal become (table) "companions of the demons." It would, as Paul puts it, be no less than provoking or defying the Lord (cf. Deut. 32:21), who makes the church his table companions and does not allow it to become at the same time table companions of the demons.

In view of the Supper understood in this way, i.e., as sacrificial meal, we are also to understand the warning in 1 Corinthians 11:27ff. against "unworthy" eating and drinking, being "guilty of the body and blood of the Lord," and "not discerning the body." Whether one chooses to take these expressions as specific "sacral-judicial terminology,"[82] or as qualifications bearing the stamp of Paul himself, it is again a matter of making oneself guilty of the body and blood of Christ as they are eaten and drunk, i.e., as they enable the church to participate at the table of the Lord in the sacrifice of Christ.[83]

(b) Spiritual food and drink

The manner in which in 1 Corinthians 10:1-3 the privilege and disobedience of ancient Israel in the wilderness are described from the perspective and with the terminology of the sacraments of the New Testament still deserves separate attention in this context. In discussing baptism we have already encountered this phenomenon ("baptized into Moses," etc.); here in treating the Lord's Supper verses 3 and 4 are especially to be pointed out: ". . . and all ate the same spiritual food and drank the same spiritual drink; for they drank of the spiritual rock that followed them; and the rock was Christ."

There is every reason to think that the words "spiritual food and drink" are borrowed from the terminology of the Supper. Not only does Paul in the preceding verse qualify the redemptive significance of the cloud and the sea as the "baptism" of old Israel, but, as we have seen, he also sets over against this eating and drinking of spiritual food and drink eating and drinking at the idolatrous sacrificial meal in the wilderness. He then says of all this that it has a typical significance (v. 11), and it serves him as the basis ("therefore, my beloved . . ." [v. 14]) for the contention that sitting down to the heathen sacrificial meal is not to be reconciled with the table of the Lord. The Old Testament situation is thus clearly intended to serve as a (warning) example to the New Testament, and in order to give as cogent expression to this as possible Paul describes the Old Testament gift in New Testament terminology.

If we assume with good reason therefore that "spiritual food and drink" is the terminology of the Supper[84] (whether already current

---

82. So Aalen, *ibid.*, pp. 143ff.; cf. G. Bornkamm, "On the Understanding of Worship," in *Early Christian Experience*, pp. 174ff.

83. See further below, Section 67.

84. Thus, e.g., Käsemann, *Essays on New Testament Themes*, pp. 113ff.; also Goppelt, *TDNT*, VI, p. 146, i.a., with a reference to Did. 10:3, where in relation

or coined in this manner by Paul), then so far as the Old Testament situation is concerned nothing more needs to be said than that this food and drink (the manna from heaven and water from the rock) bore a "spiritual," that is to say, a divine, miraculous character,[85] and one is under no necessity of having to attach to it the conclusion that according to Paul with the manna and water from the rock Israel received the gift of the Holy Spirit.[86] Yet the rock is thereby expressly called "Christ." What Israel was given to eat and to drink was not merely an incidental miraculous food and drink, but was taken up in the great context of the divine work of redemption in Christ. Considered in this light, the deliverance in Moses through the sea can be called Israel's baptism, and the feeding with manna and water from the rock, Israel's Supper, and the eating and drinking of spiritual food and drink, Christ (cf. John 6:31ff., 35, 51ff., where Jesus also calls himself the bread from heaven and further defines this as his flesh and blood, which are to be eaten and drunk).

Conversely, this redemptive-historical analogy also casts clear light on the New Testament Supper. As Israel was in Moses once led out of Egypt and further kept alive in the wilderness by God's miraculous power, so for the church not only does its once-for-all deliverance lie in Christ's death, but its continual food and drink as well. The Lord's Supper, as communion in the body and blood of Christ delivered up in death, is also spiritual food and drink. The sacrificial gift becomes sacrificial food, the receiving of bread and wine from the hand of the Lord, in liberation and rejoicing. Therefore this food and drink may also be called "spiritual," pneumatic, not only because it is from heaven, but because it makes us live out of Christ's self-surrender and thus imparts his Spirit (Rom. 5:5). The Supper is, also and precisely as sacrificial meal, a means of salvation with regard to all the gifts of Christ, and as spiritual food and drink (unlike baptism[87]) has a significance that is repeated again and again and accompanies the whole Christian life. There is every reason therefore to understand the pronouncement of 1 Corinthians 12:13b: "and were all made to drink of one Spirit," after the reference to baptism in verse 13a, of the Lord's Supper. However much the Supper is communion with the body and blood of the Lord, i.e., with his self-surrender on the cross, it also makes the church share in the gift of the Spirit of the exalted Lord. One cannot here separate the one from the other. For he who gave himself up for his own as an atoning sacrifice is also the Lord of his own table who in the communion of his body and blood declares himself to his church as the living Lord, that is to say, as the Lord who is the Spirit (2 Cor. 3:17).

---

to the Supper *pneumatikēn trophēn kai poton* is spoken of. Others repudiate this conception (e.g., Schweizer, *RGG*, I, col. 589; Grosheide, *1 Cor.*, p. 261).

85. Cf. Grosheide, *ibid.*, p. 261; Schweizer, *TDNT*, VI, p. 437 ("which comes directly from God's sphere and gives divine power").

86. Thus Käsemann, *Essays on New Testament Themes*, p. 113. On the other hand see Goppelt, *TDNT*, VI, p. 147, n. 17, and Schweizer, *TDNT*, VI, p. 437, n. 705.

87. See below, pp. 424f.

(c) The anamnesis

Further, the command to anamnesis in the words of institution: "this do in remembrance of me," stands in the closest relationship to the character of the Supper as a sacrificial meal. Others, to be sure, seek the background of this *anamnesis* in the like-named observance of the anniversaries of deaths in the Hellenistic world.[88] But in the first place, from a purely phenomenological point of view the *anamnesis* intended in the Supper is something different from and more than keeping in remembrance one deceased.[89] And so far as the terminology is concerned, there is much more to be said for a link with the element of *anamnesis* in the ritual of the Jewish feast days, especially in the Passover meal,[90] on the occasion of which after all the Supper was instituted.[91] The Lord's Supper is herewith qualified as a redemptive-historical commemorative meal. It is not a question here only of the commemoration of what has once taken place in the past, but no less of its abiding, actual redemptive significance. Christ's self-surrender is now, as hitherto the exodus of Israel out of Egypt, the new and definitive fact of redemption which in the eating of the bread and in the drinking of the wine the church may accept as such again and again[92] from the hand of God.[93]

---

88. For the materials see, e.g., Lietzmann, *Cor.*, p. 273; Jeremias, *The Eucharistic Words of Jesus*, 2nd ed., pp. 159f. (3rd ed., pp. 238ff.); B. Reicke, *Diakonie*, pp. 257ff.

89. Cf. Käsemann as well (*Essays on New Testament Themes*, pp. 120f.); and Schweizer, *RGG*, 3rd ed., I, col. 10. If one seeks the origin of this qualification in the Hellenistic remembrance of the dead, he must also question the genuineness of the *anamnesis* command as spoken by Jesus himself. The arguments of B. Reicke for nevertheless ascribing it to Jesus are not convincing. On the other hand, the fact that Paul relates the *anamnesis* specifically to the death of Christ (v. 26) need not argue in favor of this conception, as Reicke apparently supposes (*ibid.*, p. 257). This finds sufficient explanation in the repeated mention of his body and blood (see above).

90. Cf. Jeremias, *The Eucharistic Words of Jesus*, 2nd ed., p. 161 (3rd ed., pp. 244ff.); cf. also Douglas Jones, "[*Anamnēsis*] in the N.T.," *The Journal of Theological Studies*, VI, 1955, pp. 188f. The latter also points to the correspondence between *katangellete* and *higgid*: "the recitation of the death of Jesus as act of redemption corresponding exactly to the recitation of the Exodus in the Passover Haggada" (p. 189); the same idea is found in W. D. Davies, *Paul and Rabbinic Judaism*, 2nd ed., 1955, p. 252.

91. See my *The Coming of the Kingdom*, Section 41, pp. 418-432.

92. That from *hosakis ean pinēte* (v. 25) one could infer that wine was not always used in the Supper and *hosakis* would therefore be an indication of the celebration with bread alone (cf. Jeremias, *The Eucharistic Words of Jesus*, 2nd ed., p. 29, n. 1; 3rd ed., p. 52, n. 3, following Schlatter), is foiled already by the repetition of *hosakis* in v. 26, where it goes as well with *esthiēte* as with *pinēte*.

93. That it is not the congregation but God who is thought of here as the subject of the *anamnesis* ("that God may remember me ... by bringing the consummation to pass"), as Jeremias wishes (*ibid.*, 2nd ed., pp. 163, 165; 3rd ed., pp. 252, 254), seems unacceptable in this context in which everything speaks of the redemptive significance of the Supper for the church (cf. also Exod. 12:14; 13:9; Deut. 16:3; Ps. 111:4; Jub. 49:15). Against this view see Douglas Jones, in *The Journal of Theological Studies*, VI, p. 190, and W. C. van Unnik, "Kanttekeningen bij een nieuwe verklaring van de Anamnese-woorden," *Nederl. Theol. Tijdschr.*, 1950, p. 6.

For the development of the *anamnesis* element in such early church writers

How this *anamnesis* is otherwise intended to be understood may appear further from verse 26: "as often as you eat this bread . . . you proclaim the Lord's death till he come." This verse no longer pertains to the Supper tradition, but serves to confirm the foregoing admonition.[94] In accordance with the command to *anamnesis* the eating and drinking at the Supper take their start from the death of Christ, and the Corinthians are to remain conscious of this. Hence the indicative: you proclaim. By these words the character of the *anamnesis* is further described.[95] It is not merely a subjective recalling to mind, but an active manifestation of the continuing and actual significance of the death of Christ. "Proclaim" in this respect has a prophetic, declaratory significance. As often as the church observes the Supper, the preaching[96] of the redemptive significance of Christ's death goes out from it. And this proclamatory character of the Supper has an abiding significance; it is a proclamation "till he come." As it was instituted by Christ in the night in which he was delivered up, so it retains its power until his appearing in glory. It is a matter here not simply of the *termini a quo* and *ad quem* as chronological data, but of the redemptive character of the Supper that commenced with his death and obtains till his return. It spans the time between the great redemptive times, it is the connecting link between the last supper of Jesus and the glorified eating and drinking in the kingdom of God (Mark 14:25; Matt. 26:29; Luke 22:16). It characterizes not only the Supper, but also the time in which it is to be celebrated and the place of the congregation in it. Everything is directed not only toward the past, but also toward the future. It is the proclamation that in the death of Christ the new and eternal covenant of grace has taken effect, if still in a provisional and not yet consummated sense. It is that

---

as Hippolytus and Justin see, e.g., N. A. Dahl, "Anamnesis," *Studia Theologica,* I, 1958, p. 83, which development may not, however, be projected back into the Pauline texts. Dahl describes the *anamnesis* as "a commemoration . . . of the death of Jesus and of his resurrection, when the history of salvation becomes present anew by the sacramental commemoration" (*ibid.,* p. 83). Much depends on how one chooses to understand this "becoming present anew."

94. This is at least the most probable; cf., e.g., Grosheide, *1 Cor.,* p. 311.

95. One will therefore not have to see two distinct facets in the Supper in *anamnēsis* and *katangellein.* Rather, the *anamnēsis* consists in the *katangellein.* It is apparent from this, too, that analogy with the Hellenistic meals in remembrance of the deceased is fundamentally lacking; cf. also Lessig, *Abendmahlsprobleme,* p. 224.

96. There is a difference of opinion whether by this proclamation is meant the "actual act," the *drōmenon* of eating and drinking (so, e.g., Lietzmann), or specifically the accompanying, explanatory word (so, e.g., Schniewind, *TDNT,* I, p. 72). The latter is then related to the recitation of the Passover Haggadah during the Passover meal; cf. also Käsemann, *Essays on New Testament Themes,* pp. 120f., and Jones, in *The Journal of Theological Studies,* pp. 188f. In our view the one need not exclude the other. While *katangellete* makes one think of a proclamation with words, the sentence structure of v. 26, as well as the repeated *touto poieite* in vv. 24 and 25, certainly appears to include eating and drinking in the proclamation. The later development that increasingly made a drama of the Supper, in which the sacrifice of Christ on the cross was purportedly repeated in the actions with bread and wine or *in mysterio* was realized anew in the present (cf. also Lessig, *Abendmahlsprobleme,* p. 226), finds no support in the conception of *katangellein* mentioned above and conversely cannot be urged as an objection against it.

consummation toward which on the ground of Christ's death the church is reaching out and which in every observance of the Supper is, as it were, drawn nearer, because the certainty of that consummation has been given to the church in the death of the Lord.

(d) The Lord's Supper and the church

A separate aspect of the redemptive significance of the Lord's Supper — regarded by some[97] as the most typical of the Pauline doctrine of the Supper — is the close relationship established by Paul between the Supper and the church. In particular the remarkable transition in 1 Corinthians 10:16, 17 is pointed out, where the words "the bread which we break, is it not the communion with the body of Christ?" are followed by: ". . . because there is one bread, we who are many are one body; for we all partake of the one bread."

In the preceding chapter[98] we have already mentioned the, in our opinion, inadmissible identification of the church as the body of Christ with the body of Christ presented in the Supper. What function this pronouncement has in the course of the argument of 1 Corinthians 10:14ff. was also discussed there. In this context we have to pay heed particularly to the positive side of the matter, namely, to the close relationship that Paul establishes between the Supper and the church as the body of Christ, and then especially between the unity of the two.

In the whole Pauline (and New Testament!) doctrine of the Lord's Supper the general relationship between the Supper and the church is not something unusual, but rather is self-evident. The abuses surrounding the Supper in Corinth are therefore termed not only making oneself guilty of the body and blood of the Lord (1 Cor. 11:27), but also despising the church (v. 22). And what is more, the cup is called "the New Covenant in my blood." As in the making of the covenant at Sinai the shedding of blood was of foundational significance (Exod. 24:8), so the new relationship between God and his people, promised in prophecy, rests on the sacrifice of Christ in which the church receives a share in the Supper. In the Supper, therefore, the foundations of the church are laid bare. The Supper is no personal affair between the individual believer and Christ. It is the covenant meal, the congregational meal *par excellence*. And it points to the sacrifice made by Christ, the reconciliation that has taken place in his blood, as the only ground of this communion between God and his people and of the unity of the church. Only in the eating of the body thus understood and in the drinking of this cup representing the reconciling power of his blood is the church one. In that sense, therefore, the Supper is the foundation and criterion for the unity of the church as the new people of God.

When in the words of 1 Corinthians 10 quoted above Paul infers the unity of the church as the body of Christ from partaking of the one

---

97. See, e.g., G. Bornkamm, "Lord's Supper and Church in Paul," in *Early Christian Experience*, pp. 123ff.; Käsemann, *Essays on New Testament Themes*, p. 110.

98. See above, pp. 373ff.

bread, it is fundamentally the same matter. The apostle undoubtedly expresses himself here in a way that is characteristic for him, and his special conception of the unity of "the many" in the one underlies the wording "we who are many are one body." But the bond and along with it the ground of this unity are here indicated in the Supper. This bond does not lie in the fact that the church in a mysterious fashion eats the physical body of Christ or receives a share in his divine-human nature and thus itself becomes this body of Christ.[99] It is the partaking of the one bread, in the one gift and blessing of the meal, that constitutes the unity.[100] That means here partaking of the offering, communion in the body of Christ delivered up to death. That this unity of the body does not only or first come into being in the Supper is, from all that we have already discussed with respect to baptism as the rite of incorporation, perfectly clear.[101] But in the common eating of the bread the unity of "the many" in Christ is constituted, manifested, and experienced anew again and again, a unity that binds the diversity together within the one body, which keeps the "strong" and the "weak" together, and which is exclusive with respect to those who unite themselves about the idols. The continued observance of the Supper is the incomparable means for bringing the unity of spiritual Israel and of the body of Christ to revelation in its deepest and only ground: communion in the body and blood of Christ. It contains within it at the same time the imperative criterion for safeguarding the church, as in Corinth, against every alien and false unity.

(e) The Lord's Supper and baptism

All this brings us to the question as to the relationship of the Lord's Supper and baptism as means of salvation. How closely these two are linked together and what an entirely unique significance they have as means of salvation is evident from the manner in which Paul again and again occupies himself with them both in the same context of thought (1 Cor. 10:2, 3; 12:13), but especially from the specific significance he ascribes to both within the framework of his conception of the church as the body of Christ. With all their fundamental unity, however, the modal distinction emerges.

Both of them, baptism and the Lord's Supper, according to the nature of the means of salvation concomitant with preaching,[102] establish contact with the death of Christ — baptism as baptism-into-his death, the Supper as communion with the body and blood of Christ. As such the unity of the church as the body of Christ attaches to both, baptism as entrance to and incorporation into the body, the Supper as the unity of the body repeatedly received and manifested afresh in eating one bread. Implicit in this are the distinct functions baptism and the Lord's

---

99. See above, Section 60.
100. Cf. Jeremias, *The Eucharistic Words of Jesus*, 2nd ed., pp. 153f. (3rd ed., p. 232).
101. See above, Section 64, under c.
102. Cf. above, pp. 409ff.

Supper have as means of salvation, likewise with respect to the body of Christ. Baptism incorporates, represents the transition from "dead to sin" to "alive to God" (Rom. 6:11), and from the old to the new man; it is therefore once-for-all as the incorporating means of salvation and is not capable of repetition. The Supper is the continuing proclamation of the redemptive significance of Christ's death; it is spiritual food and spiritual drink for the time between the times, as manna and water from the rock after the exodus out of Egypt and before the entrance into Canaan; in its constant repetition it spans life in the present world, until he come. It represents both the "already" and the "not yet"; it is already celebrated as the fulfilled sacrificial meal of the New Testament with bread and wine, but is yet to be celebrated both in remembrance and in expectation, in unceasing care for abiding in the fellowship of Christ, for the holiness of God's people, and the eschewing of idols (1 Cor. 10:14). Baptism, therefore, opens up the way along which the church is to go with the Supper; incorporates into the communion that the church may celebrate in the Supper, as the communion of the New Covenant, of the body of Christ, under the dominion of his Spirit. But both have the same root, proclaim the same death, and enable participation in its redemptive significance. For this reason they also demand the same faith, the same "discerning of the body." Paul speaks of the latter in particular with respect to the Lord's Supper because in it the genuineness of the transition once effected by baptism must be confirmed and authenticated.

SECTION 67. THE CRITICAL SIGNIFICANCE OF THE LORD'S SUPPER. SELF-EXAMINATION

The paraenetic purport of both pericopes in 1 Corinthians in which Paul speaks of the Lord's Supper involves the fact that along with the redemptive content of the Supper its critical significance is emphatically brought to the fore. This also takes place — it would be difficult to anticipate anything else in the same epistle to the same congregation — in both these pericopes in a manner that is in many respects the same, so that we are again able to combine the discussion. Once more we begin with the pericope of 1 Corinthians 11 as the more directly concerned with the observance of the Supper.

After having indicated the significance of the Lord's Supper according to the institution of Christ in the manner described above, Paul concludes that everyone who eats the bread and drinks the cup of the Lord in an "unworthy" manner will stand guilty of the body and blood of the Lord. The word "unworthy" here can scarcely reproduce the meaning. For every idea as though by merit or legal claim one would have to or were able to make himself "worthy" of eating the bread is to be excluded. The thought is rather that of inadequate, inappropriate eating and drinking, in a manner that is unsuited to it and not in harmony with it. It is a question of respect for the true character of what is here called the bread and cup of the Lord, i.e., the sanctity of his table fellowship (cf. 1 Cor. 10:21). In verse 29 this is expressed in a slightly different way, as "not discerning the body," that is to say, not recognizing the offering in its separatedness and sanctity and not recognizing the sacrifice of Christ itself.[103] Whether or not one chooses to see in these words a reflection of sacral legal terminology against desecration (and chooses to connect the punishment mentioned in v. 30 with the rooting out of the people[104]), it is apparent here again how close the connection is between the bread and cup on the one hand and the body and blood of the Lord on the other. This relationship does not rest — we may now say: of course — on the physical constitution of the elements of the Supper, but arises from the nature of the fellowship of the Supper as a sacrificial meal. Thereby the elements are the bread and cup of the Lord, i.e., by virtue of his institution and the living relationship in which Christ as Lord of his table stands to his own gifts. Whoever does not respect the sanctity of this table fellowship, therefore, will be guilty of Christ's body and blood, that is to say, sin against the sacrifice made by him (cf. Heb. 10:29; 6:6).[105] For this reason also he[106] eats and drinks judgment to himself; for by eating and drinking he enters into the holy presence of him whose self-surrender in death he evidently does not respect and who is not only the Savior, but also the judging *Kyrios* (cf. vv. 31, 32). However much everything is concentrated on bread and cup, body and blood, this does not mean that it is only a question of things and material relationships. He who enters into communion with the thing also enters into communion with the person. For the Crucified One is the Living One, and he who at the table of the Lord does not respect the sacrifice of the Crucified falls under the judgment of the exalted Lord. We have to do here with the same thought that we have already met above[107] in 1 Corinthians 10, that communion with the body and blood of the Lord means that one enters into Christ's holy sphere of life and power and that whoever therefore wishes to combine the table of the Lord with the table of the demons may wonder whether he does not wish to defy the Lord and fancy himself stronger than he.

Thus the use of the Supper in no way automatically communicates

---

103. Here again some wish by "the body" to understand the church; so, e.g., B. Reicke, *Diakonie*, pp. 253, 254; Lietzmann-Kümmel, *Cor.*, p. 186; H. M. Matter, *De kerk als Lichaam van Christus*, 1962, p. 29. But in view of the foregoing "body and blood" (v. 27), and considering the whole terminology oriented as it is to the sacrificial meal, this is highly improbable.

104. Cf. Aalen, [*CHARIS KAI SOPHIA*], pp. 144ff.

105. For this and other parallels see C. F. D. Moule, "The Judgement Theme in the Sacraments," in *The Background of the N.T. (Studies in Honour of C. H. Dodd)*, p. 471.

106. Käsemann incorrectly posits (*Essays on New Testament Themes*, pp. 126ff.) that *krima heauto esthiei* must be applied to every communicant, because everyone has to do with the judgment of the Judge of the world present in the Lord's Supper. But it is a question here only of those who "do not discern the body." The absence of *anaxiōs* in v. 29 in the best mss. says little because the whole sentence is determined by *mē diakrinōn to sōma*; against the view of Käsemann cf. Kümmel in Lietzmann-Kümmel, *Cor.*, p. 186, and Schweizer, *TLZ*, 1954, col. 589, n. 81.

107. See p. 417.

the salvation given in Christ and the gift of the Holy Spirit to the members of the church,[108] and on the other side it is not vain or empty for those who partake of it in an apostate or "unworthy" manner. The fate of Israel in the wilderness, although they were all baptized into Moses and all received the same spiritual food and drink, is a (warning) example for the one as well as for the other. The origin of this judging power of the Supper does not, however, inhere in a magical or spiritual "potency" of the elements of bread and wine. There is no other gift in the sacrament than from the hand of the Giver, nor are the elements in themselves either for blessing or for judgment. But it is the living presence of Christ, in accordance with the arrangement established in his own words of institution, which in the elements effects communion with the sacrifice once made by him and which can transform the gift in the Supper into a judgment, and the blessing into a curse.

This does not mean, of course, that the nature and content of the sacrament are twofold, and that salvation and judgment both pertain to it in an equally essential way. The *manducatio indignorum* and the judgment to which they expose themselves do not abrogate the gracious character of the sacrament. The rock Christ, the sacrificial meal of ancient Israel, the Supper of the Lord, are in their essence and intent not to be understood otherwise than on the basis of the saving activity of God in Christ, and without this last they would not be. For this reason there is also differentiation in the judgment one can eat to himself in the Lord's Supper. Its purpose is not always nor immediately to condemnation. Paul points to the judgment of Christ within the congregation of Corinth in the great number of cases of sickness and death that had occurred in it (v. 30). These, however, do not serve to condemnation with the world, but are intended precisely to warn against it (v. 32). They serve now as the gracious pedagogy *(paideuometha;* 1 Cor. 11:32) of God who does not will to wreck the church, but to bring it back again from the wrong pathway. Here again blessing and curse are not automatically given with the elements nor are both joined to them in an equally essential way, but it is the living Lord himself who, also in the food and drink of his table, deals with the church according to his gracious and righteous redemptive will.

The conclusion for the church is that everyone should examine himself and so (that is, after having examined himself) eat of the bread and drink of the cup (1 Cor. 11:28). The purport of this self-examination is further elucidated by the play on words in verse 31 (cf. v. 29): "if we, however, rightly judged ourselves,[109] we should not be judged." It is a question

---

108. To what extent such a conception of the Supper as an automatic means of salvation of indefectible power was prevalent (as supposed by Käsemann, for example, who here recalls the *pharmakon athanasias* [*Essays on New Testament Themes*, pp. 116f.; cf. Bornkamm, *loc. cit.*]) is difficult to decide for lack of clear data.

109. *Diekrinōmen*, the same word as in v. 29; in v. 31 it has the sense of a critical self-examination and has reference to (one's own) imperfection; in v. 29

here of self-examination before one eats and drinks. The intention is not that everyone institute an inquiry as to whether he will in fact eat and drink, but that he not do so before having examined himself. It is an examination that is to prevent "unworthy" eating and drinking, and is to clear away that which impedes the observance of the Supper. It is, in other words, an examination that is to lead to right eating and drinking: "but let a man examine himself, and so let him eat. . . ." The same thing is to be found in verse 31. Here, too, the apostle does not warn against the Supper itself, but against a lack of self-criticism in partaking of it. To discern the body of Christ, that is to say, to recognize it in its holy and saving significance, also means to discern oneself, that is, to make oneself pass through the judgment and criticism that are in conformity with the holiness of Christ's body. We are not to think here of a self-appraisal that even in the slightest degree would darken the gracious character of that which is given in the Supper, but rather of such a self-scrutiny as does full justice to the divine and holy character of this grace.

The conclusion with which Paul closes this pericope in verses 33 and 34 is accordingly not negative, but positive, that is, it does not keep back the church from the Lord's Supper, but stirs it up to the observance of the Supper as commanded by Christ and worthy of God.

---

it signifies: to appreciate rightly, to judge according to its unique significance, and has reference to the holiness (of Christ's body).

XI

THE UPBUILDING OF THE CHURCH

SECTION 68. THE CHURCH AS EDIFICE

In addition to what has been treated in the foregoing chapters concerning the nature of the New Testament church, the epistles of Paul also contain a great deal concerning the practice and the organization of the church. One can perhaps best gather this up in the concept occurring so frequently in Paul of the upbuilding of the church. Its presupposition is on the one hand that the New Testament church did not immediately reach its final goal and perfection; on the other hand that therein it is the abiding object of God's care over it and has itself been called to progress, extension, consolidation, in a word, to its own self-upbuilding. Another concept that runs parallel to this and could be employed for the same thing is that of the growth or increase of the church. Both conceptions, as we shall see still further, have always been closely coupled together, both have a clear redemptive-historical background, and each represents a viewpoint of its own. The figure of upbuilding predominates, however, so that we take our point of departure in it.

The idea of upbuilding rests on the concept often occurring in the New Testament of the church as the "house," the "temple," the "building" of God, as does that of growth on the representation of the church as "planting," "field," etc. Just as "body of Christ," they constitute a further definition of the church as the people of God and make us see that one may not grant one of the several "images" of the church an exclusive significance and absolutize it at the expense of the others.

What first of all concerns the representation of the church as "house," "temple," or "building" is its broad Old Testament basis. This has already been demonstrated frequently.[1] Applied to the true eschatological Israel, this imagery had its point of departure primarily in the prophetic promise of the gracious restoration of the people who had been given up to exile, of the reconstruction of their devastated houses and walls, of their cities and temple.[2] The concept upbuilding thus becomes a symbol of the gracious dealings of God with the remnant of his people, and is found in this sense in later Judaism's expectation for

---

1. Cf., e.g., Michel, *TDNT*, V, pp. 120f.; and the monographs on this idea by P. Vielhauer, *Oikodome, Das Bild vom Bau in der christlichen Literatur vom Neuen Testament bis Clemens Alexandrinus*, 1940; P. Bonnard, *Jésus-Christ édifiant son Église*, 1948; J. Pfammatter, *Die Kirche als Bau. Eine exegetisch-theologische Studie zur Ekklesiologie der Paulusbriefe*, 1960; J. H. Roberts, *Die Opbou van die Kerk volgens die Efese-brief*, 1963.
2. Cf. Roberts, *ibid.*, pp. 22ff.

the future.[3] In this redemptive-historical and eschatological sense it is applied in the whole of the New Testament and especially in Paul to the Christian church as well.

In doing so the church can be represented both in general as a building, and in particular as the temple of God. The place of the Old Testament temple and worship is taken, according to 1 Peter 2:5, by "the spiritual house," into which the church is built as "living stones." The same thought underlies Paul's qualification of the church as the temple of God (1 Cor. 3:16, 17; 2 Cor. 6:16; Eph. 2:21), just as he speaks of the new life as the spiritual worship in which believers are to dedicate themselves to God as a living sacrifice (Rom. 12:1; cf. 15:16).

Closely bound up with this is the thought of the indwelling of God, and this also sheds light on the nature of the church. Here, too, the Old Testament background of the dwelling of God among his people in his temple is plain (cf. 2 Cor. 6:16). Now this dwelling is further described as an indwelling of the Spirit of God, who is at the same time the Spirit of Christ (Rom. 8:9-11; 1 Cor. 3:16; Eph. 2:21; 2 Tim. 1:14). The order of ideas is again that by belonging to Christ the church is the temple of God in which the Spirit of Christ dwells, which can also be described therefore as the dwelling of Christ in their hearts (Eph. 3:17; cf. Rom. 8:10).

Along with that — perhaps in close connection with it — the idea of the divine "house" or "building" recurs again and again — however, without direct allusion to the temple. The church is God's building (1 Cor. 3:9), the house of God, the pillar and bulwark of the truth (1 Tim. 3:15); believers are members of the household of God (Eph. 2:19; cf. Gal. 6:10); and the apostles and elders are God's stewards (1 Cor. 4:1; Tit. 1:7; Eph. 3:2; Col. 1:25; 1 Tim. 1:4ff.). In harmony with this we find in Paul a whole series of figures and expressions that are borrowed from the building of a house, whereby the conception is not always the same. In 1 Corinthians 3:10 Paul calls himself the architect who lays the foundation on which others go on to build (cf. Rom. 15:20). In the same context Christ is called the foundation (1 Cor. 3:11; cf. Col. 2:7), and there is mention of the differing quality of the structure erected on it ("gold," "silver," etc.), whereby it is evidently not the church itself but the labor bestowed on it by later preachers or office-bearers that is thought of. Elsewhere the apostles and prophets are called the foundation (Eph. 2:20), and the church itself, especially in the paraenetic sections, is represented as the subject of the upbuilding (e.g., Eph. 4:16). This last idea finds application in various connections and from a great many points of view, and is among the most typical features of Paul's preaching (see below). The most inclusive "building terminology" that is applied to the church is found in Ephesians 2:19-22. It is said here of the gentile Christians that they are no longer strangers and sojourners, but fellow-citizens and members of the household of God. Here the idea of the church as the house of God is closely bound up therefore with the

---

3. Clear light is shed on this point in the Qumran writings; cf. especially Pfammatter, *Die Kirche als Bau*, pp. 155ff.

spiritual citizenship of the true Israel, the redemptive-historical people of God (cf. v. 12). This house is now entirely determined by Christ and his work of redemption. It has its foundation in the apostles and prophets designated by him to that end; Christ himself is its supporting ground, the cornerstone[4] of the whole building (cf. Isa. 28:16 [LXX]; Ps. 118:22). In him — thus Ephesians 2:21 — the whole structure,[5] fitly joined together, grows into a holy temple in the Lord, and in him the gentiles, too, are built up together into a habitation of God in the Spirit. Thereby belonging to the building also becomes a dynamic thing. The temple is the point of departure, but also the goal. Everyone who is in Christ is built up together in this building in order thus to belong to the house in which God will dwell with his Spirit.[6]

All this may enable us to see as well how closely connected are the conceptions of the church as the body of Christ and as the house or dwelling of God. The imagery sometimes flows together.[7] The same words that express the inner coherence of the body of Christ also apply to the consolidation of the house of God (cf. Eph. 4:16 and 2:21). It is said of the house of God that it *grows up,* as a living organism (Eph. 2:21), and of the body that it is *built,* as a house (Eph. 4:12, 16). A third idea blended together with these is that of the church as the planting of God. Already in the Old Testament "to build" and "to plant" go together (respectively, "to pull down" and "to pluck out") (cf. Jer. 24:6). The New Testament church, too, is at the same time God's field and God's building (1 Cor. 3:9); and "planting" and "watering," just as laying the foundation and building, are the labors of the apostles and their fellow-workers (1 Cor. 3:6ff.). Thus receiving a share in the privileges of the people of God can be called being grafted into the olive tree (Rom. 11:17ff.). To be incorporated into the church is therefore "to be rooted" in Christ, which again is a synonym of "to be grounded" and requires further "upbuilding" (Eph. 3:17; Col. 2:7). These figures and representations are mingled together in all sorts of ways, so that one may even ask whether the growth of the church as building and body is oriented to the idea of the body or to that of planting (cf. 1 Cor. 3:6; 2 Cor. 9:10

---

4. *Akrogōniaios,* following Jeremias, *Angelos,* I, 1925, pp. 65-70; *ZNW,* 1930, pp. 264-280; *TDNT,* I, pp. 792f., is taken as "keystone" by many recent exegetes. There are also serious objections against this translation, however, so that in our view the old translation still has much to be said for it; cf., e.g., Percy, *Probleme,* pp. 328-332, 485-488. See the detailed discussion in Roberts, *Die Opbou,* pp. 61ff.

5. *Pasa oikodomē* (some mss. insert *hē* after *pasa*) is usually taken as: all that is built. There are also important arguments, however, for the translation "the whole building"; cf. Hanson, *The Unity of the Church in the New Testament,* 1946, p. 132; Dibelius, *Col., in loc.;* see also Bl.-Debr., Par. 275, 3; Roberts, *Die Opbou,* pp. 167ff.

6. *En pneumati* in v. 22 gives a further definition of *katoikētērion.* The thought is that of 1 Pet. 2:5: *oikos pneumatikos;* cf. 1 Cor. 12:13.

7. Some accordingly wish to assume gnostic influences in relation to *oikodomē* in Eph.; cf. e.g., Vielhauer, *Oikodome,* pp. 141ff.; Käsemann, *Leib Christi,* pp. 171ff.; Michel, *TDNT,* V, pp. 145f.; Schlier, *Christus und die Kirche,* 1930, pp. 57ff.; but see also Percy, *Probleme,* p. 329; Hanson, *The Unity of the Church,* pp. 129ff.

with Eph. 4:15, 16; Col. 2:19). It is also said of believers themselves that they grow up, increase in the knowledge of God (Col. 1:10; cf. 2 Cor. 10:15). It is evident from all this therefore how much for Paul the conception originating in the Old Testament of the church as the people of God, house of God, temple of God, and planting of God has become thoroughly bound up with the idea characteristic of his own world of thought of the church as the body of Christ, so that what holds for the one can also be said of the other, and what is to occupy us still further in Paul's preaching concerning the church we can treat as a unity.

In summary[8] the following can be said of the building up of the church as Paul speaks of it in his epistles:

(a) In accordance with the redemptive-historical character of the church this upbuilding must be seen first of all as the continuing work of God with his people (Rom. 14:19, 20), whose temple and dwelling place it is. This continuing and consummating work consists both in the bringing in of those who till now have been without (cf. Rom. 15:20ff.) and in the inner strengthening and perfecting of all who in Christ now belong to it (1 Cor. 14:3; 1 Thess. 5:11, et al.).

(b) This upbuilding takes place on Christ the foundation once laid (1 Cor. 3:10, 11), and the apostles and prophets ordained by him to that end (Eph. 2:20, 21; cf. Rom. 15:20). It accordingly bears the character of a continuing confirmation and consolidation on this foundation (Col. 2:7), by which the church receives a character of its own, comes more and more to adulthood, and is safeguarded and cleansed from all alien powers and doctrine that darken its character and throw it into confusion (cf. Eph. 4:12-14; Col. 2:6-8).

(c) For the sake of this upbuilding God equips the church with all sorts of gifts and powers that he places at its disposal, as also with various kinds of ministries that must further its upbuilding (Eph. 4:11ff.; 2 Cor. 10:8; 13:10; cf. Rom. 12:3, 6ff.; 1 Cor. 12:4ff., 28ff.). In particular the gathering of the church serves this upbuilding (1 Cor. 14:26); it is most closely bound up with the proclamation of the Word of God (1 Cor. 14:3; Rom. 15:20), and is directed toward the right corporate manifestation of the church in the world.

(d) The apostle devotes particular attention as well to the mutual upbuilding of the church, whereby it is primarily a question of the right relationship of community and individual, of the induction of the individual into and his functioning in the whole, but whereby each one is ever to place the good of the church above his own preference and ability (cf. 1 Cor. 8:1; Rom. 14:15, 19; 12:3ff.).

Several of these general aspects merit further consideration.

SECTION 69. EXTENSIVE AND INTENSIVE UPBUILDING

The nature of the upbuilding thus described, as the continuing and con-

---

8. On this see further G. Friedrich, "Erbauung," RGG, II, 3rd ed., col. 538.

summating redemptive work of God with his church, is such that both the increase and the inner consolidation of the church pertain to it; one could speak of the enlargement and preservation, of the extensive-missionary and the intensive-confirmatory element of this upbuilding, which in the work of God are one.

That the extensive-missionary point of view, which is so closely bound up with the redemptive-historical background of the divine building, is frequently present in the New Testament concept of upbuilding,[9] appears a single time from the Pauline usage as well (Rom. 15:20). The extension and progress of the church, in a qualitative as well as in a geographical sense, is in his train of thought among the essential characteristics and conditions of the Christian church in the time between Christ's ascension and future appearing. All his own missionary work, which drove him on from one place to another, from Jerusalem to Illyria and from Illyria to Rome and Spain (Rom. 15:19ff.), is the proof of it. Accordingly he sees the progress of the church in the world in the same way: as the result of the gospel that in the whole world is bearing fruit and increasing (Col. 1:6; cf. v. 23).[10] Beyond this one cannot speak of a completed missionary "theology" in Paul. The key motif of his missionary thought is the breakthrough of the proclamation of the gospel to all the nations (Rom. 1:16; 3:22ff.; 15:9ff.); with that the catholicity of the church has been given in principle (Gal. 3:28; Col. 3:11; 1 Cor. 12:13); there are no spatial boundaries set to the proclamation of the gospel and to the church; everything works toward the *pleroma,* the full number intended by God both of Jews and gentiles (Rom. 11:12, 25), a perspective with which for Paul also the end of history coincides (Rom. 11:25, 26).

This grand vision of the world-encompassing significance of the gospel and of the expansion of the church causes him furthermore to involve the church that has already been brought to salvation in this missionary work in a great many ways, and to awaken the church itself to a missionary attitude.[11] The church enters into it, and rejoices when people elsewhere come to conversion (1 Thess. 1:9; 2 Thess. 1:4). Its intercession for Paul and his missionary labor is repeatedly requested (2 Thess. 3:1; Eph. 6:18; Col. 4:3). This intercession is a striving together with the apostle (Rom. 15:30; Col. 4:12). The church is also called to tangible assistance. With a view to his work Paul often makes an appeal to the church for assistance, in which a specific term[12] is repeatedly employed, which we can translate by "to help on one's way,"

---

9. So rightly D. van Swigchem, *Het missionair karakter van de Christelijke gemeente volgens de brieven van Paulus en Petrus,* 1955, p. 108.

10. See also E. Schweizer, "The Church as the Missionary Body of Christ," *NTS,* 1961, pp. 1-11.

11. For the following see also the detailed and exact analyses of van Swigchem, *Het missionair karakter van de Christelijke gemeente.*

12. *Propempein;* in general: accompany, see a person off (Acts 20:38; 21:5); specifically: equipping one for the journey by giving him money, provisions, companions (cf. 3 John 6; Acts 15:3).

sometimes also by "to send out" (cf. 1 Cor. 16:6, 11; 2 Cor. 1:16; Rom. 15:24; Tit. 3:13).

All this does not mean merely an incidental rendering of assistance, in which the church shows its sympathy for the work of the apostle; rather, its own mode of existence as a missionary church is reflected in it.

This missionary posture consists on the one hand, more indirectly, in the sanctification of the life of the church. It must be mindful of what is good, acceptable, and commends itself to all men (Rom. 12:17); its friendliness and gentleness of spirit must be known to all men (Phil. 4:5); it must walk in wisdom toward those who are without, not permit a good opportunity to slip by. Its word is always to be gracious, seasoned with salt (Col. 4:5). The members of the church are to mind their own affairs and to work with their hands, that they may walk decently, respectably, before those who are without, having no need of anything (from others) (1 Thess. 4:12). They must be in the forefront in good deeds, for these are good and profitable to men (Tit. 3:8). The whole life of the church is to be such that an opponent to his shame has nothing adverse to say of us (Tit. 2:8). This motif recurs throughout all the epistles of Paul in various nuances and elaborations:[13] the life of the church must be a recommendation of its faith, in conformity with, "worthy of," the Lord (Col. 1:10) and the gospel of Christ (Phil. 1:27). In this last point the missionary element is very clear.

Along with this, however, there is a more direct, deliberate missionary calling of the church. If one examines what Paul says about it in his epistles, the yield does not appear to be great. The church is indeed stirred up to imitate the apostles and Christ (1 Cor. 4:16; 11:1; 1 Thess. 1:6). These passages again have reference in the first place to the conduct of the church, but then surely with the conscious and deliberate intention of saving others thereby.[14] More direct stimuli to missionary activity are found, for example, in Colossians 4:5, 6 (once again in close conjunction with conduct). Elsewhere, in Ephesians 6:15, Paul speaks of "the readiness of the gospel of peace" as necessary for the church, and he urges it to join in the struggle for the faith in the gospel (Phil. 1:27). It is evident also from other statements that the churches responded to this admonition of the apostle. Such passages as 1 Thessalonians 1:7ff., Romans 1:8, and Philippians 1:5, 12ff. show clearly that the sound that went forth from them had a good ring to it. They lent themselves to the end that the word quickly spread abroad, and that their faith was spoken of by others. They had a warm, active involvement (koinōnia; Phil. 1:5) in the progress of the gospel. One may even think that so little is expressly said on the missionary stance of the church because it was not so much

---

13. See van Swigchem at length (Het missionair karakter, pp. 88ff.); also W. C. van Unnik, "Die Rücksicht auf die Reaktion der Nicht-Christen als Motiv in der altchristlichen Paränese," in Judentum. Urchristentum. Kirche (Festschr. Jeremias), 1960, pp. 221ff.

14. For this meaning of the example see also W. P. De Boer, The Imitation of Paul, 1962, pp. 213ff.

necessary to stimulate it to activity, as that this be manifested in the right manner, i.e., not in words only, but above all in good works.[15] However this may be, that it was part of the existence of the church to give testimony to the gospel in word and deed, directly and indirectly, can scarcely be disputed on the ground of Paul's epistles, but finds corroboration everywhere in them. And the deepest motives for this, just as for the work of the apostle himself, lie in the consciousness that the church is included in the great world-encompassing work of God in Jesus Christ. It is not the church itself that is the ultimate object, not its numbers and prestige, but the revelation of the full eschatological salvation in Christ, of whom the church is the *pleroma*, that is to say, the bearer of the glory of Christ (Eph. 1:23; 4:13, 16).

It is in the closest connection with this that what is said time and again in the epistles of Paul concerning the inner confirmation and upbuilding of the church is to be understood. On the ground of the great redemptive-historical perspectives of Paul's preaching there can scarcely be question of any priority or preponderance of what is called indeed the "preserving" and the "increasing" of the church; nor can one posit as a dilemma whether the nature and destiny of the church are situated in its missionary calling or in its inner consolidation.[16] As the people of God and as the body of Christ the goal and destiny of the church lie in its *pleroma*, in the extensive as well as in the intensive sense of the word. For this reason Paul can at one time give expression to the fact that the purpose of the divine economy of redemption for the church is situated in the coming in of the fullness of the gentiles as well as that of the Jews (Rom. 11:25-32); and this all to the praise of God, from whom and through whom and unto whom are all things. But he is also able to say that all the gifts of Christ to his church serve to build up the body of Christ, the destiny of which he then describes as follows: "till we all attain to the unity of the faith, and of the knowledge of the Son of God, to mature manhood, to the measure of the stature of the fulness of Christ" (Eph. 4:13). It is thus the intensive "fulness," the adulthood and maturity of the church, toward which the entire process of upbuilding is directed.[17]

If we look more closely at what Paul understands by this inner upbuilding, growth, and adulthood of the church, then in addition to what has already been said in another context concerning the "perfec-

---

15. So van Swigchem, *Het missionair karakter*, pp. 140, 144.

16. For this problem, in addition to van Swigchem, *ibid.*, pp. 247ff., see G. Brillenburg Wurth, "Het apostolaat der kerk," in *De apostolische kerk*, 1954, pp. 98-133; H. Berkhof, "Tweeërlei ekklesiologie," in *Kerk en Theologie*, 1962, pp. 145ff.

17. For Eph. 4:12ff. see also the full and penetrating exegesis of Roberts, *Die Opbou*, pp. 170ff. He wants here to distinguish the missionary as well as the consolidating motif; that is, he takes *hoi pantes* in v. 13 as the "full total" of those who will come to the knowledge of Christ; on the other hand, v. 14 would then speak of the consolidating element in the upbuilding. A serious objection to this conception is that the subject of *katantēsōmen* in v. 13 and that of *ōmen* in v. 14 would vary in meaning (cf. pp. 173 and 177).

tion"[18] and "fulness"[19] of the church, the following are still to be pointed out:

(a) In the upbuilding of the church it is a question first of all of its establishment in Christ, of the certainty that it may and must ever increasingly draw from the fact that Christ is its foundation and the source of its life. Paul speaks of this being founded and rooted in Christ in terms of an accomplished fact. Christ is the foundation and corner-stone (1 Cor. 3:11; Eph. 2:20), the church is once-and-for-all grounded *(tethemeliōmenoi)* and rooted *(errizōmenoi)* in him (Eph. 3:17; Col. 2:6, 7), and on this ground the upbuilding is now to go on as an actual reality.[20] This being rooted and grounded consists in having "received" Christ, a *terminus technicus* for the acceptance of the authoritative apostolic tradition concerning Christ (1 Cor. 11:23; 15:1, 3; Gal. 1:9; Phil. 4:9; Col. 2:6; 1 Thess. 2:13; 4:1; 2 Thess. 3:6). It is now of utmost importance for the upbuilding of the church that, as it has "received" and "learned" Christ (Col. 2:6; Eph. 4:20, 21), so it should walk in him and abide in him. Paul never wearies of stressing this binding character of the "tradition," in the authoritative, apostolic[21] sense of the word, even in the words in which the church has received it (1 Cor. 15:1, 2). Only thus will it be safeguarded against instability, being moved up and down, tossed to and fro by every wind of doctrine, in the game that men play with it, in the deceit of false doctrine (Eph. 4:14). He sets this tradition, which is "according to Christ," over against "the tradition of men and the principles of the world," falling prey to human wisdom (Col. 2:7, 8). This concern for the church's remaining rooted and grounded in Christ, in accordance with the holy, apostolic (Eph. 3:5) tradition and doctrine, is found in all the epistles of Paul, and not only in the Pastoral Epistles, although there the contrast with rising heresy and the admonition to continue in "sound" doctrine come particularly to the fore (cf., e.g., 1 Tim. 1:10; 6:3; 2 Tim. 1:13; 4:3; Tit. 1:9, 13; 2:1, 2), and the expression "that which has been entrusted" *(parathēkē, depositum)* takes the place of "tradition" *(paradosis)*, otherwise with the same meaning (1 Tim. 6:20; cf. 2 Tim. 1:12, 14; 2:2).

(b) This being rooted and grounded in Christ as the church has "received" and "learned" him does not, however, signify a static condition, but precisely the foundation for a progressive upbuilding and growth from this root. One is also not to think here only or in the first place of a quantitative extension, but of inner, qualitative upbuilding and growth. It is a question here of remaining immature and underage *(nēpios, nēpiazō;* cf. 1 Cor. 3:1; Gal. 4:3; Eph. 4:14) as contrasted with progress toward perfection, manly maturity. What is intended by this is the appropriation of the full Christ. Although Paul thus distinguishes between being underage and full-grown in Christ (cf. 1 Cor. 3:1, 2; 2:6; Eph. 4:14), he does not wish thereby to introduce a classification

---

18. See above, Section 44.
19. See above, Section 62.
20. *Epoikodomoumenoi* and *bebaioumenoi* — present participles.
21. Cf. above, p. 240.

within the church, but rather he sets himself against the religious immaturity of some.[22] The whole church is to live out of the abundance and fullness of Christ, in order with all the saints to be able to apprehend what are the dimensions (of what has happened and been given in Christ); it must learn to know his love which surpasses knowledge and thus be filled unto all the fullness of God (Eph. 3:18, 19).

It is a matter here, as is again and again apparent particularly in Ephesians and Colossians, of the full awakening of consciousness, knowledge, insight into the all-embracing significance of Christ. What is intended is not a purely theoretical or speculative knowledge, but an ever more profound awareness and an increasing clarity of insight with regard to all the implications of the salvation given in Christ.[23]

(c) This is accompanied by still another aspect of this upbuilding, that of mutual unity and love, which is no less a proof of maturity than is knowledge. For the truth must be practiced in love, and only so does growth take place (Eph. 4:15), just as the hearts of believers are to be united together in love unto all insight and knowledge (Col. 2:2). The building up of the church accordingly consists in this, that all may come to the unity of the faith and the knowledge of the Son of God and may attain to mature manhood (Eph. 4:13). On the one hand this means therefore a common growth and upbuilding to greater perfection. On the other, Paul's admonition, precisely in the texts on upbuilding, is directed toward this, that mutual harmony, the right relationship of community and individual, be preserved. It is accordingly here that his warnings apply against spiritual individualism and self-complacency.[24] For this reason he also cautions against a knowledge that is not directed toward the whole and refuses to place itself at the service of others; this knowledge puffs up, but love builds up (1 Cor. 8:1). Therefore it is precisely those who have come to a deeper insight and spiritual maturity who must bear with those who are not yet so far along. For each one must wish not to please himself, but his neighbor, for good, for edification (Rom. 15:1, 2). With every spiritual gift that arises in the church the question should therefore be asked as to its "value for upbuilding,"[25] its value for the church (1 Cor. 14:3, 5, 26), so that he who aspires to spiritual gifts must do so with a view to this upbuilding (1 Cor. 14:12). It is repeated again and again that love is the secret of upbuilding (Rom. 14:15, 19; 1 Cor. 8:1), of all gifts is the most excellent (1 Cor. 13), constitutes the bond that alone makes the church "perfect" (Col. 3:14). Positively this upbuilding consists in mutual admonition, encouragement, warning, patience (1 Thess. 5:11; cf. v. 14; 1 Cor. 14:3). The continuing upbuilding of the church means that not only in its individual members, but

22. This also holds for the striking usage of 1 Cor. 2:6 (cf. P. J. Du Plessis, [TELEIOS], The Idea of Perfection in the New Testament, 1959, p. 178).

23. On this see above, Section 41.

24. Cf. above, p. 295.

25. For this peculiar and repeated use of oikodomeō in 1 Cor. 8ff. also see Michel, TDNT, V, p. 141. He surmises that Paul here associates himself with certain expressions current in the church of Corinth.

above all in its unity as the body of Christ it reaches perfection, i.e.,
brings to revelation the fullness it possesses in Christ, in keeping what it
has once received, in the increase of the knowledge of faith and wisdom,
in love and mutual fellowship.

Furthermore, the *charismata* Christ wills to give for the edification of his church, both in their diversity among themselves and in their
collective tendency toward the upbuilding of the one church, are to be
appreciated in the right way. This "chapter" on the *charismata* in Paul's
epistles requires a separate treatment, however.

SECTION 70. THE SPIRITUAL EQUIPMENT OF THE CHURCH. CHARISMA AND MINISTRY (OFFICE)

If one can therefore say that the pronouncements on the upbuilding of
the church are plain in their general purport and give us a clear insight
into the meaning of the apostle, we are placed before many difficulties
when we attempt to form a picture of the structure and organization of
the church, as that in part is presupposed in the Pauline epistles, in part
also emerges in all kinds of concrete instructions and prescriptions. In
general, we have to do here with the special spiritual equipment of the
church, which is necessary for its upbuilding and which, as we shall see
still further, is given expression particularly in the concepts *charismata*
and ministries.

The treatment of the problem involved here is also of such great
consequence for the reason that in the history of investigation it has
been thought possible to appeal especially to Paul for a very specific
conception of the character and organization of the early Christian
church. This conception is said to have been determined to a very considerable degree by incidental and individual operations of the Spirit,
consisting above all in prophetic and ecstatic *charismata* and still to have
been entirely "free" from the later institutional and official organization
of the church. In this conception we have to do with what was presented
in great style by the jurist Rudolf Sohm around 1900, a position that no
longer finds supporters in its totality, but which nevertheless makes
itself felt and exercises influence in a great many respects in the New
Testament literature on this subject, especially in connection with the
interpretation of the Pauline texts.

Sohm's basic thesis[26] was that every form of ecclesiastical polity is in flagrant
conflict with the essence of the church. He started from the church as an absolutely spiritual reality, the invisible body of Christ, the church whose citizenship is in heaven, which is held together only by common faith and pneumatic
charismata, which has an external organization therefore neither locally nor
otherwise, but is present as the church wherever only two or three are present
in Christ's name. This church receives its leadership and government immedi-

---

26. Defended especially in his principal work, *Kirchenrecht*, I, 1892; later
summarized and repeated in his *Wesen und Ursprung des Katholizismus*, 1909.

ately from God by the Spirit, who makes his will known to persons appointed
to that end. The church is to pay heed to it, but cannot itself produce this government, nor designate certain persons for that purpose. The prophets, too, are
dependent on the Spirit in their speaking. There can be no question therefore
of any office or legal order instituted by the church. Everything is dependent on
the immediate influence of the Spirit.

Although Sohm appealed chiefly to Paul, he thought that with the above
he had sketched the whole structure of the early Christian church. In this respect
his conception has met with much opposition. For as was very quickly demonstrated by Harnack[27] and later by Holl,[28] in the remaining books of the New
Testament, as in the Pastoral Epistles (which it was usually thought could not
be attributed to Paul), there are so many direct and indirect data that clearly
point to an institutional organization — if still elementary — of the early Christian church that one certainly cannot all along the line conclude a pneumatic-
charismatic organization of the church. On the basis of a detailed analysis of
the New Testament data Harnack especially has thrown light on the untenableness of Sohm's extreme spiritualism. In so doing he contended that the church
as a sociological entity simply requires an organizational formation, which
becomes church-law as soon as it is applied to ecclesiastical affairs.[29] On the
other hand, the spiritualism of Sohm was opposed by Harnack, but not at
heart overcome. Both started from a specific, liberal view of the church, of
which the religious-individual and the personal-pneumatic relation between
Christ and the individual believer was the governing point of view. For Harnack, too, therefore, the institutional and juridical aspect of ecclesiastical
organization was a concern alien to the essence of the church; he would
have nothing to do with what he termed a "religious" determination of law
in the church.[30] Church law, office, ecclesiastical connection, in short, everything in the church that does not rest on the free impulse of the Spirit, but
bears an institutional character, does not touch the inner essence of the
church, has an administrative significance, and is based on agreement. On
the ground of this view he arrived at his well-known distinction between
religious (or charismatic) ministries, which are founded on the free impulse
of the Spirit and were not bound to a local church, and administrative, local
ministries.[31] Particularly in Paul the individual-charismatic purportedly comes
strongly to the fore, and only gradually was what for him was still pneumatic
superseded by the institutional and administrative, when the eldership came
in the place of glossolalia and prophecy. Others have posited, especially following in the footsteps of Holl, that Paul from the outset stood in sharp contrast
with the church at Jerusalem. Whereas the traditional and institutional was
of dominant significance in the early Jewish-Christian church, Paul is said to
have placed much more emphasis on the personal and pneumatic discernment
of individual believers; in regard to that, too, the independent significance

27. For Harnack's conception see especially his *The Constitution and Law
of the Church in the First Two Centuries*, ET 1910. His extensive criticism of Sohm's
work is included there (pp. 175ff.).

28. Cf. his essay, "Der Kirchenbegriff des Paulus in seinem Verhältnis zu
dem der Urgemeinde," 1921, included in Karl Holl, *Gesammelte Aufsätze zur
Kirchengeschichte*, II, 1928, pp. 44-67.

29. *The Constitution and Law of the Church*, pp. 215f.

30. *Ibid.*, p. 214: "This [that is, the relative character of every administration
of justice] means that ecclesiastical law cannot include religious regulations in the
proper sense because these are thereby deprived of their value, and indeed are called
in question."

31. See for this already Harnack's *Die Lehre der zwölf Apostel*, 1884, pp. 145ff.

of the local church is said through him to have come very much to the foreground, and the importance Jerusalem initially had in the primitive Christian
church is said thereby to have been broken.[32]

The whole problem, particularly as it was posed by Sohm, came to
stand in an entirely different light, however, when a more adequate approach
to the New Testament idea of the church took the place of the spiritualistic
and individualistic views of theological liberalism,[33] and the redemptive-
historical conception of the church as the people of God made possible a
better apprehension of the relationship between the nature and manifestation
of the church. Only then could the antithesis posited by Sohm between the
spiritual character of the church on the one hand and the institutional,
ecclesiastical organization on the other, be overcome in principle, and one did
not need to stop at the essentially hybrid solution of Harnack, who thought
he could wed the spiritual essence of the church to a secular organization alien
to that essence. With this development the groundlessness also emerged of the
constant appeal which it was thought might be made to Paul for this conception.[34] For with Paul the Spirit not only represents the invisible and heavenly
existence of the church, but is given to the church precisely as earnest and
firstfruits in the provisional character of its temporal existence, so that the
church should reveal itself therein as the people of God directed toward the
future and as the historical-visible communion of the body of Christ. Every
dualism of visibleness and invisibleness, of form and Spirit, is alien to the
New Testament, as also to the Pauline, idea of the church. On this account
the historical and visible upbuilding and instrumentation of the church are
pointed out as also the object and the fruit of the Spirit, not only elsewhere
in the New Testament but in the epistles of Paul as well, and the *charismata*
and ministries given to the church are to be viewed in this light.

These general points of view do not, however, release us from the task
of entering further into the concrete data in Paul's epistles that have a
bearing on this spiritual equipment and organization of the church. In so
doing we encounter a multiplicity of descriptions and distinctions, at the
root of which there is apparently no fixed, systematic arrangement.

As summary, general qualifications for all that serves the upbuilding and equipment of the church the apostle primarily employs two
words, gifts *(charismata;* Rom. 12:6; 1 Cor. 1:7; 12:4, 9, 28, 30, 31; 1 Tim.
4:14; 2 Tim. 1:6; in a single instance also called *domata* [Eph. 4:8; cf.
v. 11], in accordance with the quotation from Ps. 68:19) and ministries
(diakoniai; Rom. 11:13; 12:7; 1 Cor. 12:5; 16:15; 2 Cor. 4:1; 6:3; 11:8;
Eph. 4:12; Col. 4:17; 1 Tim. 1:12; 2 Tim. 4:5, 11). In addition to these
we meet with still other descriptions, such as workings *(energēmata;*
1 Cor. 12:6, 19), work *(ergon;* Eph. 4:12; 1 Thess. 5:13; 1 Tim. 3:1;
2 Tim. 4:5), administration, stewardship *(oikonomia;* 1 Cor. 9:17; Eph.

---

32. Holl, *Gesammelte Aufsätze,* II, pp. 62ff.

33. For this whole development see, for example, O. Linton, *Das Problem
der Urkirche in der neueren Forschung,* 1932; F. M. Braun, *Neues Licht auf die Kirche,*
1946, pp. 29ff.; W. G. Kümmel, *The New Testament: The History of the Investigation
of Its Problems,* ET 1972, pp. 212ff. Especially with a view to church polity, W. Maurer,
"Vom Ursprung und Wesen kirchlichen Rechts," in *Zeitschr. für evang. Kirchenrecht,*
1956, pp. 5ff.; he points especially to the significance of H. von Campenhausen. For his
standpoint see below.

34. Cf., e.g., the summary in Holl, *Gesammelte Aufsätze,* II, pp. 62ff.

3:2; Col. 1:25; 1 Tim. 1:4; cf. 1 Cor. 4:2; Tit. 1:7), service (*leitourgia;* 2 Cor. 9:12; Phil. 2:17, 30; cf. Rom. 15:16). None of these words has carefully defined boundaries, and more often than not they are used in a broader sense rather than as a denotation of specific gifts or activities in the life of the congregation. The most striking thing is surely that these words have no sacral connotation and that, conversely, the words that are used in the LXX and in Hellenism for the sacral ministry in temple or sanctuary are not employed in Paul and in the New Testament generally for any service in the Christian church.[35] In that fact is expressed the entirely new manner in which Paul understands the intercourse between God and the church as his people.[36]

Although each of these qualifications has its own special significance, the words *charisma* and *diakonia* most characterize this spiritual equipment, the first as a denotation of what Christ by his Spirit grants to the church in diversity and freedom, the second as a general delineation of how this functions in the church.[37] It is especially important thereby to give the concept *charisma,* which may be said to be highly characteristic for Paul's theological usage,[38] the large content that it has for him. To be sure, he distinguishes[39] in 1 Corinthians 12 between *charismata,* "ministries," and "workings" (vv. 4-6), and he understands *charismata* especially of gifts of healing (vv. 9, 28, 30); in the same context, however, *charisma* also means all that Christ works in the church to its upbuilding and fulfillment (v. 31). Elsewhere all the "workings" and "ministries" stand under one denominator — *charismata* (Rom. 12:6), just as in Ephesians 4 *domata* (gifts) is the key word. This general significance of *charisma* is corroborated by the use of *charisma* in a less specific context: in Romans 1:11 Paul expresses the hope that in his visit to the church he may impart to it "some spiritual *charisma*" for its strengthening, which clearly has a general meaning. And in 1 Corinthians 7:7 he says, with reference to the questions concerning marriage, that "each man has his own *charisma* from God, the one of one kind, the other of another," which does not refer to the married or unmarried state itself,[40] but surely gives expression to the fact that the *charisma* of

---

35. Paul does use the word *leitourgia* — occurring outside the N.T. frequently in a sacral sense — a few times, but then in the general, non-sacral sense of mutual service (2 Cor. 9:12 — of a collection [cf. Rom. 15:27]; Phil. 2:25, 30). The only time that *leitourgos* has a sacral connotation in Paul is Rom. 15:16 (in connection with *hierourgein*). But here he speaks in a figurative sense (cf. below, p. 481).

36. See further below, p. 481.

37. *Charisma* can also in general denote the gift of God in Christ (Rom. 5:15, 16; 6:23; 11:29; 2 Cor. 1:11), and the particularization of it for all believers (Rom. 1:11); *diakonia* can also have a general, more abstract meaning of ministry (cf. 2 Cor. 3:7ff.; 5:18); on the other hand, of one definite kind of ministry or assistance, e.g., of the collection for Jerusalem (Rom. 15:31; 2 Cor. 8:4ff.; cf. Rom. 12:7).

38. Cf., e.g., E. Käsemann, "Ministry and Community in the New Testament," *Essays on New Testament Themes,* p. 64: "We can establish with the maximum degree of historical certainty that it was Paul who was the first to use it in this technical sense and who indeed introduced it into the vocabulary of theology."

39. See further below, pp. 446ff.

40. So, e.g., Käsemann, *Essays on New Testament Themes,* pp. 70ff., who

the Spirit can consist in being able to abstain from marriage (cf. v. 7a).

It is evident even from this general use of *charisma* that one may not restrict the content of this idea to the unusual and spectacular, such as the performance of healings, speaking in tongues, being in a condition of ecstasy, etc. For, while these special *charismata* get particular (critical) attention in 1 Corinthians 12-14, in Romans 12 and Ephesians 4 they are not mentioned at all. In the church at Corinth great value was apparently attached to them, and perhaps these unusual phenomena were intended by "the *pneumatica*" with which in 1 Corinthians 12:1 Paul introduces the whole subject of the *charismata*. Paul begins by setting these *pneumatica* over against heathenism and what occurred there, too, in the way of ecstatic phenomena (of a demonic nature; vv. 2, 3). He gives a warning against the latter to the Corinthians, who were apparently particularly susceptible to "*pneumatica*" (but also to derailment in them). Nevertheless he accepts these miraculous powers, ecstasy, and even glossolalia as gifts of the Spirit of Christ. But in doing so he makes a double reservation: in the first place, they must serve the upbuilding of the church. "They are validated not by the *fascinosum* of the praeternatural but by the edification of the community."[41] And in the second place, he elucidates with great clarity the diversity of the *charismata*. The pneumatic and charismatic is not only that which is spectacular and unusual, or which touches the inwardness of the religious life. *Charisma* is everything that the Spirit wishes to use and presses into service for equipping and upbuilding the church, what can serve for instruction and admonition and for ministering to one another, or even the effective direction and government of the church. The whole distinction between charismatic and non-charismatic ministries in the church therefore cannot be reconciled with the Pauline conception of *charisma*.[42] In discussing the several gifts we have still to return to the particulars. But the general purport of the "*charismata* chapter," 1 Corinthians 12, is simply to reject any hierarchical distinction between what is to be valued in the gifts and service in the church as more and less "pneumatic." For "it is the same Spirit" and "the same Lord" (1 Cor. 12:4, 5) who works all

wishes to understand the contrasts mentioned in Gal. 3:28; Col. 3:11 (male-female, slave-free, etc.) as *charismata,* not to be sure in the mere fact of their existence, taken by themselves, but because each of them (maleness, femaleness, familial and social relationships, etc.) can become a *charisma* ("when it is overshadowed by the *monon en Kyriō* of I Cor. 7:39"). But however true it is that *charisma* has to do with the whole of life because "the field of the Church's operation must be the world in its totality" and "the secular is no longer abandoned to demons and demonic energies" (p. 72), the Pauline usage of *charisma* is plainly narrower. It does not have reference to marriage, etc., itself, but to the special and varied spiritual possibilities God gives to believers in every area of life in order thereby to build his church and glorify his name.

41. Käsemann, *Essays on New Testament Themes*, p. 67. With regard to these special *pneumatica* he writes: "He can hardly go further in his approach to his opponents at Corinth and to the world of Hellenistic mystery religion which lies beyond them. But this is precisely the point at which he diverges most sharply from his environment."

42. Against this distinction introduced by Harnack (see above, p. 439) see also E. Schweizer, *Church Order in the New Testament,* ET 1961, pp. 145, 181ff.

things. There is differentiation, of course, and every *charisma* is not of equal worth. Apostles, prophets, and teachers are expressly listed first in the enumeration ("first," "second," etc.) (1 Cor. 12:28; cf. Eph. 4:11). Paul also speaks of "the best *charismata*" (1 Cor. 12:31), and he puts prophecy highest (1 Cor. 14:1). But this distinction is other than that of more or less ecstatic or spectacular. For the apostles are also the governors who order practical affairs, who occupy themselves with the collection and with the care of the poor (2 Cor. 8ff.). In 1 Corinthians 12:28 the ability to help and to govern stands between the gifts of healing and glossolalia, and in Romans 12:6 the last two are entirely lacking. Each has his own *charisma* from God. All stands under his sovereign will (1 Cor. 12:11, 18), and is to be directed "according to the measure of faith" that God will assign (Rom. 12:3; Eph. 4:7). And everyone has to live and to act therein according to the nature of his *charisma,* and not according to that of another (Rom. 12:3, 6ff.).

The second fundamental idea in which the equipment of the church is spoken of in a summary way[43] is that of ministries. Decisive for the significance of the concept ministry — thus Beyer writes — is that young Christianity learned to consider and to characterize every activity in the church important for its upbuilding as *diakonia.*[44] Generally, therefore, the *charisma* acts in the church as a ministry and finds its destiny and its criterion only in its character as ministry (cf. 1 Pet. 4:11). By this designation the congregational character of all the gifts conferred by Christ and of all the activities these gifts enable is thus denoted. For all these gifts have been placed at the service of the body of Christ, with the ultimate object of the service and glorification of God himself in Christ (cf. Eph. 4:12; 1 Cor. 14:26; Col. 3:16, 17).

Wherein these different gifts and ministries consist will have to appear further in the following section. It is of importance for what occupies us here to observe that as little as one may make a spiritualistic antithesis between "charismatic" and "administrative" ministries, so little is one to want to see a distinction in principle in an actualistic sense between the *charisma* as a gift of Christ active *in concreto* on the one hand, and the institutional, ordered ministries or offices in the church on the other.[45] And it is the more necessary to take a position against this because interpreters who are fully alive to the unwarrantedness of this first antithesis and repudiate in it the spiritualism of Sohm (and Harnack), yet with respect to the latter remain stuck halfway along in this one-sided conception of *charisma* and *diakonia*. In particular it is a question here again of the interpretation of the Pauline conception. This is said to have been incompatible in principle with the later institutional conception of office and ministry in the church, so that we

---

43. Sometimes *diakonia* is also used for one specific ministry (cf. Rom. 12:7; see also above, p. 441, n. 37).

44. *TDNT,* II, p. 87.

45. For the preceding and the following see also my essay "Kerkelijke orde en kerkelijk recht in de brieven van Paulus," in *Ex auditu verbi (Festschr. G. C. Berkouwer),* 1965, pp. 194-215.

have to draw a sharp distinction between Paul and the church at Jerusalem as well as between Paul and the later development, as this is said
to be met with particularly in the Pastoral Epistles and in the writings
of Luke.[46]

It is our conviction that the contrast between the charismatic and
institutional is at bottom just as false as that between charismatic and
non-charismatic ministries in the church.[47] It is no doubt true and it has
its significance that in the enumerations in Romans 12, 1 Corinthians 12,
and Ephesians 4 it is not the institutional, but the qualitative aspect in
these *charismata* that comes to the fore. It is not presbyters, bishops, or
deacons who are spoken of there, but the *charisma* of giving leadership,
helping, showing mercy. This points to the fact that even if some of the
charismata mentioned here are denotations of specific offices,[48] yet it is
not the official-institutional as such, but the material significance of the
office that is brought to the forefront. But he who wishes to seek a contrast here between the institutional and the charismatic is on the wrong
track. For one thing, Paul reckons his own apostolic office among the
gifts Christ has given to his church (1 Cor. 12:28; Eph. 4:11). The apostolic office is undoubtedly distinguished from all other offices and
ministries in that its bearers have been immediately called by Christ,
and have a wholly unique, fundamental significance for the church.[49]
But it is nevertheless apparent from this office how little reason there is
for making a contrast between office and *charisma*, between institute and
Spirit, and how wrong the categories are with which one is at work if he
wishes here to place the actual, concrete, *Ereignis*-like (that is, having

---

46. For this antithesis, in addition to the older conception of Holl *et al.*
already mentioned, see also Käsemann, *Essays on New Testament Themes*, pp. 83ff.,
who, among other things, denies with great decisiveness that the Pauline church at
the time of the apostle would already have known a *presbyterium* and who characterizes the development as it emerges in the Pastoral Epistles as an abandonment
(dictated by the circumstances) of the "Pauline conception of a church order based
on charisma" (p. 88). Schweizer, too, regards an ordination, in general an appointment at the beginning of a specific ministry, an impossibility with Paul (*Church
Order in the New Testament,* p. 101). Such an appointment or ordination would be
for him "a subsequent recognition of a ministry that had been bestowed previously"
(p. 207). Here again all the emphasis falls on *charisma* and ministry as event *(Ereignis).*
For this same actualizing conception of office see Käsemann, *ibid.,* p. 83: "The Apostle's
theory of order is not a static one, resting on offices, institutions, ranks, and dignities;
in his view, authority resides only within the concrete act of ministry as it occurs,
because it is only within the concrete act that the *Kyrios* announces his lordship and
his presence." H. von Campenhausen, *Ecclesiastical Authority and Spiritual Power in
the Church of the First Three Centuries,* ET 1969, is also of the opinion that, though
certain regulations were observed, every ministry that was performed in the church
did not for Paul rest on such human regulations, but "it is the employment of a
gift which the Spirit bestows" (p. 68). For von Campenhausen here the antithesis
between Spirit and "law" especially plays a great part (cf. pp. 56ff.). For this whole
problem see also J. L. Leuba, *Institution und Ereignis,* 1957.

47. See P. Menoud, *l'Église et les ministères selon le Nouveau Testament,*
1949, p. 12; also Bultmann, *Theology,* II, pp. 97ff.

48. See below, pp. 446ff., 455ff.

49. See further below, pp. 448ff.

the character of event or happening) as a distinguishing feature of *charisma* over against the continual, regular, and institutional character of office.

Furthermore, in Paul's epistles along with the special office of the apostles we see the clear signs of stability, institutionality, and orderedness of specific ministries and *charismata* in the church. In addition to what is to be said later in more detail on their differentiation, in the general qualification of "ministry" there is already a clear stabilizing tendency. To think here only of incidental and concrete service is not only an unnatural conception of the reality, but is also in conflict with the Pauline usage, where "ministry," even though it does not yet have the special significance of "diaconate," can denote a definite, "fixed" activity in the church that is discharged by specific persons.[50] Paul accordingly speaks not only of the *charisma* of governing (1 Cor. 12:28), but also of "the leaders" of the church (Rom. 12:8), to whom authority was due and submission owed. One thinks in this context, too, of "the firstfruits" (Rom. 16:5; 1 Cor. 16:15), persons who in a certain locality or a certain area had first come to the faith and in consequence enjoyed a special position of trust. That all this may be said to point only to moral and not to "official" authority or that from these specific charismatic endowments or personal positions of authority certain qualifications to act as leader resulted *a posteriori*,[51] can indeed indicate the historical course of events, but even so does not distinguish the official and institutional qualitatively from the charismatic or justify even an antithesis between the two. For it is in the nature of certain *charismata* that they have not merely an incidental, but a continual significance, and therefore of themselves might lay claim to continuing and regular recognition (for which reason the *charismata*, too, are not only denoted as powers, etc., but also as persons; cf. 1 Cor. 12:28; Eph. 4:8, 11). The *charisma* tends, therefore, to the institutional and consists in the fact that the church not only here and now, but as far as this is needed, receives a fixed instrumentation and "articulation," as once again with a figure borrowed from the body Paul describes the healthy functioning of the church endowed with the gifts of Christ (Eph. 4:16; cf. vv. 11, 12). It is therefore a false antithesis to set the charismatic and institutional as "spiritual authority" *(Vollmacht)* and "human rule" over against each other.[52] For not only does this "human rule," where, as for example in the Pastoral Epistles, it is active in establishing and institutionalizing, stand in the closest relation to *charisma* and "spiritual authority" (cf. 1 Tim. 4:14; 1:18; 2 Tim. 1:6; 1 Tim. 3:1ff.; Tit. 1:6ff.; 2 Tim. 2:24), but in this whole antithesis between "human" and "spiritual" the "spiritual" character of the church and the choice, appointment, and

---

50. "The discharge of certain obligations in the community" (Beyer, *TDNT*, II, p. 88). In addition to the "ministry" of the apostles (the office of apostle) (Rom. 11:13; 2 Cor. 4:1; 6:3ff.; 11:8), reference is to be made to Col. 4:17 (cf. 1 Tim. 1:12; 2 Tim. 4:5, 11). For the apostolate *oikonomia* is also employed, which perhaps comes closest to our "office" (cf. 1 Cor. 9:17; Eph. 3:2; Col. 1:25).

51. As Schweizer puts it (see above, p. 444, n. 46).

52. As von Campenhausen does (see above, p. 444, n. 46).

ordination of certain persons for certain ministries going out from it are eliminated or ignored — a view that is certainly not in agreement with Paul's conception of the church's character and its own competence (cf. 1 Cor. 3:21, 22, *et al.*). However striking it may therefore be that in the enumerations of 1 Corinthians 12:28 and Ephesians 4:11 apostles, prophets, and teachers do occur, but not presbyters and deacons, this need not only mean that in the Pauline congregations at the time of the apostle there was not yet a *presbyterium*[53] (as is clearly evident also from the Epistle to the Philippians, written in the same period as that to the Ephesians; Phil. 1:1[54]), but likewise it in no way distinguishes this ministry of presbyters and deacons from that which Christ has given to the church as *charisma*.

The sequel will have to teach us to what extent it is possible from the data of Paul's epistles to reach an insight into the actual state of affairs in the congregations addressed by him. Everything is certainly not going to become clear to us thereby. But with full allowance for what is uncertain here, we shall have to be very careful indeed with the argument from silence, especially when this is pressed into the service of certain preconceived opinions with respect to the manner in which the Spirit works and equips the church. We may rather, on the basis of what has so far become apparent to us, ascertain that for a right understanding of the spiritual equipment of the church the distinction between the charismatic and institutional sooner leads us astray than that it could serve us as a directive for what follows. If one chooses to regard the enumerations in 1 Corinthians and Ephesians 4 from the viewpoint of office and *charisma*, then only one conclusion is possible, namely, that the office is itself a *charisma*.[55] Every attempt to construct an antithesis here betrays a conception of the work of the Spirit that was indeed for a long period of time characteristic of a certain interpretation of the New Testament idea of the church, but which finds as little support in the Pauline conception of the building up of the church as it does in that of the remainder of the New Testament.

SECTION 71. DIVERSITY OF GIFTS

So far as the several gifts, ministries, etc., are concerned, Paul gives them no systematization, but rather places emphasis on the great diversity in

53. As Käsemann interprets it (see above, p. 444, n. 46).

54. For the attempt to eliminate Phil. 1:1 from the discussion see below, n. 85.

55. Cf. Bultmann, *Theology*, II, p. 104: "According to Paul's view the tasks and activities within the compass of congregational life (the 'varieties of service,' the 'helps' and 'administrations'; 1 Cor. 12:5, 28) are also gifts of the Spirit. To that extent it may be justified to term the offices of 'presbyter' and 'episkopos' charismatic, but in so doing one must be aware that although this corresponds to Paul's specific understanding of the matter it nevertheless does not agree with the oldest usage of Hellenistic Christianity" (cf. I, p. 154). So Kümmel as well in Lietzmann-Kümmel, *Cor.* (p. 188): "for Paul all the functions of the church bear a charismatic character."

the gifts and ministries God has given to the church (cf. Rom. 12:6; 1 Cor. 12:4),[56] a diversity, however, which must find its harmony in the unity of the body and its general well-being (pros to sympheron; 1 Cor. 12:7).

When one examines the lists as they occur in Romans 12:6-8; 1 Corinthians 12:8-10, 28-30; Ephesians 4:11, he repeatedly meets with gifts and ministries — some of which are the same, some of which are different.[57] The following are to be mentioned in summary:

(1) apostles (1 Cor. 12:28, expressly mentioned "first"; Eph. 4:11);
(2) prophets (Rom. 12:6; 1 Cor. 12:10, 28: "secondly"; Eph. 4:11);
(3) teachers (Rom. 12:7; 1 Cor. 12:28: "thirdly"; Eph. 4:11: "pastors and teachers");
(4) evangelists (Eph. 4:11; cf. 2 Tim. 4:5);
(5) service (diakonia [Rom. 12:7], here intended therefore in a special sense, probably to be understood to the same effect as antilēmpseis in 1 Cor. 12:28);
(6) distributing, showing mercy (Rom. 12:8);
(7) giving leadership (ho pro-histamenos [Rom. 12:8]; cf. kybernēseis in 1 Cor. 12:28);
(8) the gift of exhortation (Rom. 12:8: ho parakalōn);
(9) the word of wisdom (logos sophias; 1 Cor. 12:8);
(10) the word of knowledge (logos gnōseōs; 1 Cor. 12:8);
(11) powers (dynameis; 1 Cor. 12:10, 28; cf. "faith" [1 Cor. 12:9; see 1 Cor. 13:2]);
(12) gifts of healing (1 Cor. 12:9, 28);
(13) glossolalia (1 Cor. 12:10, 28);
(14) interpretation (of the speaking in tongues; 1 Cor. 12:10, 28);
(15) distinguishing of spirits (1 Cor. 12:10).

Elsewhere one finds indications that coincide with the above; for example, he who gives instruction in the Word (Gal. 6:6 — see under 3), those who give leadership in the Lord (1 Thess. 5:12; cf. 1 Tim. 5:17 —

---

56. There is a difference of opinion on the question whether diaireseis in I Cor. 12:4ff. speaks of "diversity" in gifts, etc., or of "distribution." It is usually translated by the former. Schlier, however, defends the latter in TDNT, I, p. 185, and is followed, among others, by Kümmel (Lietzmann-Kümmel, Cor., p. 187), departing from Lietzmann (p. 60). Schlier appeals (a) to the plural, (b) to the contrast with to de auto pneuma, (c) to the parallel with the "basic concept" hē phanerōsis tou pneumatos (v. 7). One could point further to v. 11 where diairoun undoubtedly means "distribute." Nevertheless the element of diversity in this expression is unmistakable. The contrast with to de auto pneuma obviously stands over against the dissimilarity, the differences among the gifts of the Spirit; and in v. 7 the accent is placed on what is of service for all (pros to sympheron), once again in contrast to the gift allotted to each one separately. However, in the word diaireseis the thought of bestowing (in variety) certainly also has a part (cf. vv. 11, 8). We do not, however, have a word that (as diairein, etc.) embraces the one as well as the other: "distribution" insufficiently indicates the differentiation. One will perhaps have to be content with a circumscription: "there is a variegated distribution of charismata," etc.

57. For a full and illuminating survey see Joseph Brosch, Charismen und Ämter in der Urkirche, 1951, pp. 38-41.

see under 7), and admonish (*nouthetountes;* 1 Thess. 5:12 — see under 8). Finally, the following are still to be mentioned separately:

(16) overseers (*episkopoi;* Phil. 1:1; 1 Tim. 3:2; Tit. 1:7), whether or not to be taken together with

(17) presbyters (*presbyteroi;* 1 Tim. 5:17, 19; Tit. 1:5);

(18) deacons (Phil. 1:1; 1 Tim. 3:8, 12).

In addition to what we have already brought together under one denominator (cf., e.g., under 5 and 7), there are certainly all kinds of designations here that are not to be kept apart rigidly, but coincide in the same person or ministry. Thus, for example, the gift of exhortation[58] (8) in 1 Corinthians 14:3, 31 is specifically reckoned as being part of the prophetic activity (2). Similarly, it is difficult to distinguish between the "word of knowledge" (10) and the "word of wisdom" (9). Both also occur in close connection with prophecy (2) and teaching (3) (1 Cor. 13:2; 14:6; Col. 1:28).[59] Likewise that which is mentioned under 5 and 6 obviously lies close together, just as what is mentioned under 11 and 12 and under 13 and 14. Furthermore, one has to consider to what extent the "pastors" mentioned in Ephesians 4:11 are the same as the teachers mentioned there, or whether they are more to be identified with those who give leadership (7, 16) (cf. Acts 20:28). This brings us finally to the question as to what the relationship is between the gifts mentioned in Romans, 1 Corinthians, and Ephesians, and the offices of overseers, presbyters, and deacons intended in Philippians 1:1 and the Pastoral Epistles. In general the gifts and ministries enumerated by Paul do not denote a differentiation of persons, but rather represent and particularize the fullness of the grace given by Christ to his church; finally, they clearly demonstrate that the whole instrumentation and upbuilding of the church has not been committed to a number of *charismatici* added to the church, whether or not in an official relationship, but rather has its matrix in the church itself as the body of Christ. Not a few only, but all by incorporation into the one body have been baptized into the one Spirit (1 Cor. 12:13).

On the several gifts, ministries, offices, the following remarks are to be made.

(1) Apostles

They stand first in the lists (1 Cor. 12:28; Eph. 4:11). The apostolate (Rom. 1:5; 1 Cor. 9:2; Gal. 2:8) is distinguished from all the other gifts and ministries because it does not belong to the continuing, repeatedly renewed equipment of the church, but bears a foundational and once-for-all character (Eph. 2:20). Apostles, in the sense of 1 Corinthians 12:28;

---

58. One is to think of pastoral admonition and encouragement (cf. *paramythia;* 1 Cor. 14:3; 1 Thess. 2:12; 5:14; Phil. 2:1), often difficult to distinguish from *paraklēsis* (see Stählin, *TDNT,* V, p. 817).

59. Cf. Bultmann, *TDNT,* I, p. 708, n. 73.

Ephesians 4:11,[60] are those who have beheld Christ himself, the eye-witnesses of the redemptive event lying at the foundation of the church, who have been called by Christ himself to this special ministry. Paul, too, appeals for his apostolate to the fact that he has seen the Lord, the Risen One (1 Cor. 9:1; cf. 15:8, 15). Together with being an eye-witness the special divine calling and sending also pertain to the essence of the apostolate (cf., e.g., Gal. 1:1). The apostleship is the privilege (charis; Rom. 1:5; 15:15) conferred by Christ himself on those who have been witnesses of his resurrection. They are therefore the heralds of salvation authorized by Christ (Rom. 10:15; 1 Cor. 1:23; 9:27; 1 Tim. 2:7 [apostle and herald]; cf. 2 Tim. 1:11); and their word is the kerygma (1 Cor. 15:14). Through this special position with respect to Christ as well as to the church, the apostolate according to its nature is unrepeatable and untransferable. The apostles, as the first gift of Christ to his church, therefore form a closed group, the bounds of which in Paul are not to be determined with certainty,[61] but of which he knew himself to be the last (1 Cor. 15:8; cf. 3:10).

The concept apostle is determined first of all by the idea of appointment and authorization. As apostles of Jesus Christ their word has absolute authority in the church, and they lay claim to obedience (Rom. 1:5; 2 Cor. 2:9; Phil. 2:12, et al.). They are the receivers and bearers of the tradition, the foundational gospel (1 Cor. 15:3-7; 11:23; 1 Thess. 2:13), the guarantors of the depositum fidei (1 Tim. 6:20; 2 Tim. 1:12, 14), the layers of the foundation of the church (1 Cor. 3:10; Eph. 2:20; 1 Cor. 9:1, 2); their writings are intended for liturgical reading in the church (Col. 4:16; 1 Thess. 5:27), the canon for the church to come.[62]

---

60. The effort of Brosch, Charismen und Ämter in der Urkirche, pp. 98ff., to distinguish the apostles mentioned in 1 Cor. 12 and Eph. 4 from the apostles appointed by Jesus and to conceive of this apostolate as a temporary phenomenon, which in its "circles of duties and manners of applications showed similarities with the stable office of the apostle, but was of a purely charismatic nature" (p. 109), rests, as is apparent from his whole argument, far too much on (Roman Catholic) dogmatic presuppositions and leads to very arbitrary exegeses of the passages involved.

61. The question is whether Paul knew other apostles in addition to the twelve in the sense of founders of the church. In 2 Cor. 8:23; Phil. 2:25 there is mention of apostles of the church(es), by whom are simply meant authorized (apostle = one having full powers) of one or more specific churches. And in 2 Cor. 11:5, 13; 12:11, it is a question of people who apparently called themselves apostles, but are called by Paul "false apostles who pose as apostles of Christ." Did Paul, however, know still other apostles of Christ than the twelve and himself? It is of special importance who are intended by tois apostolois pasin in 1 Cor. 15:7 (after the twelve; v. 5!). Holl has made it perfectly clear that one cannot understand here Christian missionaries in general (Gesammelte Aufsätze, II, pp. 47ff.). Only to think of the twelve, however — as Harnack, e.g., wished to do — is, after v. 5, also difficult; that the twelve plus James were intended (so Holl) does not appear from the context. Although the circle of "all the apostles" can only have been very small, yet more seem to have belonged to it than the twelve (cf. also Rom. 16:7; see also Grosheide, 1 Cor., p. 389; Lietzmann, Cor., pp. 77, 78; and for the whole question of 1 Cor. 15:7 at length W. G. Kümmel, Kirchenbegriff und Geschichtsbewusstsein in der Urgemeinde und bei Jesus, 1943, pp. 4ff.). Whether James also belonged to it is not to be proved with certainty from Gal. 1:19; 2:9.

62. On the significance of the apostolate see further my "De apostoliciteit

From the significance of the apostolate understood in this way it is clear that the apostles, unlike those invested with other ministries in the church, do not come forth from the church, but that the church rather owes its genesis to them (cf. Gal. 4:19; 1 Cor. 4:14, 15; 2 Cor. 6:13; 1 Thess. 2:11; Philem. 10); also that the significance of the apostles is not restricted to one congregation but that they exercise a universal ministry in the gospel. On the other hand, their task does not remain restricted to the foundation of the church. Although Paul places all the emphasis on this fundamental work and leaves the continuing upbuilding of the church to others (1 Cor. 3:10; cf. 1:17; cf. also Rom. 15:20, 21), yet he exercises a permanent authority over the churches founded by him. He stands by the church with counsel and admonition, with instruction and warning. He also occupies himself not only with the further unfolding of the gospel and with the combatting of false doctrine, but with the institution and maintenance of right order (*taxis;* Col. 2:5) in the church (cf. 1 Cor. 4:15; 9:1ff.; 2 Cor. 3:1-3; Gal. 6:6, *et al.*). The Pastoral Epistles in this respect represent a somewhat later stage in the development of the church and put all the stress on this regulative authority of the apostle and his fellow-workers; yet at a later time the organization of individual churches was not wrongly taken back to the apostles.[63] The apostles are not only the founders of the church; they also exercise authority over the whole church. One can speak of "an ecumenical function of the apostles."[64] Their significance for the upbuilding of the church, therefore, in addition to being unique and unrepeatable, is in part exemplary as well, directed toward imitation and succession, as is evident so far as Paul is concerned particularly from the Pastoral Epistles.

(2) Prophets

Along with the apostles the prophets occupy an important place in the enumerations given by Paul (1 Cor. 12:28 ["secondly" prophets]; Eph. 4:11; cf. Rom. 12:6; 1 Cor. 12:10). He devotes special and separate attention to the prophetic *charisma* (1 Cor. 14). Of all the *pneumatica* one must strive most after prophecy (1 Cor. 14:1). Paul places it above speaking in tongues (1 Cor. 14:5). Whereas the speaker in tongues edifies himself and is intelligible only to God, the prophet is concerned to build the church, to exhort, to encourage (14:3, 31). It holds for prophecy, in distinction from the language of tongues, that it takes place not only with the spirit, but also with the understanding, just as for public prayer in the church, the singing of psalms, and the giving of thanks (1 Cor. 14:13-19). Unbelievers and interested auditors,[65] too, will be brought to

---

der kerk in het N.T." in *De Apostolische Kerk*, 1954, pp. 39-97 and the literature cited there; *The Authority of the New Testament Scriptures*, pp. 13ff.; and especially B. Gerhardsson, *Memory and Manuscript*, 1961, pp. 262ff.

63. Cf. Bultmann, *Theology*, II, p. 106.

64. Menoud, *l'Église et les ministères*, p. 32.

65. *Hoi idiōtai;* see Arndt-Gingrich-Bauer, p. 371, *s.v.;* cf. also *ho topos tou idiōtou* (v. 16).

true self-knowledge only by prophecy (and not by glossolalia). For glosso-lalia must impress them as madness; prophecy, on the other hand, is addressed to them and can lead them to repentance and worship.

Prophecy is a special form of the Spirit given to and working in the church. For this reason the speaking of the prophets can also be called revelation (1 Cor. 14:30, cf. v. 26; v. 6, cf. Eph. 3:15), and they are mentioned together with the apostles (Eph. 3:5; cf. 2:20).[66] This character of prophecy as revelation is to be sought in speaking under the direct impulse of the Spirit (cf. 1 Cor. 14:30), but also in the content of what is spoken in this way. The prophet receives an insight into the mysteries of God (cf. 1 Cor. 13:2); he explains the meaning and progress of the divine redemptive activity (Eph. 3:5). When in Romans 11:25; 1 Corinthians 15:51; 1 Thessalonians 4:13, Paul announces and inter-prets to the church the redemptive work of God still to be expected, he also speaks in virtue of prophetic endowment. Yet prophecy does not only or primarily have reference to the future. It consists as well in pointing out the will of God (1 Tim. 1:18; 4:14), serves the church for exhortation, encouragement, and instruction (1 Cor. 14:3, 31; cf. vv. 24, 25). Prophets are the Spirit-impelled proclaimers of the Word of God to the church, who unfold God's plan of redemption, as well as elucidate and impress upon it the significance of the work of God in Christ in a pastoral and paraenetic sense.[67]

This prophecy and revelation is not to be understood, however, as an exceptional gift in which the church as such has no share and which it has to receive only as an infallible message of the Spirit coming to it from without. However much Paul sees the work of the Spirit in this prophecy and therefore warns the church not to quench the Spirit and not to despise the prophesyings (1 Thess. 5:19, 20), on the other hand the church is constantly to put prophecy to the test as to its genuine-ness and truth (1 Thess. 5:21; cf. 1 Cor. 14:36-38). It is a gift given to and in the church, which ought to be discerned by the church itself therefore and secured against abuse and degeneration (1 Cor. 12:10; 14:29). In Romans 12:6 it is said that prophecy must take place in conformity with the faith (kata tēn analogian tēs pisteōs). It is not only said here that every prophet must prophesy according to the measure of the faith allotted him,[68] for this would be too general a standard and difficult to understand. Evidently a more objective norm is intended here, namely, the faith according to its content,[69] or, in general, Christian doctrine. Any prophecy that no longer takes place in the faith of the Christian church, any prophetic enthusiasm gone astray,[70] must continually be averted. It is in agreement with this that in 1 Corinthians 14:29ff. Paul gives clear

---

66. For the view that Old Testament prophets are intended here, see, e.g., Roberts, *Die Opbou*, pp. 124ff.

67. Cf. such definitions as those of Friedrich, *TDNT*, VI, p. 848, and P. Menoud, *l'Église et les ministères*, p. 41.

68. So, e.g., Brosch, *Charismen und Ämter*, p. 86.

69. Cf. H. Greeven, "Propheten, Lehrer, Vorsteher bei Paulus," *ZNW*, 1952/3, p. 10; von Campenhausen, *Ecclesiastical Authority*, p. 62.

70. So Friedrich, *TDNT*, VI, p. 851.

directions on the manner in which prophecy is to take place in the church. This, too, is to be done not in confusion, but in peace and in mutual harmony. Several are not to speak at the same time, but sepa-rately, and one is to be prepared at once to give place to others. There is to be opportunity not only for prophesying, but also for judgment of the others. Whether by "the others" the whole congregation[71] is meant, or the others who were prophetically gifted,[72] prophecy is to be tested as to its content. For as the Spirit gives prophecy to the church, so he gives it the ability to discern the true and the false or inferior. It is not a question of the self-realization of the few, but of what is able to build and exhort the whole church. For this reason the spirits of the prophets are subject to the prophets (v. 32). Some take this as a mutual giving heed to one another and a submitting to one another on the part of the prophets;[73] most, however, as an indication of the self-control a prophet is to have over himself. In any case it is a matter of benefit for all and of the prophets putting themselves at the service of all. To that end they have need of self-control as well as an openness to mutual criticism. This same motive causes Paul in 1 Corinthians 13:2 to make prophecy conditional on love. Here again it is a question of being subservient to the church (love; cf. 1 Cor. 8:1) and against pneumatic individualism, no matter with what splendid gifts it may be adorned.

This prophecy, which is an evidence of the riches of the New Testament church, not only makes its appearance during the worship service as a gift here and now, but also qualifies certain persons to be prophets, that is to say, as permanent bearers of the gift of prophecy (1 Cor. 12:28; Eph. 4:11).[74] The prophetic gift certainly gave them a position of leadership and will also have brought them to recognition in the church as designated leaders, whether in a more or in a less official sense.[75]

(3) Teachers

Teachers are mentioned in 1 Corinthians 12:28 under "thirdly," in Ephesians 4:11 in one breath with pastors. As Paul ascribes the prophetic gift to himself (1 Cor. 14:6), so also that of the teacher (cf. 1 Cor. 4:17; 2 Thess. 2:15; Col. 1:28; 1 Tim. 2:7; 2 Tim. 1:11). In 1 Corinthians 14 (cf. Rom. 12), "teaching" occurs as a *charisma* that manifests itself freely in the church (1 Cor. 14:26). Yet just as in the case of apostles and prophets, a clearly delimited group of persons with a definite spiritual quality is apparently to be thought of with teachers as well (1 Cor. 12:28; cf. Eph. 4:11). They might as such lay claim to a certain recognition and count on the liberality of others (Gal. 6:6). This points to a continuing, methodical activity. We do not read of a distinct office of teacher, that is

---

71. So Lietzmann, *Cor., in loc.*
72. So Greeven, *ZNW*, p. 6; Büchsel, *TDNT*, III, p. 947, n. 8; Brosch, *Charis-men und Ämter*, p. 76; von Campenhausen, *Ecclesiastical Authority*, p. 62.
73. Greeven, *ZNW*, p. 13.
74. Cf. Bultmann, *Theology*, I, pp. 161f.
75. See Greeven, *ZNW*, p. 8, and the literature cited there.

to say, appointment as teacher in and by the church. It is required of the leading figures in the church, for example, of the overseers, that they be *didaktikos,* apt to teach (1 Tim. 3:2; cf. 2 Tim. 2:24; Tit. 1:9), and of the elders those are to be held in highest honor who are charged especially with preaching and instruction (1 Tim. 5:17; cf. 1 Thess. 5:12; 2 Tim. 2:2). Women are forbidden to teach (1 Tim. 2:12).

It is no simple matter to distinguish precisely the activity of these teachers from those of the other *charismatici,* for example, the prophets. Their teaching seems to go back less than prophecy to the direct inspiration and impulse of the Spirit, but rather to have consisted in instruction and in transmitting the apostolic tradition, both as concerns its great redemptive-historical content and the paraenesis arising from it. As "teaching" and "tradition" are concepts that in Paul lie very closely together (cf. Rom. 6:17; Gal. 1:12; 2 Thess. 2:15; Col. 2:6, 7), so one will have to understand by "teachers" those who were competent to instruct others in the Christian tradition and precepts (cf. 1 Cor. 4:17; 2 Tim. 2:2). One is not therefore to restrict the activity of these teachers to a certain part of Christian doctrine, for example, to the paraenesis, but rather to extend it to the whole content of the proclamation.[76] Hence at one time "the gospel" in an all-embracing sense, then again the manner in which one is to live from it, is denoted as the content of the "doctrine" (Gal. 1:11, 12; Col. 1:23; 3:16, *et al.*). One will therefore be permitted to suppose that in the time when oral tradition was still the primary source for knowledge of the Christian faith, the teachers provided an important ministry for the propagation of that tradition. In this connection the corresponding use of the name of teacher in the Synoptic Gospels as a designation of the Jewish teachers is also to be pointed out. They, too, had the task of transmitting the fixed material of tradition, whereby in particular the tradition concerning the Old Testament played a great part. If, as could appear from the close connection of "tradition" and "doctrine," one may consider the name of the Christian teachers to have originated by analogy with that of the Jewish, in this way the activity of these Christian teachers is also to be further understood.[77] The labor of these teachers will have been of particular significance for the catechumenate and the instruction of those who wished to be baptized. On the other hand, as appears from the close conjunction of "pastors and teachers" in Ephesians 4:11, their teaching activity had a broader scope as well. While the modality of prophets and teachers was different, therefore, the former representing more the current, the latter the traditional aspect of the preaching of the gospel, the function of both lay in upbuilding, comforting, and giving spiritual direction to the church. It is consequently not easy to locate exactly the line of demarcation and to determine with respect to the "word of wisdom" and "word of knowledge," for example, whether these are

---

76. Cf. Greeven, *ZNW*, pp. 18ff., and W. Schrage, *Die konkreten Einzelgebote in der paulinischen Paränese,* 1961, pp. 136ff.

77. Cf. Greeven, *ZNW*, p. 28; von Campenhausen, *loc. cit.*

specifically prophetic or didactic qualities.[78] When one reads Colossians 2:1-8, for example, it is clear that the treasures of knowledge and wisdom that are hidden in Christ exhibit prophetic as well as didactic aspects, both of which are necessary for the upbuilding of the church and require interpretation by persons who are differently gifted.

(4) Evangelists

In the enumerations of the gifts given to the church the evangelists are mentioned only in Ephesians 4. Elsewhere in Paul we find this qualification in 2 Timothy 4:5, where he exhorts Timothy: "do the work of an evangelist." Because of the sparing use of this word — elsewhere in the New Testament only in Acts 21:8, where there is mention of the evangelist Philip — it is not easy to determine its content accurately. Most often the thought is that of men who set out to proclaim the gospel, such as Philip (Acts 8:4ff., 12, 35, 40), or of helpers of the apostles. Thus Paul calls Timothy his fellow-worker in the gospel of Christ (1 Thess. 3:2). Their number was perhaps greater therefore than is to be gathered from the scanty use of the name evangelist[79] (cf., e.g., Col. 4:11; 2 Cor. 8:18; Phil. 4:3). Here again a specific office in the sense of a regular appointment is not to be spoken of with certainty. Certain persons being regularly employed in this ministry will surely have been qualified as such. That one is to regard them not only as missionaries but also as leaders of already established churches, as Friedrich, also on the ground of 2 Timothy 4:5, thinks himself able to posit,[80] is doubtful. Certainly the evangelists will not have confined themselves to the proclamation of the gospel, but also have baptized and given directions for the establishment of the organization of the church (cf. 1 Tim. 2:2; Tit. 1:5; Acts 8:12). Yet their proper work, so far as we are able to conclude from the few examples, apparently lay not so much in the government of the church as in the continuing proclamation of the gospel.[81] In the first period they frequently formed the link between the apostles and the leading figures in the church. With the dying out of the apostles the evangelists disappear as well.[82]

(5) Pastors

So far as the pastors in Ephesians 4:11 are concerned, these are mentioned together with the teachers with the same article, which does not to be sure imply an identity, but does seem to point to a close relationship between the work of pastors and teachers. One may infer the nature of the ministry of these pastors from the metaphorical mode of expression, as that of the leadership and care of the church. In 1 Peter 2:25

---

78. On this see also Brosch, *Charismen und Ämter*, p. 115 (cf. pp. 80, 91, 92).
79. Cf. Friedrich, *TDNT*, II, p. 737.
80. *Loc. cit.*
81. Cf. E. K. Simpson, *The Pastoral Epistles*, 1954, p. 154.
82. See also J. L. Koole, *Liturgie en ambt in de apostolische kerk*, 1949, pp. 81, 82.

Christ is spoken of as pastor and overseer (episkopos); in Acts 20:28 the presbyters of Ephesus are charged to take heed to the flock (cf. 1 Pet. 5:1, 2). Pastors therefore do the work that is elsewhere committed to presbyters and bishops. Ephesians 4:11 qualifies "pastors and teachers" more as an activity than as an office, though the office of overseer can very well be alluded to (cf. Phil. 1:1). That "pastors and teachers" are so closely linked points to what they have in common in their ministry as leaders of the church, whereby the teachers especially take upon themselves the task of instruction, the pastors the general guidance of the church (cf. 1 Tim. 5:17).

In close connection with this ministry of the pastor we shall also have to understand the other qualifications that point to gifts of leadership in the church. Thus Romans 12:8 exhorts the pro-histamenos[83] (he who gives leadership) to exercise this charisma with zeal. The same word is employed in 1 Thessalonians 5:12, and in the same context there is mention of "those who admonish you." In 1 Timothy 3, again with the same word, the demand is made of the overseers that they are to rule their own house well (pro-histamenon [v. 4]; prostēnai [v. 5]); for how shall a man who cannot do this be able to take care of (epimeleisthai) the church of God? And in 1 Timothy 5:17 the same quality is ascribed to the presbyters (hoi kalōs proestōtes presbyteroi). Although the point of view in Romans and 1 Timothy is different (what is there called charisma is here made a condition for the office), the one does not exclude the other, and with those who give leadership in Romans 12 Paul can very well be alluding to presbyters or bishops.[84] The same applies to the enumerations in 1 Corinthians 12:28-30. There he uses the word "qualities of government" (kybernēseis) in the same sense. Here, too, he certainly has in view specific persons in the church, who in virtue of the capacities given to them occupy a position of leadership and to whom others are obligated to submit themselves (cf. 1 Cor. 16:16). Once again the qualities and not the official powers are mentioned here. But this need not mean that in these churches no such offices as that of presbyter had (yet) been instituted[85] (cf. Phil. 1:1).

---

83. Ho pro-histamenos; variant — stanomenos.

84. Brosch is of the opinion that by those who give leadership in Rom. 12 are meant those who were entrusted with the work of mercy. The same would hold for the kybernēseis in 1 Cor. 12:28. But this is, also in view of the use of prostēnai, etc., in 1 Tim. 3:4, 5; 5:17, a too restricted view; see also B. Reicke, TDNT, VI, p. 702.

85. Some are of the opinion that in Rom. and 1 Cor. the presence of elders and deacons must simply be presupposed. Who other than the elders would have written Paul the letter to which he responds in 1 Cor.? Thus A. M. Farrer, The Apostolic Ministry, 1947, p. 153. He thinks also that in 1 Cor. 6:2 an allusion is made to Isa. 24:21-23 (LXX), where there is mention of God's judgment (episkopē) and of his glory before his elders. There would be in this a hint that in 1 Cor. 6 Paul thought of the supervision of the elders over the church. Schweizer, Church Order in the New Testament, p. 99, n. 379, terms this argumentation "unconvincing." But as much interested as (the Anglican) Farrer appears to be in the early episcopate, so much is Schweizer at pains to give as little "chance" as possible to the institutional in Paul. In practice he plays down Phil. 1:1, mentions this passage only once, states that Schmithals regards the words syn episkopois kai diakonois in Phil. 1:1 as a gloss (for which there is otherwise no textual critical or material basis

(6) Mutual service

The *charismata* that refer to mutual service in the church are yet again of a somewhat different character. When believers are admonished in Romans 12 that everyone is to put the gift conferred on him into practice in the right manner, Paul comes to the following pronouncements, among others: "if it is [the gift of] service, [let it appear] in serving *(eite diakonian, en tē diakonia)*, . . . he who distributes *(ho metadidous)* of his own, [let him do it] in simplicity, . . . he who does acts of mercy *(ho eleōn)*, [let him do it] with cheerfulness . . ." (Rom. 12:7, 8). And the expression "mutual acts of service" or "ability to serve" *(antilēmpseis)* in 1 Corinthians 12:28 will have to be classed in the same category.

It is no simple matter to form a clear idea of all these descriptions and to make a precise distinction, for example, between distributing and doing acts of mercy. The first perhaps has aid to the poor in view, the second the work of mercy in a more general sense.[86] The acts of service of 1 Corinthians 12:28 could then embrace the one as well as the other.[87] Still more difficult is the interpretation of the general denotation "service" and "serving" in the context of Romans 12:7. Perhaps the word that in general can denote every act of service, in Romans 12:7, where the point is just that of specialization, has the significance of helping work of love, practical rendering of service, as it is also employed elsewhere in Paul (cf. Rom. 15:31; cf. v. 25; 1 Cor. 16:15; 2 Cor. 8:4ff.; 9:12ff.). In Romans 12:7 it would then have about the same meaning as that which we have taken as "acts of service" in 1 Corinthians 12:28. In any case, it is clear that among the various *charismata* the apostle also emphatically designates those which lie in the province of the practical rendering of assistance to one another.

(7) Presbyters, bishops

If so far we have had to do chiefly with those *charismata* whereby it was especially the qualitative character of the ministries that was in the foreground, and if the boundaries between these ministries and the offices to be occupied in behalf of the church are not always clearly to

---

whatever), and then acknowledges in passing — after he has first written that in Paul the absence of presbyters "is . . . a demonstration in which he throws overboard everything that is merely conservative and retrospective, and stresses the vitality of the ever-present Spirit in the Church of the last days" *(ibid.,* p. 99) — that inasmuch as Paul recognizes the *antilēmpseis* and the *kybernēseis* as *charismata,* it "is quite possible that such services were part of the order later too" (p. 103, n. 395). But, as appears from Phil. 1:1, this then occurred already in a church founded by Paul in his own lifetime (for that matter also entirely in harmony with Acts 14:23), so that there can be no question of a demonstration that there were no elders, etc. In fact, all that Paul writes on giving leadership, etc., is applicable to the office of elder, however remarkable it may be that outside the Pastoral Epistles only in Phil. 1:1 does he speak explicitly of bishops and deacons.

86. Cf. my *Rom.,* p. 280. Bultmann, *TDNT,* II, p. 483, speaks of "loving-kindness in general."

87. Delling, *TDNT,* I, p. 376, writes: "The reference is obviously to the activity of love in the dealings of the community."

be distinguished, it is otherwise with the offices of presbyter, bishop, and deacon, mentioned in Philippians 1:1 and the Pastoral Epistles.

So far first of all as the presbyters and bishops are concerned, it should be stated at once that we have to do here with one and the same office. The names, of course, have a different significance. Presbyter, eldest, certainly has a patriarchal background and originated in Judaism, where it is the designation of a certain status. That in the Pastoral Epistles it is "a specification not of office but of age," as Jeremias supposes,[88] is in view of Titus 1:5 not to be accepted.[89] The *episkopos* is not so easily identified as the counterpart of a pre-Christian figure, whether from the Jewish or from the Greek world.[90] But even so both words must denote the same kind of office-bearers, from different points of view. For not only are the demands that are made of the good presbyter in Titus 1:5-9 very much akin to what is said of the *episkopos* in 1 Timothy 3:2ff., but also the designations are used interchangeably in Titus 1:7 without there being a transition to other persons.[91]

The significance of the office of presbyter or bishop is not expressly mentioned in the Pastoral Epistles. It is assumed to be well known. The necessary prerequisites of the presbyter or *episkopos* respec-

---

88. J. Jeremias, *Die Briefe an Timotheüs und Titus (NTD)*, p. 33.

89. In Tit. 1:5 there is mention of *katastēnai* of presbyters, which it is surely difficult to understand of older men.

90. See the discussion of the various views in Beyer, *TDNT*, II, pp. 614ff., particularly that of Goetz, who finds the Jewish *archisynagōgos* with his *hypēretēs* in the *episkopos* with the *diakonos;* and that of Jeremias, who connects the *episkopos* with the *mebaqqēr*, the leader of the church of the New Covenant according to the Damascus Document. From thence the conclusion would be back to the office of the leader of a Pharisaic community. But, without regard now to the linguistic issue, the question is whether one can speak of such a material correspondence, that the office intended in the Qumran literature can in a broader ("Pharisaic") context have been the pattern for the New Testament bishop; see also Schweizer, *Church Order in the New Testament*, p. 201, n. 763; and B. Reicke in Krister Stendahl, *The Scrolls and the New Testament*, 1958, p. 150.

91. See, e.g., Beyer, *TDNT*, II, p. 617; Bultmann, *Theology*, II, p. 102. To be sure, others wish to know nothing of an identification of presbyter and *episkopos;* so, e.g., Bornkamm, *TDNT*, VI, pp. 666f., *s.v. presbys*. He points out that *episkopos* in the Pastoral Epistles always occurs in the singular, while the presbyters form a college. He thinks then that they represent two different principles of church organization, and that the *episkopos* has originally a more monarchical tendency. One will have to think of the bishops in the Pastoral Epistles, according to Bornkamm, as the *presbyteroi proestōtes*, which he then conceives as "presbyters who come to the fore"; cf. also J. L. Koole, *Liturgie en ambt in de apostolische kerk*, p. 93. Spicq, too, in his commentary on the Pastoral Epistles, will know nothing of an identification. The *episkopos* is the *primus inter pares*, the *presbyteros kat' exochēn*. In this way, in the *episkopos* of the New Testament the transition is established to the monarchical episcopate. But altogether incorrectly. When the *episkopos* is spoken of in the singular this is undoubtedly to be taken generically, just as occurs with the presbyter in 1 Tim. 5:1; cf. Bl.-Debr., Par. 139 (for the singular) and Par. 252, 263 (for the particle). In Phil. 1:1 they are in fact mentioned in the plural. Furthermore, that in 1 Tim. 3:1-7 and 8-13 the *episkopos* and the deacon are indeed spoken of, but not the presbyter mentioned elsewhere in 1 Tim., is no evidence of two different offices, but only of a varying use of language (cf. also Acts 20:17, 28). Titus 1:5-8 is in this respect certainly highly illustrative and conclusive. The shifting of the monarchical episcopacy to the New Testament is therefore arbitrary.

tively in 1 Timothy 3:1-7 and Titus 1:6ff. are of a general, for the most
part ethical nature and only intimate obliquely anything of the character
of the office, for example, in 1 Timothy 3:4, 5, where there is mention
of "to be at the head of" *(pro-histasthai, prostēnai)*, "to keep under
discipline" *(echein en hypotagē)*, "to take care of" *(epimeleisthai)*. It can
be gathered from this, therefore, that the task of the presbyter-*episkopos*
consists particularly in giving leadership to, and seeing to it that things
go well in, the church, just as there is mention in 1 Timothy 5:17 of the
elders who "rule well," and in Titus 1:7 the *episkopos* is called "God's
steward" *(Theou oikonomos)*. A special point, moreover, is his ability to
advocate and defend the Christian doctrine. The bishop is to be *didaktikos* (1 Tim. 3:2), which we shall surely have to take as "apt to teach."
According to Titus 1:9 he must "hold fast to the trustworthy word in
accordance with the teaching, so that he may be able also to exhort upon
the ground of the sound doctrine and to confute those who contradict
it." Similarly there is mention in 1 Timothy 5:17 of the honor[92] that is
due to the elders who rule well, "particularly to those who labor in
[the preaching of] the word and in teaching" *(hoi kopiōntes en logō kai
didaskalia)*. It is to be inferred from this that the elders had the leadership of the church not only in terms of administration and church order,
but also in a spiritual and essential sense.[93] Within and without they had
to advocate and defend the Christian faith in its pure and original meaning. In this respect their labor in part coincided with that of "the
teachers." As is evident from 1 Timothy 5:17, however, not all elders
were equally directly and specifically involved in "labor in the word and
in teaching." For some the center of gravity was more general leadership, from which, however, one cannot dissociate the teaching aspect; for
others it was more proclamation and teaching, without it being possible
simply to identify them with "teachers" or "prophets." It appears from
this that the boundaries between the official and non-official *charisma*
are fluid. The *charisma* of government and leadership (Rom. 12:9; 1 Cor.
12:28) was indispensable and in that sense a prerequisite for the
presbyter-bishop. Nor, moreover, could aptness to teach be lacking, for
it was the men with those special gifts who were called to leadership in
the church. The *charisma* tends to the office, and the office cannot lack
the *charisma*. That there was furthermore a development toward the
official is not to be denied, and is altogether in the nature of the case,
both when one views it from the side of the *charisma* and from that of
the office. From the side of the *charisma*: certain qualities given by the
Spirit of themselves made the persons qualified thereby to come to the
fore; and the recognition and appointment of these persons as official
leaders, elders, bishops, lay in the line of development and was negatively
advanced by the fact that the church had to distinguish between that
which was genuine and edifying and that which was spurious and de-
structive in what were said to be *pneumatica*. On the other hand, the

---

92. *Timē* is also thought of in the sense of *honorarium* (cf. 1 Tim. 5:18).
93. So now Dibelius-Conzelmann, *A Commentary on the Pastoral Epistles*,
pp. 54ff.

appointment of general leaders in the official sense was not a novelty for the Christian church, but in harmony with its Jewish-synagogical background, and in general with the demands of practical reality. That in so doing not every individual *charisma* became an office is clear from this practice and is likewise understandable from the nature of the case. The presbyter-bishops were not intended to take the place of the non-official *charismatici*. The meaning and structure of their office had a more general significance: to give leadership to the organizational and spiritual life of the church. They were indeed recruited from among the persons endowed by the Spirit with special gifts, but did not deprive the latter of the freedom and the room to go on building the church in a non-official sense. The general character of the office of the elders as giving leadership did involve the fact that certain *charismata* (e.g., that of the ability to teach, to govern, to speak) were more essential and conducive to commendation than others that contributed less to this leadership (e.g., the gift of healing, speaking in tongues, *et al.*). It is to be understood in this way that where the official aspect begins to come more into prominence, as, for example, in the Pastoral Epistles, some *charismata* are discussed, others are not. This development is not to be called one-sided in the sense that the office came to thrust aside or over-shadow the *charisma*.[94] As congregational life consolidated itself on the foundation of the apostolic tradition and doctrine (formation of the canon), the church had greatest need of those *charismata* which Paul designates as the foundation of, and as indispensable for, the office of the presbyter-*episkopos:* the gift of government, the ability to teach, the correct distinguishing of what is in conflict with sound doctrine, and a good posture toward those without. It is primarily this office, therefore, to which he entrusts the church in its further upbuilding and develop-ment when the time draws to a close during which the apostles and their immediate helpers stood by and governed the churches.

(8) Deacons

In close connection with the presbyter-*episkopos* Paul speaks of deacons (Phil. 1:1; 1 Tim. 3:1, 8; in Tit. 1 he mentions only the former). From the "deacons'-mirror" in 1 Timothy 3:8-13 very little is evident con-cerning the nature of the office intended there. The demands made of deacons are of a more general kind. It is to be gathered from the re-mainder of the New Testament that the office of the deacon especially provided for (the direction of) mutual assistance in the church and will therefore have had reference in particular to what Paul describes in Romans 12 as the *charisma* of serving, sharing, showing mercy (vv. 6-8), and in 1 Corinthians 12:28 as the gift given by God to the church of the "capacity to help" *(antilēmpseis)*. It is clear from the manner in

---

94. G. Delling, *Worship in the New Testament,* ET 1962, pp. 40f., also shows that the differences that occur with respect to the operation of the Spirit in worship between the Pastoral Epistles and the earlier epistles do not touch the essence of the matter (see further above, p. 444).

which he speaks of these *charismata* that he does not attribute to all this activity a subordinate or dependent significance among the *charismata* as a whole, but rather brings into prominence their peculiar and independent character. If, as surely seems obvious, we may now assume that the office of deacon was instituted for the regular supervision of this mutual assistance, it can also be concluded from this that the deacon is not to be viewed merely as an assistant elder, or as a subordinate of the overseers,[95] but as an office-bearer to whom a peculiar task was assigned in the proper functioning of the life of the church as the body of Christ and that he was to be acknowledged as such. That for this work a separate office came into being will have to be judged in the same way as the rise of the office of elder. It applies to the office of deacon, too, that it did not come in place of the charismatic ministries, but that it rather rested on them, but nevertheless proved to be necessary for regular and assured order in this work. That room remained and had to remain alongside it for the gifts of the Spirit that were not being employed in the way of office is plain when one is able to distinguish the office of deacon, just as the office of the presbyter-*episkopos,* in terms of its own reason for existence, namely, as a means of giving direction to the church in an ordered way in the right administration of the gifts and powers given it by Christ, which it needed for its continuing and regular upbuilding.

(9) Women

The position the woman occupies in the upbuilding and equipment of the church constitutes a separate question. We must confine ourselves here to what is most important.[96] Generally Paul's pronouncements on the place of women in the church exhibit the same two viewpoints we have already been able to observe in his precepts for marriage:[97] on the one hand the woman shares fully in the salvation given in Christ, and there is complete equality between man and woman in that respect, just as between Jew and Greek, master and slave, etc. (Gal. 3:28; Col. 3:11; cf. 1 Cor. 11:11, 12); on the other hand, fellowship in Christ does not remove the natural distinction between man and woman, and man's position of leadership with regard to woman. Considering the place women occupied in Paul's day, both in antiquity in general and in

---

95. Some indeed want to relate the office of deacon to those who performed certain services for the apostles (cf. Acts 19:22; 13:5); possibly the deacons would then in a similar way be the servants of the bishops (cf. Schweizer, *Church Order in the New Testament,* p. 199). But this interpretation of the deacon's office projects back the later development. Paul speaks of the deacons as servants of the church and their ministry as a *charisma* given to the church and not as servants or a *charisma* for the benefit of the apostles or bishops.

96. For the following see also the detailed studies of G. Delling, *Paulus' Stellung zu Frau und Ehe,* 1931; F. J. Leenhardt, *La place de la femme dans l'église après le N.T.,* 1948; N. J. Hommes, *De vrouw in de kerk. Nieuwtest. perspectieven,* 1951; G. Huls, *De dienst der vrouw in de kerk,* 1952; K. H. Rengstorf, "Die neutest. Mahnungen an die Frau," etc., in *Festschrift für O. Schmitz,* 1953, pp. 131-145; L. Hick, *Die Stellung des hl. Paulus zur Frau im Rahmen seiner Zeit,* 1957; Else Kähler, *Die Frau in den paulinischen Briefen,* 1960.

97. Above, Section 50.

Judaism in particular,[98] the first point of view certainly meant nothing less than a revolution for the position of women in the church as well. This equality of man and woman in Christ emerges in a great many ways in his epistles. Although he frequently addresses the church as "brethren," he often directs himself expressly to the women as well; and that not merely, as also happened in the synagogue, with commandments, but in other ways, too, as is evident, for example, from the large place women take up in the lists of greetings (cf. Rom. 16). The gift of prophecy for the benefit of the church he attributes to women as much as to men (1 Cor. 11:5), just as "praying," by which what is intended in this context is certainly not only personal, private prayer, but prayer in the presence and to the edification of others. Along with that such women are to be pointed to as Priscilla, whom with her husband Paul calls his fellow-worker (cf. Acts 18:2); and as Mary (Rom. 16:6), of whom he testifies, with a word that specifically denotes work in the gospel and in the church (kopian), that she "worked" hard. The same applies to Tryphena and Tryphosa and Persis (Rom. 16:12). He attributes to such a woman as Phoebe in Romans 16:1ff. specific ministries and qualities in his own and the church's behalf, which are certainly to be classed among the charismata of assistance and serving in Romans 12:7ff. and 1 Corinthians 12:28. Even if Phoebe were not a deaconess in the "official" sense of the word,[99] there is in that fact, as we have repeatedly contended,[100] no fundamental difference whatever from official appointment to the occupancy of such a ministry by the church. Nor is there any argument whatever to be derived from Paul's epistles that it was only the non-official charisma that was extended to the woman and not regular office. In 1 Timothy 5:9ff. there is in any case mention of an ordered task for widows in the church and of a ministry or office to which some of them were to be admitted and others were not.[101]

On the other hand, Paul also imposes certain restrictions on women, particularly so far as their behavior in the meeting of the church is concerned. In 1 Corinthians 14:34 it is expressly required of them that they keep silence in the church (gatherings). It is no simple matter to reconcile this commandment to silence with the gift (and liberty) granted them in 1 Corinthians 11 of praying or prophesying. According to some it is only asked of the women in 1 Corinthians 14:34ff. that they be silent in the judging of others (prophecy);[102] others wish to regard verses 34 and 35 as later additions;[103] still others are of the

---

98. See, e.g., Strack-Billerbeck, III, pp. 467ff., 558ff., 610ff.

99. The text does not in our view permit firm conclusions (cf. my Rom., in loc.). There is also a difference of opinion on the question whether in 1 Tim. 3:11ff. there is mention of the wives of the deacons or of deaconesses. The former is the more probable; but see, e.g., also Schweizer, Church Order in the New Testament, p. 86, n. 334.

100. Above, Section 70.

101. Chēra katalegesthai: be enrolled, be considered, as "widow."

102. Cf. Koole, Liturgie, p. 101.

103. Schweizer, Church Order in the New Testament, p. 203, n. 783. But in terms of textual criticism there is not the slightest ground for this.

opinion that a satisfactory solution has so far not been found.[104] It seems difficult to escape the conclusion, however, that to "keep silence in the church" means the same thing as the words in 1 Corinthians 14:28: to be silent in the meeting of the church. One is to think of this praying and prophesying of the women as restricted to pneumatic utterances outside the official gathering. The proscription apparently applies to women speaking in public.

Paul motivates this command to silence in various ways. In 1 Corinthians 14:34 he says it is not permitted women to speak[105] but that they "must remain subordinate," must conform to the rule or order appointed them (hypotassesthai; cf. Eph. 5:22), "as" — so he adds to this — "the law also says." What is meant apparently is the rule or order relating to the place of woman with respect to man. It follows accordingly that if there is anything a woman desires to know she is to ask it of her own husband at home. For, thus Paul goes on, "it is shameful (aischron) for a woman to speak in the church [gathering]." We meet with a similar pronouncement in 1 Timothy 2:11. A woman is — in the church meeting, for which directions are given here — to keep quiet in all subordination (hypotagē). It is therefore not permitted a woman to teach, nor "to have authority[106] over the man,"[107] but she is to keep still, to be quiet. Here again an appeal follows to what is in 1 Corinthians 14 called the law, in other words, to the history of the beginning: Adam was created first, then Eve. And Adam was not deceived, but the woman.

It is clear that in this argumentation two different motives are very closely coupled together: (a) what "the law" says or is inferred from the history of the beginning, and (b) what according to standards current in Paul's day was considered unbecoming for a woman. The latter he denotes with the words "it is shameful" in the same manner that he speaks in 1 Corinthians 11:5-13 of "proper" (prepon; v. 13) and "shameful" (aischron; v. 6) with a view to whether or not a woman prays or prophesies with uncovered head. In this last instance, too (in a way the sense of which is difficult for us any longer to fathom[108]), the intention was to give expression to the distinction between man and woman and perhaps also to the subjection of woman to man. The deeper motive, i.e., the place that from the beginning God chose to ascribe to woman in her relationship to man, therefore finds its concrete form in the manner in which it is proper according to custom that a woman conduct herself in public and is to know her place with respect to man. So

---

104. Schrage, Die konkreten Einzelgebote, p. 126.

105. Lalein. One can still consider whether this is intended in the sense of "to teach," as in Tit. 2:1. But v. 35 points in another direction.

106. Authentein, a word that seldom occurs.

107. In spite of the exegesis of some who have wanted to curtail the significance of this passage as much as possible, andros cannot here mean specifically "her husband," as though it were only a question of "the woman wanting to lord it over her own husband." We have to do here not with a household rule, but with a liturgical prescription.

108. For the various opinions with respect to this still unresolved question, see the commentaries, especially Lietzmann-Kümmel.

far as this is concerned Paul is here apparently apprehensive, just as he is elsewhere, lest in the consciousness of its new freedom the church give offense to others, and he admonishes the Corinthians, who in this respect evidently permitted themselves more liberties than did other churches, to keep within the general line of conduct (cf. 1 Cor. 14:33, 36ff.). On the other hand, it is clear that there is also a relativizing element in this appeal to custom and the "commune mesure," insofar, that is, as the (sub-*ordinated*) position of woman with respect to man is to be given expression in a manner that must be considered appropriate for a certain time and culture.

(10) Extraordinary powers, glossolalia

While there is an unmistakable connection between the gifts and ministries in the church with which we have dealt so far and the offices more clearly discernible in the later epistles of Paul, the apostle still mentions a few other *charismata*, in particular in 1 Corinthians 12 and 14, which bear a character in many respects to be distinguished from them. It is here a question first of all of the *charismata* mentioned under 11-15 in the enumeration given above, namely, "powers," "faith," the gift of healing, glossolalia, and its interpretation.

As regards the "powers" mentioned first (1 Cor. 12:10, 28), one will have to think here, just as with the "faith" spoken of in 1 Corinthians 12:9 (cf. 1 Cor. 13:2), of the gift conferred by the Spirit on some persons of performing unusual deeds, miracles in the broadest sense of the word (cf. 1 Cor. 13:2), of which the gift of healing will surely have constituted a very prominent part. Paul speaks of these special powers not only in this catalogue of the *charismata*. In more than one place he testifies that his own appearance was accompanied with these miracles; so, for example, in Romans 15:18, 19, where he speaks of what Christ has wrought through him for the obedience of the gentiles, "by word and deed, in the power of signs and wonders, by the power of the Spirit." And in 2 Corinthians 12:12 he mentions expressly "the signs of the apostle," which were wrought in the church of Corinth "by signs and wonders and powers" (cf. also Gal. 3:5 and 1 Thess. 1:5). There is a confirmation here of what we read from the reports of Paul's conduct in Acts 13:11; 14:3, 10, *et al.*, and in general of that which according to Mark 16:17 the risen Christ promised to his disciples as evidence of his communion with them.

Paul describes these powers, etc., in 1 Corinthians 12 therefore as *charismata*, given by God in the church, not to all, however, but to some (1 Cor. 12:29, 30). When he speaks to the same effect here of "faith," this will have to be understood in a special sense, that is, as the confidence worked by the Spirit in the miraculous help of God, which enables the performance of miracles (cf. Mark 4:40; 9:23ff.; 11:22ff.; Matt. 17:20; Luke 17:6),[109] a gift that is distinguished from the others and is not

---

109. For this meaning of *pistis*, see Bultmann, *TDNT*, VI, pp. 206f. Brosch defines this gift as "a supernatural ability to discern that God is going to reveal

peculiar to every believer (cf. 1 Cor. 13:2: "if I have all faith ..."). Because of this last the question as to the nature of this *charisma* thrusts itself the more forcefully upon us. For faith as trust in the wonder-working omnipotence of God is not only given to some, but, as appears from Romans 4:17-20, also defines the essence of that which distinguishes every believer as a child of Abraham from unbelievers. With this *charisma* it is accordingly not only a question of the certainty of what God will do in his time and way in the fulfilling of his promises, but of the certainty of being enabled by God at a specific moment to perform a miracle. Christ reproaches his disciples for their unbelief or little faith when they appear to be incapable of doing such mighty acts (Matt. 17:20). Paul speaks of these in particular as "the signs of the apostle" (2 Cor. 12:12). We shall thus have to view this *charisma* in close connection with the coming of the kingdom of God manifesting itself in the proclamation of the gospel, as a gift that Christ confers and wants to see used in the upbuilding of his church, however without every believer knowing himself gifted with this *charisma* of faith or empowered to the performance of miracles. And we shall have to judge the "gifts of healing" in the same way, though in 1 Corinthians 12:9 they are again distinguished from "faith." Neither do all have those gifts (v. 30), nor may there be jealousy of or contempt for one another in the church with respect to this diversity of gifts (1 Cor. 12:14ff.; Rom. 12:4ff.). But here again the Spirit works extraordinary powers. There is otherwise no further reflection on these healings in the epistles of Paul. They do not signify an end of sickness, suffering, and death in this world, nor do they constitute the means for being released from temporal suffering for everyone who simply believes (cf. Rom. 8:22, 23; 2 Cor. 12:7ff.; 2 Tim. 4:20). They are rather signs of the mighty power of Christ and of the all-embracing significance of his kingdom, which the Spirit works in the service of the proclamation of the gospel. They clearly have an extraordinary significance, however, and do not in Paul's epistles receive a permanent place in the continuing life of the church and in its upbuilding, as may also be concluded from the lack of any official form of this *charisma*.

Further, the manner in which Paul speaks in 1 Corinthians 12-14 of glossolalia is no less striking and much more elaborate, partly, as we have already seen, in connection and comparison with prophecy. Just as gifts of healing and miraculous powers, glossolalia only occurs as a *charisma* in Paul in the catalogue of 1 Corinthians 12, and in the express discussion of the value of glossolalia in 1 Corinthians 14. Although this need not mean that the phenomenon was not to be found in other churches, it was evidently especially prominent in Corinth. Paul considers it necessary to say something about it. He calls it by the name of speak-

---

his might, justice, and mercy in a very definite, concrete case. Should another person, who does not possess this charisma, wish to induce a similar miracle of God in a similar case, one would have to say, 'He is tempting God' " (*Charismen und Ämter*, p. 50).

ing or praying in tongues,[110] and for those who possessed the *charisma* ascribes a God-glorifying significance to it (1 Cor. 14:2ff.). And in 1 Corinthians 13:1 he mentions speaking in the tongues of men and of angels, with a clear allusion to glossolalia. It may be therefore that glossolalia was regarded as a kind of "heavenly language." Paul thus has a positive attitude toward it. In glossolalia he recognizes the working of the Spirit in the church. He himself lays claim to the possession of this gift, even to a greater degree than all in Corinth. On the other hand, he values prophecy more highly, and of that fact he also gives a full account. He would wish indeed that all spoke in tongues, but rather that they prophesied (1 Cor. 14:5); and he concludes his discussion with the characteristic pronouncement: "desire earnestly to prophesy, and do not forbid speaking in tongues."

From the manner in which prophecy and glossolalia are placed over against each other in 1 Corinthians 14 we get a somewhat clearer picture still of what is intended here. Glossolalia is speaking to God in a language unintelligible to others (1 Cor. 12:2, 28). This speaking can have a varied significance: praying, singing psalms, praise, thanksgiving (cf. vv. 14ff.). The one who thus by the Spirit speaks hidden things is not beside himself in the sense that he would no longer be conscious of his own speech and action. On the contrary, he speaks to God and to himself (v. 28), and he edifies himself (v. 4); he must also, if necessary, be able to impose silence on himself (v. 28). Paul, moreover, makes the distinction that he who prays, sings, etc., in glossolalia does this indeed with his[111] spirit *(pneuma)*, but not with his understanding *(nous)* (vv. 14ff.). This surely indicates that the state of consciousness is otherwise than it is ordinarily; the "I" is consciously active to be sure, but what is spoken, prayed, or sung does not admit of being controlled or put into words by the understanding.[112] It is said of the understanding therefore that with glossolalia it is unfruitful (v. 14), that is to say, is not involved in it and thus cannot be the intermediary for enabling others to share in what the one speaking in ecstasy is saying. As regards the sounds themselves that are produced in glossolalia, Paul demonstrates their unintelligibility in the example of musical instruments, if these were to give forth sounds with no difference in tone. In that case no

---

110. *Genē glōssōn* (1 Cor. 12:10, 28); *lalein glōssais* (1 Cor. 12:30; cf. 13:1), also with the singular *glōssē* (1 Cor. 14:2), *proseuchesthai glōssē* (1 Cor. 14:14). It is not entirely clear how one is to take *glōssa* in this usage. The meaning "tongue," in view of the plural, seems hardly to fit. One is rather to think of *glōssa* in the sense of unknown, unintelligible word (so, e.g., Lietzmann). Behm thinks that one must start from the meaning "language," but then as a technical expression for one or another uncommon language (*TDNT*, I, p. 725). Nevertheless the plural seems to point more to the individual words or sounds. The expression has, however, acquired a stereotyped significance.

111. *To pneuma mou* is (among others, by Lietzmann, *Cor.*, and by Bultmann, *Theology*, I, p. 207) not understood of the human spirit, but of the divine Spirit given to men. To be sure, the possession of the Spirit, so far as we see, is nowhere denoted by the possessive pronoun. But *pneuma* does surely have a very specific significance here, related to the divine Spirit. See also above, pp. 117f., n. 68.

112. "Intelligent and intelligible speech" (Bultmann, *Theology*, I, p. 211).

one is able to distinguish what is played on the flute or harp, or what the meaning is of the sound of the trumpet. Just so does glossolalia lack a clear sense (*eusēmos logos;* v. 9); one cannot understand the meaning of the sounds (*hē dynamis tēs phōnēs;* v. 11); for this reason one can compare glossolalia with "speaking into the air," that is to say, no one comprehends it, no one is reached by it; one remains unintelligible to others, just as when he speaks in an alien language not familiar to others (vv. 9-11). Indeed, those who so speak even give others who have no acquaintance with this glossolalia the impression that they are mad (v. 23).

It is this lack of communication that Paul urges as the great objection against glossolalia and by which he estimates its worth as lower than that of prophecy, for example, unless what is said be interpreted and the church built thereby. Of glossolalia that is not interpreted, however, nothing is to be expected. The ignorant auditor cannot say "amen" to it. For unbelievers it can only be a sign of their hardening, namely, that God permits them to be spoken to in this unintelligible manner, as Paul makes known with a peculiar use of a pronouncement from Isaiah 28:11ff. (1 Cor. 14:21, 22). For this reason he also determines that one is not to express himself in glossolalia unless there is someone to interpret it. If there is not, he is to be silent; further, there shall not be more than two, at most three, who speak thus, and then each one in his turn (vv. 27, 28). It holds here, too, that everything must be done decently and in order.

Reference is still to be made in this context to the interpretation of glossolalia, listed as a separate *charisma* (cf. 1 Cor. 12:10). This interpreter can himself be the one who speaks in sounds (1 Cor. 14:5, 13); it may also be another (v. 28).[113] The gift of interpretation is not given with the gift of glossolalia, however. He who possesses the first must pray God that he may also receive the second (14:13). Only then does his gift become fruitful for others. In the light of all this, therefore, we shall have to understand the glossolalia of which Paul speaks as a psychological or parapsychological phenomenon,[114] in which the power of the Spirit manifested itself in certain persons, perhaps also in connection with what occurred elsewhere in a specific locality,[115] and enabled them thus to give utterance to their religious feelings in a special manner. The extraordinary character of this gift is clearly pointed out by Paul.

---

113. Cf. Grosheide, *1 Cor.*, p. 374, n. 63.

114. To what extent one may speak here of a natural predisposition is outside the reach of our judgment. It is surely clear that Paul does not regard the *charisma* as lying in the special state of consciousness or the strange sounds — therein is just the limitation of the *charisma* — but in the manner in which the Spirit makes this the medium of a peculiar religious experience. For the "natural" aspect see also Schweizer, *Church Order in the New Testament*, p. 184.

115. W. Keilbach writes in *RGG*, VI, 3rd ed., col. 1941, that in the history of heathen religions glossolalia was neither a very frequent nor a very important phenomenon. He adds to this, however: "However, it assumed impressive form in the Greek cultus and in the ecstatic mysticism of Hellenism." In this connection it would not be strange that the glossolalia found an unusual matrix in the spiritualistically tinted church at Corinth.

It is an attendant phenomenon, not salvation itself, that (some) believers received in it. The highly personal character of this *charisma* explains the unmistakable caution with which Paul judges it and the very incidental attention he devotes to it.

SECTION 72. ECCLESIASTICAL ORDER AND DISCIPLINE

Not only do *charismata* and the persons gifted with them pertain to the upbuilding of the church, but also the observance of a certain order and the acknowledgment of a certain law in the church. We touch here once more, and now indeed in the most direct manner, the relationship of the charismatic and the institutional in the upbuilding of the church, and the controversy about it that has manifested itself time and again in the history of interpretation.[116] In the more recent literature on this subject[117] Sohm's conception that for Paul in particular "church" and "law" constitute an inner contradiction has been overcome; likewise scholars are no longer satisfied with the conception of Harnack that insofar as ecclesiastical order and law can be spoken of already in Paul and in the whole of the New Testament, this is nothing other than the adaptation of worldly categories and legal forms for the external upbuilding of ecclesiastical life. From the manner in which Paul wishes to see order and discipline maintained in the church it is clear that to his mind this must answer to the essence of the church as the holy people of God and as the body of Christ visibly manifesting itself. The question now is what this involves and to what extent one can arrive at a clearly outlined idea of the upbuilding of the church thus understood in terms of church order.

It can here be posited first that for the furtherance of this upbuilding Paul does not seek his strength in as many regulations and legalistic rules as possible, but wants above all to make the church conscious of its own being in order thereby *in concreto* to test the organization of the ecclesiastical life and make it answer to that. We have already seen[118] that in his paraenesis he repeatedly appeals to its own faculty of discernment as full-grown church (Rom. 15:14; Col. 2:5; Phil. 1:5, 6, 9ff.). This does not hold only for the Christian life in general, but also for the organization of congregational life in the narrower sense of the word. In so doing he continually exercises the greatest care not to usurp the church's own powers (1 Cor. 5:4; 2 Cor. 8:18, 23; 1 Cor. 16:3).

---

116. Cf. Section 70. For what follows here note 45 is also relevant in part.

117. See, e.g., besides the literature already mentioned earlier, E. Käsemann, "Sentences of Holy Law in the New Testament," *New Testament Questions of Today*, pp. 66ff.; H. von Campenhausen, *Die Begründung kirchlicher Entscheidungen beim Apostel Paulus*, 1957; by the same author together with H. Bornkamm, *Bindung und Freiheit in der Ordnung der Kirche*, 1959; W. Maurer, "Vom Ursprung und Wesen kirchlichen Rechts," in *Zeitschrift für evangelisches Kirchenrecht*, 1956; R. Bohren, *Das Problem der Kirchenzucht im Neuen Testament*, 1952; F. W. Grosheide, *Wat leert het Nieuwe Testament inzake de tucht?*, 1952.

118. Above, pp. 287ff.

But this liberty and independence may not be abstracted from the great principle that in the church a well-ordered condition is to prevail, just because it is the people of God. All things must be done decently and in good order. God is not a God of confusion, but of peace, that is to say, of a condition of well-being (1 Cor. 14:40, 33). The church is to set itself rules, and Paul also establishes them for it in a great many ways. He requires this order *(taxis)* where it is lacking, he commends it where it is present (Col. 2:5), and he wants the church to subject itself to it (1 Cor. 16:16; Eph. 5:21). Every appeal against this to the liberty of the Spirit is misplaced, for the *charisma* that is of God is incompatible with disorder (1 Cor. 14). It has rightly been said that all his life Paul opposed the arbitrariness of the *charismatici* and set limits to them on the basis of sound understanding, custom, love, and the cross of Christ, and therewith placed the very *charismata*, too, under the liberty and discipline of Christ and his Spirit as the ground and strength of a truly ordered church.[119] But the arbitrariness is accordingly shown of the conception that is able to discover the *charisma* of Christ and of his Spirit in the free, spontaneous, and concrete, and not in the institutional, fixed, and regulated.[120] Paul does not confine himself therefore to the giving of specific "advice," which he offers to the church for consideration (as, e.g., in 1 Cor. 7:6[121]), but his instructions bear the character of commands *(parangelia, parangellein;* 1 Thess. 4:2; 1 Tim. 1:18; cf. v. 5; 1 Cor. 7:10; 11:17; 1 Thess. 4:11; 2 Thess. 3:4, 6, 10, 12; 1 Tim. 1:3; 4:11; 5:7; 6:13, 17) or, with another word characteristic in this connection, of ordinances *(diatassein, diatassesthai;* 1 Cor. 7:17; 11:34; 16:1; Tit. 1:5). Similarly the word "exhort" *(parakalein),* usually employed in a general pastoral sense, can sometimes have the significance more in the area of church order of "charge," "ordain"; very clearly, for example, in 1 Timothy 2:1; cf. 6:2; Titus 2:15; also with this connotation, however, in Romans 16:17; 2 Corinthians 8:6; 9:5; 2 Thessalonians 3:12. But without this special terminology, too, this character of Paul's pronouncements as ordinances sometimes emerges very clearly, for example, in 1 Corinthians 14, where in the form of these prescriptions a certain stereotyped quality is to be observed: in the first member of the sentence a specific situation or possibility is repeatedly posited, whereupon in the second "in the decretal jussive"[122] Paul's ordinance follows (1 Cor. 14:13, 30, 35, 37).

Such ordinances as these, rules for congregational life, are to be met with incidentally in most of the epistles of Paul, not systematically, but according as there was occasion or necessity for them. In 1 Corinthians this also occurs apparently as an answer to certain questions that

---

119. Käsemann, *Essays on New Testament Themes,* pp. 84f.

120. Cf. Bultmann, who posits against the spiritualistic conception that in this way one takes for normal what Paul in 1 Cor. 12 and 14 combats precisely as dangerous or at least limits *(Theology,* II, p. 98).

121. *Kata syngnōmēn, ou kat' epitagēn:* "by way of advice, not by way of command."

122. Käsemann, *New Testament Questions of Today,* p. 74.

have come to him: 1 Corinthians 7:1 on marriage; 1 Corinthians 8:1 on the attitude one is to take toward meat sacrificed to idols; 1 Corinthians 12:1 on the *charismata*. But he also speaks with a regulatory effect of the manner in which a woman is to conduct herself in the church (1 Cor. 11:2ff.), of the right observance of the Lord's Supper (1 Cor. 11:17ff.), elsewhere of the obligation to provide those who instruct others in the Word with a subsistence (Gal. 6:6; 1 Cor. 9:14; cf. Rom. 15:27), of vigilance over against teachings that produce discord and the duty of turning aside from men who disseminate such doctrine (Rom. 16:18); on the other hand, of honoring those who exert themselves for the gospel and being amenable to them (1 Cor. 16:15ff.). All this serves to induce the church to preserve its own character, to cause it to live together in order and harmony, to bring it to a distinctive and responsible common service of God, to secure it against error and schism.

Although these regulations constitutive of rule and order for the life of the church lend themselves with difficulty to a systematic treatment because in Paul's epistles they mostly bear an incidental character and are connected to what is already presumed to be familiar, it cannot be said — as seems for some to hold as a kind of indisputable truth — that there is a profound or fundamental difference on this point between the older epistles of Paul and those to Timothy and Titus. In particular the contrast is to be rejected here, according to which in the former the ordinances given by Paul are to be directly attributed to Christ and to his Spirit, while in the latter the Spirit acts as the Spirit of a certain principle, namely, as the power of the holy and apostolic tradition.[123] The difference consists in this, that in the Pastoral Epistles Paul "commands" and takes regulatory action via his fellow workers (1 Tim. 1:3, 18; 4:11; 5:7; Tit. 2:1, 15, *et al.*), for which indeed parallels are also to be adduced in the older epistles (cf., e.g., 2 Cor. 8:6ff.). That thereby the personal and situational recedes more into the background and a pattern of more stabilized prescriptions and ordinances develops is obvious. With regard to the content of these prescriptions, however, this does not in itself as yet make any essential difference. If, for example, in 1 Timothy 2:1-3:13 specific prescriptions are given for the gatherings and the organization of the church and indeed one has spoken here of "the oldest church order,"[124] even so this bears no other character than what Paul ordains, for example, in 1 Corinthians 11 and 14 with a view to the gathering of the church and promises to regulate still further when he comes (1 Cor. 11:34). The point in both cases is that men shall know how they ought to behave themselves in the house of God (1 Tim. 3:15). And these prescriptions in the Pastoral Epistles have a character that arises no less from the nature of the church than in the older epistles (cf. 1 Tim. 2:3ff.; 3:15ff.; Tit. 2:11ff.; 3:4ff.); while in the latter Paul

---

123. To that effect Käsemann, *Exegetische Versuche und Besinnungen*, I, p. 255.

124. Cf. J. Jeremias, *Die Briefe an Timotheüs und Titus (NTD)*, p. 13.

enters no less into detail, when the occasion exists, than is the case in the former (cf., e.g., 1 Cor. 14 *passim;* 1 Cor. 16:2; 1 Tim. 5:9ff.).

So far furthermore as the content of this order to be observed by the church is concerned, in addition to what has already been said regarding it with respect to the gatherings, ministries, and offices, what Paul writes on the mutual and ecclesiastical exercise of discipline is still to be mentioned in particular. In so doing he not only speaks of admonishing one another[125] (Rom. 15:14; Col. 3:16; 1 Thess. 4:18), whereby they were to attempt to reclaim the disorderly (1 Thess. 5:11, 14; Gal. 6:1, 2, *et al.*), but he also requires that the congregation act in the way of church order or church law against the one who pays no attention to admonition or by his gross aberration can no longer be suffered as a member of the church. Passing by such a passage as 2 Corinthians 2:6, 7, where the picture is less clear, reference is to be made first of all to 2 Thessalonians 3:6, where Paul commands the church in the name of Christ to "withdraw" themselves from every brother who walks disorderly and not according to the authoritative doctrinal tradition of the apostle. And in verse 14, evidently with a view to the same case, it is added that if anyone is not obedient to the word of Paul's epistle, the church is to "mark"[126] such a one and have nothing "to do" with him, that he may be ashamed. The question that arises here is whether what is intended by all this is expulsion from the church or a measure within the congregation, whereby normal intercourse with such a person was suspended and in this way the unacceptableness of his behavior was made clear to him, but brotherly admonition was not withheld. In view of the probable nature of the sin in view here (cf. v. 11) and Paul's addition that one must continue to consider the persons intended here as brothers and must go on admonishing them (v. 15), this latter view is surely the more probable. They did not as yet break with him entirely. It is evident, however, what a stress the apostle lays on the holiness and blamelessness of the church in the world and how much he wishes to see ascribed to the prescriptions given by him not only an ethical or "medical" significance, but also a significance in terms of church government. Where this is flouted, action is to be taken by the church, if in the case of 2 Thessalonians 3 not immediately in the definitive sense of expulsion from the church, yet surely in such a brotherly manner that the one implicated is confronted with the consequence of his acts.

Paul wishes to see a severer sentence passed in the case of 1 Corinthians 5. There he reproaches the church with the fact that it has not yet removed from its midst a member living in grave immorality, and he demands that it execute on him the sentence that the apostle has

---

125. On this at greater length see Bohren, *Das Problem der Kirchenzucht im Neuen Testament,* pp. 91ff.; Grosheide, *Wat leert het Nieuwe Testament inzake de tucht?,* pp. 8ff.

126. *Sēmeiousthe:* to be thought of as communication in one way or another to the church. For similar measures in the exercise of discipline in the synagogue, see, e.g., Strack-Billerbeck, IV, 1, p. 309.

already determined concerning him,[127] that is, "to deliver such a one to Satan for the destruction of his flesh, that his spirit may be saved in the day of the Lord" (1 Cor. 5:5). It is plain that formal expulsion from the church is meant here. This is then qualified, however, as a delivering to Satan in the name of the Lord Jesus. When it has gathered in the name of Christ (cf. Matt. 18:20), the church is to understand itself as the executor of the full power of the Lord to hand the sinner over from Christ's saving dominion to the sphere of the power of Satan (cf. Gal. 1:4; Col. 1:13). This handing over means for the sinner that his flesh is abandoned to "destruction." This is often so taken that being delivered over to Satan will result in death for the sinner.[128] But it cannot then be made clear[129] how the words that follow — "that [his] spirit be saved" — are to be understood. If death follows, there is no longer any place for such a salvation. It is much more probable, therefore, that with this "destruction of the flesh" a grave physical affliction, at least affecting the temporal life, is to be thought of,[130] which is to strike the sinner who has been delivered up to Satan (cf. 2 Cor. 12:7; Luke 13:16; Job 1, where suffering, too, is attributed to the working of Satan). The latter part of the sentence then denotes a possible spiritual turning and salvation arising from this; cf. the similar pronouncement in 1 Timothy 1:20.

Here again expulsion from the church has a double purpose: first, to cleanse the church of those who desecrate it by their conduct. The sequel (vv. 9ff.) goes into this still further, once more (just as in 2 Thess. 3:14) with the admonition not to associate with people who, though they may be called brothers, give themselves up to all manner of sins, and even not to want to eat with them. It is required here, however, otherwise than is presupposed in the first instance in 2 Thessalonians 3, that the guilty be put away, out of the church. The second purpose is expressed here also as the conversion of the sinner, though the remedy be one that goes much further: to deliver him up to the evil power of Satan.[131]

---

127. On this see also below, p. 473.

128. So, e.g., Lietzmann-Kümmel on 1 Cor. 5:5; Büchsel, *TDNT*, II, p. 170, n. 9; Schneider, *TDNT*, V, p. 169; Käsemann, *New Testament Questions of Today*, p. 71; Bohren, *Das Problem der Kirchenzucht*, p. 110, and the literature mentioned there in note 135.

129. Cf., e.g., Bohren, *ibid.*, pp. 111ff.

130. Various Greek fathers also understood it in that sense (cf. K. Staab, *Pauluskommentare aus der griechischen Kirche*, 1933, pp. 178, 243ff.); Grosheide (*1 Cor.*, pp. 143, 144) understands *olethros tēs sarkos* as "destruction of the sin" in the way of a process of purification. But it is difficult to understand the expression with *olethros* only of the sin.

131. One can also think here of the anathema-formula frequently employed by Paul (Rom. 9:3; 1 Cor. 16:22; Gal. 1:8, 9; cf. 1 Cor. 12:3). Anathema, however, at least in the LXX, is being abandoned not to Satan, but to the judgment of God (cf. Behm, *TDNT*, I, pp. 354f.); in general: that which by God or in God's name has been abandoned to destruction (cf. Strack-Billerbeck, III, p. 260). Paul does not use the word, so far as we see, in the context of the congregational exercise of discipline. Some have indeed wished to infer from a comparison of 1 Cor. 16:22 and Did. 10, 6 that the anathema was pronounced at the beginning of the celebration

Finally, the ordinance in Titus 3:10 ought still to be mentioned with reference to "a heretical man," that is to say, one who by false doctrine jeopardizes the unity of the church. Paul commands that Titus, after the first and second admonition, shall reject such a man. Here too expulsion, removal from the church, is intended, as also appears from the very negative judgment of this sinner in verse 11. The question is then what is meant by the first and second admonition. Reference is usually made here to Matthew 18:15-17, and indeed justly. A further background is very likely to be sought in the synagogical disciplinary practice, where likewise the practice was not to proceed to excommunication before repeated warnings had been given.[132] The distinction was also known in the synagogue between provisional and radical expulsion, from which the difference between the procedure followed in 2 Thessalonians 3 and that in 1 Corinthians 5 and Titus 3 can possibly be further elucidated.

All this does not for our purpose need to be further investigated in detail. It is to be concluded from the above that with regard to church discipline, too, Paul wanted to see clear regulations followed in the church, and in so doing perhaps found correspondence in certain measures in the Jewish congregation from which he had come. So far is it removed from any such notion as that for him church and law, Spirit and canon, were incompatible. However much in the exercise of discipline the church must also have the salvation of the sinner at heart, this may not result in any obliteration within it of the boundary between what is and what is not lawful and with that also between the church itself and the world.[133] This boundary is rather to be maintained by the application of clear regulations and has its standard not only with respect to the moral life but also with respect to the doctrine received in the church in what has been handed over to it and its leaders as the apostolic *paradosis* (2 Thess. 3:6, 14; 1 Tim. 6:20; 2 Tim. 1:14; Tit. 3:10; cf. 1 Tim. 4:7). And all this speaks the more forcefully because in the epistles that have been preserved to us these surely very radical regulations and measures are mentioned only incidentally and without detailed explanation. This confirms the impression we have already received repeatedly that with reference to the order in the churches required by Paul one must be very cautious with the argument from silence and

---

of the Supper against possible unbelievers or the unworthy (cf. G. Bornkamm, "The Anathema in the Early Christian Lord's Supper Liturgy," in "On the Understanding of Worship," *Early Christian Experience*, pp. 169ff.). To want to conclude from this that in the early Christian church there was an "open" Lord's Supper, which was, e.g., also accessible for those who had not been baptized (cf. Bornkamm, pp. 171f.), is unjustified (cf. also Did. 9, 5). If the anathema had a place in the Supper liturgy, then it was certainly as a summons to self-examination for the church itself (cf. 1 Cor. 11:28).

132. For expulsion from the synagogue, see Bohren, *Das Problem der Kirchenzucht*, pp. 23ff., and the literature cited there; also Strack-Billerbeck, IV, 1, p. 298; A. Edersheim, *The Life and Times of Jesus the Messiah*, 29th ed., II, 1934, p. 183.

133. See also Schrage, *Die konkreten Einzelgebote in der paulinischen Paränese*, pp. 159ff.

that the church had already been much more fully informed about such things than we can gather from these epistles.

Of importance furthermore are those in whom these powers in the church are vested and by whom the order of church government is to be maintained. We are faced here with a somewhat complicated problem; it is worthwhile to go into it a little more deeply.

In what we have dealt with so far we have already seen a clear twofold tendency. On the one hand the church itself must be aware of its responsibility for order and discipline in its midst. On the other hand, the church is to know that it is itself subject to this order and to obey it as an order given it by God.

So far as the first is concerned the important fact to be pointed out is that in his epistles the apostle is constantly addressing the church, with the exception only of Philippians 1:1, where the bishops and the deacons also occur in the address (and the Pastoral Epistles). Nowhere does he direct himself over the head of the church to the office-bearers. Even in so severe a case of discipline as that intended in 1 Corinthians 5 he reproves the church that it has not taken action, and he wants the exercise of discipline still to take place "when we are assembled, you and my spirit with the power of our Lord Jesus Christ," etc. (1 Cor. 5:4). Although the interpretation of this pronouncement presents us with certain difficulties,[134] it is surely clear that the church, together with the apostle, is the executor of the sentence against the sinner, which Paul had already determined (v. 3); at the same time this execution must not only take place with an appeal to the command once given by Christ, but also in the consciousness of Christ's own presence in the church and thus of the authority and spiritual power to act with which the church in consequence is invested.

That the church does not have to submit itself as an underage or dependent multitude under the authorities set over it, but has the power and calling to upbuild itself, is fundamental for a correct insight into the Pauline concept of the church and of the order and law that are to obtain in its midst. And where the church is not aware of this and does not conduct itself as "perfect" in Christ but as novices and minors, Paul reproaches it for this; particularly when people appeal over against each other to him or to Apollos, as if they were anything other than the means by which the church has come to conversion. Therefore they must know that they are not the work of Paul or Apollos, nor are they to name themselves for them, and much less still are the factions in the church to attempt to cover themselves with their authority. The church is God's building, a temple in which God dwells. Its boast and its authority do not lie in the fact that it can appeal to men. All things are the

---

134. This holds in particular for the "coming together" of the church with "the spirit" of the apostle. All kinds of interpretations have been attempted; see, e.g., in Lietzmann-Kümmel, *Cor.* In our view one will, also considering v. 3, have to understand by this a (surely very) graphic way of speaking with which Paul gives expression to his authority and cooperation with respect to the sentence to be executed.

church's, whether Paul, or Apollos, or Cephas ... , and it is Christ's (1 Cor. 3:1ff., 21ff.).

The second point of view is no less clear and important, however: the church is itself subject to the authority and order that have validity in its midst and owes obedience to them. And this not merely by way of mutual arrangement and as an agreement of the ecclesiastical community, but because this is the authority and the order that Christ has set over it. Nor is this authority and this order an *abstractum*, but it assumes concrete shape in the persons in the church who are invested with these full spiritual powers and in the control they exercise.

That Paul is himself conscious of bearing this authority and on that ground requires obedience of the church to his ordinances has already been sufficiently evident to us. But he does not restrict this authority to himself. He also ascribes it to those who in virtue of the *charismata* given them or their position in the church from the beginning give leadership and stand in the forefront. However little the outlines of office stand out as having been fixed in his early epistles, already in the first epistle to the newly established church at Thessalonica he points his readers to those whom they are to acknowledge and esteem highly (5:12ff.). And in the same epistle to Corinth in which he makes all gifts and ministries to be understood in the organic relationships of the body of Christ, it is said as well that the church is to be in subjection, that is to say, to respect the order *(hypotassesthai)* that is represented by those who place themselves at the service of the saints, exert themselves and labor for it (1 Cor. 16:16, 18; cf. Phil. 2:29). There is thus a twofold relationship in which the church is the subject as well as the object. The church that has been taught of God is itself the bearer of the gifts, ministries, and full powers that Christ has conferred on it, and at the same time the object of this authority. And this twofold aspect — one could perhaps say: this reciprocal dependence — does not comprise an internal contradiction, but arises from the essence of the New Testament church and can be understood in particular when one grasps the significance of the body of Christ. For it is in this communication, in this corporate communion between Christ as the Head and the church as his body, that all the *charismata*, ministries, and offices are given to the church. It is itself their bearer, and all these gifts do not function outside or above, but in the body, and belong to the parts and articulations that knit together and nourish the body (Eph. 4:16).

It is God, therefore, it is Christ, it is the Spirit, who "appoints," "gives," "assigns," and "entrusts" apostles, prophets, and teachers in the church (1 Cor. 12:28; Rom. 12:3; Eph. 4:7, 8, 11; Rom. 12:6; Gal. 2:7, *et al.*). They are God's builders, vine-dressers, stewards (1 Cor. 3:6ff.; Rom. 15:20; 1 Cor. 4:1, 2; Tit. 1:7). The ministry of the Spirit and the indwelling of Christ in his body become visible in them. For this reason the exercise of office and the functioning of gifts and powers in the church are never only a mutual service of the members of the church to one another, and discipline never only a supervision one of another. It is the gift of Christ, it is the truth and the law of the Lord; the full powers of Christ are administered and vested in them. Thus the authority and those who hold it are given by Christ for the upbuilding of the church, and thus the church has to acknowledge, honor, and subject itself to them, and obey them.

But it is no less essential that in this equipping of the church with *charismata*, ministries, and full powers, an authority or level is not created that could place itself between the church and its Lord. For whatever may be due the church through the apostles, prophets, and teachers given it by Christ, whether instruction, or admonition, or discipline, or comfort, it is always due it as the body of Christ, in the communion of which all official gifts and full powers also function. There is no power or office apart from the church; and these contain nothing in themselves that has been withheld from the church itself. The question whether the church is the subject or the object of the full powers that are held by certain persons in its midst falls away as soon as one catches sight of the church as the *corpus Christi*. The church labors and struggles with them in watching and praying (2 Cor. 1:11; Eph. 6:18; Phil. 4:3; Col. 4:3; 1 Thess. 5:25; 2 Thess. 3:1, *et al.*). The church has to place itself under the spiritual powers, discipline, office. But, conversely, all these stand under the judgment of the church. Paul says this expressly with a view to the prophets. Not only are the spirits of the prophets to be subject to the prophets themselves in self-criticism, but the other prophets are also to judge when one of them speaks (1 Cor. 14:32, 29). Competent criticism, but criticism even so! And that does not only apply to fellow-prophets, but to the whole church. As little as they are allowed to despise prophecy and to quench the Spirit, so much are they to test everything and hold fast that which is good (1 Thess. 5:19ff.; cf. 1 John 4:1). Moreover, it is not only the non-official *charismata* that are at issue here, but equally the official. For between them there is no difference in principle. In the Pastoral Epistles the institutional character of certain ministries is much more clearly to the fore than elsewhere, and the *Gegenüber* of office with respect to the church. But nowhere are the prerequisites for office more fully and more earnestly pointed out than there: prerequisites that are not only to be respected by the office-bearer in his ministry, but which are also to be, and to continue to be, insisted on by those who choose the overseers and deacons and call them to the office.

From all this it may also appear that, though we do not find any clearly developed doctrine of office in Paul's epistles, yet the premises for such entirely conform to what we meet with elsewhere in the New Testament on investiture with certain powers or ministries. It may be at first glance that a diverse mixture presents itself here, which does not immediately seem capable of being combined and unified. Thus, for example, the election of Matthias in Acts 1 takes place with prayer and the casting of lots, after two names were first put forward by the assembled church (1:15, 23ff.). The church offers two candidates, the Lord himself designates. In Acts 6 the church chooses the seven and presents them to the apostles. These pray and lay their hands on them. The Spirit says to the prophets and teachers: "Separate for me Barnabas and Saul." After fasting and prayer hands are laid on them, and they are sent forth. Although it is not altogether settled who does the fasting and praying (the church or the prophets and teachers), it is clear that while the Spirit, Christ himself, is the Person acting, who calls to specific offices and tasks, its execution takes place by means of fasting and prayer in and by the church (cf. 14:23). Thus it can simply be said elsewhere to the overseers of Ephesus: "the Holy Spirit has placed you in the church" (Acts 20:28), whereas in Acts 14:23 it is said than Barnabas and Paul appointed elders. Similarly, as appears from 1 Timothy 4:14, Timothy received his special calling through the agency of a prophecy (cf. 1:18) and with the laying on of the hands of the body of elders, but the appointment of elders from city to city is in Titus 1:5 without more ado charged to Titus.

At first sight it may appear that all sorts of ideas run through each other here and that on this ground one could now defend apostolic succession, then again direct calling by the Spirit, in a third instance designation to office by means of prophetic voices, finally also investiture with office as the act of the church only.

When one surveys the whole, however, it is evident that in each investiture with and acceptance of official power to act and authority two different elements are present: first, Christ himself, who will not only have the office established and maintained in the way of the transference of the power once given, but works in the church through his Spirit, so that the work of the Lord on earth may be done, his church be built up, and his power to act invested in persons qualified to that end. Second, the church itself, which designates and chooses these persons and in the name of the Lord enables them to enter upon the work charged to them.

For the rest, so far as the emergence of office-bearers in the early Christian churches is concerned, one will have to take into account the different situations and gradations in the independence of the churches and the more or less consolidated conditions. While most of the epistles are addressed directly to the churches themselves, in the Pastoral Epistles it is Paul's closest fellow workers who under his instructions are to act with regulatory authority, are to appoint elders where these are lacking (Tit. 1:5), and must put affairs in order where abuses are threatening (cf., e.g., 1 Tim. 5:5ff.). That the increasing dangers that menaced the church from the side of heresy will have constituted a powerful reason for a stricter order and tighter upbuilding of the church may also be gathered from these epistles. On the other hand, the view that in these persons delegated by the apostle (who then appear in the guise of Timothy and Titus) we should have to see an intermediate link between the apostolate and the monarchical episcopate in which then the apostolic succession would demonstrate itself[135] is in many respects in conflict with the real situation, to be taken as history, that is described in the Pastoral Epistles. Timothy and Titus function as *temporary* leaders of the churches in Ephesus and Crete (cf. 1 Tim. 1:3; 3:15; 2 Tim. 4:9ff.; Tit. 1:5; 3:12ff.). The purpose of their appearance and of the epistles addressed to them is precisely to bring the church and the office coming to development in it to greater independence, in view of Paul's absence and approaching demise and their own impending departure. The

135. So Käsemann, *Essays on New Testament Themes*, p. 87.

letters directed to them are accordingly to be read in the meetings of the church itself, as is evident, among other things, from the concluding benediction, and were thus intended for the church as apostolic *paradosis* and included as such in the canon. And the authority is indeed given to Timothy and Titus to appoint office-bearers (1 Tim. 5:22; Tit. 1:5), but this is not to say that this took place without cooperation or designation by the church and that they themselves may already be said to represent an "intermediate level" between the apostolate and the "laity." Timothy himself is repeatedly reminded of his own ordination, which had come to him not only in the name of the apostle, but also in the name of the church (cf. 2 Tim. 1:6 and 1 Tim. 4:14; 6:12). Furthermore, he is encouraged in a great many ways not to conduct himself in too unassuming a fashion, not to feel ashamed of his youth, to show his progress in the work committed to him, etc. (cf. 1 Tim. 4:11, 15, *et al.*). Every trace of an incipient hierarchical order or "apostolic succession" is lacking here. Nor can the *episkopos* to be appointed by them be interpreted as a *primus inter pares*, who would then represent the incipient hierarchy.[136] However clearer in these epistles than in the older ones are the contours with which the ordering of the church is marked, no fundamental shifting is to be found here that would justify the qualification of (transition to) "early catholicism," or which would consist in the transition from the liberty of the Spirit to a principle of tradition and legitimacy.[137] For on the one hand even in the older epistles all authority and order in the church has its norm in (the "principle" of) the apostolic tradition, and on the other hand it is difficult to say in what respect the brief "mirrors" of the elders and deacons in the Pastoral Epistles contain anything that did not as yet hold for "those who give leadership," etc., in the previous epistles. For these prescriptions are put so generally, and in a certain sense so primitively, that there can as yet be no question of an even in some degree elaborated official instruction or legitimation, to say nothing of a thorough-going distinction between clergy and laity.

Neither can the ordination mentioned in the Pastoral Epistles ("laying on of hands"; 1 Tim. 4:14; 5:22; 2 Tim. 1:6) serve as evidence for such a development in a hierarchical direction. As is also apparent elsewhere in the New Testament (cf., e.g., Acts 13:3), the laying on of hands is here not (as with the Jews[138]) to be taken as conveying the grace of office and incorporating one into an unbroken succession that perpetuates itself via this ordination; it is rather to be thought of detached from that, as the (whether or not temporary) designation and equipping to a specific ministry or office. It does not create an institute standing above the church, but places one in the service of the church, at its direction (1 Tim. 1:18; 4:14), and with its cooperation (1 Tim.

---

136. As C. Spicq, *Les Epitres Pastorales,* 1947, pp. 86ff., 232, tries to make plausible; see also above, p. 457, n. 91.

137. So Käsemann, *Essays on New Testament Themes,* p. 89. Against this "modern-protestantischer Vorurteil," which in every church order that is not placed under an explicit reservation (leaving everything unsettled again) sees an attack on the liberty of the Spirit and of the sovereign Word of God, see also von Campenhausen, *Bindung und Freiheit in der Ordnung der Kirche,* pp. 18ff.

138. Cf. Strack-Billerbeck, II, pp. 647-661.

5:22), in order in this way as well to invest with the full powers that have been given to the church. This laying on of hands therefore does not represent a stage of authority and office in the ancient Christian church that is different in principle from Paul, even though in the remaining epistles such an ordination is not explicitly mentioned.

In summary, all the authorities and ordinances that have been placed in the church to build up and keep pure the body of Christ have been given it by Christ and as such require submission and obedience from the side of the church; at the same time, these powers are held by those who have been placed in the church and have been given to the church to that end. In the persons who have been endowed with these *charismata* and ministries, too, Christ is equipping the church. But this equipping does not take place without its own cooperation, insofar, that is, as those who hold the authority of Christ in the church do so on its designation or at least under its supervision and judgment. The office — in a single formula — is from Christ and through the church.

If, therefore, in the organization of the local churches a transition is to be observed in Paul from the apostolic to the congregational-presbyterial stage that comes about only gradually, this applies still more strongly to the interrelationship of the local congregations.

We have already been able to ascertain[139] that *ekklesia* in Paul usually denotes the local church. This is not of course to say — one need only think of Colossians and Ephesians — that Paul may be said to think in terms of "local congregations" and to consider the church as a whole only as something secondary; the cause of this phenomenon is to be found in the fact that he had in practice primarily to do with individual churches and the questions and problems arising in them.

This does not alter the fact, however, that in various ways he makes the local congregations also realize their fellowship among each other and wishes to promote among them as large a degree of agreement in their actions as possible. Time and again he points the churches to what is taking place elsewhere. They are to be conscious of the cosmic ("ecumenical") relationships in which the gospel involves them (Col. 1:6, 23; 1 Tim. 3:16; cf. Eph. 1:10). What happens in other congregations must have their full interest (cf. 2 Cor. 9:2ff.; Col. 4:16); they are to participate in that which is undertaken elsewhere (1 Cor. 16:1ff.); they must allow themselves to be guided by the same line of conduct. Paul accordingly stresses that he gives the same directives in all the churches (1 Cor. 7:17; 4:17; 14:33); he wants them to pay heed to each other's ecclesiastical rules; and he reprimands the Corinthians for their individualizing and independent attitude: "Did the Word of God originate with you, or are you the only ones it has reached?" (1 Cor. 14:14, 36).[140]

The basis for this interrelationship does not lie only in the practical desirability or necessity of cooperation, exchange of ideas,

---

139. See above, Section 54.
140. Cf. von Campenhausen, *Bindung und Freiheit,* pp. 14ff.

mutual assistance, or brotherly advice, but above all in the nature of the church, the unity of which is not the product of the component parts, but rather underlies them.[141] In the local congregation the universal church of Christ manifests itself. Therein lies its independence, on the one hand; on the other, the necessity for allowing itself to be determined by and amenable to other congregations. For as the figure of the multiplicity of the members and the one body (Rom. 12; 1 Cor. 12) forms a directive for life in the local congregations, so no less for the relationship of these congregations to each other. For Christ does not have many bodies, but the one body of Christ must manifest itself in the unity and harmony of the whole church, local and general (cf. Eph. 4:1-6).

It is provisionally here again the apostle himself who gives guidance to this interrelationship. The apostolate represents not only the foundation, but also the unity and the ecumenical character of the church. But in the same sense in which in the local congregations the apostolic powers of government and superintendence are continued in the competence, adulthood, and self-sufficiency of the congregations themselves and in the government of the leaders given to them and designated by them, the church in its larger connections will also have to preserve its unity, exercise the authority of Christ given to it, and subject itself to it. The fundamental structures of the church as the body of Christ here also constitute clear directives for the whole church. For this reason no vacuum arose with the disappearance of the last apostle, and the local congregations do not break apart as separate "bodies," but they have to preserve their interconnection and authority in harmony with the being and calling of the church as the body of Christ.

Paul's epistles (and the whole of the New Testament) give still less detailed prescriptions for this than for the organization of the local congregations. Provision is not made by apostolic succession or by the beginning of a hierarchical upbuilding corresponding with it. The "succession," if that is here to be spoken of, lies in the churches themselves and in the apostolic *paradosis* given in them. This does not mean for the church in general (any more than for the local congregations themselves), however, that in this interrelationship no regulations and no ordering of the authority given to the church would apply. Nor that outside the context of the local church this would only bear the character of a charismatic or ethical authority in the sense of the "twofold organization" of Harnack.[142] Here again every opposition of the pneumatic and charismatic and of church order and institution is in conflict with the nature of the church, and it lies exactly in the line of what was evident to us with regard to the local upbuilding of the churches that the churches themselves must bear the responsibility for seeing that, insofar as this is necessary and in harmony with the being of the church,

---

141. See also Bultmann, *Theology*, II, p. 96.
142. See above, p. 439.

the authority of Christ be given expression and be made to function in the sense of church order in the broader connections as well.

Because in the New Testament no new apostles succeed the initial ones and likewise no distinct offices are created to rule the church in its broad relationships, it is most in harmony with the development perceptible in Paul's epistles (and in the New Testament as a whole) for these broader connections, too, that the church receive the government it needs in certain organs designated by the several congregations themselves. However one chooses to conceive of such ecclesiastical organs, whether, as in the first instance is certainly the most obvious, as church assembly (cf. Acts 15; Gal. 2) or otherwise, the principal thing is that they are designated by the congregations themselves in order, on the analogy of the government of the local congregation, to invest the authority conferred on them by Christ in the larger ecclesiastical relationships as well.[143]

Along with this the manner in which Paul himself exercises his authority over the local congregations can constitute a clear directive. He is aware of having been vested by Christ with authority and power, but he does not hesitate to say: "All things are yours . . . , whether Paul, or Apollos." He does not act without the church and apart from it, therefore, even when the church itself is in default, but rather stirs it up to be conscious of its own calling and authority, to know its own independence and adulthood (1 Cor. 5:5; Rom. 15:14, 15). But at the same time he takes action when it forsakes its calling as the church in unspiritual leniency or passivity, in order to cleanse it of the alien blemish and to make it to be "the fresh dough" in accordance with its belonging to Christ, the paschal lamb who has been sacrificed for it (1 Cor. 5:3, 7). For this holy and Christian character of the church transcends everything else and in consequence requires preserving and upholding, if those who were first designated to that end should forsake their calling.

Although, in keeping with the incipient character of the church to which Paul addresses himself and in view of the peculiar significance of his writings as epistles, a systematic exposition of the precepts regarding church order is lacking, these epistles contain a multitude of motives and directives that are of great and abiding significance for correct insight into the structure, connection, and government of the Christian church and thus for its organizational upbuilding as the people of God and the body of Christ.[144]

SECTION 73. WORSHIP

It may be asked finally what place worship occupies in the whole of Paul's ecclesiological pronouncements and what significance is to be attached to it for the upbuilding of the church.

---

143. See also my essay "De apostoliciteit van de kerk volgens het Nieuwe Testament," in the volume *De Apostolische Kerk*, 1954, pp. 39-97, especially 93ff.

144. See, e.g., also von Campenhausen, *Die Begründung kirchlicher Entscheidungen beim Apostel Paulus.*

It is surely of fundamental importance that where Paul directly or indirectly makes mention of the meetings of the church he does not speak of them in sacral concepts. Twice he employs the term "worship" (*latreia*), once as a denotation of the Old Testament worship of God (Rom. 9:4), and once of the life of New Testament believers (Rom. 12:2). But he does not apply it to the meetings, but to the daily walk of the church. And the same holds for sacrificial terminology. Attention has rightly been called to the fact that after the sacrifice made by Christ, the priest as pontifical mediator between God and men is entirely missing in the world of the New Testament.[145] All of life is spiritual worship, every believer a priest (Rom. 12:1; cf. Rom. 1:9; Phil. 3:3; 2 Tim. 1:3). So far as priestly leadership has to be given in this sacrificial service, it consists in the apostolic instruction and admonition as to how the spiritual sacrifice of the church can be acceptable to God (Rom. 15:16; cf. Phil. 2:17). With this a fundamental change has been ushered in with regard to the Old Testament. The New Testament knows no holy persons who substitutionally perform the service of God for the whole people of God, nor holy places and seasons or holy acts, which create a distance between the cultus and the life of every day and every place. All members of the church have access to God (Rom. 5:2) and a share in the Holy Spirit; all of life is service to God; there is no "profane" area.[146]

On the other hand, for Paul the meeting of the church nevertheless has a specific and highly important significance. In it the revelation of the church takes place in what distinguishes it from the world; in the common participation in the one bread it is disclosed as the body of Christ (1 Cor. 10:17). Especially in its coming together the church is to be conscious of its priestly and prophetic task in behalf of and, in a certain sense, as substitute for the world: in its intercession for all men (1 Tim. 2:1ff., 8), in being the demonstration for unbelievers and observers that God is with it (1 Cor. 14:24, 25). For this reason adoration, prophecy, confession, the preaching of God's Word are also to take place. This does not create a new distance between life in the cultus and that of every day, for that is also and precisely to be cultus. But in these meetings the peculiar character of the church in the world is disclosed in an exemplary way, just as the indwelling of Christ in his church becomes manifest through the proclamation of the gospel, the observance of the Lord's Supper, the promise given, and the benediction pronounced in his name (cf., e.g., 2 Cor. 1:20; Col. 3:16; 2 Cor. 13:14, *et al.*).[147]

---

145. P. A. van Stempvoort, *Decorum, orde en mondigheid in het Nieuwe Testament*, 1956, p. 11; see also P. Menoud, *l'Église et les ministères selon le Nouveau Testament*, 1949, pp. 16ff.

146. On this see also the essay by Käsemann, "Worship in Everyday Life," *New Testament Questions of Today*, pp. 188ff.

147. For the significance of the "liturgy" in the New Testament church see also Käsemann, *Essays on New Testament Themes*, pp. 78f.

Now so far as these gatherings[148] of the church are concerned, it is far from the case that in Paul we have received detailed information or prescriptions. In the epistles that have been preserved to us he writes of them incidentally, more often than not in connection with certain abuses and with the presupposition of much that is often not clear to us and about which we should be glad to know more.

Thus at the very outset it is difficult on the ground of the Pauline epistles to answer the question as to whether and to what extent these gatherings of the church were under the guidance of specific persons designated for that purpose.

This question is of course closely bound up with that of the presence of office-bearers in the church in general. If one starts from such a passage as 1 Corinthians 11:17ff., very little is evident of a fixed order; rather, there seems to be a shortage of leadership. And the same thing applies to 1 Corinthians 14, where Paul is obliged to impress on the church that God is after all not a God of confusion (v. 33). On the other hand, all this is certainly no proof that in the meetings of the church there was in general no leadership, even in the church at Corinth, which was apparently inclined to spiritualism and licentiousness. When Paul elsewhere exhorts this church to be subject to certain persons who occupy a special place in its midst (16:13ff.), it is difficult to accept that this leadership took place exclusively outside the meetings of the church and did not also have influence on the organization of these gatherings.[149] Similarly, the prescriptions with regard to speaking in tongues, prophesying, etc., presuppose that certain rules had to be observed, something that is scarcely to be imagined apart from leadership.[150] With all this we may certainly consider more to have been presupposed than is expressed in so many words. Yet it is evident from the manner in which in this respect, too, Paul continually addresses himself to the church, and not to a few who occupy positions of leadership or to office-bearers, how much the gatherings of the church are not a hierarchical affair or one to be discharged by a few "holy" persons, but bear a fully congregational character.

This is not, of course, to say that these meetings would have significance as the mutual exercise of fellowship and not also and above all as "liturgy" and the worship of God. The contrary is the case. Although there are again more indirect than direct data, the following are to be pointed out.

(a) The proclamation of the Word in the assembly of the church. The church has not only to thank the preaching of the gospel for its origin, but its continued existence is dependent on the inviolate preservation of this preaching (cf. 1 Cor. 15:1, 2; Col. 2:7; 1 Tim. 6:14, et al.). That it was especially the meeting of the church where the continuation of preaching in its various shapes occurred is obvious and appears as well

---

148. *Synerchesthai*, whether or not with *epi to auto* (1 Cor. 11:17, 18, 20, 33, 34; 14:23, 26).
149. Cf. Bultmann, *Theology*, II, pp. 109ff.
150. See also G. Delling, *Worship in the New Testament*, pp. 34f.

from the direct pronouncements of the apostle. Thus he commands that his own epistles be read aloud in the assembly of the church (1 Thess. 5:27; Col. 4:16). The word that is employed for this *(anaginōskō, anagnōsis)* is the technical term for the cultic reading aloud of the Old Testament in the synagogue (cf. Luke 4:16; Acts 13:15, 27; 15:21; 2 Cor. 3:14, 15). By applying this terminology to the reading of his own epistles he not only ascribes the same authority to the apostolic word as to the Old Testament writings (as in 1 Tim. 5:18 he also combines a quotation from the Old Testament with a word of Jesus and introduces the whole with the familiar formula: "for the Scripture says"), but he also intends that they function as such in the gathering of the church. Elsewhere this "public reading" apparently has reference to the continued reading of the Old Testament in the gatherings of the church[151] (1 Tim. 4:13), just as, evidently once again with a view to teaching activity in the meeting of the church, Paul says of the God-inspired Scripture of the Old Testament that it is profitable for teaching, for reproof, etc. (2 Tim. 3:16; cf. Rom. 15:4; 1 Cor. 9:9, 10). Accordingly, just as in the synagogue (cf. Acts 13:15; Luke 4:20), the congregation was exhorted and taught from this "reading." All this comes clearly to the fore especially in the Pastoral Epistles. In the absence of Paul Timothy is to apply himself to public reading, exhortation, and teaching, understood, as appears from the repeated article, as fixed constituent parts of his work in the assembly of the church, for which he must prepare himself diligently.[152] Moreover, by the "exhortation" one is to understand not only the critical-paraenetic word, but all that is able to serve for religious awakening and upbuilding; "teaching" refers especially to the tradition, including its interpretation and application to the present (cf. Rom. 15:4). The church had increasing need of the reading of Scripture and instruction in the tradition in proportion as error arose that also appealed to Scripture (1 Tim. 1:7). In various ways in the Pastoral Epistles this "labor in the Word and in the doctrine" (1 Tim. 5:17) is insisted on (cf. 1 Tim. 4:11; 6:3; 2 Tim. 4:2) with the employment of different terminology (cf. 2 Tim. 2:14, 15; Tit. 3:1), whereby again and again the assembly of the church is presupposed as the place of this activity (cf. 1 Tim. 4:16; 2 Tim. 2:14).

In the older epistles more attention is devoted to the non-official prophetic utterances. Here, too, it is a matter of the continuing activity of the exalted Lord through his Spirit in the church, even if not everything that announced itself as a *charisma* of the Spirit was to be accepted, but was rather to be judged on its worth and authenticity (1 Thess. 5:21; cf. Rom. 12:6). As the gift of prophecy and of teaching was more and more restricted to certain persons, these also will have interpreted the Word of God in the assembly of the church, as is apparent from such designations as: to teach the Word (Gal. 6:6) and to labor in the Word and doctrine (1 Tim. 5:17). Yet the "free word" not bound to a specific

---

151. See J. L. Koole, *Liturgie en ambt in de apostolische kerk*, pp. 29ff.; cf. also, however, with greater reserve, Delling, *ibid.*, pp. 92ff.

152. Cf. W. Lock, *The Pastoral Epistles*, 1959, p. 53.

office also continues to characterize the meeting of the church (cf. Eph. 4:29; Col. 3:16; 1 Tim. 2:8ff.). But this freedom will increasingly have been exercised under the guidance of specific persons.

(b) In addition to the Word of God going forth to the church in its various forms, Paul speaks further of the observance of the Lord's Supper as an event recurring time and again in the assembly of the church. Here again in the epistles more is presupposed than is prescribed. How frequently the Supper was observed, or in the judgment of the apostle ought to be observed, can no longer be concluded with certainty from the way in which he writes of it (cf. 1 Cor. 11:25, 26), though one does get the impression here that the observance of the Supper took place in close connection with a non-cultic meal preceding it and thus was perhaps among the regular constituents of the church assembly.[153] Nor is the manner in which the Supper took place and in which the *anamnesis* element was given further expression, for example, by the recitation of certain parts from the tradition, described in the epistles of Paul. He does apparently feel the need of more rule in the church at Corinth. But he saves these additional regulations until he is there in person (1 Cor. 11:34).

So far further as the administration of baptism is concerned, it incorporates into the church and will therefore certainly have taken place in the presence of the church (cf. 1 Cor. 12:13). That baptism by immersion may be inferred from Romans 6:4[154] is, in our view, not simply to be posited without further ado. For baptism is not a symbol of going down in death and rising to life.[155] Baptism in Paul symbolizes cleansing and washing (1 Cor. 6:11; Eph. 5:26). This does not alter the fact that the "water bath" thus intended can have taken place in the form of immersion, which the word "baptize" originally means. Baptism for Paul is baptism into Christ and thus the appropriation of the redemptive event realized in Christ, and one can think to that effect of a baptismal song in such a passage as Ephesians 5:14.[156]

Through whom baptism took place and with whom the decision lay as to admission to baptism do not arise. It is surely worthy of remark that Paul says of himself that Christ has not sent him to baptize, but to preach the gospel (1 Cor. 1:17), and that he more or less glories in the fact that he baptized only a few of the Corinthians (1 Cor. 1:14). One is not to see here a depreciation of the liturgical act, and baptism is not set over against the gospel as a matter of secondary importance.[157] Paul only wants in this way to deprive the partisans in Corinth of every

---

153. See Delling, however (*Worship in the New Testament*, p. 148), who sees in the meal of 1 Cor. 11 a festive affair, which in his opinion "speaks in support of its infrequency." But a common weekly meal may very easily be thought of as a communion meal.

154. As Delling thinks (*ibid.*, p. 130, n. 5). He also refers to Col. 2:12 and 1 Cor. 10:2.

155. Cf. above, p. 402.

156. As, e.g., Dibelius-Greeven do (*Col.*).

157. So Lietzmann, *Cor.*, p. 9; on the other hand, see Kümmel, however, in the annotations of the same work.

argument for calling themselves after him as the party of Paul. Yet it remains striking that he explicitly divided the commission to proclaim the gospel and to baptize from each other. Baptism thus evidently pertains to the competence of the church itself, as soon as it has been established, substantially of the persons designated by it to that end.

(c) In addition to the ministry of the Word in its various forms of reading, prophecy, teaching, and the administration of baptism and the Supper, we find mentioned in the Pauline epistles the singing of psalms, hymns, and spiritual songs as an element of the assemblies (Col. 3:16; cf. Eph. 5:19). Although we are not further informed as to the content and character of these songs, it is apparently a question here of the songs to be sung in the meeting of the church, whether prepared by an individual member and rendered in the church (cf. 1 Cor. 14:26, 15), or, what is no less likely, sung by the whole congregation. The designations "psalm," "hymn," and "spiritual song" do not give much to go on for a further distinction, unless with "psalms" one chooses to think of the psalms of the Old Testament, for which no decisive arguments are to be adduced, however, and against which there are also objections to be urged.[158] That in such passages as Ephesians 5:14; Philippians 2:6ff.; 1 Timothy 3:16, we have to do with examples or fragments of Christian song, as is often supposed, is not improbable, though we shall have to be cautious in our judgment here because direct indications for it are lacking. The same thing holds for other expressions, formulae, stereotyped phrases, in which it is thought that liturgical elements can be pointed out, as, for example, the salutation with which Paul begins his epistles and in which a formula for the commencement of the gatherings of the church could possibly be seen;[159] similarly, the thanksgiving and intercession that follow on this prescript in almost all of the Pauline epistles; likewise doxologies and eulogies; and non-Greek expressions such as Maranatha (1 Cor. 16:22), Abba (Gal. 4:6; Rom. 8:15), and Amen (2 Cor. 1:20; 1 Cor. 14:16, et al.). That this last did in fact involve a form of agreement on the part of the church is evident from the passages cited. Further, in 1 Corinthians 16:20-25 one can find allusions to the liturgy of the Supper; [160] reference is also to be made to the "holy kiss," repeatedly mentioned in Paul (Rom. 16:16; 1 Thess. 5:26; 2 Cor. 13:12).[161] To examine all this at length, whereby the origins of the congregational confession of faith ought also to be discussed as well as congregational prayer, the place of the Lord's Prayer, the observance of the first day of the week, etc., does not belong to an investigation into the content of Paul's preaching.[162] From all that has been mentioned it

---

158. See also my Col., p. 222, and especially Delling, Worship in the New Testament, p. 87. Koole thinks of psalms from the O.T. (Liturgie, p. 60).

159. Cf. Delling, Worship in the New Testament, p. 56.

160. See the above-mentioned (n. 131) essay by Bornkamm, in Early Christian Experience, pp. 169ff.

161. Cf. K. M. Hofmann, Philema hagion, 1938.

162. On this see the special studies that have been mentioned, such as those of Koole, Delling, and further O. Cullmann, Early Christian Worship, ET 1953; A. Cole, The New Temple, 1950, et al.

may appear, however, how significant for Paul, too, the meetings of the church were for its upbuilding. However much the "liturgy" must be seen as a spiritual worship of God embracing the whole of life (Rom. 12:1, 2), this does not alter the fact that the indwelling in and communion of Christ with the church have their point of concentration and special realization in its unity as assembled congregation.

XII

THE FUTURE OF THE LORD

SECTION 74. THE LIFE OF EXPECTATION. THE "NEARNESS"

In the preceding study it has been apparent time and again how much the whole of Paul's preaching is determined by the all-important fact that in Christ's advent and work, especially in his death and resurrection, the divine work of redemption in history has reached its fulfillment and the redemptive dispensation of the great future promised by God and foretold by prophecy has become present time: "Behold, now is the acceptable time; behold, now is the day of salvation" (2 Cor. 6:2). We have been able to trace how all the central subjects of Paul's proclamation of redemption — the revelation of the righteousness of God, the new life of believers, the gift of the Holy Spirit, the church as the new people of God and as the body of Christ — must be understood in the light of this central motif of fulfillment and thus in their fundamentally eschatological and redemptive-historical determination. Along with that, however, we have been able to observe repeatedly that this promise of redemption fulfilled in Christ and the great day of salvation that has dawned with his death and exaltation as yet bear a character that is only in principle and provisional. They do not yet signify the end of the expectation of redemption and do not yet render the Christian hope superfluous. For this reason the "already" and the triumphant "but now" of the fulfillment are always coupled with the "not yet." The revelation of the righteousness of God does indeed guarantee the hope of the glory of God (Rom. 5:2), but does not yet signify the obtaining of this glory in the present time. Nor does the redemptive indicative of having died and having been raised with Christ make the necessity of the imperative in the struggle against sin superfluous. And the Spirit, however much the evidence of deliverance given in Christ from slavery under the law and sin, is still only the earnest and the firstfruits of the perfect redemption. In a word: the certainty that in Christ the day of salvation, the acceptable time, has dawned does not mean the end of redemptive expectation, but only makes it increase in intensity.

This expectation of the coming of the Lord and what accompanies it is one of the most central and powerful motifs of Paul's preaching. There are passages in which, in discussing specific questions or conditions in the church, he devotes deliberate and detailed attention to it — especially in 1 and 2 Thessalonians, but also in 1 Corinthians 15. We shall have to return to them. But in addition to these passages, the extent to which Christ's parousia determines his attention and preaching appears in many ways. He can define the content of conversion and of the Christian life as "waiting for his [God's] Son from heaven, whom he raised from the dead, Jesus who delivers us from the wrath to come" (1 Thess. 1:10), or as "a godly life in this world, in expectation of the blessed hope and the appearing of the glory of our great God and Savior, Christ Jesus" (Tit. 2:13). In 1 Corinthians 1:7 he further defines the confirmation of the gospel in the church as "not lacking in any spiritual gift," and as "waiting for the revelation of our Lord Jesus Christ" (cf. Phil. 3:20). This expectation, which can be called the content of the apostolic testimony (2 Thess. 1:10), is also a powerful motive for the Christian life (1 Thess. 2:12). Again and again the apostle confronts the church with the day of Christ, on which it will have to appear before its Lord pure and blameless (Phil. 1:10; 1 Thess. 3:13; 5:23; 1 Cor. 1:8). This motive is the more urgent because by this church Paul evidently does not mean the church in its already glorified mode of existence after the resurrection, but simply in its historical appearance, directed toward the parousia. Its calling to holiness and blamelessness he places in the very concrete light of the expected coming of the Lord, and it is the church with whom as his glorying he hopes to enter into the presence of the Lord at his coming (2 Cor. 1:14; Phil. 2:16), indeed it is his hope, his joy, and crown of honor before his Lord (1 Thess. 2:19, 20). It is with a view to that approaching day that believers are to cast off the works of darkness and to put on the armor of light. It is now time to awaken out of sleep; salvation is already nearer than when they first believed. The night is far spent, and the day is at hand. One is therefore to walk becomingly as in the day and no longer in the sins of darkness (Rom. 13:11-13). One meets with the same motifs in 1 Thessalonians 5:2-8. It is clear both that the motif of fulfillment, of already belonging to the day, finds expression here, and on the other hand that, as the great day of the Lord, this day is coming and with its beams is illuminating the present.

The coming of the Lord can for this reason not only be a motive for sanctification, but also a source and ground of comfort in the present "affliction," a word that does not merely refer to an incidental setback or difficulty, but very definitely characterizes the last phase of the present world preceding the coming of Christ.[1] Therefore the revelation of the Lord Jesus from heaven also signifies rest for those who are now in that distress (2 Thess. 1:6ff.). Because of this hope of the glory of God the church may glory in this affliction (Rom. 5:2-5). Affliction, suffering, and glory frequently occur in one context (Rom. 8:18), indeed in the former lie the announcement and proof of the latter (Rom. 8:19-23). Hope in the appearing of Christ (Tit. 2:13) is accordingly the distinguishing mark of the Christian life (Rom. 8:24; Gal. 5:5). As the one who will appear, Christ is the hope of glory (Col. 1:27), or in the absolute sense "our hope" (1 Tim. 1:1), with whose manifestation the church, too, will be manifested in glory (Col. 3:4). It is this glory which is time and again held out in prospect to the church that now finds itself in distress and suffering (1 Cor. 15:43; 2 Cor. 3:18; 4:17; Eph. 1:18; Phil. 3:4; 2 Thess. 2:14; 2 Tim. 1:10), and on which its hope is set

---

1. Cf. Rigaux, *Th.*, and Schlier, *TDNT*, III, pp. 143ff., *s.v. thlibō.*

(Col. 1:5; 1 Thess. 5:8; Tit. 1:2; 2:13; 3:7). And with what intensity this expectation is charged all those passages prove in which the apostle strongly accentuates the "not yet" of the present. There the sparks shoot, as it were, to and fro between the two poles (Rom. 8:18ff.; 2 Cor. 4:16-18); there it is evident what a living and fervent longing supports and glows through all the preaching of the apostle (cf. Rom. 7:24, 25; 8:23, *et al.*).[2]

In view of the important place the future expectation occupies in Paul's preaching and the actual significance he ascribes to it, it is no wonder that the query as to the eschatological perspective in a temporal respect has frequently been raised. In so doing the question in particular that has been dealt with repeatedly is whether he considered the parousia of the Lord as an event still to be experienced by him, or by his generation, and proceeds from that idea in his epistles. It is not a matter of a simple yes or no answer to this specific question, but above all of that which is closely bound up with it as to how Paul viewed the present life and its development in the light of the coming parousia.

Now in our opinion it is difficult to doubt that not only the ancient Christian church, but Paul, too, in the epistles that have come down to us, did not make allowance for a centuries-long continuing development of the present world order. The manner in which he speaks, for example, in Romans 13:11ff., of the approaching of salvation (that is to say, the parousia of Christ — "salvation is nearer to us now than when we first believed") points to the fact that the apostle did not expect Christ's coming to be in the distant future.[3] This may also appear from the words of Philippians 4:5, likewise to be understood to a temporal effect: "The Lord is at hand." Further, reference is to be made to the pronouncement in 1 Corinthians 7:29: "I mean this, brethren, the time is short."[4] In view of what follows this, in which the church is exhorted not to cling to the present life, because "the outward form of this world"[5] is passing away (vv. 29ff.), the "shortness" of the time is to be taken as the remaining temporal duration of this world and not merely of the individual life of believers.[6] Although the quali-

---

2. Cf. Berkouwer, *The Return of Christ*, pp. 115ff.

3. On the basis of certain Jewish speculations on "the days of the Messiah" (the time between the first appearing of the Messiah and the transcendent dawning of the new aeon), Schoeps thinks that Paul reckoned with an interval of forty years. When he wrote the Epistle to the Romans approximately twenty-five years of this total had elapsed, so that fifteen years still separated him from the parousia (*Paul*, pp. 100f.). But irrespective of what Paul writes elsewhere about ignorance concerning the time, it must be urged against the application of this speculation to his expectation for the future that it attempts to press Paul's "eschatology" into one or another contemporaneous Jewish schema. Against this method (followed by Schweitzer as well) see above, pp. 52ff.

4. *Ho kairos synestalmenos estin*, properly: has been drawn together, shortened. Some wish to understand this of a divine act of shortening. But it is more probable that the expression simply means "short" (cf. Arndt-Gingrich-Bauer, p. 802, *s.v. systellō*).

5. *To schēma tou kosmou toutou*: "This world in its distinctive manifestation (or form)" (Schneider, *TDNT*, VII, p. 956, *s.v. schēma*).

6. Cf. G. Vos, *The Pauline Eschatology*, p. 81, who rejects as "unrealistic" the

fication "short" (compressed) does not any more than "at hand" give a precise definition and can be taken more or less broadly, it is nevertheless clear that Paul sees in this "shortness" an urgent motive even for his readers of that day. The shortness of the time, the nearness of salvation, is a matter of great relevance, which heightens the earnestness of the paraenesis (cf. Phil. 4:5ff.).

And not only does the apostle see the life of the church from this point of view, when he warns it not to continue to cleave to the present life and to be holy in view of the nearness of the day of the Lord (Phil. 1:10; 1 Thess. 3:13; 5:23; 1 Cor. 1:8), but it also determines his view of the world around him. He hears in the whole creation a groaning for redemption, which has the character of an eager longing[7] of the creature[8] subjected to death and perishableness, of being already in travail, reaching out in pain toward a new birth (Rom. 8:19, 20, 22). He also sees in all this the approaching end of the power of darkness, which still appears as the world-ruling principle (Eph. 6:12). For God will soon *(en tachei)* crush Satan under the feet of the church, in accordance with the promise given at the ejection of man from Paradise (Rom. 16:20).

Interpreters frequently go further and suppose that Paul counted on himself still living to see the parousia of Christ, and that he awakened that expectation in the church. Appeal is made to two passages in particular for that purpose, namely, 1 Thessalonians 4:13ff. and 1 Corinthians 15:51. In 1 Thessalonians 4:13 Paul goes into the anxiety that has arisen in the church concerning those among them who have died and had thus not lived to see the coming of Christ. This is said to point to the fact that during his time in Thessalonica he had not spoken of this possibility, that Christians should die before the parousia. It is also supposed to be clearly evident, when in 1 Thessalonians 4:13 he attempts to remove this anxiety, that neither he himself nor his readers have thought of their own dying before the parousia. Appeal is then made especially to the "we" in the words: "we who are alive, who are left until the coming of the Lord [or: we who continue to live until the coming of the Lord], shall in no case precede those who have fallen asleep" (1 Thess. 4:15; cf. v. 17).[9] And a similar conclusion is attached to 1 Corinthians 15:51: "Behold, I tell you a mystery: we all shall not sleep, but we shall be changed." Paul is said to have declared herewith that not all Christians of his time, nor he himself, would die before the parousia. And it is alleged that this cannot be set aside, for example, by referring the fact that all shall not sleep, not to Paul and

---

exegesis according to which one is not to take *sōtēria* in Rom. 13 in an eschatological sense or has to understand the shortness of the time in 1 Cor. 7:29 of the nearness of death for every individual person. For the various Roman Catholic conceptions of the *Naherwartung* in Paul, see the survey of Rigaux, *Th.*, p. 223.

7. *Apokaradokia,* from *kara* (head) and *dekomai* (expect), not "with uplifted head," but "with outstretched neck," "eager longing."

8. For *ktisis* see my *Rom.*, pp. 185, 186.

9. See, e.g., Dibelius, *Th.*, pp. 23, 24; also Cullmann, *Christ and Time*, p. 76.

those whom he addresses themselves, but just to those who are alive at the parousia.[10]

Now in the light of the "nearness" pronouncements that have already been cited, one can hardly contend that personally living to see the parousia was a thought that was far removed from Paul's mind; rather, the reverse seems to be the case. Likewise the fact that the church at Thessalonica could place the death of believers before Christ's coming only with difficulty points out how relevant it had found the announcement of the parousia in the apostolic preaching and how much that event had come, as it were, to fill its whole horizon (cf. 1 Thess. 1:9, 10). It is something else again, however, whether Paul, either in his preaching or in his epistles, may be said to have left no place for another possibility, so that one would be permitted to take the words "we who are left alive," etc., in 1 Thessalonians 4:15, 17, only in a positive and not in a hypothetical or at least a facultative sense ("so far as we," etc.). And this is, on further reflection, surely a contention that is difficult to maintain. First of all, it is not in any sense apparent from Paul's answer to the church that the death of members of the congregation before the parousia constituted a problem for him. Rather his answer is evidence to the contrary. He is able indeed to appeal to a word of the Lord in which the fate of those who died (before the parousia) as well as that of survivors had been foreseen. In addition, if it had been the presupposition of Paul's preaching that believers continue to live till the parousia, he would already have attributed a certain immortality to himself and his fellow believers, something that is altogether in conflict with the manner in which he generally speaks of his own life and death and that of his fellow-believers (cf., e.g., 1 Thess. 5:10; Rom. 14:7-9; 8:10, 11, to say nothing of such passages as Phil. 1:22ff.; 2:17; 2 Cor. 4:11; 5:1ff.; 2 Tim. 4:6, in which the possibility, in part even the expectation, of dying before the coming of Christ is explicitly posited).

This scarcely deniable fact has accordingly given rise to the theory that a certain contradiction exists in Paul's pronouncements on death; there is said to be a juxtaposition of the eschatological expectation of the parousia and an individual hope in the period after death, which would in a sense give expression to the peculiarity of Paul's faith.[11] More radical and in a certain respect more plausible is the view that as time went on Paul changed his mind.[12] Inasmuch, however, as the "old" standpoint is seen to emerge in 1 Corinthians 15 and the "new" in 2 Corinthians 5:1ff., one is surely obliged to reach the bold assertion that that change came about in the one- or two-year interval between the first and second epistles to the Corinthians.[13] But all these theories are untenable. How could Paul have been able to "introduce"

10. So, e.g., Kümmel in Lietzmann-Kümmel, *Cor.*, p. 196. In so doing he directs himself against Allo.

11. So Dibelius in his excursus on Phil. 1:23 (*An die Philipper*, 3rd ed., 1937, p. 69).

12. See, e.g., Cullmann, *Christ and Time*, p. 88.

13. So Schoeps, *Paul*, p. 103.

these sweeping "alterations" in his epistles to Corinth, written in such rapid succession, without speaking so much as one word of justification concerning them, while both in 1 Corinthians 15 and 2 Corinthians 5 he deals with death explicitly and at length? But then, how could he persist so long (up to the writing of 2 Cor.) in this "old" conception? How many believers had he, who wrote his epistles twenty years and more after his conversion, already seen pass away? And how could he then, whether in his preaching or in his first epistles, have given people the impression that they were no longer to die? That he himself would thereby occupy an exceptional position is just as incapable of being made plausible. In the passages to which appeal is made, in 1 Thessalonians 4:15ff. as well as in 1 Corinthians 15:51, he speaks of "we." This "we" can accordingly signify nothing other than a general designation that has a facultative thrust: "we," insofar as we are permitted to experience this and insofar as this will be found to apply to us (cf., e.g., Rom. 15:1). One will thus be allowed to conclude that living to see the parousia was for Paul indeed a real possibility, we may perhaps say the object of his hope and expectation, but that both for his own faith and for his paraenesis this expectation was in no way a *conditio sine qua non*. The force of his expectation for the future and of his paraenesis is to be sure dependent on the appearing of Christ in glory, and on its significance for the present, but not on still being alive to see this appearing.

This ascertainment, however important it may be, does not, however, alter the fact that Paul's preaching and particularly the paraenesis resulting from it was, as we have seen, very strongly conditioned by the nearness of Christ's parousia. And the question can arise whether this motif does not in a decisive way make the validity of the pronouncements and exhortations conditioned by it dependent on the shortness of the time still remaining to the world. One will certainly have to keep fully in view that in Paul also every computation of the time of the parousia is entirely lacking, and that furthermore, as we shall see in greater detail, he also takes a strong position against the failure to observe what is yet to take place in the interval that remains (cf., e.g., 2 Thess. 2:3ff.). One can certainly say, therefore, that the connection between the nearness and the incalculability of the end is highly essential for understanding the Pauline *Naherwartung*.[14] On the other hand, this may not lead to such a relativizing of the "nearness" that the moment of time situated in it would scarcely play a part any longer and one would find in the "nearness" only the expression of the earnestness of the preaching or something of that sort. For however much the nearness pronouncements lie outside the sphere of calculation and numerical speculation, it does not alter the fact that this nearness is not to be eliminated as a category of time or to be converted into a general denotation of mystical or transcendental "nearness."

Another consideration seems to us to be no less important, therefore, for a correct understanding of this nearness and for the continuing

---

14. See Berkouwer, *The Return of Christ*, p. 90.

validity of the pronouncements and paraenesis motivated by it: the indissoluble unity of the perfect tense and the future tense of the New Testament eschatology in general and of the Pauline in particular. This element becomes clear to us when we get a better view of the ground for these nearness pronouncements in Paul and along with that of the nature of this nearness. For it is plain that Paul does not derive the nearness of Christ's parousia from any special knowledge or insight concerning the time within which this parousia is to be expected — it is precisely with respect to that that he acknowledges his ignorance (1 Thess. 5:1, 2) — but rather from the overwhelming significance of the eschatological time of redemption that has already been entered upon with Christ's first advent. The certainty of standing in this all-embracing turning point of the times for him makes the parousia, too, such a relevant reality filling the whole of his horizon. Time and again we accordingly see that both these motifs — that of the "realized" and that of the still "prospective" eschatology — are brought into immediate relation with each other and, as it were, flow over into one another; and that the paraenesis that points toward the nearness of Christ's coming is borne by what the church already is and already has in Christ. When, for example, it is said to the church in 1 Thessalonians 5:4: "but you, brethren, are not in darkness, that that day should overtake you as a thief," this does not mean that the church in distinction from others is in fact informed as to "the times and the seasons" and that it does not apply to it that the day of the Lord "so comes as a thief in the night." It means instead that as standing in the light that has already appeared and as "sons" of the day that has already dawned (cf. v. 5), the church is no longer able carelessly to put off the day of the Lord, but rather goes to meet it and expects it in soberness and watchfulness (vv. 6ff.). Similarly, when it is said to believers in Romans 13:12 that the night is far gone and the day is at hand, there is not here in the first place a reference to the light that is still to come, but to that which already has come. "Children of the light" in the New Testament and with Paul does not mean merely: destined for the coming light, but in the first place: standing in the light that has already appeared. And "the day," of which there is mention in Romans 13 ("the day is at hand ... let us walk becomingly as in broad daylight"), is to be understood, therefore, not only as the day of the judgment or of the parousia, but as the redemptive dispensation that has already dawned in Christ. In the inseparable and reciprocal linking of the perfect with the future and of the future with the perfect, the real motivation and the nature of the nearness pronouncements are to be sought, and the perfect- and future-aspect of Christ's coming time and again encroach upon each other. The one cannot exist without the other, cannot be thought of without the other, and automatically summons the other therefore as an indispensable complement to itself.

As a result, Paul's preaching with regard to the character or meaning of the interval (between Christ's ascension and parousia) exhibits a remarkable ambivalence. Starting from the entrance of what has already taken place, proclaimed with so much force, the conclusion seems to be obvious that for this present world, too, an entirely new future, a new basis of life has opened up. Yet this conclusion is not drawn in the temporal sense. There is no new perspective forcing its way through as a view of the future or of the mandate of the church spanning the ages. Rather the new present thus understood remains in respect of time most closely bound to the future. An adequate period of time scarcely appears to be left over for a development of the kingdom of Christ in the present world. And this is the more striking because the universality — preached with such great power especially by Paul — of the salvation that has made its appearance in Christ and its proclamation in the world seem to make an extension of the temporal and spatial horizon of this world, as it were, inevitable. This spatial and even cosmic perspective is accordingly abundantly present in Paul, but yet not in the sense that it would form the foundation for an accompanying expansion of the time of the present world. Rather, the universal preaching to all nations and in the whole world is seen as a matter the execution of which may already be pointed out, but not as the beginning of a new path the end of which is as yet unforeseeable (cf. Col. 1:6; 1 Tim. 3:16; Rom. 15:19, 23). Undoubtedly its fulfillment, too, is not to be calculated by human standards, and the apostle here makes everything conditional on the fullness determined in God's counsel of redemption (cf. Rom. 11:12, 25). But acknowledging that does not prevent him from concentrating on the nearness of the parousia and wakening the church to it.

On the other hand, it is of no less importance to observe that this eschatological determination of Paul's preaching and paraenesis nowhere asserts itself as a depreciation of life in the present world. Even in the oldest epistles there is no trace whatever of that; rather, he resists precisely those who from the early coming of the Lord want to infer a lesser evaluation of the present life (2 Thess. 3:6ff.). Opposition and suffering in this world do weigh heavily on him, especially with a view to the church. He sees this "affliction" in an eschatological light and, as we have already seen in another context, because this distress is evaluated eschatologically, in a specific situation he makes a strong reservation in the unqualified acceptance, for example, of married life (1 Cor. 7:29ff.). But on the other hand it is just this distress which is for him the motive for stirring up the church to stand positively in the world. Because the days are evil, the church is to make the most of the opportunity (still) given it (Eph. 5:15, 16; Col. 4:5). What is meant by this "opportunity" is not merely a favorable point of time in general, but the continuance of the time of the present life. It is this opportunity which is now to be made the most of (literally: "to buy up"); all the possibilities present in it are to be used. And to what purpose? To walk carefully and wisely (Eph. 5:15), in particular toward those who are without (Col. 4:5, 6), to do good toward all men and especially toward those who are of the household of faith (Gal. 6:10). Again and again this *kairos* is pointed to (cf. Rom. 13:11) as the critical juncture, as the special opportunity, in which the church is to place the insight that has been given it into the will of God (Eph. 5:15) at the service of others, and is to know its special responsibility. This consists also in acknowledging and maintaining the ordinance God has given for the continued existence and organization of natural life. The passage on the authorities in Romans 13 immediately precedes: you know the *kairos*, being faced with the coming of the Lord (Rom. 13:11). The same holds for the admonition to a regular and orderly life in 1 Thessalonians 5:14 and 2 Thessalonians 3:6ff. And in 1 Timothy 4:1ff. the apostle warns that "in the last times," as the Spirit expressly says, some will fall away from the faith, among other things, by forbidding to marry and demanding abstinence from foods that God has created. Whereas in 1 Corinthians 7, therefore, the view of the impending distress and the shortness of the time leads him to great reserve with respect to entering into marriage, here he warns, likewise with an appeal to "the last days," against all kinds of self-willed religion and ascetic practices that bring marriage into discredit. The one is not in conflict with the other. Both together give us a correct insight into the eschatological determination of Paul's paraenetic preaching for the interim period. The eschatological motive, the consciousness of the coming of the Lord as near at hand, has not a negative, but a positive significance for life in the present time. It does not make the responsibility for that life relative, but rather elevates it. It is consequently not so that in a prolongation of the present world time this eschatological preaching and paraenesis would lose its validity or meaning. The contrary is rather the case. There is nothing that makes believers aware with greater seriousness of their responsibility for the present life than the manner in which the motive of the nearness of the parousia functions in Paul's preaching.

On account of this not only material, but also temporal connection of the perfect tense and the future tense, there is in Paul's nearness pronouncements, according to the nature of prophecy,[15] a clear proleptic element. In spite of all its provisional character that cries out for the consummation, the perfect would appear, even for the present existence of life and the world, to have a more inclusive significance and to span a larger period than could be perceived *a priori* at the turning point of the times. For that matter, as we have already seen, all the conditions for such a protracted development are implicit in Paul's preaching itself. Not only does the preaching of the gospel itself, in its character of inviting, enlisting, compelling to decision, in its proclamation of God's will to reconciliation and of his longsuffering toward all men, ask time and again, as it were, for more space and more time, before the irrevocableness of the end that accompanies the parousia enters in (cf., e.g., Luke 13:8).[16] But further, one is to think here of the depth of God's wisdom, the unsearchableness of his judgments, and the inscrutableness of his ways, again and again confessed by Paul (cf. Rom.

15. On this point see also T. van der Walt, *Die koninkryk van God — naby!*, 1962, pp. 208ff.
16. For this motif in the preaching of Jesus and the provisional modality of the coming of the kingdom of God bound up with it see my *The Coming of the Kingdom*, pp. 148ff.

11:33), or, as it is called in Ephesians 3:18: the breadth and length and height and depth of God's work of redemption and of the love of Christ that surpasses all knowledge. These universal dimensions of what has taken place in Christ, embracing the whole creation, contain a multiplicity of viewpoints also for the regenerating power of the gospel in the present world and for the continuing unlocking of the plan of God's counsel with respect to history. The result of all this has accordingly been that with the prolongation of the time of the present world Paul's preaching has not become unintelligible,[17] but for the church has ever and again been full of positive guidance and direction in its course through history. For this preaching is and remains, even when it draws the future of the Lord, as it were, within the boundaries of the present, preaching of the victory that Christ has already gained over the powers of darkness. Therefore every reflection on what has been called the meaning of history or of the interim time is not to start from "the problem of the delay of the parousia," but rather from this all-embracing motif of fulfillment.[18]

When this takes place in the spirit and power of the Apostle Paul, the nearness of Christ's coming will not thereby fade into the background as an expectation becoming ever more obscured. For Christ is one, and it holds with respect to the problem of the relevance of the "at hand" that Christ is not divided. In the final analysis the "at hand" does not involve a question of the importance of the length of the intervening period, but of the inseparability of the future from the perfect. This "at hand" is not only the expression therefore of individual human "understanding of Being" (Seinsverständnis), in which the meaning of history would be swallowed up by eschatology;[19] it rather, first and foremost, gives testimony to the irresistible progress and haste of the divine work in its all-embracing sense (cf. Luke 18:8). But "at hand" thus understood will not be able to find its standard only in the unity and inseparability of present and future, as faith, standing on the turning point of the times, prophetically takes them together in one glance; it will also have to be understood ever and again out of the divine dimensions indicated by the gospel itself of the counsel of God

---

17. For this viewpoint see also the writings of Cullmann in his criticism of the consistent eschatology (cf. above, p. 43); also Berkouwer, *The Return of Christ*, pp. 73ff., 91ff. For his part Schweitzer, too, recognizes with respect to Paul's ethics: "As though he had an intuition that it might be the fate of Christianity to have to make terms with the continuance of the natural world, he reaches by his spirituality that attitude towards earthly things by means of which Christianity must henceforth maintain its place in the world. Though living and thinking in his own day, he is at the same time preparing the future" (*The Mysticism of Paul the Apostle*, p. 332).

18. See also H. Berkhof, *Christ the Meaning of History*, pp. 78f.

19. Cf. Bultmann, *History and Eschatology*, p. 43: "But although the history of the nation and the world had lost interest for Paul, he brings to light another phenomenon, the historicity of man, the true historical life of the human being, the history which everyone experiences for himself and by which he gains his real essence." Against this existentialistic interpretation of eschatology see, e.g., N. Q. Hamilton, *The Holy Spirit and Eschatology in Paul*, pp. 71ff.; also C. Müller, *Gottes Gerechtigkeit und Gottes Volk*, pp. 104ff.; and Käsemann, "On the Subject of Primitive Christian Apocalyptic," *New Testament Questions of Today*, pp. 130ff.

and of its realization in history. It is only in this sense that "at hand" retains its relation to history, and at the same time does not lose its significance in the relativity of human historical consciousness.

SECTION 75. DEATH BEFORE THE PAROUSIA. THE "INTERMEDIATE STATE"

Before going further into Paul's expectation for the future in general, we have to give attention here also to the question frequently treated in recent years whether there is a place in this expectation for the so-called intermediate state between death and the resurrection, and if so, in what this state consists.[20] In the preceding section we have seen that the death of believers before the parousia is not an "unforeseen thing" in Paul's preaching, so that one may anticipate that the church is not left in doubt concerning the fate of deceased believers. Paul prefers to speak of this dying as "falling asleep" (koimasthai; cf. 1 Cor. 11:30; 15:6, 18, 20; 1 Thess. 4:13ff.). Likewise he denotes having already died as "sleeping" (katheudein; Eph. 5:14; 1 Thess. 5:10).[21]

The question has indeed been asked whether by this description the condition of deceased believers before the parousia is also thought of as a sleep in which all activity and consciousness cease and from which they will only awaken at the resurrection.[22] But it is certainly incorrect to take the words "to fall asleep" and "to sleep" as an explication of the manner of continued existence after death. For first of all, this expression is not a distinctive characteristic only of the preaching of Paul and of the New Testament as a whole. It also occurs in all sorts of places outside the sphere of the Bible.[23] And in the second place, there are other pronouncements in Paul that define the significance of this intermediate state in a manner much more his own.

---

20. See, e.g., P. H. Menoud, Le sort des trespassés, 1945; J. N. Sevenster, "Einige Bemerkungen über den 'Zwischenzustand' bei Paulus," NTS, I, 1955, pp. 291ff.; the same author, "Some remarks on the [gymnos] in 2 Cor. V. 3," in Studia Paulina, 1953; J. Dupont, [SYN CHRISTŌ], l'Union avec le Christ suivant Saint Paul, I, 1952, pp. 171ff.; O. Cullmann, "Unsterblichkeit der Seele und Auferstehung der Toten," TZ, 1956, pp. 126ff.; E. E. Ellis, "The Structure of Pauline Eschatology (II Corinthians V.1-10)," in Paul and His Recent Interpreters, pp. 35ff. (see also the literature given there, p. 35, n. 2); B. Telder, Sterven ... en dan?, 1960; G. C. Berkouwer, The Return of Christ, pp. 32ff. See also the study of G. Vos, important for the entire Pauline "eschatology," The Pauline Eschatology; and K. Dijk, Tussen sterven en opstanding, 2nd ed., 1955.

21. For both concepts see also O. Michel, Die Christliche Hoffnung, 1936, pp. 40ff.

22. Cf., e.g., Bultmann, TDNT, III, p. 17: "On the intermediate state between death and the resurrection the NT gives us no explicit information. It is thought of as a sleep unless the various authors suggest other conceptions."

23. Cf. P. H. Menoud, Le sort des trespassés, p. 46: "But one must take care not to construct an entire psychology of the deceased on the basis of this expression 'those who sleep,' considering that it is an old image in the world, a euphemism employed as well by those who have no hope whatever of an 'awakening' of the deceased...." See also Vos, The Pauline Eschatology, pp. 142ff.

Besides this, these pronouncements are of an indirect sort, and one cannot speak of a doctrine concerning the intermediate state in Paul. The clearest passage is surely Philippians 1:20ff. The apostle here posits the possibility that he will not survive his imprisonment. The chief thing for him, however, is that Christ be glorified in his body (his present existence), "whether by my life, or by my death" (v. 20). He can speak in this way because, as he adds in verse 21, for him living is Christ and dying gain. What he means by this is clarified further along when he says that he does not know what he ought to choose and that he is hard pressed between the two: his desire is "to depart and be with Christ; for it is better by far"; yet for the church it is more profitable that he remain.

On the relation of verses 20 and 21 there is much difference of opinion.[24] The most natural view is that by "living" and "dying" in verse 21 Paul is reflecting on "whether by my life or by my death" in verse 20. The difficulty lies in this, however, that both predicates in verse 21, "Christ" and "gain," seem to lend themselves less well to a description of the distinction between living and dying. For this reason some choose to take verse 21 as a further explication of the last three words in verse 20: for inasmuch as for me to live is Christ, therefore to die for me is only gain. Verse 22 would then hark back to the possibility posited in verse 20 of continuing to live on earth and throw light on its importance.[25] Others think that verse 21 does not have reference so much to Paul's own lot as indeed to what he calls in verse 20 the magnifying of Christ. This would take place by his life as well as by his death. For the life of Paul is a demonstration of the glory of Christ. If he must die for Christ, then this applies still more, and this is to be taken as "gain" in that sense, whether with a view to the proclamation of the gospel, or as a gain for Paul when he has to render an account of his work before God. In both cases "gain" would not be a description of what was in store for Paul immediately after death and thus not be a qualification of the intermediate state.[26]

However one is to understand precisely the transition from verse 20 to verse 21, the words "to die is gain" will have to be taken in the first place as a denotation of what applies to Paul himself.[27] The words "to me" are emphatically put first and go with the whole sentence.[28] In them he also harks back to what has gone before, in which it is not only a question of the continuing proclamation of the gospel but of his own lot as well (cf. vv. 12, 20a). Both members of verse 21 are thereby certainly not to be taken as an antithetic parallelism, in the sense that they set life and death over against each other. The intention is simply to say that (continuing) to live or to die makes no fundamental difference. Living (Christ) and dying (gain) are accordingly not placed

---

24. See, e.g., the discussion of the various opinions in Greijdanus, *De brief van den Apostel Paulus aan de Gemeente te Philippi*, 1937, pp. 137ff.

25. In this sense Dibelius, *An die Philipper*, p. 87.

26. Cf. for these conceptions P. Bonnard, *l'Épitre de Saint Paul aux Philippiens*, 1950, p. 28.

27. So correctly W. Michaelis as well (*Der Brief des Paulus an die Philipper*, 1935, p. 25).

28. This is wrongly denied by Telder, *Sterven ... an dan?*, pp. 93ff.

over against each other, but the latter is rather a result of the former. That he nevertheless can call dying "gain" is because life in the flesh presents all kinds of trouble, trials, and limitations with regard to what Christ means for him. To that effect one will also have to understand the pronouncement in verses 23 and 24, that he desires to depart (to die) and to be with Christ; for that is better by far. The words "be with Christ" denote therefore what dying means for Paul. He employs the same expression in 1 Thessalonians 4:17. There it has reference, however, to the existence of believers after the parousia, that is to say, after the resurrection and the union with those who are then still alive. In Philippians 1:23 something else is apparently intended, however, namely, a transition that takes place at death, and one will not therefore be allowed to regard the resurrection as tacitly presupposed. For then the alternative of remaining with you or being with Christ is no longer a genuine alternative, and "no longer to remain with you" would not mean at once "to be with Christ." To be with Christ therefore denotes the condition of believers immediately after their death.[29] (Concerning the "how" see below, p. 505.)

Another passage that demands further examination for the idea of the intermediate state in Paul's epistles is 2 Corinthians 5:1-10. The exegesis is difficult, and there is much difference of opinion concerning the main point as well as the various parts. Referring to what he has said in the preceding passage about the eternal glory in which believers are to share and which makes them consider their temporary affliction as slight, however grievous it may seem (2 Cor. 4:17), the apostle comes first of all to the statement: "For we know that if our earthly tent-house is destroyed, we have a building from God, a house in the heavens which is not made with hands and is eternal" (v. 1).

---

29. So rightly also Dibelius, *An die Philipper,* p. 69; cf. Greijdanus as well (*De brief aan de Gemeente te Philippi,* pp. 144, 145), against Michaelis, who considers the condition "on the other side of the resurrection" to be spoken of (*Der Brief an die Philipper,* p. 27). According to Michaelis Paul thought of the "intermediate state" as a sleep (1 Thess. 5:10), and as a continuation of the *tou Kyriou einai.* J. N. Sevenster writes that Paul must certainly have conceived of an intermediate state. He does not wish, however, to say with absolute certainty that the *syn Christō einai* (Phil. 1:23) or the *endēmēsai pros ton Kyrion* (2 Cor. 5:8) has reference to this intermediate state: "It could also be — although I consider it improbable — that Paul is speaking in a certain sense proleptically of the glory of the day of the Lord," in *NTS,* I, p. 296; see also his *Leven en dood in de brieven van Paulus,* 1954, p. 133, where he considers it more probable that Paul sees the time immediately after death as the beginning of the full glory. Grosheide expresses himself in passing (in a note) as follows; "I prefer to view it so, that dying for Paul means to experience the return" (*I Cor.,* p. 140, n. 2; cf. p. 142). He thus apparently assumes no conscious intermediate state. Bultmann, *Theology,* I, p. 346, thinks that Paul "gets into contradiction with the resurrection doctrine when he hopes in Phil. 1:23 that his 'being with Christ' will begin immediately after his death" and that "this contradiction betrays how little difference it makes what images are used." But that Paul (in one and the same epistle; cf. Phil. 1:6; 3:20ff.) should have become entangled in contradictory ideas at such a basic point is surely difficult to accept. The *syn Christō einai* must have had for Paul a specific content immediately after death and thus before the resurrection. Otherwise, H. M. Matter as well (*De brief aan de Philippenzen,* 1965, p. 33).

The words "for we know," etc., give a further motivation to what has been said before about not looking to the visible, which is temporal, but to the invisible and eternal. "Temporal" and "eternal" are then more fully defined, the former as "our earthly tent-house." However one chooses to explain this expression further,[30] it is clear from the whole context that what is meant here is the temporal mode of existence of man in the earthly body. Its dissolution commences already in the present assaults and afflictions mentioned by Paul in the preceding passage (the decay of the outward man; 4:16), and has its completion in death.[31] Being in that destruction and looking to the death that ever threatens him, Paul then gives testimony to what he knows by faith concerning the invisible and eternal, the building he expects from God, not made with hands but eternal in the heavens.

The question directly arises along with this as to whether what is meant here is something that believers are to receive immediately at their death (whether as an "intermediate state"[32] or as a definitive mode of existence taking effect at once after death[33]), or whether there is mention here of what is to be realized at the parousia, that is, the new body. For the first conception appeal is made to the words "we have," and these are then so taken that as soon as our earthly house, etc., is

---

30. Cf., e.g., J. Dupont, [SYN CHRISTŌ], pp. 145ff. (as dwelling place of God); W. D. Davies, *Paul and Rabbinic Judaism*, 2nd ed., 1955, p. 313, who finds an allusion here to dwelling in tabernacles, following T. W. Manson.

31. R. Bultmann, *Exegetische Probleme des zweiten Korintherbriefes*, 1947, pp. 9ff., thinks that *kataluthēnai* can also refer to the moment of the parousia (cf. Bachmann in Zahn's commentary). But after all that has been said in the foregoing (2 Cor. 4) about death, this is not very credible, irrespective of the unusualness of the terminology, if this should have reference to what takes place at the parousia.

32. So Schlatter, *Erläuterungen (Kor.)*, 1920, pp. 194ff. He takes "house" not as new body, but as abode in heaven before the resurrection. Likewise Grosheide, who with "tent-house" does not wish to think of the earthly body, but of the "outward man" of 4:16, and under the "building in the heavens" the "inward man." In our view, especially so far as the latter is concerned, a not very transparent idea.

33. This goes much further than the conception mentioned in note 32. It presupposes that in our text the whole idea of the parousia and the resurrection of the body has been relinquished and that in its place appears that of the glorified continued existence of souls in heaven. In this a "development" of the Pauline eschatology in the direction of Greek thought would then reveal itself. So especially some of the older "liberal" exegetes, but also W. L. Knox, *St. Paul and the Church of the Gentiles*, 1939, pp. 128ff.; different again, W. D. Davies, *Paul and Rabbinic Judaism*, pp. 308-332. The latter speaks of a "juxtaposition of two different views" in Paul. The first would be represented by 1 Cor. 15. Here there is mention of the resurrection of the body at the parousia. On the other hand 2 Cor. 5 would speak of the heavenly body that is given to believers immediately at death. Davies thinks that both representations hark back to similar ideas in Judaism, and that the latter in Paul would thus not arise directly from Greek thought. However, against this whole view of a twofold eschatology in 1 Cor. 15 and 2 Cor. 5 see already Lietzmann, *Cor.*, pp. 118, 119, and A. Plummer, *A Critical and Exegetical Commentary on the Second Epistle of St. Paul to the Corinthians*, 1951 (1915), pp. 160ff. Further also Wendland, *Cor.*, pp. 129ff.; J. Dupont, [SYN CHRISTŌ], *l'Union avec le Christ suivant Saint Paul*, pp. 137-139; J. N. Sevenster, *Leven en dood in de brieven van Paulus*, pp. 124ff. It is, i.a., rightly pointed out that it would surely be very strange were Paul in the time between 1 Cor. and 2 Cor. to have come to this "development," and then to have returned, e.g., in Rom., to his original idea.

demolished, we "have" and also obtain our heavenly house forthwith. But in the first place just such a "forthwith" is missing.[34] And further, from the correlation between "building from God," "heavenly house," and "earthly tent-house" as well as from what follows it is to be concluded with certainty that what is meant by this "new building" is the glorified counterpart of the earthly body, and in the whole of Paul's proclamation this is to be understood in no other way than as that which will take place at Christ's coming. The pronouncement of verse 1 will thus denote the whole future in which believers share in Christ (cf. 4:17); "have" thus has an anticipatory[35] significance;[36] it can also be understood as having something coming to them in heaven, a gift that has been prepared and hidden for them there and in which at the manifestation of Christ believers will also be manifest (Col. 3:3, 4).[37]

This knowledge concerning the building to be expected from God is further motivated as follows: "For in this [in this respect, or in this temporal existence] we groan, longing to be clothed upon with our habitation which is from heaven; inasmuch as [only] after having put it on we shall not be found naked" (2 Cor. 5:2, 3).

There is in the present "groaning," negatively, a clear indication and confirmation of what believers may expect (cf. Rom. 8:19ff.). Their suffering merely stirs up even more their eager longing "to be covered over" with the habitation from heaven. The words employed here also express that what is intended is not life in heaven before the parousia, but receiving *from* heaven a new dwelling or new garment in the sense of a new body. This takes place at the parousia.[38] Regarding verse 4 many are of the opinion that by "being covered over" Paul is not thinking of the resurrection of the dead, but of the transformation of those who will still be alive at the parousia. There would then be mention not of putting off the body, being unclothed, but of putting on the new body, as it were, over the old.[39] But this conception is too limited.[40] It is a question here in general of the new body, becoming conformed to the glorified body of Christ (1 Cor. 15:51; Phil. 3:21), when "the mortal shall be swallowed up by life" (v. 4; cf. 1 Cor. 15:53, 54).

Verse 3 can perhaps best[41] be taken as the motivation of the

---

34. Cf. Bultmann, *loc. cit.*

35. Plummer writes: "The present tense is often used as a future, which is absolutely certain" (*Commentary on Second Corinthians*, p. 144).

36. Cf. E. E. Ellis, *Paul and His Recent Interpreters*, pp. 41ff.: Paul here is thinking not in the first place of individual bodies, but of what believers have together in Christ and will receive at the parousia.

37. So, e.g., Wendland, *Cor.*, p. 127.

38. So Schlatter as well, in contrast with his interpretation of v. 1. Grosheide takes v. 2 in the same sense as v. 1 (see n. 32).

39. They wish to read this from *ependysasthai:* not to be "clothed," but "clothed over."

40. See also the counter-arguments of Bultmann, *Exegetische Probleme,* pp. 11, 12.

41. The interpretation of v. 3 is exceedingly difficult. The text also is not certain, although *eiper* in place of *ei ge* makes little difference, and the reading *ek-* instead of *en-dysamenoi* is very likely not original. *Ei ge*, translated causally by us (Bl.-Debr., Par. 493, 2, here gives the meaning *siquidem*), is taken concessively or even

longing described in verse 2;[42] it says then that only when investiture with the dwelling from heaven takes place shall we not be found naked, that is to say, shall we no longer be subject to the threatened character and destruction of the present mode of existence.[43]

Verse 4 harks back to "the groaning" of verse 2: ". . . for we who [still] dwell in the tent groan, being oppressed, not for the reason that we would be unclothed, but clothed, so that the mortal may be swallowed up by life."

It is still more evident here than in verse 2 that the concern in this pericope is indeed with the present and the future life, not merely in the anthropological sense of old and new corporeality, but in the qualitative-existential sense of whether or not subject any longer to death. That "to be unclothed" has reference here to the perishing of the present existence in the body (cf. 4:16) and not to condemnation in the judgment,[44] appears from the contrast in the final clause where

---

conditionally by others. The concessive translation "although" (so, e.g., Reitzenstein, Allo, G. Vos), if it is even possible, offers little to go by. Paul would then wish to say that believers in any case, that is to say, irrespective of this clothing from heaven, will not be found "naked." But the meaning of it is difficult to understand (Vos therefore decides for *ekdysamenoi* and thinks thereby of dying; cf. also H. Bavinck, *Geref. Dogmatiek*, IV, 4th ed., 1930, p. 596); it consists in a reserve that we do not expect after the heavily charged words of v. 2. The conditional meaning "if at least" (so, e.g., Oepke, *TDNT*, I, p. 774; Schlatter, *Erläuterungen*, p. 196; Schrenk, *TDNT*, I, p. 560; Kümmel, in Lietzmann-Kümmel, *Cor.*, p. 203) is to be rejected, if a condition were made with it, which possibly could not be fulfilled and the longing expressed in v. 2 thus would not be brought to fulfillment; for that Paul is still uncertain for himself and his own with respect to such a nakedness (however that may be taken) is not to be squared with the certainty of v. 1 (cf. vv. 5ff.). There is indeed a certain condition in v. 3, but one that will assuredly be fulfilled according to the conviction of Paul's faith (cf. the *eiper* in Rom. 8:9 and the *ei* in Col. 3:1). Decisive, however, is the causal "for because only so" (cf. the translation of Lietzmann, *Cor.*, p. 120, and of Wendland, *Cor.*, p. 126). Bultmann, too, takes *ei ge kai* causally. He thinks, however, that this only gives a good sense if one reads, not *en-*, but *ekdysamenoi* (*Exegetische Probleme*, p. 11). But to the much more trustworthy reading *endysamenoi* a good sense can be attached; see the translation above.

42. "V. 3 states again the actual basis of the longing" (Bultmann, *Exegetische Probleme*, p. 11).

43. Some take this as the fate of the damned; so, e.g., Schlatter, *Erläuterungen*, p. 196; Ellis, *Paul and His Recent Interpreters*, p. 43 ("the fate of unbelievers"); Schrenk, *TDNT*, I, p. 560, *s.v. bareō;* Oepke, *TDNT*, I, pp. 774f., *s.v. gymnos* ("the final destiny of unbelievers, for whom there will be no heavenly body"). But what is the motive for which Paul would at once posit this possibility for himself and believers? Most accordingly think here only of the condition of "being without body," without the additional significance of "being condemned." This "being naked" would in consequence already apply to the state between death and the parousia. Then *gymnos* would be an anthropological qualification, in a dichotomistic sense. In our view, Paul is here thinking, however, in other, more qualitative categories; see further at v. 4.

Grosheide wishes to take *endysamenoi* as "clothed with the righteousness of Christ," and *gymnos* as the unchanged man (*Cor.*, pp. 144, 145), with an appeal to Rom. 13:14 and Gal. 3:27. But *endysamenoi* is nowhere used absolutely in this meaning. In the context of 2 Cor. 5 this would also be a *metabasis eis allo genos:* Paul is here speaking of other things.

44. So Oepke, *TDNT*, II, p. 318 (cf. above, n. 43).

there is mention of the swallowing up of the mortal in the sense of the weak, perishable, threatened life (cf. 1 Cor. 15:53, 54). To be "unclothed" and to be "clothed" therefore refer to the perishing of the old and the "putting on" of the new existence.

Now it has been contended that by to "be unclothed" Paul cannot mean death. For how could he who elsewhere speaks of it as "gain" and calls the (intermediate) state that follows "being with Christ" (Phil. 1:23) here describe this condition as a "dreadful nakedness"?[45] But this line of reasoning will not hold up. For first of all, it would then surely not be the "intermediate state" following death, but death itself that he terms "being unclothed."[46] But one is thinking altogether too much in abstract anthropological notions when he speaks of a "bodiless continued existence," etc. Paul here is thinking much more pregnantly. He does not speak of the body *per se* and his contrast is not: to be with or without body. It is for him a matter of two different modes of existence, qualified to be sure by the body, but then in the sense of the "body of our humiliation" (as he puts it in Phil. 3:21), that is, the imperfect mode of existence subject to affliction and death, and the glorified body, sharing in the glory of God (for this contrast cf. also 4:17). For this reason "to be unclothed" also includes more than death alone. It has reference to all that has already been said in the preceding pericope on the vulnerability, affliction, being threatened with death in the present body, "bearing about in the body the putting to death of Jesus," "always being given up to death," "the working of death in our mortal flesh," the "wasting away of the outward man" (cf. 4:7-17). Out of this body of death he sighs for the glory of God in the new body. "To be unclothed" (v. 4) does not mean therefore merely "to be bodiliess," as an anthropological (Greek!) denotation, but to be given up to death in the comprehensive sense of the word. Conversely, "not to be found naked" and "to be clothed" (vv. 2-4) mean not only: no longer to be bodiless, but: to share in the full glory of God, undoubtedly because of receiving the new glorified "body." In this contrast the "intermediate state" recedes entirely into the background.[47] In verses 1-5 it is a matter only of the contrast between the believer's being demolished in his temporal mode of existence and the share to be expected in the glory of God in the resurrection.

In this train of thought it can be understood how in verses 5-10 Paul is able to present the "intermediate state" finally as a (temporary) deliverance over against life in the present body:

> But he who has prepared us for this very thing [i.e., for this being clothed, etc.] is God, who has given us the earnest of the Spirit. We

---

45. Oepke, *TDNT*, I, p. 774; cf. II, p. 318.
46. So, e.g., Schrenk, *TDNT*, I, p. 560, *s.v. bareō.*
47. Cf. J. N. Sevenster, "Some remarks on the [*gymnos*] in 2 Cor. V. 3," in *Studia Paulina*, p. 207, who, however, still takes the *gymnos* too much as "the state between death and resurrection." Is this not still too Greek (however much Sevenster places the emphasis on the contrast beween Plato, Philo, *et al.*, and Paul)? In our view *gymnos* here does not denote a state of incorporeality, but the lacking (still) of the glory of God, even in this body.

are always therefore of good courage, even though we know that as
long as we reside in the body, we live away from the Lord; for we walk
by faith and not by sight. But we are of good courage, and are willing
rather to depart from the body and to take up abode with the Lord.
Wherefore we also make it our aim, whether by our remaining or our
departing, to be well pleasing to him. For we must all appear before
the judgment seat of Christ . . . (2 Cor. 5:5-10a).

These words hark back to what has been said previously (cf.
4:16) of perseverance and good courage in the midst of all decay and
affliction. Because God has destined us for the coming glory, and given
us his Spirit as an earnest of it, there is every reason to be of good
courage, even though we know that as long as we are yet in this body,
we live away, absent from the Lord. For we still walk in faith. Nevertheless there is that good courage, and, if we were to be faced with the
choice, we are the more ready[48] to accept death and thus to break up
residence in the body and to take up abode with the Lord. Because
of that expectation and the earnest given of it, we see also as the
real purpose of life to be well pleasing to the Lord, whether by staying
or by departing. "For we must all appear before the judgment seat
of Christ. . . ."

The question arises here anew whether by this "breaking up"
and "taking up abode" Paul means the transition that is to be carried
into effect in the resurrection, or that which already takes place before
the resurrection, at death. In the latter case what is intended by "to
take up abode with the Lord" is therefore the intermediate state. And
the purport of 2 Corinthians 5:1-10 is then, to summarize it in a few
words: In the certain expectation of the life of the resurrection and the
new body promised by God, we do not lose heart in the midst of all
the assaults and peril of death, and we are also more willing, if this
should be the will of God, to leave our bodily existence and even now
to be united by death with Christ. Paul wishes to say therefore that with
a view to the great future he is prepared to continue to endure affliction
and, even more, to accept death for Christ's sake.

Although because of the varying imagery the mode of expression
can occasion confusion,[49] this conception which by "to take up abode

---

48. *Eudokoumen mallon.* In this construction of *eudokein* plus the infinitive
it is a question of what in a choice clinches the decision, if the better deserves the
preference (cf. Schrenk, *TDNT*, II, p. 741; see also Arndt-Gingrich-Bauer, p. 319,
s.v.: "wish rather, prefer"; and Liddell-Scott, *Greek-English Lexicon, s.v.:* "c. inf.,
consent, agree to do . . . to be ready, willing" [cf. 1 Thess. 2:8]). Cf. also Plummer,
Second Corinthians, pp. 152, 153, who speaks of "goodwill, contentment," and then
continues: "This goodwill and contentment is not quite the same as [*thelomen*] (v. 4)
or [*epipothountes*] (v. 2). It is possible to long for one thing, and yet be content
with, or even prefer, another, because one knows that the latter is well worth
having and perhaps better for one." The *ekdēmēsai ek tou sōmatos,* etc., is thus not
simply something desirable, but a matter to which Paul, on account of the hope
that is in him, would give preference, if he were put to the choice.

49. In v. 6 *endēmountes* refers to life in the body, *ekdēmoumen* to being
away from Christ; in v. 8 *ekdēmēsai* refers to dying and *endēmēsai* to taking up abode
with Christ. In v. 9, finally, *endēmountes* means: to continue to live (as in v. 6);
ekdēmountes: to die (as in v. 8). The translation of the Dutch Bible Society (and

with the Lord" understands the intermediate state (that sets in when the "breaking up" of the body takes place) seems most worthy of recommendation. For first of all, these expressions are less suited to indicate the transition from this body to the body of the resurrection. There is mention of leaving the body (v. 8) — not of moving into another body, but of "taking up abode with the Lord." As long as at the breaking up of the earthly tent-house the new bodily dwelling is not there, living with the Lord takes place. This expression in itself can hardly as yet denote the resurrection;[50] it enables us to know in any case what occurs when the body is abandoned.

But in the second place, the expression in verse 9 — "whether by remaining or by departing" — can scarcely be understood otherwise than as: whether by our living or by our dying. Paul does not place his own preference above everything else, but the manner in which he can best serve God and be well pleasing to him. This "whether . . . or" apparently has the same significance as the corresponding expressions in 1 Thessalonians 5:10; Romans 14:8; cf. Philippians 1:23, 24. And with that it is said therefore that, in expectation of the glorified life of the resurrection, he sees as his highest desire whether by his life or by his death[51] to be well pleasing to God; though if he were put to the choice he would choose the latter because it means at the same time to be permitted to take up abode with Christ.

If this exegesis is, as we think, the correct one, then the intermediate state is in fact spoken of in 2 Corinthians 5:8 and that indeed as "taking up abode with the Lord." That an entirely new idea would herewith be introduced into this pericope, which first speaks of the resurrection, is only correct when one starts from the view that Paul is here giving instruction on the future of believers. He is speaking, however, out of a concrete situation and says what it is that comforts and stirs him in it. Above and beyond all else it is the hope of the resurrection. God will substitute the new body for that which is now being demolished. But though that day should not yet dawn, he would

---

the ASV and RSV), "whether at home or away," does not, in our view, touch the specific character of the pronouncement and is therefore unclear: what is meant here by "at home"?

50. Cf. Vos, *The Pauline Eschatology*, p. 194: ". . . he would scarcely have expressed himself precisely thus, had he meant that immediately another body would be substituted, for the state in such a new body would hardly be describable as the state of one absent from the body" (*ekdēmēsai ek tou sōmatos*).

51. If one will not understand *ekdēmountes* of dying, then one comes (in view also of the function this *ekdēmein* is intended to have: to be well pleasing to God!) to all manner of tortuous explanations. Lietzmann takes it as the possibility *after* death of preparing oneself for the judgment, a thought that not only is not implied in this word, but with which we meet nowhere in Paul. Pop paraphrases *ekdēmountes* as the new mode of existence of one who has been raised from the dead (*De tweede brief van Paulus aan de Korinthiërs*, 2nd ed., 1962). But this is too far removed from the meaning of the words. Wendland translates *ekdēmountes* "in der Fremde" and then understands by that "full fellowship with the Lord," the "life of the consummation," after the resurrection (*Cor.*, p. 129), however without thinking of a preparation for the judgment. But then there is no connection with v. 10. If on the other hand one takes *ekdēmountes* in direct connection with v. 8 as dying, then there is no difficulty and the pronouncement acquires a clear sense.

nevertheless be of good courage, even in the affliction he had now, to surrender his life in death. Indeed, he would even prefer it above this life of trials and persecutions in the earthly body. For then he might already take up his abode with the Lord. The idea of the "intermediate state" is no *Fremdkörper* here. It comes to the fore of itself, as it were, when the great future is still waiting and death is nevertheless an immediate reality. The idea is the more acceptable because it entirely corresponds with the pronouncement of Philippians 1:20ff. (also as regards the climate of the context, living under pressure, giving preference to death). What there is called "to be with the Lord" is here described as "taking up abode with the Lord," two expressions of which one cannot deny that they can easily mean the same thing and admit of easily being bound together.

If within the framework of Paul's preaching there is thus no doubt of the reality of believers being with Christ immediately after their death, much more difficult is the answer to the question as to what significance is to be ascribed to this reality and what place it occupies in the whole of the salvation proclaimed by Paul.

So far as the latter is concerned, first of all, one may undoubtedly say that in the epistles preserved to us separate and deliberate attention is not devoted to the state of deceased believers after death and before the parousia. In both passages that have been discussed this reality is mentioned with a single word, a word that indeed is to the point but is not further explained. And this is all the more striking because it is the great future that begins with the resurrection that so frequently has Paul's attention. The intermediate state is not spoken of as a separate ground of comfort. However much the certainty with which "to be with Christ" is posited as an indication of the bond between Christ and believers that cannot be broken even by death, yet this expectation apparently does not have an "independent existence" for Paul, but is entirely taken up in the hope of the resurrection, and would not exist without it (cf. 1 Cor. 15:18; 1 Thess. 4:13ff.). Some have wanted indeed to conclude from this that Paul knew nothing of a provisional state of blessedness. Otherwise — so it is said — he would surely have comforted the church with it.[52] But this conclusion is not compelling.[53] All that can be inferred from Paul's reasoning is that without the resurrection there is no hope at all for deceased believers.

It is certainly true therefore that to be with Christ after death and before the resurrection does not have the full redemptive significance in Paul's epistles that the resurrection has. For this reason all hope is focused on the resurrection and not on death, death before the resurrection can be a cause of sorrow and bewilderment for the church, and Paul can explain the death of members of the church as a chastisement on the part of the Lord (1 Cor. 11:30ff.). But this does not mean that deceased believers can only be spoken of before the resurrection

---

52. Telder, *Sterven . . . en dan?*, pp. 30, 31.
53. For the correct view of these passages see also Vos, *The Pauline Eschatology*, p. 146.

in terms of death and not of life. Without question any appeal is lacking here to an immortality that would be native to man or to anything in man. The massive point of view is here again the christological one. There is mention not only of those who have "fallen asleep in Christ" (1 Cor. 15:18),[54] but also of "the dead in Christ" (1 Thess. 4:16). The bond with Christ, having been included in him and sharing in him, does not therefore cease with death (cf. Rom. 8:38; 14:8). Just as believers, whether they live or die, are the Lord's, so Christ also, because he died and came to life again, is Lord both of the dead and of the living (Rom. 14:9). From this all-embracing viewpoint of the belonging of believers to Christ, their communion with him, their inclusion in him, we are also to understand the fact of believers being with Christ directly after their death (Phil. 1:23), as well as after the resurrection (1 Thess. 4:17; 5:10). Only, that which is first in order of time does not stand first in order of faith. But it is on that account no less real and essential.

To the question as to how we must conceive of this "being with Christ" immediately after death we receive no further answer. Anthropologically it is not explained, not even in 2 Corinthians 5 and in Philippians 1. Negatively it is called departing or moving out of the body (ekdēmēsai ek tou sōmatos; 2 Cor. 5:8), and it is placed over against "remaining in the flesh" (Phil. 1:24); the transition is described as "taking up abode with the Lord." We have already questioned[55] the view that suggests that the "nakedness" of 2 Corinthians 5:3 is a designation of the state between death and the resurrection. The soul is nowhere spoken of in this context as the subject of continued existence after death, however frequently 2 Corinthians 5 and Philippians 1 have been interpreted in this way.[56] Even of living believers Paul says in Colossians 3:3 that their life is hid (in heaven) with Christ in God. The question is whether we are able to say anything more about being with Christ after death than that it is an existence hidden with Christ in heaven, which is one day to be revealed with him. It is to be no longer in the earthly body and therefore freed from all imperfection, sin, and affliction in this body. For that reason it can also be described by Paul as "gain," which therefore is to be preferred above the trials, the "putting to death in the body," always being given up to death in this life (2 Cor. 5:8; cf. 4:10, 11). "From this perspective death is a gain by comparison with present life."[57] On the other hand, it is not yet to be in the glorified body and thus for us an inconceivable mode of human existence. Yet the expressions "to be with Christ" and "to take up abode with the Lord" lead us to think of more than a negative no-longer and not-yet. Greijdanus notes, in connection with Philippians 1:23, that to be with Christ indicates not only presence, but close union and fellow-

---

54. Whether we are to take dia tou Iēsou in 1 Thess. 4:16 with koimēthentas or with axei is a question that exegesis has not decided; see, e.g., the detailed discussion by Rigaux, Th., pp. 535ff.; cf. further below, n. 125.

55. Cf. p. 503.

56. See the critical discussion of Sevenster, Studia Paulina, p. 211.

57. Menoud, Le sort des trépassés, p. 41.

ship as well, and he defines this then as "to be personally with the Lord, to see him, to be permitted to share in his company, to live in his presence,"[58] though a little further along he adds (when writing on "for this is better by far") that these words do not give a description, but awaken a supposition, give an impression.[59] Others express themselves in still other ways.[60] We can give no other expression to it than that which Paul says in another connection: nothing will separate us from the love of Christ (Rom. 8:35, 38ff.). As he there explicitly declares, this holds for death as well. It will bring about no separation between Christ and us. This presupposes continuity not of love only, but also of the object of love. It means that we are kept in the omnipotence of God's love in Christ, and for this reason, even when death comes, we are more than conquerors (Rom. 8:36, 37).

SECTION 76. THE REVELATION OF THE MAN OF LAWLESSNESS

(a) Sequence and delay in eschatological occurrence

In addition to what has already been said in general in Section 74 of the intervening period between Christ's coming in the flesh and his expected parousia, certain events are still to be dealt with in particular, events that, likewise according to the epistles of Paul, precede the parousia. It is not a question here of the continuation of history in general, but in a more restricted sense of eschatological phenomena in which a "program" established by God with respect to the great end time manifests itself. Just as a "fulness of the time" can be spoken of regarding Christ's advent in the flesh (Gal. 4:4; cf. Eph. 1:10), that is to say, a fulfillment of the divine plan of redemption "in its own time"

---

58. *Cor.*, pp. 144, 145; cf. Calvin on Phil. 1:23: "Paul openly declares that we enjoy Christ's presence on being set free" (against the doctrine of soul sleep); see Berkouwer, *The Return of Christ*, pp. 48ff.

59. Greijdanus, *ibid.*, p. 146; G. Vos, *The Pauline Eschatology*, p. 145, concludes from this that here at the least a conscious continued existence must be thought of and not a soul sleep or something of that sort: "the whole contrast of 'worse' or 'better' loses its significance, if consciousness, the only organ of difference in appraisal, be denied."

60. On this point Cullmann speaks of "a particular nearness to Christ," in which those who die in Christ find themselves before the end (the resurrection). They are "in Abraham's bosom" (Luke 16:23) or, according to Rev. 6:9, "under the altar" or "with Christ." All these are only figures for "proximity to God." "The most familiar image, however, is: 'they are sleeping.' " With this, according to Cullmann, not only is the "impression" reproduced that the survivors receive. The expression says more — so Cullmann — and "actually refers, like the 'rest' of Rev. 14:13, to the *state* in which those who die before the parousia are." Besides this, he too denies that on the ground of the New Testament one can come to certain speculations on this intermediate state. One cannot say more of it than that this state exists and that it already signifies "being joined with Christ (by virtue of the Holy Spirit)" (O. Cullmann, "Unsterblichkeit der Seele und Auferstehung der Toten," *TZ*, pp. 150, 151). Vos rightly maintains that the thought of absolute "rest" can scarcely lend anything desirable to death, unless from the viewpoint of "a morbidly pessimistic appraisal of life" (p. 146).

(1 Tim. 2:6; Tit. 1:3; Rom. 5:6), so also with respect to the parousia of the Lord not only has a specific time been fixed, but also an order of events that must come to fulfillment at the appointed moment of time and thus "in their own times" (cf. 2 Thess. 2:6). In the epistles of Paul, as elsewhere in the New Testament, this is also denoted with the term "must" (take place) (cf. 1 Cor. 15:25, 53), whereby expression is not given to a certain deterministic view of history, but reflection is focused on the order of events established in God's counsel of redemption. We come into contact with that most clearly in Paul in 2 Thessalonians 2:1-12, where he says, among other things, that the day of the Lord is not coming before certain other events have "first" taken place.

We have to do here with a phenomenon that one may perhaps call the essence of the (Old and) New Testament apocalyptic.[61] It is a matter there of the revelation of what according to its nature, i.e., because of belonging to the hidden counsel of God, is a "mystery." These secrets or mysteries are "revealed" when by their realization at the time appointed they are manifested. But their revelation also takes place in the a priori divine announcement to those who have been privileged to that end (cf. Dan. 2:28 [LXX]; Rev. 1:1; Eph. 3:3). In this sense, in relation to the future of the Lord, we have to do with apocalyptic passages in Paul's epistles as well (cf., e.g., 1 Cor. 15:51ff.; 1 Thess. 4:13-18). And these also have reference in part to what precedes the parousia of the Lord (2 Thess. 2:1-11; cf. Rom. 11:25).

All this is not concerned with a computation of the time of the parousia or with a "reportorial eschatology" presently so much controverted in the footsteps of K. Rahner.[62] As has already been observed, immediately after the great apocalyptic passage on the parousia in 1 Thessalonians 4:13-18, Paul writes with reference to "the times and the seasons"[63] that the church "knows accurately" that the day of the Lord is coming as a thief in the night. In this respect he associates himself entirely with ideas from the prophecies and the teaching of Jesus, in which the fact that the day of the Lord is unknown and the sudden and surprising character of its coming are frequently pointed out (cf. Isa. 13:6-8; Matt. 24:38; Luke 21:34; cf. also Acts 1:7; Luke 12:39ff.; 2 Pet. 3:10; Rev. 3:3; 16:15). The unknown time of the day of the Lord, as appears from what follows 1 Thessalonians 5:1, is for Paul no occasion for computation or speculation,[64] but for paraenesis to be watchful and sober.

---

61. Cf. M. A. Beek, Inleiding in de Joodse Apokalyptiek van het oud- en nieuwtestamentische tijdvak, 1950, p. 73.

62. K. Rahner, "The Hermeneutics of Eschatological Assertion," in Theological Investigations, IV, ET 1966, pp. 323ff.

63. The expression hoi chronoi kai hoi kairoi is in this context a set phrase, more or less in the form of a hendiadys (cf. Acts 1:7). See further Rigaux, Th., pp. 553ff.

64. It is well known that all kinds of calculations have been made from the numbers in the Book of Daniel, in Jewish as well as in later Christian circles. Not only did Augustine urge serious objections against that — because the computation of the end of the world in his view did damage to the readiness of Christians daily to face the judgment — but the rabbis also warned against such a "ḥeshbôn haqqēṣ" and even denied those who made themselves guilty of this a share in the world to

It is another matter, however, that the church may have knowledge of certain events that are antecedent to the day of the Lord and from which it can in a certain respect be gathered whether the way for the coming of the Lord is already "free." What is intended here is not only the eschatological or apocalyptic "interpretation," for example, of catastrophic events in nature or in the history of the nations, in which the all-encompassing and crisis-producing character of the day of the Lord is already "recognized" by faith, but also an attentiveness to such events or situations, without the realization of which the end "cannot" yet come. This does not mean that one is thus informed as to the precise facts of the history of the end and on that ground is able to arrive at a sketch or "photographic likeness" of what is yet to take place. It does imply that, also with regard to Christ's parousia, the fullness of the time is determined by factors or developments that must first come to the fulfillment set for them in the counsel of God.

This element in the eschatology of the New Testament — with which we meet in Jesus as well as in Paul (cf., e.g., Mark 13:7, 10; Luke 21:9; 2 Thess. 2:3) — introduces a certain delay into the end event and the expectation corresponding with it, and prevents such an actualization of the "signs of the times," etc., whereby all temporal differentiation and shading in the "at hand" is practically removed. There are definite sequences here, by which the one thing cannot occur before something else has "first" taken place.[65] One can here again feel strongly the problem of the *Naherwartung* and ask himself what the permanent theological significance is of the developments in history apparently expected on a short-term basis; on the other hand, one will have to be on his guard against the illusion that he is able to maintain the significance of the apocalyptic when he fails to do justice to this element of delay. Such a "de-apocalypticizing" of the New Testament eschatology is hardly to be reconciled any longer at least with the reiterated "first," "then," "thereafter," in the apocalyptic passages in the teaching of Jesus and Paul (cf. Luke 21:12; 1 Cor. 15:23, 24; 2 Thess. 2:3).

Now although, so far as we can see, Paul does not speak of precursory "signs" of the day of the Lord, there are in him, too, all kinds of direct and indirect indications that further define and in part limit the proximity of the day of the Lord. Such an indirect datum, for example, underlies the train of thought in Romans 11, where the future

---

come (cf. Beek, *Inleiding*, p. 75; Strack-Billerbeck, IV, 2, p. 1013). That these calculations were nevertheless zealously practiced is certainly evident from the detailed survey in Strack-Billerbeck, IV, 2, pp. 977-1015.

65. For this *prōton* cf. Michaelis, *TDNT*, VI, p. 870: *prōton* serves frequently "to emphasize the observance of the divinely established sequence of eschatological events." For this whole deferment of the *eschaton* see Cullmann, *Christ and Time*, e.g., on pp. 66f.: "The time character of the future becomes especially clear from the fact that the eschatological drama, as it is pictured in the Apocalypses, including the New Testament ones, takes place in a thoroughly chronological progression.... In these writings we hear of 'afterward' and 'then,' and this occurs not merely in the book of Revelation, but particularly in Paul." For the "rehabilitation" of apocalyptic thus conceived (against a one-sided actualistic or existentialistic interpretation) see also the survey of the relevant newer literature in Cullmann, *Salvation in History*, pp. 57ff.

of Israel is spoken of and in conjunction with it the coming in of "the fulness [the full number] of the gentiles" (Rom. 11:25), just as in verse 12 there is mention of the "fulness" of Israel. In both instances we have to do in the word "fulness" *(plērōma)* with an eschatological notion, that is to say, with a "full number" determined by God in his redemptive counsel, of the gentiles and Jews respectively, who will share in the salvation of the Lord and "come into" it.[66] It is here implied therefore that history cannot meet its end before this fullness has been reached. At the same time a very close relation is clearly established between the progress and fruit of the preaching of the gospel on the one hand and the parousia of Christ on the other. One can also ask to what extent the universal character of the preaching of the gospel and the worldwide character of the mandate of Paul himself, as he speaks of it, for example, in Colossians 1:6, 23; 1 Timothy 3:16; cf. Romans 15:23, 24, also determined the time of Christ's parousia for his own consciousness (cf. Matt. 24:14; Rev. 6:1-8; Acts 1:6ff.; Mark 16:15; Matt. 28:19). Though he does not allude to this in so many words, one may certainly regard such a connection as present also in the Pauline view of history and the future.[67]

A very direct and express indication of what must yet precede the parousia and still stands in the way of its coming is contained in the well-known pericope on "the man of lawlessness" or "of sin" in 2 Thessalonians 2:1-12. Here the apostle deals directly with an overstrung *Naherwartung* that cropped up in the church, perhaps in consequence of what he had written in his first epistle (cf. 1 Thess. 4:13-17), and which he qualifies as being quickly shaken in mind and troubled, as though the (time of the) day of the Lord were come (already).[68] Against such a conception, according to which nothing more would stand in the way of the coming of the day of the Lord, Paul now sets the fact that

---

66. That *plērōma* does not here denote merely a quantitative limit, but rather has a qualitative significance that is further defined by the expression *pas Israēl* in 11:26 can here be left out of consideration (cf. above, pp. 357ff. and my *Rom.*, pp. 254ff.).

67. Cf. above, p. 494. On this point see J. Munck, *Paul and the Salvation of Mankind*, pp. 39ff., following Cullmann. Munck's exposition is forced here and there, however, also in connection with his view of *ho katechōn* in 2 Thess. 2; see below, pp. 523f.

68. *Hōs hoti enestēken hē hēmera tou Theou.* The expression *enestēken* denotes the present. For this reason many translate: "as if the day of the Lord had already dawned"; see, e.g., Rigaux, *Les Épitres aux Thessaloniciens*, p. 653; R. Schippers, *Mythologie en Eschatologie in 2 Thess. 2:1-17*, 1961, p. 7. The latter thinks that Paul here alludes to a gnostic heresy. But in this case we might expect another kind of opposition from the side of Paul, namely, not an emphasizing of the "not yet" (as is now the case), but of the reality of the still to be expected parousia (as in 1 Cor. 15 with reference to the resurrection). Paul's answer, in other words, is not anti-spiritualistic, but directed against a conception that was unable to give content to the interim before the parousia and led to all kinds of disturbance and over-excitement. Therefore *enestēken* must here surely have a somewhat broader meaning; cf., e.g., Oepke, *TDNT*, II, p. 544, n. 2, who (i.a., with an appeal to Bl.-Debr., Par. 323, 3) translates by "in process of coming" and appeals for that also to the non-spiritualizing character of the heresy.

other things must take place "first." He mentions here (1) the revelation of "the man of lawlessness," (2) the "falling away" that accompanies this, and (3) the one who (or that which) "restrains."

(b) The man of lawlessness

The central datum of this announcement is of course the figure of the man of lawlessness,[69] or of sin.[70] Paul speaks of him in eschatological, apocalyptic terminology. Three times there is mention of his "revelation" (vv. 3, 6, 8), further described in verse 6 as to "be revealed in his own time," also of his "parousia" (v. 9). The reverse side is that he is now still "hidden." The meaning of this terminology is not that the man of lawlessness enters into history from a kind of pre-existence, but that the time appointed by God for this appearance has not yet come, and the man of lawlessness is therefore still "hidden," that is to say, has not yet materialized.[71]

The question of course arises as to whether anything further is to be said on the origin of this eschatological expectation and representation in Paul. Of particular importance here, first of all, is the clear reflection of Daniel 11:36. This applies especially to the words "exalts himself against all that is called God," ascribed to the man of lawlessness. The words "takes his seat in the temple of God" will also have to be explained in this light. Although they do not occur elsewhere in this connection, they are apparently meant to describe with other words what is said in Daniel on the profanation of the temple (cf. 11:31), a passage that is also cited in Matthew 24:15 and Mark 13:14. Finally, the falling away or apostasy to be discussed still further is also a term from Daniel 11:32.

If we look farther about us into the pre-Christian tradition, then it must be ascertained that in the Jewish expectation for the future the figure from Daniel as an anti-divine eschatological appearance apparently played no further part. While falling away from God and from the law as a distinguishing feature of the time preceding the advent of the Messiah is frequently spoken of in the Jewish writings,[72] Judaism at approximately the beginning of the Christian era did not know the expectation of a man of sin in whom unrighteousness is concentrated and of whom Satan makes use as the anti-Messiah in the final revelation of ungodliness. In the nationally slanted Jewish expectation the last ruler of Rome sometimes does appear as the great antagonist of the anticipated Messiah (so, e.g., in the Apocalypse of Baruch[73]). Mention is also made a few times of a tyrant in the great end time who is described in obscure words and is difficult to identify further. Thus, for

---

69. *Ho anthrōpos tēs anomias.* For *anomia* as an eschatological datum see Schippers, *Mythologie en Eschatologie,* pp. 11, 12.

70. *Tēs hamartias,* in other, mostly later, textual witnesses.

71. For this use of *apokalyphthēnai,* etc., see, e.g., Rom. 1:17; 8:18; 1 Cor. 3:13; Gal. 3:23, *et al.* Cf. above, pp. 46ff.

72. Cf., e.g., Strack-Billerbeck, III, p. 637; IV, 2, pp. 977ff.

73. Strack-Billerbeck, IV, p. 638. For discussion of this passage from Baruch see also B. Rigaux, *l'Antéchrist,* 1932, p. 189.

example, in 4 Ezra 5, 6, where in the description of the great all-embracing revolution in the last time a ruler is spoken of "whom the inhabitants of the earth do not expect." Some think they detect in this figure, whose shape otherwise remains very vague, the features of the antichrist.[74] In the pre-Christian writing *Assumption of Moses*, cap. 8, too, a tyrant makes his appearance in the great end time, not however as the anti-Messiah.[75] In these tyrannical figures and shapes in whom the portrayal of Antiochus IV possibly lingers on (although this is not very clearly demonstrable), the enmity of the devil against God is manifested, which reaches its peak in the great end time. However, one cannot simply identify these tyrants of the nations with the man of sin in 2 Thessalonians 2. The latter bears much more the character of a false prophet who leads men astray not so much with outward force as with lying wonders, and whose character is defined above all by his godlessness and immorality carried to an extreme.[76]

If therefore the pre-Christian tradition (apart from Daniel) does not yield much for the "genealogy" of the expectation enunciated by Paul with so much certainty in 2 Thessalonians 2, on the other hand it is clear that this expectation in 2 Thessalonians 2 is not to be traced back exclusively to the prophecies of Daniel. The delineation of Paul bears a much too shaded character for that; it also allows other expressions from the Old Testament to have a part in it (cf. Isa. 14:13, 14; Ezek. 28:2; Isa. 11:4), and will in any case have to be understood in the context of a broader Christian tradition. What is said in 1 John 2:18, 22; 4:3; 2 John 7 about the antichrist is to be pointed out in particular, where the features of an anti-Christian seducer also stand out (and not those of a military tyrant) (cf. Rev. 13:11-18); while the motif of craving for divine honor and worship by the man of sin, likewise missing outside the New Testament, perhaps underlies the delineation of Matthew 24:15 and Mark 13:14.[77] In its turn this broader Christian tradition is unquestionably dependent on Daniel 11 (cf. Matt. 24:15; Rev. 13:5) and the Old Testament motifs, even though it is apparent in 2 Thessalonians 2 as well as elsewhere that the expectation that there emerges had acquired an existence of its own and bears a specifically Christian signature.[78]

Furthermore, so far as the entrance of these ideas into the Christian expectation for the future is concerned, one can point out first of all that the figure sketched in Daniel 11, although having reference in the first place to Antiochus Epiphanes, is placed in a clearly eschato-

---

74. So, e.g., W. Bousset and H. Gressmann, *Die Religion des Judentums im späthellenistischen Zeitalter*, 3rd ed., 1926, p. 255; Rigaux, *l'Antéchrist*, p. 184.

75. Cf. Bousset-Gressmann, *ibid.*, pp. 254, 255; Strack-Billerbeck, III, p. 638.

76. Bousset-Gressmann also write: "This idea is of course only indirectly preserved by Christian evidences"; they add, however, that "it probably stems from Judaism" (*ibid.*, p. 256).

77. The masculine form of the participle *hestēkota* in Mark (in Matt. the neuter *hestos*) could also point to this; see, however, my *The Coming of the Kingdom*, pp. 488ff., 533, n. 105.

78. For a comparison of the Synoptic motifs and 2 Thess. 2 see Rigaux, *Th.*, p. 101.

logical context (cf., e.g., Dan. 11:40), and thus continued to retain its position in the apocalyptic literature.[79] To what extent the prophecy of Daniel 11 already intended to refer beyond Antiochus to a more distant future is a question that need not be decided in this context.[80] In view of the great significance the prophecy of Daniel occupied from the very outset in the proclamation of Jesus (in particular the figure of the Son of Man; Dan. 7:13), it is not strange that other eschatological-apocalyptic features from Daniel have also passed over into the Christian expectation for the future. And that this was the case in particular with the figure from Daniel 11 can also be explained by the fact that his appearance constitutes the ending of the eschatological perspective of Daniel.

At the same time all the Old Testament prophecies that have reference to the war waged ever since Paradise between God and Satan have come to stand in an entirely new light through the advent of Jesus Christ, and have acquired the highest possible relevance (cf. Rom. 16:20 — with an obvious allusion to Gen. 3:15). Paul accordingly makes use of the language of prophecy by applying what is said there of God's triumph over his enemies to Christ: "whom [the lawless one] the Lord will slay with the breath of his mouth" (cf. Isa. 11:4).

The most striking thing of course is that this power inimical to God is concentrated here in the figure of what Paul calls *the man* of lawlessness. Undoubtedly this also finds its explanation in the anti-God appearance of certain human figures in Israel's history and in the eschatological-apocalyptical delineation of them in prophecy, particularly in that of Antiochus IV in the prophecy of Daniel. Furthermore, it is certainly indicated as well in the denotation "the man of lawlessness" that this man is not merely a pre-eminently godless individual, but that in him the humanity hostile to God comes to a definitive, eschatological revelation. In this striking qualification Paul's corporate way of thinking unquestionably plays a part. Just as elsewhere he places Adam and Christ over against one another as the first and second "man," as the great representatives of two different orders of men, so the figure of "the man of lawlessness" is clearly intended as the final, eschatological counterpart of the man Jesus Christ, who was sent by God to overthrow the works of Satan. The traits with which the man of lawlessness is described in 2 Thessalonians 2 provide the clearest evidence that not only the prophecy of Daniel, but the appearance and the glory of the man Jesus Christ himself as well determined the representation of the man of sin. His coming, just as that of Christ, is called a parousia; it is marked by all manner of powers, signs, and wonders, like those of Christ in the past; indeed, whether deliberately or not, in his wicked ambition he can even be called by the name that is given to the betrayer Judas: "son of perdition" (v. 3; cf. John 17:12). All his striving directed toward destruction and evil likewise presupposes the

79. For the phenomenon of the continuing actualizing of certain apocalyptic ideas, see, e.g., also M. A. Beek, *Inleiding in de Joodse Apokalyptiek van het oud- en nieuwtestamentische tijdvak*, pp. 74ff.
80. On this see, e.g., Rigaux, *l'Antéchrist*, pp. 172, 173.

coming of Christ and the nature of his redeeming activity: it has effect with those who have not received "the love of the truth" (of the gospel) and works itself out in "faith in the lie" in those who "did not believe the truth." What the lie is here is defined by the truth of Christ; what faith is here stands over against faith in the gospel. "Without Christ [the antichrist] is absolutely unthinkable ... he exists by fighting against everything Christ means in the world."[81] "This apostasy ... cannot be depicted as an isolated moral phenomenon. Like the antichrist, it always stands in relation to Him who is the First and the Last."[82] However much the appearance of the man of lawlessness was prefigured in the Old Testament prophecy therefore, its Pauline specification, as also the denotation "the man of lawlessness" itself, is clearly oriented to the fundamental lines of his whole theology: the man of sin is the last and highest revelation of man (humanity) inimical to God,[83] the human adversary of the man Jesus Christ, in whom the divine kingdom and the divine work has become flesh and blood. The antithesis between God and Satan that dominates history is decided on the human plane, but then not merely in every man individually, but in those who as *the man* represent humanity in the great junctures of history (beginning, "middle," and end) in a decisive way for salvation or destruction.

In the light of the foregoing the question is also to be considered as to whether it is possible to say anything more about the identity of the man of sin sketched out in 2 Thessalonians 2.

First of all one will be permitted to take it as certain that in Paul's train of thought it is not a *collectivum* but a person who is intended by this man. Though elsewhere in the New Testament in the end of the days pseudo-prophets and pseudo-christs (not the same as antichrist) are foretold (Matt. 24:24; cf. 1 John 4:1), and there is mention of "many antichrists" already in the present (1 John 2:18 — evidently as precursors[84] of *the* antichrist), a fact that also leads to a more collective use of the name antichrist (1 John 2:22; 4:3; 2 John 7), the conception in 2 Thessalonians 2 is certainly a different one. Here it is said specifically that the man of sin has not yet appeared. Nor can one posit that Paul has only the "last" or "real" antichrist in view. We do not find such a distinction here.[85]

This does not alter the fact, however, that in Paul, too, the antichrist is not to be thought of apart from the whole power and disposition in history that is hostile to God and to Christ. In 2 Thessalonians 2:7 the mystery of lawlessness now already at work is placed in the

---

81. H. Berkhof, *Christ the Meaning of History*, p. 115.

82. G. C. Berkouwer, *The Return of Christ*, pp. 283f.

83. *Ho anthrōpos tēs anomias* is therefore more than a usage "in Semitic fashion to express relationship to something abstract" (Jeremias, *TDNT*, I, p. 364). Rather, the specific character of the expression lies in the representative significance of *ho anthrōpos*, further qualified by the genitive *tēs anomias*.

84. See also below, p. 517.

85. Cf. the very elaborate discussion of and opposition to the contrary standpoint (of Allo and Bury) by Rigaux in *l'Antéchrist*, pp. 270-287 and in *Th.*, p. 269. See also R. J. van der Meulen, "Veractualisering van de Antichrist," in *Arcana Revelata*, 1951, p. 75.

closest relationship with the revelation of the man of lawlessness. For this reason the representation given elsewhere (1 John, 2 John) of many "antichrists" need not be in conflict with that of 2 Thessalonians 2. Here again we may certainly judge by analogy with the person and work of Christ, of whom after all the antichrist constitutes the opponent. As Christ is a person, but at the same time one with all who believe in him and are under his sovereignty, so the antichrist is not only a godless individual, but a concentration of godlessness that already goes forth before him and which joins all who follow him at his appearance into a unity with him. It is just on this account that not the mystery of lawlessness, but indeed the man of godlessness is still kept under, because at his appearance unbelief, lawlessness, and godlessness will attempt to set themselves as an organic unity over against God and Christ. And in proportion as his precursors manage to bring godlessness the more to a coherent unity they will also the more exhibit the image of the antichrist and the caricature of the image of Christ. Therefore, finally, the restrainer will also "get out of the way" and give the antichrist opportunity to reveal himself, in order that in him, as in the man of lawlessness, Christ shall do away at once with all of the godlessness put into the field against him by Satan. For with the destruction of the antichrist there is no longer any place on earth for sin.

In this train of thought the antichrist is clearly more than a single person who makes his appearance at the end of the ages. What makes him the antichrist is all the lawlessness, the mystery of which is already at work and of which others (as his precursors) are already the bearers and organizers. On the other hand it is altogether in the line of Paul's eschatological and redemptive-historical thinking that he does not stop with an "it," with an idea, or with a force, but that the organic and corporate unity of human life finds its bearer and representative, as in Adam and Christ, so also in the antichrist, in a specific person. The antichrist would be no antichrist if he were not the personal concentration point of lawlessness, if he were not *the man* of lawlessness.

I arrive here at a somewhat different view from that which has been defended in two important works of recent years, namely, G. C. Berkouwer's *The Return of Christ,* and R. Schippers' monograph, *Mythologie en Eschatologie in 2 Thessalonicensen 2:1-17,* 1961.

Berkouwer starts from the passages in 1 and 2 John and posits that "we ought not to read and interpret John on the basis of Paul" (2 Thess. 2) (p. 265). He then points out that John sees the antichrist in the present and that according to 1 John 2:22 he is the antichrist who denies the Father and the Son. One may not, in his opinion, resolve the difficulty that the antichrist is spoken of in 1 John both in the plural and in the singular by speaking of (present) "precursors" of the (future) antichrist. "There is no hint here of two concepts concerning present and future" (p. 265). The one antichrist makes his appearance in the reality of the great heresy. Berkouwer associates himself with Althaus when the latter says that (with the antichrist) it is and must be a matter of a present actuality of battle. He also thinks that there is reason to call into question the *personal* character of the man of lawlessness. The fact that in 2 Thessalonians 2 he is spoken of so "personally" cannot in his view be determinative. This speaking of him as a person also occurs in John, and there it is a question of "antichrist already present" (p. 270). For Berkouwer, too, it is primarily a matter of the present relevance of the antichrist. If room were to come in for a long development up until the "end time," then one would fail to appreciate the "actuality that Paul is trying to preserve" (pp. 270f.). In his view there is accordingly "no reason to posit with certainty on the basis of the New Testament that the antichrist as portrayed there is a person of the end of history" (p. 271). He qualifies his exposition as that of a "continuous actuality and reinterpretation" and writes that one must be more apprehensive of weakening the earnestness of this preaching when one thinks of the antichrist as of a future figure, whereby we then only have to do with "precursors," than when one thinks of the anti-Christian power (p. 282).

In this manner 1 John is to be sure not interpreted according to Paul, but Paul according to a certain interpretation of 1 John. It is questionable, however, whether within the limits drawn by this interpretation 2 Thessalonians 2 can as yet be given its full weight. For irrespective of the undoubtedly personal character of the "man of lawlessness" drawn here, it is a question in 2 Thessalonians precisely of a figure who is not yet and cannot yet be because of the "restrainer." It is striking that Berkouwer does not in this context speak further of "this restrainer." He deals with the question earlier in his book. There he writes (in my view quite correctly) that a "not yet" of the coming of the man of sin "and the continuity of time are here mentioned in one breath" (p. 125); even though we do not know exactly what Paul meant by this restraining, "a case can undoubtedly be made for a retardation . . . a restraining of the manifestation of lawlessness" (p. 127). It is not clear how Berkouwer wishes to link this postponement of the coming of the man of sin with his opposition to a conception whereby the antichrist would not yet fully be an actual reality. One can say of course that if the preaching with reference to the antichrist intends to be relevant in the sense of 1 John 2, this restraint and this postponement cannot be shifted to a distant future; but this is a matter that touches the whole *Naherwartung*, that is to say, not only the parousia of the antichrist, but also that of Christ. For both the restraint and the coming of the two stand in immediate relation to each other. Paul's concern in 2 Thessalonians 2 does not accordingly consist in the first place in that he wishes to "protect" the present relevance of the antichrist, but that, with all pastoral care for the seriousness of the present, he wants to counter the overstrung *Naherwartung* with respect to the parousia of Christ. And he does that by pointing to "the retardation," "the delay." The mystery of lawlessness is already at work. The "power" is already busy, "the man" is not yet there. A "reconciliation" with 1 John 2 is not only possible here, but also entirely obvious. And is there still, even though one need not attach any special value to the word, any real ground for rejecting the idea of "precursors" of the antichrist? Does it not lie altogether in the line of the Johannine train of thought to make the great future (the resurrection, the judgment, etc.) present, without denying therewith the future reality of the resurrection, etc., as an incisive and (in its significance of consummation) once-for-all event, to be distinguished from it? And is there not on this account more that argues for the present tense of 1 John 2 — "this is the antichrist," to be understood in that sense — than that out of a certain absolutizing of this present tense one would leave no room for a definitive parousia that has not yet appeared of the man of lawlessness in Paul (and of the antichrist in John)? Why must one offer resistance to the idea that what is now a "power" could in the future be a person as well? And that the power even now manifesting itself will in the future bear the character of a final, decisive defiance concentrated in one person?

This is not of course to say that in 2 Thessalonians we receive an exactly sketched "plan" of the future, or have to do with "reportorial eschatology." In the continuing interpretation of these apocalyptic ideas one will also have to take account of the fact that they were viewed, as it were, at short range and thereby understood as well within the framework of a time now past. That undoubtedly makes necessary a continuing reinterpretation, or a " 'pneumatic-historic' view of the antichrist" (p. 275). But in so doing all the knots of delay (of "already" and "not yet" and "first" and "then" or "thereafter") nevertheless cannot be undone.

The views of Schippers are also of importance here. He writes that "the biblical apocalypses, deriving from Old Testament prophecy and, if one wish, also from Old Testament apocalyptic, illuminate the permanent eschatological character of history, that is to say, its character as precursory sign, in which the eschaton of the consummation of the future is permanent or at least present again and again anew" (p. 14). And further: "... there is an only but acute 'future,' threatening and redeeming in this 'present,' with a near removal of the temporal distance." "It is not so that in the biblical apocalypses an 'organic' process is foretold with final products as results of an historical development" (against Berkhof). "One may not spread out what was expected by the first generation as very near future over a world history with a separate 'end of the times,' to which then the suggestion is always joined that the apex of a development long past must still come" (p. 14). "The object of Jesus and Paul was no other — when they spoke of the apostasy and of the personalized lawlessness — than radically to cut off the idea that He had returned or that there was still time before He came back" (p. 15).

Likewise with what is said in 2 Thessalonians 2 of "the mysterious factor" of the restraint one must be careful not to introduce "the long pathways of history" into the text of Paul. The restraining is highly relevant to the present. It consists in the divine holding back, and "it is present as often as the temptations of apostasy shall touch the people of God in their theocratic solidarity, and the man of lawlessness reveals himself with his sacrilegious demonstrations" (p. 23).

In our opinion one must ask whether in this view of the significance of history between the present and the consummation justice is still done to the deferment of that which must "yet" take place, the programmatic character of New Testament eschatology as the realization of the divine mystery. In Schippers this is also to be felt most clearly in his paraphrase of what is intended by the restraint in 2 Thessalonians 2. This restraint is not there defined as that which separates us from the man of lawlessness who has not yet come, but as the detaining power of God, which is present whenever and as often as the man of lawlessness (already now) reveals himself. That this last is something other than what is said in 2 Thessalonians 2 on the restraint needs no further demonstration.

That the biblical apocalypses elucidate the permanently eschatological character of history is undoubtedly a correct and valuable typification. But one will have to take account of the prophetic-proleptic character of the "nearness" of Christ's parousia in order to continue to understand anything of the "meaning" of the progression of history. The New Testament approaches this meaning from the redemptive-historical perfect tense as well as from the apocalyptic deferment of that which must "yet" and "first" take place before the end has come and can come. 2 Thessalonians 2 is the *locus classicus* for this last, and therefore does not permit itself to be melted down into an undifferentiated concept of nearness, with whatever justice the latter lays emphasis on the present, eschatological seriousness of the here and now of history. It pertains precisely to the essence of the New Testament apocalypses that they indicate the articulations in the consummating work of God in history. Theological exegesis of these apocalypses will consequently not be able to pass this by if it does not wish, in place of falling on the Scylla of a "reportorial-eschatology," to suffer shipwreck on the Charybdis of a "de-apocalypticizing" in which the coming of the *eschaton* is detached from the progress of history.

All this, in the second place, is to say that it is a matter here of a human person, and that it is not, for example, the devil himself who is intended. The question: "Who is this? Perhaps Satan?" was already answered by Chrysostom in the negative, with a reference to verse 9 where it is surely said that the lawless one is to derive his power and appearance from Satan.[86] Some point, to be sure, to the figure of Belial in the later Jewish apocalyptic writings and think they see an indication of the antichrist in this; but Paul in any case distinguishes Belial clearly from the man of sin (cf. 2 Cor. 6:15).[87]

Furthermore, all kinds of speculations have been devoted to the origin of the man of sin. According to some the antichrist was thought of as a pseudo-messiah of the Jews.[88] Paul's sharp condemnation of the Jews in 1 Thessalonians 2:14-16, sitting in the temple (of Israel), and other traits are said to point to that.[89] Moreover, according to some of the early Christian writers, the antichrist would be descended from the tribe of Dan. Bousset chose to see in that the cropping up of a pre-Christian Jewish tradition.[90] But to our knowledge no evidence has so far been adduced from the Jewish literature for it. This conception is usually related to the absence of the tribe of Dan in Revelation 7:5ff., and to the allegorizing exegesis of certain unfavorable qualifications of Dan in the Old Testament (cf. Gen. 49:16, 17; Deut. 33:22, *et al.*).[91] The great objection to this whole identification of the antichrist with a Jewish messiah, however, lies in the fact that the latter can scarcely be conceived of as one who as God's great adversary could let divine honor be paid him in the temple. There are of course a great many (anti-)messianic features in the delineation of 2 Thessalonians 2 (see above), but that he would represent himself as the Messiah sent by God is simply in conflict with the presentation of 2 Thessalonians.

Others have attempted the *zeitgeschichtliche* interpretation here. Starting from the fact that in Daniel 11 a heathen usurper is intended, they have wished to find a similar figure of a later time again in 2 Thessalonians 2. Some have wanted to establish a connection with the

---

86. Cf. Dibelius, *Th.*, p. 48. For this identification (among others by Celsus) see Rigaux, *Th.*, p. 270; for its refutation, see the detailed argument of Vos, *The Pauline Eschatology*, pp. 112ff.

87. For Belial (or Beliar) see Beek, *Inleiding*, pp. 100ff.

88. So, e.g., Dibelius, with a reference to 2:11, 12.

89. See the detailed exposition in Vos, *The Pauline Eschatology*, pp. 114ff., who himself rejects this opinion, however.

90. W. Bousset, *Der Antichrist*, 1895, pp. 108ff.

91. Cf. Vos, *The Pauline Eschatology*, p. 119.

antichrist in the Revelation of John, which is again identified with the legend of *Nero redivivus* that lived on among the people. This implies, of course, that 2 Thessalonians 2 did not come from the pen of Paul, inasmuch as Nero died in A.D. 68. But this view, which has no foundation whatever in the text and can point out no literary agreement between Revelation and 2 Thessalonians, has again been abandoned by the later radical criticism itself.[92] The whole notion that Paul would have assigned the role of the man of sin to (a representative of) the Roman *imperium* has no basis in the words of the text and in the apostle's whole world of thought. And the same thing applies to every *zeitgeschichtliche* political explanation.

Another view still is that the man of sin is not to be a Jew or a gentile, but an apostate Christian: the antichrist cannot arise out of heathenism, but only out of a Christianized-dechristianized world.[93] Appeal is then made especially to the fact that there is mention in 2 Thessalonians 2:3 of "the" falling away, by which the falling away from Christ is understood, as well as to the a-theistic (not heathen) character of the godlessness unleashed by the antichrist. The pronouncement that the man of lawlessness will "take his seat in the temple of God" (2 Thess. 2:4) has likewise frequently been seen as an indication that the antichrist will magnify himself in the church, and that the danger therefore will come "from within."[94]

It is questionable, however, whether with such an exegesis one does justice to the apocalyptic character of the pronouncements in 2 Thessalonians 2. The particulars in the portrayal of the man of sin obviously do not have the purpose of foretelling definite historical particulars and giving indications concerning the concrete manifestation of the man of the future. These particulars are too general and too traditionally determined for that. The concept "falling away" stems from Daniel 11:32 and on that account, at least in its origin, is not a specifically Christian concept. Nor is the "atheism" of the man of sin a proof that it would here have to be a matter of post-Christian nihilism, for the words that describe this atheism are drawn from the portrayal of Antiochus IV in Daniel 11. And as regards "sitting in the temple," no more than one is able to say on this ground that Paul expected the man of sin in the temple at Jerusalem is one able to let this datum refer to the appearance of the man of sin in the church after the destruction of the temple. With the temple certainly the temple at Jerusalem is in the first instance to be thought of. One must not, however, fail to appreciate the apocalyptic character of the delineation. That which is still hidden, which as future event is still incapable of description, is denoted with the help of available notions borrowed from the present. To sit in the temple is a divine attribute, the arrogating to

---

92. See, e.g., H. J. Holtzmann, *Neutestamentliche Theologie*, II, 2nd ed., 1911, p. 214; A. Jülicher-E. Fascher, *Einleitung in das Neue Testament*, 7th ed., 1931, p. 64.

93. Berkhof, *Christ the Meaning of History*, pp. 115f.

94. For this interpretation, in the Reformers (the antichrist is papal power) as well as in some later writers, see Berkouwer, *The Return of Christ*, pp. 268ff.

oneself of divine honor. No conclusions are to be drawn from that for the time and place in which the man of sin will make his appearance.[95]

This is not to say of course that the man of sin and the apostasy unleashed by him will not be able in one way or another to answer to the interpretations mentioned above; still less, that already in the course of history there are not all sorts of phenomena of apostasy and opposition to God in the manner of 1 John 2 in a personifying sense that would have been or would yet be recognizable. The question is only whether in 2 Thessalonians 2 this apostasy and opposition to God would already be denoted in all kinds of concrete future manifestations. One will have to maintain a clear distinction here between what is (or is not) to be determined on the basis of the text about the manifestation and recognition of the man of sin and the mystery of lawlessness in all kinds of present, concrete phenomena.

In keeping with this apocalyptic character of the delineation, the answer to other questions that one would like to ask about a purely historical announcement[96] remains obscure. Thus, for example, the manner in which the man of sin will "appear" and will be destroyed by Christ. The sketch of the man of sin, however much described as a person, admits of no further "historicizing" explanation. It is part of the character of the apocalyptic to speak in images, to repeat traditional descriptions, by which the historical reality announced continues and must continue to lie under the veil of "mystery."[97]

(c) The restraint

Furthermore, the old question[98] regarding the restraint or the restrainer in 2 Thessalonians 2:6, 7 is deserving of separate discussion. For after the man of lawlessness is spoken of in the first verses, the argument proceeds as follows:

> Do you not remember that when I was still with you I told you this? And you know what is restraining him now, so that he may be revealed in his own time. For the mystery of lawlessness is already at work.

---

95. See Rigaux, *Th.*, p. 661; and Vos, *The Pauline Eschatology*, p. 124: "The 'sitting in the temple of God' only sums up in one terse image that unholiest offense offered to the Holiest of Beings."

96. See, e.g., in Vos, *The Pauline Eschatology*, pp. 126ff.

97. Cf. Rigaux, *Th.*, pp. 267ff.: "Paul has used these themes and texts according to the rule of the genre and the character of his writing.... The genre is apocalyptic. Consequently, we know that recourse to certain previous descriptions is natural, that the borrowings from the past retain a connotation from their origin to color the present, but that they ought to be interpreted in the light of the particular intent of the author who turns to them. Moreover, we know that borrowing the formulas causes words to lose the tie with reality that they have in ordinary language. In the language of the apocalypses, images abound and give the descriptions a stamp of mystery and majesty which it is not necessary to translate in terms of realities that are adequate to the words expressed.

98. For the older literature see, e.g., the detailed survey of G. Wohlenberg, *Der erste und zweite Thessalonicherbrief*, 2nd ed., 1909, pp. 177ff. For the more recent literature, e.g., the detailed discussion in the above-mentioned monograph of Schippers.

[Everything waits] only until he who now restrains shall have got out of the way. And then will the lawless one be revealed . . . (2 Thess. 2:5-8).

Although because of the difficult sentence structure not everything is entirely clear, yet the train of thought can surely be followed. When he was in Thessalonica Paul prepared the church for the coming of the man of lawlessness. For this reason the church could also know what still checks the lawless one,[99] so that he cannot reveal himself before the time appointed to him. For the mystery of lawlessness is even now at work. But all this still bears only a provisional character, until the one who now restrains shall have got out of the way, have disappeared from the scene.

The question now is, who or what is meant by this restraint? At the very outset the alternate use of the masculine and the neuter is striking. Notwithstanding a few divergent opinions, scholars are generally in agreement that in both cases the meaning is essentially the same. The verb *katechein* too (in both cases used absolutely, which seems to point to a current terminology) can be translated in more than one way: to restrain, hold fast, keep under. The thought is apparently that there is a power or a person that now still prevents the man of lawlessness from appearing. In the main the following conceptions exist on this point.

(1) That which restrains is the Roman *imperium* and the re-

---

99. On the *nyn* before *to katechon* in v. 6 there is much difference of opinion. In the main three views are to be distinguished: (a) *nyn* belongs with *to katechon* and thus stands over against *en tō autou kairō;* (b) *nyn* belongs with *oidate* and stands over against *eti* in v. 5. Meaning: now you know what you did not know when I was still with you; (c) *nyn* stands indeed over against *eti ōn* in v. 5, but without involving *oidate* in this contrast. *Kai nyn* is more or less independent and indicates the difference in circumstances between Paul's time at Thessalonica and now. Translation: "and now, you know what restrains," etc. Between (b) and (c) there is no essential difference. In both cases it is presupposed that since Paul's first instruction (v. 5), new light had been cast on the matter because a new development had occurred, by which the church was now informed of the restraint of the revelation of the man of lawlessness. In our opinion, however, there is more to be said for linking *nyn* with *to katechon.* Grammatically there is no objection against it (cf. Bl.-Debr., Par. 474, 5, under c). It also concurs very well with v. 5, where Paul appeals to the instruction he has given, which indicates the ground for *oidate.* In this way we need not make the difficulties greater than they are already, namely, by having still to give an answer to the question as to what would have occurred as the new element in the time between Paul's stay in the church and the moment at which he wrote the epistle. In the context of our text this is not alluded to further with so much as a word. We take it therefore that *nyn* belongs with *to katechon* and that with *oidate* Paul has in view the knowledge that the church already possessed or had received from him during his stay with it. To be sure, it is urged against this conception that if the apostle had earlier spoken to the church about this restraint, it is not clear why it had not kept to this knowledge and nevertheless expected the coming of the Lord at once. But this applies not only with respect to *to katechon* but also to the first appearance still to be expected of the man of lawlessness. For that matter, in both cases the apostle presupposes knowledge of *to katechon* now in the church, and its anticipatory posture thus remains equally unclear. We shall have to assume that the expectation of the immediate commencement of the parousia made it take too little account of the intermediate events that must still precede the parousia.

strainer is the person of the emperor as the representative of this *imperium*. This view is already to be found in Tertullian, and was subsequently followed by a great number of exegetes.[100] It is supported by Paul's positive attitude toward government (Rom. 13; 1 Tim. 2). As *civis Romanus* he more than once appealed to the Roman legal order that protected him (Acts 16:37ff.; 22:25, 29). This conception is able to explain the alternate masculine and neuter use of restrain. An allusion has even been seen in the word "to restrain" *(katechein)* to the name of the then reigning emperor Claudius *(claudo*=to shut, to close, to prevent).[101]

But on further reflection this view has nevertheless not proved to be sound. In the first place, unless one wants to speak of an unfulfilled prophecy, he has to shift over from the Roman government to government in general as the restrainer of the antichrist, whereby the alternation of neuter and masculine is obscured. For who then is "the" restrainer? Furthermore, the whole idea of government as restrainer is not in harmony with the character ascribed to the antichrist. The man of lawlessness does not make his appearance as a usurper of power who only would get opportunity if the legal order represented by the government were done away with; he is rather a religious seducer. And is one able then to say that the government, here to be thought of in particular as the Roman government, was the great opponent and restrainer of such an anti-God appearance? It did not champion the rights of the true God, but provided for tranquillity and order. From the viewpoint of arrogating divine honor to themselves many Roman emperors were rather allies than restrainers of the antichrist (Rev. 13). The character of the antichrist as false prophet in our view really makes this political explanation impossible.

(2) Another view is one that is already to be met with in some church fathers, and in Calvin, and which has subsequently been defended especially by Cullmann[102] and in his footsteps by Munck.[103] It finds the restraining of the antichrist in the fact that the gospel must first be proclaimed to all peoples. Only when this has happened can the end come. Interpreters point for this to all sorts of data in the New Testament that relate the end of the world to the progress of the preaching of the gospel. Cullmann and Munck go so far here that in the

100. See, e.g., E. Stauffer, *New Testament Theology*, p. 84; J. A. C. van Leeuwen, *Paulus' zendbrieven aan Efeze, Colosse, Filémon en Thessalonica*, 1926, p. 432. See also O. Betz, "Der Katechon," *NTS*, 1963, pp. 284ff.

101. Cf. W. Neil, *The Epistle of Paul to the Thessalonians* (Moffatt Comm.), 1950, p. 167. Cf. also E. von Dobschütz, *Die Thessalonicher-Briefe* (Meyer Comm., 7th ed.), 1909, p. 283.

102. First in his essay "Le caractère eschatologique du devoir missionaire et de la conscience apostolique de S. Paul. Étude sur le [*katechon(ōn)*] de 2 Thess. 2:6-7" (*Revue d'Histoire et de Philosophie réligieuses*, 1936, pp. 210ff.); often repeated in his later writings.

103. J. Munck, *Paul and the Salvation of Mankind*, p. 40. See Berkhof, *Christ the Meaning of History*, pp. 130f. For that matter one finds this conception defended already by some exegetes of the last century, as, e.g., G. Lüdemann, in the Meyer Commentary on Thess., 1878.

restrainer they wish to discover Paul himself, who after all viewed himself in a special sense as the apostle of the gentiles.

But however much may be attached to this significance of the preaching of the gospel elsewhere in the New Testament, there is no indication whatever that this is the case in 2 Thessalonians 2.[104] If it were, Paul has surely spoken of it in very obscure terms. This objection itself, which has been urged against the conception time and again since Chrysostom, makes it difficult to accept. And it is still more improbable that Paul looked on himself as the great restrainer, and viewed his own death as the removal of the obstacle in the way of the antichrist. For where does it appear that he attributed such a significance to himself? And when he speaks elsewhere of the possibility of his approaching death, could he have kept silent about the startling consequences bound up with it? That Paul considered himself (and then, as the issue showed, entirely wrongly) to be the restrainer is thus without more ado to be rejected. Even if one leaves this last out of consideration (and the question of *the* restrainer thus remains open), the idea that the preaching of the gospel is intended by the restraining is nevertheless not simply to be accepted. For then, regardless of the obscurity of the description, the close of verse 7 remains unintelligible. How can it be true of the preaching or the preacher of the gospel that it (he) "disappears from the scene" or "gets out of the way"? Does Paul then foresee a time when the proclamation of the gospel comes to an end?

These and similar objections make it impossible to follow explanations formerly adhered to, according to which the Holy Spirit, the good teachers, the apostles, etc., were meant by the restraint (restrainer).[105] Both so far as the choice of words in 2 Thessalonians and the matter itself are concerned, in no way whatever can all this be made probable.

(3) The question may be put as to whether interpretation is on the right track when it seeks the cause of the restraint in specific demonstrable historical factors. As is also evident from the subsequent "revealed in his own time," we have to do here with typical apocalyptic terminology.[106] This "restraint" is in general to be defined as that which, in virtue of the counsel of God applying to it, checks the outbreak of satanic godlessness in the man of sin before the time appointed for it by God. What is said in Revelation 20:2 about the shutting up and binding of Satan has not unjustly been called to mind[107] (cf. Luke

---

104. Cf. Rigaux, *Th.*, p. 276.

105. Cf., e.g., the explanation of Severianus of Gabala: *to katechon phēsi tēn tou hagiou pneumatos charin* (in K. Staab, *Pauluskommentare aus der Griechischen Kirche*, 1933, p. 334).

106. In the Jewish literature, too, there is mention of the "holding back" or retarding of the coming of the Messiah. Various answers are given to the question: who then holds it back? See Strack-Billerbeck, III, pp. 640ff.; II, pp. 588ff. Cullmann appeals to this terminology for his conception; cf. Schippers, *Mythologie en Eschatologie*, pp. 21ff. Betz thinks he finds some support in the Qumran writings (*NTS*, 1963, pp. 279ff.).

107. Cf. Dibelius, *Th.*, p. 48; Neil, *Thessalonians*, pp. 169ff.

8:31). It is also remarkable that papyri have been found in which, with the employment of the same word ("restrain," or "keep under"), there is mention of the keeping in check of the mythological dragon by the deity or by the angel Michael.[108] This last may bring us back once again to Daniel in which Michael is spoken of in more than one place, who in the final struggle stands by the people of God (cf. Dan. 10:13, 21; 12:1).[109]

Without identifying all these representations we can nevertheless form an idea of what that which restrains or the restrainer could mean: a supernatural power or a ruler ordained by God (in Rev. 20 "a strong angel") who checks the final revelation of the power of Satan,[110] until the time set for the man of sin has come. One may perhaps also think of God himself.[111] In any case, it is a matter of a specific act in the eschatological drama planned in the counsel of God, whereby the "time" belonging with it is also determined by all the factors that are at work in the divine economy of redemption with regard to the end of things (e.g., the progress of the gospel). But there is no basis for wishing to be specific here, nor is it in harmony with the apocalyptic character of the text to do so.[112] Paul does not allude here — so we think — to specific historical phenomena or events, but speaks in apocalyptic language of the supernatural factors that determine the restraining of the last things.

One can still consider whether *katechein* is to be translated by "restrain" or by "hold fast," "keep in check." In the latter case one has surely to arrive at the idea that "the man of sin" already exists, but must yet be kept in check. Although this idea, as long as it is concerned with the operation of the power of Satan himself, is very apposite, and in verse 7 where the person in question is closely related to "the mystery of iniquity" would certainly be in place, yet in verse 6 the object of "that which restrains" is apparently the man of sin. And that in one way or another he would have to be and could be kept in check before his revelation (appearance in history) is a thing difficult to imagine. As the man of sin he is hardly conceivable outside history. For this reason one will perhaps have to give preference to the translation "to restrain" because this allows a more figurative interpretation and can be understood not so much of the checking of the man of sin himself as indeed of his appearance and revelation. But it is also possible that in the apocalyptic language the apostle here employs all this is not to be so rigidly distinguished, and that the man of sin is spoken

---

108. See the reference to a late Egyptian prayer in Arndt-Gingrich-Bauer, pp. 423f., *s.v. katechō*, in which the god Horus is called the *katechōn drakonta*, and from one of the so-called *Zauberpapyri*, in which there is mention of *Michaēl... katechōn hon kaleousi drakonta megan*. Dibelius refers to *Acta Pilati* 22, 2, where Christ delivers up Satan to Hades with the words: *labōn auton kateche asphalōs achri tēs deuteras mou parousias* (*Th.*, p. 46).

109. Vos, too, makes a connection with Michael, a conception that was already advocated by Von Hofmann; see in Vos, *The Pauline Eschatology*, pp. 131ff. Cf. also V. Hepp, *De Antichrist*, 1919, p. 168.

110. Cf. Hanse, *TDNT*, II, pp. 829f.

111. Schippers, *Mythologie en Eschatologie*, p. 22.

112. Cf. above, p. 521.

of as a figure who is now still held back, kept in check, without this presupposing a "pre-existence." The vivid and realistic representation that is proper to the apocalyptic does indeed argue in some degree for this conception, in which the divine moment of power receives somewhat more emphasis.[113]

(d) The apostasy

Finally, as concerns the godlessness that is to reach its peak in the man of lawlessness, Paul speaks of it in two typical eschatological terms, "the falling away" (apostasy, v. 3) and "the mystery of godlessness" (v. 7). This is usually so interpreted that the reality denoted by "the apostasy" coincides with the time of the lawless one and therefore at the moment that he writes this has not yet, at least not yet fully, taken effect. There is much to be said for this explanation, for it is said in verse 3 that the day of the Lord will not come except the apostasy come first. And this — thus the reasoning — is not yet the case. Whether, as some do, one is simply to identify the apostasy with the man of godlessness[114] is still another question. In Daniel 11:32 there is also mention of "the falling away," but there more as the consequence and effect of the appearance of the great adversary than as this appearance itself. In our opinion, this is in any case included in the apostasy. It follows from the manner in which the appearance of the man of lawlessness is described. Because Satan will place his power at his disposal, he will be able to do powers, signs, and lying wonders. What is meant by this is that the wonders of the lawless one have a mendacious, deceitful purpose. They lead men astray. In concurrence with that it is said that his appearance is attended with all kinds of unrighteous deceit for those who are perishing. Those who are already on the road to ruin are totally beguiled and misled by the deceptive delusions of God's arrogant adversary and the manifestations of his power, so that they will no longer escape the destruction toward which they are bound. This does not remove their responsibility, for that they are delivered up to this destruction is the consequence of the fact that they "have not received the love of the truth, that they might be saved. Therefore God sends them the working of error that they should believe the lie, so that all should be judged who have not believed the truth, but had pleasure in unrighteousness" (vv. 10-12). Here Paul makes a close connection between the working of the man of sin and the gospel. Not believing the truth of the gospel is the cause for which men fall prey to the fascination of the satanic power through the man of lawlessness. In this link between unbelief in the gospel and falling into the power of the godless seducer the old prophetic predictions of the struggle between God and Satan are given new relevance for the church (cf. 1 John 2:18, 22; 4:3; 2 John 7).

This falling away, the apostle now writes, has at present not yet come to its full unfolding. Although unbelief and godlessness are even now present, another revelation is to be expected, an explosion of

---

113. Cf. Schippers, *Mythologie en Eschatologie*, p. 23.
114. See on this point, e.g., Rigaux, *Th.*, pp. 265ff.

sin, still to be distinguished from the present godlessness in compass, design, and consequence. That is *the* apostasy. But "the mystery of lawlessness" is even now at work. "Mystery," just as "revelation," is to be understood here in relation to the eschatological event determined by God. Insofar as this has not yet come to realization, it is "mystery," that is to say, has not yet appeared. That applies in general to the apostasy or lawlessness intended here. Yet the working of the *anomia,* which is nothing other than the apostasy mentioned in verse 3, has already begun. It is to be sought in opposition and enmity to the gospel and in the means employed to that end. For just as the final decision falls in the encounter of Christ with the man of lawlessness, so the enmity revealing itself against the gospel of Christ also bears an eschatological character. No further decision is reached other than that which must already be made now with respect to Christ and his gospel. Therefore this decision discloses even now what the issue is to be in the final stage between God and Satan, between Christ and the antichrist. It is consequently to that that Paul directs the church's attention, and wants to teach it thus to understand the character of the time in which it lives.

In summary, we may ascertain that the passage preserved to us in 2 Thessalonians 2 on the revelation of the man of lawlessness signifies a remarkable and important contribution for our insight into Paul's expectation for the future and his view of history. So far as the former is concerned, in no respect does it mean a breaking through or abrogation of the pronouncements on nearness. What is said about the restraining is also to be understood in the framework of these nearness pronouncements. What is said on the still to be expected revelation of the man of lawlessness does confirm what we have already been able to determine in general on the perspective for the future. It embraces all manner of universal elements, the temporal and spatial implications of which are *a priori* incalculable, and which give the words "at hand" a strongly proleptic-prophetic character. This applies to the *pleroma* of the gentiles and of Israel; it also applies to the man of lawlessness, if one is, as we think, to attribute a representative significance to this denotation. All that has been said earlier, therefore, on the nature of this future expectation and this future perspective also applies to the expectation of this last and universal revelation of the mystery of lawlessness and finds further confirmation in it.

For understanding Paul's view of history, too, the pericope of 2 Thessalonians 2 is of paramount importance. It gives us some insight into the strongly dramatic and antithetic character of Paul's conception of history. It is dominated by the great opposition between God and Satan, between the power of the truth and that of the lie. In that struggle the coming of Christ signifies the decisive turning point. But for this reason his coming also evokes the parousia of the man of lawlessness. The mystery of lawlessness has therefore already come into operation as the beginning of the final struggle, and Christ's parousia is not to be thought of apart from the antecedent parousia of the man of lawlessness. The thing itself and the perspective are indissolubly bound up with each other, and together they determine Paul's view of history as well as that of the New Testament as a whole.

This look at the future and history bears an apocalyptic character. Therein on the one hand is its possibility, on the other its limitation. The possibility: for this apocalyptic "works" with the last and most powerful motifs of the prophecy of Israel and applies them to the history of the world. And the Christian apocalyptic brings these all under the denominator of the new and all-embracing revelation of the divine work of redemption in Christ. This is the possibility, the strength, and the imperishable worth of the New Testament apocalyptic. It comprises for the church the "final" comfort and hope and certitude of victory. On the other hand, in the apocalyptic character of the New Testament expectation for the future is also its limitation. The limitation of clarity, of concrete knowledge, of the possibility of being able to survey history in its factual progress. Here accordingly lies the failure of every interpretation that sees in the apocalyptic a means to becoming "informed" about this concreteness and factualness of the future event. Here, too, lies the justice of the criticism of "reportorial-eschatology." For the knowledge of the prophet is something other than sharing in divine omniscience. Nevertheless, this prophecy joins the kingdom of God with history, and it teaches us to see history under the decisive points of view. This insight into the Christian apocalyptic can also make us understand in the proper light the abiding significance of 2 Thessalonians 2 for the church. It elevates the church above the level on which only individual decisions take place and teaches it to understand something of the dimensions that define the work of Christ and with it the time of his parousia.

SECTION 77. THE PAROUSIA

In Paul's epistles we are given no complete or rounded off "doctrine" or description of the parousia of Christ and of the great events that are to take place along with it. On the one hand, this is certainly bound up with the apocalyptic character of this event, hidden in the counsel of God, which does not as an existing event admit of being narrated or described by means of human historiography. On the other hand, account is also to be taken here of the already frequently observed character of Paul's epistles as occasional writings, even if there is differentiation with respect to this character of his epistles. As regards the description of the "last things" (taken in the narrower sense), this "situational" element of the preaching and instruction contained in his epistles holds very clearly indeed. In only a few epistles does he go into this more fully, in connection with specific questions and situations in the churches. Here too, however, it does not amount to a "systematic" exposition, but to an elucidation of the great events of the end from a specific point of view, frequently also with an appeal to the preaching that has preceded the epistles (cf. 1 Thess. 5:2; 2 Thess. 2:5), and to that which the church "knows" or at least ought to "know" (cf., e.g., 1 Cor. 6:2, 3), without the content and origin of this knowledge thereby being fully explained. All this means that we can speak of a "doctrine of the last things" in Paul only in a fragmentary sense, even where it concerns the manner of the parousia itself and the events attending it. This fragmentary character will also have to make us very careful, therefore, in drawing conclusions and in bringing the separate data together.

Of importance for a correct conception of the matter, first of all, is the terminology with which Paul describes the coming of the Lord. This in the main is the following.

(a) The coming *(parousia)* of Christ (1 Cor. 15:23; cf. the variant in 1:8), or of our Lord Jesus (1 Thess. 2:19; 3:13; 4:15; 5:23; 2 Thess. 2:1, 8). The word "parousia" means[115] coming, arrival, and presence. It is employed in an entirely neutral sense without technical or special significance. In Hellenism, however, it also serves frequently to denote the visit of dignitaries, kings, generals, etc., as well as the coming, the appearance of gods. The term "parousia" has this technical meaning in Paul — but then, of course, with a content entirely its own[116] — especially in 1 and 2 Thessalonians. There and in 1 Corinthians 15:23 it very definitely does not mean "return,"[117] nor is parousia used in Paul (or elsewhere in the New Testament) of the first advent of Christ. The parousia of the Lord denotes the expected manifestation of Christ, as the definitive, ultimate revelation of his glory. "Coming" therefore has the connotation of the revelation of glory, the glorious coming and the presence linked with it.

(b) A second term with which Paul denotes the great future is that of the epiphany of our Lord Jesus Christ (1 Tim. 6:14); of our Savior Jesus Christ (2 Tim. 1:10); his epiphany and his kingdom (2 Tim. 4:1; cf. v. 8); the epiphany of the glory of our great God and Savior (Tit. 2:13). Finally, the combination of epiphany and parousia is still to be mentioned (2 Thess. 2:8: "whom [the lawless one] the Lord Jesus will bring to nought by the epiphany of his parousia"). Although epiphany, otherwise than parousia, does once allude to Christ's first coming (2 Tim. 1:10), it is generally employed exclusively for Christ's definitive[118] coming in glory. The word was particularly suited for this purpose because in the Hellenistic world it had acquired the additional

115. For this idea see the extensive study of P. L. Schoonheim, *Een semiasologisch onderzoek van Parousia met betrekking tot het gebruik in Mattheüs 24*, 1953. Further Oepke, *TDNT*, V, pp. 859ff.; Rigaux, *Th.*, pp. 196ff.

116. For the connection of this idea, stemming from the Greek world, with the Jewish-apocalyptic representation, see M. Sabbe, "De Paulinische beschrijving van de Paroesie," in *Collationes Brugenses et Gandavenses*, IX, 1961, pp. 105ff., as well as the conception mentioned there of R. de Langhe, according to whom *parousia* has not been taken over from the Greek usage, but is linked philologically with "day of the Lord"; in our view a rather labored explanation.

117. It only acquires this significance later when one came to speak of a first and second parousia; so, e.g., Justin Martyr.

118. In 2 Tim. 1:10 *epiphaneia* also alludes to the revelation of the glory of Christ at his first coming, in particular to his resurrection.

significance of a solemn, glorious appearance or entrance, as, for example, of the Hellenistic rulers.

(c) In the third place, the word "revelation" *(apokalypsis)* is likewise used for Christ's coming in glory (2 Thess. 1:7: "at the revelation of our Lord Jesus Christ from heaven"; cf. 1 Cor. 1:7: "waiting for the revelation of our Lord Jesus Christ from heaven"). In these combinations it is not Christ who reveals "something," but he is himself revealed, that is to say, he emerges from the hiddenness in which he now is. In that same sense, although with another word *(phaneroō),* there is mention in Colossians 3:4 of the manifestation of Christ, with which then the manifestation of the church with him in glory is joined. In distinction from the first two words there is in "revelation" the thought of a preceding period of concealment or hiddenness.

(d) Finally, those expressions are still to be mentioned in which the coming of Christ is denoted as "the day," sometimes used absolutely (1 Thess. 5:4: "you are not in darkness, that the day should overtake you as a thief"; likewise 1 Cor. 3:13: "each man's work shall be made manifest; for the day shall declare it, because it is revealed with fire"); compare also the expression "that day" (2 Tim. 1:12, 18; 4:8). In Romans 2:5, too, one finds the combination of "day" and "revelation" ("the day of wrath and of the revelation of the righteous judgment of God"). Again, the day is further qualified as "the day of the Lord" (1 Thess. 5:2; 2 Thess. 2:2; 1 Cor. 5:5 [in the reading followed by most]; cf. 1 Cor. 1:8; 2 Cor. 1:14), or "of Christ Jesus" (Phil. 1:6; cf. 1:10; 2:16). This term stems from the Old Testament, where the day of Yahweh is frequently spoken of as the future revelation of his power. In some of the passages we have cited "the day of the Lord" can still be understood as the day of God; in view of the further additions in other passages it is more probable, however, that by "the Lord" all along Christ must be understood. Here again we have proof of the extent to which the great future is in the epistles of Paul entirely concentrated about Christ, even though the terminology is not originally Messianic, but theological.[119] However, while in the Old Testament and especially in the late Jewish usage some degree of diversity presents itself with respect to the content and temporal delimitation of the expression "the day of the Lord," in the epistles of Paul the day of the Lord is given with the revelation or coming *(parousia)* of Christ, whereby then with the expression "day of the Lord," in harmony with the usage of the Old Testament, it is a matter especially of the judgment[120] to be executed by Christ. Yet in 1 Thessalonians 5:2 and 2 Thessalonians 2:2 it is not specifically the judgment, but the coming of the Lord, his parousia in general, that is to be understood by the day of the Lord. In all these descriptions it is

---

119. It is also thought that the Pauline expression "the day of our Lord Jesus Christ" does not directly have its origin in the Old Testament "day of Yahweh," but is derived from the theology of the Son of Man, where it denotes the enthronement of the Son of Man invested by God with all power (cf. S. Mowinckel, *He That Cometh,* 1956, p. 392).

120. Cf. Delling, *TDNT,* II, p. 952, *s.v. hēmera.*

a matter of a general denotation of the great future that dawns with Christ's coming.

The passages where the parousia and its significance come up for discussion more fully and directly are 1 Thessalonians 4:15-18 and 2 Thessalonians 1:7-10. Although certain features of this epiphany are also mentioned a few times elsewhere — so, for example, in 2 Thessalonians 2:8, already discussed, where it is said that the Lord Jesus will slay the lawless one by the breath of his mouth and bring him to nought by the epiphany of his coming; as well as in 1 Thessalonians 3:13, where the parousia of Christ "with all his saints" is spoken of — yet the above-mentioned passages are in this respect much more detailed. Both passages, however, have an exceedingly practical purport, which can also account for the fact that at one time the judging and punishing character of the parousia comes to the fore (2 Thess. 1), while at another light is cast on the appearing of Christ's coming exclusively in its saving significance (1 Thess. 4).

In 2 Thessalonians 1 the apostle goes into the difficult situation in which the church finds itself, particularly into the affliction to which it is exposed from the side of its enemies. He declares then that God will openly give it justice by requiting with affliction those who now afflict it, and rest to those who are afflicted at the parousia of Christ, which he then describes as follows: "... at the revelation of the Lord Jesus from heaven with the angels of his power, in flaming fire, inflicting punishment upon those who do not know God and do not obey the gospel of our Lord Jesus; they shall pay the penalty with an eternal destruction, far from the face of the Lord and from the glory of his might, when he comes to be glorified in his saints, and to be marvelled at in all who have believed ... in that day" (vv. 7ff.).

If one looks more closely at this description, it appears to represent the parousia of Christ as a descent from heaven, together with his holy angels, in the same manner as elsewhere (cf. 1 Thess. 3:13; 4:16; Matt. 24:31). This description already associates itself closely with that of the Old Testament theophanies (cf., e.g., Zech. 14:5; Jude 14 with a quotation from En. 1:9). This applies in still greater measure to the succeeding words, borrowed from various passages in the Old Testament where the appearing of God is described and his punitive judgment on his enemies is announced (cf. Exod. 3:2 — the flame of fire in the appearance of the Lord to Moses at Horeb; Isa. 66:4, 15; Jer. 10:25; Ps. 68:36; Isa. 2:11, 17). It is apparent from this, therefore, how much the parousia of Christ is linked to the coming of Yahweh in judgment according to Old Testament prophecy, both as regards its substance and its representation.[121]

In 2 Thessalonians 1:7-10, moreover, the discriminating significance of the parousia is in the foreground. Although, as is evident elsewhere, the judgment is also to concern believers and the fire is also to prove their work (see Section 79), here the separation between be-

---

121. For these Old Testament (and late Jewish) parallels also see the full article by M. Sabbe cited above, *Collationes Brugenses*, IX, pp. 105ff.

lievers and unbelievers is especially alluded to. Christ's appearing in majesty and glory means punitive judgment, eternal ruin for those who do not know God and who are disobedient; and this is then denoted as an exclusion from the presence of the Lord and from participation in his glory (cf. Matt. 7:23, et al.). This in absolute contrast with the lot of those who belong to Christ and whose glory will consist in that they will always be with the Lord (1 Thess. 4:17).[122] Here, in 2 Thessalonians 1, this is expressed in words in which Psalm 67 (68):36 and 88 (89):8 (LXX) sound through, namely, that the Lord comes to be glorified in his saints (believers, his own) and to be beheld with wonder by all who have believed. For them his coming means to share in his glory, above all reverent and worshipful amazement at the glory with which he himself is clothed. Thus at his coming the division is carried into effect, and the roles are to be reversed: there will be retribution on the heads of the afflicters, relief and rest for the afflicted (vv. 6, 7). The revelation of Christ also means the revelation of righteousness, both in its redeeming and in its retributive significance.

Of no less importance for insight into this discriminatory significance of the parousia is the well-known pericope of 1 Thessalonians 4:13-18. Here again the church does not receive a complete description in sequence of all that is to take place at the coming of the Lord, but further instruction with respect to the lot of believers who have fallen asleep before the parousia. Uncertainty and anxiety had apparently arisen about them. The church itself still hoped to be permitted to experience the parousia of Christ as a whole. But how must one conceive of the fate of those who have already died, if in the great moment of Christ's appearance they were no longer able to go to meet him with the church?

It is apparently not a question here, as in 1 Corinthians 15, of upholding the reality of the resurrection, but of the manner in which deceased believers are to be involved directly and at the first appearing of Christ at the parousia.[123] Would those who are dead have to miss the great moment of Christ's appearing, which they, too, so earnestly anticipated? It may be that for the consciousness of the church the parousia and the resurrection of the dead still lay far apart, and the latter was conceived of as a final phase, entered on only much later (after the parousia and the reign of Christ on earth beginning with it).[124] Or perhaps the whole fate of deceased believers was an obscure matter for the church.

However this may be, Paul's instruction is here directed toward

---

122. Neil, *Thessalonians*, correctly writes: "In its deepest sense punishment is separation from God and reward is fellowship with Him" (p. 145).

123. So rightly Dibelius, *Th.*, p. 25, and Neil, *Thessalonians*, p. 95.

124. On this in detail cf. Dupont, [*SYN CHRISTŌ*], *l'Union avec le Christ suivant Saint Paul*, I, pp. 40ff., 84. With other writers he thinks of a possible Jewish idea present among the Thessalonians, according to which the resurrection only takes place at the end of the Messianic reign on earth. We have no certainty on this, but will surely be permitted to conclude from the answer that the dead at once and together with those still alive will go to meet Christ, that the church needed further instruction on this point.

convincing the church that deceased believers will from the very outset share in the glory of Christ's parousia no less than those who are still alive. Here again the point of departure of the line of reasoning lies in the bond that joins Christ with all his own, even with those who have died: "for if we believe that Jesus died and rose again, even so them also that are fallen asleep through Jesus[125] will God bring with him" (1 Thess. 4:14). That which is especially in view in this pronouncement lies in the final words: "bring with him." They say something still more than "will cause them to arise with him," for with that the share of deceased believers in the parousia would not yet have been elucidated. The meaning is no less than that God will make them appear with Christ in his parousia, that is to say, they will be in his company, at his side, when Christ appears. How this is intended only becomes clear from the following verses. For the apostle explains what goes before with "a word of the Lord" in this way, that "we who are alive, who are left until the parousia of the Lord, will not precede those who have fallen asleep." This (not) preceding apparently has reference to the same occurrence as that which is expressed in verse 14 with the words "bring with him" or "cause to come with him." It is a question of the way in which believers, both those who have died and survivors, are to be involved at the parousia and will share in its glory. How this is to take place is then explained as follows, in the description of the parousia itself: "For the Lord himself will descend from heaven with a cry of command, with the voice of the archangel, and with the trumpet of God; and the dead in Christ will rise first; then we who are alive, who are left, shall be caught up together with them in the clouds to meet the Lord in the air. And so we shall always be with the Lord" (vv. 16ff.).

This description of the parousia — the most detailed we are given in the epistles of Paul — bears a pronouncedly apocalyptic character, partly making use of features that occur elsewhere in the delineations of theophanies. The representation describes occurrences that fall outside the present mode of human existence. In the manner of apocalypses it places these within the framework of the world picture of that day, and thus gives human vividness to the divine occurrence, which, however, no longer admits of being interpreted in the manner of human history. There is mention of a "shout of command" (going out over the whole earth), the "voice of the archangel," and "the trumpet of God." So far as the meaning of this representation is concerned, one can ask whether we have to do here with a threefold act in the divine event, or whether the same thing is intended in three different ways, namely, the signal for the commencement of the great event. Is the "shout of

---

125. The question is whether one is to connect the words *dia tou Iēsou* with the preceding *tous koimēthentas,* or with the following *axei.* For the arguments pro and con see, e.g., Rigaux, *Th.,* pp. 535ff., and Neil, *Thessalonians,* pp. 94ff. With the majority we choose for the former view, in part because with *axei* one gets a double prepositional apposition, which both times has reference to Christ. To be sure, it is not easy to put into words what is meant by *koimēthentas dia tou Iēsou.* The expression will very likely have to be understood by analogy with *hoi nekroi en Christō* (cf. Dupont, [*SYN CHRISTŌ*], p. 42, n. 2).

command" the voice of God or of Christ? Does this command apply to the descent of Christ himself, or is it already addressed to the dead? One can ask similar questions about "the voice of the archangel and the trumpet of God."[126] The expressions employed here also form the regular material of descriptions of theophanies, of the day of the Lord, and of the coming of Christ related to it.[127] Angels are always present in the eschatological occurrence, as accompanying attendants of Christ, as co-executors of the final events (cf., e.g., Matt. 13:39, 49; 16:27; Mark 8:38; Matt. 25:31, et al.; Luke 12:8ff.; 2 Thess. 1:7).[128] Elsewhere Paul speaks of the coming of Christ "with all his saints" (1 Thess. 3:13), among whom angels are also to be understood. "The trumpet" also has a specifically eschatological significance. Some think that the blast of the trumpet in theophanies denotes the indescribable voice of God.[129] However this may be, as already in the Old Testament the theophany at Mt. Sinai (Exod. 19:16) and the day of Yahweh must be announced with the blast of the trumpet and also consist in the sound of the trumpet (cf. Joel 2:1; Zeph. 1:16; Isa. 27:13; Zech. 9:14), so in the New Testament the Apocalypse is full of trumpets, angels with trumpets, etc. (cf. also Matt. 24:31). Paul speaks of it in 1 Corinthians 15:52 as the last trumpet that announces the resurrection. Likewise in 1 Thessalonians 4:16 the blast of the trumpet and the raising of the dead must be understood in close relation to each other.[130] Who it is that blows the trumpet is not said; it is "the great trumpet" (Matt. 24:31), the "last trumpet" (1 Cor. 15:32), the "trumpet of God" (1 Thess. 4:16).[131] All this, however, does not have an independent significance in the description of 1 Thessalonians 4. It is the eschatological-apocalyptic entourage of what is meant to be said here of the parousia: that all believers, those who have died as well as those who remain alive, will share at once and together in the glory of Christ's parousia. This is also the meaning of the resurrection of the dead here indicated in only a few words. The mention of it serves only to remove any suggestion as though deceased believers would not immediately be there and as though their redemptive and glorification were unclear or must still await a further order. Rather, their resurrection will take place first of all, when the appearing of Christ is announced by voices and trumpet blast. Only thereafter will the collective meeting and uniting with Christ of the dead and the

---

126. Cf., e.g., Lothar Schmid, *TDNT*, III, p. 658.

127. For the materials with respect to *archangelos,* see Kittel, *TDNT*, I, p. 87; Sabbe, *Collationes Brugenses,* IX, pp. 89ff.

128. For the rabbinic and pseudepigraphical literature, see, e.g., Strack-Billerbeck, I, pp. 672ff., 973ff.

129. Cf. Friedrich, *TDNT*, VII, p. 80.

130. The same is the case in the Jewish writings: "God will take a great horn in his hand.... At the first blast the whole earth shakes; at the second the dust is sifted out; at the third the bones are brought together; at the fourth the limbs are warmed; at the fifth their skin is put on; at the sixth the spirits and the souls enter their bodies; at the seventh they come to life and stand on their feet in their clothes, as it is said: The almighty Yahweh will blow the horn (Zech. 9:14), Alphabet-Midr. of R. Aqiba, 9." Quoted by Friedrich, *TDNT,* VII, p. 84.

131. For these ideas in detail see Vos, *The Pauline Eschatology,* pp. 138ff., and especially Sabbe, *Collationes Brugenses,* pp. 89ff.

living take place. In what way the latter are to experience this meeting, that is to say, in what mode of existence, is not said. To wish to infer from this that in 1 Thessalonians Paul had not yet come to the idea of the "change" of which he speaks in 1 Corinthians 15:52 is altogether without foundation; just as it is to wish to assume that the resurrection of those already dead would take place in the same body as that in which they had lived before. All this is not further spoken of here. One will have to interpret Paul with Paul, however, and not with all sorts of ideas that are to be found here and there in the late Jewish literature; and one will furthermore have to bear in mind that the apostle is not concerned here with a rounded off "eschatology," but only with upholding the simultaneous and collective involvement of the dead and the living in the parousia of Christ.

This is done then in the remarkable words of verse 17, which speak of being "caught up in the clouds to meet the Lord in the air." This denotes a supernatural translation, of which there is likewise mention elsewhere in an apocalyptic context (Rev. 12:5), also indeed in the sense of a visionary translation (2 Cor. 12:2, 4; cf., however, Acts 8:39). The clouds, too, form a fixed apocalyptic motif. Of the Son of Man it is said continually that he is to come on or with the clouds, referring to Daniel 7:13 (cf. Mark 13:26; 14:62; Matt. 26:64; Luke 21:27; Rev. 1:7; 14:14ff.). In the Old Testament theophanies, too, the cloud occurs repeatedly as manifestation, seat, vehicle of God (cf. Ps. 97:2; Isa. 19:1; Exod. 19:9, 16, *et al.*). In 1 Thessalonians 4 the cloud constitutes the manifestation of the glory of Christ, in which his own are permitted to participate. What is meant then is the beginning of this union, the meeting. In the descent of Christ from heaven his own are taken up in his transcendent appearance ("in the air"), certainly not to remain there,[132] or from thence to return to heaven, but to be by him and with him when he appears on earth.

Where the origin of this idea is to be sought is disputed. It is often thought that the ceremony of the "bringing in" of Hellenistic princes in connection with their visit to a specific city or region was of influence in the description of the parousia. One finds both the word *parousia* and *eis apantēsin* in the descrip-

---

132. G. Vos, *The Pauline Eschatology*, pp. 136ff., thinks that the union of Christ and his own in the air does not denote a provisional place as preparation for a further descent to the earth, but the beginning of their abode with him "in the supernal regions" (p. 138). He writes: "A position of some remoteness from the surface of the earth is after all most natural to assume in this connection. The far reach and universal scope of the tremendous event here set in motion are in better accord with some central elevated place in the air than a standpoint on the flat surface on the ground" (p. 136). In our view it is difficult to debate about the spatial implications of these apocalyptic ideas. But that the place of glorified believers would be with Christ in the air appears to us a thought that finds no basis elsewhere. However inconceivable the coming of Christ on earth and all that is connected with it may be for us (so that one may ask himself whether discussions on the spatial "standpoint" of where Christ will act really make sense), yet the earth is the real object and in the representation the terrain of the eschatological drama. The meeting in the air has the significance of the "bringing in" of Christ by his own and of their fellowship with him when he shall come to the earth; see also Sabbe, *Collationes Brugenses*, IX, pp. 90ff.

tions of these joyous entries. The inhabitants of the city, insofar as they had no bad conscience, went to meet the ruler in order then to march into the city in his retinue or otherwise to observe his entry. Likewise the figure of the crown of which Paul speaks in connection with the parousia of 1 Thessalonians 2:19, 20 ("What is ... our crown of glorying [*stephanos kaucheseos*] before our Lord Jesus at his parousia? Is it not you?") is often explained from this context. For they presented the ruler with crowns or garlands, or adorned themselves with them when they went to meet him (cf., e.g., Deissmann, *Licht vom Osten*, 4th ed., 1923, p. 315, and especially E. Peterson, "Die Einholung des Kyrios," *ZST*, 1929/30, pp. 682ff.; the same author in *TDNT*, I, p. 380; see also Sabbe, in *Collationes Brugenses et Gandavenses*, IX, pp. 97ff.). This explanation is followed by many and does indeed offer striking points of contact.

Others, however, are of the opinion that the background is to be sought entirely in the apocalyptic ideas of the Old Testament and Judaism. In his extensive discussion of this question Dupont, [*SYN CHRISTŌ*], pp. 64ff., has pointed in particular to the description of the theophany at Mt. Sinai (Exod. 19:10-18), where there is also mention (LXX) of *hai phōnai kai hai salpinges*, which were heard at the coming of the Lord. On the third day — so it follows — there were voices and lightning and a thick cloud *(nephele)*, and the sound of the trumpet *(phōne tes salpingos)* rang out loudly. And Moses led the people forth to meet God *(exegagen M. ton laon eis synantesin tou Theou,* etc.). Dupont is of the opinion that in this whole apocalyptic-eschatological context (of I Thess. 4) "the point of departure is to be found in the story of the theophany at Sinai, which inspires the apocalyptic context of this passage of Paul's letter" *(ibid.,* pp. 71, 73). Although the comparison with the bringing in of the Hellenistic princes is striking and was also, for example, employed by Chrysostom as an explanation, the apocalyptic character of the description in 1 Thessalonians 4 and the Old Testament elements undoubtedly to be found in it argue not a little in favor of Dupont's mode of interpretation. Sabbe has worked this out still further and provided a number of additions (*Collationes Brugenses,* IX, pp. 99-113).

It is plain that this going of believers to meet the Lord has the meaning of being placed at Christ's side at his coming, the open demonstration of belonging to him and being his people. The same thing is intended in 2 Thessalonians 2:1 when "our joining together"[133] with Christ at his parousia is spoken of, and in Colossians 3:4: "your being manifested with him in glory." With that the expression in 1 Thessalonians 4:14 — "them ... will God bring with him" — has been sufficiently explained. God will make them come with Christ in his triumphant appearance. It cannot mean "bring with him from heaven," for they are simply to go to meet him. Likewise there is no thought of a return to heaven.[134] For Christ's parousia is directed just toward the earth. It is being included in his company, moving in his retinue, coming with Christ in his glory. It means also to be separated forthwith from those for whom Christ's parousia is unto condemnation and therefore deliverance "from the wrath to come" (1 Thess. 1:10).

133. *Episynagōge;* literally "being gathered" to him.
134. As Rigaux apparently thinks: "God will lead them to heaven with him" (*Th.,* p. 537; cf. Frame, *Thessalonians, in loc.*). Otherwise Dupont, [*SYN CHRISTŌ*], pp. 42f.: "They will constitute the train of the Lord when he arrives on the earth."

How all this is to be realized and what follows on this union is not further explained here. The description ends with the words: "and so we shall always be with the Lord." This is the summary and climax of all that has gone before. When this point has been reached, the apostle breaks off, and he says that the church is to comfort itself with it, both for its dead and for itself. The christological viewpoint constitutes the new integrating point of the age-old involvement of the people of God in the revelation of the glory of the Lord. Christ is the central point, the certainty, the ground for the hope of glory. The old is not thereby set aside, however, but used and illuminated in view of its capacity for expression.[135] But the hope is directed toward Christ, toward always being with him. That is the new qualification, concentrated in one word, of the salvation of the future of the Lord for his people described in all kinds of grandiose forms and conceptions but still always indescribable.

SECTION 78. THE RESURRECTION

As has already been apparent in the preceding section, the redemptive significance of the parousia of Christ for the church above everything else lies in the fact that immediately with Christ's appearing believers who have fallen asleep will arise and — this we may add at once[136] — those who then remain alive will be changed.

Whereas other events connected with the great future come up for discussion in Paul's epistles only in part or incidentally, the resurrection of the dead and the renewing of the body are part of the central substance of his proclamation of the gospel. To be sure, one can term 1 Corinthians 15 in a special sense "the" chapter of the resurrection — both of Christ and of believers — but this does not alter the fact that the resurrection of believers is set before the church time and again in many different contexts as the great redemptive occurrence of the future. It springs directly from and has its explanation in the reality of the resurrection of Christ, the center of the Pauline proclamation (Rom. 8:11; 1 Cor. 6:14; 2 Cor. 4:14). His own people were already included in Christ's resurrection, and baptism is the sacramental incorporation into

---

135. Cf. Vos, *The Pauline Eschatology*, p. 142: "It were wrong undoubtedly to reduce all the things mentioned to the rubric of figurative language, in regard to which the author is aware of painting freely, rather than of copying the solid content of prophecy given him by the Spirit. On the other hand we should not overlook the equally obvious fact, that in painting by words, even with the fullest intention of accuracy, the Apostle had to avail himself of a fixed medium of language, which left room for a margin of over-literalism, and whose interpretation by others, while seemingly in full accord with the words recorded, nevertheless may introduce an ingredient of inadequacy when compared with the actual intent of Paul. We have here before us a striking example of the possibility of over-stressing the literalness of the language and imagery used, and yet, while thus seeming to do justice to the writer's speech, missing in reality the deeper and finer qualities and objectives of his true conception."

136. Cf. above, pp. 534f.

this redemptive event (Rom. 6:4ff.; Col. 2:12; 3:1). The actual renewal of their life is the likeness of Christ's resurrection (Rom. 6:5); in it the resurrection of Christ is already working itself out (Rom. 6:8; 2 Cor. 4:10ff.), and will work itself out more and more (2 Cor. 3:18). It is this having been raised with Christ, this being permitted to know oneself alive for God in Christ (Rom. 6:11), this having already put on the new man (of the resurrection) (Col. 3:10), which has its consummation in the resurrection from the dead at Christ's parousia. And in proportion as believers may be the more forcefully aware of having been included in this spiritual event of renewal, they will also be the more fervent for its full outworking in the resurrection of the dead (Phil. 3:11ff.).

Because of this all-controlling significance of Christ's resurrection for the future of his people, Christ can also be called the Firstfruits (*aparchē*) of those who have fallen asleep (1 Cor. 15:20, 23). "Firstfruits" is a qualification borrowed from the harvest. The firstfruits represent the whole of the anticipated and still to be ingathered crop, are the evidence that the new harvest, that is to say here, the new aeon, has come. To the same effect there is mention in Colossians of the Beginning, the Firstborn from the dead (cf. Rom. 8:29). Both terms do not say only that in order of time Christ is the beginning of the resurrection, but also that the beginning made by him was decisive and opened the way for the "many brethren" who belong to this Firstborn.[137] He has robbed death of its power (2 Tim. 1:10), given his own victory over death (1 Cor. 15:57). His resurrection and that of his people form an unbreakable unity.

From this exclusively christological approach to the resurrection of believers is also to be understood the connection Paul makes repeatedly between the resurrection and the Holy Spirit.[138] For it was the Spirit who in Christ's resurrection was overpoweringly at work. Christ was also endowed with the Spirit before his resurrection, and he was driven and led by the Spirit (Matt. 3:16; 4:1, *et al.*).[139] But before the resurrection Christ's existence was also determined by the fact that he was "in the flesh" (Rom. 1:3; 1 Tim. 3:16). And while this "flesh" meant for Christ the subjection to death of the old aeon — for God sent him "in the likeness of the flesh of sin" (Rom. 8:3) — the Spirit is the Author of the redeemed and imperishable life of the new aeon (2 Cor. 3:17, 18). For this reason the resurrection of Christ is particularly related to the Spirit. In the resurrection he was "justified by the Spirit" (1 Tim. 3:16), that is to say, in the sight of all declared to be right. The glory and power of God according to "the Spirit of holiness" were given to Christ at his resurrection (Rom. 1:4).[140] However, this does not mean that he no longer had any part in the corporeal — precisely his resurrection is

---

137. Cf. above, Section 9.
138. On this point see, e.g., K. Deissner, *Auferstehungshoffnung und Pneumagedanke bei Paulus*, 1912; G. Vos, "The Eschatological Aspect of the Pauline Conception of the Spirit," *Princeton Biblical and Theological Studies*, 1912, pp. 211-259; N. Q. Hamilton, *The Holy Spirit and Eschatology in Paul*; Ingo Hermann, *Kyrios und Pneuma*, 1961, pp. 114ff.
139. Cf. my *The Coming of the Kingdom*, pp. 86ff.
140. Cf. Hamilton, *The Holy Spirit and Eschatology in Paul*, p. 12.

proof to the contrary — but that he has been freed from the weakness and humiliation of the flesh, and he himself is given disposal over the Spirit, so that his new mode of existence can be identified with that of the Spirit (2 Cor. 3:17; 1 Cor. 15:45). For this reason, by way of a synonym and equivalent of the work of the Spirit in the resurrection, there can also be mention of Christ's being raised from the dead "by the glory of the Father" and of his life "from the power of God" (Rom. 6:4; 2 Cor. 13:4).

In this regime of the power and glory of the Spirit as the Creator of the new life believers are now included in virtue of their belonging to Christ (Rom. 8:9). Therefore their temporal-corporeal existence (just as that of Christ) is indeed subject to death because of sin (condemned in the body of Christ), but in its place the Spirit gives life because of righteousness (wrought in Christ) (Rom. 8:10).[141] And that also means for them, therefore, the quickening of their mortal bodies by the Spirit of Christ, who dwells in them (Rom. 8:11).

All this can enable us better to understand that Paul, particularly in 1 Corinthians 15, so forcefully upholds the resurrection of the dead over against those, apparently even in the church, who denied it. At the present time[142] it is often assumed that in this denial of the resurrection we are to see a spiritualistic heresy that is perhaps also in view in 2 Timothy 2:18 (men who contended that "the resurrection is past already"). It was not the resurrection of Christ that was denied, nor that believers shared in it, but it was said that the latter is to be understood in an exclusively spiritual sense, and to consist in the perfection to be attained already in this life, whereupon no resurrection of the body need follow. However one chooses further to assess the spiritual background of this heresy, the denial of the bodily resurrection of believers is the cardinal point on which the argument of the apostle is concentrated.[143]

Its construction[144] is very clear and impressive. After the explicit repetition and confirmation of the apostolic *paradosis* concerning the

---

141. For this exegesis of Rom. 8:10 also see Bultmann, *Theology*, I, pp. 208f.; *TDNT*, IV, p. 894, n. 29, *s.v. nekros;* and my *Rom.*

142. On the nature of this Corinthian heresy all kinds of hypotheses exist. The Tübingen school thought of Judaizers. Later on scholars sought the explanation more in the direction of a spiritualistic heresy. See, e.g., the exensive discussion of this question by J. Schniewind, "Die Leugner der Auferstehung in Korinth," in *Nachgelassene Reden und Aufsätze*, 1952, pp. 110ff.; W. Bieder, "Paulus und seine Gegner in Korinth," in *TZ*, 1961, pp. 319ff.; E. Brandenburger, *Adam und Christus*, 1962, pp. 70ff., according to whom it was primarily the resurrection of the dead as a future event that was at issue.

143. H. Riesenfeld contends that the principal theme of 1 Cor. 15 really is not "the resurrection of the dead" but "death as the presupposition for resurrection" ("Paul's Grain of Wheat Analogy," in *The Gospel Tradition*, ET 1970, p. 174). But this statement of the problem is incorrect. Paul does not argue the necessity of death (cf. v. 51), but the impossibility of receiving in this body the full salvation of Christ (vv. 19, 50ff.).

144. For what follows see also J. Jeremias, "Flesh and Blood Cannot Inherit the Kingdom of God," *NTS*, II, 1955/56, pp. 151ff.

resurrection of Christ as the foundation stone and basis of all that must be said in what follows, Paul comes in verse 12 to the assertion of those who say that there is no resurrection of the dead. Over against that he first maintains with great force the *that* (*hoti*; v. 12) and thereafter discusses, beginning with verse 35, the *how* (*pōs*) of the resurrection. In the first part he posits plainly that the denial of the resurrection of the dead would bring the resurrection of Christ into question (which was apparently not denied by the heresy), indeed, all the content of the apostolic preaching and of the Christian faith. Already here he places Christ over against Adam in order to make clear the indissoluble connection between Christ and his own, likewise so far as the resurrection is concerned (vv. 22ff.). In so doing he already goes into the sequence of events at the parousia (vv. 23-29), to return thereafter to the consequences that the omitting of the resurrection would have for himself as well as for the church; it would make all his life-and-death struggle for the gospel senseless, and it could, if death after all means the end of everything, only give occasion to libertinism: "let us eat and drink . . ." (vv. 30-34). In this context he speaks also of being "baptized for the dead" (v. 29), an allusion to a practice of which, despite all the research that has been devoted to it,[145] it cannot be said that its meaning is clear to us. In this context this allusion serves, however, as (supplementary) argument against those who denied the resurrection and did apparently consider this baptism for the dead meaningful. The main thing in the whole argument is, however: (a) Christ's unquestioned resurrection implies the resurrection of his own; and (b) without the hope of the resurrection at Christ's parousia the Christian life and the Christian life-struggle lose their meaning. And he adds to this in verse 34, with a not indistinct recollection of Christ's answer to the Sadducees (Matt. 22:29, 33), that those who deny the resurrection have no idea who God is.[146]

In verse 35, then, he begins his exposition of the *how*, referring to the questions of those who opposed it (introduced in the manner of the diatribe): "but — someone will say — how are the dead raised? and with what kind of body do they come?" It appears from the answer that this "how" has yet again a twofold aspect. In verses 36-50 the quality of the resurrection body is first dealt with, and then, in verses 51ff., the manner in which the resurrection event takes place.[147] So far as the former

---

145. One of the most recent comprehensive investigations is that of M. Rissi, *Die Taufe für die Toten*, 1962. Rissi himself thinks of letting oneself be baptized in the place of believing, but unbaptized deceased persons, in order thus to bear witness as yet to the faith of these who have died in the resurrection. Jeremias, following up M. Raeder (*ZNW*, 1955, pp. 258-260), wants to take *hyper* not in a substitutionary, but in a final sense. He thinks then of heathen who let themselves be baptized, with the intention of in this way becoming united with their Christian relatives or connections at the resurrection (*NTS*, 1955/56, pp. 155ff.). But neither the one nor the other is very convincing; see also above, p. 25.

146. *Agnōsian gar Theou tines echousin.*

147. Jeremias thinks that in vv. 36-49 and 50-54 Paul deals with the two questions of v. 35 in a strict chiastic order. This is bound up with his conception of v. 50a; see below.

is concerned, Paul makes use of a double analogy. First of all, he employs that of the seed.[148] It is also true of seed that it comes to new life only if it has first died (v. 36). And one can learn from it at the same time that the quality of what shall be must not be measured by what one sees die. For it applies to sowing, too, that it is not "the future body," but only the single ("naked") grain, whether of wheat or of something else, that is sowed. Here the almighty and absolute power of God prevails, who not only gives each seed its own (future) "body," but also gives men and animals, birds and fish, another "flesh," i.e., their own earthly manner of existence. So great and unimaginable are the riches God has at his disposal for giving each a "body" as he has chosen. And that holds not only for what is on earth, but also for what appears in the heavens. Their glory is of another order than that which is on earth, but the heavenly bodies differ again among themselves (vv. 37-41).

When in conclusion the apostle now adds: "so is it also with the resurrection of the dead," he not only elucidates the possibility and quality of the resurrection body with a reference to the various modes of existence God in his omnipotence has bestowed on his creatures, but he has already, and certainly not without design, placed the heavenly[149] and the earthly over against each other, a contrast to which he shortly returns in the analogy of the first and second Adam (cf. vv. 47ff.).

The transition from the first analogy (that of the seed) to the second forms the fourfold contrast between what is sown and raised.

> It is sown in corruption,
>   it is raised in incorruption;
> it is sown in dishonor,
>   it is raised in glory;
> it is sown in weakness,
>   it is raised in power;
> it is sown a psychical body,
>   it is raised a pneumatic body.

With this last contrast (psychical-pneumatic) we have come to a new crucial point in the argument which is elucidated with a new appeal to the analogy between Christ and Adam (vv. 44bff.). Only hence can the psychical-pneumatic contrast be understood in its proper meaning.[150] That which comes about anthropologically in the believer (in being "sown" and "raised") derives its significance from the fact that the mode of existence of his body before death is determined by that

---

148. That he hereby employs an analogy that in Jewish thinking had a certain tradition is proved not only by John 10:24, but also the rabbinic literature; cf. Hauck, *TDNT*, III, p. 132, *s.v. therizō;* see further at length on this metaphorical language H. Riesenfeld, "Paul's Grain of Wheat Analogy," *loc. cit.*

149. In so doing he has already introduced the word *doxa,* as denotation of the mode of existence of *ta epourania,* after *sarx* as denotation of that of the *epigeia.* Yet in v. 40 he also applies *doxa* to *ta epigeia;* see also H. Clavier, "Brèves remarques sur la notion de [*SOMA PNEUMATIKON*]," in *The Background of the N.T. and Its Eschatology* (in honor of C. H. Dodd), 1956, pp. 342-362, especially p. 348.

150. For the confusing multiplicity of interpretations of this antithesis in the history of the investigation see the article by Clavier *(ibid.).*

of the first Adam (and is therefore "psychical") and that in being raised it is determined by the second Adam (and is therefore "pneumatic"). In this light the pronouncement, which at first glance is not very transparent, is to be understood: "if there is a psychical body, there is also a pneumatic body," as also that the psychical is first and only then the pneumatic. All this is not in the nature of the human in itself — for why from the existence of a psychical and mortal body should that of a pneumatic and immortal body coming later have to follow? — but springs from the succession of the first Adam by the second and from the two different modes of existence pertaining to them. For this reason the psychical mode of existence (participating in the existence of the first Adam) is followed by the pneumatic (sharing in the second Adam). The anthropological contrast is anchored in the redemptive-historical.

The content of this psychical and pneumatic contrast is accordingly — in the second place — explained from the first man Adam and the last or second Adam, Christ. If "psychical" means belonging to the first Adam, "pneumatic" to the second, the one as well as the other is to be further elucidated on the ground of what is known concerning these two "men."[151]

As regards the first Adam Paul is able to appeal directly to Scripture: because God breathed into him the breath of life (Gen. 2:7), he became "living soul," he received life, which is therefore qualified as psychical (v. 46), a little further along as "from the earth, earthy" (once again referring to Gen. 2:7), and to which then the qualifications "flesh and blood" (v. 50), and "mortal" and "perishable" (v. 53) have reference.[152] All the descendants of the first Adam are sharers of this life. For as was the earthy, such are those who are earthy (v. 48).

---

151. Meanwhile scholars think very differently about the origin of the contrast employed in this context. Those who are of the opinion that Paul borrowed the thought of the two "men," the earthy and the heavenly, from certain gnostic influences, think that the contrast psychical-pneumatic had already been given therein (cf. E. Brandenburger, *Adam und Christus*, p. 74 [he can appeal for that already to Reitzenstein]; cf. also Arndt-Gingrich-Bauer, p. 902, s.v. *psychikos*). But just as the whole of this reduction of the Adam-Christ parallel to pre-Christian, mythological thought (with which Paul is said to have had to do in the heresy at Corinth) is a very uncertain matter, so also the Hellenistic-gnostic derivation of the psychical-pneumatic antithesis. Dupont in particular has argued forcefully that this contention lacks any substantial basis and that here rather a Jewish antithesis is normative; see his detailed discussion of this theme in *Gnosis*, 1949, pp. 151-181; cf. also Schweizer, *TDNT*, VI, pp. 395f., s.v. *pneuma*. Paul in any case connects *psychikos* here with Gen. 2:7; cf. also the use of *psychikos* in Jas. 3:15.

152. It has rightly been pointed out that Paul here does not speak of the existence of the first man as it has been disfigured by sin, but of man in his original state (cf., e.g., G. Vos, *The Pauline Eschatology*, p. 167: "The passage is unique... in that it contrasts not the body affected by sin... with the future body, but the primordial body of Adam ['the first Adam'] and the body of the consummation"). This body was susceptible to death, perishable, whereby it is not said that man *had* to die. It does appear from this pronouncement that the pneumatic resurrection is more than the restoration of the original "psychical" man; cf. also H. Bavinck, *Gereformeerde Dogmatiek*, II, p. 525; H. Berkhof, *De Mens Onderweg*, 1960, p. 95. But one cannot say that *psychikos* here has "a pejorative sense" and that "the psychic

Now over against this first Adam as living soul stands Christ, the second and last Adam, as life-giving Spirit, as well as the pneumatic body determined by him over against the psychical that is derived from the first Adam. It is clear from the manner in which the pneumatic is here connected to Christ that psychical and pneumatic do not stand over against each other as the lower and higher in the sense of a dualistic anthropology,[153] but as two modes of bodily existence, of which the resurrection of Christ forms the turning point. Paul therefore does not in general set Christ as "living Spirit" over against Adam as living soul, but says that Christ has *become* life-giving Spirit. Just as with Adam, this last denotes a beginning, which in this context is scarcely to be understood otherwise than of Christ's resurrection. From then on Christ not only "had" the Spirit, but he himself "was" the Spirit (cf. 2 Cor. 3:17), which is not to say that there would no longer be a distinction between the subject of Christ and of the Spirit, but that not only for himself but also for his own he has the Spirit at his disposal.[154] Therefore Paul speaks of Christ as the life-giving Spirit, by which he again establishes the relation between the Spirit and the resurrection in Christ. For this reason belonging to Christ not only consists in the gift of the *pneuma* in this life, but reaches out to the still to be expected quickening in accordance with Christ's resurrection (cf. v. 22). Therefore Paul also follows this up by saying in verse 46 that the spiritual (body) is not first, but the psychical, and then the spiritual. One is again not to see in this a broad pronouncement on what has priority in a general anthropological respect,[155] but rather a rejection[156] of the view that the pneumatic represents a primal datum that would be antecedent to a psychical existence sunk away from it or opposed to it and in which man does not receive a share till through Christ's coming and resurrection. Paul sets against that precisely the redemptive-historical character of the body given in Christ and of the life-giving power of the Spirit. The first and second Adam do not represent two timeless, dualistic "principles" or modes of existence standing over against each other, but stand to each other in a redemptive-historical (typical-antitypical; Rom. 5:14) relation, whereby Adam is "the first" and Christ "the second" or "the last" in the divine economy of redemption. Therefore it also applies to believers that they will bear the image of the latter, just as they have borne the image of the former (cf. v. 49). Thus when in this

body, participating in this degradation, is not only living body but fallen body," as Clavier thinks (*The Background of the N.T. and Its Eschatology*, p. 351).

153. Over against other spiritualistic conceptions of *sōma pneumatikon*, see Schweizer, *TDNT*, VI, p. 420.

154. Cf. Schweizer on 2 Cor. 3:17 (*TDNT*, VI, pp. 418f.). He correctly writes that it is plain from v. 17b that "v. 17a is not asserting the identity of two personal entities. *Pneuma* is defined as the mode of existence of the *Kyrios* ... and this means the power in which He encounters His community. In so far as Christ is regarded in His significance for the community, in His powerful action upon it, He can be identified with the *pneuma*. In so far as He is also Lord over His power, He can be differentiated from it.

155. Against this see also Berkouwer, *The Return of Christ*, pp. 191f.

156. For the polemic significance of v. 46 see Brandenburger, *Adam und Christus*, p. 74, and the literature cited there; and Schweizer, *TDNT*, VI, p. 420.

context it is said of Christ that he is the second man from heaven[157] and he is for this reason called the heavenly (v. 48), that is not an allusion to his heavenly pre-existence, nor a characteristic datum of Christ's whole human existence. Not only would it be difficult to reconcile that with what is said, for example, in Romans 8:3 of Christ's coming in the likeness of sinful flesh,[158] but also his own could not be called "the heavenly," as is done in verse 48, without contradiction with what is here first said of their earthly origin. The expression "from heaven" or "heavenly" gives a further qualification of the second man as the Risen One. It indicates that as the second Adam and as the Inaugurator of the new life of the resurrection Christ lives from the power of the heavenly, divine Spirit. In that sense accordingly those who belong to him can be spoken of as "the heavenly." They are not such because they come from heaven, or are going to heaven, but because they belong to Christ as the one living from divine power and in this way will bear the image of the heavenly, as they have once borne the image of the earthy. This future, heavenly image can now also be called the pneumatic body.[159] *Pneuma* and pneumatic thus do not denote a new substance, but a new determination or origin. The new body does not "consist of" *pneuma,* but is brought forth and determined by the divine, heavenly power.[160] For that reason (and not on the ground of

---

157. It is of particular importance to keep in view that in the expression *ho deuteros anthrōpos ex ouranou* the last *two* (and not the last *three*) words are to be taken predicatively ("the second man is from heaven," and not: "the second is the man from heaven"). That this is the only acceptable translation is evident especially from the parallel with v. 47a ("the first man is from the earth, earthy," and not: "the first is the earthy man from the earth"). It follows from this that the repeated predicative speaking of "the man from heaven" in all kinds of literature on this subject (cf., e.g., Traub, *TDNT,* V, pp. 528f.) is not Pauline. It also forms a continuous obstacle to the right explanation of 1 Cor. 15:47; see Traub, *loc. cit.,* who, despite the correct insight that Christ's exaltation is spoken of here, regards the pre-existence of Christ intended "secondarily" (!).

158. Vos, too, writes justly that if "from heaven" refers to Christ's pre-existence, Paul contradicts himself; for this would reverse the order he indicates in v. 46, namely, that it is not the pneumatic but the psychical that is first. This would also make the pneumatic "the constituent principle of the human nature in Christ before the resurrection," of which thought no trace is elsewhere to be found in Paul (*The Pauline Eschatology,* pp. 167, 168).

159. In the same manner in 1 Cor. 10:3, 4, there is mention of the pneumatic food and the pneumatic drink, which is elsewhere called the bread "from heaven" (John 6:31, 32; cf. Ps. 78:24).

160. Cf. Clavier, *The Background of the N.T. and Its Eschatology,* p. 361: "The essential characteristic of the *sōma pneumatikon* according to Paul is not being or not being a body with spirit, but an organ of the spirit, controlled by the Spirit, by the Holy Spirit." Yet he thinks (in my opinion on the basis of too "Greek" a conception of *pneumatikos*) that the formula *sōma pneumatikon* was not entirely satisfactory and that Paul therefore uses it only once (p. 355). Cf. Schweizer: "Thus the *sōma pneumatikon* of either Redeemer or believer is to be understood, not as one which consists of *pneuma,* but as one which is controlled by the *pneuma.* It must be realized, however, that this applies only to the concern of Paul. It is obvious in his terminology that like any Hellenist he thinks of power in terms of substance. Hence the matter in Paul is Jewish, his vocabulary Hellenistic" (*TDNT,* VI, p. 421). Vos writes more radically: "Every thought of immateriality or etherealness or absence of physical density ought to be kept carefully removed from the term. What-

what is inherent in the pneumatic "substance") it can now be said of this body that it is imperishable, immortal, the very model of glory and power (vv. 42, 43, 48, 53).

Paul can also write in Philippians 3:21 therefore that Christ will change our humiliated body so that it becomes conformed to his glorified body, according to the power whereby he is able even to subject all things to himself. Here again Christ himself is the one who — as life-giving Spirit — will change the body of his people. The relation between Christ's mode of existence as the Risen One and that of believers is expressed very clearly. What in 1 Corinthians 15:49 is called "bearing the image of the heavenly," is called here "becoming conformed to his [Christ's] glorified body" (cf. Rom. 8:29, where the combination of both elements occurs: "becoming conformed to the image of his [God's] Son"). One will thereby have to take the word "conformed" not only as a likeness in appearance or shape, but in mode of existence. It is a question of receiving a share in the glory of Christ, the bearing of his image. Although the first man is also called the image and the glory of God (1 Cor. 11:7), he was this nevertheless within the limits of his original mortal existence derived from the earth. Over against that, becoming conformed to the glorified body of Christ (or, as Rom. 8:29 says, to the image of God's Son) signifies sharing in the glory of God in the re-creation by the Spirit, the imperishable and immortal body of the resurrection.

Still deserving of separate discussion are verses 50-54, where the preceding argument essentially comes to its conclusion:

> Now this I say, brethren, that flesh and blood cannot inherit the kingdom of God; neither does corruption inherit incorruption.
> Behold, I tell you a mystery: we shall not all sleep, but we shall all be changed,
> in a moment, in the twinkling of an eye, at the last trumpet: for the trumpet will sound, and the dead will be raised incorruptible, and we shall be changed.
> For this corruptible must put on incorruption, and this mortal must put on immortality.
> But when this corruptible shall have put on incorruption, and this mortal shall have put on immortality, then shall come to pass the saying that is written, Death is swallowed up in victory.

There is much dispute as to whether verse 50 adds a new element to what has gone before or summarizes and confirms it. Some suppose that in verse 50 Paul dissociates himself from the materialistic, Jewish conception of the resurrection in order thereafter to come to speak of the lot of those who will still be alive at the parousia of Christ and thus will not rise from the dead.[161] In a detailed essay Jeremias has

---

ever in regard to such qualifications may or may not be involved, it is certain that such traits, if existing, are not described here by the adjective in question" (*The Pauline Eschatology*, pp. 166, 167).

161. So, e.g., Wendland, *Cor.*, pp. 103, 104; Lietzmann-Kümmel, *Cor.*, p. 86.

contended that verses 50-54 were devoted to the twofold significance that the parousia has for those who are then dead and for those who have not yet died. Already in verse 50 there is said to be a distinction between the two. By "flesh and blood" those are then intended who are alive at the parousia, by "the corruptible" the bodies in decay of those who have fallen asleep.[162] So verse 50 would already reach out to verses 51 and 52. Verses 53 and 54 also would not contain a synonymous but a synthetic parallelism: the "corruptible" are the dead, the "mortal" that which is still confronted with death, the living. The whole then forms a further answer to the *how?* in verse 35, that is, of the first question: how are the dead raised up? after the second question of verse 35 has been dealt with in verses 36-49: with what body will they come?[163] And the effect of it would be that, in divergence from the Jewish expectation and from 1 Thessalonians 4 (where nothing is said of the transformation of the survivors), Paul here pronounces as a new revelation that the change of the living and the dead takes place immediately at the parousia.

In our opinion, however, the whole interpretation that beginning with verse 50 Paul is turning against a Jewish-materialistic conception of the resurrection is incorrect. In 1 Corinthians 15 Paul is not dealing with a materialistic, but with a spiritualistic conception of the resurrection. Over against this idea, according to which the resurrection has taken place already in this life (cf. v. 19) and thus in this body, Paul, after first elucidating the manner of the resurrection and with the aid of the analogy of the seed and of the redemptive-historical contrast of Adam and Christ, establishes the necessity of this resurrection with great force, beginning with verse 50. "Now this I say" (v. 50) thus does not usher in a contrast, nor an entirely new thought, but brings to the fore the heart of the matter that is at stake in 1 Corinthians 15 with great force and with a final, conclusive argument, i.e., that of its necessity and indispensability.

He first puts the argument negatively (in v. 50). That in so doing he is already distinguishing between those still alive ("flesh and blood") and those who have already died ("the corruptible") is hardly plausible on the ground of the terms employed. "This" perishable, as he expresses it in verse 53, obviously refers, just as "this" mortal, to the existing earthly life and earthly body, and not to that which is in process of decomposition in the grave. In addition this conception is the consequence of the idea that Paul's special object in these verses is a further revelation about what is to take place at the parousia — on the one hand with the survivors, on the other with those who have died. This is the point of view of 1 Thessalonians 4, as we have seen. But it is not the point of view here. It is a matter in general of maintaining the future resurrection of the body over against those who denied it. Verse 51 is also

---

Often the further thought is attached that here in Paul a more spiritual conception of the resurrection reveals itself (in comparison, e.g., with 1 Thess. 4); see further below, n. 165.

162. "Flesh and Blood Cannot Inherit the Kingdom of God," *NTS*, II, 1955/56, p. 152; indeed following A. Schlatter, *Paulus der Bote Jesu*, 1934, pp. 441ff.

163. *Ibid.*, p. 157.

in that line of thought. It carries on the reasoning of verse 50. Even though all will not sleep[164] — the first clause of verse 51 has a concessive force — what is said in verse 50 also applies to the survivors. To that end the apostle discloses a "mystery," something that is still concealed in the veils of the divine counsel, but is to be realized before long. How he is in a position to speak thus he does not explain further. In 1 Thessalonians 4:15 he makes a similar pronouncement on the ground of "a word of the Lord." It is possible that the mystery in 1 Corinthians 15:51 is also to be understood in this way. It is also possible, however, that "mystery" here denotes that which has not yet been realized, but for one who has insight into the way of the Lord, as the apostle and the prophet, is even so not unknown (cf. Rom. 11:25; 1 Cor. 13:2). But, in any case, the announcement of this mystery is not intended only as an announcement, but serves to elucidate further what is expressed in verse 50; no one, not even those who are alive at the parousia, can in this body inherit the kingdom of God. When the last trumpet sounds, those who have died will be raised imperishable (that is, in a new body) and we, insofar as we have not fallen asleep, shall be changed. For — so verse 53, with the adducing of the ground for which this is to take place thus — this corruptible must put on incorruption and this mortal immortality. This is the positive statement of what is expressed negatively in verse 50. It is a question of "must," of the necessity laid down by God of the resurrection (c.q., of the change) and of the new body. And then (only), when this all shall have taken place, the prophecy of the swallowing up of death in victory will be fulfilled.

In this train of thought, which fits entirely in the framework of the argument of 1 Corinthians 15 carried on to this point and forms its impressive conclusion, there is no need whatever to think of some implied alteration or another in the Pauline expectation for the future.[165]

---

164. It is presupposed that the text *pantes ou koimēthēsometha, pantes de allagēsometha* is original. There are many variants. But that the text we have followed (of Nestle) is original is hardly contested any longer, and has already been frequently elucidated in detail; cf., e.g., Lietzmann-Kümmel, *Cor.*, pp. 195, 196, and the literature cited there. That one need not take *pantes ou* as a negation holding for all, but can also take it in the sense of "not all" has been demonstrated, e.g., by Bl.-Debr., Par. 433, 2*. *Pantes* is first because it is so also in the second half. There is also something to be felt, to be sure, for the conception of Grosheide, who wishes to place *ou koimēthēsometha* between dashes and to translate: "we shall all — not sleep indeed — but all be changed." The exegesis, however, comes to the same thing. One can posit that Paul here — if in a concessive clause — expresses the expectation that he and his contemporaries will not all sleep. It only depends on how narrowly one wants to take "we." Elsewhere he says that God will raise "us" up (from the dead) (1 Cor. 6:14), or "will quicken your mortal bodies" (Rom. 8:11). This does not intend to say that the future perspective in Paul's pronouncements is unrestricted, but that he is not able to draw a line of demarcation between who would and who would not live to experience the parousia. He does not in any case promise this experience to any one of his contemporaries; such a promise does not pertain to his proclamation of redemption. See further above, Section 74, pp. 490f.

165. Jeremias points here to the influential publication of E. Teichmann, *Die paulinischen Vorstellungen von Auferstehung und Gericht*, 1896. He thinks that the spiritualistic conception of 1 Cor. 15:50a has played a "disastrous role" in New Testament theology. He attempts to counter this influence by his new conception of 1 Cor. 15:50a (according to which in the first part of v. 50 there is no mention

When there is mention here of a "change" of those still alive at the parousia, this is not to be regarded as the breaking through of a new insight taking the place of a Jewish conception still maintained in 1 Thessalonians 4, according to which the dead would appear in their former bodies and there would as yet be no question of a "change" of the survivors. For there is no reason whatever to think that when Paul speaks of the resurrection in 1 Thessalonians 4:16, he intends another resurrection than that in 1 Corinthians 15; and just as little that the "change" of the survivors signifies something new with respect to 1 Thessalonians 4. Although it is true that this "change" is not mentioned in 1 Thessalonians 4, the *argumentum e silentio* says nothing because in 1 Thessalonians 4 something entirely different is under discussion, i.e., the lot of those who have died before the parousia. This whole reasoning rests on the incorrect conception that in 1 Corinthians 15:50 ("flesh and blood will not inherit the kingdom of God") Paul is dissociating himself from a "materializing" conception of the resurrection body that he himself once held (in part), whereas it was, as everyone must recognize, precisely the spiritualizing heresy in Corinth that he combats in this chapter. That without any further indication he would in verse 50 suddenly change front is even in itself difficult to suppose, but also finds no support whatever in the clearly anti-spiritualizing purport of verses 50-54. The contrary is rather the case.

One can ask finally whether anything further is to be said in an anthropological respect about the bodily resurrection that Paul so vigorously upholds. This question also touches the manner in which the apostle gives expression to the continuity of the present and future life.

So far as the first is concerned, it is of importance to keep in view that Paul constantly denotes the future resurrection as the being raised, the glorifying of the body. The manner in which he expresses himself in so doing signifies a clear corroboration of what we have already been able to observe in general with regard to the Pauline use of "body."[166] There is mention here of "body" and not, for example, of "flesh." "Flesh," even when it is not used in the sense of sinful existence, always has the meaning of that which is only temporal. It denotes man in his weakness and mortality.[167] "Body," on the other hand, typifies man as

---

of the resurrection). But by understanding 1 Cor. 15:50a of the surviving and with respect to these still alive then assuming in Paul a certain (spiritualizing) turn with regard to 1 Thess. 4 (in the manner of Teichmann), his opposition to this spiritualizing interpretation of the close of 1 Cor. 15 (according to him "a commonplace in New Testament scholarship" [*ibid.*, p. 158]) contains something half-hearted, especially in view of the unsatisfactory distinction he makes between v. 50a and v. 50b. One can get further only by taking v. 50 precisely as a continuation of the opposition to spiritualism; see above, the text. For the unwarrantedness of this "change of position" of Paul in the matter of the resurrection see further Section 74, pp. 491ff.

166. Cf. above, Section 19, pp. 115ff.

167. It has therefore rightly been observed by various interpreters that the confessional expression "resurrection of the flesh" is not in harmony with the Pauline usage and would not be possible in it. On this question in detail see W. Bieder, "Auferstehung des Fleisches oder des Leibes," *TZ*, 1945, pp. 105-112; cf. Cullmann,

he has been created by God, for God's glory, and to his service and therefore as he is raised from the dead and saved by God. This is not of course to say that the human body as it now exists is not to die and perish or be changed. In that sense it applies to the present body no less than to "flesh and blood" that it cannot inherit the kingdom of God. But what is raised and changed is nevertheless denoted as "body."

Furthermore, it is of paramount importance that "body" in this context, too, does not denote the material "part" of man, to be distinguished from the "soul" or the "spirit," in the sense of the Greek dichotomy, but rather man's whole mode of existence, before as well as after the resurrection. Insofar as there is mention of "soul" in the pronouncements discussed here, this serves simply as a further qualification of man in his temporal and perishable existence. And insofar as there is mention of the "spiritual," it is the glorified character of the new body originating from the Holy Spirit that is denoted, and the question as to whether or not it is material remains entirely out of consideration. That "body" here denotes the whole man is apparent also from the practically synonymous use of "raising of the body" in 1 Corinthians 15:44 with "resurrection of the dead" in verse 42; just as it is said in verse 52 that "the dead" will be raised and that "we" shall be changed. On the other hand, a distinction is again made in verse 35 between the subject of the risen man and his body ("with what kind of body do they come?"), and it is said in verse 49 that "we" have borne the image of the earthy (the natural body of v. 44) and that "we" shall bear the image of the heavenly (the spiritual body of v. 44). However difficult it may be to come to adequate distinctions here, it can be ascertained that the "I" of man can at one time be identified with his body, then again distinguished from it. The body thus denotes the total mode of existence of man, before and after his resurrection, but then in such a way that man himself (the "I"), as the bearer (v. 49) respectively of the image of the earthy and of the heavenly, is once again to be distinguished from it. In the same manner it can at one time be said that "we" shall all be changed (1 Cor. 15:51, 52), then again that "our body" will be changed[168] (Phil. 3:21).

If nothing other is here the object of the raising of the body than man himself in the totality of his functions and capacities and if that which is raised is not to be restricted to the material and visible aspects of the present man, then the question emerges as to the con-

---

"Unsterblichkeit der Seele und Auferstehung der Toten," TZ, 1956, p. 147; see also Schweizer, TDNT, VII, pp. 128f. G. C. Berkouwer, The Return of Christ, denies that one is allowed to call the words "resurrection of the flesh" un-Pauline. He appeals to 1 Cor. 15:53, where Paul says that this corruptible puts on incorruption (pp. 192ff.; see also his Man the Image of God, p. 232, n. 47). This corruptible is undoubtedly the same as the "flesh and blood" in v. 50. But it has not been proved therewith that, according to the Pauline usage, one could still call the corruptible, when it shall have put on incorruption, flesh. This does apply to "body," but (in Paul) certainly not to "flesh." Otherwise this is a question of usage. There need not be a material difference here between "resurrection of the body" and what the church means by "resurrection of the flesh." So Berkouwer, too (loc. cit.).

168. To be sure, another word is employed in Phil. 3:21 (metaschēmatizō) than in 1 Cor. 15:51 (allattō).

tinuity and identity of life before and after the resurrection. The figure employed by Paul of the seed and sowing is often related to this, and the conclusion drawn from it that just as "the germ" of the seed is continued in the life of the new plant, so a continuity and identity of the natural and spiritual body is capable of being vindicated.[169]

But a more than superficial consideration of the text teaches that the whole metaphor of the seed and sowing is not intended to establish such a connection, and in any case is not so applied. It is just said that what is sown dies and is made alive. Of a kernel or germ that remains alive there is therefore not only no mention, but also no presupposition. The thought is rather that the one is substituted for the other. It is not being reaped or harvested that stands over against being sown, but being raised. The first represents the old that died, the second the new that is raised by the omnipotence of God; and for the latter, reference is then made to the sovereignty of God in giving every being its own body and its own glory. The continuity and identity is consequently not to be sought in something that passes from the old body into the new body, but in the miraculous power of God. The same thing is implied in 1 Corinthians 15:47. In the first clause it is said indeed of what "material" the first man consists (of the earth earthy); but in the second clause it is said of "the second man" and the humanity derived from him that he is "from heaven," whereby not his "substantiality," but his divine origin, his miraculous character, is denoted.[170] In this miraculous power of God the continuity and the identity between the psychical and the pneumatic body is guaranteed. And it is on that ground that Paul can say that "the dead" will be raised and that "we" shall be changed. Although this "we" cannot be made transparent anthropologically, he nevertheless confesses the identity in anthropological terms as well.

He is also able to express it in a christological way. It is the dead-in-Christ who will rise, and it is in virtue of that corporate unity with Christ that those who die in him will be raised by him. Not only does the identity lie in this belonging to him, but also the continuity, which is not (temporarily) abrogated even by death, and this also holds for those who have fallen asleep before the parousia. Here the reality of the "intermediate state"[171] fits in, although Paul does not say a word about it in 1 Corinthians 15. It consists in being "of the Lord" and "with Christ" and "with the Lord," for those who have died also. As those who in this way belong and continue to belong to the Lord they will rise.

Finally, there is again the pneumatological viewpoint. For what is true of being joined to Christ is also true of believers as being "in the Spirit," that is to say, living under his regime (Rom. 8:9). The same Spirit, in virtue of whose omnipotence the body of the resurrection is a "spiritual body," even now dwells and works in believers as living souls.

---

169. On this see, e.g., the old exegeses cited by Clavier, *The Background of the N.T. and Its Eschatology*, pp. 342, 347; also Berkouwer, *The Return of Christ*, pp. 188ff.

170. Cf. Schweizer, *TDNT*, VI, p. 421.

171. Cf. above, Section 75.

What establishes the connection between life before and after the resurrection and what "passes over" from the one into the other is the Spirit and being under the rulership of the Spirit. Insofar as man is flesh and blood he will not inherit the kingdom of God (1 Cor. 15:50), but the kingdom of God is nevertheless already present time in righteousness, peace, and joy through the Holy Spirit (Rom. 14:17). What "abides" is faith, hope, and love (1 Cor. 13:13). That undoubtedly presupposes the human mode of existence, a future "ontological" structure of man, in virtue of which even after the resurrection he can believe, hope, and love. On that account the resurrection of the body pertains to the inalienable content of the Christian kerygma. Believers will bear the image of the heavenly as men and not as other beings. The Spirit not only works in man, therefore, but also renews his manhood. But the secret of the continuity does not lie in the human "being," but in the Spirit. And the firm ground of the belief that the mortal will one day put on immortality is in conformity with it. He who has prepared us to that end is God, who has given us the Spirit as an earnest (2 Cor. 5:5). In that sense the renewing and working of the Spirit in believers during their present life can also be understood as a beginning of the resurrection of the body, and be described by Paul in this way (cf. 2 Cor. 3:18; 4:10, 11, 16, 17; Eph. 5:14; Phil. 3:10, 11). So the shining of the glory of the future life illuminates them even now (2 Cor. 3:18; 4:6), a firstfruit and earnest in the present time of their resurrection from the dead (cf. Gal. 6:8; Rom. 8:23; 2 Cor. 5:5).[172]

The apostle does not give a further representation of this resurrection body or life. It is a "body of glory" (Phil. 3:21; 1 Cor. 15:43), the mirroring in perfection of the glory of the Lord, being transformed after his image from glory to glory (2 Cor. 3:18). It is, likewise in sharing in the gifts of the Spirit, a doing away with and putting off of that which is still "in part" (1 Cor. 13:9, 10). It is no longer to walk in faith but in sight (2 Cor. 5:7), no longer to see by a mirror in riddles but face to face; knowing as we ourselves are known (1 Cor. 13:12). This existence can also be described in the expression "to be always with the Lord" (1 Thess. 4:18).

SECTION 79. THE JUDGMENT

In Paul's expectation for the future the last judgment is closely connected with the parousia of the Lord and the resurrection of the dead. We have already mentioned[173] the qualification of the parousia

---

172. On this point also see Hamilton, *The Holy Spirit and Eschatology in Paul*, pp. 19ff.; G. Vos, *The Pauline Eschatology*, pp. 200ff.; K. Deissner, *Auferstehungshoffnung*, p. 69; Behm, *TDNT*, I, p. 475, *s.v. arrabōn*; E. Schweizer, "Gegenwart des Geistes und eschatologische Hoffnung," in *The Background of the New Testament and Its Eschatology*, pp. 504ff.

173. Cf. Section 77, p. 530.

as "the day of the Lord" and the thought of the judgment linked with it. Paul here stands entirely in the tradition of the Old Testament and of Judaism, in which the day of the Lord signifies both redemption and judgment (cf. Amos 5:18ff.). That God will one day judge the world is for him an axiom. When in Romans 3:5ff. he repudiates the thought that God could act unjustly he appeals to the fact that God is after all to judge the world. This he will do without respect of persons (Rom. 2:11); he will bring the hidden things to light (Rom. 2:16); and he will render to every man according to his works (Rom. 2:6). This general expectation is now, as in the whole of the New Testament, linked with that of the parousia of Christ. Paul charges Timothy by God and by Jesus Christ, who will judge the living and the dead (2 Tim. 4:1). That which in the Old Testament has reference to God's judging and punishing righteousness is in quoting simply applied to Christ (cf., e.g., 2 Thess. 1:8ff.; 2:8). There is mention at one time of appearing before the judgment seat of God (Rom. 14:10), then again before that of Christ (2 Cor. 5:10). There is thus no consistent and exclusive usage. The theological and christological viewpoints go together. But what is said about the coming judgment and the day of the Lord is concentrated even so about the work and the parousia of Christ. Therein lies the stronger pregnance of judgment in Paul (and in general in the New Testament) in comparison with that of the Old Testament and later Jewish apocalyptic.[174]

We have already seen[175] that the judgment and the revelation of the wrath of God are not spoken of only in a future sense, but that Paul draws the attention of his readers to the fact that this wrath — that is to say, the judgment — is already revealing itself (Rom. 1:18ff.). Therein the restraint is already broken that God has exercised till now and which is intended to lead men to repentance (Rom. 3:26; 2:4); just as already in the death of Christ he shows his righteousness, both judging and acquitting (Rom. 3:25, 26).[176] Likewise the present revelation of God's judgment can be spoken of with reference to the affliction and persecution to which the church must presently be exposed. In 2 Thessalonians 1:5 Paul terms that an "evidence of the righteous judgment of God." The meaning is that these persecutions[177] disclose the share of believers in the coming kingdom, just as for their opponents they are an evidence of their judgment (Phil. 1:28).

The judgment of Christ, too, is sometimes spoken of already in a present sense, especially with reference to the church. The apostle points this judgment out in the cases of sickness and death that occurred in the church of Corinth as a result of the profanation of the Lord's Supper[178]

---

174. So Delling, *TDNT*, II, p. 952, *s.v. hēmera*.

175. Cf. above, Section 18, pp. 109ff.

176. Cf. above, Section 28, p. 169.

177. Others seek this evidence in their patience and faith; cf., e.g., Frame, *Thessalonians*, p. 226. But the context points clearly in another direction; see also Dibelius, *Th.*, p. 41; cf. Phil. 1:28.

178. See above, Section 67, p. 427. For the element of judgment appearing here see Leon Morris, *The Biblical Doctrine of Judgment*, 1960, p. 45; C. F. D. Moule,

(1 Cor. 11:30, 31). It does not have a definitive, condemnatory significance, but is intended simply to warn the church against it (v. 32). It is
meant as a chastisement and as a stimulus for subjecting itself to a
searching examination. Elsewhere Paul speaks to a still stronger effect of
the judgment on sinners in the church even now coming about in the
power of Christ; here again, however, as a judgment that must have the
goal of salvation and not only destruction (1 Cor. 5:4ff.).[179]

The proper focus of the Pauline pronouncements on the judgment lies, however, in the parousia of Christ. We have already seen[180]
how the separative significance of Christ's parousia governs its description in the great passage of 2 Thessalonians 1:5-10. That which now
becomes knowable of this judgment in the opposition to the church
(cf. Phil. 1:28) points toward the great reversal of all things to be expected at the coming of Christ (2 Thess. 1:6ff.).

So far, first of all, as the representation of the great judgment at
Christ's coming is concerned, this is done from various points of view
that are not always easy to combine. At one time all the accent is placed
on the common significance of the judgment, applying to all in the same
way. So, for example, in Romans 2:1-16, where against Jewish self-conceit
Paul with great emphasis sets the fact that on the day of wrath and of
the revelation of his righteous judgment God will render to every man
according to his works. For there is no acceptance of persons with God.
Not the hearers, but the doers of the law will be justified in the day
when God judges the secrets of men. That Paul here does not merely
occupy "pre-evangelical" ground in order to carry the idea of righteousness from works *ad absurdum*[181] appears sufficiently clearly from such a
pronouncement as Romans 14:10, 11, where against the inclination to
discrimination within the church he points to the coming judgment:
"for we shall all stand before the judgment seat of God." And in 2 Corinthians 5:10, where the judgment seat of Christ is mentioned in the
same terms, the general warning follows: "so that each one may receive
good or evil, according to what he has done in the body." For this universality of the judgment Paul in Romans 14:11 appeals to the prophetic
words of Isaiah 49:18 and 45:23: "As I live, says the Lord, every knee
shall bow before me."

Elsewhere, however, it is not the commonness but the separation
in the coming judgment that is to the fore. Already at the appearing
of Christ the great separation is carried into effect. For the unbelieving
and ungodly Christ's coming signifies judgment and destruction. He
reveals himself with flaming fire to execute judgment on those who are
unbelieving and disobedient and to exclude them from his blessed
presence; while in that day he will be glorified in his saints and be
marvelled at in them (2 Thess. 1:8ff.). For his saints, in distinction from

---

"The Judgment Theme in the Sacraments," in *The Background of the New Testament and Its Eschatology*, pp. 476ff.

179. See above, Section 72, p. 471.
180. Above, Section 77.
181. So Lietzmann, *Rom.*, pp. 39, 40.

those who do not belong to him, will at once be caught up to meet him at his appearing (1 Thess. 4:17). Of an antecedent common act of judgment there is no mention.

There need, of course, be no contradiction between the two. We have to do here with two different points of view: believers will not come to the judgment in the same manner as unbelievers and the ungodly, but rather are secured against it by Christ (1 Thess. 1:10); on the other hand, God will do justice to all and according to the same standard (cf. also Eph. 6:9; Col. 3:24, 25). Here again it appears that the presentation of the eschatological reality is fragmentary, is not intended to be nor can be a source of information, but under all kinds of traditional figures and phrases makes the church understand the absolute significance of being *with* or *against* Christ, not only with an eye to the present, but also to the great future. So there can be mention in two different senses of the fire with which the day of the Lord will appear (1 Cor. 3:13). On the one hand there is in this fire an indication of the inexorableness of punishment and the irretrievableness of those who fall under the judgment of God (2 Thess. 1:8), a punishment and a fate from which Christ will keep and deliver his own (1 Thess. 1:10; 5:9; Rom. 5:9); on the other hand, the fire of the judgment as a refining fire concerns all human work, even that of those who have built on the foundation of Christ. The fire will burn away and consume all that is shoddy in it. However, it will not devour the believer himself. He will be saved, but as through fire (1 Cor. 3:13-15).

How much we have to do here with realities the presentation of which in a great many respects bears a fragmentary and inadequate character is evident surely from the impossibility of coming from the various elements and moments of this preaching of judgment to an at all rounded off and systematic conception. Paul's pronouncements here bear the character of flashing, prophetic warnings, which illuminate for an instant the awful seriousness of the great future, not of a doctrine that in fixed order and piece by piece indicates the component parts of the picture of the future and combines them with each other into an integral unity. This applies in particular to the punitive judgment on unbelievers and the ungodly. Paul declares the certainty of this judgment in an unmistakable way, in many respects with words that have been derived from the Old Testament preaching of judgment. He speaks of it as ruin, death, payment with an eternal destruction (1 Thess. 5:3; 2 Thess. 1:9; Phil. 1:28; 3:19; Rom. 6:21); wrath, indignation, tribulation, anguish (Rom. 2:8, 9). But nowhere is the how, the where, or the how long "treated" as a separate "subject" of Christian doctrine in the epistles of Paul that have been preserved to us. Thus the question can be asked, for example, whether the judgment on unbelievers and the ungodly, as that on believers, presupposes a resurrection and whether one can thus extend what Paul says in 1 Corinthians 15 about the resurrection of the body to unbelievers as well. On the one hand such a resurrection seems essential when one takes into consideration that the judgment appears to be effected with the coming of Christ on earth and, according to the presentation, in the sphere of what is visible and in the full sense human. On the other hand it is indisputable that the whole maintenance of the resurrection against the contradiction of it in Corinth rests on the unity of Christ and his own and is therefore applicable only to the latter. It is also difficult to draw a conclusion on the ground of 2 Thessalonians 1:8ff. For here it is apparently only those alive at Christ's coming who are in view. We cannot therefore conclude otherwise than that, although the thought of a general resurrection of the dead seems most to correspond to the nature of the judgment that is to take place with the parousia and is also in harmony with what is communicated to us in Acts 24:15 as a pronouncement of Paul, his epistles neither directly nor indirectly contain any data on the basis of which we could come to know further the expectation and thought of the apostle with respect to it.

As concerns the judgment on those who belong to Christ by faith, the thought is here certainly that the resurrection precedes the judgment. Yet here again every programmatic description of a sequence of events and how it is to happen is lacking. What gives Paul's judgment pronouncements a character of their own is that Christ forms the point of concentration and integration of all the traditional ideas, as we find them also in the Old Testament and in part in later Judaism as well, and that the preaching of the judgment therefore is preaching of Christ. This means that life as it now stands has, to be sure, already found its initial criterion in Christ, but still awaits its definitive judgment in his future revelation. Only when Christ is revealed in glory will his own also be manifested (Col. 3:3, 4). His coming is the revealing of the sons of God, for which the whole creation waits with outstretched neck (Rom. 8:19). But at the same time this revelatory character of the parousia is a cause for watchfulness and self-examination. This thought of revelation or disclosing is one of the dominating motifs in Paul's preaching of judgment. Every man's work will then become manifest *(phaneron genēsetai)*. For the day will declare it *(deloō)*, because it will be revealed *(apokalyptō)* with fire, and the fire will prove *(dokimazō)* of what sort every man's work is (1 Cor. 3:13). Therefore no one is to judge before the time, that is, before the Lord has come who will bring to light *(phōtizō)* the things now hidden in darkness and will disclose the purposes of the heart; and then each man will receive his commendation from God (1 Cor. 4:5). Then the great unmasking of that which is now done in secret is also to take place. For all this becomes visible *(phaneroō)* when it is exposed *(elenchō)* by the light, for all that becomes visible is light. Therefore it is said: "awake thou that sleepest and arise from the dead, and Christ will shine *(epiphauō)* upon thee" (Eph. 5:13, 14).

On the one hand this central place of Christ in the Pauline preaching of judgment does not, as we have already been able to ascertain in another context,[182] abolish the reality of the judgment as the divine judgment on every man's deeds and as reward according to works.

---

182. Cf. above, Section 31.

For God has created his own in Christ Jesus for good works (Eph. 2:10), and therefore their belonging to him must be manifested in good works. Hence Paul's pronouncements on the judgment as the receiving of what each one has done, the reaping of what he has sown, etc. (cf. 2 Cor. 5:10; Gal. 6:7ff.; Eph. 6:8). On the other hand the comfort and certainty of believers also lie in the fact that Christ will judge the world. They will be manifested in their belonging to him, and no one will be able to bring any charge against them (Rom. 8:33). They will be placed at his side and with him judge the world, and even the angels (1 Cor. 6:2, 3).

SECTION 80. THE CONSUMMATION. THE ETERNAL STATE

The parousia of Christ with the accompanying resurrection of the dead and execution of the judgment at the same time forms the transition to the consummation of all things and the eternal state. The work of Christ is then completed and through him all things return to God (cf. 1 Cor. 15:28; Rom. 11:36; 1 Cor. 8:6).

Scholars have not infrequently thought themselves able to observe further in Paul a final interim phase between that which is to take place at Christ's parousia and the end of all things, namely, that of an "intermediate kingdom" after the (first) resurrection and before the consummation. They appeal for this in particular to 1 Corinthians 15:23ff., and in conjunction with that to 1 Thessalonians 4:13-18. Without mentioning the word, Paul is said here to give expression to what is called in the Apocalypse of John the millennial kingdom.

This conception is very old and has often been refuted.[183] Nevertheless it emerges time and again and also has defenders in more recent literature.[184] The view is presented in more than one way. They go farthest who consider that in 1 Corinthians 15 not only is an "intermediate kingdom" indicated, but also two resurrections. Appeal is then made to the familiar passage in 1 Corinthians 15:22ff.:

> For as in Adam all die, so also in Christ shall they be made alive.
> But each in his own order *(tagmati):* Christ as the firstfruits; then *(epeita)* they that are Christ's at his parousia;
> thereafter *(eita)* the end, when he delivers the kingdom to God the Father, when he shall have abolished all rule and authority and power....

First of all, those who hold this view appeal for the idea of a

---

183. It is discussed at length and rejected by G. Vos, *The Pauline Eschatology*, pp. 226-260; cf. J. Héring, "Saint Paul a-t-il enseigné deux résurrections?," *Revue d'Histoire et de Philosophie religieuses*, 1931, pp. 300-320; W. Masselink, *Why Thousand Years?*, 2nd ed., 1930, pp. 187ff.

184. See, e.g., H. Bietenhard, *Das tausendjährige Reich*, 1955, pp. 55ff.; G. Schrenk, *Die Weissagung über Israel im Neuen Testament*, 1951, pp. 54ff., 71. A detailed discussion of the new conceptions is also to be found in Berkouwer, *The Return of Christ*, pp. 301ff.

double resurrection to the words: all shall be made alive in Christ. This would already presuppose more than the resurrection of believers at Christ's parousia. They think that with the words "then" and "thereafter" in verses 23 and 24, there is mention not of one, but of two resurrections (after that of Christ). On this account some[185] wish to translate the words "thereafter the end" by "thereafter the rest," whereby the remaining persons (unbelieving Jews and gentiles[186]) not yet made alive at the first resurrection are to be understood. Others who shrink from this translation are nevertheless of the opinion that by "the end" the end of the event of the resurrection is denoted.[187] Finally, in harmony with all this, instead of the translation "order" in verse 23 the word is also rendered by "class" or "division,"[188] whereby once again the two groups of those who have been made alive are said to be intended. The second resurrection would then come at the close of the "intermediate kingdom," in which the final battle is fought against the powers (v. 24). Some also suppose, finally, that they find support for this conception in 1 Thessalonians 4: the anxiety there discussed with respect to deceased believers would then have no reference to their resurrection in general, but to their share in the first resurrection.[189] This accordingly is alleged to be the reason why Paul says in 1 Thessalonians 4:15 that those who are alive will in no case "precede" those who have fallen asleep.

This whole conception is untenable, however. Not only does it rest on the introduction of the idea (taken from Rev. 20) of the millennial kingdom into the context of 1 Corinthians 15:22ff.,[190] but it is also not to be reconciled with the clear meaning of this passage. In the first place, how could one understand the expression "all in Christ shall be made alive" other than of "those who are Christ's"? It would be altogether in conflict with the continuous significance of this typical Pauline corporate usage.[191] "All" can here mean only: all who belong to Christ. Of another resurrection Paul does not mean to speak in 1 Corinthians 15. There is therefore no reason for, but indeed a great objection against, thinking of different groups of persons (to be raised) in verses 23ff. and to that end translating *tagma* in verse 23 by "division," "class," and *telos* in verse 24 by "rest." Not only do these words lend themselves very little to that and is *telos* in particular very clearly robbed of its obvious sense (see below), but there is also no occasion in the course of the argument to think of any such successive series of quickenings or resurrections. The apostle certainly wants to fix the church in a specific sequence or order *(tagma)* in the resurrection event, but this concerns (a) Christ as firstfruits and (b) those who are Christ's in his parousia. When the words "thereafter *(eita)* the end" follow, it is not at all neces-

185. So, e.g., Lietzmann, *Cor.,* p. 193.
186. So Lietzmann, *in loc.*
187. Bachmann (in Zahn's commentary) takes *to telos* as *to telos tou zōopoieisthai.*
188. E.g., in Lietzmann.
189. Cf. J. Dupont, [*SYN CHRISTŌ*], p. 84.
190. Cf. Kümmel in the "Anhang" to Lietzmann, *Cor.,* p. 193.
191. Cf. above, pp. 340ff.

sary to see in this "thereafter" a continuation of the "then" (*epeita*) in verse 23, in the sense that the words "thereafter the end" denote the final phase of the resurrection event. The intention is exclusively that the church continue to distinguish between the order in the resurrection of Christ and that of believers at his parousia; and that "thereafter" or "then"[192] the end comes. One must surely keep the purport of the whole argument in view here. Paul polemicizes against those who as members of the church (cf. 1 Cor. 15:12) apparently did believe in the resurrection of Christ but no longer expected a resurrection of the dead. Over against this error Paul sets the divine order: Christ as the firstfruits; thereafter, at the parousia, those who are Christ's. In this train of thought not only is there no occasion for a third category following that, but it also falls entirely outside the sphere of thought. The words "thereafter the end" are intended to say that "then and not before" will the end, the consummation, have come. The church may and must now still live in expectation, therefore. Christ will only have completed his work with and after the resurrection of believers in his parousia. Thus by "end" in this context is not to be understood the outcome of things, but, as the use of this word in an eschatological context also teaches elsewhere: the consummation of the world, the completion that at the same time signifies a new beginning of what has thus been completed and which is described in verse 28 with the words "that God may be all in all."[193]

If in the interpretation of 1 Corinthians 15:22ff. one will therefore have to abandon entirely the idea of a second resurrection, the less extreme conception of an "intermediate kingdom" between the parousia (v. 23) and the end (v. 24) is likewise not to be derived from the text, but is clearly read into it. In recent years this conception has been advocated especially by Cullmann. He lays the emphasis on the last part of verse 24, in which there is mention of the transfer of the kingship from Christ to the Father, when he shall have destroyed all the powers. Cullmann thinks that therewith the last phase of Christ's work is denoted, namely, the destruction of the already conquered powers, and this would then take place in a "final act" falling between "parousia" and "end," which is elsewhere called the millennial kingdom.[194]

The great objection to this view is that one would have to assume

---

192. Vos writes correctly that *eita* "can be used as well as [*tote*] to express momentary sequence of events" (*The Pauline Eschatology*, p. 243); cf. Arndt-Gingrich-Bauer, p. 233, *s.v. eita*: "In enumerations [*eita*] often serves to put things in juxtaposition without reference to chronological sequence."

193. P. J. Du Plessis, [*TELEIOS*], *The Idea of Perfection in the New Testament:* "the eschatological connotation of *telos* is an association and identification with the Parousia" (p. 163). And on p. 166, with an appeal to the investigations of A. Feuillet: "there is every reason to disregard [*telos*] and [*synteleia*] as synonyms." With respect to 1 Cor. 15:24 he writes: "One might say [*eita to telos*], but then begins a new order of things with the subjection of every possible opposing power until the final state [*hina hē ho Theos panta en pasin*] (15:28). Christological mediation remains until this stage."

194. Cf. O. Cullmann, "The Kingship of Christ and the Church in the New Testament," in *The Early Church*, 1956, p. 112; *Christ and Time*, pp. 151f.

this entire "intermediate kingdom" only on the ground of the words "thereafter (the end)." We have already set forth above that these words find a very natural explanation if one takes the parousia as the overture of the end setting in immediately thereafter. On the other hand, great objections against this conception of the intermediate kingdom arise out of the text as well. It is difficult to conclude otherwise from 1 Corinthians 15:50ff. than that the parousia itself and the resurrection taking place with it signify the end of the power of death. And inasmuch as death is the last enemy, the destruction of the remaining powers ("when he shall have destroyed all rule and authority and power") will have to be understood not as a final struggle beginning after the parousia, but as the definitive victory of Christ that has already begun in his cross and resurrection and exaltation (cf., e.g., Col. 2:15), and is now finally settled at, and in virtue of, his parousia[195] (cf. 2 Thess. 2:8). This view seems to us, at least on the ground of the Pauline pronouncements, much more acceptable than that one still has to conceive of a battle for the destruction of the powers and of death, which would in the parousia have only its beginning and point of departure. Such a final phase or intermediate kingdom must in any case be introduced into the text as a presupposition,[196] and has no basis in all Paul's preaching of the last things, so far as that is known to us.[197]

If 1 Corinthians 15:23ff. thus furnishes no ground for the view that with the parousia only a provisional objective has as yet been reached, on the other hand there is here a further explication of the condition ushered in by the parousia and the resurrection of the dead: the consummation, the delivering up by Christ to the Father of the kingdom now no longer challenged by any power whatever, the fact that God is all in all.

In these pronouncements the theocentric point of view comes to the fore with particular force. Elsewhere the condition of consummation dawning for believers is described more in christocentric categories. The most inclusive description surely, as we have already been able to observe, is that of 1 Thessalonians 4:17: "to be always with the Lord." This being with Christ denotes a communion that, as has been pointed out by Dupont in particular,[198] must be taken in a very comprehensive way. The content of this being-with-Christ is accordingly elucidated and explained in other pronouncements in a great many ways. In 2 Timothy 2:12 this "living with him" is further defined as "reigning with him." And the same idea is present in Romans 5:17, where there is mention of the justified "reigning in [eternal] life through the One Jesus Christ." Elsewhere this "being with Christ" finds explanation in the expressions: "be glorified with him," "joint-heirs with Christ" (Rom. 8:17), and "having an inheritance in the kingdom of Christ" (Eph. 5:5).

---

195. See also R. Schnackenburg, *God's Rule and Kingdom*, ET 1963, p. 296.

196. So also C. H. Lindijer, *Kerk en Koninkrijk*, 1962, p. 35.

197. For the appeal to 1 Thess. 4 see the cogent refutation by G. Vos, *The Pauline Eschatology*, pp. 246ff.

198. J. Dupont, [*SYN CHRISTŌ*], pp. 79-113.

In general there is of course no contradiction in this twofold (theocentric and christocentric) point of view. All things are from God and through God and unto God (Rom. 11:36). The new life of the resurrection is for those who are Christ's, therefore, a life before God, at his disposal and to his glory (Rom. 6:11, 13). What they receive in communion with Christ is the riches of the glory of God, which he gives to his saints as their inheritance (Eph. 1:18). In being joint-heirs with Christ they are joint-heirs of God (Rom. 8:17; Col. 1:12). And this inheritance in Christ's kingdom (Eph. 5:5) is nothing other than to share in the kingdom of God (Rom. 14:17). But on the other hand, the fundamental thought of all Paul's preaching of salvation is that they do not receive this otherwise than in communion with Christ, that they have been chosen in him from before the foundation of the world to live holy and blameless lives before God and to be conformed to his image that he might be the firstborn among many brethren (Eph. 1:4; Rom. 8:29ff.).

One may ask, to be sure, whether the transfer of the kingship by Christ to the Father so expressly declared in 1 Corinthians 15:24 must be seen as an end of Christ's dominion,[199] and further whether this is still in harmony with the pronouncements (also of Paul) in which the consummation is described as a ruling or kingship together with Christ. Some [200] have consequently wished to explain these latter pronouncements as alluding to the "intermediate kingdom." But this rests merely on the *a priori* of the to be rejected chiliastic view of 1 Corinthians 15:23ff., and is refuted by the passages in question themselves.[201]

In our opinion we encounter here again the frequently signalized phenomenon that Paul's "eschatology," at least in its terminology, does not form a closed system and that he gives expression to the same matter in various ways, even though this sometimes involves the appearance of mutual contradiction. This also applies to what is called in 1 Corinthians 15 the delivering up of the kingship of Christ to the Father and the subjection of the Son to the one who has subjected all things to him. Here the thought of the conclusion of the economy of redemption carried out by Christ is at the fore. The purpose for which he was sent by God

---

199. Cullmann in particular has made this passage the point of departure for the conception that Christ's rule will finally end in that of God; that accordingly Christ's Messiahship will come to an end and that in general there is here a very radical indication for the functional character of the Pauline (and New Testament) Christology (cf. his *Christ and Time*, p. 109; "The Kingdom of Christ and the Church in the New Testament," *loc. cit.; The Christology of the New Testament*, pp. 268, 293). After the transfer of the kingdom and the subjection of the Son there would no longer be any sense in distinguishing between the Father and his Word of revelation, the Son. Others see in 1 Cor. 15:28 an indication for a definitive and exclusive incision in Christ's person and work. For this whole discussion (i.a., in connection with the views of Marcellus of Ancyra, Calvin, A. A. van Ruler), see Berkouwer, *The Return of Christ*, pp. 426ff. For Cullmann's "functional" Christology, also see above, p. 69.

200. So Lietzmann, *Cor.*, p. 81.

201. In 2 Tim. 2:10 "eternal glory" is explicitly spoken of, and in Rom. 5:17 "reign in (eternal) life with Christ."

(cf., e.g., Rom. 8:3ff.; Gal. 4:4ff.) and for which he has been invested with divine authority will then have been attained. The giving back of the accomplished commission and the authority pertaining to it, the commencement of the now undisturbed dominion of God over all things, is therefore no strange or startling idea. It rather throws light on the fact that Christ has completed his task in perfection and that the glory of God, no longer clouded by the power of sin and death, can now reveal itself in full luster.

One can thereby ask himself whether in the context of 1 Corinthians 15 there was for Paul a special occasion for regarding the consummation from this point of view. If we rightly proceed from the presupposition that in 1 Corinthians 15 the apostle is pleading against an anticipating and spiritualizing heresy, this could provide the explanation for his expressing himself in this particular way. For this heresy apparently had no eye for the still provisional character of Christ's victory and for the consummation still to be awaited. Only then — so the Corinthians had to learn to understand — will the consummation and the perfection have come, when in all the world nothing any longer raises itself against God, and Christ has subdued all the enemies, finally even death; for this is the word in which Christ's power and commission are described: "he [God] has put all things in subjection under his feet" (vv. 25-27a). But this word also implies that God was himself the great Initiator and Authorizer and that therefore the state of perfection (to telos) cannot be spoken of before God himself again fills all things with his glorious presence (vv. 27b-28). The manner in which in the consummation of his work Christ is thereby made subordinate to the Father is thus not to be regarded as an eschatological extra of 1 Corinthians 15,[202] but rather as a specific aspect of the great future, which was of particular importance for Paul's argumentation in 1 Corinthians 15 and was therefore formulated by him in this pregnant way.

On the other hand it must be clear that this transfer of kingship and this self-subjection of the Son to the Father does not mean that from that moment on he is really no longer to be spoken of as the Son, or that no power or dominion is any longer due him. Just as he, as the Son, was in his pre-existence clothed with the glory of God (Phil. 2:6ff.; Col. 1:15, et al.), so also the honor and glory he received at his exaltation are not of a temporary nature (Phil. 2:9ff.; Eph. 1:21). Therefore in him all things have their purpose and subsistence, as they also have their existence through him (Col. 1:16, 17). And for this reason the glory of those whom God has destined to be conformed to his image (Rom. 8:29) can also consist in the fact that they may share in his power and in his dominion (cf. Rom. 5:17; 2 Tim. 2:12). To see in this a contradiction with 1 Corinthians 15:24, 28, would signify a failure to appreciate the considerable nuances that characterize biblical language. Christ's kingly power need not end at the point at which he transfers to God the sub-

---

202. Cf. Berkouwer, who denies that in 1 Cor. 15:24 we have to do with an "exclusive aspect of the eschatological fulfilment" (The Return of Christ, p. 438, n. 37).

jection of all powers as a thing accomplished by him. Different but not contradictory points of view are under discussion here, a fact that — even though one cannot perceive it in every respect — one will the more easily accept if he grasps what realities are here at issue. These are not to be spoken of in one all-embracing look, but now from this, then again from another point of view.

With this twofold point of view, namely, that God will be all and in all and that we shall always be with the Lord, everything has really been said that can be said on the consummation commencing with Christ's parousia. Paul's attention for what is to be in the coming kingdom is always concentrated on this twofold viewpoint. This does not alter the fact that he gives expression to the content of this life with Christ and the "all" with which God will fill all in various ways: it is being saved by his life (Rom. 5:10); salvation with eternal glory (2 Tim. 2:10); honor and immortality (Rom. 2:7; 1 Cor. 15:42ff.; 2 Tim. 1:10); eternal glory (2 Cor. 4:17); seeing face to face (1 Cor. 13:12); fulfillment of righteousness and peace and joy in the Holy Spirit (Rom. 14:17); perfect knowing (1 Cor. 13:12). All are concepts of salvation, descriptions of God's imperishable gift, every one of which has its own context, origin, and nuance, and offers its own special contribution in order to make what is unutterable (2 Cor. 12:4) nevertheless known even now in part. But all these words, likewise as qualifications of the life of the consummation, receive their particular meaning and content only from the gospel of the revelation of the mystery preached by Paul in an incomparable multiplicity of aspects.

INDEX OF PRINCIPAL SUBJECTS

INDEX OF PERSONS

INDEX OF SCRIPTURES